CLYMER™

HARLEY-DAVIDSON

FX/FL SOFTAIL BIG-TWIN EVOLUTION • 1984-1994

INTERTEC PUBLISHING
P.O. Box 12901, Overland Park, Kansas 66282-2901

Copyright ©1995 Intertec Publishing Corporation

FIRST EDITION
First Printing August, 1992
Second Printing November, 1993

SECOND EDITION
First Printing June, 1995

Printed in U.S.A.

ISBN: 0-89287-637-9

Library of Congress: 94-77641

MEMBER

Technical photography by Ron Wright.

Technical illustrations by Steve Amos.

Technical assistance provided by:
   American Motorcycle Institute
   3042 International Speedway Blvd.
   Daytona Beach, FL 32124

   A special thanks goes out to the American Motorcycle Institute without whose help this book would not
   have been possible. We would also like to acknowledge the following individuals:
   • AMI president Lamar Williams for allowing us to work in the well-equipped AMI shops.
   • AMI program director James Watts.
   • AMI instructor David A. Walker for going the extra mile in organizing the entire photo and teardown
     shoot. His preparation and assistance helped to make this the best book possible.
   • The AMI Harley-Davidson specialty program.
   • AMI graduate Bill Eaton for his tuning expertise.

Robison Harley-Davidson Sales
508 International Speedway Blvd.
Daytona Beach, FL 32114

   A special thanks goes out to Joe Robison and his mechanics for allowing us to photograph in their shop.

COVER: Photographed by Mark Clifford, Mark Clifford Photography, Los Angeles, California.

629.2877
C62

CONTENTS

QUICK REFERENCE DATA

TIRE PRESSURE*

	Front		Rear	
	psi	kg/cm²	psi	kg/cm²
1984				
Rider only	30	2.1	28	1.9
With passenger	30	2.1	36	2.5
1985-on FLST (all models)				
Rider only	36	2.5	36	2.5
With passenger	36	2.5	40	2.8
1985-1990 FXST (all models)				
Rider only	30	2.1	32**	2.2
With passenger	30	2.1	32	2.2
1991-on FXST (all models)				
Rider only	30	2.1	36	2.5
With passenger	30	2.1	40	2.8

* Tire pressures listed in this table are for original equipment tires. See your dealer or tire manufacturer when equipping your model with non-stock tires.
** If you have an early model 1985 FXST with K101 A rear tires, set the tire pressure to 28 psi (1.9 kg/cm²).

ENGINE OIL

Type	HD rating	Viscosity	Ambient operating temperature
HD Multigrade	HD 240	SAE 20W/50	20° F to 100° F
HD Regular Heavy*	HD 240	SAE 50	60° F to 100° F
HD Extra Heavy*	HD 240	SAE 60	80° F to 100° F

* Not recommended for use when ambient temperature is below 50° F.

RECOMMENDED LUBRICANTS AND FLUIDS

Brake fluid	DOT 5
Fork oil	HD Type E or equivalent
Battery top up	Distilled water
Transmission	HD transmission or equivalent
Clutch	HD lubricant or equivalent
Fuel	Leaded or unleaded gasoline with a pump octane rating of 87 or higher

ENGINE, CLUTCH AND TRANSMISSION OIL CAPACITIES

Oil tank	3 U.S. qts. (2.8 L, 2.5 imp. qts.)
Primary chain case	
1984-1989	1.5 U.S. qts. (1.4 L, 1.2 imp. qts.)
1990-on	Approximately 30-36 U.S. oz. (887-1,065 ml, 31.3-37.5 imp. oz.)*
Transmission	
4-speed	Approximately 1.5 U.S. pints (710 ml, 25 imp. oz.)*
5-speed	
1985-1990	Approximately 1 U.S. pint (473 ml, 13.3 imp. oz.)*
1991-on	Approximately 1.25-1.5 U.S. pints (590-710 ml, 20.9-25 imp. oz.)*

* See text for correct check and refill procedure.

FUEL TANK CAPACITY

	Total			Reserve		
	U. S. gal.	Liters	Imp. gal.	U. S. gal.	Liters	Imp. gal.
1984 FXST	5.0	18.9	4.2	1.2	4.5	1.0
1985-on						
FXSTC & FLSTN	5.2	19.7	4.3	1.2	4.5	1.0
FXSTS & FLSTC/F	4.2	15.9	3.5	0.75	2.8	0.6

FRONT FORK OIL CAPACITY

	Wet			Dry		
	oz.	cc	Imp. oz.	oz.	cc	Imp. oz.
1984	9.25	273.5	9.6	10	295	10.42
1985-on						
FXST/C	10.2	301	10.6	11.2	331	11.7
FLST/C/F	11.5	340	12.0	12.5	370	13.0

ENGINE TUNE-UP SPECIFICATIONS

Engine compression	90 psi (6.3 kg/cm^2)
Spark plugs	
Type	HD 5R6A or equivalent
Gap	0.038-0.043 in. (0.96-1.09 mm)
Ignition timing	
Type	Electronic
Timing specifications	
Early 1984	
Range	5°-50° BTDC
Start	5° BTDC
Fast idle	35° BTDC
@ 1,800-2,800 rpm	50° BTDC
Late 1984-on	
Range	0°-35° BTDC
Start	5° BTDC
Fast idle	35° BTDC
@ 1,800-2,800 rpm	50° BTDC

CARBURETOR IDLE SPEED SPECIFICATIONS

1984	
Slow idle	900-950 rpm
Fast idle	1,500 rpm
1985-1989	
Slow idle	1,000-1,050 rpm
Fast idle	1,500-1,550 rpm
1990-on	
Idle	1,000-1,050 rpm

CARBURETOR SPECIFICATIONS

	Main jet	Pilot jet
1984	160	50
1985	165	50
1986	170	50
1987	165	50

(continued)

CARBURETOR SPECIFICATIONS (continued)

	Main jet	Pilot jet
1988-1989		
49-state models	165	52
California	140	42
1990-1991		
49-state models	185	45
California	165	42
1992		
49-state models	165	40
California	160	40
1993		
49-state models	175	42
California	160	42
HDI*	165	40
1994		
49-state models	165	42
California	165	42
HDI*	165	42

* Harley-Davidson international models.

ELECTRICAL SPECIFICATIONS

Battery capacity	12 volt, 19 amp hr.
Ignition coil	
Primary resistance	
1984	3.3-3.7 ohms
1985-on	2.5-3.1 ohms
Secondary resistance	
1984	16,500-19,500 ohms
1985-1992	11,250-13,750 ohms
1993-on	10,000-12,500 ohms
Alternator	
Stator coil resistance	
1984-1988	0.2-0.4 ohms
1989-on	0.1-0.2 ohms
AC voltage output	
1984-1988	19-26 VAC per 1,000 rpm
1989-on	16-20 VAC per 1,000 rpm
Voltage regulator	
Voltage output @ 3,600 rpm	13.8-15 volts @ 75° F
Amperes @ 3,600 rpm	
1984-1988	22 amps
1989-on	32 amps
Starter current draw test	
1984-1988	45 amps max.
1989-1992	150 amps max.
1993-on	200 amps max.

STARTER SPECIFICATIONS

	in.	mm
Starter brush length		
1984-1988	0.438	11.1
1989-1990	0.354	8.9
1991-1992	0.413	10.5
1993-on	0.354	8.9
Commutator diameter wear limit (minimum OD)		
1984-1988	—	—
1989-on	1.141	28.9

CIRCUIT BREAKER RATINGS

Circuit	Rating (amps)
Main (battery)	30
Ignition	15
Lights	15
Accessory	15

DRY CLUTCH SPECIFICATIONS

Item	Specification
Type	Dry, multiple disc
Spring adjustment	1 1/32-1 7/8 in. (26.2-47.6 mm) from spring collar edge
Spring free length	1 47/64-1 45/64 in. (44.04-43.26 mm)
Friction plates	
Minimum lining thickness	1/32 in. (0.8 mm)
Warpage limit	0.010 in. (0.25 mm)
Steel disc warpage limit	0.010 in. (0.25 mm)
Clutch screw adjustment	See text
Clutch hand lever free play	1/16 in. (1.59 mm)

WET CLUTCH SPECIFICATIONS (1985-1989)

Type	Wet, multiple disc
Clutch hand lever free play	1/8-3/16 in. (3.17-4.76 mm)
Steel disc	
Minimum lining thickness	0.044 in. (1.12 mm)
Warpage limit	0.011 in. (0.30 mm)
Friction plate	
Minimum thickness	0.078 in. (1.98 mm)

WET CLUTCH SPECIFICATIONS (1990-ON)

Type	Wet, multiple disc
Clutch hand lever free play	
1984-1990	1/8-3/16 in. (3.2-4.8 mm)
1991-on	1/16-1/8 in. (1.6-3.2 mm)
Steel disc	
Warpage limit	0.006 in. (0.15 mm)
Friction plate assembly	
Minimum lining thickness (assembly)*	0.661 in. (16.8 mm)

* See text for procedures on measuring friction plates.

BRAKE SPECIFICATIONS

	in.	mm
Brake pad minimum thickness		
Front and rear	0.062	1.57
Brake disc (front and rear)		
Minimum thickness	0.205	5.21
Outside diameter	11.50	292.1

FRONT WHEEL TIGHTENING TORQUES (NON-SPRINGER)

	ft.-lb.	N·m
Front axle		
1984	50	69
1985-on	45-50	62-69
Slider cap nuts	9-13	12-18

(continued)

FRONT WHEEL TIGHTENING TORQUES (NON-SPRINGER) (continued)

	ft.-lb.	N·m
Front brake caliper		
1984	115-120 in.-lb.	13.2-13.8
1985-on	25-30	34.5-41.4

FRONT WHEEL TIGHTENING TORQUES (SPRINGER)

	ft.-lb.	N·m
Front axle	60-65	81-88
Slider cap nuts	11	15
Front brake caliper		
Top bolt	42-46	57-62
Bottom bolt	25-30	34-41

REAR WHEEL TIGHTENING TORQUES

	ft.-lb.	N·m
Rear axle		
1984	65-70	88-96.6
1985-on	60-65	82.8-88
Sprocket bolts		
1984	35	48.3
1985-1991	65-70	88-96.6
1992-on	55-65	75-88

CHAPTER ONE

GENERAL INFORMATION

This Clymer shop manual covers all Harley-Davidson 1340 cc Softail models from 1984-1994.

Troubleshooting, tune-up, maintenance and repair are not difficult, if you know what tools and equipment to use and what to do. Step-by-step instructions guide you through jobs ranging from simple maintenance to complete engine and suspension overhaul.

This manual can be used by anyone from a first time do-it-yourselfer to a professional mechanic. Detailed drawings and clear photographs give you all the information you need to do the work right.

Some of the procedures in this manual require the use of special tools. The resourceful mechanic can, in many cases, think of acceptable substitutes for special tools—there is always another way. This can be as simple as using a few pieces of threaded rod, washers and nuts to remove or install a bearing or fabricating a tool from scrap material. However, using a substitute for a special tool is not recommended as it can be dangerous to and may damage the part. If you find that a tool can be designed and safely made, but will require some type of machine work, you may want to search out a local community college or high school that has a machine shop curriculum. Shop teachers sometimes welcome outside work that can be used as practical shop applications for advanced students.

Table 1 lists model coverage.

General specifications are listed in Table 2 while gross vehicle weight ratings are listed in Table 3. Fuel tank capacity is listed in Table 4.

U.S. to metric conversion is given in Table 5.

Critical torque specifications are found in table form at the end of each chapter (as required). The general torque specifications listed in Table 6 can be used when a torque specification is not listed for a specific component or assembly.

Inch tap drill sizes can be found in Table 7.

A wind chill chart is found in Table 8 that can be used to better prepare yourself when riding your Harley in cold weather.

MANUAL ORGANIZATION

This chapter provides general information useful to Harley vehicle owners and mechanics. In addition, information in this chapter discusses the tools and techniques for preventive maintenance, troubleshooting and repair.

Chapter Two provides methods and suggestions for quick and accurate diagnosis and repair of problems. Troubleshooting procedures discuss typical symptoms and logical methods to pinpoint the trouble.

Chapter Three explains all periodic lubrication and routine maintenance necessary to keep your

Harley operating well. Chapter Three also includes recommended tune-up procedures, eliminating the need to consult other chapters constantly on the various assemblies.

Subsequent chapters describe specific systems, providing disassembly, repair, assembly and adjustment procedures in simple step-by-step form. If a repair is impractical for a home mechanic, it is so indicated. It is usually faster and less expensive to take such repairs to a dealer or competent repair shop. Specifications concerning a specific system are included at the end of the appropriate chapter.

NOTES, CAUTIONS AND WARNINGS

The terms NOTE, CAUTION and WARNING have specific meanings in this manual. A NOTE provides additional information to make a step or procedure easier or clearer. Disregarding a NOTE could cause inconvenience, but would not cause damage or personal injury.

A CAUTION emphasizes areas where equipment damage could occur. Disregarding a CAUTION could cause permanent mechanical damage; however, personal injury is unlikely.

A WARNING emphasizes areas where personal injury or even death could result from negligence. Mechanical damage may also occur. WARNINGS *are to be taken seriously*. In some cases, serious injury and death has resulted from disregarding similar warnings.

SAFETY FIRST

Professional mechanics can work for years and never sustain a serious injury. If you observe a few rules of common sense and safety, you can enjoy many safe hours servicing your own machine. If you ignore these rules you can hurt yourself or damage the equipment.

1. Never use gasoline as a cleaning solvent.

> *WARNING*
> *Gasoline should only be stored in an approved safety gasoline storage container, properly labeled. Spilled gasoline should be wiped up immediately.*

2. Never smoke or use a torch in the vicinity of flammable liquids, such as cleaning solvent, in open containers.

3. If welding or brazing is required on the machine, remove the fuel tanks to a safe distance, at least 50 feet away.

4. Use the proper sized wrenches to avoid damage to fasteners and injury to yourself.

5. When loosening a tight or stuck nut, be guided by what would happen if the wrench should slip. Be careful; protect yourself accordingly.

6. When replacing a fastener, make sure to use one with the same measurements and strength as the old one. Incorrect or mismatched fasteners can result in damage to your Harley and possible personal injury. Beware of fastener kits that are filled with cheap and poorly made nuts, bolts, washers and cotter pins. Refer to *Fasteners* in this chapter for additional information.

7. Keep all hand and power tools in good condition. Wipe greasy and oily tools after using them. They are difficult to hold and can cause injury. Replace or repair worn or damaged tools.

8. Keep your work area clean and uncluttered.

9. Wear safety goggles during all operations involving drilling, grinding, the use of a cold chisel or *any* time you feel unsure about the safety of your eyes. Safety goggles (**Figure 1**) should also be worn when solvent and compressed air is used to clean parts.

> *WARNING*
> *The improper use of compressed air is very dangerous. Using compressed air to dust off your clothes, bike or workbench can cause flying particles to be blown into your eyes or skin. **Never** direct or blow compressed air into your skin or through any body opening (in-*

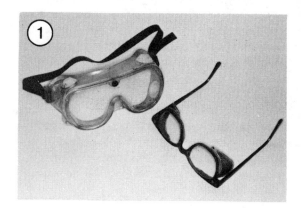

cluding cuts) as this can cause severe injury or death. Compressed air should be used carefully; never allow children to use or play with compressed air.

10. Keep an approved fire extinguisher nearby (**Figure 2**). Be sure it is rated for gasoline (Class B) and electrical (Class C) fires.

11. When drying bearings or other rotating parts with compressed air, never allow the air jet to rotate the bearing or part. The air jet is capable of rotating them at speeds far in excess of those for which they were designed. The bearing or rotating part is very likely to disintegrate and cause serious injury and damage. To prevent bearing damage when using compressed air, hold the inner bearing race (**Figure 3**) by hand.

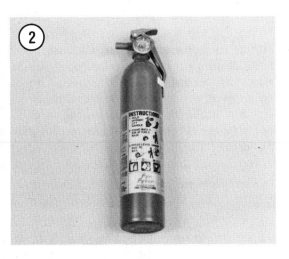

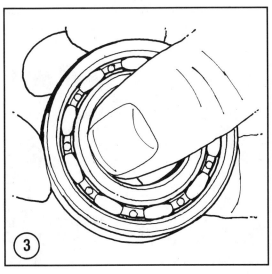

12. Never work on the upper part of the bike while someone is working underneath it.

13. Never carry sharp tools in your pockets.

14. There is always a right way and wrong way to use tools. Learn to use them the right way.

SERVICE HINTS

Most of the service procedures covered are straightforward and can be performed by anyone reasonably handy with tools. It is suggested, however, that you consider your own capabilities carefully before attempting any operation involving major disassembly.

1. "Front," as used in this manual, refers to the front of the motorcycle; the front of any component is the end closest to the front of the motorcycle. The "left-" and "right-hand" side refer to the position of the parts as viewed by a rider sitting on the seat and facing forward. For example, the throttle control is on the right-hand side. These rules are simple, but confusion can cause a major inconvenience during service.

2. Whenever servicing the engine or transmission, or when removing a suspension component, the bike should be secured in a safe manner. If the bike is to be parked on its jiffy stand, check the stand to make sure it is secure and not damaged. Block the front and rear wheels if they remain on the ground. A small hydraulic jack and a block of wood can be used to raise the chassis or you can use a commercial type of stand. If the transmission is not going to be worked on and the drive chain or drive belt is connected to the rear wheel, shift the transmission into first gear.

3. Repairs go much faster and easier if the bike is clean before you begin work. There are special cleaners for washing the engine and related parts. Spray or brush on the cleaning solution, following the manufacturer's directions. Rinse parts with a garden hose. Clean all oily or greasy parts with cleaning solvent as you remove them.

> *WARNING*
> ***Never*** *use gasoline as a cleaning agent. It presents an extreme fire hazard. Be sure to work in a well-ventilated area when using cleaning solvent. Keep a fire extinguisher, rated for gasoline fires, handy in any case.*

4. Much of the labor charged for by mechanics is to remove and disassemble other parts to reach the defective unit. It is usually possible to perform the preliminary operations yourself and then take the defective unit to the dealer for repair.

5. Once you have decided to tackle the job yourself, read the entire section *completely* while looking at the actual parts before starting the job. Make sure you have identified the proper procedure. Study the illustrations and text until you have a good idea of what is involved in completing the job satisfactorily. If special tools or replacement parts are required, make arrangements to get them before you start. It is frustrating and time-consuming to get partly into a job and then be unable to complete it.

NOTE
Some of the procedures or service specifications listed in this manual may not be applicable if your Harley has been modified or if it has been equipped with non-stock equipment. When modifying or installing non-stock equipment, file all printed instruction or technical information regarding the new equipment in a folder or notebook for future reference. If your Harley was purchased second hand, the previous owner may have installed non-stock parts. If necessary, consult with your dealer or the accessory manufacturer on components that may change tuning or repair procedures.

6. Simple wiring checks can be easily made at home, but knowledge of electronics is almost a necessity for performing tests with complicated test gear.

CAUTION
Improper testing can sometimes damage an electrical component.

7. Disconnect the negative battery cable (**Figure 4**) when working on or near the electrical, clutch or starter systems and before disconnecting any wires. On all models covered in this manual, the negative terminal will be marked with a minus (–) sign and the positive terminal with a plus (+) sign.

WARNING
Never disconnect the positive battery cable unless the negative cable has been disconnected. Disconnecting the positive cable while the negative cable is

still connected may cause a spark. This could ignite the hydrogen gas given off by the battery, causing an explosion.

8. During disassembly, keep a few general cautions in mind. Force is rarely needed to get things apart. If parts are a tight fit, such as a bearing in a case, there is usually a tool designed to separate them. Never use a screwdriver to pry parts with machined surfaces such as crankcase halves. You will mar the surfaces and end up with leaks.

9. Make diagrams (or take a Polaroid picture) wherever similar-appearing parts are found. For instance, crankcase bolts are often not the same length. You may think you can remember where everything came from—but mistakes are costly. There is also the possibility that you may be sidetracked and not return to work for days or even weeks—in which the time carefully laid out parts may have become disturbed.

10. Tag all similar internal parts for location and mark all mating parts for position (A, **Figure 5**). Record number and thickness of any shims as they are removed; measure with a vernier caliper or micrometer. Small parts such as bolts can be identified by placing them in plastic sandwich bags (B, **Figure 5**). Seal and label them with masking tape.

11. Place parts from a specific area of the engine (e.g. cylinder head, cylinder, clutch, primary drive, etc.) into plastic boxes (C, **Figure 5**) to keep them separated.

12. When disassembling transmission shaft assemblies, use an egg flat (type that restaurants get their eggs in) (D, **Figure 5**) and set the parts from the shaft in one of the depressions in the same order in which they were removed.

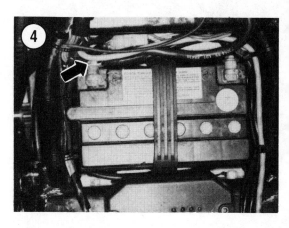

13. Wiring should be tagged with masking tape and marked as each wire is removed. Again, do not rely on memory alone, especially if the wiring was changed by a previous owner.

14. Finished surfaces should be protected from physical damage or corrosion. Keep gasoline off painted surfaces.

15. Use penetrating oil on frozen or tight bolts, then strike the bolt head a few times with a hammer and punch (use a screwdriver on screws). Avoid the use of heat where possible, as it can warp, melt or affect the temper of parts. Heat also ruins finishes, especially paint and plastics.

16. No parts removed or installed (other than bushings and bearings) in the procedures given in this manual should require unusual force during disassembly or assembly. If a part is difficult to remove or install, find out why before proceeding.

17. Cover all openings after removing parts or components to prevent dirt, small tools, etc. from falling in.

18. Recommendations are occasionally made to refer service or maintenance to a Harley-Davidson dealer or independent Harley-Davidson repair shop. In these cases, the work will be done more quickly and economically than if you performed the job yourself.

19. In procedural steps, the term "replace" means to discard a defective part and replace it with a new or exchange unit. "Overhaul" means to remove, disassemble, inspect, measure, repair or replace defective parts, reassemble and install major systems or parts.

20. Some operations require the use of a hydraulic press. It would be wiser to have these operations performed by a shop equipped for such work, rather than to try to do the job yourself with makeshift equipment that may damage your machine.

21. When assembling parts, be sure all shims and washers are replaced exactly as they came out.

22. Whenever a rotating part butts against a stationary part, look for a shim or washer.

23. Use new gaskets if there is any doubt about the condition of the old ones.

24. If it becomes necessary to purchase gasket material to make a gasket, measure the thickness of the old gasket (at an uncompressed point) and purchase gasket material with the same approximate thickness.

25. Heavy grease can be used to hold small parts in place if they tend to fall out during assembly. However, keep grease and oil away from electrical and brake components.

26. Never use wire to clean out jets and air passages. They are easily damaged. Use compressed air to blow out the carburetor only if the diaphragm has been removed first.

27. A baby bottle makes a good measuring device. Get one that is graduated in fluid ounces and cubic centimeters. After it has been used for this purpose, do *not* let a child drink out of it as there will always be an oil residue in it.

28. Take your time and do the job right. Do not forget that a newly rebuilt engine must be broken in just like a new one.

SERIAL NUMBERS

Harley-Davidson makes frequent changes during a model year, some minor, some relatively major. All Harley models in this manual can be identified by their individual 17 digit Vehicle Identification Number (VIN); for example, 1HD1BJL11LM110001. This number is stamped into the steering head (**Figure 6**) and recorded on a label placed on the right front frame downtube. The engine is identified with an abbreviated VIN number stamped onto the left-hand crankcase at the base of the rear cylinder block (**Figure 7**); for example, BJLM110001.

NOTE
When Harley-Davidson makes a running change during a production year, the bikes, depending on where they are produced during production, are identified as an early or late model for that year. For example, if a production

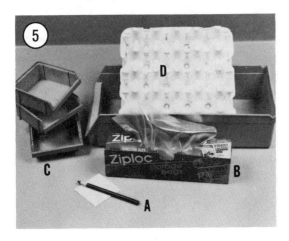

change was made during the 1985 production run, the bikes, depending on where they were manufactured during the actual run, would be referred to as an Early 1985 or Late 1985 model. If you run across this type of designation in this manual that pertains to your model, give your Harley-Davidson dealer a call and have them identify your model with its 17 digit VIN number.

PARTS REPLACEMENT

When you order parts from the dealer or other parts distributor, always order by the full 17 digit VIN number. Compare new parts to old before purchasing them. If they are not alike, have the parts manager explain the difference to you.

TORQUE SPECIFICATIONS

Torque specifications throughout this manual are given in foot-pounds (ft.-lb.) as well as the metric equivalent in newton-meters (N•m).

Table 6 lists general torque specifications for nuts and bolts that are not listed in the respective chapters. To use the table, first determine the size of the bolt or nut. Use a vernier caliper and measure the inside dimensions of the threads of the nut (**Figure 8**) and across the threads for a bolt (**Figure 9**).

FASTENERS

The materials and designs of the various fasteners used on your Harley are not arrived at by chance or accident. Fastener design determines the type of tool required to work the fastener. Fastener material is

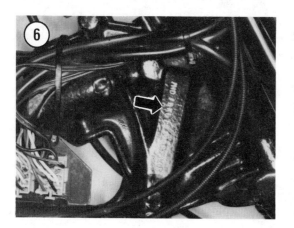

carefully selected to decrease the possibility of physical failure.

Nuts, bolts and screws are manufactured in a wide range of thread patterns. To join a nut and bolt, the diameter of the bolt and the diameter of the hole in the nut must be the same. It is just as important that the threads on both be properly matched.

The best way to tell if the threads on 2 fasteners are matched is to turn the nut on the bolt (or the bolt

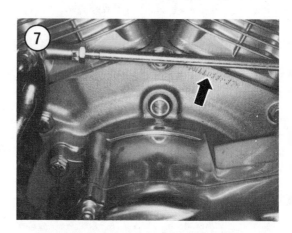

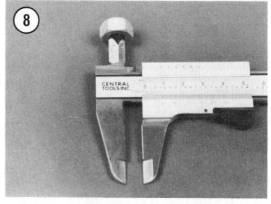

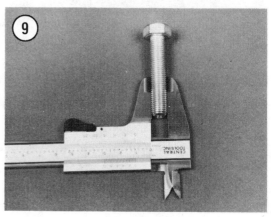

into the threaded hole in a piece of equipment) with fingers only. Be sure both pieces are clean. If much force is required, check the thread condition on each fastener. If the thread condition is good but the fasteners jam, the threads are not compatible. A thread pitch gauge (**Figure 10**) can also be used to determine pitch. Harley-Davidson motorcycles are manufactured with American standard fasteners. The threads are cut differently than metric fasteners (**Figure 11**).

Most threads are cut so that the fastener must be turned clockwise to tighten it. These are called right-hand threads. Some fasteners have left-hand threads; they must be turned counterclockwise to be tightened. Left-hand threads are used in locations where normal rotation of the equipment would tend to loosen a right-hand threaded fastener.

American Threads

American threads come in a coarse or fine thread. Because both coarse and fine threads are used for general use, it is important to match the threads correctly so you do not strip the threads and damage one or both fasteners.

American fasteners are normally described by diameter, threads per inch (TPI) and length; **Figure 12** shows the first 2 specifications. For example, 3/8-16 × 2 indicates a bolt 3/8 in. in diameter with 16 threads per inch, 2 inches long. The measurement across 2 flats on the head of the bolt or screw (**Figure 13**) indicates the proper wrench size to be used. **Figure 9** shows how to determine bolt diameter.

Markings found on American bolt heads indicate tensile strength. For example, a bolt with no head marking is usually made of mild steel, while a bolt with 2 or more markings indicates a higher grade material. **Figure 14** indicates the various head markings with SAE grade identification. When torquing SAE bolts not listed in a torque specification table, refer to the head marking (**Figure 13**) and then to **Table 6** for the torque specification.

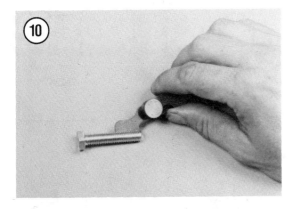

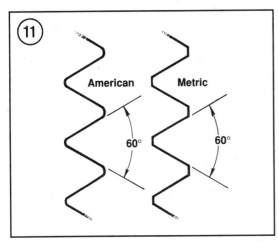

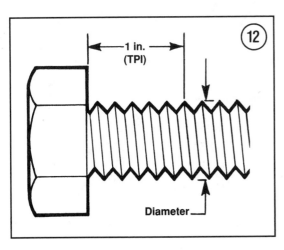

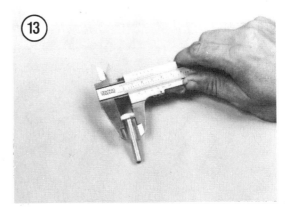

Determining Bolt Length

When purchasing a bolt from a dealer or parts store, it is important to know how to specify bolt length. The correct way to measure bolt length is to measure the length starting from underneath the bolt head to the end of the bolt (**Figure 15**). Always measure bolt length in this manner to avoid purchasing bolts that are too long.

Machine Screws

Machine screw refers to a numbering system used to identify screws smaller than 1/4 of an inch. Machine screws are identified by gauge size (diameter) and threads per inch. For example, 12-28 indicates a 12 gauge screw with 28 threads per inch.

There are many different types of machine screws. **Figure 16** shows a number of screw heads requiring different types of turning tools. Heads are also designed to protrude above the metal (round) or to be slightly recessed in the metal (flat). See **Figure 17**.

Bolts

Commonly called bolts, the technical name for these fasteners is cap screw. Refer to *American Threads* in this section for additional information.

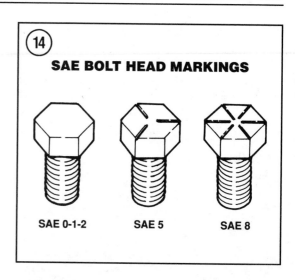

(14) **SAE BOLT HEAD MARKINGS**

SAE 0-1-2   SAE 5   SAE 8

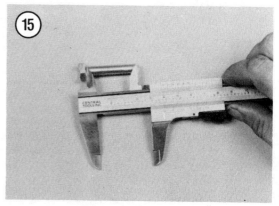

(15)

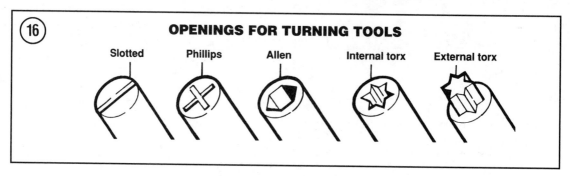

(16) **OPENINGS FOR TURNING TOOLS**

Slotted   Phillips   Allen   Internal torx   External torx

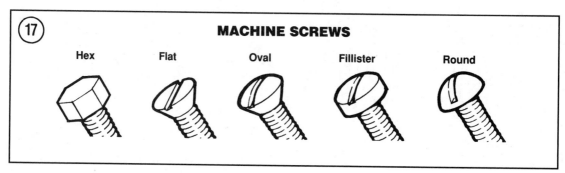

(17) **MACHINE SCREWS**

Hex   Flat   Oval   Fillister   Round

Nuts

Nuts are manufactured in a variety of types and sizes. Most are hexagonal (6-sided) and fit on bolts, screws and studs with the same diameter and pitch.

Figure 18 shows several types of nuts. The common nut is generally used with a lockwasher. Self-locking nuts have a nylon insert which prevents the nut from loosening; no lockwasher is required. Wing nuts are designed for fast removal by hand. Wing nuts are used for convenience in non-critical locations.

To indicate the size of a nut, manufacturers specify the diameter of the opening and the thread pitch. This is similar to bolt specifications, but without the length dimension. The measurement across 2 flats on the nut (**Figure 19**) indicates the proper wrench size to be used.

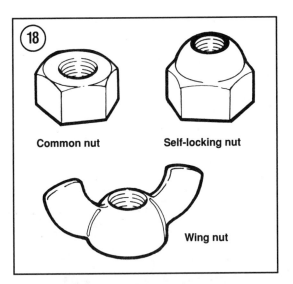

Common nut   Self-locking nut

Wing nut

Self-locking Fasteners

Several types of bolts, screws and nuts incorporate a system that develops an interference between the bolt, screw, nut or tapped hole threads. Interference is achieved in various ways: by distorting threads, coating threads with dry adhesive or nylon, distorting the top of an all-metal nut, using a nylon insert in the center or at the top of a nut, etc.

Self-locking fasteners offer greater holding strength and better vibration resistance. Some self-locking fasteners can be reused if in good condition. Others, like the nylon insert nut, form an initial locking condition when the nut is first installed; the nylon forms closely to the bolt thread pattern, thus reducing any tendency for the nut to loosen. When the nut is removed, the locking efficiency is greatly reduced. For greatest safety, it is recommended that you install new self-locking fasteners whenever they are removed.

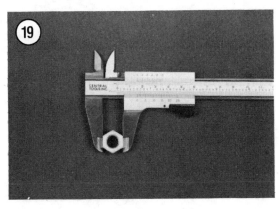

Washers

There are 2 basic types of washers: flat washers and lockwashers. Flat washers are simple discs with a hole to fit a screw or bolt. Lockwashers are designed to prevent a fastener from working loose due to vibration, expansion and contraction. Lockwashers should be installed between the bolt head or nut and a flat washer (**Figure 20**). **Figure 21** shows several types of washers. Washers are also used in the following functions:

    a. As spacers.

    b. To prevent galling or damage of the equipment by the fastener.

    c. To help distribute fastener load during torquing.

    d. As fluid seals (copper or laminated washers).

Note that flat washers are often used between a lockwasher and a fastener to provide a smooth bearing surface. This allows the fastener to be turned easily with a tool.

NOTE
As much care should be given to the selection and purchase of washers as that given to bolts, nuts and other fasteners. Beware of washers that are made of thin and weak materials. These will deform and crush the first time they are used in a high torque application.

Cotter Pins

Cotter pins (**Figure 22**) are used to secure fasteners in a special location. The threaded stud, bolt or axle must have a hole in it. Its nut or nut lock piece has castellations around its upper edge into which the cotter pin fits to keep it from loosening. When *properly* installed, a cotter pin is a positive locking device.

The first step in properly installing a cotter pin is to purchase one that will fit snugly when inserted through the nut and the mating thread part. This should not be a problem when purchasing cotter pins through a Harley-Davidson dealer; you can order them by their respective part numbers. However, when you stop off at your local hardware or automotive store, keep this in mind. The cotter pin should not be so tight that you have to drive it in and out, but you do not want it so loose that it can move or float after it is installed.

Before installing a cotter pin, tighten the nut to the recommended torque specification. If the castellations in the nut do not line up with the hole in the bolt or axle, tighten the nut until alignment is achieved. Do not loosen the nut to make alignment. Insert a *new* cotter pin through the nut and hole, then tap the head lightly to seat it. Bend one arm over the flat on the nut and the other against the top of the axle or bolt (**Figure 22**). Cut the arms to a suitable length to prevent them from snagging on clothing, or worse, your hands, arms or legs; the exposed arms will cut flesh easily. When the cotter pin is bent and its arms cut to length, it should be tight. If you can wiggle the cotter pin, it is improperly installed.

Cotter pins should not be reused as their ends may break and allow the cotter pin to fall out and perhaps the fastener to unscrew itself.

Circlips

Circlips can be of internal or external design. They are used to retain items on shafts (external type) or within tubes (internal type). In some applications, circlips of varying thicknesses are used to control the end play of parts assemblies. These are often called selective circlips. Circlips should be replaced during installation, as removal weakens and deforms them.

Two basic styles of circlips are available: machined and stamped circlips. Machined circlips (**Figure 23**) can be installed in either direction (shaft or housing) because both faces are machined, thus

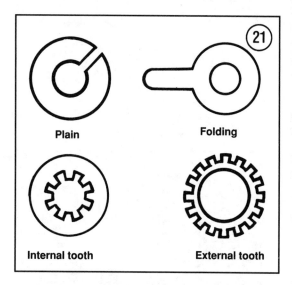

Plain   **Folding**

Internal tooth   **External tooth**

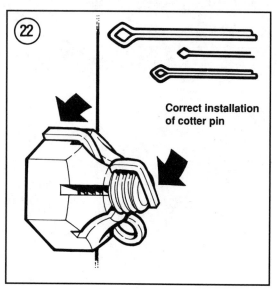

Correct installation of cotter pin

creating two sharp edges. Stamped circlips (**Figure 24**) are manufactured with one sharp edge and one rounded edge. When installing stamped circlips in a thrust situation, the sharp edge must face away from the part producing the thrust. When installing circlips, observe the following:

a. Circlips should be removed and installed with circlip pliers. See *Circlip Pliers* in this chapter.

b. Compress or expand circlips only enough to install them.

c. After the circlip is installed, make sure it is completely seated in its groove.

Transmission circlips become worn with use and increase side play. For this reason, always use new circlips whenever a transmission is to be reassembled.

LUBRICANTS

Periodic lubrication assures long life for any type of equipment. The *type* of lubricant used is just as important as the lubrication service itself, although in an emergency the wrong type of lubricant is better than none. The following paragraphs describe the types of lubricants most often used on motorcycle equipment. Be sure to follow the manufacturer's recommendations for lubricant types.

If any unique lubricant is recommended by Harley-Davidson, it is specified in the service procedure.

Generally, all liquid lubricants are called "oil." They may be mineral-based (including petroleum bases), natural-based (vegetable and animal bases), synthetic-based or emulsions (mixtures). "Grease" is an oil to which a thickening base has been added so that the end product is semi-solid. Grease is often classified by the type of thickener added; lithium soap is commonly used.

Engine Oil

Four-cycle oil for motorcycle and automotive engines is graded by the American Petroleum Institute (API) and the Society of Automotive Engineers (SAE) in several categories. Oil containers display these ratings on the top or label (**Figure 25**).

API oil grade is indicated by letters; oils for gasoline engines are identified by an "S."

Viscosity is an indication of the oil's thickness. The SAE uses numbers to indicate viscosity; thin oils have low numbers while thick oils have high numbers. A "W" after the number indicates that the viscosity testing was done at low temperature to simulate cold-weather operation. Engine oils fall into the 5W-30 and 20W-50 range.

Multi-grade oils (for example 10W-40) are less viscous (thinner) at low temperatures and more viscous (thicker) at high temperatures. This allows the oil to perform efficiently across a wide range of engine operating conditions. The lower the number, the better the engine will start in cold climates.

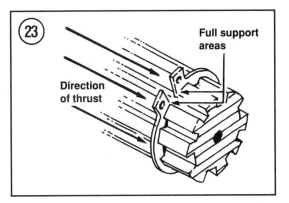

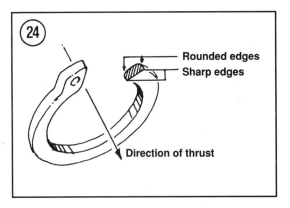

Higher numbers are usually recommended for engines running in hot weather conditions.

Grease

Greases are graded by the National Lubricating Grease Institute (NLGI). Greases are graded by number according to the consistency of the grease; these range from No. 000 to No. 6, with No. 6 being the most solid. A typical multipurpose grease is NLGI No. 2. For specific applications, equipment manufacturers may require grease with an additive such as molybdenum disulfide (MOS2).

Also recommended for axle and swing arm pivot shafts is an anti-seize lubricant (**Figure 26**). This is necessary to prevent the pivot points from corroding and locking up.

RTV GASKET SEALANT

Room temperature vulcanizing (RTV) sealant is used on some pre-formed gaskets and to seal some components. RTV is a silicone gel supplied in tubes and can be purchased in a number of different colors.

Moisture in the air causes RTV to cure. Always place the cap on the tube as soon as possible when using RTV. RTV has a shelf life of one year and will not cure properly when the shelf life has expired. Check the expiration date on RTV tubes before using and keep partially used tubes tightly sealed.

Applying RTV Sealant

Clean all gasket residue from mating surfaces. Surfaces should be clean and free of oil and dirt. Remove all RTV gasket material from blind attaching holes, as it can cause a "hydraulic" effect and affect bolt torque.

Apply RTV sealant in a continuous bead. Circle all mounting holes unless otherwise specified. Torque mating parts within 10 minutes after application.

THREADLOCK

A chemical locking compound should be used on all bolts and nuts, even if they are secured with lockwashers. A locking compound will lock fasteners against vibration loosening and seal against

leaks. Loctite 242 (blue) and 271 (red) are recommended for many threadlock requirements described in this manual (**Figure 27**).

Loctite 242 (blue) is a medium strength threadlock and component disassembly can be performed with normal hand tools. Loctite 271 (red) is a high strength threadlock and heat or special tools, such as a press or puller, may be required for component disassembly.

Applying Threadlock

Surfaces should be clean and free of oil, grease, dirt and other residue; clean threads with an aerosol electrical contact cleaner before applying the Loctite. When applying Loctite, use a small amount. If too much is used, it can work its way down the threads and stick parts together not meant to be stuck.

GASKET REMOVER

Stubborn gaskets can present a problem during engine service as they can take a long time to re-

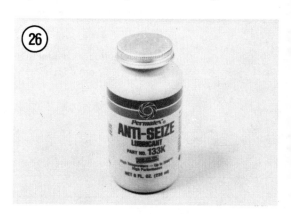

move. Consequently, there is the added problem of secondary damage occurring to the gasket mating surfaces from the incorrect use of gasket scraping tools. To quickly and safely remove stubborn gaskets, use a spray gasket remover. Spray gasket remover can be purchased through automotive parts houses. Follow the manufacturer's directions for use.

EXPENDABLE SUPPLIES

Certain expendable supplies are required during maintenance and repair work. These include grease, oil, gasket cement, wiping rags and cleaning solvent. Ask your dealer for the silicone lubricants, contact cleaner and other products which make maintenance simpler and easier. Cleaning solvent or kerosene is available at some service stations or hardware stores.

BASIC HAND TOOLS

Many of the procedures in this manual can be carried out with simple hand tools and test equipment familiar to the average home mechanic. Keep your tools clean and in a tool box. Keep them organized with the sockets and related drives together, the open-end combination wrenches together, etc. After using a tool, wipe off dirt and grease with a clean cloth and return the tool to its correct place.

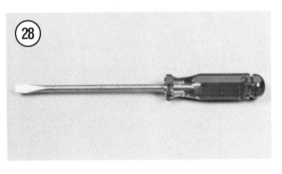

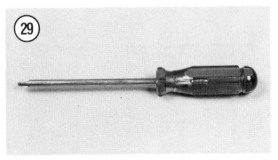

Top quality tools are essential; they are also more economical in the long run. If you are now starting to build your tool collection, stay away from the "advertised specials" featured at some parts houses, discount stores and chain drug stores. These are usually a poor grade tool that can be sold cheaply and that is exactly what they are—*cheap*. They are usually made of inferior material, and are thick, heavy and clumsy. Their rough finish makes them difficult to clean and they usually don't last very long. If it is ever your misfortune to use such tools, you will probably find out that the wrenches do not fit the heads of bolts and nuts correctly and damage the fastener.

Quality tools are made of alloy steel and are heat treated for greater strength. They are lighter and better balanced than cheap ones. Their surface is smooth, making them a pleasure to work with and easy to clean. The initial cost of good quality tools may be more but they are cheaper in the long run. Don't try to buy everything in all sizes in the beginning; do it a little at a time until you have the necessary tools.

The following tools are required to perform virtually any repair job. Each tool is described and the recommended size given for starting a tool collection. Additional tools and some duplicates may be added as you become familiar with your Harley. Harley-Davidson motorcycles are built with American standard fasteners. If you are starting your collection now, buy American sizes.

Screwdrivers

The screwdriver is a very basic tool, but if used improperly it will do more damage than good. The slot on a screw has a definite dimension and shape. Through improper use or selection, a screwdriver can damage the screw head, making removal of the screw difficult. A screwdriver must be selected to conform to the shape of the screw head used. Two basic types of screwdrivers are required: standard (flat- or slot-blade) screwdrivers (**Figure 28**) and Phillips screwdrivers (**Figure 29**).

Note the following when selecting and using screwdrivers:

    a. The screwdriver must always fit the screw head. If the screwdriver blade is too small for the screw slot, damage may occur to the screw slot and screwdriver. If the blade is too large, it cannot engage the slot properly and will result in damage to the screw head.

b. Standard screwdrivers are identified by the length of their blade. A 6-inch screwdriver has a blade six inches long. The width of the screwdriver blade will vary, so make sure that the blade engages the screw slot the complete width of the screw.

c. Phillips screwdrivers are sized according to their point size. They are numbered one, two, three and four. The degree of taper determines the point size; the No. 1 Phillips screwdriver will be the most pointed. The points become more blunt as their number increases.

NOTE
You should also be aware of another screwdriver similar to the Phillips, and that is the Reed and Prince tip. Like the Phillips, the Reed and Prince screwdriver tip forms an "X" but with one major exception, the Reed and Prince tip has a much more pointed tip. The Reed and Prince screwdriver should never be used on Phillips screws and vice versa.Intermixing these screwdrivers will cause damage to the screw and screwdriver. If you have both types in your tool box and they are similar in appearance, you may want to identify them by painting the screwdriver shank underneath the handle.

d. When selecting screwdrivers, note that you can apply more power with less effort with a longer screwdriver than with a short one. Of course, there will be situations where only a short handled screwdriver can be used. Keep this in mind though, when having to remove tight screws.

e. Because the working end of a screwdriver receives quite a bit of abuse, you should purchase screwdrivers with hardened-tips. The extra money will be well spent.

Screwdrivers are available in sets which often include an assortment of common and Phillips blades. If you buy them individually, buy at least the following:

a. Common screwdriver—5/16 × 6 in. blade.

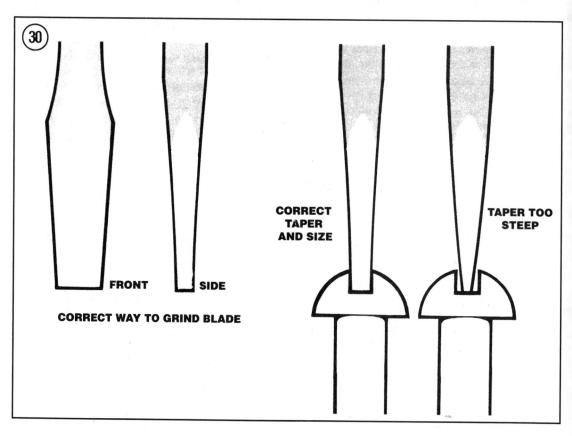

FRONT   SIDE
CORRECT WAY TO GRIND BLADE

CORRECT TAPER AND SIZE

TAPER TOO STEEP

b. Common screwdriver—3/8 × 12 in. blade.

c. Phillips screwdriver—size 2 tip, 6 in. blade.

d. Phillips screwdriver—size 3 tip, 6 and 8 in. blade.

Use screwdrivers only for driving screws. Never use a screwdriver for prying or chiseling metal. Do not try to remove a Phillips, Torx or Allen head screw with a standard screwdriver (unless the screw has a combination head that will accept either type); you can damage the head so that the proper tool will be unable to remove it.

Keep screwdrivers in the proper condition and they will last longer and perform better. Always keep the tip of a standard screwdriver in good condition. **Figure 30** shows how to grind the tip to the proper shape if it becomes damaged. Note the symmetrical sides of the tip.

Pliers

Pliers come in a wide range of types and sizes. Pliers are useful for cutting, bending and crimping. They should never be used to cut hardened objects or to turn bolts or nuts. **Figure 31** shows several pliers useful in repairing your Harley.

Each type of pliers has a specialized function. Slip-joint pliers are general purpose pliers and are used mainly for holding things and for bending. Needlenose pliers are used to hold or bend small objects. Water pump pliers can be adjusted to hold various sizes of objects; the jaws remain parallel to grip around objects such as pipe or tubing. There are many more types of pliers.

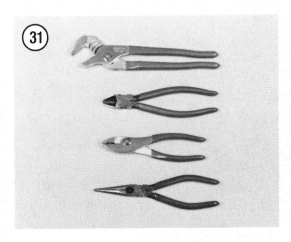

> *CAUTION*
> *Pliers should not be used for loosening or tightening nuts or bolts. The pliers's sharp teeth will grind off the nut or bolt corners and damage it.*

> *CAUTION*
> *If slip-joint or water pump pliers are going to be used to hold an object with a finished surface, wrap the object with tape or cardboard for protection.*

Vise-grip Pliers

Vise-grip pliers (**Figure 32**) are used to hold objects very tightly while another task is performed on the object. While vise-grip pliers work well, caution should be followed with their use. Because vise-grip pliers exert more force than regular pliers, their sharp jaws can permanently scar the object. In addition, when vise-grip pliers are locked into position, they can crush or deform thin-walled material.

Vise-grip pliers are available in many types for more specific tasks.

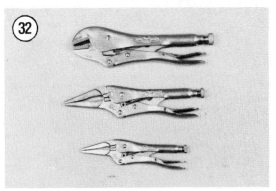

Circlip Pliers

Circlip pliers (**Figure 33**) are special in that they are only used to remove or install circlips. When purchasing circlip pliers, there are two kinds to choose from. External pliers (spreading) are used to remove circlips that fit on the outside of a shaft. Internal pliers (squeezing) are used to remove circlips which fit inside a housing.

> *WARNING*
> *Because circlips can sometimes slip and "fly off" during removal and installation, always wear safety glasses when servicing them.*

Box-end, Open-end and Combination Wrenches

Box-end and open-end wrenches (**Figure 34**) are available in sets or separately in a variety of sizes. The size number stamped near the end refers to the distance between 2 parallel flats on the hex head bolt or nut.

Box-end wrenches are usually superior to open-end wrenches. Open-end wrenches grip the nut on only 2 flats. Unless a wrench fits well, it may slip and round off the points on the nut. The box-end wrench grips on all 6 flats. Both 6-point and 12-point openings on box-end wrenches are available. The 6-point gives superior holding power; the 12-point allows a shorter swing.

Combination wrenches which are open on one side and boxed on the other are also available. Both ends are the same size.

No matter what style of wrench you choose, proper use is important to prevent personal injury. When using a wrench, get into the habit of pulling the wrench toward you. This technique will reduce the risk of injuring your hand if the wrench should slip. If you have to push the wrench away from you to loosen or tighten a fastener, open and push with the palm of your hand; your fingers and knuckles will be out of the way if the wrench slips. Before using a wrench, always think ahead as to what could happen if the wrench should slip or if the fastener strips or breaks.

Adjustable Wrenches

An adjustable wrench can be adjusted to fit nearly any nut or bolt head which has clear access around its entire perimeter. Adjustable wrenches are best used as a backup wrench to keep a large nut or bolt from turning while the other end is being loosened or tightened with a proper wrench. See **Figure 35**.

Adjustable wrenches have only two gripping surfaces which makes them more subject to slipping off the fastener and damaging the part and possibly your hand. See *Box-end, Open-end and Combination Wrenches* in this chapter.

These wrenches are directional; the solid jaw must be the one transmitting the force. If you use the adjustable jaw to transmit the force, it will loosen and possibly slip off.

Adjustable wrenches come in all sizes but something in the 6 to 8 inch range is recommended as an all-purpose wrench.

Socket Wrenches

This type is undoubtedly the fastest, safest and most convenient to use. Sockets which attach to a ratchet handle (**Figure 36**) are available with 6-point

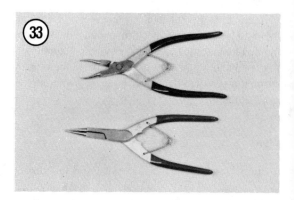

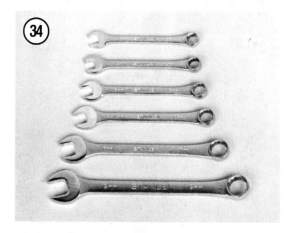

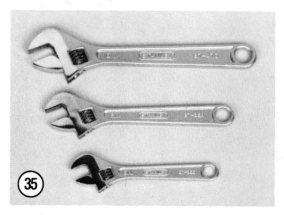

or 12-point openings and 1/4, 3/8, 1/2 and 3/4 in. drives. The drive size indicates the size of the square hole which mates with the ratchet handle.

Torque Wrench

A torque wrench (**Figure 37**) is used with a socket to measure how tightly a nut or bolt is installed. They come in a wide price range and with either 3/8 or 1/2 in. square drives. The drive size indicates the size of the square drive which mates with the socket.

Impact Driver

This tool makes removal of tight fasteners easy and eliminates damage to bolts and screw slots. Impact drivers and interchangeable bits (**Figure 38**) are available at most large hardware and motorcycle dealers. Don't purchase a cheap one as they don't

work as well and require more force than a moderately priced one. Sockets can also be used with a hand impact driver. However, make sure the socket is designed for use with an impact driver or air tool. Do not use regular hand type sockets, as they may shatter during use.

Hammers

The correct hammer (**Figure 39**) is necessary for repairs. Use only a hammer with a face (or head) of rubber or plastic or the soft-faced type that is filled with buckshot. These are sometimes necessary in engine teardowns. *Never* use a metal-faced hammer on engine or suspension parts, as severe damage will result in most cases. Ball-peen or machinist's hammers will be required when striking another tool, such as a punch or impact driver. When striking a hammer against a punch, cold chisel or similar tool, the face of the hammer should be at least 1/2 in. larger than the head of the tool. When it is necessary to strike hard against a steel part without damaging it, a brass hammer should be used. A brass hammer can be used because brass will give when striking a harder object. Brass hammers are used when truing crankshafts.

When using hammers, note the following:

a. *Always* wear safety glasses when using a hammer.

b. Inspect hammers for damaged or broken parts. Repair or replace the hammer as required. Do *not* use a hammer with a taped handle.

c. Always wipe oil or grease off of the hammer *before* using it.

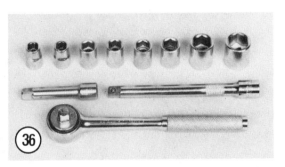

36

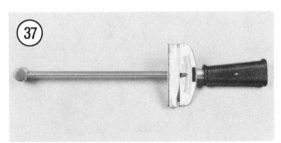

37

38

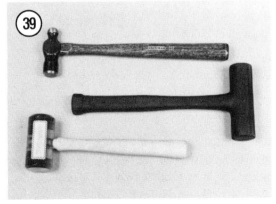

39

d. The head of the hammer should always strike the object squarely. Do not use the side of the hammer or the handle to strike an object.

e. Always use the correct hammer for the job.

Allen Wrenches

Allen wrenches (**Figure 40**) are available in sets or separately in a variety of sizes. These sets come in SAE and metric size, so be sure to buy a SAE set. Allen bolts are sometimes called socket bolts.

Harley-Davidson uses Allen bolts throughout the bike. Some times the bolts are difficult to reach and it is suggested that a variety of Allen wrenches be purchased (e.g. socket driven, T-handle and extension type) as shown in **Figure 40**.

Tap and Die Set

A complete tap and die set (**Figure 41**) is a relatively expensive tool. But when you need a tap or die to clean up a damaged thread, there is really no substitute. Be sure to purchase one for American Standard (SAE) threads when working on your Harley.

Tire Levers

When changing tires, use a good set of tire levers (**Figure 42**). Never use a screwdriver in place of a tire lever; refer to Chapter Ten for tire changing procedures using these tools. Before using the tire levers, check the working ends of the tool and remove any burrs. Don't use a tire lever for prying anything but tires. **Figure 42** shows a regular pair of 10 in. long tire levers. However, for better leverage when changing tires on your Harley, you may want to invest in a set of 16 in. long tire irons. These can be ordered through your dealer.

Bike Stand

Because Harley-Davidson motorcycles are not equipped with centerstands, you will need some safe means of raising your Harley's wheels off of the ground during many of the service procedures described in this manual. And when raising your Harley, you do not want to improvise a bike stand with available materials to just get you by. Consider the

physical damage that can occur if your bike falls onto a cement floor.

There are a number of accessory bike stands that can be used to raise and support your Harley safely during service. Most are designed for shop use only. The bike stand shown in **Figure 43** was made out of heavy duty pipe. Aftermarket stands are available that are both useful and innovative. Along with using it in your shop or garage, some stands can be folded into a compact size and packed with your other travel gear and taken along for emergency use on the road. When selecting a bike stand, make sure that it can be used on Harley-Davidson motorcycles. Al-

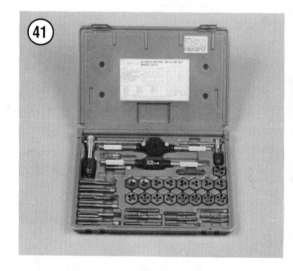

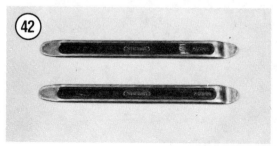

ways check the stability of the bike stand before walking away from the bike or when working it.

Drivers and Pullers

These tools are used to remove and install oil seals, bushings, bearings and gears. These will be

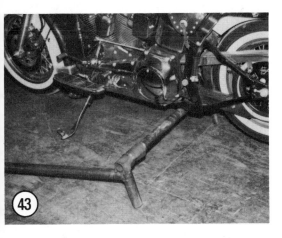

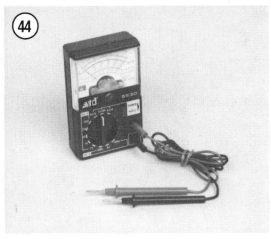

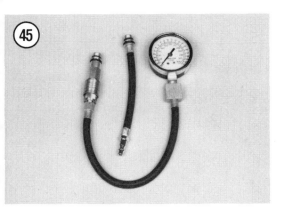

called out during service procedures in later chapters as required.

TEST EQUIPMENT

Multimeter or Volt-ohm Meter

This instrument (**Figure 44**) is invaluable for electrical system troubleshooting and service. A few of its functions may be duplicated by homemade test equipment, but for the serious mechanic it is a must. Its uses are described in the applicable section of the book.

Compression Gauge

An engine with low compression cannot be properly tuned and will not develop full power. A compression gauge measures engine compression. The one shown in **Figure 45** has a flexible stem with an extension that can allow you to hold it while cranking the engine over. Press-in rubber tipped types (**Figure 46**) are also available. Open the throttle all the way when checking engine compression. See Chapter Three.

Cylinder Leak Down Tester

By positioning a cylinder on its compression stroke so that both valves are closed and then pressurizing the cylinder, you can isolate engine problem areas (eg. leaking valve, damaged head gasket, broke, worn or stuck piston rings) by listening for escaping air through the carburetor, exhaust pipe,

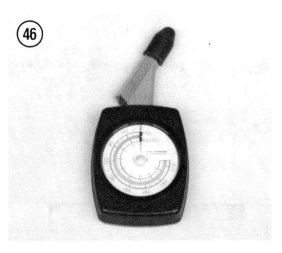

cylinder head mating surface, etc. To perform this procedure, a leak down tester and an air compressor are required. This procedure is described in Chapter Three as it pertains to the Harley Evolution engines. Cylinder leak down testers can be purchased through Harley-Davidson dealers, accessory tool manufacturers and automotive tool suppliers.

Battery Hydrometer

A hydrometer (**Figure 47**) is the best way to check a battery's state of charge. A hydrometer measures the weight or density of the sulfuric acid in the battery's electrolyte in specific gravity.

Portable Tachometer

A portable tachometer is necessary for tuning (**Figure 48**). Ignition timing and carburetor adjustments must be performed at specified engine speeds. The best instrument for this purpose is one with a low range of 0-1,000 or 0-2,000 rpm and a high range of 0-4,000. Extended range (0-6,000 or 0-8,000 rpm) instruments lack accuracy at lower speeds. The instrument should be capable of detecting 25 rpm on the low range.

Timing Light

Suitable timing lights range from inexpensive neon bulb types to powerful xenon strobe lights (**Figure 49**). A light with an inductive pickup is recommended to prevent any possible damage to ignition wiring.

PRECISION MEASURING TOOLS

Measurement is an important part of servicing your Harley. When performing many of the service

procedures in this manual, you will be required to make a number of measurements. These include basic checks such as engine compression and spark plug gap. As you become more involved with engine disassembly and service, measurements will be required to determine the condition of the piston and cylinder bore, crankshaft runout and so on. When

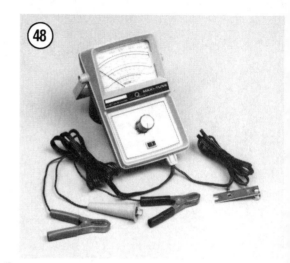

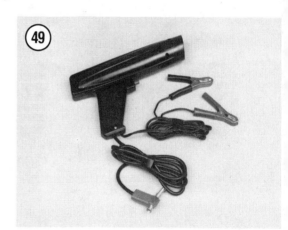

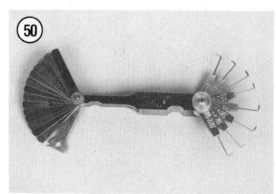

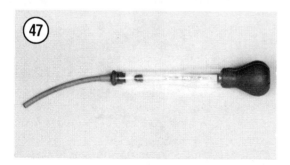

making these measurements, the degree of accuracy will dictate which tool is required. Precision measuring tools are expensive. If this is your first experience at engine service, it may be more worthwhile to have the checks made at a dealer. However, as your skills and enthusiasm increase for doing your own service work, you may want to begin purchasing some of these specialized tools. The following is a description of the measuring tools required during engine overhaul.

Feeler Gauge

The feeler gauge (**Figure 50**) is made of either a piece of a flat or round hardened steel of a specified thickness. Wire gauges are used to measure spark plug gap. Flat gauges are used for all other measurements.

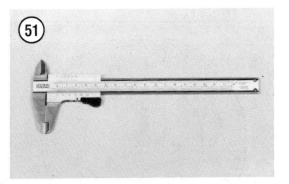

Vernier Caliper

This tool (**Figure 51**) is invaluable when it is necessary to measure inside, outside and depth measurements with close precision. It can be used to measure the thickness of shims and thrust washers. It is perhaps the most often used measuring tool in the motorcycle service shop. Vernier calipers are available in a wide assortment of styles and price ranges.

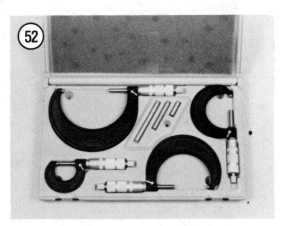

Outside Micrometers

The outside micrometer (**Figure 52**) is used for very exact measurements of close-tolerance components. It can be used to measure the outside diameter of a piston as well as for shims and thrust washers. Outside micrometers will be required to transfer measurements from bore, snap and small hole gauges. Micrometers can be purchased individually or in a set.

Dial Indicator

Dial indicators (**Figure 53**) are precision tools used to check crankshaft and drive shaft runout limits. For motorcycle repair, select a dial indicator with a continuous dial (**Figure 54**).

Cylinder Bore Gauge

The cylinder bore gauge is a very specialized precision tool. The gauge set shown in **Figure 55** is comprised of a dial indicator, handle and a number of length adapters to adapt the gauge to different bore sizes. The bore gauge can be used to make cylinder bore measurements such as bore size, taper and out-of-round. An outside micrometer must be used together with the bore gauge to determine bore dimensions.

Telescoping Gauges

Telescoping gauges (**Figure 56**) can be used to measure hole diameters from approximately 5/16 in. to 6 in. Like the small hole gauge, the telescoping gauge does not have a scale gauge for direct readings. Thus an outside micrometer is required to determine bore dimensions.

Small Hole Gauges

A set of small hole gauges (**Figure 57**) allows you to measure a hole, groove or slot ranging in size up to 1/2 in. An outside micrometer must be used together with the small hole gauge to determine bore dimensions.

Screw Pitch Gauge

A screw pitch gauge (**Figure 58**) determines the thread pitch of bolts, screws, studs, etc. The gauge is made up of a number of thin plates. Each plate has a thread shape cut on one edge to match one thread pitch. When using a screw pitch gauge to determine a thread pitch size, try to fit different blade sizes onto the bolt thread until both threads match.

Surface Plate

A surface plate can be used to check the flatness of parts or to provide a perfectly flat surface for minor resurfacing of cylinder head or other critical gasket surfaces. While industrial quality surface plates are quite expensive, the home mechanic can improvise. A thick metal plate can be put to use as a surface plate. The metal surface plate shown in **Figure 59** has a piece of sandpaper glued to its surface that is used for cleaning and smoothing cylinder head and crankcase mating surfaces.

> *NOTE*
> *Check with a local machine shop on the availability and cost of having a metal plate resurfaced for use as a surface plate.*

CLEANING SOLVENT

With the environmental concern that is prevalent today concerning the disposal of hazardous solvents, the home mechanic should select a water soluble, biodegradable solvent. These solvents can be purchased through dealers, automotive parts houses and large hardware stores.

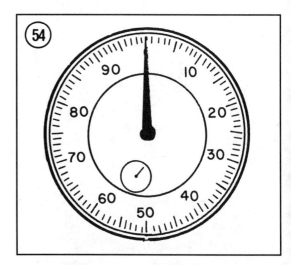

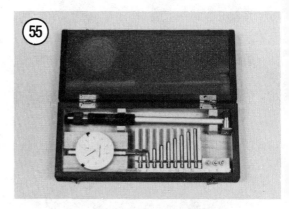

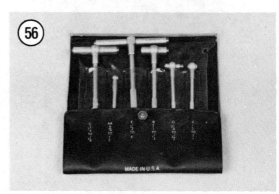

Selecting a solvent is only one of the problems facing the home mechanic when it comes to cleaning parts. You need some type of tank to clean parts as well as to store the solvent. There are a number of manufacturers offering different types and sizes of parts cleaning tanks. While a tank may seem a luxury to the home mechanic, you will find that it will quickly pay for itself through its efficiency and convenience. When selecting a parts washer, look for one that can recycle and store the solvent, as well as separate the sludge and contamination from the clean solvent. Most important, check the warranty, if any, as it pertains to the tank's pump. Like most tools, when purchasing a parts washer, you get what you pay for.

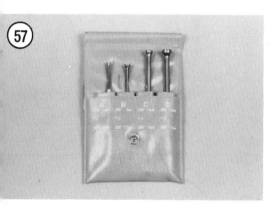

WARNING
Having a stack of clean shop rags on hand is important when performing engine work. However, to prevent the possibility of fire damage from spontaneous combustion from a pile of solvent soaked rags, store them in a lid sealed metal container until they can be washed or discarded.

NOTE
To avoid absorbing solvent and other chemicals into your skin while cleaning parts, wear a pair of petroleum-resistant rubber gloves. These can be purchased through industrial supply houses or well-equipped hardware stores.

OTHER SPECIAL TOOLS

A few other special tools may be required for major service. These are described in the appropriate chapters and are available from Harley-Davidson dealers or other manufacturers as indicated.

MECHANIC'S TIPS

Removing Frozen Nuts and Screws

When a fastener rusts and cannot be removed, several methods may be used to loosen it. First, apply penetrating oil such as Liquid Wrench or WD-40 (available at hardware or auto supply stores). Apply it liberally and let it penetrate for 10-15 minutes. Rap the fastener several times with a small hammer; do not hit it hard enough to cause damage. Reapply the penetrating oil if necessary.

For frozen screws, apply penetrating oil as described, then insert a screwdriver in the slot and rap the top of the screwdriver with a hammer. This loosens the rust so the screw can be removed in the normal way. If the screw head is too chewed up to use this method, grip the head with vise-grip pliers and twist the screw out.

Avoid applying heat unless specifically instructed, as it may melt, warp or remove the temper from parts.

Remedying Stripped Threads

Occasionally, threads are stripped through carelessness or impact damage. Often the threads can be cleaned up by running a tap (for internal threads on nuts) or die (for external threads on bolts) through the threads. See **Figure 60**. To clean or repair spark plug threads, a spark plug tap can be used.

If an internal thread is damaged, it may be necessary to install a Helicoil (**Figure 61**) or some other type of thread insert. These kits have all of the necessary parts to repair a damaged internal thread.

If it is necessary to drill and tap a hole, refer to **Table 7** for SAE tap drill sizes.

Removing Broken Screws or Bolts

When the head breaks off a screw or bolt, several methods are available for removing the remaining portion.

If a large portion of the remainder projects out, try gripping it with Vise-grip pliers. If the projecting portion is too small, file it to fit a wrench or cut a slot in it to fit a screwdriver. See **Figure 62**.

If the head breaks off flush, use a screw extractor. To do this, centerpunch the exact center of the remaining portion of the screw or bolt. Drill a small hole in the screw and tap the extractor into the hole. Back the screw out with a wrench on the extractor. See **Figure 63**.

Removing Broken or Damaged Studs

If a stud is broken or the threads severely damaged, perform the following. A tube of Loctite 271 (red), 2 nuts, 2 wrenches and a new stud will be required during this procedure (**Figure 64**).

NOTE
*The following steps describe general procedures for replacing a typical stud. However, if you are replacing cylinder studs, refer to **Cylinder Stud Replacement** in Chapter Four. Do **not** use the following steps to replace cylinder studs. The improper installation of cylinder studs can cause cylinder head leakage.*

1. Thread two nuts onto the damaged stud. Then tighten the 2 nuts against each other so that they are locked.

NOTE
If the threads on the damaged stud do not allow installation of the 2 nuts, you

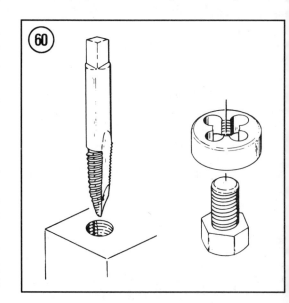

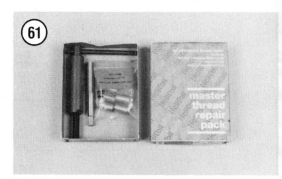

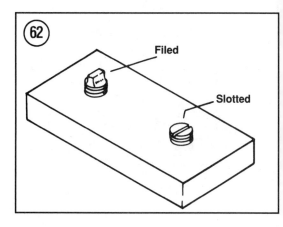

will have to remove the stud with a pair of Vise-grip pliers.

2. Turn the bottom nut counterclockwise and unscrew the stud.

3. Threaded holes with a bottom surface should be blown out with compressed air as dirt buildup in the bottom of the hole may prevent the stud from being torqued properly. If necessary, use a bottoming tap to true up the threads and to remove any deposits.

4. Install 2 nuts on the top half of the new stud as in Step 1. Make sure they are locked securely.

5. Coat the bottom half of a new stud with Loctite 271 (red).

6. Turn the top nut clockwise and thread the new stud securely.

7. Remove the nuts and repeat for each stud as required.

8. Follow Loctite's directions on cure time before assembling the component.

BALL BEARING REPLACEMENT

Ball bearings (**Figure 65**) are used throughout your Harley's engine and chassis to reduce power loss, heat and noise resulting from friction. Because ball bearings are precision made parts, they must be maintained by proper lubrication and maintenance. When a bearing is found to be damaged, it should be replaced immediately. However, when installing a new bearing, care should be taken to prevent damage to the new bearing. While bearing replacement is described in the individual chapters where applicable, the following can be used as a guideline.

NOTE
Unless otherwise specified, install bearings with the manufacturer's mark or number on the bearing facing outward.

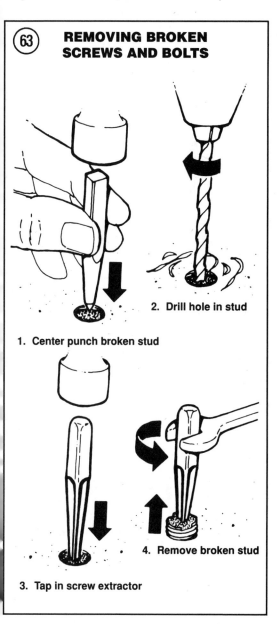

63 REMOVING BROKEN SCREWS AND BOLTS

2. Drill hole in stud

1. Center punch broken stud

3. Tap in screw extractor

4. Remove broken stud

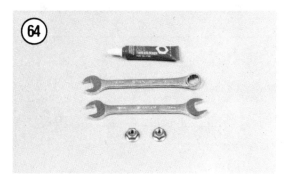

64

65

Bearing Removal

While bearings are normally removed only when damaged, there may be times when it is necessary to remove a bearing that is in good condition. Depending on the situation, you may be able to remove the bearing without damaging it. However, bearing removal in some situations, no matter how careful you are, will cause bearing damage. Care should always be given to bearings during their removal to prevent secondary damage to the shaft or housing. Note the following when removing bearings.

1. When using a puller to remove a bearing on a shaft, care must be taken so that shaft damage does not occur. Always place a piece of metal between the end of the shaft and the puller screw. In addition, place the puller arms next to the inner bearing race. See **Figure 66**.

2. When using a hammer to remove a bearing on a shaft, do not strike the hammer directly against the shaft. Instead, use a brass or aluminum spacer between the hammer and shaft (**Figure 67**). In addition, make sure to support *both* bearing races with wood blocks as shown in **Figure 67**.

3. The most ideal method of bearing removal is with a hydraulic press. However, certain procedures must be followed or damage may occur to the bearing, shaft or case half. Note the following when using a press:

    a. Always support the inner and outer bearing races with a suitable size wood or aluminum

spacer ring (**Figure 68**). If only the outer race is supported, the balls and/or the inner race will be damaged.

    b. Always make sure the press ram (**Figure 68**) aligns with the center of the shaft. If the ram is not centered, it may damage the bearing and/or shaft.

    c. The moment the shaft is free of the bearing, it will drop to the floor. Secure or hold the shaft to prevent it from falling.

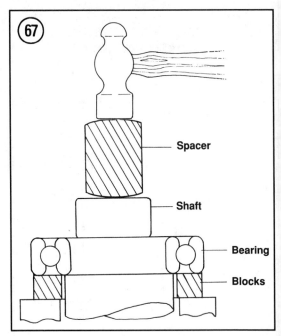

67

Spacer

Shaft

Bearing

Blocks

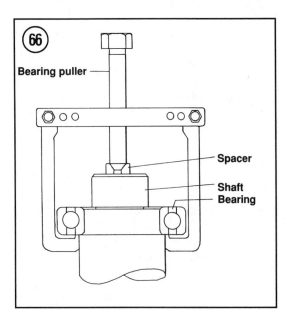

66

Bearing puller

Spacer

Shaft
Bearing

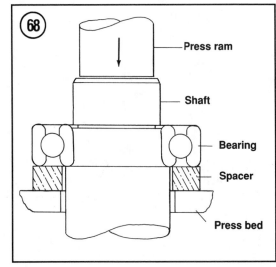

68

Press ram

Shaft

Bearing

Spacer

Press bed

Bearing Installation

1. When installing a bearing in a housing, pressure must be applied to the *outer* bearing race (**Figure** 69). When installing a bearing on a shaft, pressure must be applied to the *inner* bearing race (**Figure 70**).

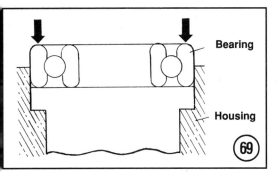

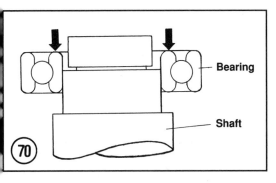

2. When installing a bearing as described in Step 1, some type of driver will be required. Never strike the bearing directly with a hammer or the bearing will be damaged. When installing a bearing, a piece of pipe or a socket with an outer diameter that matches the bearing race will be required. **Figure 71** shows the correct way to use a socket and hammer when installing a bearing over a shaft.

3. Step 1 describes how to install a bearing in a case half and over a shaft. However, when installing a bearing over a shaft and into a housing at the same time, a snug fit will be required for both outer and inner bearing races. In this situation, a spacer must be installed underneath the driver tool so that pressure is applied evenly across *both* races. See **Figure 72**. If the outer race is not supported as shown in **Figure 72**, the balls will push against the outer bearing track and damage it.

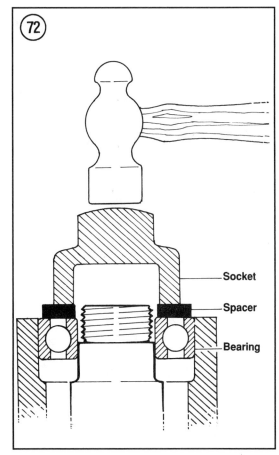

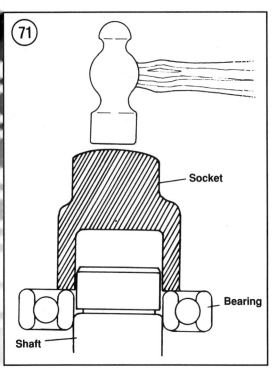

Shrink Fit

1. *Installing a bearing over a shaft*: When a tight fit is required, the bearing inside diameter will be smaller than the shaft. In this case, driving the bearing on the shaft using normal methods may cause bearing damage. Instead, the bearing should be heated before installation. Note the following:

   a. Secure the shaft so that it can be ready for bearing installation.
   b. Clean the bearing surface on the shaft of all residue. Remove burrs with a file or sandpaper.
   c. Fill a suitable pot or beaker with clean mineral oil. Place a thermometer (rated higher than 248° F) in the oil. Support the thermometer so that it does not rest on the bottom or side of the pot.
   d. Remove the bearing from its wrapper and secure it with a piece of heavy wire bent to hold it in the pot. Hang the bearing in the pot so that it does not touch the bottom or sides of the pot.
   e. Turn the heat on and monitor the thermometer. When the oil temperature rises to approximately 248° F, remove the bearing from the pot and quickly install it. If necessary, place a socket on the inner bearing race and tap the bearing into place. As the bearing chills, it will tighten on the shaft so you must work quickly when installing it. Make sure the bearing is installed all the way.

2. *Installing a bearing in a housing*: Bearings are generally installed in a housing with a slight interference fit. Driving the bearing into the housing using normal methods may damage the housing or cause bearing damage. Instead, the housing should be heated before the bearing is installed. Note the following:

> *CAUTION*
> *Before heating the crankcases in this procedure to remove the bearings, wash the cases thoroughly with detergent and water. Rinse and rewash the cases as required to remove all traces of oil and other chemical deposits.*

   a. The housing must be heated to a temperature of about 212° F in an oven or on a hot plate. An easy way to check to see that it is at the proper temperature is to drop tiny drops of water on the case as it heats; if they sizzle and evaporate immediately, the temperature is correct. Heat only one housing at a time.

> *CAUTION*
> *Do not heat the housing with a torch (propane or acetylene)—never bring a flame into contact with the bearing or housing. The direct heat will destroy the case hardening of the bearing and will likely warp the housing.*

   b. Remove the housing from the oven or hot plate and hold onto the housing with a kitchen pot holder, heavy gloves or heavy shop cloths—*it is hot.*

> *NOTE*
> *A suitable size socket and extension works well for removing and installing bearings.*

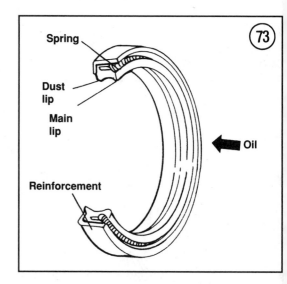

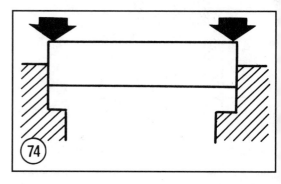

c. Hold the housing with the bearing side down and tap the bearing out. Repeat for all bearings in the housing.

d. While heating the housing halves, place the new bearings in a freezer if possible. Chilling them will slightly reduce their overall diameter while the hot housing assembly is slightly larger due to heat expansion. This will make installation much easier.

NOTE
Always install bearings with the manufacturer's mark or number facing outward.

e. While the housing is still hot, install the new bearing(s) into the housing. Install the bearings by hand, if possible. If necessary, lightly tap the bearing(s) into the housing with a socket placed on the outer bearing race. *Do not* install new bearings by driving on the inner bearing race. Install the bearing(s) until it seats completely.

OIL SEALS

Oil seals (**Figure 73**) are used to contain oil, water, grease or combustion gasses in a housing or shaft. Improper removal of a seal can damage the housing or shaft. Improper installation of the seal can damage the seal. Note the following:

a. Prying is generally the easiest and most effective method of removing a seal from a housing. However, always place a rag underneath the pry tool to prevent damage to the housing.

b. Grease should be packed in the seal lips before the seal is installed.

c. Oil seals should always be installed so that the manufacturer's numbers or marks face out.

d. Oil seals should be installed with a socket placed on the outside of the seal as shown in **Figure 74**. Make sure the seal is driven squarely into the housing. Never install a seal by hitting against the top of the seal with a hammer.

Table 1 MODEL IDENTIFICATION

1984	**1990**
FXST	FXST
1985	FXSTC (Custom)
FXST	FXSTS (Springer)
1986	FLST
FXST	FLSTC (Classic)
FXST (Custom)	FLSTF (Fat Boy)
1987	**1991**
FXST	FXSTC (Custom)
FXSTC (Custom)	FXSTS (Springer)
FLST	FLSTC (Classic)
1988	FLSTF (Fat Boy)
FXST	**1992**
FXSTC (Custom)	FXSTC (Custom)
FLST	FXSTS (Springer)
FLSTC (Classic)	FLSTC (Classic)
1989	FLSTF (Fat Boy)
FXST	**1993-on**
FXSTC (Custom)	FXSTC (Custom)
FXSTS (Springer)	FXSTS (Springer)
FLST	FLSTC (Classic)
FLSTC (Classic)	FLSTF (Fat Boy)
	FLSTN (Heritage Softail Special)

Table 2 GENERAL SPECIFICATIONS

Item	in.	mm
Wheel base		
1984-1992		
FXST (all)	66.30	1684
FLST/F & FLSTC	62.50	1587
1993-on		
FXSTC	66.50	1689
FLSTF/N	63.89	1623
FLSTC	63.90	1623
FXSTS	64.41	1636
Length		
1984-1992		
FXST (all)	94.30	2395
FLST/F & FLSTC	93.80	2382
1993-on		
FXSTC	94.92	2411
FLSTF/N	93.85	2384
FLSTC	94.02	2388
FXSTS	92.52	2350
Width		
1984-1992		
FXST (all)	29.00	736
FLST/F & FLSTC	38.00	965
1993-on		
FXSTC & FXSTS	29.00	736
FLSTF/N & FLSTC	38.00	965
Height		
1984-1992		
FXST (all)	47.00	1194
FLST/F	49.00	1245
FLSTC	59.40	1509
1993-on		
FXSTC & FXSTS	47.00	1194
FLST/F	49.00	1245
FLSTC	59.40	1509
	lbs.	kg.
Weight		
1984-1992		
1984 FXST	612	278
1985-on FXST/C	618	281
FXSTS	625	284
FLST/F	650	295
FLSTC	710	323
1993-on		
FXSTC	618	281
FLSTF/N	710	323
FLSTC	710	323
FXSTS	625	284

Table 3 GROSS VEHICLE WEIGHT RATINGS

Gross vehicle weight rating (GVWR)	1,085 lbs. (493 kg)
Gross axle weight ratings (GAWR)	
Front	390 lbs. (177 kg)
Rear	695 lbs. (316 kg)

*GVWR is the maximum allowable vehicle weight. This weight will include combined vehicle, rider(s) and accessory weight.

Table 4 FUEL TANK CAPACITY

	Total			Reserve		
	U. S. gal.	Liters	Imp. gal.	U. S. gal.	Liters	Imp. gal.
1984 FXST	5.0	18.9	4.2	1.2	4.5	1.0
1985-on						
FXSTC & FLSTN	5.2	19.7	4.3	1.2	4.5	1.0
FXSTS & FLSTC/F	4.2	15.9	3.5	0.75	2.8	0.6

Table 5 DECIMAL AND METRIC EQUIVALENTS

Fractions	Decimal in.	Metric mm	Fractions	Decimal in.	Metric mm
1/64	0.015625	0.39688	33/64	0.515625	13.09687
1/32	0.03125	0.79375	17/32	0.53125	13.49375
3/64	0.046875	1.19062	35/64	0.546875	13.89062
1/16	0.0625	1.58750	9/16	0.5625	14.28750
5/64	0.078125	1.98437	37/64	0.578125	14.68437
3/32	0.09375	2.38125	19/32	0.59375	15.08125
7/64	0.109375	2.77812	39/64	0.609375	15.47812
1/8	0.125	3.1750	5/8	0.625	15.87500
9/64	0.140625	3.57187	41/64	0.640625	16.27187
5/32	0.15625	3.96875	21/32	0.65625	16.66875
11/64	0.171875	4.36562	43/64	0.671875	17.06562
3/16	0.1875	4.76250	11/16	0.6875	17.46250
13/64	0.203125	5.15937	45/64	0.703125	17.85937
7/32	0.21875	5.55625	23/32	0.71875	18.25625
15/64	0.234375	5.95312	47/64	0.734375	18.65312
1/4	0.250	6.35000	3/4	0.750	19.05000
17/64	0.265625	6.74687	49/64	0.765625	19.44687
9/32	0.28125	7.14375	25/32	0.78125	19.84375
19/64	0.296875	7.54062	51/64	0.796875	20.24062
5/16	0.3125	7.93750	13/16	0.8125	20.63750
21/64	0.328125	8.33437	53/64	0.828125	21.03437
11/32	0.34375	8.73125	27/32	0.84375	21.43125
23/64	0.359375	9.12812	55/64	0.859375	22.82812
3/8	0.375	9.52500	7/8	0.875	22.22500
25/64	0.390625	9.92187	57/64	0.890625	22.62187
13/32	0.40625	10.31875	29/32	0.90625	23.01875
27/64	0.421875	10.71562	59/64	0.921875	23.41562
7/16	0.4375	11.11250	15/16	0.9375	23.81250
29/64	0.453125	11.50937	61/64	0.953125	24.20937
15/32	0.46875	11.90625	31/32	0.96875	24.60625
31/64	0.484375	12.30312	63/64	0.984375	25.00312
1/2	0.500	12.70000	1	1.00	25.40000

Table 6 GENERAL TORQUE SPECIFICATIONS*

Thread size	N·m	ft.-lb.
Bolt		
6 mm	6	4.5
8 mm	15	11
10 mm	30	22
12 mm	55	40
14 mm	85	61
16 mm	130	94
Nut		
10 mm	6	4.5
12 mm	15	11
14 mm	30	22
17 mm	55	40

Table 6 GENERAL TORQUE SPECIFICATIONS* (continued)

Thread size	N·m	ft.-lb.
Nut (continued)		
19 mm	85	61
22 mm	130	94

* Use these torque figures for all fasteners not individually listed.

Table 7 AMERICAN TAP DRILL SIZES

Tap thread	Drill size	Tap thread	Drill size
#0-80	3/64	1/4-28	No. 3
#1-64	No. 53	5/16-18	F
#1-72	No. 53	5/16-24	I
#2-56	No. 51	3/8-16	5/16
#2-64	No. 50	3/8-24	Q
#3-48	5/64	7/16-14	U
#3-56	No. 46	7/16-20	W
#4-40	No. 43	1/2-13	27/64
#4-48	No. 42	1/2-20	29/64
#5-40	No. 39	9/16-12	31/64
#5-44	No. 37	9/16-18	33/64
#6-32	No. 36	5/8-11	17/32
#6-40	No. 33	5/18-18	37/64
#8-32	No. 29	3/4-10	21/32
#8-36	No. 29	3/4-16	11/16
#10-24	No. 25	7/8-9	49-64
#10.32	No. 21	7/8-14	13/16
#12-24	No. 17	1-8	7/8
#12-28	No. 15	1-14	15/16
1/4-20	No. 8		

Table 8 WINDCHILL FACTOR

Estimated Wind Speed in MPH	Actual Thermometer Reading (° F)*											
	50	40	30	20	10	0	−10	−20	−30	−40	−50	−60
	Equivalent Temperature (° F)*											
Calm	50	40	30	20	10	0	−10	−20	−30	−40	−50	−60
5	48	37	27	16	6	−5	−15	−26	−36	−47	−57	−68
10	40	28	16	4	−9	−21	−33	−46	−58	−70	−83	−95
15	36	22	9	−5	−18	−36	−45	−58	−72	−85	−99	−112
20	32	18	4	−10	−25	−39	−53	−67	−82	−96	−110	−124
25	30	16	0	−15	−29	−44	−59	−74	−88	−104	−118	−133
30	28	13	−2	−18	−33	−48	−63	−79	−94	−109	−125	−140
35	27	11	−4	−20	−35	−49	−67	−82	−98	−113	−129	−145
40	26	10	−6	−21	−37	−53	−69	−85	−100	−116	−132	−148
**	Little Danger (for properly clothed person)				Increasing Danger			Great Danger				
						• Danger from freezing of exposed flesh •						

* To convert Fahrenheit (°F) to Celsius (°C), use the following formula: °C = 5/9 × (°F - 32).
** Wind speeds greater than 40 mph have little additional effect.

CHAPTER TWO

TROUBLESHOOTING

Every motorcycle engine requires an uninterrupted supply of fuel and air, proper ignition and adequate compression. If any of these are lacking, the engine will not run.

Diagnosing mechanical problems is relatively simple if you use orderly procedures and keep a few basic principles in mind.

The troubleshooting procedures in this chapter analyze typical symptoms and show logical methods of isolating causes. These are not the only methods. There may be several ways to solve a problem, but only a systematic approach can guarantee success.

Never assume anything. Do not overlook the obvious. If you are riding along and the bike suddenly quits, check the easiest, most accessible problem spots first. Is there gasoline in the tank? Has a spark plug wire fallen off?

If nothing obvious turns up in a quick check, look a little further. Learning to recognize and describe symptoms will make repairs easier for you or a mechanic at the shop. Describe problems accurately and fully. Saying "it won't run" isn't the same thing as saying "it quit at high speed and won't start," or "it sat in my garage for 3 months and then wouldn't start."

Gather as many symptoms as possible to aid in diagnosis. Note whether the engine lost power gradually or all at once. Remember that the more complicated a machine is, the easier it is to troubleshoot because symptoms point to specific problems.

After the symptoms are defined, areas which could cause problems are tested and analyzed. Guessing at the cause of a problem may provide the solution, but it can easily lead to frustration, wasted time and a series of expensive, unnecessary parts replacements.

You do not need fancy equipment or complicated test gear to determine whether repairs can be attempted at home. A few simple checks could save a large repair bill and lost time while the bike sits in a dealer's service department. On the other hand, be realistic and do not attempt repairs beyond your abilities. Service departments tend to charge heavily for putting together a disassembled engine that may have been abused. Some won't even take on such a job—so use common sense, don't get in over your head.

Table 1 (electrical specifications) is at the end of the chapter.

OPERATING REQUIREMENTS

An engine needs 3 basics to run properly: correct fuel/air mixture, compression and a spark at the correct time (**Figure 1**). If one or more are missing, the engine will not run. If all three engine basics are present, but one or more is not working properly, the engine may start, but it will not run properly.

The electrical system is the weakest link of the 3 basics. More problems result from electrical breakdowns than from any other source. Keep that in mind before you begin tampering with carburetor adjustments and the like.

If the machine has been sitting for any length of time and refuses to start, check and clean the spark plugs and then look to the gasoline delivery system. This includes the fuel tanks, fuel shutoff valve and fuel line to the carburetor. Gasoline deposits may have formed and gummed up the carburetor jets and air passages. Gasoline tends to lose its potency after standing for long periods. Condensation may contaminate the fuel with water. Drain the old fuel (fuel tanks, fuel lines and carburetor) and try starting with a fresh tankful.

TROUBLESHOOTING INSTRUMENTS

Chapter One lists the instruments needed and gives instruction on their use.

TESTING ELECTRICAL COMPONENTS

Most dealers and parts houses will not accept returns on electrical parts purchased from them. When testing electrical components, make sure that you perform the test procedures as described in this chapter and that your test equipment is working properly. If a test result shows that the component is defective but the reading is close to the service limit, have the component tested by a Harley-Davidson dealer to verify the test result before purchasing a new electrical component.

EMERGENCY TROUBLESHOOTING

When the bike is difficult to start, or won't start at all, it doesn't help to wear down the battery using the starter or your leg and foot on kickstart models. Check for obvious problems even before getting out your tools. Go down the following list step by step. If the bike still will not start, refer to the appropriate troubleshooting procedures which follow in this chapter. As described under *Operating Requirements*, the engine requires 3 basics before it will start

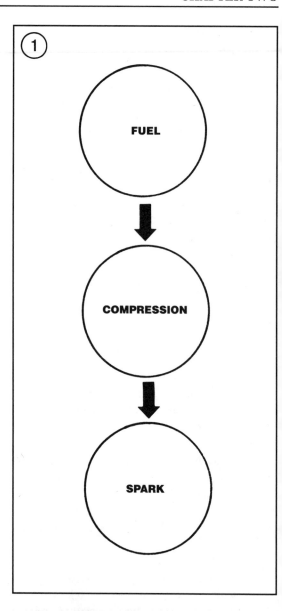

and run properly. The following procedure will illustrate steps for checking each of the 3 basic engine principles.

1. Visually inspect the bike for gas or oil leakage, loose wires or other abnormal conditions. If you did not find anything that could cause a starting problem, proceed with the following.

2. Make sure the engine STOP switch is not in the OFF position (**Figure 2**).

WARNING
*Do **not** use an open flame to check the tanks. A serious explosion is certain to result.*

3. Is there fuel in the tanks? Open the filler caps (**Figure 3**) and rock the bike. Listen for fuel sloshing around.

NOTE
If the engine has not been run for some time, gasoline deposits may have gummed up carburetor jets and air passages. In addition, gasoline tends to lose its potency after standing for long periods or you may find water in the tank. Drain the old gas and try starting with a fresh tankful.

4. Is the fuel supply valve (**Figure 4**) in the ON position? If the fuel level in the tanks is low, turn the valve to RESERVE to be sure you get the last remaining gas.

5. Is the choke (**Figure 5**) in the correct position? The choke knob should be pulled out when starting a cold engine and pushed in when restarting a warm or hot engine. If the choke does not seem to be operating correctly, adjust it as described in Chapter Three.

NOTE
The condition of your engine's spark plugs is a deciding factor in its performance and an important reference point during troubleshooting and general maintenance. To avoid mixups when removing the spark plugs in Step 6, make sure to identify each plug so that you know from which cylinder it came from.

6. After attempting to start the engine, immediately remove the spark plugs (**Figure 6**) and check their firing tips. Refer to Chapter Three for information on reading spark plugs. Fuel should be present on both plugs firing tips; this indicates that fuel is being pumped from the fuel tank to the engine. If there is no sign of fuel on the plugs, suspect a fuel delivery problem; refer to *Fuel System* in this chapter. If it appears that there is water on the plugs, water has probably entered the engine from contaminated fuel or there is water in the crankcase.

7. Perform a spark test as described under *Engine Fails to Start (Spark Test)* in this chapter. If there is a strong spark, perform Step 8.

8. Check cylinder compression as follows:

   a. Turn the fuel valve OFF.

   b. Remove and ground the spark plugs against the cylinder head. The spark plugs must be grounded when performing the following steps or the ignition system will be permanently damaged.

WARNING
When grounding the spark plugs, make sure the plugs are placed away from the spark plug holes in the cylinder head. Because you will be placing your fingers over the cylinder head spark plug holes, you could be shocked if you accidentally touch a plug while cranking the engine.

   c. Put your finger over one of the spark plug holes.

   d. Crank the engine with the starter button. Rising pressure in the cylinder should force your finger off of the spark plug hole. This indicates that the cylinder probably has sufficient cylinder compression to start the engine.

   e. Repeat for the opposite cylinder.

   f. Lack of cylinder compression indicates a problem with that cylinder. This could be worn or damaged piston rings or valve(s). Refer to *Engine* in this chapter.

NOTE
Engine compression can be checked more accurately with a compression gauge as described in Chapter Three.

   g. Reinstall the spark plugs.

Engine Fails to Start (Spark Test)

Perform the following spark test to determine if the ignition system is operating properly.

1. Remove the spark plugs.

2. Connect the spark plug wire and connector to the spark plug and touch the spark plug base to a good ground like the engine cylinder head. Position the spark plug so you can see the electrodes. See **Figure 7**. Repeat for the other spark plug.

3. Crank the engine over with the starter. A fat blue spark should be evident across the spark plug electrodes.

WARNING
Do not hold the spark plug, wire or connector or a serious electrical shock may result. If necessary, use a pair of insulated pliers to hold the spark plug or wire. The high voltage generated by the ignition system could produce serious or fatal shocks.

4. If the spark is good, check for one or more of the following possible malfunctions:

   a. Obstructed fuel line or fuel filter.

   b. Leaking head gasket(s).

   c. Low compression.

5. If the spark is not good, check for one or more of the following:

   a. Loose electrical connections.

   b. Dirty electrical connections.

   c. Loose or broken ignition coil ground wire.

   d. Broken or shorted high tension lead to the spark plug.

   e. Discharged battery.

f. Disconnected or damaged battery connection.

g. Damaged ignition system component.

Engine is Difficult to Start

Check for one or more of the following possible malfunctions:

a. Fouled spark plug(s).

b. Improperly adjusted choke.

c. Intake manifold air leak (**Figure 8**).

d. Contaminated fuel system.

e. Improperly adjusted carburetor.

f. Weak ignition unit.

g. Weak ignition coil(s).

h. Poor compression.

i. Engine oil too heavy.

Engine Will Not Crank

Check for one or more of the following possible malfunctions:

a. Discharged battery.

b. Defective starter motor.

c. Seized piston(s).

d. Seized crankshaft bearings.

e. Broken connecting rod.

ENGINE PERFORMANCE

In the following check list, it is assumed that the engine runs, but is not operating at peak performance. This will serve as a starting point from which to isolate a performance malfunction.

Engine is Difficult to Start

a. Carburetor incorrectly adjusted.

b. Fouled or improperly gapped spark plug(s).

c. Leaking head gasket(s).

d. Obstructed fuel line or fuel shutoff valve.

e. Obstructed fuel filter.

f. Battery nearly discharged.

g. Loose battery connection.

h. Incorrect ignition timing.

i. Faulty ignition components.

j. Choke stuck open.

k. Sticking valves.

l. Faulty vacuum operated electric switch (VOES).

m. Plugged fuel tank vent hose.

n. Plugged vapor valve (if so equipped).

Engine Runs but Misses

a. Fouled or improperly gapped spark plugs.

b. Improper carburetor main jet selection.

c. Incorrect ignition timing.

d. Faulty ignition components.

e. Obstructed fuel line or fuel shutoff valve.

f. Obstructed fuel filter.

g. Clogged carburetor jets.

h. Battery nearly discharged.

i. Loose battery connection.

j. Short circuit due to damaged wiring or insulation.

k. Water in fuel.

l. Weak or damaged valve springs.

m. Damaged valve(s).

n. Dirty electrical connections.

o. Faulty vacuum operated electric switch (VOES).

Engine Overheating

a. Incorrect carburetor adjustment or jet selection.

b. Ignition timing retarded. This could be due to improper adjustment or defective ignition component(s).

c. Faulty vacuum operated electric switch (VOES).

d. Improper spark plug heat range.

e. Damaged or blocked cooling fins.

f. Oil level low.

g. Oil not circulating properly.

h. Valves leaking.

i. Heavy engine carbon deposit.

Smoky Exhaust and Engine Runs Roughly

a. Clogged air filter element.

b. Carburetor adjustment incorrect—mixture too rich.

c. Choke not operating correctly.

d. Water or other contaminants in fuel.

e. Clogged fuel line.

f. Spark plugs fouled.

g. Ignition coil defective.

h. Ignition module or sensor defective.

i. Loose or defective ignition circuit wire.

j. Short circuit from damaged wire insulation.

k. Loose battery cable connection.

l. Cam timing incorrect.

m. Intake manifold or air cleaner air leak.

Engine Loses Power

a. Carburetor incorrectly adjusted.

b. Engine overheating.

c. Ignition timing incorrect due to faulty ignition component(s).

d. Incorrectly gapped spark plugs.

e. Obstructed muffler.

f. Dragging brake(s).

Engine Lacks Acceleration

a. Carburetor mixture too lean.

b. Clogged fuel line.

c. Ignition timing incorrect due to faulty ignition component(s).

d. Dragging brake(s).

Front or Rear Cylinder Spark Plug Fouls Consistently

a. Worn valve guide(s).

b. Damaged valve guide(s).

c. Worn or damaged valve guide oil seal(s).

d. Worn piston rings.

e. Damaged piston rings.

f. Incorrect spark plug heat range.

g. Incorrect fuel mixture.

h. Incorrect enrichener (choke) operation.

STARTING SYSTEM

The starting system consists of the battery, starter motor, starter relay, solenoid, start switch, starter mechanism and related wiring.

When the ignition switch is turned on and the start button pushed in, current is transmitted from the battery to the starter relay. When the relay is activated, it in turn activates the starter solenoid which mechanically engages the starter with the engine.

Starting system problems are relatively easy to find. In most cases, the trouble is a loose or corroded electrical connection.

Troubleshooting Preparation

Before troubleshooting the starting system, make sure that:

a. The battery is fully charged.

b. Battery cables are proper size and length. Replace cables that are damaged, severely corroded or undersize.

c. All electrical connections are clean and tight.

d. The wiring harness is in good condition, with no worn or frayed insulation or loose harness sockets.

e. The fuel tank is filled with an adequate supply of fresh gasoline.

f. The spark plugs are in good condition and properly gapped.

g. The ignition system is correctly timed and adjusted.

Troubleshooting is intended only to isolate a malfunction to a certain component. If further bench testing is required, remove the suspect component and test it further.

Troubleshooting (1984-1988)

Perform the steps listed under *Troubleshooting Preparation*. When making the following voltage checks, test results must be within 1/2 volt of battery voltage.

> *CAUTION*
> *Never operate the starter motor for more than 30 seconds at a time. Allow the starter to cool for approximately 2 minutes before reusing it. Failing to allow the starter motor to cool after continuous starting attempts can damage the starter.*

1984 and late 1985-1988 models

When making the following voltage tests, you will be isolating individual components to check voltage flow into a component (input side) and then checking voltage through the component (output side).

1. Turn on the ignition switch and depress the start button. If the solenoid and relay do not click, perform Step 2. If only the solenoid clicks, perform Step 3. If only the relay clicks, perform Step 4.

2. If the solenoid and relay did not click when performing Step 1, perform the following checks. When making the following checks, first connect the black voltmeter lead to a good ground, then connect the red voltmeter lead to the point in the circuit described in each of the following tests. When both voltmeter leads are connected, turn the ignition switch ON and depress the start button while observing the voltmeter scale. Turn the ignition switch OFF and disconnect the voltmeter after making the test. Refer to **Figure 9** for typical starter relay terminal contact numbers.

   a. Connect the black voltmeter lead across the No. 85 starter relay terminal (ground). Then connect the red voltmeter lead across the No. 86 starter relay terminal. If the voltage reading is low, check for loose or damaged wiring at the starter relay and start switch. If battery voltage is indicated, the starter relay is defective. Confirm by bench testing the starter relay as described in this chapter.

   b. Connect the black voltmeter lead to ground, then connect the red voltmeter lead separately across the start switch input and output sides; battery voltage should be shown during each test. Low input voltage indicates a damaged

stop switch. Low output voltage indicates a damaged start switch.

   c. Connect the black voltmeter lead to ground, then check input and output voltage at the stop switch; battery voltage should be shown during each test. Low input voltage indicates damaged or faulty wiring to the ignition switch. Low output voltage indicates a faulty stop switch.

   d. Connect the black voltmeter lead to ground, then connect the red voltmeter lead to the ignition circuit breaker input side (copper stud). Repeat to check voltage on circuit breaker output side. Battery voltage should be shown when making each test. If the input voltage is low, there is a problem in the wiring from the ignition switch and circuit breaker. If the output voltage is low, the ignition circuit breaker is faulty.

   e. Connect the black voltmeter lead to ground, then connect the red voltmeter lead to the main circuit breaker input side (copper stud). Repeat to check voltage on output side. Battery voltage should be shown when making each test. If the input voltage is low, there is a problem in the wiring from the main circuit breaker to the battery. If the output voltage is low, the main circuit breaker is faulty.

   f. Connect the black voltmeter lead to ground, then connect the red lead to the ignition terminal on the ignition switch. If the reading is low, the ignition switch is damaged.

   g. Connect the black voltmeter lead to the battery terminal on the ignition switch. If the voltage is low, there is a problem in the wiring from the main circuit to the switch.

3. If only the solenoid clicked when performing Step 1, perform the following checks. When making the following checks, first connect the black voltmeter lead to a good ground, then connect the red voltmeter lead to the point in the circuit described in each of the following tests. When both voltmeter leads are connected, turn the ignition switch ON and depress the start button while observing the voltmeter scale. Turn the ignition switch OFF and disconnect the voltmeter after making the test.

   a. Connect the black voltmeter lead to ground, then connect the red lead to the starter wire at the starter; battery voltage should be indi-

9   **STARTER RELAY INTERNAL WIRING (1984-1988 EXCEPT EARLY 1985)**

87

85   86

87A

30

cated. If the reading is low, there is a problem in the wiring from the solenoid to the starter.

b. Connect the black voltmeter lead to ground, then connect the red lead to the *long* solenoid terminal; battery voltage should be indicated. If reading is low, there is a problem in the wiring from the battery to the solenoid.

c. Connect the black voltmeter lead to ground, then connect the red lead to the *short* solenoid terminal; battery voltage should be indicated. If reading is low, the solenoid is damaged or there is a problem in the starter drive system.

4. If only the starter relay clicked when performing Step 1, perform the following checks. When making the following checks, first connect the black voltmeter lead to a good ground, then connect the red voltmeter lead to the point in the circuit described in each of the following tests. When both voltmeter leads are connected, turn the ignition switch ON and depress the start button while observing the voltmeter scale. Turn the ignition switch OFF and disconnect the voltmeter after making the test.

a. Connect the black voltmeter lead to ground, then connect the red lead to the starter relay No. 30 terminal; meter should read battery voltage. If reading is low, there is a problem in the main circuit breaker wiring.

b. Connect the black voltmeter lead to ground, then connect the red lead to the starter relay No. 87 terminal; meter should show battery voltage. A low reading indicates a damaged starter relay. Confirm by bench testing the starter relay as described in this chapter.

c. Connect the black voltmeter to ground, then connect the read lead to the center solenoid terminal; meter should show battery voltage. If the reading is low, there is a problem in the wiring between the solenoid and starter relay.

Early 1985 models

When making the following voltage tests, you will be isolating individual components to check voltage flow into a component (input side) and then checking voltage through the component (output side).

1. Turn on the ignition switch and depress the start button. If the solenoid and relay do not click, perform Step 2. If only the solenoid clicks, perform Step 3. If only the relay clicks, perform Step 4.

2. If the solenoid and relay did not click when performing Step 1, perform the following checks. When making the following checks, first connect the black voltmeter lead to a good ground, then connect the red voltmeter lead to the point in the circuit described in each of the following tests. When both voltmeter leads are connected, turn the ignition switch ON and depress the start button while observing the voltmeter scale. Turn the ignition switch OFF and disconnect the voltmeter after making the test. Refer to **Figure 10** for starter relay test points.

a. Connect the black voltmeter lead across the starter relay base (ground) and the red lead across the small starter relay terminal; note voltmeter reading. A low reading indicates a problem in the wiring at the relay base (ground), small terminal or at the start switch. If battery voltage is indicated, the starter relay is defective. Confirm by bench testing the starter relay as described in this chapter.

b. Connect the black voltmeter lead to ground, then connect the red voltmeter lead separately across the start switch input and output sides; battery voltage should be shown during each test. Low input voltage indicates a damaged stop switch. Low output voltage indicates a damaged start switch.

c. Connect the black voltmeter lead to ground, then check input and output voltage at the stop switch; battery voltage should be shown during each test. Low input voltage indicates damaged or faulty wiring to the ignition

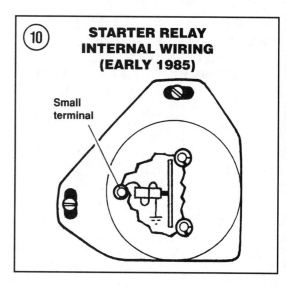

10 **STARTER RELAY INTERNAL WIRING (EARLY 1985)**

Small terminal

switch. Low output voltage indicates a faulty stop switch.

d. Connect the black voltmeter lead to ground, then connect the red voltmeter lead to the ignition circuit breaker input side (copper stud). Repeat to check voltage on circuit breaker output side. Battery voltage should be shown when making each test. If the input voltage is low, there is a problem in the wiring from the ignition switch and circuit breaker. If the output voltage is low, the ignition circuit breaker is faulty.

e. Connect the black voltmeter lead to ground, then connect the red voltmeter lead to the main circuit breaker input side (copper stud). Repeat to check voltage on output side. Battery voltage should be shown when making each test. If the input voltage is low, there is a problem in the wiring from the main circuit breaker to the battery. If the output voltage is low, the main circuit breaker is faulty.

f. Connect the black voltmeter lead to ground, then connect the red lead to the ignition terminal on the ignition switch. If the reading is low, the ignition switch is damaged.

g. Connect the black voltmeter lead to the battery terminal on the ignition switch. If the voltage is low, there is a problem in the wiring from the main circuit to the switch.

3. If only the solenoid clicked when performing Step 1, perform the following checks. When making the following checks, first connect the black voltmeter lead to a good ground, then connect the red voltmeter lead to the point in the circuit described in each of the following tests. When both voltmeter leads are connected, turn the ignition switch ON and depress the start button while observing the voltmeter scale. Turn the ignition switch OFF and disconnect the voltmeter after making the test.

a. Connect the black voltmeter lead to ground, then connect the red lead to the starter wire at the starter; battery voltage should be indicated. If the reading is low, there is a problem in the wiring from the solenoid to the starter.

b. Connect the black voltmeter lead to ground, then connect the red lead to the short/large solenoid terminal; battery voltage should be indicated. If reading is low, the solenoid may be damaged. Confirm by bench testing the solenoid as described in this chapter. If the

solenoid tests okay, check the starter drive system for damage.

4. If only the starter relay clicked when performing Step 1, perform the following tests. During testing, first connect the black voltmeter lead to a good ground, then connect the red voltmeter lead to the point in the circuit described in each of the following tests. When both voltmeter leads are connected, turn the ignition switch ON and depress the start button while observing the voltmeter scale. Turn the ignition switch OFF and disconnect the voltmeter after making the test.

a. Connect the black voltmeter lead to ground, then connect the red lead to the starter relay battery terminal; meter should show battery voltage. A low reading indicates a problem in the wiring between the starter relay and battery.

b. Connect the black voltmeter lead to ground, then connect the red lead to the starter relay-to-solenoid terminal at the starter relay. If battery voltage is not recorded, suspect a faulty starter relay.

c. Connect the black voltmeter lead to ground, then connect the red lead to the long/large solenoid terminal. Low battery voltage indicates a problem in the wiring from the solenoid to the starter relay.

d. Connect the black voltmeter lead to ground, then connect the red lead to the small solenoid terminal. A low voltage reading indicates a problem between the jumper wire at the solenoid.

Troubleshooting
(1989-on)

The basic starter-related troubles are:

a. Engine cranks very slowly or not at all.

b. Starter spins but does not crank engine.

c. Starter will not disengage when start button is released.

d. Loud grinding noises when starter runs.

Perform the steps listed under *Troubleshooting Preparation*. When making the following voltage checks, test results must be within 1/2 volt of battery voltage.

CAUTION
Never operate the starter motor for more than 30 seconds at a time. Allow the starter to cool for approximately 2 minutes before reusing it. Failing to allow the starter motor to cool after continuous starting attempts can damage the starter.

Engine cranks very slowly or not at all

1. If the starter does not work, check the intensity of the headlight with the ignition switch turned on. If the headlight dims or does not come on at all, the battery or connecting wires are most likely at fault. Check the battery with a hydrometer as described in Chapter Nine. Check wiring for breaks, shorts and dirty connections. If the battery is okay, check the starter connections at the battery, solenoid and start switch. Check continuity between the battery and ignition switch with an ohmmeter.

2. If the headlight is bright but dims or goes out when the start button is pressed, check for a corroded or loose connection at the battery. Wiggle the battery terminals and recheck. If the starter turns over, you've found the problem. Clean and/or replace corroded or damaged cables as required.

3. If the headlight remains bright or dims only slightly when cranking, the trouble may be in the starter, solenoid or wiring. Check the start switch, engine stop switch, starter relay and the solenoid. Check each switch by bypassing it with a jumper wire. If the starter spins, check the solenoid and wiring to the ignition switch.

4. If the headlight dims severely when the start button is pressed, the battery is nearly dead or the starter is shorted to ground.

Starter spins but does not crank engine

1. Remove the starter. See Chapter Nine.

2. Check the starter pinion gear. If the teeth are chipped or worn, inspect the clutch flywheel ring gear for the same problems.

3. If the pinion gear and overrunning clutch are in good condition, disassemble the starter and check the armature shaft for corrosion. See Chapter Nine.

4. If there is no corrosion, suspect a damaged overrunning clutch assembly:

   a. The overrunning clutch rollers and/or compression spring is damaged.

   b. The overrunning clutch, idler gear and solenoid gear teeth are damaged.

   c. Pinion gear shaft does not slide smoothly during engagement.

   d. The overrunning clutch assembly fails to operate after the engine has started.

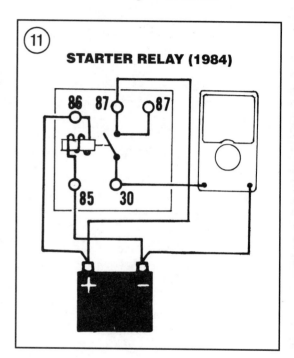

STARTER RELAY (1984)

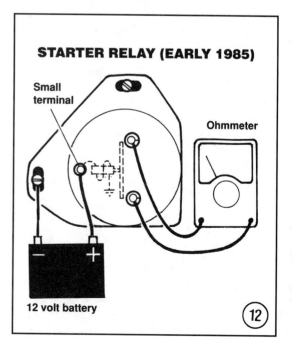

STARTER RELAY (EARLY 1985)

Starter will not disengage when start button is released

1. A sticking solenoid can cause this problem, which may be due to a worn solenoid return spring or other internal damage. If the solenoid is damaged, it must be replaced as a unit.

2. On high-mileage models, the pinion gear can jam on a worn clutch ring gear. Unable to return, the starter will continue to run. This condition usually requires ring gear replacement.

3. Check the start switch and starter relay for internal damage.

Loud grinding noises when starter runs

This can be caused by improper meshing of the starter pinion and clutch ring gear or by a broken overrunning clutch mechanism. Remove and inspect the starter as described in Chapter Nine.

Component Testing

This section describes testing of individual starting system components. Refer to Chapter Nine for starter service.

Starter Relay Testing (All Models)

You can check starter relay operation with an ohmmeter, jumper wires and a fully charged 12-volt battery.

1. Disconnect and remove the starter relay from the starting circuit on the bike.

2. Connect an ohmmeter and 12-volt battery between the relay terminals as shown in **Figure 11** (1984), **Figure 12** (early 1985), **Figure 13** (late 1985-1988) or **Figure 14** (1989-on). This setup will engerize the relay for testing.

> *CAUTION*
> *On 1991-on models, the No. 85 terminal must be connected to the negative battery terminal as shown in* **Figure 14***. Otherwise, the diode connected across the relay winding will be damged.*

3. Check for continuity through the relay contacts with the ohmmeter while the relay coil is energized. The ohmmeter should read 1 ohm or less (continuity). If there is no continuity, replace the relay.

Starter Current Draw Test

This test will determine whether current is flowing in the starter circuit, and whether the current flow is excessive because of a short in the circuit or from a mechanical problem in the starter drive mechanism. An induction ammeter will be required for this test. Current draw specifications are listed in **Table 1**.

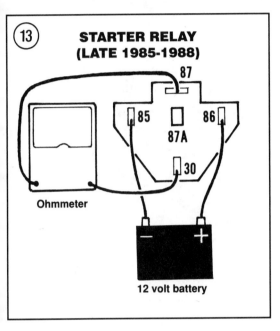

(13) **STARTER RELAY (LATE 1985-1988)**

87
85   87A   86
30
Ohmmeter
12 volt battery

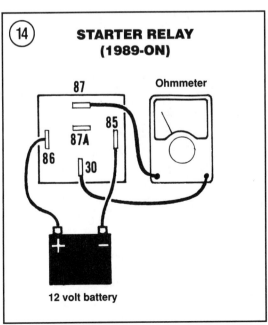

(14) **STARTER RELAY (1989-ON)**

87   Ohmmeter
85
87A
86   30
12 volt battery

NOTE
The battery should be fully charged when performing the following test.

1. Shift the transmission into NEUTRAL.

2. Disconnect the 2 spark plug caps at the spark plugs. Then ground the plug caps with 2 spark plugs. Do not remove the spark plugs in the cylinder heads.

3. Connect a jumper cable to the battery terminal and then to the ammeter lead. Connect a second jumper cable to the short heavy solenoid stud, then connect the cable to the ammeter. See **Figure 15** (1984-1988) or **Figure 16** (1989-on).

4. Turn the ignition switch ON and press the start button for approximately 10 seconds. Note the ammeter reading.

NOTE
Initially, the current draw will be very high when the start button is first pressed, then it will drop and hold at a lower level. This second level or reading is the one you should refer to during this test.

5. If the current draw exceeds the specified current draw rating listed in **Table 1**, suspect a faulty starter or starter drive mechanism. Remove and service these components as described in Chapter Nine.

6. Disconnect the ammeter and the 2 jumper cables.

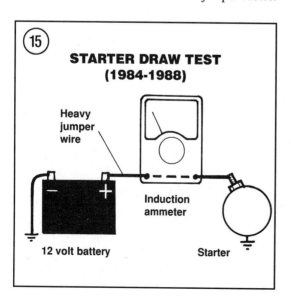

**Solenoid Testing
(1984-1988)**

The solenoid can be tested while mounted on the motorcycle. The solenoid terminals are identified in **Figures 17-19**. An ohmmeter will be required to perform the following tests.

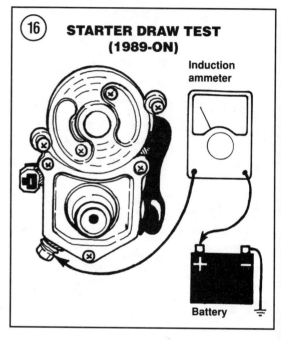

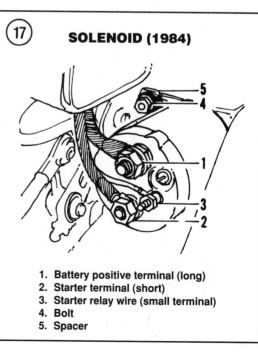

1. Disconnect the negative battery cable.

2. Locate the solenoid on your bike. Then label and disconnect all of the cables at the solenoid. See **Figure 17**, **Figure 18** or **Figure 19**.

> *NOTE*
> *The ohmmeter should be set on the R ×
> 1 scale when performing the following
> tests. In addition, make sure to calibrate
> the meter by crossing the test leads and
> adjusting the meter needle until it reads
> zero.*

3. Connect an ohmmeter between the 2 large coil terminals (**Figure 20**). There should be continuity (no measurable resistance).

4. *Pull-in coil test*: Connect an ohmmeter between the small and the short/large terminal on the solenoid (**Figure 21**). There should be continuity (no measurable resistance).

5. *Hold-in coil test*: Connect one ohmmeter lead to the small diameter solenoid terminal. Then touch the opposite lead next to the solenoid body (**Figure 22**). There should be continuity (no measurable resistance).

6. Replace the solenoid if it failed any one test in Steps 3-5.

7. Reverse Steps 1 and 2 after testing or replacing the solenoid.

**Solenoid Testing
(1989-on)**

A fully charged 12-volt battery and 4 jumper wires will be required to make the following tests.

1. Remove the starter motor as described in Chapter Nine. The solenoid must be installed on the starter during the following tests. Do not remove it.

2. Disconnect the "C" wire terminal at the starter motor (**Figure 23**) before performing the following tests.

> *CAUTION*
> *Because battery voltage will be applied
> directly to the solenoid and starter in the
> following tests, do not leave the jumper*

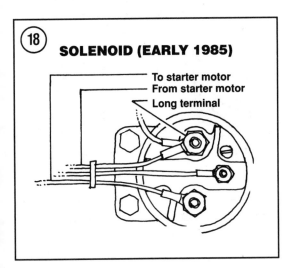

(18) **SOLENOID (EARLY 1985)**

To starter motor
From starter motor
Long terminal

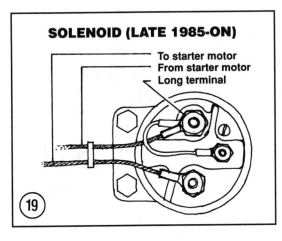

SOLENOID (LATE 1985-ON)

To starter motor
From starter motor
Long terminal

(19)

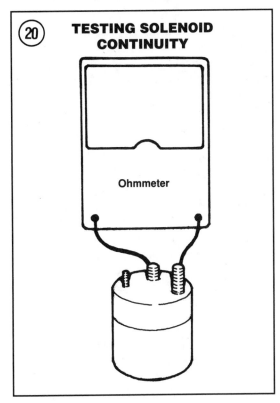

(20) **TESTING SOLENOID CONTINUITY**

Ohmmeter

cables connected to the solenoid for more than 3-5 seconds. Failure to observe this caution can cause solenoid damage.

3. Connect a battery to the starter motor as shown in **Figure 23**. The starter shaft should *pull* into the housing. Then disconnect the jumper wire at the "C" starter terminal (**Figure 24**). The starter shaft should *remain* in the housing. Quickly reconnect the jumper wire at the "C" starter terminal and disconnect the jumper wire at the "50" starter terminal (**Figure 25**); the starter shaft should *return* to its original position. Disconnect the jumper wires from the starter and solenoid.

4. Replace the solenoid if the starter shaft failed to operate properly as described in Step 3.

Free Running Current Draw Test (1989-on)

A fully charged 12-volt battery, induction ammeter, 14 gauge jumper cable and 3 heavy jumper cables (6 guage minimum) will be required to make the following tests.

1. Remove the starter motor as described in Chapter Nine. The solenoid must be installed on the starter during the following test. Do not remove it.

2. Mount the starter motor in a vise with soft jaws.

3. Connect a heavy jumper cable between the positive battery terminal and the induction ammeter (**Figure 26**).

4. Connect a heavy jumper cable between the positive battery terminal and the induction ammeter (**Figure 26**).

5. Connect another cable between the induction ammeter and the "M" terminal on the starter solenoid (**Figure 26**).

6. Connect a 14 gauge jumper cable between the positive battery terminal and the solenoid "50" terminal.

7. Read the current indicated on the ammeter. Ammeter should read 90 amps maximum. If current reading exceeds 90 amps, disassemble starter as described in Chapter Nine. Check for severely worn or damaged parts.

CHARGING SYSTEM

The charging system consists of the battery, alternator and a solid state rectifier/voltage regulator.

The alternator generates an alternating current (AC) which the rectifier converts to direct current (DC). The regulator maintains the voltage to the battery and load (lights, ignition, etc.) at a constant

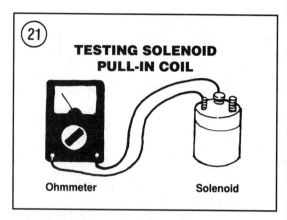

TESTING SOLENOID PULL-IN COIL

Ohmmeter   Solenoid

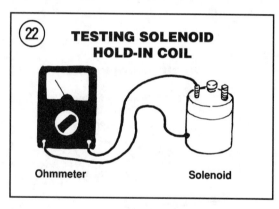

TESTING SOLENOID HOLD-IN COIL

Ohmmeter   Solenoid

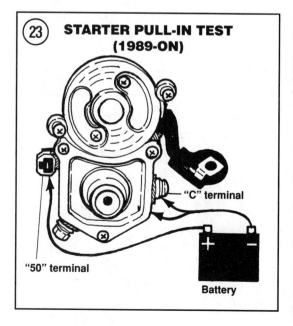

STARTER PULL-IN TEST (1989-ON)

"C" terminal

"50" terminal

Battery

voltage regardless of variations in engine speed and load.

A malfunction in the charging system generally causes the battery to remain undercharged.

Service Precautions

Before servicing the charging system, observe the following precautions to prevent damage to any charging system component.

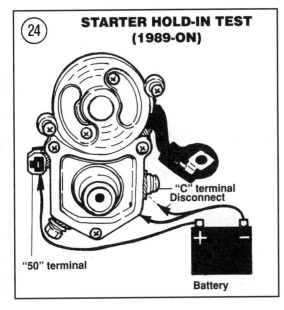

STARTER HOLD-IN TEST (1989-ON)
(24)
"C" terminal Disconnect
"50" terminal
Battery

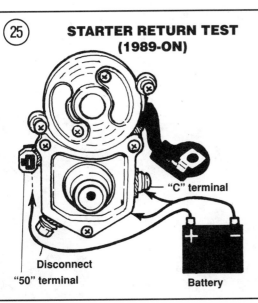

STARTER RETURN TEST (1989-ON)
(25)
"C" terminal
Disconnect
"50" terminal
Battery

1. Never reverse battery connections. Instantaneous damage may occur.
2. Do not short across any connection.
3. Never attempt to polarize an alternator.
4. Never start the engine with the alternator disconnected from the voltage regulator/rectifier, unless instructed to do so in testing.
5. Never start or run the engine with the battery disconnected.
6. Never attempt to use a high-output battery charger to assist in engine starting.
7. Before charging battery, remove it from the motorcycle.
8. Never disconnect the voltage regulator connector with the engine running.
9. Do not mount the voltage regulator/rectifier unit at another location.
10. Make sure the battery negative terminal is connected to both engine and frame.

Testing

Whenever the charging system is suspected of trouble, make sure the battery is fully charged before

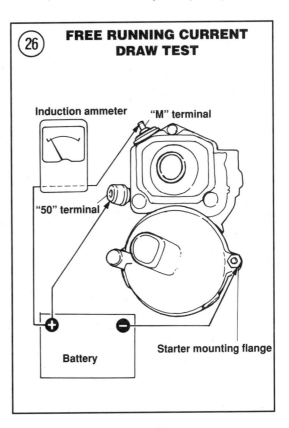

FREE RUNNING CURRENT DRAW TEST
(26)
Induction ammeter   "M" terminal
"50" terminal
Battery
Starter mounting flange

going any further. Clean and test the battery as described in Chapter Nine. If the battery is in good condition, test the charging system as follows.

If your battery runs down when riding the motorcycle, perform the *Current Draw Test*. If the battery runs down when the motorcycle is not being used, perform the *Voltage Regulator/Rectifier Test* in this chapter.

Current Draw Test

This test will check your electrical systems current draw. An induction load tester will be required for this test; see **Figure 27**, typical. If you do not have the proper test equipment, have the test performed by a Harley-Davidson dealer or an independent service shop familiar with Harley-Davidson service.

1. To perform this test, the battery must be fully charged. Use a hydrometer to check the specific gravity as described in Chapter Nine, and bring the battery up to full charge, if required.

> *NOTE*
> *Follow the manufacturer's instructions closely when using their test equipment. As a rule, you do not want to leave the load switch ON for more than 20 seconds at a time, or tester damage may occur from overheating.*

2. Connect an induction load tester into your bike's electrical circuit as shown in **Figure 28**.
3. Turn the ignition switch on. Then turn on all electrical accessories and switch the headlight beam to HIGH.
4. Read the amp reading (current draw) on the induction load tester and compare it to the voltage regulator/rectifier amp reading for your model listed in **Table 1**. If the voltage regulator/rectifier amp reading does not exceed the amp reading shown on the load tester scale by a minimum of 3.5 amps, your bike's existing current draw exceeds the charging system output. Under this condition, the battery will continually run down. Excessive current draw can be caused by an excessive number of electrical accessories (added to your bike) or by a short circuit.
5. If you have installed one or more electrical accessories to your bike's electrical system, their current draw combined with the current draw from your bike's stock electrical components may be the cause

of the excessive current draw. You can check this by disconnecting all of the accessory equipment and repeating this test; if the current draw is now within specifications (Step 3), you have found the problem. However, if you have not added any electrical accessories to your bike, the excessive current draw may be due to a short circuit.

> *NOTE*
> *If the charging system on your bike is working correctly but your bike is experiencing excessive current draw from added-on electrical accessories, consider adding a power reducer to your bike's electrical system. Contact Kriss Mfg. & Machine Inc., P.O. Box 35331, Tucson, AZ, 85740.*

Voltage Regulator/Rectifier Test

1. Turn the ignition switch and all electrical accessories OFF when performing this test.
2. Connect an ammeter between the battery positive terminal and the regulator. See **Figure 29**.
3. With the ammeter connected as shown in **Figure 29**, the reading should not exceed 1 milliamp (1984) or 3 milliamps (1985-on).
4. If the amp reading is excessive, the regulator/rectifier is damaged and must be replaced.
5. Remove all test equipment and reconnect all electrical leads.

Voltage Regulator Bleed Test

> *NOTE*
> *The voltage regulator must be connected to the battery when performing this test.*

1. Disconnect the voltage regulator connector at the crankcase.

2. Using a test light, touch one probe to a good engine ground and the other probe to the regulator pins, one at a time.

3. If the light comes on during any test, replace the voltage regulator.

Charging System Output Test

An induction load tester will be required for this test procedure.

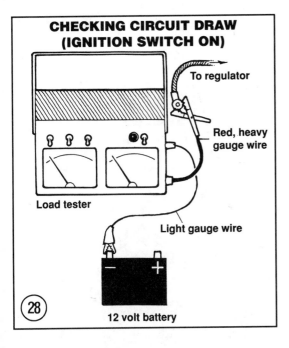

CHECKING CIRCUIT DRAW (IGNITION SWITCH ON)

To regulator

Red, heavy gauge wire

Load tester

Light gauge wire

28

12 volt battery

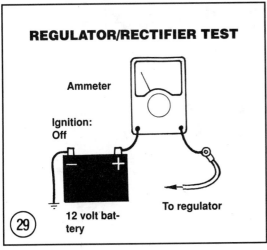

REGULATOR/RECTIFIER TEST

Ammeter

Ignition: Off

To regulator

29 12 volt battery

1. To perform this test, the battery must be fully charged. Use a hydrometer to check the battery specific gravity as described in Chapter Nine, and bring the battery up to full charge, if required.

> *NOTE*
> *Follow the manufacturer's instructions closely when using their test equipment. As a rule, you do not want to leave the load switch ON for more than 20 seconds at a time, or tester damage may occur from overheating.*

2. Connect an induction load tester to your bike as shown in **Figure 30**.

3. Start the engine and slowly bring its speed up to 2,000 rpm while reading the load tester scale. With the engine idling at 2,000 rpm, operate the load tester switch until the voltage scale reads 13.0 volts. Then read the current output scale. For the charging system output to be correct, it must read as follows:

   a. *1984*: 14 amps minimum.
   b. *1985-1988*: 19-23 amps.
   c. *1989-on*: 29-33 amps.

4. With the engine still running at 2,000 rpm, turn the load switch off and read the load tester voltage scale. Battery voltage must not exceed 15 volts. Turn the engine off and then disconnect the load tester from the bike.

5. An incorrect reading in Steps 3 and 4 indicates one of the following:

   a. The voltage regulator/rectifier unit is damaged.
   b. There is a short circuit in the bikes wiring system.

Stator Check

1. With ignition turned off, disconnect the regulator/rectifier connector from the stator at the crankcase. See **Figure 31**.

2. Connect an ohmmeter between either stator pin and ground (**Figure 32**). Set the ohmmeter to the R × 1 scale. The ohmmeter should read infinity (no continuity). If the reading is incorrect, the stator is grounded and must be replaced.

3. Connect an ohmmeter between both stator pins. Set the ohmmeter to the R × 1 scale. The ohmmeter should read 0.2-0.4 (1984-1988) or 0.1-0.2 (1989-on) ohms. If no needle movement was noticed, or if

the resistance is higher than specified, the stator must be replaced.

4. Check the stator AC output as follows:

   a. Connect an AC voltmeter across the stator sockets as shown in **Figure 33**.

   b. Start the engine and slowly increase idle speed to 3,000 rpm (1984) or 2,000 rpm (1985-on). Meter should read 60 volts minimum for 1984 models, 38-52 AC volts for 1985-1988 or 32-40 AC volts for 1989 and later models.

   c. A reading lower than that indicated in sub-step b indicates a faulty stator or rotor.

5. Reconnect the regulator/rectifier connector (**Figure 31**).

IGNITION SYSTEM

All Harley-Davidson softail models are equipped with a solid state transistorized ignition system that uses no breaker points. This system provides a longer life for the components and delivers a more efficient spark throughout the entire speed range of the engine than breaker point systems.

Most problems involving failure to start, poor driveability or rough running are caused by trouble in the ignition system.

Note the following symptoms:

   a. Engine misses.

   b. Stumbles on acceleration (misfiring).

   c. Loss of power at high speed (misfiring).

   d. Hard starting or failure to start.

   e. Rough idle.

Most of the symptoms can also be caused by a carburetor that is dirty, worn or improperly adjusted.

Precautions

Several precautions should be strictly observed to avoid damage to the ignition system.

1. Do not reverse the battery connections. This reverses polarity and can damage the ignition components.

2. Do not "spark" the battery terminals with the battery cable connections to check polarity.

3. Do not disconnect the battery cables with the engine running. A voltage surge will occur which will damage the ignition components and possibly burn out the lights. A spark may occur which can cause the battery to explode and spray acid.

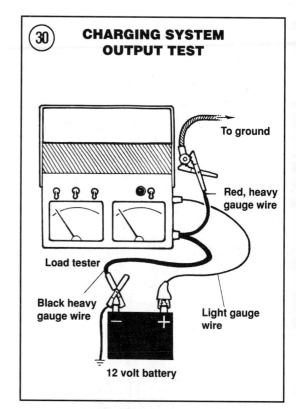

30 **CHARGING SYSTEM OUTPUT TEST**

To ground

Red, heavy gauge wire

Load tester

Black heavy gauge wire

Light gauge wire

12 volt battery

31

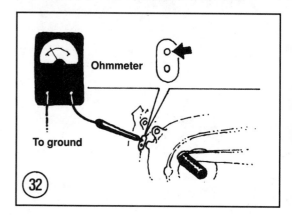

Ohmmeter

To ground

32

4. Do not crank the engine if the ignition module is not grounded to the frame. The black wire leading out of the ignition module is the ground wire. Check the end of the wire for corrosion or damage.

5. Whenever working on any part of the ignition system, first turn the ignition switch OFF or disconnect the battery negative (–) lead (**Figure 34**). This is done to prevent damage to the ignition system components from an accidental short circuit.

6. Keep all connections between the various units clean and tight. Be sure that the wiring connections are pushed together firmly to help keep out moisture.

7. Make sure all ground wires are properly attached and free of oil and corrosion.

Troubleshooting Preparation

If you suspect a problem with the ignition system, perform the following procedures in order.

1. Check the wiring harness and all plug-in connections to make sure that all terminals are free of corrosion, all connectors are tight and the wiring insulation is in good condition.

2. Check all electrical components that are grounded to the engine for a good ground. See wiring diagrams at the end of this book for ground connections for your model. These will include the ignition module, battery-to-frame and engine-to-frame ground wires and straps.

3. Make sure that all ground wires are properly connected and that the connections are clean and tight. Clean connectors with electrical contact cleaner.

4. Check remainder of the wiring for disconnected wires and short or open circuits.

5. Check the ignition circuit breaker to make sure it is not defective.

6. Make sure the fuel tank has an adequate supply of fuel and that the fuel is reaching the carburetors.

7. The battery must be fully charged. Use a hydrometer to check the specific gravity as described in Chapter Nine, and bring the battery up to full charge, if required.

8. Check spark plug cable routing. Make sure the cables are properly connected to their respective spark plugs. If cable routing is correct, perform the *Engine Fails to Start (Spark Test)* in this chapter. If there is no spark or only a weak one, recheck with a new spark plug(s). If the condition remains the same with new spark plugs and if all external wiring connections are good, the problem is most likely in the ignition system; perform the following tests. If a spark is obtained, the problem is not in the breakerless ignition or coil. Check the fuel system.

Performance Testing (1984)

Refer to **Figure 35** for this procedure.

1. Check the battery charge as described in Chapter Three. If battery is okay, proceed to Step 2.

2. Remove the outer ignition cover (**Figure 36**) as described in Chapter Nine.

3. Check that the ignition module (located on frame above regulator) black lead is fastened securely. Check also that the battery ground lead is fastened and in good condition.

NOTE
When performing the following tests, a voltmeter with an input resistance of

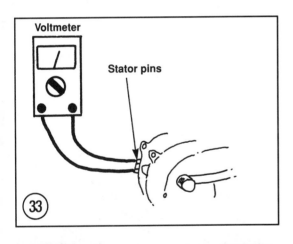

Voltmeter

Stator pins

33

34

20,000 ohms/volts or higher is required. A lower resistance meter may give a faulty reading.

4. Turn the engine over so that the sensor is located between the 2 rotor slots. **Figure 37** shows the sensor. **Figure 38** shows the rotor.

NOTE
The ignition switch must be turned ON and the stop switch turned to RUN when performing Steps 5 and 6.

5. Connect a voltmeter between the ignition positive coil terminal (white wires) and a good engine

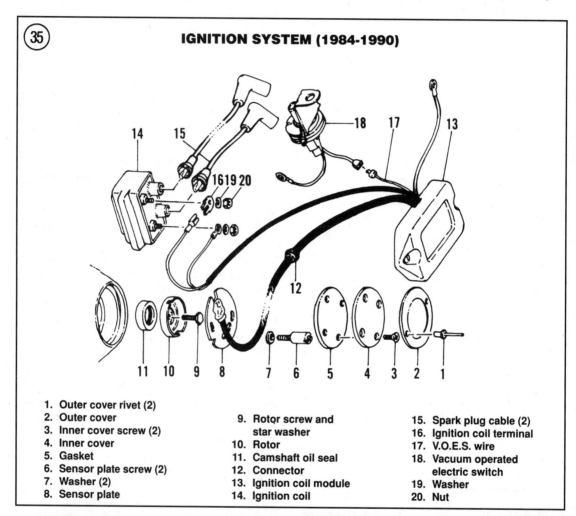

IGNITION SYSTEM (1984-1990)

1. Outer cover rivet (2)
2. Outer cover
3. Inner cover screw (2)
4. Inner cover
5. Gasket
6. Sensor plate screw (2)
7. Washer (2)
8. Sensor plate
9. Rotor screw and star washer
10. Rotor
11. Camshaft oil seal
12. Connector
13. Ignition coil module
14. Ignition coil
15. Spark plug cable (2)
16. Ignition coil terminal
17. V.O.E.S. wire
18. Vacuum operated electric switch
19. Washer
20. Nut

ground. The voltmeter should read 11.5 ±0.5 volts. Interpret results as follows:

    a. If the voltage is incorrect, the problem is in the battery-to-ignition coil circuit. Check the wiring connectors at the circuit breakers and at the ignition switch. See **Figure 39**.

    b. If the voltage is correct, proceed to Step 6.

6. Disconnect the ignition coil negative connector (blue). Connect a voltmeter between the coil negative connector and a good engine ground. Turn the ignition switch ON. The voltmeter should read 11.5 ±0.5 volts. Interpret results as follows:

    a. If the voltage is incorrect, the problem is in the ignition coil primary circuit. Replace the ignition coil and perform the *Engine Fails to Start (Spark Test)* in this chapter.

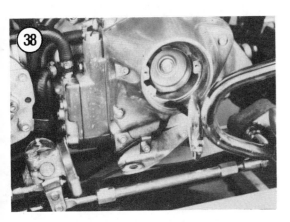

    b. If the voltage is correct, check the control module and sensor beginning with Step 7.

    c. Turn the ignition switch OFF.

    d. Reconnect the ignition coil negative connector (blue).

7. Disconnect the sensor plate from the control module at the connector (12, **Figure 35**).

8. Install an ignition test adapter (HD-94465-81) and a voltmeter as shown in **Figure 40**.

CAUTION
When using the ignition test adapter, make sure the exposed terminal connector does not touch another connector or to ground or the ignition module may be damaged.

9. Turn the ignition switch and the stop switch ON and measure the voltage between the No. 1 pin (red wire) and the No. 2 pin (black wire) as shown in **Figure 40**.

10. The meter should read 5.4-5.5 volts. If it does not, the control module is defective and should be replaced as described in Chapter Nine.

11. To test the sensor operation, connect the voltmeter to the ignition test adapter as shown in **Figure 41**.

12. Turn the ignition switch and the stop switch ON.

13. Turn the engine so that the rotor slots are not present at the sensor. Measure the voltage reading. It should be 4.5-5.5 volts.

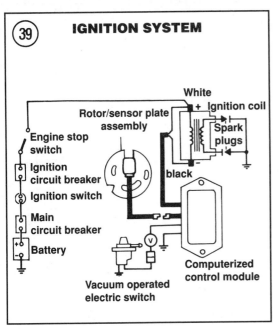

IGNITION SYSTEM

White
+ Ignition coil
Rotor/sensor plate assembly
Spark plugs
Engine stop switch
Ignition circuit breaker
Ignition switch
black
Main circuit breaker
Battery
Computerized control module
Vacuum operated electric switch

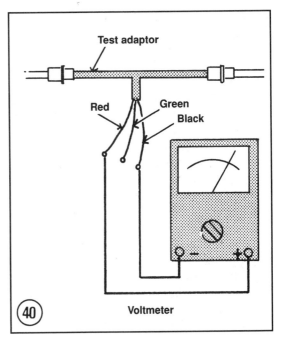

Test adaptor
Red
Green
Black
Voltmeter

14. Turn the engine so that the center of the sensor is between the 2 rotor slots. The voltmeter should read 0-1 volts.

15. If the voltage readings in Steps 13 and 14 are incorrect and the control module passes the previous test, the sensor is faulty and should be replaced as described in Chapter Nine.

16. Turn the ignition switch off. Remove the ignition test adapter and reconnect the module connectors.

**Ignition Test
(No Spark at Spark Plug)
(1985-on)**

Refer to **Figure 35** (1985-1990) or **Figure 42** (1991-on) when performing these procedures.

1. Check the battery charge as described in Chapter Nine. If battery is okay, proceed to Step 2.

2. Check that the black ignition module ground lead is fastened securely. Check also that the battery ground lead is fastened and in good condition.

NOTE
When performing the following test procedures, it will be necessary to fabricate a test jumper from 2 lengths of 16 gauge wire, 3 clips and a 0.33 MFD capacitor; see ***Figure 43***. *The test jumper should be long enough to reach from the ignition coil to a good engine ground.*

NOTE
A voltmeter is required to perform the following tests.

3. Perform the following:
   a. Connect the red voltmeter lead to the white ignition coil wire and the black voltmeter lead to ground (**Figure 44**).
   b. Turn the ignition switch ON. The voltmeter should read 11-13 volts. Turn the ignition switch OFF. Interpret results as follows.
   c. Voltage correct: Proceed to Step 4.
   d. Voltage incorrect: Check the main and ignition circuit breakers. Also check for loose or damaged ignition system wiring.

4. Perform the following:
   a. Disconnect the blue (1985-1990) or pink (1991-on) wire from the ignition coil terminal (**Figure 45**).
   b. Turn the ignition switch ON.

   c. Connect the black voltmeter lead to ground. Then connect the red voltmeter lead to the white and blue or pink ignition coil terminals separately (**Figure 45**). The voltmeter should read 12 volts at both terminals. Turn the ignition switch OFF. Interpret results as follows.
   d. Voltage correct: Proceed to Step 5.
   e. Voltage incorrect: Check the ignition coil resistance as described in this chapter. If the resistance is okay, proceed to Step 5.

5. Perform the following:
   a. Disconnect the blue (1985-1990) or pink (1991-on) wire from the ignition coil terminal (**Figure 46**).
   b. Remove one of the spark plugs. Then connect the spark plug wire and connector to the spark plug and touch the spark plug base to a good ground like the engine cylinder head. Position the spark plug so you can see the electrodes.
   c. Turn the ignition switch ON.
   d. Connect the 2 jumper wires to a good engine ground (**Figure 46**). Then momentarily touch the jumper wire with the capacitor to the ignition coil blue or pink terminal while observing the spark plug firing tip. The spark plug should spark. Turn the ignition switch OFF and remove the jumper wire assembly. Interpret results as follows.
   e. Spark: Proceed to Step 6.

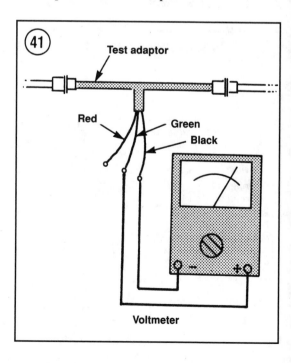

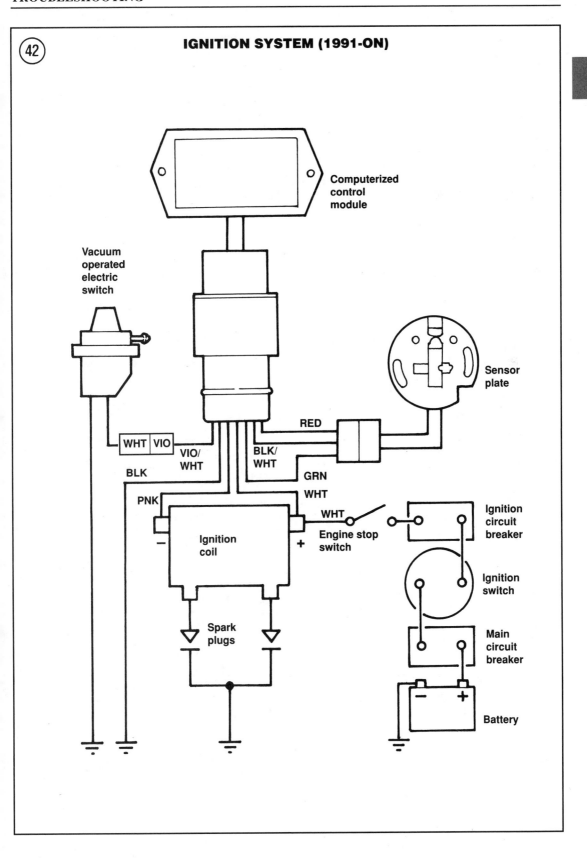

(42)

IGNITION SYSTEM (1991-ON)

2

Computerized
control
module

Vacuum
operated
electric
switch

Sensor
plate

WHT | VIO

VIO/
WHT

BLK

BLK/
WHT

RED

GRN

WHT

PNK

Ignition
coil

Spark
plugs

WHT

Engine stop
switch

Ignition
circuit
breaker

Ignition
switch

Main
circuit
breaker

Battery

f. No spark: Replace the ignition coil.

g. Do not reinstall the spark plug at this time.

6. Perform the following:

a. Reconnect the ignition coil blue (1985-1990) or pink (1991-on) wire to its terminal on the ignition coil.

b. Turn the ignition switch ON.

c. Disconnect the sensor plate electrical connector.

d. Connect the red voltmeter lead to the ignition module red wire socket and the black voltmeter lead to the ignition module black (1985-1990) or black/white (1991-on) pin (**Figure 46**). The voltmeter should read 11.5-12.5

volts. Disconnect the voltmeter and turn the ignition switch OFF. Interpret results as follows.

e. Voltage correct: Proceed to Step 7.

f. Voltage incorrect: Check the ignition module ground wire and the module for loose connections or damage. If okay, proceed to Step 7.

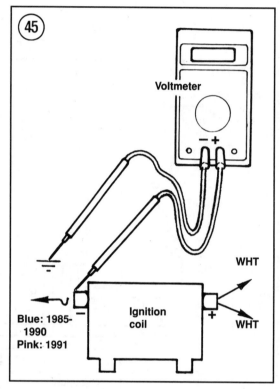

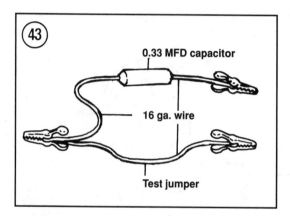

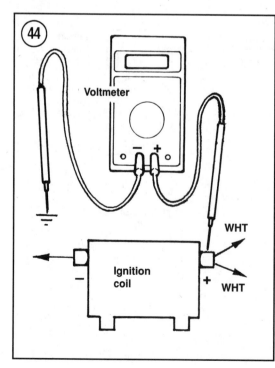

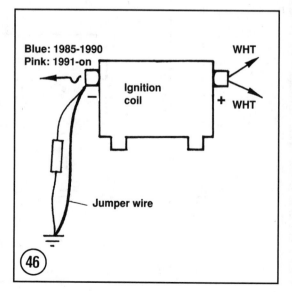

7. Turn the ignition switch ON. Then momentarily ground a screwdriver across the ignition module green and black connector pins (**Figure 48**) while observing the spark plug firing tip. There should be strong spark at the spark plug firing tip as the screwdriver is *removed*. Interpret results as follows:

a. Spark: Check the sensor resistance as described in this chapter.

b. No spark: Check the ignition module resistance as described in this chapter.

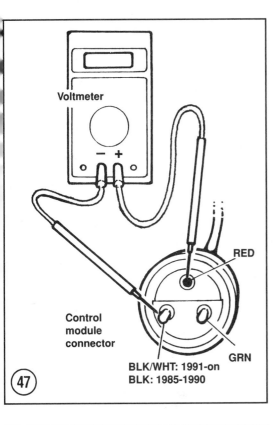

Voltmeter

RED

Control
module
connector

GRN

BLK/WHT: 1991-on
BLK: 1985-1990

47

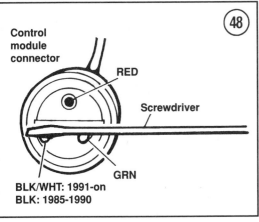

48

Control
module
connector

RED

Screwdriver

GRN

BLK/WHT: 1991-on
BLK: 1985-1990

8. Install and reconnect all parts removed for this procedure. If there is still no spark, either retest or have a Harley-Davidson dealer check the ignition system.

Ignition Test
(Intermittent Ignition Problems)

Intermittent problems are usually caused by temperature or vibration variances. Perform the following.

Temperature test

NOTE
Steps 1-4 must be performed with the engine cold.

1. Remove the outer timing cover as described in Chapter Nine.

2. Remove the inner timing cover and gasket (**Figure 49**).

3. Start the engine.

4. Spray the sensor (**Figure 50**) with an electrical component cooler (available at electronic supply

49

50

stores). If the engine dies, replace the sensor as described in Chapter Nine.

5. Allow the engine to warm to normal operating temperature. Then apply heat to the sensor with a blow dryer. If the engine dies, replace the sensor as described in Chapter Nine.

6. Remove the left-hand side cover. With the engine running, apply heat to the ignition module with a blow dryer or heat gun. If the engine dies, replace the module as described in Chapter Nine.

7. Install the inner timing cover, gasket and outer timing cover as described in Chapter Nine.

Vibration test

Read this procedure completely through before starting. Refer to **Figure 51**.

1. Check the battery connections (**Figure 34**). Retighten or repair as required.

2. Check the module ground wire connection. If necessary, remove the ground wire at the frame and scrape all paint at the mounting point. Reinstall the ground with a star washer.

3. Start the engine and retest. If there is still an intermittent problem, proceed to Step 4.

4. Disconnect the white *ignition stop switch* wire terminal at the ignition coil.

NOTE
Do not disconnect the white module wire at the ignition coil. See the wiring diagram at the end of this book and **Figure 51**.

5. Connect a 16 gauge jumper wire from the positive battery terminal to the white ignition coil terminal.

WARNING
Steps 4 and 5 have by-passed the ignition stop switch. When performing Step 6, the engine can only be stopped by removing the jumper wire. Test by re-

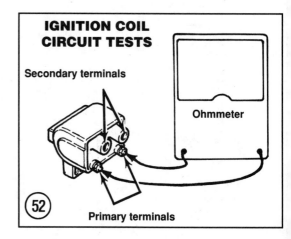

1. IGNITION COIL CIRCUIT TESTS

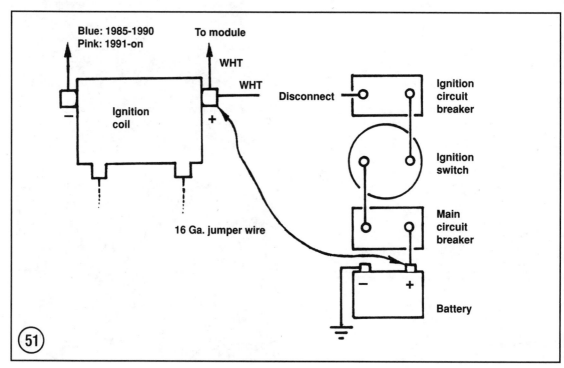

moving the jumper wire before riding the bike. It is suggested to test ride the bike on a paved surface in a secluded area away from all traffic. If you do not feel that you can perform this test safely or if you do not have access to a safe riding area, refer testing to a Harley-Davidson dealer.

6. Test ride the bike. If the intermittent problem has stopped, there is a problem with the ignition kill switch. If the problem continues, the vibration may be caused by loose connections in the starter circuit safety switches.

7. Remove the jumper wire and reconnect the white wire at the ignition coil terminal.

Ignition Coil Testing

If the coil condition is doubtful, there are several checks which can be made. Disconnect the coil secondary and primary wires before testing.

NOTE
When switching between ohmmeter scales in the following tests, always cross the test leads and zero the needle to assure a correct reading.

1. Set an ohmmeter on R × 1. Measure the coil primary resistance between both coil primary terminals (**Figure 52**). Compare reading to specification listed in **Table 1**.
2. Set the ohmmeter on R × 100. Measure the coil secondary resistance between both high voltage terminals (**Figure 52**). Compare reading with **Table 1**.
3. Replace the coil if it does not test within specifications in Step 1 or Step 2.

Ignition Module and Sensor Resistance Testing

The following tests should be performed with the Harley-Davidson KMT multimeter (part no. HD-35500). If any other meter is used, the results may be different than the specified values listed in these tests. If you do not have the Harley-Davidson multimeter, it is suggested that you do not purchase replacement parts based upon your meter's test results as electrical components normally cannot be returned.

NOTE
In the following tests, the red ohmmeter lead is always considered to be the positive lead and the black ohmmeter lead is the negative lead. Refer to the instructions provided with the KMT multimeter for proper operation.

Ignition module ground test—all models

Refer to **Figure 53** (1984-1990) or **Figure 54** (1991-on) when performing this procedure.

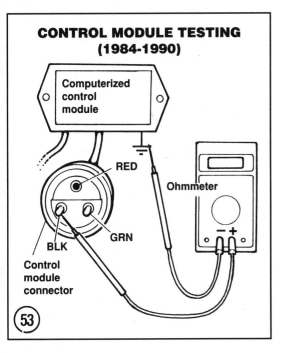

CONTROL MODULE TESTING (1984-1990)

Computerized control module

RED

Ohmmeter

GRN

BLK

Control module connector

⑤③

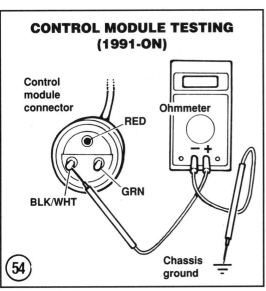

CONTROL MODULE TESTING (1991-ON)

Control module connector

RED

Ohmmeter

BLK/WHT

GRN

Chassis ground

⑤④

1. Disconnect the module to sensor connector.

2. Connect the red ohmmeter lead to the black (1984-1990) or black/white (1991-on) module pin and the black ohmmeter lead to ground.

3. The correct resistance reading should be 0-1 ohms. If the reading exceeds 1 ohm, replace the module.

4. Reconnect the connector.

Power supply diode test—1984-1990

Refer to **Figure 55** when performing this procedure.

1. Disconnect the white ignition coil-to-module connector.

2. Set the ohmmeter on the R × 100 scale.

3. Connect the red ohmmeter lead to the white ignition coil connector and the black lead to the module ground wire. The resistance should be 800-1300 ohms.

4. Switch the test leads in Step 3. The ohmmeter should indicate infinite resistance.

5. Replace the module if either reading is not within specifications.

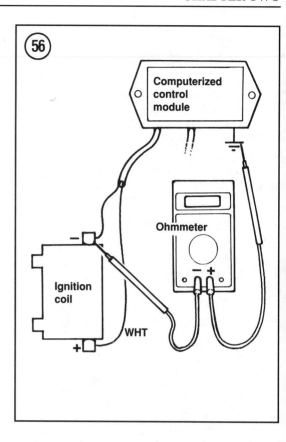

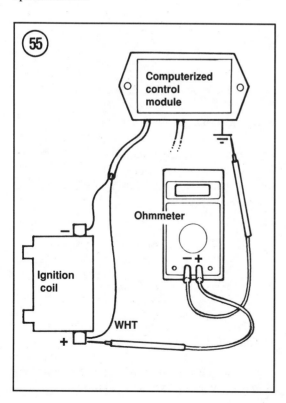

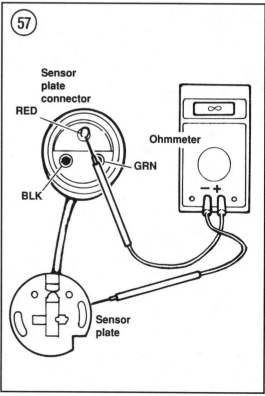

6. Remove the ohmmeter and reconnect the ignition coil-to-module connector.

Coil driver transistor check—1984-1990

Refer to **Figure 56** when performing this procedure.
1. Disconnect the blue ignition coil-to-module connector.
2. Set the ohmmeter on the R × 100 scale.
3. Connect the red ohmmeter lead to the blue ignition coil connector and the black lead to the module ground wire. The ohmmeter should indicate infinite resistance.
4. Switch the test leads in Step 3. The resistance should be 400-800 ohms.
5. Replace the module if either reading is not within specifications.
6. Disconnect the ohmmeter and reconnect the ignition coil-to-module connector.

Ignition sensor ground test—1984-1990

Refer to **Figure 57** when performing this procedure.
1. Disconnect the module to sensor connector.
2. Set the ohmmeter on the R × 1 scale.
3. Connect the red ohmmeter lead to the sensor connector red pin and the ohmmeter black lead onto the sensor plate.
4. The ohmmeter should read infinite resistance.

5. Repeat Step 3 by checking at the sensor connector black and green pins. In each case, the ohmmeter should read infinite resistance.
6. If the ohmmeter showed continuity in either test, replace the sensor plate.
7. Disconnect the ohmmeter and reconnect the module to sensor connector.

Ignition sensor output test—1984-1990

Refer to **Figure 58** for this procedure.
1. Disconnect the ignition module to sensor plate electrical connector.
2. Set the ohmmeter on the R × 100 scale.
3. Connect the red ohmmeter lead to the sensor connector green pin and the ohmmeter black lead to the sensor connector black pin. The meter should show infinite resistance.
4. Switch the test leads in Step 3. The resistance reading should be 300-750 ohms.
5. If any of the meter readings differ from the stated values, replace the sensor plate.
6. Disconnect the ohmmeter and reconnect the ignition module-to-sensor plate connector.

FUEL SYSTEM

The fuel system consists of the fuel tanks, fuel valve, fuel lines and carburetor. The throttle and choke cables and the throttle grip should also be included in the operation of the fuel system.

During engine operation, fuel will flow from the fuel tank, through the fuel valve and into the carburetor where it is mixed with air before entering the engine. If fuel flow is entering the carburetor incorrectly (too much or too little), the engine will not run properly.

Many owners automatically assume that the carburetor is at fault when the engine does not run properly. While fuel system problems are not uncommon, carburetor adjustment is seldom the answer. In many cases, adjusting the carburetor only compounds the problem by making the engine run worse.

Fuel system troubleshooting should start at the fuel tank and work through the system, reserving the carburetor as the final point. Most fuel system problems result from an empty fuel tank, sour fuel, a dirty air filter or clogged carburetor jets.

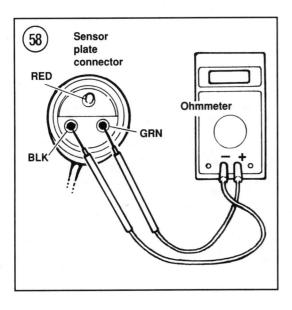

(58) Sensor plate connector
RED
Ohmmeter
GRN
BLK
− +

Identifying Carburetor Conditions

The following list can be used as a guide when distinguishing between rich and lean carburetor conditions.

When the engine is running rich, one or more of the following conditions may be present:

a. The spark plug(s) will foul.
b. The engine will miss and run rough when it is running under a load.
c. As the throttle is increased, the exhaust smoke becomes more excessive.
d. With the throttle open, the exhaust will sound choked or dull. Bringing the motorcycle to a dead stop and trying to clear the exhaust with the throttle held wide open does not clear up the sound.

When the engine is running lean, one or more of the following conditions may be present:

a. The spark plug firing end will become very white or blistered in appearance.
b. The engine overheats.
c. Acceleration is slower.
d. Flat spots are felt during operation that feel much like the engine is trying to run out of gas.
e. Engine power is reduced.
f. At full throttle, engine rpm will not be steady.

Troubleshooting

Fuel system problems should be isolated to the fuel tank, fuel valve and filter, fuel hoses, external fuel filter (if used) or carburetor. The following procedures assume that the ignition system is working properly and is correctly adjusted.

Fuel delivery system

As a first step, check the fuel flow. Remove the fuel tank caps and look into each tank. If there is fuel present, disconnect the battery ground cable as a safety precaution. Then check that the fuel valve is turned OFF (**Figure 59**). Disconnect the fuel hose at the carburetor and put the hose into a container to catch any discharged fuel.

> *NOTE*
> *Make sure there is a sufficient supply of fuel in each tank to allow the fuel valve to work in its normal operating position.*

> *WARNING*
> *Make sure there are no open flames in the area when performing the following.*

The fuel valve controls fuel flow from the fuel tanks to the carburetor. The fuel valve on all models is a 3-position valve (**Figure 59**). Because a gravity-feed type fuel delivery system is used, fuel should always be present at the fuel valve. Turn the fuel valve so that the end of the handle faces down (valve is normal operating position). Fuel should flow into the container. Turn the fuel valve so that the end of the handle faces up (valve is in RESERVE). Fuel

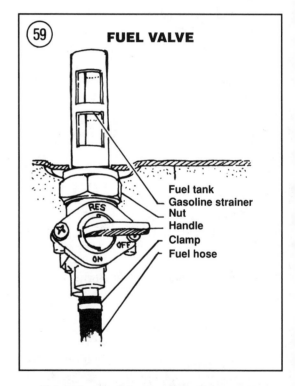

FUEL VALVE

Fuel tank
Gasoline strainer
Nut
Handle
Clamp
Fuel hose

should flow into the container. If there is no fuel from the hose:

   a. The fuel valve may be shut off or blocked by rust or foreign matter. If fuel flows in the RESERVE but not in the ON position, the fuel level in the tank may be too low. If the fuel level is high enough to flow in the ON position, the ON side of the valve is clogged. This would also hold true if the RESERVE side failed to work properly.

   b. The fuel hose may be stopped up or kinked. Remove the fuel hose and then clear the hose by passing a stiff piece of wire or a rod (less than 1/4 in. in diameter) through the hose.

> *WARNING*
> *When reconnecting the fuel hose, make sure the hose is inserted through the nylon hose insulator (**Figure 60**). Do not operate the engine without the insulator properly installed.*

   c. The fuel tank is not properly vented. Check by opening the fuel tank cap. If fuel flows with the cap open, check for a plugged vent.

If a good fuel flow is present, fuel is reaching the carburetor. Examine the fuel in the container for rust or dirt that could clog or restrict the fuel valve filter and the carburetor jets. If there is evidence of contamination, it will be necessary to clean and flush the fuel tanks, fuel valve assembly, hoses and carburetor. Refer to Chapter Eight for fuel system service.

If you are getting a good fuel flow from the fuel tank to the carburetor and the fuel is not contaminated with dirt or rust, refer to the troubleshooting chart in **Figure 61** or **Figure 62** for additional information.

Fuel level system

The fuel supply system is shown in **Figure 63** (1984-1989) and **Figure 64** (1990-on). Proper carburetor operation is dependent on a constant and correct carburetor fuel level. As fuel is drawn from the float bowl during engine operation, the float level in the bowl drops. As the float drops, the float needle moves away from its seat and allows fuel to flow through the seat into the float bowl. Fuel entering the float bowl will cause the float to rise and push against the float needle. When the fuel level reaches a predetermined level, the needle is pushed against the float seat to prevent the float bowl from overfilling.

If the float needle doesn't close, the engine will run rich or flood with fuel. Symptoms of this problem are rough running, excessive black smoke and poor acceleration. This condition will sometimes clear up when the engine is run at wide open throttle, as the fuel is being used up before the float bowl can overfill. As the engine speed is reduced, however, the rich running condition repeats itself.

Figure 61 (1984-1989) and **Figure 62** (1990-on) list several things that can cause fuel overflow. In most instances, it can be as simple a small piece of dirt trapped between the needle and seat or an incorrect float level. If you see fuel flowing out of the overflow tube connected at the bottom of the float bowl, the float valve is being held open. First check the position of the fuel valve. Turn the fuel lever OFF if it was left in the ON or RESERVE position. Then tap on the carburetor (not too hard) and turn the fuel valve back on. If the fuel flow stopped running out of the overflow tube, you may have dislodged whatever it was holding the needle off of its seat. If fuel continues to flow from the overflow tube, it will be necessary to remove and service the carburetor. See Chapter Eight.

Starter or choke system

A cold engine requires a very rich mixture. The choke used on 1984-1989 models consists of a choke valve and a fast idle cam. On 1990 and later models, a cable actuated enrichener valve is used for cold-starting.

Carburetor chokes can also present a problem by causing difficult cold starting. If your engine has become difficult to start when cold, first check the choke adjustment as described in Chapter Three. If the choke adjustment is correct, refer to the possible causes listed under "Hard Starting" in **Figure 61** or **Figure 62**.

Accelerator pump system

Because the carburetor cannot supply enough fuel during sudden throttle openings (quick acceleration), a lean air/fuel mixture will cause hesitation and poor acceleration. To prevent this condition, all of the factory Harley-Davidson carburetors are equipped with a diaphragm type accelerator pump

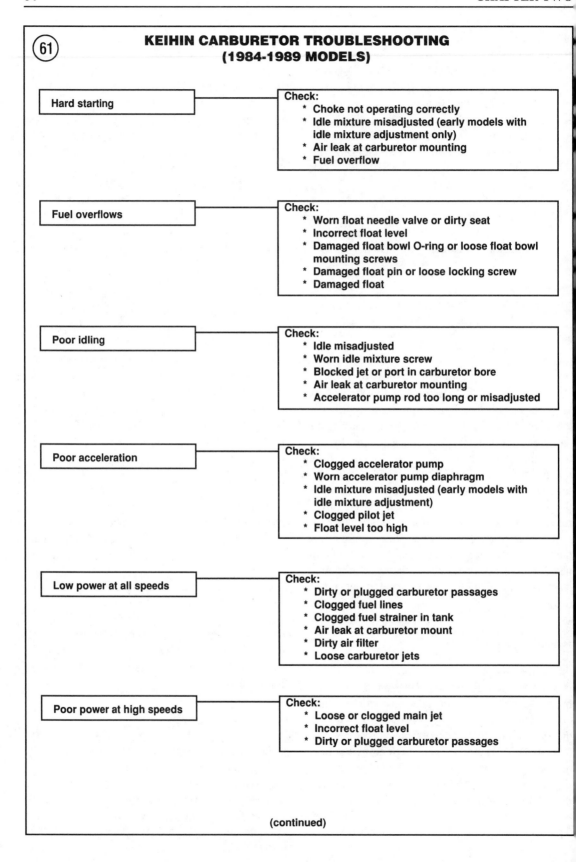

KEIHIN CARBURETOR TROUBLESHOOTING (1984-1989 MODELS)

Hard starting

Check:
* Choke not operating correctly
* Idle mixture misadjusted (early models with idle mixture adjustment only)
* Air leak at carburetor mounting
* Fuel overflow

Fuel overflows

Check:
* Worn float needle valve or dirty seat
* Incorrect float level
* Damaged float bowl O-ring or loose float bowl mounting screws
* Damaged float pin or loose locking screw
* Damaged float

Poor idling

Check:
* Idle misadjusted
* Worn idle mixture screw
* Blocked jet or port in carburetor bore
* Air leak at carburetor mounting
* Accelerator pump rod too long or misadjusted

Poor acceleration

Check:
* Clogged accelerator pump
* Worn accelerator pump diaphragm
* Idle mixture misadjusted (early models with idle mixture adjustment)
* Clogged pilot jet
* Float level too high

Low power at all speeds

Check:
* Dirty or plugged carburetor passages
* Clogged fuel lines
* Clogged fuel strainer in tank
* Air leak at carburetor mount
* Dirty air filter
* Loose carburetor jets

Poor power at high speeds

Check:
* Loose or clogged main jet
* Incorrect float level
* Dirty or plugged carburetor passages

(continued)

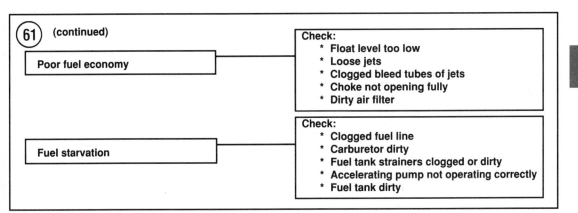

61 (continued)

Poor fuel economy

Check:
* Float level too low
* Loose jets
* Clogged bleed tubes of jets
* Choke not opening fully
* Dirty air filter

Fuel starvation

Check:
* Clogged fuel line
* Carburetor dirty
* Fuel tank strainers clogged or dirty
* Accelerating pump not operating correctly
* Fuel tank dirty

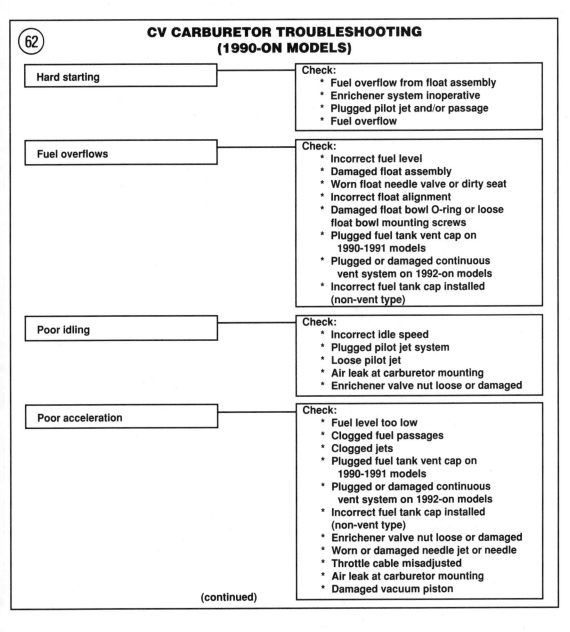

62

CV CARBURETOR TROUBLESHOOTING
(1990-ON MODELS)

Hard starting

Check:
* Fuel overflow from float assembly
* Enrichener system inoperative
* Plugged pilot jet and/or passage
* Fuel overflow

Fuel overflows

Check:
* Incorrect fuel level
* Damaged float assembly
* Worn float needle valve or dirty seat
* Incorrect float alignment
* Damaged float bowl O-ring or loose
  float bowl mounting screws
* Plugged fuel tank vent cap on
  1990-1991 models
* Plugged or damaged continuous
  vent system on 1992-on models
* Incorrect fuel tank cap installed
  (non-vent type)

Poor idling

Check:
* Incorrect idle speed
* Plugged pilot jet system
* Loose pilot jet
* Air leak at carburetor mounting
* Enrichener valve nut loose or damaged

Poor acceleration

Check:
* Fuel level too low
* Clogged fuel passages
* Clogged jets
* Plugged fuel tank vent cap on
  1990-1991 models
* Plugged or damaged continuous
  vent system on 1992-on models
* Incorrect fuel tank cap installed
  (non-vent type)
* Enrichener valve nut loose or damaged
* Worn or damaged needle jet or needle
* Throttle cable misadjusted
* Air leak at carburetor mounting
* Damaged vacuum piston

(continued)

2

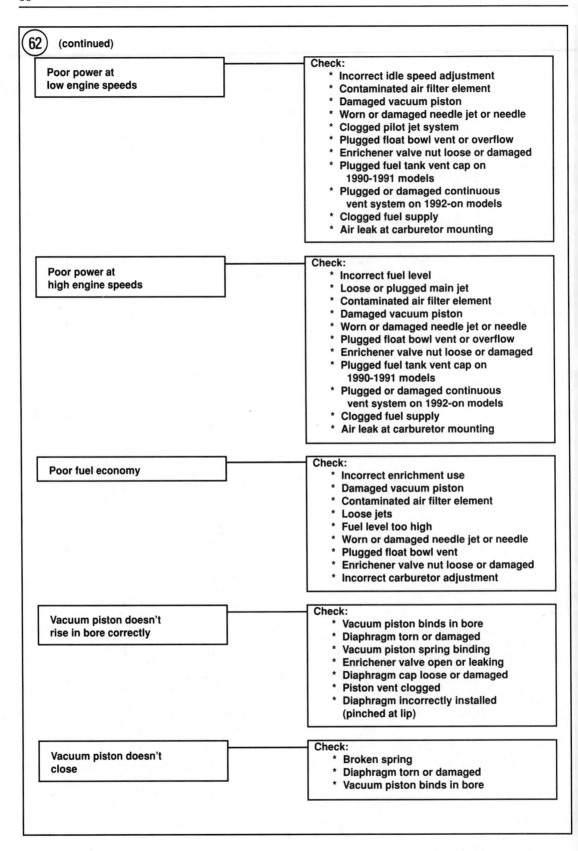

62 (continued)

Poor power at low engine speeds

Check:
* Incorrect idle speed adjustment
* Contaminated air filter element
* Damaged vacuum piston
* Worn or damaged needle jet or needle
* Clogged pilot jet system
* Plugged float bowl vent or overflow
* Enrichener valve nut loose or damaged
* Plugged fuel tank vent cap on
   1990-1991 models
* Plugged or damaged continuous
   vent system on 1992-on models
* Clogged fuel supply
* Air leak at carburetor mounting

Poor power at high engine speeds

Check:
* Incorrect fuel level
* Loose or plugged main jet
* Contaminated air filter element
* Damaged vacuum piston
* Worn or damaged needle jet or needle
* Plugged float bowl vent or overflow
* Enrichener valve nut loose or damaged
* Plugged fuel tank vent cap on
   1990-1991 models
* Plugged or damaged continuous
   vent system on 1992-on models
* Clogged fuel supply
* Air leak at carburetor mounting

Poor fuel economy

Check:
* Incorrect enrichment use
* Damaged vacuum piston
* Contaminated air filter element
* Loose jets
* Fuel level too high
* Worn or damaged needle jet or needle
* Plugged float bowl vent
* Enrichener valve nut loose or damaged
* Incorrect carburetor adjustment

Vacuum piston doesn't rise in bore correctly

Check:
* Vacuum piston binds in bore
* Diaphragm torn or damaged
* Vacuum piston spring binding
* Enrichener valve open or leaking
* Diaphragm cap loose or damaged
* Piston vent clogged
* Diaphragm incorrectly installed
   (pinched at lip)

Vacuum piston doesn't close

Check:
* Broken spring
* Diaphragm torn or damaged
* Vacuum piston binds in bore

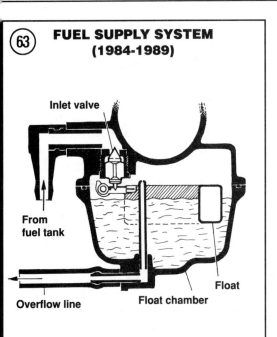

FUEL SUPPLY SYSTEM (1984-1989)

- Inlet valve
- From fuel tank
- Overflow line
- Float chamber
- Float

63

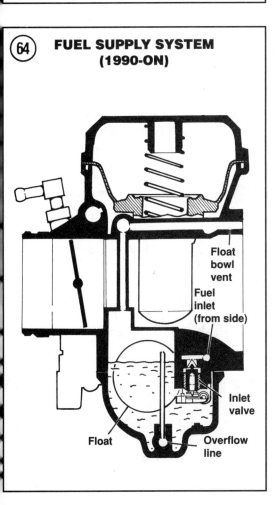

FUEL SUPPLY SYSTEM (1990-ON)

- Float bowl vent
- Fuel inlet (from side)
- Inlet valve
- Float
- Overflow line

64

system. See **Figure 65** (1984-1989) or **Figure 66** (1990-on). A spring-loaded neoprene diaphragm is installed in a pump chamber at the bottom of the float bowl. During sudden acceleration, the diaphragm is compressed by the pump lever, forcing fuel out of the pump chamber through a check valve and into the carburetor venturi. This additional fuel richens the existing air/fuel mixture to prevent engine hesitation. The diaphragm spring returns the diaphragm to its uncompressed position, allowing the chamber to refill with fuel for its next use. The check valve prevents fuel from back flowing into the chamber during pump operation.

If your bike hesitates during sudden acceleration or if it suffers from overall poor acceleration, perform the checks listed under "Poor Acceleration" in **Figure 61** or **Figure 62**. If the accelerator pump system is faulty, it will necessary to service the carburetor as described in Chapter Eight.

ENGINE NOISES

Often the first evidence of an internal engine problem is a strange noise. That knocking, clicking

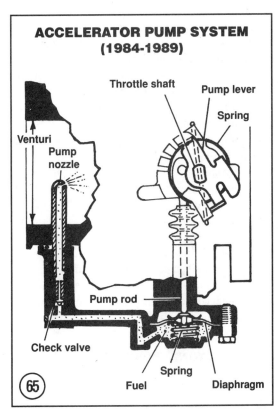

ACCELERATOR PUMP SYSTEM (1984-1989)

- Throttle shaft
- Pump lever
- Spring
- Venturi
- Pump nozzle
- Pump rod
- Check valve
- Spring
- Fuel
- Diaphragm

65

2

or tapping sound which you never heard before may be warning you of impending trouble.

While engine noises can indicate problems, they are difficult to interpret correctly; inexperienced mechanics can be seriously misled by them.

Professional mechanics often use a special stethoscope (which looks like a doctor's stethoscope) for isolating engine noises. You can do nearly as well with a "sounding stick" which can be an ordinary piece of doweling, a length of broom handle or a section of small hose. By placing one end in contact with the area to which you want to listen and the other end near your ear, you can hear sounds emanating from that area. The first time you do this, you may be horrified at the strange sounds coming from even a normal engine. If you can, have an experienced friend or mechanic help you sort out the noises.

Consider the following when troubleshooting engine noises:

1. *Knocking or pinging during acceleration*— Caused by using a lower octane fuel than recommended. May also be caused by poor fuel. Pinging can also be caused by a spark plug of the wrong heat range. Refer to *Correct Spark Plug Heat Range* in Chapter Three.

2. *Slapping or rattling noises at low speed or during acceleration*—May be caused by piston slap, i.e., excessive piston-cylinder wall clearance.

3. *Knocking or rapping while decelerating*—Usually caused by excessive rod bearing clearance.

4. *Persistent knocking and vibration*—Usually caused by worn main bearing(s).

5. *Rapid on-off squeal*—Compression leak around cylinder head gasket(s) or spark plugs.

6. *Valve train noise*—Check for the following:
   a. Bent push rod(s).
   b. Defective tappets.
   c. Valve sticking in guide.
   d. Worn cam gears and/or cam.
   e. Low oil pressure—probably caused by obstructed oil screen. Also check oil feed pump operation.
   f. Damaged rocker arm or shaft. Rocker arm may be binding on shaft.

ENGINE LUBRICATION

An improperly operating engine lubrication system will quickly lead to engine damage. The engine

oil tank should be checked weekly and the tank refilled, as described in Chapter Three. Oil pump service is covered in Chapter Four.

Oil Light

The oil light will come on when the ignition switch is turned to ON before starting the engine. After the engine is started, the oil light should go off when the engine speed is above idle.

If the oil light does not come on the when the ignition switch is turned to ON and the engine is not running, check for a burned out oil light bulb. If the bulb is okay, check the oil pressure switch as described in Chapter Nine.

If the oil light remains on when the engine speed is above idle, turn the engine off and check the oil level in the oil tank. If the oil level is satisfactory, check the following:

   a. Check for a plugged tappet screen (**Figure 67**). Remove and service the screen as described in Chapter Three.
   b. Oil may not be returning to the tank from the return line. Check for a clogged or damaged

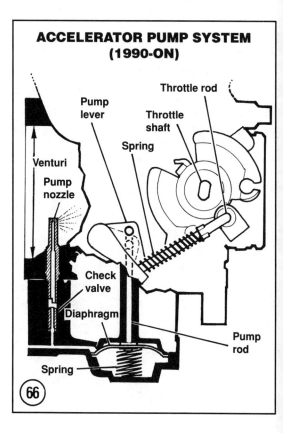

ACCELERATOR PUMP SYSTEM (1990-ON)

Throttle rod

Pump lever

Throttle shaft

Spring

Venturi

Pump nozzle

Check valve

Diaphragm

Pump rod

Spring

66

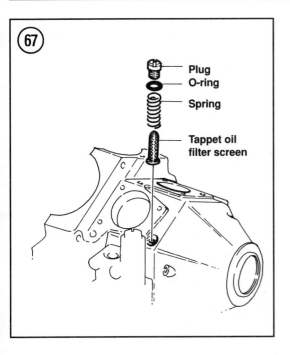

Plug
O-ring
Spring
Tappet oil filter screen

return line or a damaged oil pump. See **Figure 68** (1984), **Figure 69** (1985-1991), **Figure 70** (1992) or **Figure 71** (1993-on).

c. If you are operating your Harley in conditions where the ambient temperature is below freezing, ice and sludge may be blocking the oil feed pipe. This condition will prevent the oil from circulating properly.

NOTE
Because water is formed during combustion, it can collect in the engine if the engine is run at moderate speeds for short periods of time, especially during winter months. If you ride your bike for short trips and then turn the engine off and allow it to cool before it has reached maximum operating temperature, water that is formed each time the engine is started will begin to accumulate in the engine's lubrication system. This

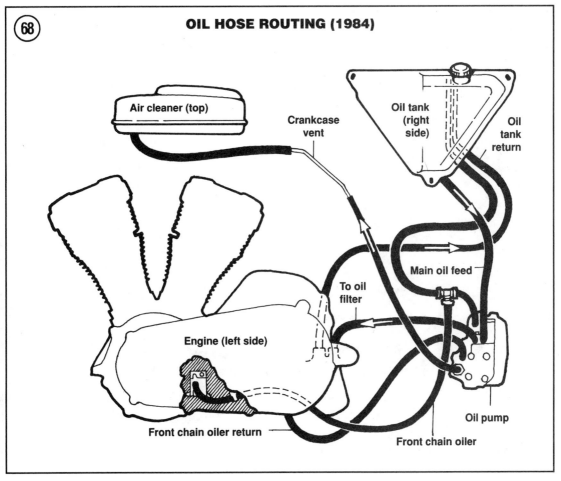

OIL HOSE ROUTING (1984)

Air cleaner (top)
Crankcase vent
Oil tank (right side)
Oil tank return
Main oil feed
To oil filter
Engine (left side)
Oil pump
Front chain oiler return
Front chain oiler

buildup of water, as it mixes with the oil, will form sludge deposits. Sludge is a thick, creamy substance that will clog oil feed and return systems (oil filter, tappet screen, lines, etc.). This can accelerate engine wear and result in engine failure. In addition, when the ambient temperature falls below freezing, water in the tank and oil lines will freeze, thus preventing proper oil circulation and lubrication. To prevent sludge buildup in your engine, note the following:

1. When operating your Harley in cold/freezing weather, be aware of how long you actually run the engine—the engine is colder in winter months and will take longer to warm up. Run the engine for longer periods so that it can reach maximum operating temperature. This will allow water that has formed in the engine to vaporize and to be blown out through the engine breather.

2. Change the engine oil more frequently. This step can prevent sludge from accumulating in sufficient quantities to prevent engine damage.

3. Flush the oil tank at each oil change. Refer to Chapter Three for oil change and tank flush procedures.

Oil Consumption High or Engine Smokes Excessively

Check engine compression and perform a cylinder leakage test as described in Chapter Three. Causes can be one or more of the following:

  a. Worn valve guides.

  b. Worn valve guide seals.

  c. Worn or damaged piston rings.

  d. Breather valve damaged or timed incorrectly.

  e. Restricted oil tank return line.

  f. Oil tank overfilled.

  g. Oil filter restricted.

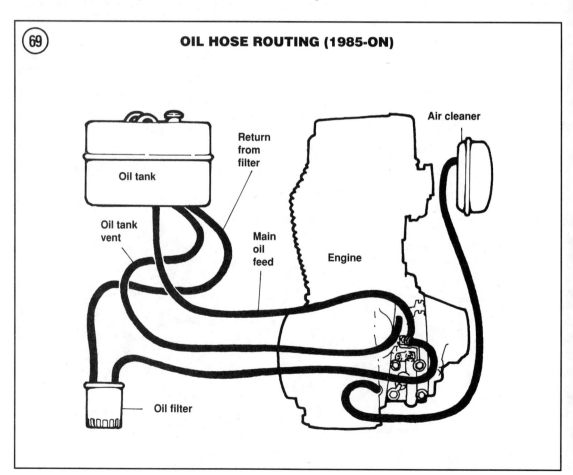

69 **OIL HOSE ROUTING (1985-ON)**

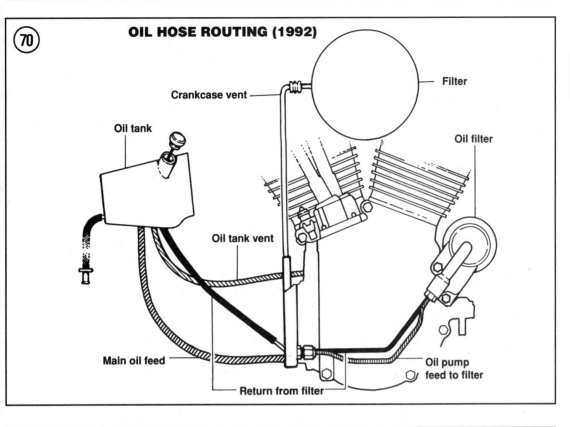

OIL HOSE ROUTING (1992)

70

Crankcase vent

Filter

Oil tank

Oil filter

Oil tank vent

Main oil feed

Oil pump
feed to filter

Return from filter

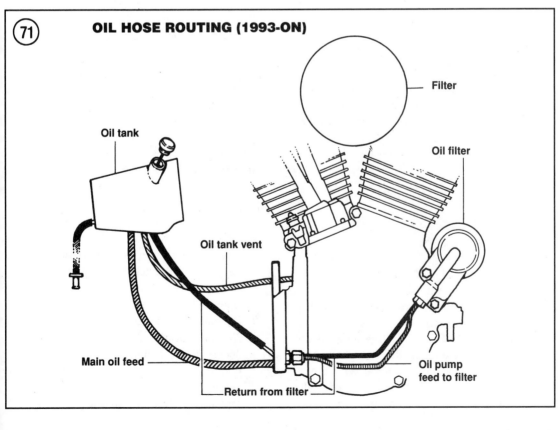

OIL HOSE ROUTING (1993-ON)

71

Filter

Oil tank

Oil filter

Oil tank vent

Main oil feed

Oil pump
feed to filter

Return from filter

2

h. Leaking cylinder head surfaces.

i. Insufficient primary chain case vacuum on dry clutch models only (early 1984). Perform the *Primary Housing Vacuum Check (Early 1984 With Dry Clutch)* as described in Chapter Five.

Oil Fails to Return to Oil Tank

a. Oil lines or fittings restricted or damaged.

b. Oil pump damaged or operating incorrectly.

c. Oil tank empty.

d. Oil filter restricted.

Excessive Engine Oil Leaks

a. Clogged air cleaner breather hose.

b. Restricted or damaged oil return line to oil tank.

c. Loose engine parts.

d. Damaged gasket sealing surfaces.

e. Restricted air cleaner breather hose.

f. Oil tank overfilled.

CLUTCH

The three basic clutch troubles are:

a. Clutch noise.

b. Clutch slipping.

c. Improper clutch disengagement or dragging.

All clutch troubles, except adjustments, require partial clutch disassembly to identify and cure the problem. The troubleshooting chart in **Figure 72** lists clutch troubles and checks to make. Refer to Chapter Five for clutch service procedures.

TRANSMISSION

The basic transmission troubles are:

a. Excessive gear noise.

b. Difficult shifting.

c. Gears pop out of mesh.

d. Incorrect shift lever operation.

Transmission symptoms are sometimes hard to distinguish from clutch symptoms. The troubleshooting chart in **Figure 73** lists transmission troubles and checks to make. Refer to Chapter Six or Chapter Seven for transmission service procedures. Be sure that the clutch is not causing the trouble before working on the transmission.

ELECTRICAL PROBLEMS

If bulbs burn out frequently, the cause may be excessive vibration, loose connections that permit sudden current surges or the installation of the wrong type of bulb.

Most light and ignition problems are caused by loose or corroded ground connections. Check these prior to replacing a bulb or electrical component.

EXCESSIVE VIBRATION

This can be difficult to find without disassembling the engine. Usually this is caused by loose engine mounting hardware. High speed vibration may be due to a bent axle shaft or loose or faulty suspension components. Vibration can also be caused by the following conditions:

a. Broken frame.

b. Severely worn primary chain.

c. Tight primary chain links.

d. Loose transmission mounting bolts.

e. Loose transmission sub-mounting plate bolts.

f. Improperly balanced wheel(s).

g. Defective or damaged wheel(s).

h. Defective or damaged tire(s).

i. Internal engine wear or damage.

FRONT SUSPENSION AND STEERING

Poor handling may be caused by improper tire pressure, a damaged or bent frame or front steering components, worn wheel bearings or dragging brakes. Possible causes for suspension and steering malfunctions are listed below.

Irregular or Wobbly Steering

a. Loose wheel axle nut(s).

b. Loose or worn steering head bearings.

c. Excessive wheel hub bearing play.

d. Damaged cast wheel.

e. Spoke wheel out of alignment.

f. Unbalanced wheel assembly.

g. Worn hub bearings.

h. Incorrect wheel alignment.

i. Bent or damaged steering stem or frame (at steering neck).

j. Tire incorrectly seated on rim.

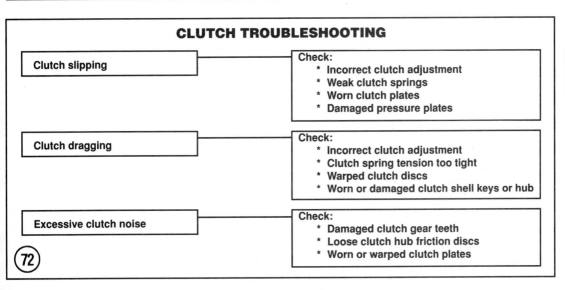

CLUTCH TROUBLESHOOTING

2

| Clutch slipping | Check:
* Incorrect clutch adjustment
* Weak clutch springs
* Worn clutch plates
* Damaged pressure plates |

| Clutch dragging | Check:
* Incorrect clutch adjustment
* Clutch spring tension too tight
* Warped clutch discs
* Worn or damaged clutch shell keys or hub |

| Excessive clutch noise | Check:
* Damaged clutch gear teeth
* Loose clutch hub friction discs
* Worn or warped clutch plates |

(72)

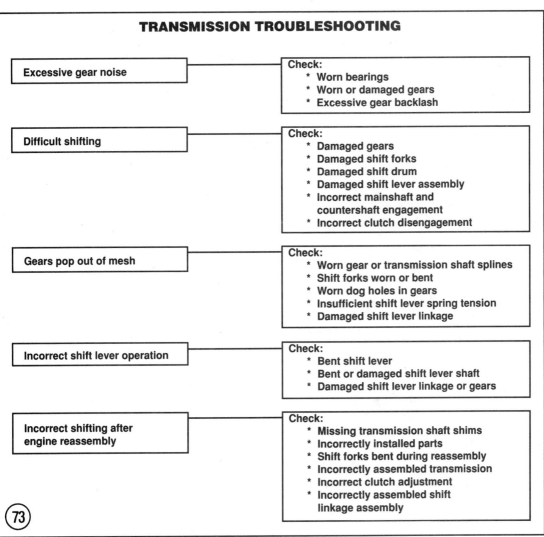

TRANSMISSION TROUBLESHOOTING

| Excessive gear noise | Check:
* Worn bearings
* Worn or damaged gears
* Excessive gear backlash |

| Difficult shifting | Check:
* Damaged gears
* Damaged shift forks
* Damaged shift drum
* Damaged shift lever assembly
* Incorrect mainshaft and countershaft engagement
* Incorrect clutch disengagement |

| Gears pop out of mesh | Check:
* Worn gear or transmission shaft splines
* Shift forks worn or bent
* Worn dog holes in gears
* Insufficient shift lever spring tension
* Damaged shift lever linkage |

| Incorrect shift lever operation | Check:
* Bent shift lever
* Bent or damaged shift lever shaft
* Damaged shift lever linkage or gears |

| Incorrect shifting after engine reassembly | Check:
* Missing transmission shaft shims
* Incorrectly installed parts
* Shift forks bent during reassembly
* Incorrectly assembled transmission
* Incorrect clutch adjustment
* Incorrectly assembled shift linkage assembly |

(73)

k. Excessive front end loading from non-standard equipment.

Stiff Steering

a. Low front tire air pressure.
b. Bent or damaged steering stem or frame (at steering neck).
c. Loose or worn steering head bearings.

Stiff or Heavy Fork Operation
(Non-Springer Front Fork)

a. Incorrect fork springs.
b. Incorrect fork oil viscosity.
c. Excessive fork oil capacity.
d. Bent fork tubes.

Poor Fork Operation
(Non-Springer Front Fork)

a. Worn or damaged fork tubes.
b. Fork oil capacity low.
c. Bent or damaged fork tubes.
d. Contaminated fork oil.
e. Incorrect fork springs.
f. Heavy front end loading from non-standard equipment.

Poor Rear Shock Absorber Operation

a. Weak or worn springs.
b. Damper unit leaking.
c. Shock shaft worn or bent.
d. Incorrect rear shock springs.
e. Rear shocks adjusted incorrectly.
f. Heavy rear end loading from non-standard equipment.
g. Incorrect loading.

BRAKE PROBLEMS

All models are equipped with front and rear disc brakes. Good brakes are vital to the safe operation of any vehicle. Perform the maintenance specified in Chapter Three to minimize brake system problems. Brake system service is covered in Chapter Fourteen. When refilling the front and rear master cylinders, use only DOT 5 brake fluid.

Insufficient Braking Power

Worn brake pads or disc, air in the hydraulic system, glazed or contaminated pads, low brake fluid level or a leaking brake line or hose can cause this problem. Visually check for leaks. Check for worn brake pads. Check also for a leaking or damaged primary cup seal in the master cylinder. Bleed and adjust the brakes. Rebuild a leaking master cylinder or brake caliper. Brake drag will result in excessive heat and brake fade. See *Brake Drag* in this section.

Spongy Brake Feel

This problem is generally caused by air in the hydraulic system. Bleed and adjust the brakes.

Brake Drag

Check brake adjustment, looking for insufficient brake pedal and/or hand lever free play. Also check for worn, loose or missing parts in the brake calipers. Check the brake disc for excessive runout.

Brakes Squeal or Chatter

Check brake pad thickness and disc condition. Make sure that the pads are not loose; check that the anti-rattle springs are properly installed and in good condition. Clean off any dirt on the pads. Loose components can also cause this. Check for:
a. Warped brake disc.
b. Loose brake disc.
c. Loose caliper mounting bolts.
d. Loose front axle nut.
e. Worn wheel bearings.
f. Damaged hub.

Table 1   ELECTRICAL SPECIFICATIONS

Battery capacity	12 volt, 19 amp hr.
Ignition coil	
Primary resistance	
1984	3.3-3.7 ohms
1985-on	2.5-3.1 ohms
Secondary resistance	
1984	16,500-19,500 ohms
1985-1992	11,250-13,750 ohms
1993-on	10,000-12,500 ohms
Alternator	
Stator coil resistance	
1984-1988	0.2-0.4 ohms
1989-on	0.1-0.2 ohms
AC voltage output	
1984-1988	19-26 VAC per 1,000 rpm
1989-on	16-20 VAC per 1,000 rpm
Voltage regulator	
Voltage output @ 3,600 rpm	13.8-15 volts @ 75° F
Amperes @ 3,600 rpm	
1984-1988	22 amps
1989-on	32 amps
Starter current draw test	
1984-1988	45 amps maximum
1989-1992	150 amps maximum
1993-on	200 amps maximum

2

CHAPTER THREE

PERIODIC LUBRICATION, MAINTENANCE AND TUNE-UP

The service life and operation of your Harley-Davidson will depend on the maintenance it receives. This is easy to understand, once you realize that a motorcycle, even in normal use, is subjected to tremendous heat, stress and vibration. When neglected, any bike becomes unreliable and actually dangerous to ride.

All motorcycles require attention before and after riding them. The time spent on basic maintenance and lubrication will provide you with the utmost in safety and performance as well as maintaining and actually increasing your Harley's monetary value. Minor problems found during these inspections are simple and inexpensive to correct. If they are not found and corrected at this time they could lead to major and more expensive problems later on. Letting things go is a bad and costly habit to get into.

Harley-Davidson motorcycles are some of the most well designed and manufactured motorcycles sold today. Maintain the image by maintaining your bike.

Regular cleaning of the bike is also very important. It makes routine maintenance a lot easier by not having to work your way through a build-up of road dirt to get to a component for adjustment or replacement. Routine cleaning also allows you to see a damaged component or leak that can be repaired or replaced as soon as the damage occurs. If a damaged part is allowed to deteriorate, it may create an unsafe riding condition that could lead to a possible accident.

If this is your first bike, start out by doing simple tune-up, lubrication and maintenance. Tackle more involved jobs as you become more acquainted with the bike.

Certain maintenance tasks and checks should be performed weekly. Others should be performed at certain time or mileage intervals. Still others should be done whenever certain symptoms appear. Some maintenance procedures are included under *Tune-up* at the end of this chapter. Detailed instructions will be found there. Other steps are described in the following chapters. Chapter references are included with these steps.

The service procedures and intervals shown in **Table 1** (1984) and **Table 2** (1985-on) are recommended by Harley-Davidson. **Tables 1-9** are located at the end of the chapter.

ROUTINE SAFETY CHECKS

The following safety checks should be performed prior to the first ride of the day.

General Inspection

1. Quickly inspect the engine for signs of oil or fuel leakage.

2. Check the tires for embedded stones. Pry them out with a suitable tool.

3. Make sure all lights work.

NOTE
At least check the brake light. It can burn out anytime. Motorists can't stop as quickly as you and need all the warning you can give.

4. Inspect the fuel lines and fittings for wetness.

5. Make sure both fuel tanks are full of fresh gasoline.

6. Check the operation of the front and rear brakes. Add DOT 5 brake fluid to the front and rear master cylinders as required.

7. Check the operation of the clutch. If necessary, adjust the clutch free-play as described in this chapter.

8. Check the throttle operation. The hand throttle should move smoothly with no sign of roughness, sticking or tightness. The throttle should snap back when released. Adjust throttle free play, if necessary, as described in this chapter.

9. Check the rear brake pedal. It should move smoothly. If necessary, adjust free play as described in this chapter.

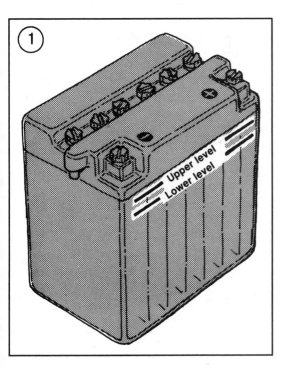

10. Inspect the front and rear suspension. Make sure they have a good solid feel with no looseness. On springer models, check for freedom of movement by holding the front brake and compressing the front end by hand.

11. Check the exhaust system for damage.

CAUTION
*When checking the tightness of the exposed fasteners on your Harley, do **not** include the cylinder head bolts in this process. Harley-Davidson lists a specific bolt tightening sequence to prevent cylinder head and cylinder distortion, head leakage and stud failure. When tightening the cylinder head bolts, follow the procedure for your model described in Chapter Four.*

Engine Oil Tank Level

Refer to *Periodic Lubrication* in this chapter.

Tire Pressure

Tire pressure must be checked with the tires cold. Correct tire pressure, listed in **Table 3**, varies with the load you are carrying. Refer to *Tire Pressure* in this chapter.

Battery

Remove the battery and check the battery electrolyte level. The level must be maintained within the MIN and MAX battery markings (**Figure 1**).

For complete details, see *Battery* in Chapter Nine.

Lights and Horn

With the engine running, check the following.

1. Pull the front brake lever and check that the brake light comes on.

2. Push the rear brake pedal down and check that the brake light comes on soon after you have begun depressing the pedal.

3. Check to see that the headlight and taillight are on.

4. Move the dimmer switch up and down between the high and low positions, and check to see that both headlight elements are working.

5. Push the turn signal switch to the left position and right position and check that all 4 turn signal lights are working.

6. Push the horn button and make sure that the horn blows loudly.

7. If the horn or any light failed to work properly, refer to Chapter Nine.

MAINTENANCE INTERVALS

The services and intervals shown in **Table 1** and **Table 2** is recommended by the factory. Strict adherence to these recommendations will go a long way toward insuring long service from your Harley. If the bike is run in an area of high humidity, the lubrication service must be done more frequently to prevent possible rust damage.

For convenient maintenance of your motorcycle, most of the services shown in **Table 1** and **Table 2** are described in this chapter. Those procedures which require more than minor disassembly or adjustment are covered elsewhere in the appropriate chapter. The *Table of Contents* and *Index* can help you to locate a particular service procedure.

CLEANING YOUR HARLEY

Regular cleaning of your Harley is important. It makes routine maintenance a lot easier by not having to work your way through built-up dirt to get to a component for adjustment or replacement. It also makes the bike look like new even though it may have many thousands of miles on it.

If you ride in a farming area or where there is a lot of rain or road salt residue in the winter, clean the bike off more often in order to maintain the painted, plated and polished surfaces in good condition. Keep a good coat of wax on the bike during the winter to prevent premature weathering of all finishes.

Washing the bike should be done in a gentle way to avoid damage to the painted and plated finishes and to components that are not designed to withstand high-pressure water. Try to avoid using the coin-operated car wash systems as the cleaning agents may be harmful to the plastic parts on the bike. Also the rinse cycle is usually fairly high pressure and will force water into areas that should be kept dry.

Use a mild detergent (mild liquid dish washing detergent) or a commercial car washing detergent available at most auto parts outlets. Be warned, these detergents will remove some of the wax that you have applied to the finish. Follow the manufacturer's instructions for the correct detergent-to-water mixture.

If the lower end of the engine and frame are covered with oil, grease or road dirt, spray this dirt with a commercial cleaner like Gunk Cycle Cleaner, or equivalent. Keep this cleaner off of the plastic components as it may damage the finish. Follow the manufacturer's instructions and rinse with *plenty of cold water*. Do not allow any of this cleaner residue to settle in any pockets as it will stain or destroy the finish of most painted parts.

Use a commercial tar-stain remover to remove any severe road dirt and tar stains. Be sure to rinse all areas thoroughly with plenty of clean water to make sure all of the tar-stain remover is rinsed off of all surfaces.

Prior to washing the plastic and painted surfaces of the bike make sure the surfaces are cool. Do not wash a hot bike as you will probably end up with streaks since the soap suds will start to dry prior to being rinsed off.

CAUTION
Do not allow water (especially under pressure) to enter the air intake, brake assemblies, electrical switches and connectors, instrument cluster, wheel bearing areas, swing arm bearings or any other moisture-sensitive areas of the bike.

After all of the heavily soiled areas are cleaned off, use the previously described detergent, warm water and a soft natural sponge and carefully wash down the entire bike, including the wheels and tires. Always wet the bike down *before* washing with a

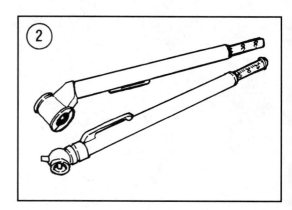

detergent soaked sponge or rag. This will remove dirt from sensitive areas and prevent scratching. Don't use too much detergent as it will be difficult to rinse off all of the soap suds thoroughly. After all areas have been washed, rinse off the soap suds with *low-pressure cold water*. Make sure all of the detergent residue is thoroughly rinsed off.

NOTE
Before washing the fuel tank, check for small pebbles, metal shavings or dirt stuck to or partially hidden in your sponge and rags. These objects may scratch and mar the tank's finish. As you wash your bike, rinse the sponge or rag frequently to remove accumulated dirt.

Straddle the bike and kick up the jiffy stand. Then lean it to both sides to allow all water to drain off the top of the cylinder block and other horizontal surfaces. If you have access to compressed air, *gently* blow excess water from areas where the water may have collected. Do not force the water into any of the sensitive areas mentioned in the previous *CAUTION*. Gently dry off the bike with a chamois, a clean soft Turkish towel or an old plain T-shirt (no transfers or hand-painted designs, these may scratch the tank).

If you have mounted a windshield on your Harley, be careful when cleaning it; windshields can be easily scratched or damaged. Do not use a cleaner with an abrasive or a combination cleaner and wax. Never use gasoline or cleaning solvent. These products will either scratch or totally destroy the surface finish of the windshield.

Clean the windshield with a soft cloth or natural sponge and plenty of water. Dry thoroughly with a soft cloth or chamois—do not press hard.

WARNING
The brake components may have gotten wet. If they are damp or wet they will not be operating at their optimum effectiveness. Be prepared to take a longer distance to stop the bike right after washing the bike. Ride slowly and lightly apply the brakes to dry off the pads.

Start the engine and let it reach normal operating temperature. Take the bike out for a *slow and careful* ride around the block to blow off any residual water. Bring the bike back to the wash area and dry off any residual water streaks from the painted and plated surfaces.

Once the bike is thoroughly dry, get out the polish, wax and Armour All and give the bike a good polish and wax job to protect the painted, plated and polished surfaces.

TIRES AND WHEELS

Tire Pressure

Tire pressure should be checked and adjusted to maintain the tire profile, good traction and handling and to get the maximum life out of the tire. A simple, accurate gauge (**Figure 2**) can be purchased for a few dollars and should be carried in your motorcycle tool kit. The appropriate tire pressures are shown in **Table 3**.

NOTE
*After checking and adjusting the air pressure, make sure to reinstall the air valve cap (**Figure 3**). The cap prevents small pebbles and dirt from collecting in the valve stem; these could allow air leakage or result in incorrect tire pressure readings.*

Tire Inspection

The tires take a lot of punishment so inspect them periodically for excessive wear, deep cuts, imbedded objects such as stones, nails, etc. If you find a nail or other object in a tire, mark its location with a light crayon prior to removing it. This will help to locate the hole for repair. Refer to Chapter Ten for tire changing and repair information.

Check local traffic regulations concerning minimum tread depth. Measure with a tread depth gauge (**Figure 4**) or small ruler. As a guideline, replace tires when the tread depth is 5/16 in. or less.

Wheel Spoke Tension

On spoked wheels, the spokes should be checked frequently for loosening or breakage. Loose spokes can cause spoke, rim and hub breakage. Spokes can be checked by one of the two following methods:

   a. Tone: Tap each spoke with a screwdriver or spoke wrench (**Figure 5**) and listen for a variation in tone between the different spokes. The higher pitch of sound it makes, the tighter the spoke. The lower the sound frequency, the looser the spoke. A "ping" is good; a "clunk" says the spoke is loose.

   b. Feel: Grab two spokes near their cross point, then squeeze and check tension. Tight spokes will not give or flex as much as loose spokes.

   c. If one or more spokes are loose, tighten them as described in Chapter Ten.

Rim Inspection

Frequently inspect the wheel rims. If a rim has been damaged, it might have been knocked out of alignment. Improper wheel alignment can cause severe vibration and result in an unsafe riding condition. If the rim portion of an alloy wheel, is damaged the wheel must be replaced as it cannot be repaired. Refer to Chapter Ten for rim service.

PERIODIC LUBRICATION

Oil

Oil is graded according to its viscosity, which is an indication of how thick it is. The Society of Automotive Engineers (SAE) system distinguishes oil viscosity by numbers. Thick oils have higher viscosity numbers than thin oils. For example, an SAE 5 oil is a thin oil while an SAE 90 oil is relatively thick.

Grease

A good quality grease (preferably waterproof) should be used (**Figure 6**). Water does not wash grease off parts as easily as it washes oil off. In addition, grease maintains its lubricating qualities better than oil on long and strenuous rides.

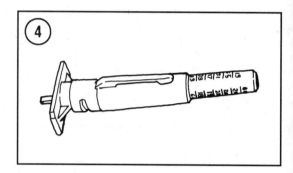

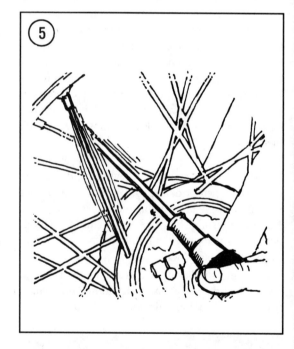

Oil Tank Inspection

Before checking the oil level, inspect the oil tank for cracks or other damage. If oil seepage is noted on or near the tank, find and repair the problem. Check all of the oil tank mounting bolts for loose or missing fasteners; replace or tighten fasteners as required. Check the hose connections on the tank. See **Figure 7A** (1984), **Figure 7B** (1985-1991), **Figure 8A** (1992) or **Figure 8B** (1993-on). Each hose should be secured with a hose clamp. Check each hose for swelling, cracks or damage; otherwise, oil leakage may occur and cause engine damage.

Oil Tank Level Check

A remote oil tank is mounted on the right-hand side of the bike. The oil level in the tank should be checked prior to each ride as oil consumption is relative to engine speed and engine tune. In addition, the engine will consume less oil and run cooler when the oil level in the tank is kept relatively high.

Engine oil level is checked with the dipstick mounted in the tank filler cap.

1. Start and run the engine for approximately 10 minutes or until the engine has reached normal

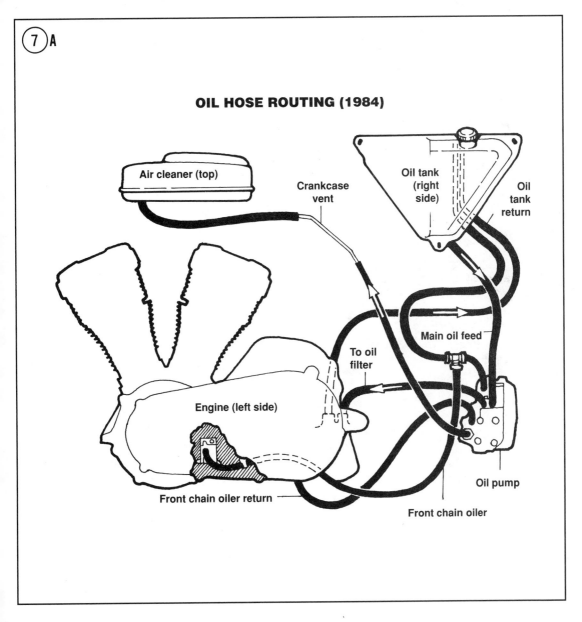

7 A

OIL HOSE ROUTING (1984)

Air cleaner (top)

Crankcase vent

Oil tank (right side)

Oil tank return

Main oil feed

To oil filter

Engine (left side)

Front chain oiler return

Oil pump

Front chain oiler

operating temperature. Then turn the engine off and allow the oil to settle in the tank.

2. Have an assistant support the bike so that is stands straight up. If the bike is supported on the jiffy stand when checking the oil level, an incorrect reading will be obtained.

3. Wipe off the oil tank filler cap and the area around the cap with a clean rag, then remove the filler cap and dipstick. Wipe the dipstick off with a clean rag and reinsert cap all the way into the oil tank. Withdraw filler cap once again and check oil level on dipstick. Oil level should be above "REFILL" dipstick mark. See **Figure 9**.

4. If the oil level in the tank is low, perform the following:

a. The dipstick on these models does not have a full or upper mark. The oil tank is full when the hot oil level in the tank is level with the bottom of the oil tank cap rubber seat (**Figure 9**).

b. Do not overfill beyond the specified point as the oil will overflow and an air space is required in the tank.

c. Add the recommended weight engine oil indicated in **Table 4** to correct the oil level.

d. Reinstall the filler cap.

5. As a safety precaution, check the oil tank drain plug or hose for tightness.

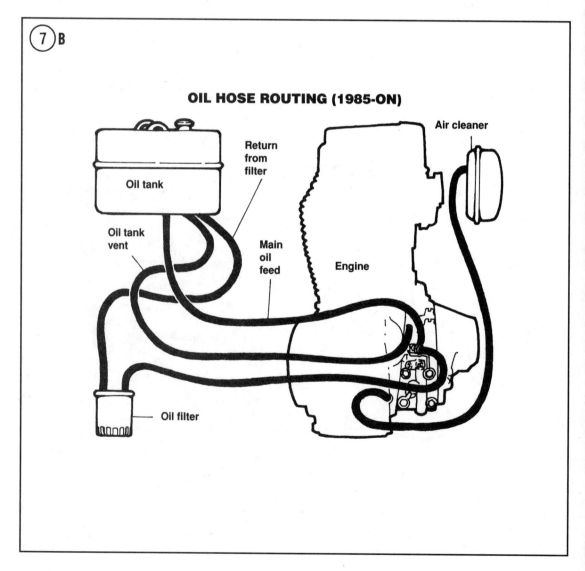

⑦ B

OIL HOSE ROUTING (1985-ON)

Engine Oil and Filter Change

The factory-recommended oil and filter change interval is specified in **Table 1** or **Table 2**. This assumes that the motorcycle is operated in moderate climates. In extreme climates, oil should be changed more often. The time interval is more important than the mileage interval because combustion acids, formed by gasoline and water vapor, will contaminate the oil even if the motorcycle is not run for several months. If a motorcycle is operated under dusty conditions, the oil will get dirty more quickly and should be changed more frequently than recommended.

Oil for motorcycle and automotive engines is graded by the American Petroleum Institute (API) and the Society of Automotive Engineers (SAE) in several categories. Oil containers display these ratings on the top of the oil can or on the bottle label (**Figure 10**).

Use only a detergent oil with an API rating of SE or SF. Try to use the same brand of oil at each change. Refer to **Table 4** for correct oil viscosity to

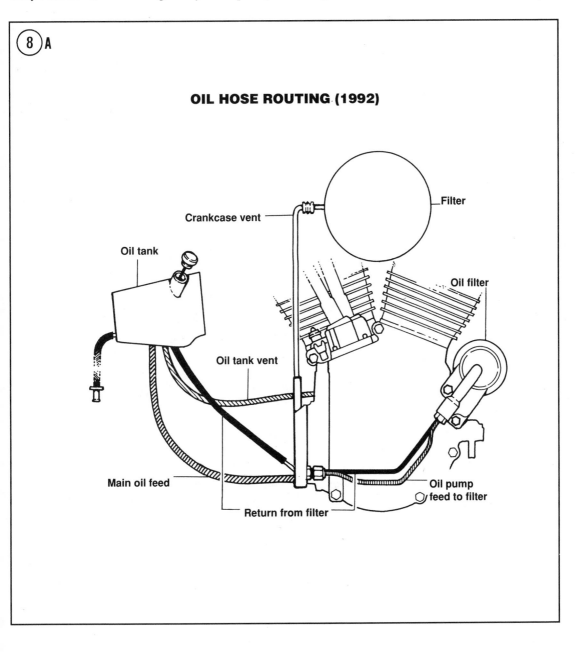

OIL HOSE ROUTING (1992)

Filter

Crankcase vent

Oil tank

Oil filter

Oil tank vent

Main oil feed

Return from filter

Oil pump feed to filter

use under anticipated ambient temperatures (not engine oil temperature).

To change the engine oil and filter you will need the following:

- a. Drain pan.
- b. Funnel.
- c. Can opener or pour spout (can-type only).
- d. Wrench (for drain plug models).
- e. 3 quarts of oil.
- f. Oil filter element.

There are a number of ways to discard the used oil safely. The easiest way is to pour it from the drain pan into a gallon plastic bleach, juice or milk container for disposal. Some service stations and oil retailers will accept your used oil for recycling. There may be a recycling center in your area that accepts oil. Do not discard the oil in your household trash or pour it onto the ground.

1. Start and run the engine for approximately 10 minutes or until the engine has reached normal operating temperature. Then turn the engine off and

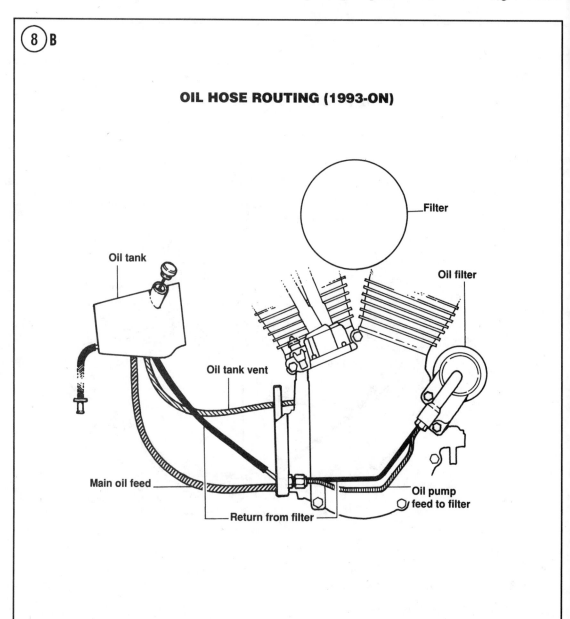

(8) B

OIL HOSE ROUTING (1993-ON)

allow the oil to settle in the tank. Support the bike so that the oil can drain completely.

NOTE
Before removing the oil tank cap, thoroughly clean off all dirt and oil around it.

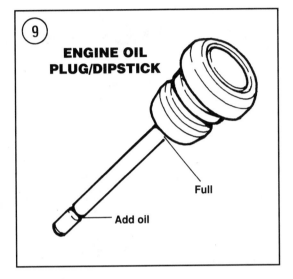

ENGINE OIL PLUG/DIPSTICK

Full

Add oil

SAE 20W-50

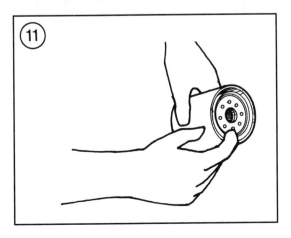

2. Place a drain pan beside the bike, then remove the oil tank drain plug and gasket or disconnect the drain hose at the oil tank or remove the drain hose plug from the oil tank drain hose. Use a funnel and drain the oil into the pan.

3. *Models with dry clutch:* Remove the primary case drain plug located underneath the clutch cover and drain the primary case. Reinstall the drain plug and washer.

4. Service the oil filter as follows:

   a. Remove the filter with a filter wrench.

   b. Discard the oil filter.

   c. Wipe the crankcase gasket surface with a clean, lint-free cloth.

   d. Coat the neoprene gasket on the new filter with clean oil (**Figure 11**).

   e. Screw the filter onto the crankcase *by hand* until the filter gasket just touches the base, i.e., until you feel the slightest resistance when turning the filter. Then tighten the filter *by hand* 1/4-1/2 turn more.

CAUTION
Do not overtighten and do not use a filter wrench or the filter may leak.

5. At the first 500 miles (new bike or after rebuilding engine), and at every second oil change thereafter, flush the oil tank as described in this chapter:

6. Reinstall the oil tank drain plug and gasket or reconnect oil drain hose or reinstall the hose plug.

7. Fill the oil tank with the correct viscosity (**Table 4**) and quantity (**Table 5**) of oil.

8. Insert the filler cap into the oil tank.

9. Clean the tappet oil screen as described under *Tappet Oil Screen Cleaning* in this chapter.

Oil Tank Flushing

At the first 500 miles (new bike or after rebuilding the engine), and at every second oil change during warm riding weather, flush the oil tank before refilling it with new oil. During colder weather, the oil tank should be flushed at each oil change.

1. Drain the oil tank as previously described.

2. ID all oil hoses at the oil tank so you don't mix them up during reassembly. Then remove the oil tank fasteners and remove the oil tank from the bike.

CAUTION
Total flushing of the oil tank while it is mounted on the bike is difficult. Sludge broken loose from the tank and not removed during flushing will pass through the main oil feed line and into the oil pump; there it will clog oil passages and cause engine seizure.

3. Reinstall the oil tank drain plug (if used) and plug all tank hose openings.

4. Fill the oil tank 3/4 full with kerosene.

5. Vigorously swish the tank from side to side to break loose sludge and sediment accumulation in the tank.

6. Remove the dipstick from the top of the tank and drain the tank. Using a small flashlight, check the tank for sludge and sediment deposits that did not drain out. Repeat this step until all of these deposits are removed. If necessary, break hard deposits loose with a wooden dowel or similar tool inserted into the tank.

7. When the tank is clean, pour some clean engine oil into the tank and shake the tank once again to cover the tank walls with the oil. Then drain and discard the oil.

8. Clean the filler cap/dipstick assembly before installing it back into the tank.

9. Remove the plugs from the oil tank hoses and reinstall the oil tank. Tighten all tank mounting bolts or nuts securely. Wipe the oil hoses off before reconnecting them onto the tank. Refer to your ID marks and Figure and reconnect the oil hoses.

Transmission Oil Check

Inspect the transmission oil level at the interval listed in **Table 1** or **Table 2**. If the bike has just been run, allow it to cool down (approximately 10 minutes), then check the transmission oil. When checking the transmission oil level, do not allow any dirt or foreign matter to enter the case opening.

1. Park the bike on a level surface and support it so that it is standing straight up. Do not support it with the jiffy stand.

2. Wipe the area around the transmission filler cap. Unscrew and remove the transmission filler cap and O-ring. See **Figure 12** (4-speed), **Figure 13** (early model 5-speed) or **Figure 14** (late model 5-speed).

3A. *4-speed with oil level plug*: Remove the oil level plug from transmission cover. The oil should be

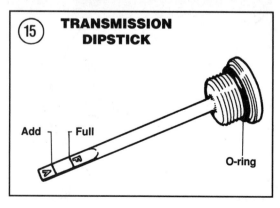

TRANSMISSION DIPSTICK

Add — Full

O-ring

level with the level plug opening. Reinstall the oil level plug.

3B. *4-speed without oil level plug*: The oil should be level with the filler cap opening.

3C. *5-speed*: Wipe the dipstick off and reinsert it back into the transmission housing; do not screw the cap in place, rest it on the housing and then withdraw it. The oil level should be between the 2 dipstick marks. See **Figure 15**.

4. If the oil level is low, add the recommended type of oil listed in **Table 6**. Do not overfill.

5. Inspect the O-ring on the filler cap. Replace if worn or damaged.

6. Install the O-ring and the oil filler cap.

7. Wipe off any spilled oil from the transmission case.

Transmission Oil Change

Change the transmission oil at the intervals specified in **Table 1** or **Table 2**.

To change the transmission oil, you will need the following:

  a. Drain pan.
  b. Funnel.
  c. Box-end wrench for drain plug.
  d. Gear oil (**Table 6**).

1. Ride the bike until the transmission oil reaches normal operating temperature. Usually 10-15 minutes of stop and go riding is sufficient. Shut the engine off.

> *NOTE*
> *There are 2 important reasons for draining the transmission oil while it is hot. First, hot oil will drain more quickly. Second, contaminants in the oil will drain with it, instead of settling in the bottom of the transmission case, ready to mix with the new oil.*

2. Park the bike on a level surface and support it so that it is standing straight up. Do not support it with the jiffy stand.

3. Wipe the area around the filler cap clean and unscrew the filler cap and O-ring. See **Figure 12**, **Figure 13** or **Figure 14**.

4. Place a drain pan underneath the transmission drain plug.

5A. *4-speed*: Remove the drain plug and gasket from the bottom of the transmission case. Allow the oil to drain for 10 minutes.

5B. *5-speed*: Remove the drain plug from the transmission side cover (**Figure 16** [early models]) or the drain plug and gasket (late models) from underneath the center of the transmission housing. Allow the oil to drain for 10 minutes.

> *WARNING*
> *Do not allow the oil to spill onto the ground where the rear tire may contact it later. Wipe up all oil spills immediately.*

6. Check the drain plug gasket for damage and replace if necessary.

7. The drain plug is magnetic. Check the plug (**Figure 17**) for metal debris that may indicate transmission wear, then wipe the plug off. Replace the plug if the head and/or threads are damaged.

8A. Install the drain plug and its gasket into the bottom of the transmission housing and tighten securely.

> *CAUTION*
> *On 5-speed models in which the drain plug screws into transmission side cover (**Figure 16**), the plug uses tapered threads. Do not overtighten this plug or you will have to drill it out the next time*

you want to drain the oil. Tighten the plug as described in Step 8B.

8B. If the transmission plug screws into the transmission side cover (**Figure 16**), install and tighten it until a distance of 0.16-0.18 in. (4.06-4.57 mm) is maintained from the top of the plug head to the side cover surface; see **Figure 18**.

9. Refill the transmission through the side cover hole (**Figure 12**, **Figure 13** or **Figure 14**) with the recommended quantity (**Table 5**) and type (**Table 6**) transmission oil.

10. Install the filler cap and O-ring and tighten securely.

11. Remove the oil drain pan from underneath the transmission and dispose the oil as outlined under *Engine Oil and Filter Change* in this chapter.

12. Ride the bike until the transmission oil reaches normal operating temperature. Then shut the engine off.

13. Check the transmission oil level as described in this chapter and readjust level if necessary.

Front Fork Oil Change (Non-Springer Models)

The fork oil should be changed at the intervals specified in **Table 1** or **Table 2**.

1. Place a drain pan beside one fork tube and remove the drain screw and washer. See **Figure 19**, typical. Apply the front brake lever and push down on the forks and release. Repeat this procedure until all of the fork oil is drained.

2. Inspect the sealing washer on the drain screw; replace if damaged in any way.

3. Reinstall the drain screw and washer. Tighten securely.

4. Repeat Steps 1-3 for the opposite fork tube.

CAUTION
Do not allow the fork oil to come in contact with any of the brake components.

5. Raise and secure the front end so that the front tire clears the ground. Both fork tubes should be fully extended.

CAUTION
Make sure the vehicle is supported securely.

WARNING
FLST models have preloaded fork springs. Early FLST fork tubes are equipped with a plug to preload the fork spring. Later models are equipped with longer fork springs. Before removing the fork cap, make sure the fork tubes are extended all the way. Remove the fork cap slowly as the spring preload can cause the parts to fly off of the fork tube unexpectedly.

6. Remove the fork cap from one fork tube. On early FLST models, remove the preload plug after removing the fork cap.

7. Insert a small funnel into the opening in the fork tube.

NOTE
*If fork has been disassembled, refill with "dry" quantity; otherwise, refill with "wet" quantity. See **Table 7**.*

NOTE
*In order to measure the correct amount of fluid, use a **discarded** baby bottle. These bottles have measurements in*

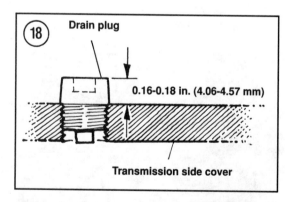

(18) Drain plug

0.16-0.18 in. (4.06-4.57 mm)

Transmission side cover

(19)

fluid ounces (oz.) and cubic centimeters (cc) imprinted on the side. Mark the bottle with "Shop Use Only" after using it.

8. Fill the fork tube with the correct viscosity and quantity of fork oil. Refer to **Table 6** and **Table 7**. Remove the small funnel.

9. Check the condition of the fork cap O-ring (if so equipped), and replace it if necessary.

10. Reinstall the fork cap and O-ring.

11. Repeat Steps 6-10 for the opposite side.

12. Road test the bike and check for leaks.

Control Cables

The control cables should be lubricated at the intervals specified in **Table 1** or **Table 2**. At this time, they should also be inspected for fraying, and the cable sheath should be checked for chafing; **Figure 20** shows a cable damaged from improper routing. Damaged cables should be replaced immediately.

They can be lubricated with any of the popular cable lubricants and a cable lubricator.

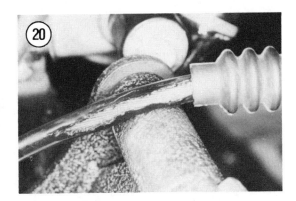

NOTE
The main cause of cable breakage or cable stiffness is improper lubrication. Maintaining the cables as described in this section will assure long cable service life.

NOTE
The enrichener cable on 1990 and later models must have sufficient cable resistance to work properly. Do not lubricate the enrichener cable or its conduit.

1. Disconnect the clutch cable from the left-hand side handlebar. Disconnect the throttle cable(s) from the throttle grip.

2. Attach a lubricator to the cable following the manufacturer's instructions (**Figure 21**).

NOTE
Place a shop cloth at the end of the cable(s) to catch all excess lubricant that will flow out.

3. Insert the nozzle of the lubricant can into the lubricator, press the button on the can and hold it down until the lubricant begins to flow out of the other end of the cable. If lubricant squirts out around the lubricator, it is not clamped to the cable properly. Loosen and reposition the cable lubricator.

NOTE
If the lubricant does not flow out of the other end of the cable, check the entire length of the cable for fraying, bending or other damage. Replace the cable if damaged.

4. Remove the lubricator, reconnect and adjust the cable(s) as described in this chapter.

Speedometer Cable Lubrication

Lubricate the cable every year or whenever needle operation is erratic.

1. Remove the speedometer cable from underneath the speedometer (**Figure 22**).

2. Pull the cable from the sheath.

3. If the grease is contaminated, thoroughly clean off all old grease.

4. Thoroughly coat the cable with a good grade of multi-purpose grease and reinstall into the sheath.

5. Make sure the cable is correctly seated into the drive unit. If not, it will be necessary to disconnect the cable at its lower connection and reattach.

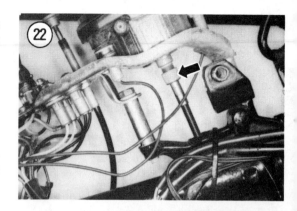

Rear Brake Pedal and Shift Linkage Lubrication

On some models, a grease fitting is installed on the brake pedal and/or shift linkage mounting bracket that allows periodic lubrication of the respective pivot shaft.

1. Wipe the grease fitting and the grease gun nozzle with a clean rag.

2. Snap the grease gun nozzle onto the fitting. Slowly pump the gun until grease starts to ooze out of the pivot shaft area.

> *NOTE*
> *If the grease fitting will not take the grease, it is probably plugged. Remove the fitting and clean or replace it.*

3. Remove the grease gun and wipe up all excess grease.

Primary Chain Lubrication (Dry Clutch Models)

The primary chain is lubricated through a metering tube (**Figure 23**) connected to an oil line attached to the oil pump. Oil flow is controlled by a fixed metering orifice; adjustment of the oil flow is not possible. Excess oil that collects in the primary cover is drawn back into the engine through the gearcase breather. Whenever the primary chain is adjusted, check to see that oil drops out of the metering tube as follows.

1. Remove the clutch inspection cover (**Figure 24**).

2. Start the engine and check that oil comes out of the metering tube (**Figure 23**).

3. Turn the engine off.

4. If oil did not flow out of the metering tube in Step 2, check and clean the oil hose and the oil fitting. See **Figure 7**.

Primary Chain Lubrication
(Wet Clutch)

Inspection

1. Park the bike on a level surface and support it so that it is standing straight up. Do not support it with the jiffy stand.

2. Remove the clutch inspection cover (A, **Figure 25**).

3. The oil level should be level with the bottom of the clutch opening or at the bottom of the clutch diaphragm spring (**Figure 26**).

4. If necessary, add Harley-Davidson Primary Chaincase Lubricant or equivalent through the opening (**Figure 26**) to correct the level.

5. Install the clutch inspection cover together with its O-ring.

Oil change

1. Ride the bike until the primary chaincase oil reaches normal operating temperature. Usually 10-15 minutes of stop and go riding is sufficient. Shut the engine off.

> *NOTE*
> *There are 2 important reasons for draining the oil while it is hot. First, hot oil will drain more quickly. Second, contaminants in the oil will drain with it, instead of settling in the bottom of the clutch case, ready to mix with the new oil.*

2. Park the bike on a level surface and support it so that it is standing straight up. Do not support it with the jiffy stand.

3. Place a drain pan under the chaincase and remove the drain plug. The drain plug is at the right-hand side of the primary chaincase. See B, **Figure 25**.

4. Allow the oil to drain for at least 10 minutes.

5. Reinstall the drain plug, making sure you do not overtighten it.

6. Remove the clutch inspection cover (A, **Figure 25**) and refill the primary housing as described under *Inspection* in this chapter.

Drive Chain Lubrication

1. Support the bike so that the rear wheel clears the ground.

2. Shift the transmission to NEUTRAL.

3. Oil the bottom run of the chain with a commercial chain lubricant. Concentrate on getting the lubricant down between the side plates, pins, bushings and rollers of each chain link. Rotate the wheel and oil the entire chain.

Miscellaneous Lubrication Points

Lubricate the clutch lever, front brake lever, rear brake lever, jiffy stand pivot and footrest pivot points. Use SAE 10W/30 motor oil.

PERIODIC MAINTENANCE

Maintenance intervals are listed in **Table 1** (1984) and **Table 2** (1985-on).

Primary Chain Adjustment

1. Disconnect the negative battery cable.

2. Remove the gearshift lever, if necessary.

3. Remove the primary chain inspection cover. See **Figure 27**, typical.

4. Loosen the chain adjuster shoe center nut (**Figure 28**) and discard the nut.

5. Move the shoe support up or down to tension chain. Free vertical movement in upper chain run (**Figure 29**) should be 5/8 to 7/8 in. (15.87-22.22 mm) (cold engine) or 3/8 to 5/8 in. (9.52-15.87 mm) (hot engine).

> *NOTE*
> *__Figure 28__ and __Figure 29__ shows the primary chain adjustment made with the primary chain cover removed for clarity. The adjustment can be made through the adjustment cover opening. See __Figure 30__.*

6. Install a new locknut (**Figure 28**) and recheck adjustment.

7. Install the inspection cover (**Figure 27**) with a new gasket.

8. Install the shift lever, if necessary.

Drive Chain Inspection/Adjustment

> *NOTE*
> *As drive chains stretch and wear in use, the chain will become tighter at one*

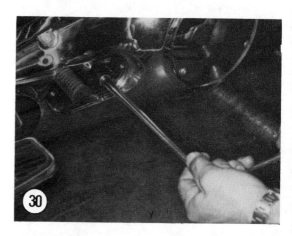

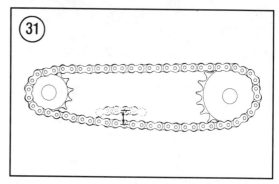

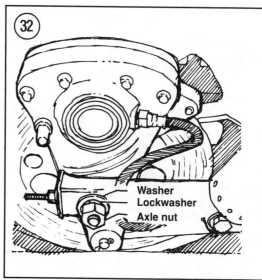

point. The chain must be checked and adjusted at this point.

1. Turn the rear wheel and check the chain for its tightest point. Mark this spot and turn the wheel so that the mark is located on the chains lower run, midway between both drive sprockets. Check and adjust the drive chain as follows:

2. Have a rider mounted on the seat.

3. Push the chain up midway between the sprockets on the lower chain run and check the free play (**Figure 31**). The free play should be 1 1/8-1 1/4 in. (28.57-31.75 mm).

4. If chain adjustment is incorrect, adjust it as follows:

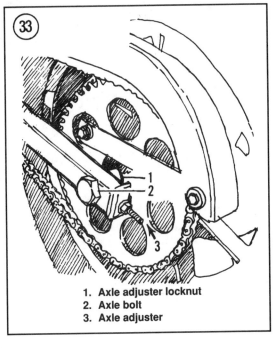

1. **Axle adjuster locknut**
2. **Axle bolt**
3. **Axle adjuster**

a. Loosen the rear brake caliper anchor nut on 1984 FXST models.

b. Loosen the rear axle nut (**Figure 32**).

c. Loosen the axle adjuster locknuts (**Figure 33**).

d. Turn each axle adjuster in or out as required, in equal amounts to maintain rear wheel alignment. The correct amount of chain free play is listed in Step 3.

e. When the chain free play is correct, check chain alignment with the tool shown in **Figure 34**; you can make the tool out of 1/8 in. (3.17 mm) aluminum or brass rod. Measure from the center of the swing arm pivot shaft bolt to the center of the axle as shown in **Figure 35**. Slide the rubber grommet along the tool until it aligns with the center of the axle. Now check alignment on the opposite side, comparing the rubber grommet position with the center of the axle. The alignment on both sides of the axle must be the same. If necessary, adjust the axle with the axle adjusters, while at the same time maintaining correct chain free play.

f. Tighten the axle nut to 65-70 ft.-lb. (89.7-96.6 N•m (1984) or 60-65 ft.-lb. (82.8-89.7 N•m) (1985-on). Tighten the chain adjuster locknuts securely.

g. On 1984 FXST, tighten the rear brake caliper anchor nut to 20-22 ft.-lb. (27.6-30.4 N•m).

5. If you cannot adjust the drive chain within the limits of the chain adjusters, it is excessively worn and stretched and must be replaced. If the chain can be adjusted, but you feel it may be worn, pull the chain away from the rear sprocket as shown in **Figure 36**. If more than 1/2 of a sprocket tooth is exposed, the chain is worn. Always replace both sprockets when replacing the drive chain; never install a new chain over worn sprockets.

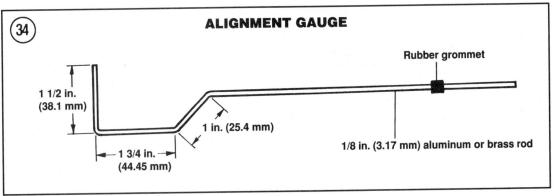

ALIGNMENT GAUGE

1 1/2 in. (38.1 mm)

1 3/4 in. (44.45 mm)

1 in. (25.4 mm)

Rubber grommet

1/8 in. (3.17 mm) aluminum or brass rod

WARNING
Excessive free play or a worn chain can result in chain breakage; this could cause a serious accident.

6. After the drive chain has been adjusted, the rear brake pedal free play must be adjusted as described in this chapter.

Drive Chain
Cleaning and Inspection

1. Remove the drive chain.
2. Immerse the chain in a pan of cleaning solvent and allow it to soak for about a half hour. Move it around and flex it during this period so that dirt between the pins and rollers may work its way out.
3. Scrub the rollers and side plates with a stiff brush and rinse away loosened grit. Rinse it a couple of times to make sure all dirt is washed out. Hang up the chain and allow it to dry thoroughly.
4. After cleaning the chain, examine it for the following conditions (**Figure 37**):
   a. Excessive wear.
   b. Loose pins.
   c. Damaged rollers.
   d. Damaged plates.
   e. Dry plates.
If any signs are visible, replace the chain.

CAUTION
Always check both sprockets every time the drive chain is removed. If any wear is visible on the teeth, replace the sprocket. Never install a new chain over worn sprockets or a worn chain over new sprockets.

Final Drive Belt
Inspection/Adjustment

The final drive belt (**Figure 38**) stretches very little after the first 500 miles of operation, but it should be inspected for tension and alignment according to the maintenance schedule (**Table 2**).

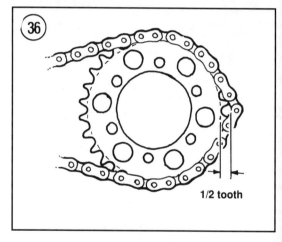

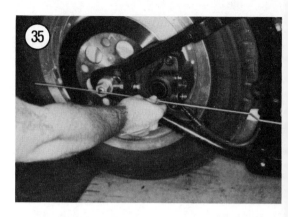

1/2 tooth

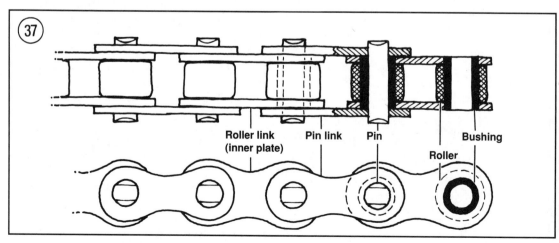

Roller link (inner plate) Pin link Pin Bushing Roller

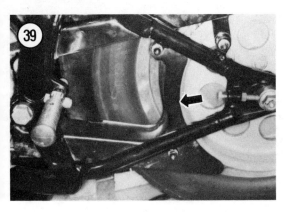

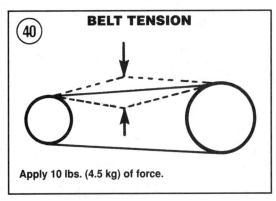

BELT TENSION

Apply 10 lbs. (4.5 kg) of force.

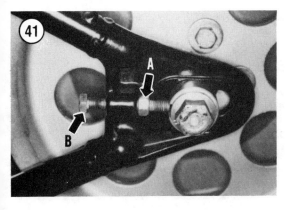

1. Remove the belt guard bolts and remove the belt guard (**Figure 39**).

2. With a force of 10 lb. (4.5 kg) applied to the middle of the upper belt strand, the top belt strand should deflect 3/8-1/2 in. (9.5-12.7 mm). See **Figure 40**.

3. If the belt tension is out of specification, adjust as follows.

NOTE
Do not loosen the rear axle nut. Belt adjustment can be made with the axle nut tightened. If the axle nut was loosened, recheck this adjustment after riding the bike 25-50 miles.

   a. Loosen the axle adjuster locknut (A, **Figure 41**). Turn each axle adjuster (B, **Figure 41**) in or out as required, in equal amounts to maintain rear wheel alignment. Recheck belt play as described in Step 2.

   b. When the belt free play is correct, check belt alignment with the tool shown in **Figure 34**; you can make the tool out of 1/8 in. (3.17 mm) aluminum or brass rod. Measure from the center of the swing arm pivot shaft bolt to the center of the axle as shown in **Figure 35**. Slide the rubber grommet along the tool until it aligns with the center of the axle. Now check alignment on the opposite side, comparing the rubber grommet position with the center of the axle. The alignment on both sides of the axle must be the same. If necessary, adjust the belt with the adjusters, while at the same time maintaining correct belt play as described in Step 2.

   c. Tighten the adjuster locknuts (A, **Figure 41**) securely.

   d. If the axle nut was loosened, tighten it to 60-65 ft.-lb. (82.8-89.7 N•m). Then recheck the adjustment after riding the bike 25-50 miles (40-80 km).

Disc Brake Inspection

The hydraulic brake fluid in the disc brake master cylinder should be checked every month. The disc brake pads should be checked at the intervals specified in **Table 1** or **Table 2**. Using a flashlight, check the brake pad friction material on each pad; see **Figure 42**, typical. If the thickness of the friction material is 1/16 in. (1.58 mm) or less, replace the brake pads as described in Chapter Fourteen.

Disc Brake Fluid Level

1A. *Front brake:* The fluid level in the reservoir should be level with the gasket surface. To check, level the master cylinder assembly by turning the handlebar assembly.

1B. *Rear brake:* The fluid level in the reservoir should be 1/8 in. (3.17 mm) below the gasket surface. To check, level the bike.

2. Wipe the master cylinder cover with a clean shop cloth.

3. Remove the cover screws and cover (**Figure 43**, typical) and lift the diaphragm out of the housing. If necessary, correct the level by adding fresh DOT 5 brake fluid.

> *WARNING*
> *Use brake fluid clearly marked DOT 5 only and specified for disc brakes. Others may vaporize and cause brake failure.*

4. Reinstall all parts.

> *NOTE*
> *If the brake fluid was so low as to allow air in the hydraulic system, the brakes will have to be bled. Refer to Chapter Fourteen.*

Disc Brake Lines and Seals

Check brake lines between the master cylinder and the brake caliper; see **Figure 44**, typical. If there is any leakage, tighten the connections and bleed the brakes as described in Chapter Fourteen. If this does not stop the leak or if a line is obviously damaged, cracked or chafed, replace the line and seals and bleed the brake.

Disc Brake Fluid Change

Every time you remove the reservoir cap a small amount of dirt and moisture enters the brake fluid. The same thing happens if a leak occurs or when any part of the hydraulic system is loosened or disconnected. Dirt can clog the system and cause unnecessary wear. Water in the fluid vaporizes at high

temperatures, impairing the hydraulic action and reducing brake performance.

To change brake fluid, follow the brake bleeding procedure in Chapter Fourteen. Continue adding new fluid to the master cylinder and bleeding at the calipers until the fluid leaving the calipers is clean and free of contaminants and air bubbles.

> *WARNING*
> *Use brake fluid clearly marked DOT 5 only. Others may vaporize and cause brake failure.*

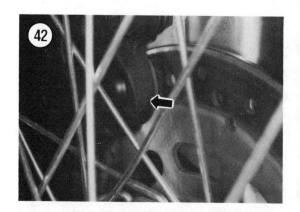

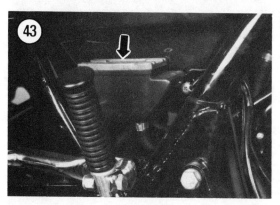

Front Disc Brake Adjustment

The front disc brake does not require periodic adjustment.

Rear Brake Pedal Adjustment (FXST)

The rear brake pedal should be adjusted anytime the rear wheel is removed or when the brake pads are replaced.

> *NOTE*
> *Many rear brake adjustments are made in relation to the brake pedal and exhaust system positions. If your model is equipped with a non-factory exhaust system, you should take your motorcycle to a Harley-Davidson dealer for rear brake adjustment.*

> *WARNING*
> *Do not ride the motorcycle until you are sure the rear brake adjustment is correct and does not interfere with the rear exhaust system or floorboard (if so equipped).*

1. Place the motorcycle on the jiffy stand.

2. Check that the brake pedal is in the at-rest position.

3. See **Figure 45**. Measure the distance between the brake pedal and the footrest. It should be 0.26-0.50 in. (6.6-12.7 mm). To adjust, loosen the locknut and adjust the stop bolt as required. Tighten the locknut and recheck.

4A. *1984-early 1987*: Work the brake pedal by hand. When the brake pedal is adjusted correctly, the pushrod will move approximately 1/16 in. (1.58 mm) before it contacts the master cylinder piston. If necessary, adjust as follows:

  a. Loosen the brake pedal locknut (**Figure 45**).

  b. Loosen the locknut and turn the clevis rod (**Figure 45**) counterclockwise to increase free play or clockwise to decrease it.

  c. Tighten the locknut and recheck the adjustment.

4B. *Late 1987-on*: Brake free play is built into the master cylinder. No adjustment is required.

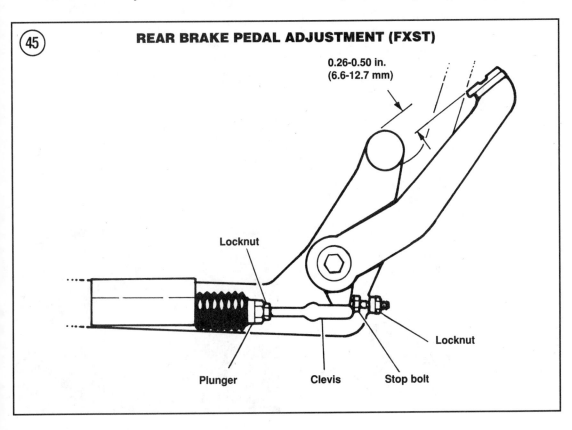

REAR BRAKE PEDAL ADJUSTMENT (FXST)

0.26-0.50 in. (6.6-12.7 mm)

Locknut

Locknut

Plunger   Clevis   Stop bolt

Rear Brake Pedal Adjustment (FLST)

The rear brake pedal on all FLST models is not adjustable. On early 1987 and earlier models, however, it is necessary to maintain a 1/16 in. (1.58 mm) free play between the stop and brake pedal. If necessary, turn the adjust screw as required. On late 1987 and later models, free play is built into the brake assembly.

Clutch Adjustment (1984 FXST with Dry Clutch)

1. Loosen the locknut (2, **Figure 46**) at the engine.
2. Turn the threaded sleeve (1, **Figure 46**) as required to produce approximately 1/16 in. (1.58 mm) free movement of the clutch hand lever before the clutch starts to release. See **Figure 47**.
3. Tighten the locknut.
4. If the sleeve adjustment has been taken up, perform the following adjustment.
5. Move the release lever on transmission as far forward as possible. See **Figure 48**.
6. Measure the clearance at the clutch release lever as indicated in **Figure 48**. Clearance should be 13/16 in. (20.6 mm). If the clearance is incorrect, perform the following.

7. Loosen the locknut (2, **Figure 46**) and turn the sleeve (1, **Figure 46**) all the way into its bracket.
8. Remove the clutch inspection cover (**Figure 49**).
9. Loosen the pushrod locknut (1, **Figure 50**).
10. Turn the clutch adjusting screw (2, **Figure 50**) counterclockwise to remove tension on the pushrod.

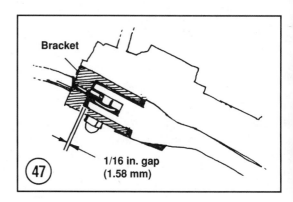

Bracket

(47) 1/16 in. gap (1.58 mm)

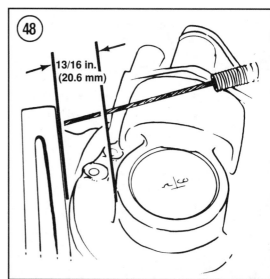

(48) 13/16 in. (20.6 mm)

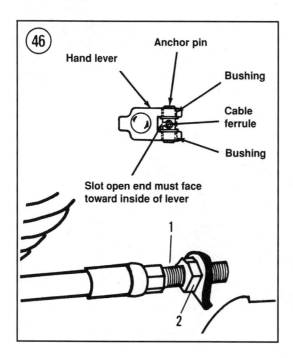

(46)

Anchor pin

Hand lever

Bushing

Cable ferrule

Bushing

Slot open end must face toward inside of lever

1

2

(49)

11. Turn the adjusting sleeve (1, **Figure 46**) until the proper clearance specified in **Figure 48** is obtained. Tighten the locknut (2, **Figure 46**).

12. Turn the clutch adjusting screw (2, **Figure 50**) clockwise until it contacts the pushrod, then back it out 1/8 turn. Tighten the locknut (1, **Figure 50**).

13. Install the clutch inspection cover.

14. Perform Steps 1-3 to adjust the clutch cable.

Clutch Adjustment
(FXST with Wet Clutch and 4-speed Transmission)

1. Park the vehicle so that it is straight up.
2. Disconnect the clutch cable at the release lever (at engine).
3. Remove the clutch inspection cover (**Figure 49**).
4. Refer to **Figure 51**. Loosen the clutch adjuster screw locknut (**Figure 52**).

NOTE
When performing Step 5, lightly push on the release lever to remove any pushrod free play.

5. Turn the adjuster screw (**Figure 51**) to position the release lever 13/16 in. (20.6 mm) from the transmission cover as shown in **Figure 48**.
6. Hold the adjuster screw in position with an Allen wrench and tighten the locknut (**Figure 51**).
7. Reconnect the clutch cable at the release lever.
8. Loosen the clutch cable adjusting screw locknut (**Figure 53**). Turn the adjusting screw (**Figure 53**)

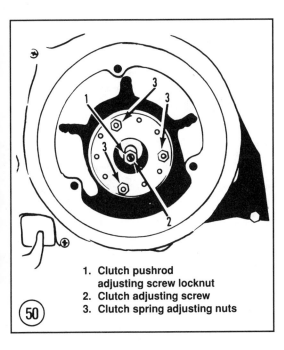

1. Clutch pushrod
   adjusting screw locknut
2. Clutch adjusting screw
3. Clutch spring adjusting nuts

50

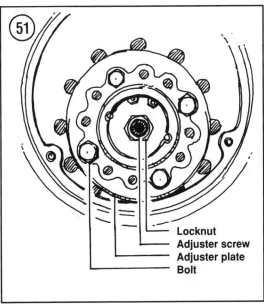

51

Locknut
Adjuster screw
Adjuster plate
Bolt

52

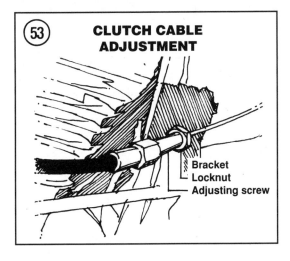

53   **CLUTCH CABLE ADJUSTMENT**

Bracket
Locknut
Adjusting screw

3

as required to obtain 1/16 in. (1.58 mm) free play at the clutch hand lever (**Figure 47**). Tighten the locknut.

9. Check the primary chaincase oil level as described in this chapter before reinstalling the clutch inspection cover.

10. Install the clutch inspection cover.

Clutch Adjustment
(1985-1986 with 5-speed Transmission)

1. Park the vehicle so that it is straight up.
2. Disconnect the clutch cable from the release lever.
3. Remove the clutch inspection cover (**Figure 49**).
4. Refer to **Figure 51**. Loosen the clutch adjuster screw locknut (**Figure 52**).
5. Turn the adjuster screw (**Figure 51**) clockwise (to remove clutch pushrod free play).
6. Turn the adjuster screw counterclockwise 3/4 turn.
7. Hold the adjuster screw in position with an Allen wrench and tighten the locknut (**Figure 52**).
8. Reconnect the clutch cable at the release lever.
9. Loosen the clutch cable adjuster screw locknut (**Figure 53**). Turn the adjuster screw (**Figure 53**) as required to obtain 1/16 in. (1.58 mm) free play at the clutch hand lever (**Figure 47**). Tighten the locknut.
10. Perform the *Clutch Diaphragm Spring Adjustment* in this chapter.
11. Check the primary chaincase oil level as described in this chapter before reinstalling the clutch inspection cover.
12. Install the clutch inspection cover.

Clutch Adjustment
(1987-1989 5-speed)

The clutch adjustment on these models is made at the clutch cable's midline adjuster.

1. Locate the clutch cable adjuster. Then slide the rubber boot away from the adjuster (**Figure 54**).
2. Loosen the cable locknut and turn the adjuster to provide as much cable slack as possible.
3. Support the bike so that it sits straight up.
4. Remove the clutch inspection cover (**Figure 49**) from the left-hand side.
5. Refer to **Figure 51**. Perform the following:
   a. Loosen the clutch pushrod adjuster screw locknut.

b. Turn the clutch adjuster screw clockwise to remove all pushrod free play.
c. Turn the clutch adjuster screw 3/4 turn counterclockwise. Then hold the screw securely and tighten the locknut.

6. Reinstall the clutch inspection cover.

NOTE
If oil drained out of the primary case, refill housing as required.

7. Pull the clutch handlebar lever 3 to 4 times to seat the clutch release mechanism.

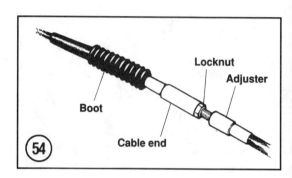

Locknut
Adjuster
Boot
Cable end

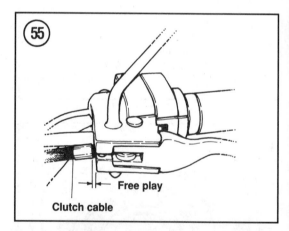

Free play
Clutch cable

NOTE
When turning the clutch cable adjuster in Step 8, pull the clutch cable away from the clutch hand lever bracket.

8. Turn the clutch cable adjuster (**Figure 54**) until there is 1/8-3/16 in. (3.17-4.76 mm) free play between the clutch hand lever bracket and the outer clutch cable end as shown in **Figure 55**.

9. Tighten the clutch cable locknut (**Figure 54**) and slide the rubber boot over the cable adjuster.

**Clutch Adjustment
(1990-on)**

CAUTION
Because the clutch adjuster screw clearance increases with engine temperature, clutch adjustment must be made when the clutch is cold (room temperature). If the clutch is adjusted when the clutch is hot (engine running), insufficient pushrod clearance will result and cause the clutch to slip.

1. Locate the clutch cable adjuster. Then slide the rubber boot away from the adjuster (**Figure 54**).

2. Loosen the cable locknut and turn the adjuster to provide as much cable slack as possible.

3. Support the bike so that it sits straight up.

4. Remove the clutch inspection cover (**Figure 49**) from the left-hand side.

5. Refer to **Figure 56**. Perform the following:

  a. Loosen the clutch pushrod adjuster screw locknut.

  b. Turn the clutch adjuster screw clockwise to remove all pushrod free play.

  c. Turn the clutch adjuster screw 1/2-3/4 turn counterclockwise. Then hold the screw securely and tighten the locknut.

6. Reinstall the clutch inspection cover.

NOTE
If oil drained out of the primary case, refill housing as required.

7. Pull the clutch handlebar lever 3 times to seat the clutch release mechanism.

NOTE
When turning the clutch cable adjuster in Step 8, pull the clutch cable away from the clutch hand lever bracket.

8. Turn the clutch cable adjuster (**Figure 54**) until there is 1/16-1/8 in. (1.58-3.17 mm) (1990) or 1/8-3/16 in. (3.17-4.76 mm) (1991) free play between the clutch hand lever bracket and the outer clutch cable end as shown in **Figure 55**.

9. Tighten the clutch cable locknut (**Figure 54**) and slide the rubber boot over the cable adjuster.

**Clutch Diaphragm Spring Adjustment
(1985-1989 Wet Clutch)**

1. Park the vehicle so that it is straight up.

2. Disconnect the clutch cable at the release lever (at engine). See **Figure 57**.

3. Remove the clutch inspection cover (**Figure 49**).

4. Refer to **Figure 51**. Loosen the clutch adjuster screw locknut (**Figure 52**) and turn the adjuster screw counterclockwise to provide clutch pushrod free play.

5. Lay a straightedge across the diaphragm spring (**Figure 58**).

6. The spring should be flat within 0.010 in. (0.25 mm). See **Figure 59**. If the spring flatness is incorrect, adjust as follows.

NOTE
*Spring compression adjustment is performed by removing the adjuster plate (**Figure 60**) and reinstalling it using one of the 3 different hole positions. The adjuster plate has been designed with 3 different hole positions that position the adjuster plate for least, middle and greatest compression. See **Figure 61**.*

7. Loosen the 4 adjuster plate bolts (**Figure 60**) in a crisscross pattern 1/2 to 1 turn. Continue until all spring tension is removed. Then remove the bolts and position the spring adjuster plate at the mounting holes that will give the correct clutch adjustment. Referring to **Figure 61**, note the following:

   a. If the spring is bowed outward more than 0.010 in. (0.25 mm), position the adjuster plate at the next hole that offers greater compression.

   b. If the spring is dished inward more than 0.010 in. (0.25 mm), position the adjuster plate at the next hole that offers less compression.

   c. The factory spring position is flat to 0.010 in. 0.25 mm) concaved; no adjustment required. See **Figure 59**.

8. Install the 4 adjuster plate bolts. Tighten them in a crisscross pattern to 6.5-8 ft.-lb. (8.9-11 N•m). Recheck the adjustment. If adjustment is correct, remove the 4 adjuster plate bolts and apply Loctite 222 (purple) to the bolt threads. Reinstall the bolts and tighten to 6.5-8 ft.-lb. (8.9-11 N•m).

9. Install the clutch inspection cover.

Throttle Cable(s)

Check the throttle cables from grip to carburetors. Make sure they are not kinked or chafed. Replace it if necessary.

Make sure that the throttle grip rotates smoothly from fully closed to fully open. Check at center, full left and full right position of steering.

Throttle Cable Adjustment

Refer to **Figure 62** for this procedure.

1. Loosen both cable adjuster locknuts (A and B, **Figure 62**), then turn the cable adjusters (C and D) clockwise as far as possible.

2. With the motorcycle's front wheel pointing straight ahead, open the throttle fully with the throttle grip and hold it in this position. Then turn the throttle cable adjuster (C, **Figure 62**) counterclockwise until the throttle cam stop just touches the stop boss cast into the carburetor body. If you are not sure if the throttle valve is fully open, turn the pulley by hand to see if there is more movement. Tighten the throttle cable adjuster locknut (A, **Figure 62**). Release the throttle grip.

3. With the motorcycle's front wheel turned all the way to the right, lengthen the throttle cable adjuster (D, **Figure 62**) until the lower end of the cable just contacts the spring in the outer cable fitting. Tighten the locknut (B, **Figure 62**).

4. Start the engine and rev it several times to be sure the engine returns fully to idle. If the engine does not return to idle, loosen the cable adjuster locknut (B, **Figure 62**) and turn the cable adjuster (D, **Figure 62**) clockwise as required. Tighten the cable adjuster (B, **Figure 62**).

5. Support the bike so that the front wheel is off the ground. Start the engine and allow it to idle, then

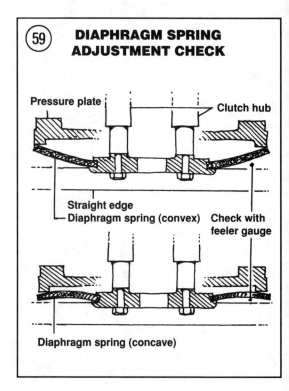

59   **DIAPHRAGM SPRING ADJUSTMENT CHECK**

Pressure plate

Clutch hub

Straight edge

Diaphragm spring (convex)

Check with feeler gauge

Diaphragm spring (concave)

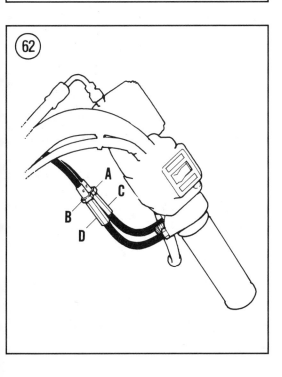

Adjuster plate

A   B   C

A: Least compression
B: Middle compression
C: Greatest compression

turn the handlebar from side to side. The engine idle speed must not rise above idle throughout the handlebar movement. If the idle speed rises, readjust the throttle cables. If this does not fix the problem, check the throttle cables for proper routing or possible damage.

WARNING
Do not ride the motorcycle until the throttle cable adjustment is correct. A sticking or improperly adjusted throttle cable can cause you to crash.

Choke Cable Adjustment (1984-1989)

1. Operate the choke lever (**Figure 63**) and check for smooth operation of the cable and choke mechanism.
2. Slide the lever (**Figure 63**) all the way to the closed position. Then pull the choke arm (**Figure 64**) at the carburetor to make sure it is at the end of its travel. If you can move the choke lever an additional amount, it must be adjusted as follows.
3. Loosen the clutch cable clamping screw (**Figure 64**) and move the cable sheath *up* until the choke lever is fully closed. Hold the choke lever in this position and tighten the cable clamping screw (**Figure 64**).
4. Slide the choke lever all the way to the fully open position.
5. If proper adjustment cannot be achieved using this procedure, the cable has stretched and must be replaced.

Enrichener/Choke Cable Adjustment (1990-on)

The enrichener knob (**Figure 65**) should move from full open to full close without any sign of binding. The knob should also stay in its fully closed or fully open position without creeping. If the knob does not stay in position, adjust tension on the cable by turning the knurled plastic nut behind the enrichener knob (**Figure 66**) as follows:

NOTE
The enrichener cable must have sufficient cable resistance to work properly. Do not lubricate the enrichener cable or its conduit.

1. Loosen the hex nut behind the mounting bracket. Then move the cable to free it from the mounting bracket slot.

2. Hold the cable across its flats with a wrench and turn the knurled plastic nut counterclockwise to reduce cable resistance so that the knob can slide inward freely.

3. Turn the knurled plastic nut clockwise so that sufficient cable resistance is maintained on the cable. Continue adjustment until the knob remains stationary when pulled all the way out while at the same time the knob movement is smooth.

4. Reinstall the cable into the slot in the mounting bracket. Tighten the hex nut to secure the cable to the mounting bracket.

Fuel Shutoff Valve/Filter

Refer to Chapter Eight for complete details on removal, cleaning and installation of the fuel shutoff valve.

Fuel Line Inspection

Inspect the fuel lines from the fuel tank to the carburetor. If any are cracked or starting to deteriorate they must be replaced. Make sure the small hose clamps are in place and holding securely.

> *WARNING*
> *A damaged or deteriorated fuel line presents a very dangerous fire hazard to both the rider and the bike if fuel should spill onto a hot engine or exhaust pipe.*

Exhaust System

Check all fittings for exhaust leakage. Do not forget the crossover pipe connections. Tighten all bolts and nuts; replace any gaskets as necessary. Removal and installation procedures are described in Chapter Eight.

Air Cleaner
Removal/Installation

A clogged air cleaner can decrease the efficiency and life of the engine. Never run the bike without the air cleaner installed; even minute particles of dust can cause severe internal engine wear.

The service intervals specified in **Table 1** and **Table 2** should be followed with general use. However, the air cleaner should be serviced more often if the bike is ridden in dusty areas.

The air filter on all models is installed on the right-hand side of the bike. See **Figure 67** (1984-1985), **Figure 68** (1986-1989) **Figure 69A** (1990) or **Figure 69B** (1991).

1. Remove the air filter cover (A, **Figure 70**) and withdraw the filter.

2. Clean the filter as described in this chapter.

3. If necessary, remove the air filter housing.

4. Installation is the reverse of these steps. If the backing plate assembly was removed, install a new carburetor gasket. Reconnect the hose to the air filter housing. See B, **Figure 70**, typical.

Air Filter Cleaning (1984-1990)

These models are equipped with a foam air filter. To work properly, the filter must be properly cleaned and oiled.

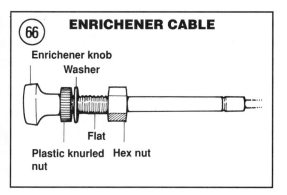

Refer to **Figure 67**, **Figure 68** or **Figure 69**A when performing this procedure.

1. Remove the air filter as described in this chapter.

2. Remove the wire mesh from inside the filter.

3. Inspect the air filter element for damage. If the filter element is torn or damaged, it must be replaced. A more thorough inspection will take place after the filter is cleaned.

WARNING
Never clean the air filter in gasoline or low flash point cleaning solvent. If this type of cleaner is used, the residual solvent or vapors could cause a fire or explosion after the filter is reinstalled and the engine started. Do not clean the filter in any type of solvent.

CAUTION
Do not wring or twist the filter when cleaning it. This harsh action could damage a filter pore or tear the filter loose at a seam. This would allow unfiltered air to enter the engine and cause severe and rapid wear.

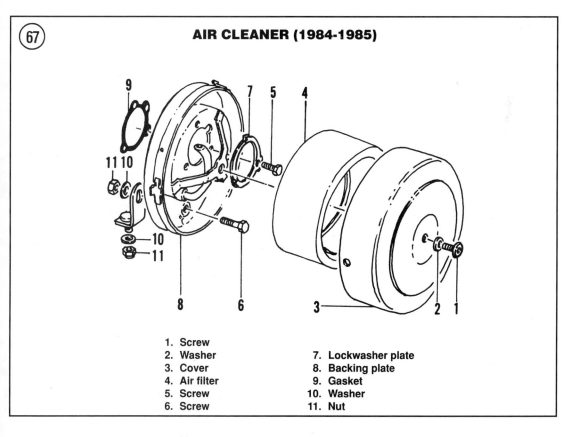

AIR CLEANER (1984-1985)

1. Screw
2. Washer
3. Cover
4. Air filter
5. Screw
6. Screw
7. Lockwasher plate
8. Backing plate
9. Gasket
10. Washer
11. Nut

4. Submerge the filter into a solution of soap and water and gently work the cleaner into the filter pores. Soak and gently squeeze the filter to clean it.

5. Rinse the filter under warm water while soaking and gently squeezing it.

6. Repeat Step 3 and Step 4 two or three times or until there are no signs of dirt being rinsed from the filter.

7. Inspect the filter; if it is torn or damaged in any area, it must be replaced. Do *not* run the bike with a damaged filter as it may allow dirt to enter the engine.

8. Set the filter aside and allow it to dry thoroughly.

CAUTION
A damp filter will not trap fine dust. Make sure the filter is completely dry before oiling it.

9. Properly oiling an air filter element is a messy job. You may want to wear a pair of disposable rubber gloves when performing this procedure. Oil the filter as follows:

   a. Purchase a box gallon size reclosable storage bags. The bags can be used when cleaning the filter as well as for storing engine and carburetor parts during disassembly.

   b. Place the cleaned filter into a storage bag.

   c. Pour engine oil onto the filter to soak it.

   d. Gently squeeze and release the filter element to soak oil into the filter's pores. Repeat until all of the filter's pores are discolored with oil.

   e. Remove the filter from the bag and check the pores for uneven oiling. This is indicated by light or dark areas. If necessary soak the filter and squeeze it again.

   f. When the filter oiling is even, squeeze the filter element a final time.

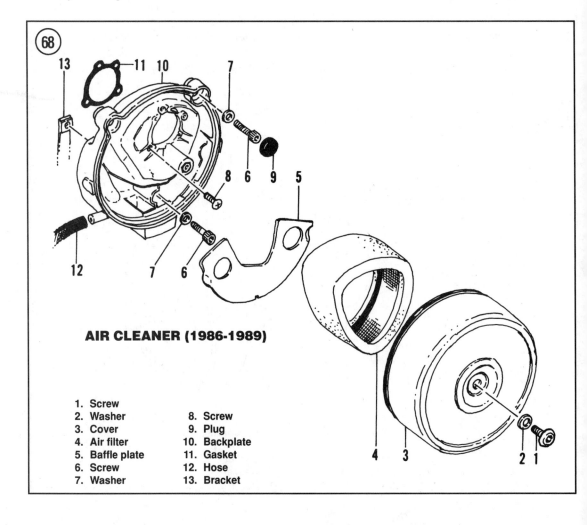

AIR CLEANER (1986-1989)

1. Screw
2. Washer
3. Cover
4. Air filter
5. Baffle plate
6. Screw
7. Washer
8. Screw
9. Plug
10. Backplate
11. Gasket
12. Hose
13. Bracket

10. Remove the filter from the bag.

11. Reinstall wire mesh frame into the filter.

12. Clean out the inside of the air box with a shop rag and cleaning solvent. Remove any foreign matter that may have passed through a torn filter.

NOTE
When cleaning the inside of air box, do not to allow any dirt or other debris to run into the carburetor.

13. Install the air filter as described in this chapter.

14. Pour the left over oil from the bag back into the oil bottle for reuse. Label the oil bottle "Air Filter Use Only."

15. Dispose of the plastic bag.

**Air Filter Cleaning
(1991-on)**

These models are equipped with a gauze air filter element.

Refer to **Figure 69**B when performing this procedure.

1. Remove the air filter as described in this chapter.

2. Inspect the element for damage. If the element is torn or damaged, it must be replaced.

WARNING
Never clean the air filter in gasoline or low flash point cleaning solvent. If this type of cleaner is used, the residual solvent or vapors could cause a fire or explosion after the filter is reinstalled and the engine started. Do not clean the element in any type of solvent.

3. Fill a pan with hot soapy water and place the filter in it for approximately 30 minutes. Swish the filter around to help removed trapped dirt and oil.

4. Remove the filter and hold it up to a strong light. Check the filter pores for dirt and oil. Repeat Step 3 until you can no longer see dirt and oil in the filter pores. If the filter cannot be cleaned by soaking, it must be replaced.

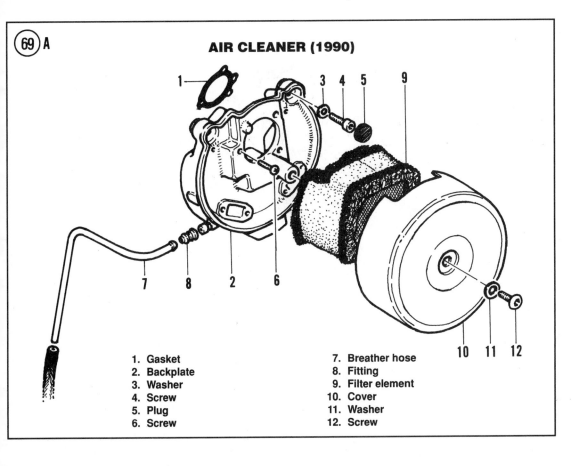

69 A

AIR CLEANER (1990)

1. Gasket
2. Backplate
3. Washer
4. Screw
5. Plug
6. Screw
7. Breather hose
8. Fitting
9. Filter element
10. Cover
11. Washer
12. Screw

CAUTION
*Do **not** use high air pressure to dry the filter, as this will damage it.*

CAUTION
In the next step, do not direct compressed air toward the outer surface of the filter. The normal air flow through the air filter, when the engine is running, is from the outer surface through the filter and out through the inner surface. Thus, during normal operation, dirt is collected on the outer filter surface. If air pressure is directed to the outer surface it will force the dirt and dust into the pores of the filter, restricting air flow.

5. *Gently* apply compressed air toward the inner surface of the element to remove all loosened dirt and dust from the filter. This is reversing the normal air flow through the filter.

6. Inspect the filter; if it is torn or damaged in any area, it must be replaced. Do *not* run the bike with a damaged filter as it may allow dirt to enter the engine.

7. Clean out the inside of the air box with a shop rag and cleaning solvent. Remove any foreign matter that may have passed through a torn filter.

NOTE
When cleaning the inside of air box, do not to allow any dirt or other debris to run into the carburetor.

8. Allow the filter to completely dry, then reinstall it as described in this chapter.

CAUTION
Running the engine with a damp air filter will allow air to pass through it. Make sure the filter is dry before installing it.

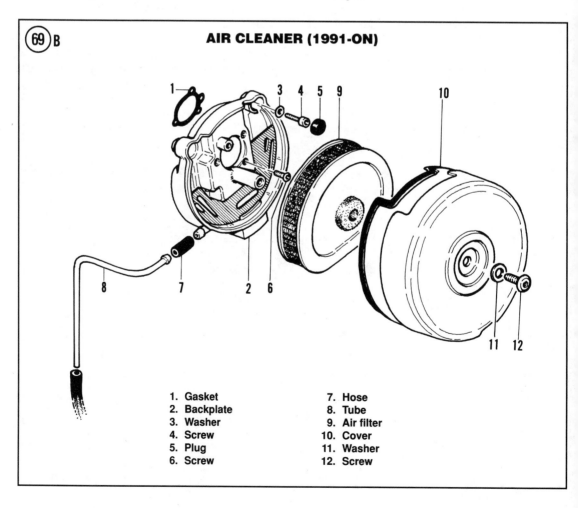

69 B — **AIR CLEANER (1991-ON)**

1. Gasket
2. Backplate
3. Washer
4. Screw
5. Plug
6. Screw
7. Hose
8. Tube
9. Air filter
10. Cover
11. Washer
12. Screw

3

Oil Tappet Screen Cleaning

After every oil change or at the intervals specified in **Table 1** or **Table 2**, remove the oil tappet screen located under the plug on the cam case near the rear cylinder tappet block. See **Figure 71**. Clean the screen in solvent. Replace the screen if damaged. Reverse to install.

Wheel Bearings

The wheel bearings should be cleaned and re-packed at the intervals specified in **Table 1** or **Table 2**.

Refer to Chapter Ten for complete service procedures.

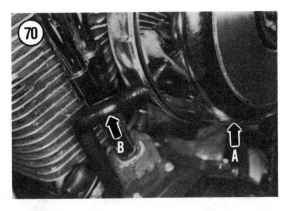

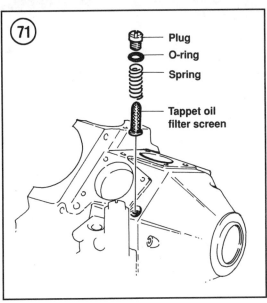

Plug
O-ring
Spring
Tappet oil filter screen

Steering Play

The steering head should be checked for loose-ness at the intervals specified in **Table 1**. Adjustment procedures are given in Chapter Eleven and Chapter Twelve.

Steering Head Bearings

The steering head bearings should be repacked at the intervals specified in **Table 1** or **Table 2**; see Chapter Eleven or Chapter Twelve.

Front Suspension Check

Periodically check the front fork mounting bolts for tightness. Refer to Chapter Eleven or Chapter Twelve for torque specifications.

Rear Suspension Check

Periodically check the rear shock absorber and rear suspension mounting bolts for tightness. Refer to Chapter Thirteen for torque specifications and procedures.

Nuts, Bolts and Other Fasteners

Constant vibration can loosen many fasteners on a motorcycle. Check the tightness of all fasteners, especially those on:

   a. Engine mounting hardware.
   b. Engine crankcase covers.
   c. Handlebar and front forks.
   d. Gearshift lever.
   e. Sprocket bolts and nuts.
   f. Brake pedal and lever.
   g. Exhaust system.
   h. Lighting equipment.

TUNE-UP

A complete tune-up restores performance and power that is lost due to normal wear and deterioration of engine parts. Because engine wear occurs over a combined period of time and mileage, the engine tune-up should be performed at the intervals specified in **Table 1** or **Table 2**. More frequent tune-ups may be required if the bike is ridden primarily in stop-and-go traffic.

Table 8 summarizes tune-up specifications.

Before starting a tune-up procedure, make sure to first have all new parts on hand.

Because different systems in an engine interact, the procedures should be done in the following order:

   a. Clean or replace the air filter element.
   b. Check engine compression.
   c. Check or replace the spark plugs.
   d. Check the ignition timing.
   e. Adjust carburetor idle speed.

To perform a tune-up on your Harley-Davidson, you will need the following tools:

   a. Spark plug wrench.
   b. Socket wrench and assorted sockets.
   c. Compression gauge.
   d. Spark plug wire feeler gauge and gapper tool.
   e. Ignition timing light.

Air Cleaner

The air cleaner element should be cleaned or replaced prior to doing other tune-up procedures, as described in this chapter.

Compression Test

At every tune-up check cylinder compression. Record the results and compare them at the next check. A running record will show trends in deterioration so that corrective action can be taken before complete failure.

The results, when properly interpreted, can indicate general cylinder, piston ring and valve condition.

1. Warm the engine to normal operating temperature. Set the choke and throttle valves so that they are completely open.
2. Remove the spark plugs (**Figure 72**).
3. Connect the compression tester to one cylinder following manufacturer's instructions (**Figure 73**).
4. Have an assistant crank the engine over until there is no further rise in pressure.
5. Remove the tester and record the reading.
6. Repeat Steps 3-5 for the other cylinder.

When interpreting the results, actual readings are not as important as the difference between the readings. Standard compression pressure is shown in

Table 8. Pressure should not vary from cylinder to cylinder by more than 10 percent. Greater differences indicate worn or broken rings, leaky or sticky valves, blown head gasket or a combination of all.

If compression readings do not differ between cylinders by more than 10 percent, the rings and valves are in good condition. If a low reading (10 percent or more) is obtained on one of the cylinders, it indicates valve or ring trouble. To determine which, pour about a teaspoon of engine oil through the spark plug hole onto the top of the piston. Turn the engine over once to clear some of the excess oil, then take another compression test and record the reading. If the compression returns to normal, the valves are good but the rings are defective on that cylinder. If compression does not increase, the valves require servicing. A valve could be hanging open but not burned or a piece of carbon could be on a valve seat.

NOTE
If the compression is low, the engine cannot be tuned to maximum performance. The worn parts must be replaced and the engine rebuilt.

3

Cylinder Leakage Test

A cylinder leakage test can determine engine problems from leaking valves, blown head gaskets or broken, worn or stuck piston rings. A cylinder leakage test is performed by applying compressed air to the cylinder and then measuring the percent of leakage. A cylinder leakage tester and an air compressor are required to perform this test.

Follow the manufacturer's directions along with the following information when performing a cylinder leakage test.

1. Start and run the engine until it reaches normal operating temperature.
2. Remove the air cleaner assembly. Then set the throttle and choke valves in their wide open position.
3. Remove the ignition timing inspection plug from the crankcase (**Figure 74**).
4. Set the piston for the cylinder being tested to TDC on its compression stroke. Reinstall the timing plug.
5. Remove the spark plugs (**Figure 72**).

NOTE
The engine may want to turn over when air pressure is applied to the cylinder. To

prevent this from happening, shift the transmission into fifth gear and lock the rear brake pedal so that the rear brake is applied.

6. Make a cylinder leakage test following the manufacturer's instructions. Listen for air leaking while noting the following:

   a. Air leaking through the exhaust pipe points to a leaking exhaust valve.
   b. Air leaking through the carburetor points to a leaking intake valve.

NOTE
Air leaking through the valves can also be caused by pushrods that are too long.

   c. Air leaking through the ignition timing inspection hole points to worn or broken piston rings, a leaking cylinder head gasket or a worn piston.

7. Repeat for the other cylinder.

Correct Spark Plug Heat Range

Spark plugs are available in various heat ranges that are hotter or colder than the spark plugs originally installed at the factory.

Select plugs in a heat range designed for the loads and temperature conditions under which the engine will operate. Using incorrect heat ranges can cause piston seizure, scored cylinder walls or damaged piston crowns.

In general, use a hotter plug for low speeds, low loads and low temperatures. Use a colder plug for high speeds, high engine loads and high temperatures.

NOTE
In areas where seasonal temperature variations are great, a "two-plug system" —a cold plug for hard summer riding and a hot plug for slower winter operation may prevent spark plug and engine problems.

The reach (length) of a plug is also important. A longer than normal plug could interfere with the valves and pistons causing permanent and severe damage. Refer to **Figure 75**. The standard heat range spark plugs are listed in **Table 8**.

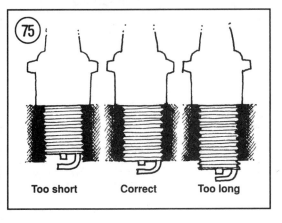

| Too short | Correct | Too long |

(76) **SPARK PLUG CONDITION**

NORMAL

- Identified by light tan or gray deposits on the firing tip.
- Can be cleaned.

GAP BRIDGED

- Identified by deposit buildup closing gap between electrodes.
- Caused by oil or carbon fouling. If deposits are not excessive, the plug can be cleaned.

OIL FOULED

- Identified by wet black deposits on the insulator shell bore and electrodes.
- Caused by excessive oil entering combustion chamber through worn rings and pistons, excessive clearance between valve guides and stems, or worn or loose bearings. Can be cleaned. If engine is not repaired, use a hotter plug.

CARBON FOULED

- Identified by black, dry fluffy carbon deposits on insulator tips, exposed shell surfaces and electrodes.
- Caused by too cold a plug, weak ignition, dirty air cleaner, too rich a fuel mixture, or excessive idling. Can be cleaned.

LEAD FOULED

- Identified by dark gray, black, yellow, or tan deposits or a fused glazed coating on the insulator tip.
- Caused by highly leaded gasoline. Can be cleaned.

WORN

- Identified by severely eroded or worn electrodes.
- Caused by normal wear. Should be replaced.

FUSED SPOT DEPOSIT

- Identified by melted or spotty deposits resembling bubbles or blisters.
- Caused by sudden acceleration. Can be cleaned.

OVERHEATING

- Identified by a white or light gray insulator with small black or gray brown spots and with bluish-burnt appearance of electrodes.
- Caused by engine overheating, wrong type of fuel, loose spark plugs, too hot a plug, or incorrect ignition timing. Replace the plug.

PREIGNITION

- Identified by melted electrodes and possibly blistered insulator. Metallic deposits on insulator indicate engine damage.
- Caused by wrong type of fuel, incorrect ignition timing or advance, too hot a plug, burned valves, or engine overheating. Replace the plug.

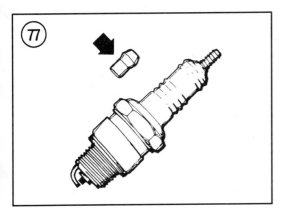

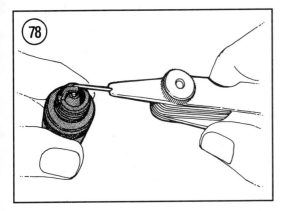

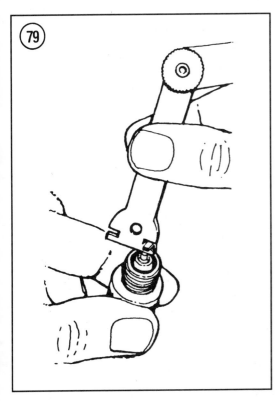

3

Spark Plug Cleaning/Replacement

1. Grasp the spark plug leads as near to the plug as possible and pull them off the plugs.

2. Blow away any dirt that has accumulated in the spark plug wells (**Figure 72**).

> *CAUTION*
> *The dirt could fall into the cylinders when the plugs are removed, causing serious engine damage.*

3. Remove the spark plugs with a spark plug wrench.

> *NOTE*
> *If plugs are difficult to remove, apply penetrating oil such as WD-40 or Liquid Wrench around base of plugs and let it soak in about 10-20 minutes.*

4. Inspect spark plug carefully. Look for plugs with broken center porcelain, excessively eroded electrodes and excessive carbon or oil fouling (**Figure 76**). Replace such plugs.

> *NOTE*
> *Spark plug cleaning with the use of a sand-blast type device is not recommended. While this type of cleaning is thorough, the plug must be perfectly free of all abrasive cleaning material when done. If not, it is possible for the cleaning material to fall into the engine during operation and cause damage.*

Spark Plug Gapping and Installation

New plugs should be carefully gapped to ensure a reliable, consistent spark. You must use a special spark plug gapping tool.

1. Remove the new plugs from the box. Screw in the small pieces that may be loose in each box (**Figure 77**).

2. Insert a wire gauge between the center and the side electrode of each plug (**Figure 78**). The correct gap is listed in **Table 8**. If the gap is correct, you will feel a slight drag as you pull the wire through. If there is no drag, or the gauge won't pass through, bend the side electrode *with the gapping tool* (**Figure 79**) to set the proper gap (**Table 8**).

3. Put a small drop of oil or anti-seize compound on the threads of each spark plug.

4. Screw each spark plug in by hand until it seats. Very little effort is required. If force is necessary, you have the plug cross-threaded or the spark plug threads in the cylinder head are damaged or contaminated with carbon or other debris; unscrew it and try again.

5. Tighten the spark plugs to 14 ft.-lb. (19.3 N•m). If you don't have a torque wrench, an additional 1/4 to 1/2 turn is sufficient after the gasket has made contact with the head. If you are reinstalling old, regapped plugs and are reusing the old gasket, only tighten an additional 1/4 turn.

> *NOTE*
> *Do not overtighten. Besides making the plug difficult to remove, the excessive torque will squash the gasket and destroy its sealing ability.*

6. Install each spark plug wire. Make sure it goes to the correct spark plug.

Reading Spark Plugs

Much information about engine and spark plug performance can be determined by careful examination of the spark plugs. This information is only valid after performing the following steps.

1. Ride bike a short distance at full throttle in third or fourth gear.

2. Turn off kill switch before closing throttle and simultaneously pull in clutch. Coast and brake to a stop. *Do not* downshift transmission while stopping.

3. Remove spark plugs and examine them. Compare them to **Figure 76**.

If the insulator is white or burned, the plug is too hot and should be replaced with a colder one.

A too-cold plug will have sooty deposits ranging in color from dark brown to black. Replace with a hotter plug and check for too-rich carburetion or evidence of oil blow-by at the piston rings.

If any one plug is found unsatisfactory, discard both.

BREAKERLESS IGNITION SERVICE

Ignition Timing
Inspection and Adjustment

1. Remove the plug from the timing hole on the left side of the engine (**Figure 74**). A clear plastic view-

ing plug is available from Harley-Davidson dealers to minimize oil spray. Make sure the plug doesn't contact the flywheel.

2. Connect a portable tachometer following the manufacturer's instructions. The bike's tach is not accurate enough in the low rpm range for this adjustment.

3. Connect an inductive clamp-on timing light to the front cylinder spark plug wire following the manufacturer's instructions.

4. Start the engine and allow to idle at 1,300-1,500 rpm. If necessary, adjust idle as described in this chapter.

5. Aim the timing light at the timing inspection hole. At 1,300-1,500 rpm, the front cylinder's advance mark should appear in the center of the inspection window. **Figure 80** shows the single drilled dot that shows full advance for the front cylinder. If the mark does not align, stop the engine and adjust the ignition timing, starting with Step 7.

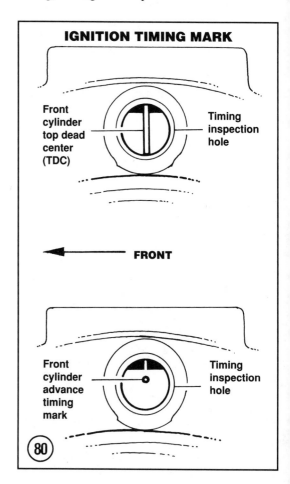

IGNITION TIMING MARK

Front cylinder top dead center (TDC)

Timing inspection hole

◄ **FRONT**

Front cylinder advance timing mark

Timing inspection hole

80

6. If the ignition timing is correct, reinstall the timing hole plug (**Figure 74**) and proceed to Step 17.

7. Drill out the 2 pop rivets (1, **Figure 81**) with a 3/8 in. (9.5 mm) drill bit. See **Figure 82**.

8. Using a punch, lightly tap the rivets out of the outer cover (**Figure 83**).

9. Remove the outer cover (**Figure 84**).

10. If necessary, lightly tap the rivets out of the inner cover (**Figure 85**).

11. Remove the inner cover screws and remove the inner cover (**Figure 86**).

12. Remove the gasket (**Figure 87**).

13. Remove any remaining rivet bits from the ignition housing.

14. Loosen the timing plate sensor plate screws (**Figure 88**) just enough to allow the plate to rotate. Start the engine and turn the plate as required so that the advanced mark is aligned as described in Step 5. Make sure idle speed specified in Step 5 is main-

3

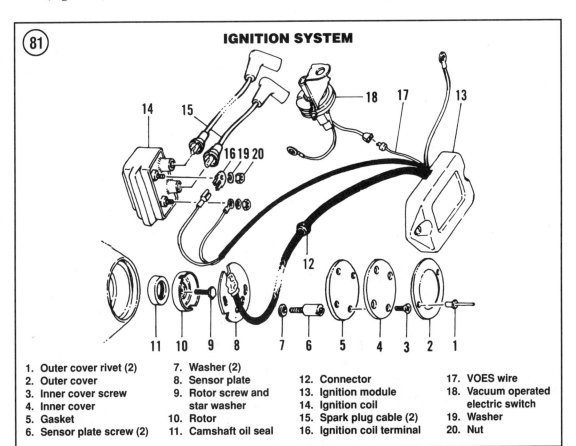

IGNITION SYSTEM

1. Outer cover rivet (2)
2. Outer cover
3. Inner cover screw
4. Inner cover
5. Gasket
6. Sensor plate screw (2)
7. Washer (2)
8. Sensor plate
9. Rotor screw and
   star washer
10. Rotor
11. Camshaft oil seal
12. Connector
13. Ignition module
14. Ignition coil
15. Spark plug cable (2)
16. Ignition coil terminal
17. VOES wire
18. Vacuum operated
    electric switch
19. Washer
20. Nut

tained when checking timing. Tighten the screws and recheck ignition timing.

15. Install the gasket and inner cover.

> *NOTE*
> *When installing pop rivets to secure the outer cover, make sure to use the headless type shown in **Figure 89**. The end of a normal pop rivet will break off on installation and damage the timing mechanism.*

16. Install the outer cover and secure with new rivets. See **Figure 90**.

17. As part of the tune-up, check the vacuum operated electric switch (VOES) as follows:

   a. Start the engine and allow to idle.

   b. Disconnect the vacuum line at the carburetor.

> *NOTE*
> ***Figure 91** (1984-1989) and **Figure 92** (1990-on) identify the VOES port with the carburetor removed for clarity.*

   c. Plug the carburetor VOES port with your finger. With the port blocked, the engine speed

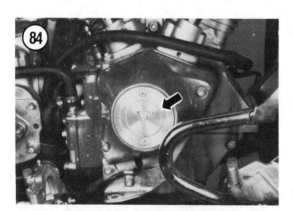

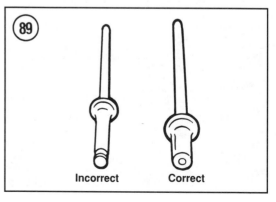

should decrease and the ignition timing should retard. When the vacuum hose is reconnected to the VOES port, the engine speed will increase.

d. If the engine failed to operate as described in sub-step c, check the VOES wire connection (**Figure 81**) at the ignition module. Also check the VOES ground wire for looseness or damage. If the wire connections are okay, have the VOES tested by a Harley-Davidson dealer.

> *CAUTION*
> *The vacuum operated electric switch (VOES) must be tested at each tune-up and replaced if malfunctioning. A damaged VOES switch will allow too high a spark advance and result with severe engine knock and damage.*

CARBURETOR ADJUSTMENTS

Slow and Fast Idle Adjustment (1984-1989)

> *NOTE*
> *The motorcycle must be parked in an upright position when performing this procedure.*

1. Attach a tachometer to the engine following the manufacturer's instructions.

2. Start the engine and warm it to normal operating temperature. Check that the choke (**Figure 93**) is off.

3. Set the slow idle speed with the throttle stop screw (**Figure 94**). See **Table 9** for specifications.

4. The idle mixture is set and sealed at the factory. It is not intended to be adjustable.

5. Rev the engine a couple of times and see if the idle speed is constant. If necessary, readjust the idle speed by turning the throttle stop screw (**Figure 94**).

6. Pull the choke knob (**Figure 93**) out to its first detent and turn the fast idle screw to set fast idle to specification listed in **Table 9**. Push the choke knob all the way in and check that idle drops to 900 rpm. If the choke does not operate correctly, adjust it as described in this chapter.

7. Disconnect and remove the tachometer.

Idle Speed Adjustment (1990-on)

NOTE
The motorcycle must be parked in an upright position when performing this procedure.

1. Attach a tachometer to the engine following the manufacturer's instructions.

2. Start the engine and warm it to normal operating temperature. Check that the enrichener valve is closed (enrichener knob all the way in).

3. Set the slow idle speed with the throttle stop screw (**Figure 95**). See **Table 9** for specifications.

4. The idle mixture is set and sealed at the factory. It is not intended to be adjustable.

5. Rev the engine a couple of times and see if the idle speed is constant. If necessary, readjust the idle speed by turning the throttle stop screw (**Figure 95**).

STORAGE

Several months of inactivity can cause problems and a general deterioration of your Harley's condition if proper care is neglected. This is especially in areas of weather extremes. Storing your bike is not difficult or time consuming, but it can become expensive if it is not done properly or avoided altogether. Proper storage is one of the most important aspects in protecting the substantial investment of time and money you've made in your Harley, as well as to prepare for the next riding season. Whether you put your Harley away for a few months or put it away for a number of winter months, you must prepare it carefully.

Preparation for Storage

Careful preparation of your Harley will minimize deterioration and make it easier to return it to service later. Use the following procedure.

1. Wash your bike thoroughly, then start and run the engine until all traces of moisture are gone. Wax all painted and polished surfaces.

NOTE
There are 2 ways to prevent the fuel system from plugging up. The first method is to drain the fuel tank and then run the engine until all of the fuel in the carburetor and fuel line is used up. The second method is to add a fuel stabilizer to the fuel tank, then following the manufacturer's directions, you basically start and run the engine long enough so that the stabilizer has a good chance to reach the carburetor float bowl, thereby stabilizing the entire fuel system. Unstabilized fuel will form gum and varnish deposits that will plug the fuel valve and carburetor passages.

WARNING
Because of the flammable nature that exists around gasoline, you should not store a motorcycle in a home garage where it is in the presence of open flames—pilot lights, electric motors, sparks, etc.

2A. If you are adding a commercial fuel stabilizer to the fuel system, fill the fuel tank and then add the stabilizer to the tank, following the manufacturer's directions. Make sure to run the engine long enough so that the stabilizer has a chance of reaching the carburetor float bowl.

2B. When draining the fuel tank, drain the fuel into a safety approved gasoline storage can.

3. Perform the lubrication procedures described in this chapter.

NOTE
Steps 5A and 5B describe two methods for protecting the engine from rust and corrosion during engine storage. Many riders avoid these steps by starting and running their bikes engine every few weeks. They feel that short term running keeps everything lubricated while at the same time preventing the carburetor from blocking up. Wrong! Because water is a by-product of combustion, short start-ups like this are probably more harmful to the engine than doing nothing at all.

4A. To fog the engine:

WARNING
The exhaust gases are poisonous. Do not run the engine in a closed area. Make sure there is plenty of ventilation.

a. Purchase a commercial engine fogging oil. Fog the engine following the manufacturer's instructions, while noting the following.

b. Start the engine and allow it to warm to normal operating temperature. If you are using a gasoline stabilizer, use it now. Turn the engine off.

c. Remove the air filter element.

NOTE
A cloud of smoke will develop in sub-step d. This is normal.

d. Start the engine once again and allow it to idle. Then spray the fogging oil into the carburetor. Do this until the engine stalls or emits smoke.

e. Turn the ignition switch off.

f. Reinstall the air filter element and its cover.

4B. To hand lubricate the engine top end:

a. Start the engine and allow it to warm to normal operating temperature. If you are using a gasoline stabilizer, use it now. Turn the engine off.

b. Remove both spark plugs.

c. Pour 1 to 2 tablespoons of engine oil into *each* spark plug hole.

d. Crank or turn the engine over five or six revolutions to distribute the oil.

e. Reinstall the spark plugs and reconnect the plug caps.

CAUTION
During the storage period, do not run the engine.

5. While the engine oil is hot, drain the oil tank and then flush it as described in this chapter. Service the oil filter and refill the oil tank as described in this chapter.

NOTE
Draining the old used oil is important because it contains moisture, acids and other contaminants that can damage the engine during storage.

6. Change the transmission oil as described in this chapter.

7. Remove the battery and coat the cable terminals with petroleum jelly; see Chapter Nine for battery service. Check the electrolyte level and refill with distilled water. Store the battery in an area above freezing temperatures and trickle charge it once a month. Keep the electrolyte level above the battery plates.

WARNING
Make sure the battery is stored where young children cannot find it.

8. Plug the exhaust pipes to prevent moisture from entering (or mice from building a nest in the pipe). Then place a note on the handlebar to remind you to remove the plugs before restarting the engine next season.

9. Spray all vinyl and rubber parts with a rubber preservative.

10. Spray the unpainted surfaces with a rust preservative.

11. Repack the wheel bearings as described in Chapter Ten.

12. Clean the brake drums and brake linings. See Chapter Fourteen.

13. Adjust the primary chain as described in this chapter.

14. Adjust the drive chain as described in this chapter.

15. Block the bike up so that the front tire is off the ground.

16. Deflate the tires to approximately 20 psi (1.4 kg/cm^2).

17. Cover the bike with a heavy cover that will provide adequate protection from dust and damage. Do not cover with a plastic tarp as moisture can collect and cause rusting.

Once A Month

1. Recharge the battery with a 1 amp charger until it is fully charged; see Chapter Nine.
2. Check the electrolyte level and keep it above the battery plates.

Removal from Storage

Preparing your Harley for use after storage should be relatively easy if proper storage procedures were followed.
1. Remove the plugs from the end of the exhaust pipes.
2. Gap and install 2 new spark plugs.
3. Service the air filter as described in this chapter.
4. Drain the oil that was installed prior to storage and fill the oil tank as described in this chapter.
5. Service the oil filter as described in this chapter.
6. Reinstall the battery, making sure the vent hose is properly attached and routed. Check the electrolyte level and refill with distilled water.
7. Check the primary and drive chain adjustments as described in this chapter. Readjust if necessary.

8. Perform the lubrication procedures described in this chapter.
9. Inflate the tires to their correct pressure for the load you will be carrying.
10. Check all of the control cables for proper adjustment.
11. Check the brake fluid level on models with rear disc brake. Refill with DOT 5 brake fluid.
12. Make sure that both brakes are working correctly.
13. Make a thorough check of the bike for loose or missing nuts, bolts or screws.
14. Without starting the engine, shift the transmission into 3rd or 4th gear, disengage the clutch and push the bike back and forth a few times. This is to make sure the clutch is disengaging properly. If not, service the clutch as described in Chapter Five.
15. If the fuel tank was drained, refill it with fresh gasoline.

WARNING
The exhaust gases are poisonous. Do not run the engine in a closed area. Make sure there is plenty of ventilation.

16. Start the engine and check for fuel or exhaust leaks. Make sure the lights and all switches work properly.

Table 1 PERIODIC MAINTENANCE (1984)*

Initial 500 miles (800 km); then every 2,500 miles (4,000 km)	Check tire pressure and tread wear Check spokes for tightness; check for broken or missing spokes Check battery electrolyte level Change engine oil and replace oil filter Inspect tappet oil screen Clean primary housing magnetic drain plug Inspect air filter for contamination; clean and reoil if necessary Check primary chain tension; adjust if necessary Lubricate drive chain Check drive chain tension; adjust if necessary Check brake fluid level; refill with DOT 5 brake fluid Check brake lines for leakage and damage Check brake pads for wear Check brake disc for wear or damage Check rear brake pedal adjustment and free play; adjust if necessary Check clutch adjustment Check external oil lines for leakage and damage Inspect fuel valve, fuel lines and all fittings for leaks Remove and clean the fuel tank filter screen Check electrical equipment and switches for proper operation Check all exposed fasteners for tightness** Check throttle operation Operate and check choke cable operation Check low and fast carburetor speed adjustments Perform general lubrication to equipment specified in this chapter
Initial 500 miles (800 km); then every 5,000 miles (8,000 km)	Change transmission oil Check steering adjustment; adjust if necessary Check swing arm bearing adjustment; adjust if necessary
Every 2,500 miles (4,000 km)	Check ignition timing Check primary case vacuum
Initial 2,500 miles (4,000 km); then every 7,500 miles (12,000 km)	Inspect spark plugs; regap or replace if necessary Check transmission oil level
Every 5,000 miles (8,000 km)	Replace spark plugs Check shock absorber rubber bushings; replace if necessary Lubricate throttle control sleeve Lubricate speedometer cable Change front fork oil
Every 10,000 miles (16,000 km)	Repack wheel bearings

* This maintenance schedule should be considered a guide to general maintenance and lubrication intervals. Harder than normal use and exposure to mud, water, high humidity, etc., will naturally dictate more frequent attention to most maintenance items.

** Except cylinder head bolts. Cylinder head bolts should be tightened by following the procedure listed in Chapter Four. Improper tightening of the cylinder head bolts may cause head leakage.

Table 2 PERIODIC MAINTENANCE (1985-ON)*

Initial 500 miles (800 km); **thereafter 2,500 miles (4,000 km)**	Check brake pad wear Check brake disc wear Inspect fuel valve, fuel lines and all fittings for leaks Check engine idle speed Check battery fluid level; refill with distilled water Check electrical equipment and switches for proper operation Check throttle operation Operate and check choke cable operation Check tire pressure and tread wear

Initial 500 miles (800 km);
thereafter every 5,000 miles (8,000 km)
	Change engine oil and replace oil filter
	Clean, inspect and reoil air filter (1985-1990)
	Inspect and clean air filter with compressed air (1991)
	Inspect tappet oil screen
	Check rear drive chain or belt tension;
	    adjust if necessary
	Inspect primary chain
	Check primary chain tension; adjust if necessary
	Change primary chaincase oil
	Check clutch adjustment; adjust if necessary
	Change transmission housing oil
	Check brake fluid level; refill with DOT 5 brake fluid
	Check rear brake pedal adjustment;
	    adjust if necessary
	Perform general lubrication to equipment
	    specified in this chapter
	Check ignition timing
	Check vacuum operated electric switch (VOES)
	Check rear swing arm pivot shaft tightness
	Check engine mount bolt tightness
	Inspect rear shock absorber
	Check all exposed fasteners for tightness**
	Lubricate rear swing arm bearing

Initial 500 miles (800 km) and **first 5,000 miles (8,000 km); thereafter** **every 10,000 miles (16,000 km)**	Check steering bearing adjustment
Every 2,500 miles (4,000 km)	Check engine oil level Check primary chaincase oil level Check transmission housing oil level

Every 5,000 miles (8,000 km)	Inspect rear brake caliper mounting pins and boots;
	    lubricate pins and boots during reassembly
	Inspect and lubricate rear brake and
	    shifter linkage assembly
	Lubricate throttle control sleeve
	Lubricate speedometer cable

Initial 5,000 miles (8,000 km); **thereafter every 10,000 miles (16,000 km)**	Inspect spark plug gap and condition
Every 10,000 miles (16,000 km)	Replace spark plugs Replace front fork oil*** Lubricate steering bearings Adjust springer rocker bearings, if so equipped Inspect and replace wheel bearings

   * This maintenance schedule should be considered a guide to general maintenance and lubrication intervals. Harder than normal use and exposure to mud, water, high humidity, etc., will naturally dictate more frequent attention to most maintenance items.
   ** Except cylinder head bolts. Cylinder head bolts should be tightened by following the procedure listed in Chapter Four. Improper tightening of the cylinder head bolts may cause head leakage.
   *** Except springer models.

Table 3 TIRE PRESSURE*

	Front		Rear	
	psi	kg/cm²	psi	kg/cm²
1984				
Rider only	30	2.1	28	1.9
With passenger	30	2.1	36	2.5
1985-on FLST (all models)				
Rider only	36	2.5	36	2.5
With passenger	36	2.5	40	2.8
1985-1990 FXST (all models)				
Rider only	30	2.1	32**	2.2
With passenger	30	2.1	32	2.2
1991-on FXST (all models)				
Rider only	30	2.1	36	2.5
With passenger	30	2.1	40	2.8

* Tire pressures listed in this table are for original equipment tires. See your dealer or tire manufacturer when equipping your model with non-stock tires.
** If you have an early model 1985 FXST with K101 A rear tires, set the tire pressure to 28 psi (1.9 kg/cm²).

Table 4 ENGINE OIL

Type	HD rating	Viscosity	Ambient operating temperature
HD Multigrade	HD 240	SAE 20W/50	20° F to 100° F
HD Regular Heavy*	HD 240	SAE 50	60° F to 100° F
HD Extra Heavy*	HD 240	SAE 60	80° F to 100° F

* Not recommended for use when ambient temperature is below 50° F.

Table 5 ENGINE, CLUTCH AND TRANSMISSION OIL CAPACITIES

Oil tank	3 U.S. qts. (2.8 L, 2.5 imp. qts.)
Primary chain case	
1984-1989	1.5 U.S. qts. (1.4 L, 1.2 imp. qts.)
1990-on	Approximately 30-36 U.S. oz. (887-1,065 ml, 31.3-37.5 imp. oz.)*
Transmission	
4-speed	Approximately 1.5 U.S. pints (710 ml, 25 imp. oz.)*
5-speed	
1985-1990	Approximately 1 U.S. pint (473 ml, 13.3 imp. oz.)*
1991-on	Approximately 1.25-1.5 U.S. pints (590-710 ml, 20.9-25 imp. oz.)*

* See text for correct check and refill procedure.

Table 6 RECOMMENDED LUBRICANTS AND FLUIDS

Brake fluid	DOT 5
Fork oil	HD Type E or equivalent
Battery top up	Distilled water
Transmission	HD transmission or equivalent
Clutch	HD lubricant or equivalent
Fuel	Leaded or unleaded gasoline with a pump octane rating of 87 or higher

Table 7 FRONT FORK OIL CAPACITY

	Wet			Dry		
	oz.	cc	Imp. oz.	oz.	cc	Imp. oz.
1984	9.25	273.5	9.6	10	295	10.42
1985-on						
FXST/C	10.2	301	10.6	11.2	331	11.7
FLST/C/F	11.5	340	12.0	12.5	370	13.0

Table 8 ENGINE TUNE-UP SPECIFICATIONS

Engine compression	90 psi (6.3 kg/cm^2)
Spark plugs	
Type	HD 5R6A or equivalent
Gap	0.038-0.043 in. (0.96-1.09 mm)
Ignition timing	
Type	Electronic
Timing specifications	
Early 1984	
Range	5°-50° BTDC
Start	5° BTDC
Fast idle	35° BTDC
@ 1,800-2,800 rpm	50° BTDC
Late 1984-on	
Range	0°-35° BTDC
Start	5° BTDC
Fast idle	35° BTDC
@ 1,800-2,800 rpm	50° BTDC

Table 9 CARBURETOR IDLE SPEED SPECIFICATIONS

1984	
Slow idle	900-950 rpm
Fast idle	1,500 rpm
1985-1989	
Slow idle	1,000-1,050 rpm
Fast idle	1,500-1,550 rpm
1990-on	
Idle	1,000-1,050 rpm

CHAPTER FOUR

ENGINE

All models are equipped with the V2 Evolution engine, an air-cooled 4-cycle, overhead-valve V-twin engine. The engine has three major assemblies: engine, crankcase and gearcase. Viewed from the engine's right side, engine rotation is clockwise.

Both cylinders fire once in 720° of crankshaft rotation. The rear cylinder fires 315° after the front cylinder. The front cylinder fires again in another 405°. Note that one cylinder is always on its exhaust stroke when the other fires on its compression stroke.

This chapter provides complete service and overhaul procedures, including information for disassembly, removal, inspection, service and reassembly of the engine. **Tables 1-3** at the end of this chapter provide complete engine specifications.

Work on the engine requires considerable mechanical ability. You should carefully consider your own capabilities before attempting any operation involving major disassembly of the engine.

Much of the labor charge for dealer repairs involves the removal and disassembly of other parts to reach the defective component. Even if you decide not to tackle the entire engine overhaul after studying the text and illustrations in this chapter, it can be cheaper to perform the preliminary operations yourself and then take the engine to your dealer. Since dealers have lengthy waiting lists for service (especially during the spring and summer season), this practice can reduce the time your unit is in the shop. If you have done much of the preliminary work, your repairs can be scheduled and performed much quicker.

General engine specifications are listed in **Table 1. Tables 1-4** are found at the end of the chapter.

SERVICE PRECAUTIONS

Whenever you work on your Harley, there are several precautions that should be followed to help with disassembly, inspection and reassembly.

1. Before beginning the job, re-read Chapter One of this manual. You will do a better job with this information fresh in your mind.

2. In the text there is frequent mention of the left-hand and right-hand side of the engine. This refers to the engine as it is mounted in the frame, not as it sits on your workbench.

3. Always replace a worn or damaged fastener with one of the same size, type and torque requirements. Make sure to identify each bolt before replacing it with another. Bolt threads should be lubricated with engine oil, unless otherwise specified, before torque is applied. If a tightening torque is not listed in **Table 3** (end of this chapter), refer to the torque and fastener information in Chapter One.

NOTE
All of the washers and fasteners used in the Evolution are hardened. Make sure to use exact replacement fasteners as described in Step 3.

4. Use special tools where noted. In some cases, it may be possible to perform the procedure with makeshift tools, but this procedure is not recommended. The use of makeshift tools can damage the components and may cause serious personal injury. Where special tools are required, these may be purchased through any Harley-Davidson dealer. Other tools can be purchased through your dealer, or from a motorcycle or automotive accessory store.

5. Before removing the first bolt and to prevent frustration during installation, get a number of boxes, plastic bags and containers and store the parts as they are removed (**Figure 1**). Also have on hand a roll of masking tape and a permanent, waterproof marking pen to label each part or assembly as required. If your Harley was purchased second hand and it appears that some of the wiring may have been changed or replaced, it will be helpful to label each electrical connection before disconnecting it.

6. Use a vise with protective jaws to hold parts. If protective jaws are not available, insert wooden blocks on either side of the part(s) before clamping them in the vise.

7. Remove and install pressed-on parts with an appropriate mandrel, support and hydraulic press. **Do not** try to pry, hammer or otherwise force them on or off.

8. Refer to the **Table 3** at the end of the chapter for torque specifications. Proper torque is essential to assure long life and satisfactory service from components.

9. Discard all O-rings and oil seals during disassembly. Apply a small amount of grease to the inner lips of each oil seal to prevent damage when the engine is first started.

10. Keep a record of all shims and where they came from. As soon as the shims are removed, inspect them for damage and write down their thickness and location.

11. Work in an area where there is sufficient lighting and room for component storage.

SPECIAL TOOLS

Where special tools are required or recommended for engine overhaul, the tool part numbers are provided. Harley-Davidson tool numbers have a "HD" prefix. These tools can be purchased through Harley-Davidson dealers. Tools unique to Harley-Davidson service can also be purchased through any number of accessory manufacturers.

SERVICING ENGINE IN FRAME

Many components can be serviced while the engine is mounted in the frame:

a. Rocker arm cover.
b. Cylinder head.
c. Cylinder and piston.
d. Camshaft.
e. Gearshift mechanism.
f. Clutch.
g. Transmission.
h. Carburetor.
i. Starter motor and gears.

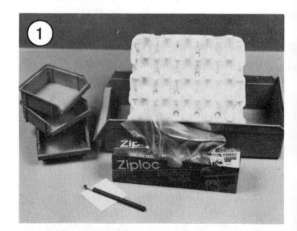

j. Alternator and electrical systems.

ENGINE REMOVAL

WARNING
Because of the explosive and flammable conditions that exist around gasoline, always observe the following precautions.
1. Disconnect the negative battery cable. See Figure 2, typical.

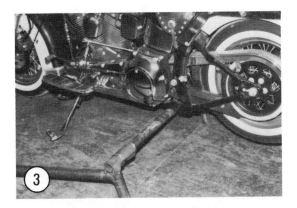

2. Gasoline dripping onto a hot engine component may cause a fire. Always allow the engine to cool completely before working on any fuel system component.
3. Spilled gasoline should be wiped up immediately with dry rags. Then store the rags in a suitable metal container until they can be cleaned or disposed of. Do not store gas or solvent soaked rags in an open container in your shop.
4. Do not service any fuel system component while in the vicinity of open flames, sparks or while anyone is smoking.
5. Always have a fire extinguisher close at hand when working on the engine.

1. Thoroughly clean the engine exterior of dirt, oil and foreign material, using one of the cleaners designed for this purpose.
2. If the engine is going to be disassembled, check engine compression and perform a leak down test as described in Chapter Three. Record the measurements so that you can refer to them later.

NOTE
Because Harley-Davidson models in this manual are not equipped with centerstands, the bike must be secured with a jack or bike stand placed underneath the frame (Figure 3). Block the front and rear wheels to prevent the bike from rolling when removing the engine.

3. Disconnect the negative battery cable (**Figure 2**).
4. Remove the fuel tank as described in Chapter Eight.
5. Remove the air cleaner assembly. See Chapter Three.
6. Remove the carburetor as described in Chapter Eight.
7. Remove the exhaust system as described in Chapter Eight.

NOTE
The upper cylinder head bracket (Figure 4) is installed with special washers between the bracket and frame. Mark these washers and install them in the same position during reassembly. Likewise, ID all electrical wire brackets and ground wires (Figure 5) at the bracket mounting bolts and nuts.

8. Remove the upper cylinder head bracket assembly. See **Figure 6**, typical.

9. Remove the rocker arm covers as described in this chapter.

10. Remove the cylinder heads and cylinders as described in this chapter.

11. On models without forward foot controls, remove the following components:

    a. Right-hand footrest assembly.

    b. Brake pedal.

    c. Master cylinder assembly (see Chapter Fourteen).

12. On wet clutch models, drain the clutch oil as described in Chapter Three.

13. Remove the primary drive system (**Figure 7**) as described in Chapter Five.

14. Remove the flywheel and stator plate as described in Chapter Nine.

15. Remove the inner primary housing-to-engine mounting bolts as described in Chapter Five. See **Figure 8**, typical.

16. Remove the clutch cable bracket at the engine.

17. Disconnect the wire at the oil pressure switch (**Figure 9**).

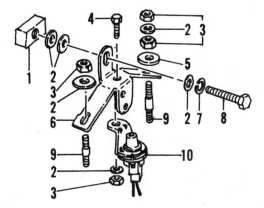

UPPER CYLINDER HEAD BRACKET (FX)

1. Block	6. Bracket
2. Washer	7. Lockwasher
3. Nut	8. Bolt
4. Bolt	9. Stud
5. Washer	10. VOES switch

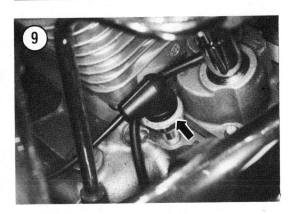

18. Drain the oil tank as described in Chapter Three.

19. Label and disconnect the engine-to-oil tank oil lines. See **Figure 10** (1984), **Figure 11** (1985-1991), **Figure 12** (1992) or **Figure 13** (1993-on).

20. Remove the front and rear engine mounting bolts. See **Figure 14**, typical.

21. Check the engine to make sure all wiring, hoses and other components have been disconnected or removed.

4

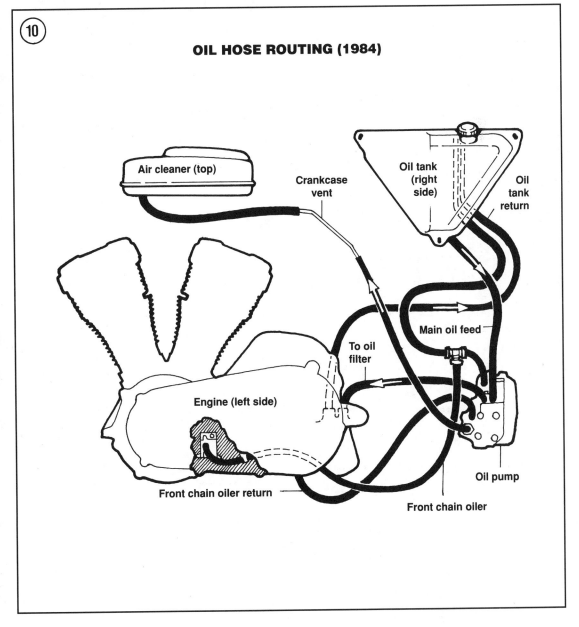

OIL HOSE ROUTING (1984)

Air cleaner (top)

Crankcase vent

Oil tank (right side)

Oil tank return

Main oil feed

To oil filter

Engine (left side)

Oil pump

Front chain oiler return

Front chain oiler

NOTE
A minimum of 2 people or an engine hoist must be used when removing the engine.

22. Remove the engine from the right-hand side.

23. Place the engine in an engine stand or take it to a workbench for further disassembly.

24. Install by reversing these removal steps. Note the following.

25. After installing the engine in the frame, install the engine mounting bolts and nuts and tighten finger-tight.

26. Install the primary housing mounting bolts and tighten finger-tight.

27. Tighten the engine mounting bolts in the following order:

   a. Tighten the rear mounting bolts to the torque specification listed in **Table 3**.

   b. Check that the front frame pad and the engine mounting boss are properly aligned (**Figure 14**).

   c. Tighten the front mounting bolts to the torque specification listed in **Table 3**.

   d. Tighten the primary housing-to-engine mounting bolts as described in Chapter Five. Install new safety wire or bend the bolt lockwasher tabs over the bolts heads as required.

   e. Install the upper cylinder head bracket and its spacers (**Figure 6**). Check the bracket align-

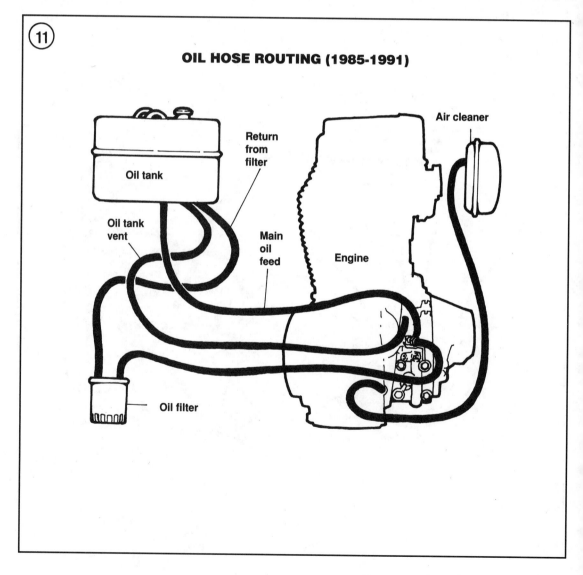

ment with the engine. Shim the bracket as required, then tighten the mounting nuts to the torque specification listed in **Table 3**.

28. Adjust the primary chain as described in Chapter Three.

29. Use new hose clamps when reconnecting the oil line hoses.

30. Install a new oil filter and refill the engine oil tank as described in Chapter Three.

31. *Wet clutch models*: Refill the primary chaincase as described in Chapter Three.

32. Adjust the choke and throttle cables as described in Chapter Three.

33. If the rear master cylinder brake hose was disconnected, bleed the rear brake as described in Chapter Fourteen.

34. Start the engine and check for leaks.

ROCKER ARM COVER/ CYLINDER HEAD

Refer to **Figure 15** and **Figure 16** when performing procedures in this section.

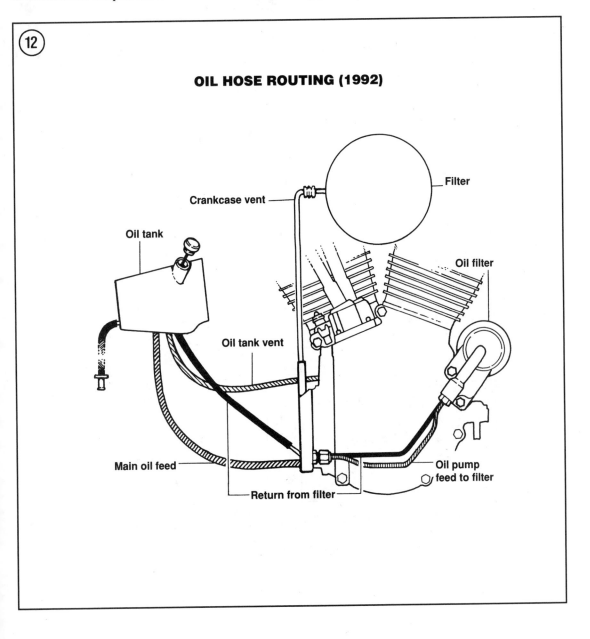

OIL HOSE ROUTING (1992)

Removal

This procedure describes rocker arm and cylinder head removal. The cylinder head can be removed with the engine in the frame.

1. Perform Steps 1-8 under *Engine Removal*.
2. Remove the spark plugs.
3. Remove the 4 upper rocker arm cover bolts, washers and the copper or fiber washers.
4. Remove the upper rocker arm cover (**Figure 17**).
5. Remove the middle rocker arm cover (**Figure 18**). Discard the gaskets.
6. Using a screwdriver (**Figure 19**), pry the spring cap retainer downward and remove it. Repeat for each pushrod.
7. Rotate the engine until both valves are closed (on the cylinder head being removed).

NOTE
Valve position can be determined by observing the rocker arm position (Figure 20).

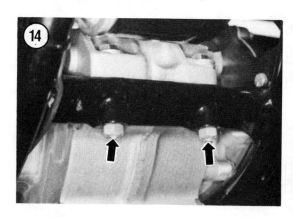

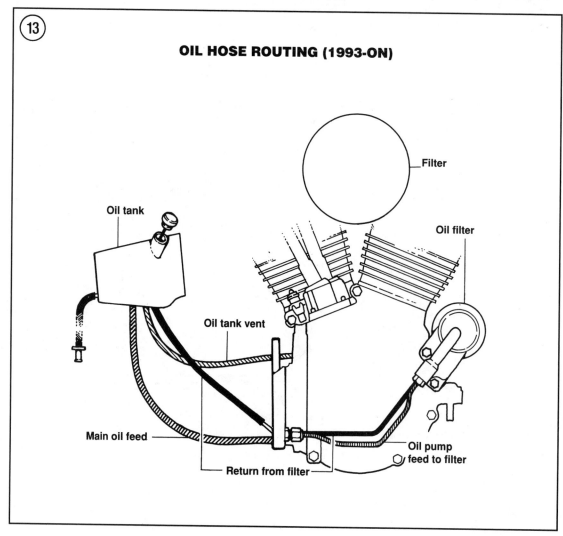

OIL HOSE ROUTING (1993-ON)

Filter

Oil tank

Oil filter

Oil tank vent

Main oil feed

Oil pump feed to filter

Return from filter

(15)

ROCKER ARM ASSEMBLY

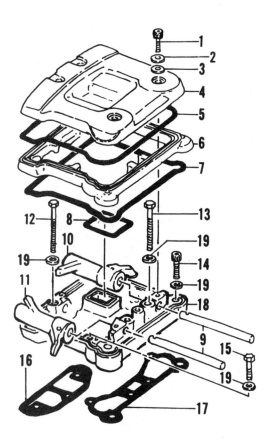

4

1. Bolts
2. Washers
3. Copper washers
4. Upper cover
5. Gasket
6. Middle cover
7. Gasket
8. Gasket
9. Rocker arm shafts
10. Rocker arm
11. Rocker arm
12. Bolt
13. Bolt
14. Bolt
15. Bolt
16. Gasket
17. Gasket
18. Lower cover
19. Washers

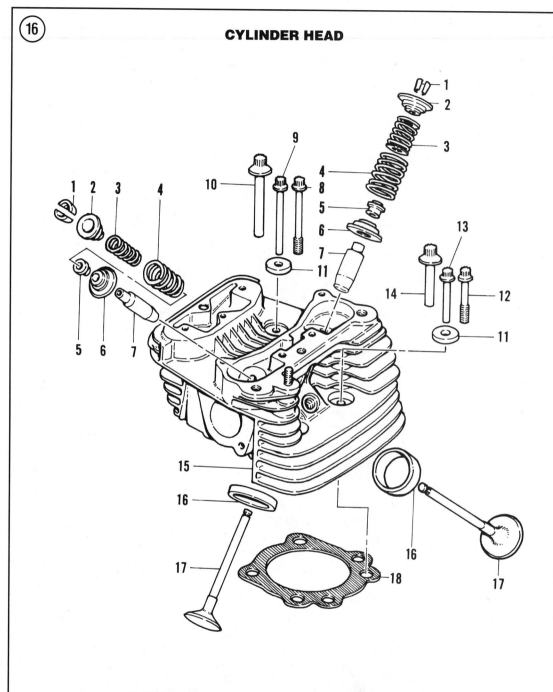

CYLINDER HEAD

1. Valve keeper
2. Upper retainer
3. Inner valve spring
4. Outer valve spring
5. Seal
6. Lower retainer
7. Valve guide
8. Bolt (1984-early 1985)
9. Bolt (late 1985-1987)
10. Bolt (1988-on)
11. Washer (1984-1987)
12. Bolt (1984-early 1985)
13. Bolt (late 1985-1987)
14. Bolt (1988-on)
15. Cylinder head
16. Valve seat
17. Valves
18. Cylinder head gasket

NOTE
While performing the following steps, mark the individual parts during removal so that they can be reinstalled into their original position.

8. Remove the rocker arm cover bolts (A, **Figure 21**) and lift the cover off of the cylinder head (B, **Figure 21**).

NOTE
Mark each pushrod as to its top and bottom position and its position in the cylinder head. The pushrods must be installed in their original position during reassembly.

9. Refer to **Figure 22**. Remove each pushrod (**Figure 23**).

10. Remove the pushrod cover assemblies (**Figure 24**).

11. Remove the upper (**Figure 25**) and lower (**Figure 26**) pushrod cover gaskets.

12. Remove the carburetor and intake manifold as described in Chapter Eight.

13. Loosen the cylinder head bolts 1/8 turn at a time in the crisscross pattern shown in **Figure 27** (1984) or **Figure 28** (1985-on).

14A. *1984-1987*: Remove the cylinder head bolts and washers. See **Figure 29**, typical.

14B. *1988-on*: Remove the cylinder head bolts.

15. Tap the cylinder head with a rubber mallet to free it. Then remove the cylinder head (**Figure 30**).

16. Repeat Steps 1-15 and remove the opposite cylinder head.

17. Disassemble and inspect the rocker arm/cylinder head assembly as described in this chapter.

4

PUSHROD ASSEMBLY

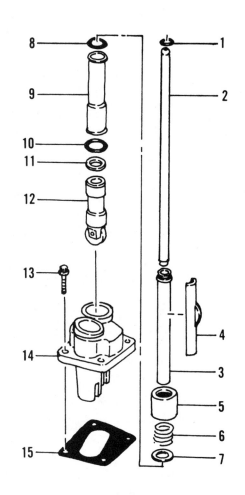

1. O-ring
2. Pushrod
3. Upper pushrod cover
4. Spring cap retainer
5. Cap
6. Spring
7. Spacer
8. O-ring
9. Lower pushrod cover
10. O-ring
11. Spacer
12. Tappet
13. Bolt
14. Tappet guide
15. Gasket

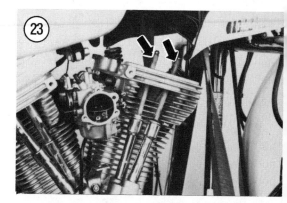

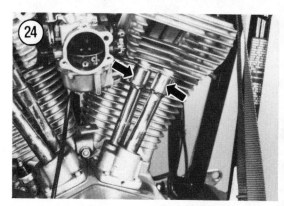

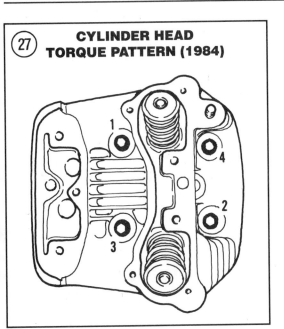

**CYLINDER HEAD
TORQUE PATTERN (1984)**

27

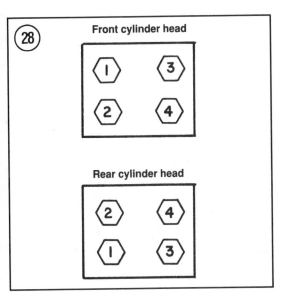

28

Front cylinder head

| 1 | 3 |
| 2 | 4 |

Rear cylinder head

| 2 | 4 |
| 1 | 3 |

29

Installation

Refer to **Figure 15** and **Figure 16** for this procedure.

1. Clean the cylinder head (**Figure 31**) and cylinder (**Figure 32**) mating surfaces of all gasket residue.

2. Install 2 new O-rings over the dowel pins in the cylinder. See **Figure 33**.

CAUTION
The cylinder dowel pin O-rings installed in Step 2 must be installed before

4

30

31

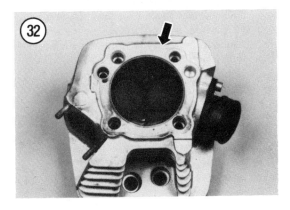

32

installing the cylinder head gasket in Step 3 to ensure correct alignment of the cylinder head gasket. If this procedure is not followed, the cylinder head gasket may leak.

3. Install a new cylinder head gasket, making sure the oil return holes in the gasket line up with the oil holes in the cylinder head. See **Figure 34**.

NOTE
Make sure the bolt holes in the cylinder head are clean and unobstructed.

4. Install the cylinder head, allowing the dowel pins to align the cylinder head as you install it onto the cylinder. See **Figure 30**.

NOTE
To ensure proper torque readings, clean all cylinder head bolts and washers (1984-1987) in solvent and then dry thoroughly. Replace damaged fasteners as required.

NOTE
The cylinder head mounting bolts are not interchangeable between certain model years. When replacing bolts, make sure to purchase the correct bolts for your Harley's model year.

5. Coat cylinder head bolt threads and the bottom face of each bolt head with oil and install them finger-tight only. Make sure to install washers on 1984-1987 models.

NOTE
*The cylinder head bolts and washers (**Figure 35,** typical) are made of Grade 8 material. Do not substitute these items with a part made of a lower grade material. If replacement is required, purchase new parts from a Harley-Davidson dealer. Late style cylinder head washers cannot be used on early style cylinder head bolts. When replacing cylinder head fasteners, have a Harley-Davidson dealer confirm the style and type of fastener required for your model.*

CAUTION
Failure to follow the torque pattern and sequence in Step 6 may cause cylinder head distortion and gasket leakage.

6A. *1984 FXST*: Tighten the cylinder head bolts in the following order:
  a. Using a torque wrench, tighten the No. 1 bolt to 7-9 ft.-lb. (9.6-12.4 N•m), Then continue and tighten bolts 2, 3 and 4 to 7-9 ft.-lb. (9.6-12.4 N•m). See **Figure 27**.

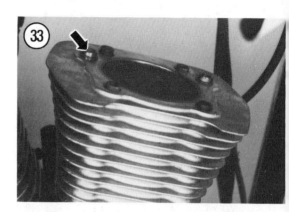

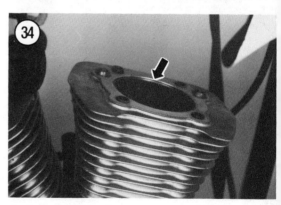

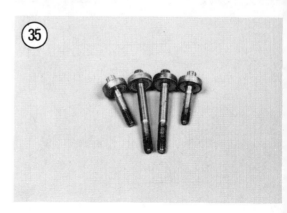

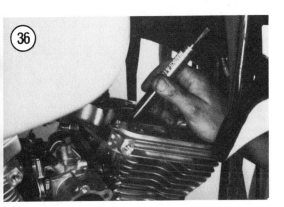

b. Tighten the No. 1 bolt to 15-17 ft.-lb. (20.7-23.5 N•m). Then continue and tighten bolts 2, 3 and 4 to 15-17 ft.-lb. (20.7-23.5 N•m). See **Figure 27**.

c. Tighten the No. 1 bolt to 24-26 ft.-lb. (33.1-35.9 N•m). Then continue and tighten bolts 2, 3 and 4 to 24-26 ft.-lb. (33.1-35.9 N•m). See **Figure 27**.

6B. *1985-on*: Tighten the cylinder head bolts in the following order:

a. Using a torque wrench, tighten the No. 1 bolt to 7-9 ft.-lb. (9.6-12.4 N•m). Then continue and tighten bolts 2, 3 and 4 to 7-9 ft-lb. (9.6-12.4 N•m). See **Figure 28**.

b. Tighten the No. 1 bolt to 12-14 ft.-lbs. (16.5-19.3 N•m). Then continue and tighten bolts 2, 3 and 4 to 12-14 ft.-lbs. (16.5-19.3 N•m). See **Figure 28**.

c. Using a pen (**Figure 36**), make a vertical mark on the No. 1 bolt head and a matching mark on the cylinder head. See **Figure 37**. Repeat for each bolt.

d. Following the torque sequence in **Figure 28**, turn each bolt head 1/4 turn clockwise, using the match marks as a guide. See **Figure 38**.

e. When all match marks are aligned as shown in **Figure 38**, the torque sequence is complete.

f. Repeat for the opposite cylinder head.

NOTE
The rocker boxes and gaskets are not interchangeable between certain model years. When installing gaskets or replacing rocker boxes, make sure to purchase parts for your Harley's model year.

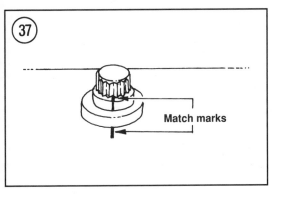

Match marks

7. Install 2 new lower rocker arm cover gaskets with the bead on the gaskets facing up. See **Figure 39**.

NOTE
If a valve train component has been replaced or if the valves and seats have been reconditioned, the length of each pushrod must be checked and adjusted by a Harley-Davidson dealer as special tools are required.

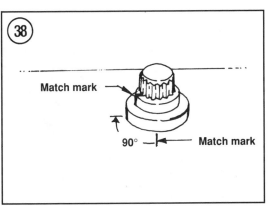

Match mark

90° — Match mark

8. Install new upper (**Figure 25**) and lower (**Figure 26**) pushrod O-rings.

9. Install the lower pushrod covers (**Figure 24**).

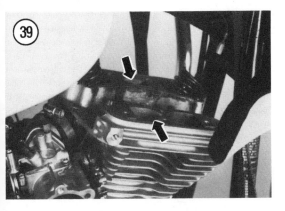

NOTE
The pushrods are color coded for proper installation: rear exhaust—purple, rear intake—blue, front intake—yellow, front exhaust—green.

10. Install the pushrods (**Figure 23**) in their original positions, using the marks made prior to removal.

NOTE
Before installing the rocker arm cover in Step 11, make sure that the cam is positioned with its face circle facing up.

11. Position the rocker arm cover (**Figure 40**) onto the cylinder head.

12. The rocker arm cover bolt sizes are different. Install the longer bolts (A, **Figure 41**) on the right-hand side.

NOTE
*If the right-hand bolts do not drop into position correctly the rocker arm shafts are not aligned properly. Refer to **Rocker Arm** in this chapter.*

13. Tighten the rocker cover bolts in a crisscross pattern to the torque specification listed in **Table 3**. Tighten the bolts in small increments to help bleed the lifters.

14. Check that the pushrods spin freely.

CAUTION
If the pushrods do not spin freely, do not start the engine as the valves could be damaged. If the valves are tight, have the pushrods gauged by a Harley-Davidson dealer.

15. Install 2 new rocker arm cork gaskets at the positions shown in **Figure 42**.

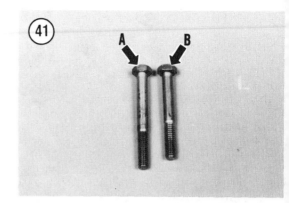

16. Position the middle rocker arm cover (A, **Figure 43**) onto the engine. Then install a new cork gasket (B, **Figure 43**).

17. Install the rocker arm cover (**Figure 44**). Then install the 4 cover screws with the steel and new copper or fiber washers.

> *NOTE*
> *The copper or fiber washers (A, **Figure 45**) must be installed under the steel washers (B, **Figure 45**).*

18. Check that the middle rocker arm cover is spaced evenly on all sides, then tighten the cover screws to 10-13 ft.-lb. (13.8-17.9 N•m) in a crisscross pattern.

19. Push the upper pushrod cover up (**Figure 46**) and seat it in the rocker arm cover (**Figure 47**). Then position the spring cap retainer as shown in **Figure 48**. Place a screwdriver under the retainer. Then lift the screwdriver up slightly and slide the retainer into position.

20. Reverse Steps 1-8 under *Engine Installation*.

Rocker Arm
Removal/Inspection/Installation

Label all parts before disassembly so they will be installed in their original positions. Refer to **Figure 15** for this procedure.

1. See **Figure 49**. Remove the rocker arm shafts (A) and remove the rocker arms (B).

2. Clean all parts in solvent. Blow compressed air through all oil passages to make sure they are clear.

3. Examine the rocker arm pads and ball sockets (**Figure 50**) for pitting and excessive wear; replace the rocker arms if necessary.

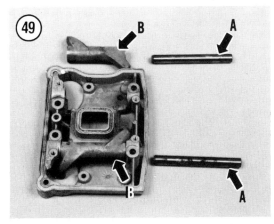

4. Measure the rocker arm shaft with a micrometer (**Figure 51**) where it rides in the lower rocker arm cover. Then measure the rocker arm shaft bore (**Figure 52**) in the lower rocker arm cover. Subtract the shaft O.D. from the bore I.D. to obtain rocker arm shaft clearance. Replace worn parts if the clearance exceeds the specifications in **Table 2**.

5. Measure the rocker arm bushing inside diameter (**Figure 53**) with a small hole gauge. Bushing replacement should be referred to a Harley-Davidson dealer as the new bushings must be reamed to size after installation.

6. After completing Steps 3-5 and replacing worn parts (if required), perform the following:

   a. Install the rocker arms and rocker arm shafts into the lower cover (**Figure 54**).

   b. Check the rocker arm end clearance with a feeler gauge (**Figure 55**).

   c. Replace the rocker arm or lower cover or both parts if the end clearance exceeds specifications (**Table 2**).

7. Inspect the upper and middle cover gasket surfaces (**Figure 56**) for damage or warpage. Replace parts as necessary.

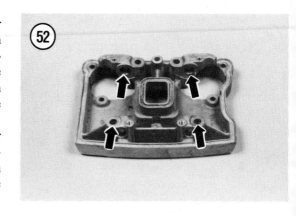

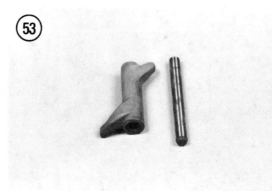

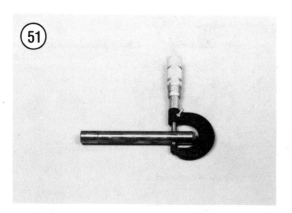

8. Assemble the rocker arm assembly as follows:

NOTE
Following the ID marks made during disassembly, install parts in their original positions.

a. Place the rocker arms into the rocker arm cover (B, **Figure 49**).

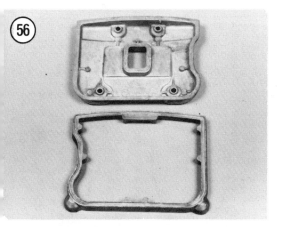

b. Install the rocker arm shafts partway so that the machined notch in each shaft faces to the right-hand side (**Figure 57**) of the cover. Then turn each shaft so that the machined notch aligns with the bolt hole slot in the cover. This allows the cover bolts to be installed correctly during cover installation. In addition, the cover bolts engage the shaft machined notch and lock the shafts in position during engine operation.

Cylinder Head Inspection

Refer to **Figure 14** for this procedure.
1. Without removing valves, remove all carbon deposits from the combustion chambers (**Figure 58**) with a wire brush.

CAUTION
If the combustion chambers are cleaned while the valves are removed, make sure to keep the scraper or wire brush away from the valve seats to prevent damaging the seat surfaces. A damaged or even slightly scratched valve seat will cause poor valve seating.

2. Examine the spark plug threads in the cylinder head (**Figure 59**) for damage. If damage is minor or if the threads are dirty or clogged with carbon, use a spark plug thread tap to clean the threads following the manufacturer's instructions. If thread damage is severe, refer further service to a Harley-Davidson dealer or machine shop.
3. After all carbon is removed from combustion chambers, valve ports and the spark plug thread holes are repaired, clean the entire head in solvent.

Use compressed air, if available, to dry the head thoroughly and to remove small debris from passages.

4. Clean away all carbon on the piston crowns. Do not remove the carbon ridge at the top of the cylinder bore.

5. See **Figure 60**. Check for cracks in the combustion chamber (A) and exhaust ports (B). A cracked head must be replaced.

6. After the head has been thoroughly cleaned, place a straightedge across the gasket surface at several points (**Figure 61**). Measure warp by inserting a feeler gauge between the straightedge and cylinder head at each location. Maximum allowable warpage is listed in **Table 2**. If warpage exceeds this limit, refer service to your dealer.

7. Check the rocker arm cover mating surface using the procedure in Step 6. There should be no warpage.

8. Check the valves and valve guides as described under *Valves and Valve Components* in this chapter.

9. Check the pushrods (**Figure 62**) for bending, wear or damage. Check the pushrod ends for wear. Replace if necessary.

10. *1984-1989*: Check the intake manifolds (**Figure 63**) for cracks or tear damage that could allow unfiltered air to enter the engine. Also check the manifold bolts for tightness. If you removed the manifold, install it with a new gasket.

VALVES AND VALVE COMPONENTS

General practice among those who do their own service is to remove the cylinder heads and take them to a dealer or machine shop for inspection and service. Since the cost is low relative to the required effort and equipment, this is the best approach, even for experienced mechanics.

Refer to **Figure 64** for this procedure.

> *CAUTION*
> *All component parts of each valve assembly must be kept together. Do not mix with like components from other valves or excessive wear may result.*

1. Remove the cylinder head(s) as described in this chapter.

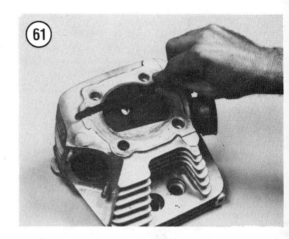

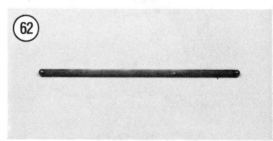

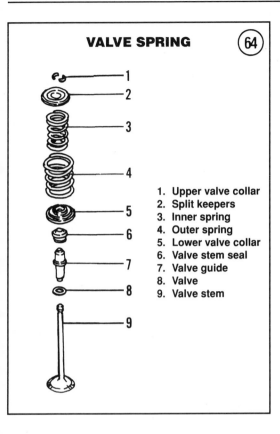

VALVE SPRING 64

1. Upper valve collar
2. Split keepers
3. Inner spring
4. Outer spring
5. Lower valve collar
6. Valve stem seal
7. Valve guide
8. Valve
9. Valve stem

2. Install a valve spring compressor squarely over the valve retainer with other end of tool placed against valve head.

3. Tighten valve spring compressor until split valve keeper separates. Lift out split keeper with needle nose pliers.

4. Gradually loosen valve spring compressor and remove from head. Lift off valve retainer.

CAUTION
*Remove any burrs from the valve stem grooves before removing the valve (**Figure 65**); otherwise the valve guides will be damaged.*

5. Remove inner and outer springs, retainer and valve.

6. Repeat Steps 2-5 and remove remaining valves.

7. Remove and discard all of the valve guide oil seals.

Inspection

1. Clean valves with a wire brush and solvent.

2. Inspect the contact surface of each valve for burning (**Figure 66**). Minor roughness and pitting can be removed by lapping the valve as described in this chapter. Excessive unevenness to the contact surface is an indication that the valve is not serviceable. The contact surface of the valve may be ground on a valve grinding machine, but it is best to replace a burned or damaged valve with a new one.

3. Inspect the valve stems for wear and roughness.

4. Measure valve stem O.D. with a micrometer (**Figure 67**). Record O.D. for each valve.

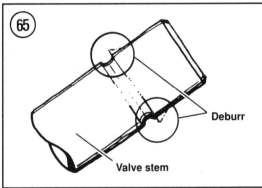

65

Deburr

Valve stem

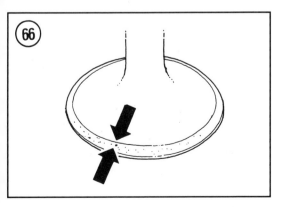

66

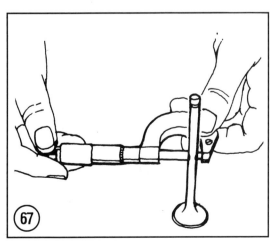

67

5. Remove all carbon and varnish from the valve guides with a stiff spiral wire brush.

> *NOTE*
> *Step 6 requires special measuring equipment. If you do not have the required measuring devices, proceed to Step 8.*

6. Measure each valve guide at top, center and bottom with a small hole gauge. Record I.D. for each valve guide.

7. Subtract the measurement made in Step 4 from the measurement made in Step 6. The difference is the valve guide-to-valve stem clearance. See specifications in **Table 2** for specified clearance. Replace any guide and valve that is not within tolerance.

8. Insert each valve in its guide. Hold the valve just slightly off its seat and rock it sideways. If it rocks more than slightly, the guide is probably worn and should be replaced. As a final check, take the head to a dealer and have the valve guides measured.

9. Measure the valve spring free length with a vernier caliper (**Figure 68**). All should be of length specified in **Table 2** with no bends or other distortion. Replace defective springs.

10. Check the valve spring retainer and split keepers. Replace worn or damaged parts as required.

11. Inspect valve seats. If worn or burned, they must be reconditioned. This should be performed by your dealer or local machine shop. Seats and valves in near-perfect condition can be reconditioned by lapping with fine carborundum paste.

Valve Guide Replacement

When guides are worn so that there is excessive stem-to-guide clearance or valve tipping, they must be replaced. Replace all, even if only one is worn. This job should only be performed by a Harley-Davidson dealer or qualified specialist as special tools are required.

Valve Seat Reconditioning

This job is best left to your dealer or local machine shop. They have the special equipment and knowledge for this exacting job. You can still save considerable money by removing the cylinder head and taking just the head to the shop.

Valve Lapping

Valve lapping is a simple operation which can restore the valve seal without machining if the amount of wear or distortion is not too great.

1. Smear a light coating of fine grade valve lapping compound on seating surface of valve (**Figure 69**).

2. Insert the valve into the head.

3. Wet the suction cup of the lapping stick (**Figure 70**) and stick it onto the head of the valve. Lap the valve to the seat by spinning tool between hands

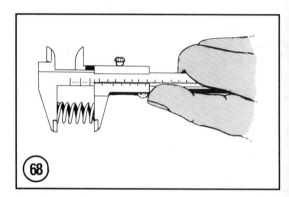

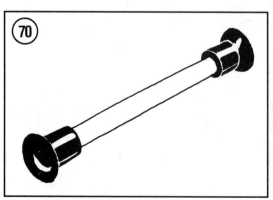

while lifting and moving valve around seat 1/4 turn at a time.

4. Wipe off valve and seat frequently to check progress of lapping. Lap only enough to achieve a precise seating ring around valve head (**Figure 71**).

5. Closely examine valve seat in cylinder head. It should be smooth and even with a smooth, polished seating "ring."

6. Thoroughly clean the valves and cylinder head in solvent to remove all grinding compound. Any compound left on the valves or the cylinder head will end up in the engine and cause premature and rapid engine wear.

7. After the lapping has been completed and the valve assemblies have been reinstalled into the head the valve seal should be tested. Check the seal of each valve by pouring solvent into each of the intake and exhaust ports. There should be no leakage past the seat. If leakage occurs, combustion chamber (**Figure 58**) will appear wet. If fluid leaks past any of the seats, disassemble that valve assembly and repeat the lapping procedure until there is no leakage.

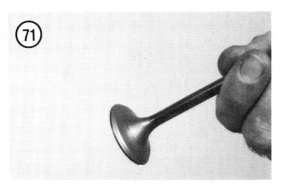

Installation

1. Lap valves as described in this chapter.

2. Coat a valve stem with oil and insert the valve into its valve guide in cylinder head.

3. Install the bottom retainer.

4. Install new valve guide seals as follows:

   a. Place a protective cover over the end of the valve stem (covering the valve keeper groove on valve stem).

   b. Apply a small amount of RC 620 Loctite (green) to the outside portion on the valve guide near the top.

CAUTION
Installing the valve guide seals without the protective cover described in sub-step c will cause seal damage.

   c. Wipe the protective cover with oil and place a new valve guide seal on the cover. Then use a socket and carefully drive the seal over the cover and onto the valve stem. Drive the seal squarely onto the valve stem until it bottoms out against the valve guide. Do not continue to drive it after it bottoms out or you will damage it.

NOTE
Harley-Davidson sells a valve seal installation tool (part No. HD-34643) and driver handle (part No. HD-34740) that can be used to install the valve guide seals accurately.

5. Install valve springs. Then install the upper valve spring retainer.

6. Push down on upper valve spring collar with the valve spring compressor and install valve keepers. After releasing tension from compressor, examine valve keepers (**Figure 72**) and make sure they are seated correctly.

7. Repeat to install the remaining valve guide seals and valves.

CAUTION
Do not remove the valve after installing it as it will damage the valve seal. If you must remove the valve, install a new seal.

CYLINDER

Removal

Refer to **Figure 73** when performing the following.

1. Remove the cylinder head as described in this chapter.

2. Remove all dirt and foreign material from the cylinder base.

3. Remove the 2 dowel pins and O-rings (**Figure 74**) from the top of the cylinder.

4. Turn the engine over until the piston is at bottom dead center (BDC).

5. Loosen the cylinder by tapping around the perimeter with a rubber or plastic mallet.

6. Pull the cylinder straight up (**Figure 75**) and off the piston and cylinder studs.

7. Stuff clean shop rags into the crankcase opening to prevent objects from falling undetected into the crankcase.

8. Install a 6 inch rubber hose over each stud. This will protect both the piston and studs from damage.

> *CAUTION*
> *While the cylinder is removed, use care when working around the cylinder studs to avoid bending or damaging them. The slightest bend could cause a stud failure later during engine operation.*

9. Repeat Steps 1-8 for the other cylinder.

Inspection

The pistons on all models cannot be accurately measured with standard measuring instruments and techniques. This is because the piston has a complex shape due to its design and manufacturing. Furthermore, the piston bore is offset. Piston-to-cylinder clearance is checked by measuring the cylinder bore only. If a cylinder is worn, the cylinder must be bored to specific factory specifications—not to match a particular piston size as with conventional methods. All service related to cylinder and piston matching should be referred to a Harley-Davidson dealer.

The following procedure requires the use of highly specialized and expensive measuring instruments. If such instruments are not readily available, have the measurements performed by a dealer or qualified machine shop.

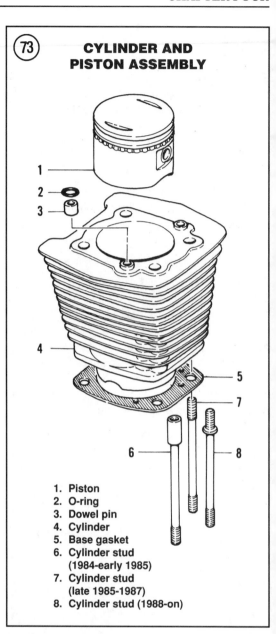

73 **CYLINDER AND PISTON ASSEMBLY**

1. Piston
2. O-ring
3. Dowel pin
4. Cylinder
5. Base gasket
6. Cylinder stud (1984-early 1985)
7. Cylinder stud (late 1985-1987)
8. Cylinder stud (1988-on)

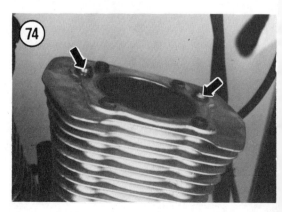

74

NOTE
*Harley-Davidson recommends clamping the cylinder between torque plates (HD-33446) (**Figure 76**) when making cylinder measurements and performing boring and honing operations. This arrangement simulates the distortion imparted on a cylinder when it is torqued down by the cylinder head and cylinder bolts. Measurements made without the engine torque plate can vary by 0.001 in. If you do not have access to the torque plates, refer service to a Harley-Davidson dealer.*

1. Thoroughly clean the cylinder with solvent and dry with compressed air. Lightly oil the cylinder bore to prevent rust after performing Step 2.

2. Check the cylinder's top (**Figure 77**) and bottom (**Figure 78**) gasket surfaces with a straightedge and feeler gauge. Replace the cylinder if the following specifications are exceeded:

   a. Top cylinder surface: 0.006 in. (0.15 mm)

   b. Bottom cylinder surface: 0.008 in. (0.20 mm)

3. Install a new cylinder head and base gasket onto the cylinder and clamp the cylinder between the torque plates (**Figure 76**). Install the torque plate bolts, making sure they engage the gaskets properly. Tighten the torque plate bolts following the procedure and torque specification given for the cylinder heads as described in this chapter.

4. Measure the cylinder bores, with a bore gauge (**Figure 79**) or inside micrometer at the points shown in **Figure 80**. Initial measurement should be made at a distance of 0.500 in. (12.7 mm) below the top of the cylinder. The 0.500 in. (12.7 mm) depth

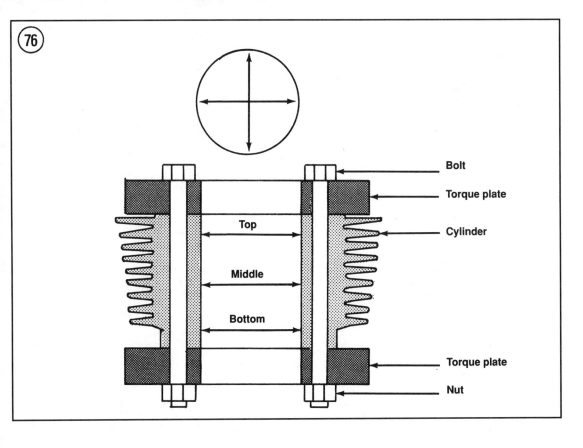

distance represents the start of the ring path area; do not take readings that are out of the ring path area.

5. Measure in 2 axes—in line with the piston pin and at 90° to the pin. If the taper or out-of-round is greater than specifications (**Table 2**), the cylinders must be rebored to the next oversize and new pistons and rings installed. Rebore both cylinders even though only one may be worn.

6. Check the cylinder walls for scuffing, scratches or other damage; if evident, the cylinders should be rebored and the pistons replaced.

7. Have your dealer confirm all cylinder measurements before you order replacement parts or have the cylinders honed or bored.

Installation

Refer to **Figure 73** when performing this procedure.

1. If the base gasket is stuck to the bottom of the cylinder it should be removed and the cylinder surface cleaned thoroughly.

2. Check that the top cylinder surface is clean of all old gasket material.

3. Install a new cylinder base gasket to the crankcase. Make sure all holes align.

4. Turn the engine over until the piston is at top dead center (TDC).

5. Lubricate the cylinder bores and pistons liberally with engine oil.

6. Compress the rings with a ring compressor (**Figure 81**) or with aircraft type hose clamps of appropriate diameter. Tighten the compressor just enough to compress the rings.

> *CAUTION*
> *Don't tighten the clamp any more than necessary to compress the rings. If the rings can't slip through easily, the clamp may gouge the rings and piston.*

7. Carefully align the cylinder over the piston and slide it down (**Figure 75**). Once the rings are positioned in the cylinder, remove the ring compressor or hose clamp installed in Step 6.

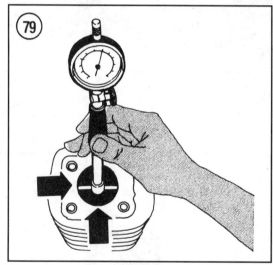

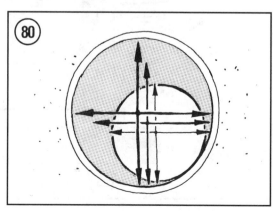

8. Rotate the cylinder as necessary and slide it over the crankcase studs.

9. Install the cylinder dowel pins, O-rings and cylinder head as described in this chapter.

PISTONS AND PISTON RINGS

Piston
Removal/Installation

1. Remove the cylinder head and cylinder as described in this chapter.

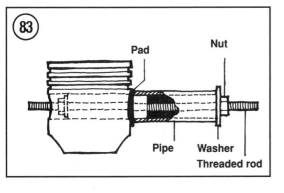

2. Stuff the crankcase with clean shop rags to prevent objects from falling into the crankcase.

3. Lightly mark the pistons with an F (front) or R (rear) so they will be installed into the correct cylinder. Also mark the piston crown with an arrow pointing to the front of the bike. Because the piston pins are offset in the pistons, the pistons must not be installed backwards.

4. Remove the piston rings as described under *Piston Ring Replacement* in this chapter.

> *WARNING*
> *Because the piston pin retaining rings are highly compressed in the piston pin ring groove, safety glasses must be worn during their removal and installation.*

5. Using an awl, pry the piston pin retaining rings (**Figure 82**) out of the piston. Place your thumb over the hole to help prevent the rings from flying out during removal.

6. Support the piston and push out the piston pin. If the piston is difficult to remove, use a homemade tool as shown in **Figure 83**.

7. Inspect the piston as described in this chapter.

8. Coat the connecting rod bushing, piston pin and piston with assembly oil.

9. Place the piston over the connecting rod, following the ID marks made prior to removal. New pistons should be installed so that the nub on the piston pin boss (**Figure 84**) faces toward the left-hand side (clutch side) of the bike. If the piston has an arrow cast into the piston crown, install it so that the arrow faces toward the front of the bike.

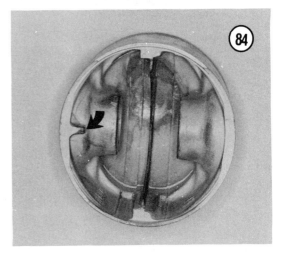

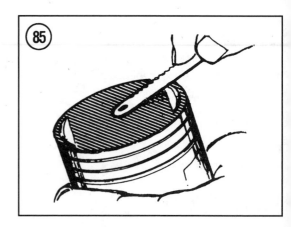

10. Insert the piston pin and tap it with a plastic
mallet until it starts into the connecting rod bushing.
Hold the rod so that the lower end does not take any
shock. If the pin does not slide easily, use the homemade tool (**Figure 83**) but eliminate the piece of
pipe. Tap the pin in until it is centered in the piston.

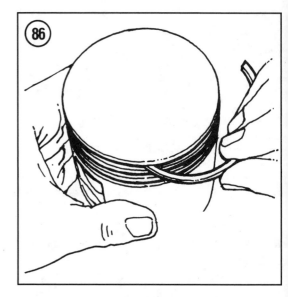

11. Install *new* piston pin retaining rings. If the
retaining rings are difficult to install, use the piston
pin retaining ring installer (HD-34623). Turn each
retaining ring so that its gap faces away from the slot
in the bottom of the piston. Make sure each retaining
ring seats fully in its piston groove.

12. Install rings as described under *Piston Ring
Replacement* in this chapter.

Piston Inspection

1. Carefully clean the carbon from the piston crown
with a soft scraper (**Figure 85**). Do not remove or
damage the carbon ridge around the circumference
of the piston above the top ring.

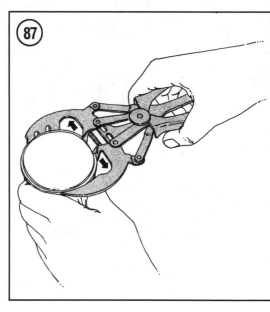

2. Using a broken piston ring, remove all carbon
deposits from the piston ring grooves (**Figure 86**).
Make sure you do not remove metal from the piston
ring grooves when cleaning them.

3. Examine each ring groove for burrs, dented edges
and wide wear. Pay particular attention to the top
compression ring groove, as it usually wears more
than the others.

4. Check cylinder clearance as described in this
chapter. Replace worn or damaged parts as required.

Piston Ring Replacement

NOTE
ID the piston rings as they are removed in Step 1 so that they can be reinstalled in their same position.

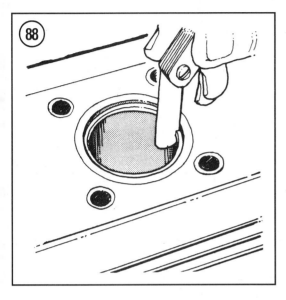

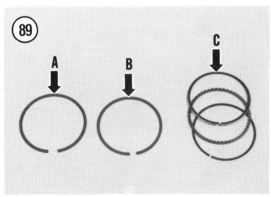

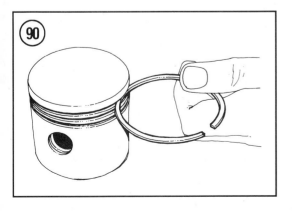

1. Remove the old rings with a ring expander tool (**Figure 87**).

2. Inspect ring grooves carefully for burrs, nicks, or broken or cracked lands. Replace piston if necessary.

3. Check end gap of each ring. To check ring, insert the ring into the top of the cylinder bore and square it with the cylinder wall by tapping it with the piston. Insert a feeler gauge as shown in **Figure 88**. Compare gap with specifications in **Table 2**. Replace ring if gap is too large.

NOTE
The piston ring end gap specifications listed in ***Table 2*** *do not apply to oversize piston rings.*

NOTE
The oil control ring expander spacer does not have a wear specification. If the oil control ring rails show wear, all 3 oil control rings (C, ***Figure 89***) *should be replaced as a set.*

4. Roll each ring around its piston groove (as shown in **Figure 90**) to check for binding.

5. Install oil ring in oil ring groove with a ring expander tool (**Figure 87**).

6. If you are installing the original rings, install them according to the ID marks made while removing them. If you are installing new compression rings, note the following:

    a. The top compression ring (A, **Figure 89**) does not have a dot. The second compression ring (B, **Figure 89**) has a dot that must face upward when installing the ring.

    b. Install the second compression ring, then install the top compression ring.

NOTE
When installing oversize compression rings, check the number to make sure the correct rings are being installed. The ring numbers should be the same as the piston oversize number.

7. Check side clearance of each ring as shown in **Figure 91**. Compare with specifications in **Table 2**.

8. Distribute ring gaps around piston as shown in **Figure 92**.

PUSHRODS

Removal/Installation

Remove and install pushrods as described under *Cylinder Head Removal/Installation.*

Inspection

Refer to **Figure 93** for this procedure.
1. Disassemble the pushrod cover as follows:
   a. Remove the lower pushrod cover (**Figure 94**).
   b. Remove the O-ring (**Figure 95**).
   c. Remove the spacer (**Figure 96**).
   d. Remove the spring (**Figure 97**).
   e. Remove the cap (**Figure 98**).
2. Check the pushrod cover assembly (**Figure 99**) as follows:
   a. Check the spring for sagging or cracking.
   b. Check the spacer for deformation or damage.
   c. Check the O-ring for cracking or wear.
   d. Check the pushrod covers for cracking or damage.
3. Check the pushrod ends (**Figure 100**) for wear.
4. Roll the pushrods on a flat surface, such as a piece of glass, and check for bending.
5. Replace all worn or damaged parts as necessary.
6. Reverse Step 1 to assemble the pushrod cover assembly. Push the lower pushrod cover into the cap to seat the O-ring. See **Figure 101**.

TAPPETS AND TAPPET GUIDES

All models are factory equipped with tappets and rollers (**Figure 93**). The tappets consist of a piston,

cylinder and check valve. During operation, tappets pump full of engine oil, thus taking up all play in the valve train. When the engine is off, the tappets will "leak down" as oil escapes from the hydraulic unit. When the engine is started, it is normal for the tappets to click until they refill with oil. If the tappets stop clicking after the engine is run for a few minutes, they are working properly.

Removal

During removal, store tappets in proper sequence for installation in their original position. Refer to **Figure 93** for this procedure.

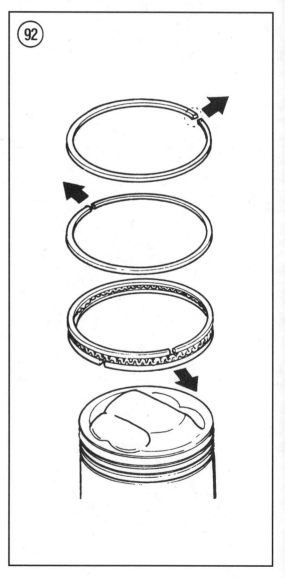

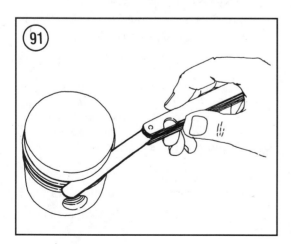

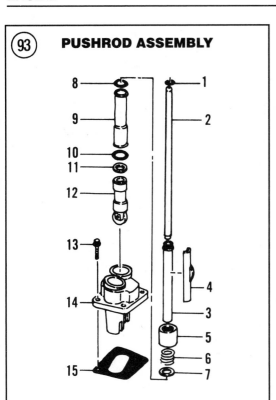

PUSHROD ASSEMBLY

1. O-ring
2. Pushrod
3. Upper pushrod cover
4. Spring cap retainer
5. Cap
6. Spring
7. Spacer
8. O-ring
9. Lower pushrod cover
10. O-ring
11. Spacer
12. Tappet
13. Screw
14. Tappet guide
15. Gasket

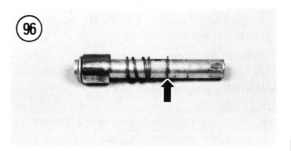

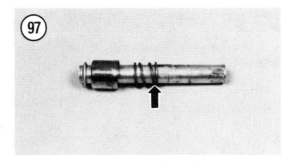

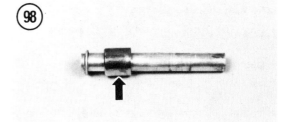

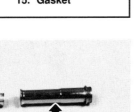

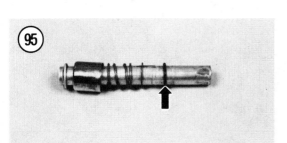

4

1. Remove the pushrods as described under *Cylinder Head Removal* in this chapter.

2. Remove the tappet guide housing bolts (**Figure 102**). Loosen the tappet guide by striking it lightly with a plastic-tipped hammer.

3. Use your fingers and push the tappet and roller assembly against the side of the tappet guide to hold it in position. Then lift the tappet guide away from the gearcase while still holding the tappets in position. This will prevent the tappets from falling into the gearcase.

4. Pull the tappet and roller assembly out from the bottom of the guide.

Disassembly/Inspection

1. Clean all of the parts, except the tappet and roller assembly, in solvent.

2. Blow out all tappet guide and hydraulic oil passages with compressed air.

3. Clean the tappet guide oil channel openings with a piece of wire.

4. Check the tappet rollers for pitting, scoring, galling or excessive wear. If the rollers are worn excessively, check the cam lobes for the same wear conditions. The cam lobes can be observed through the tappet guide hole in the crankcase. Replace the cam, if necessary, as described in this chapter.

5. Clean the roller with contact cleaner. Then check the roller end clearance. Replace if excessive (**Table 2**).

6. Measure tappet O.D. and guide I.D. to determine tappet guide fit. Compare to specifications in **Table 2** and replace parts as required.

7. If dirt has entered the tappet, replace it.

8. After inspection, soak the tappets in clean engine oil before reinstallation.

Installation

1. Slide the tappets through the bottom of the tappet guide.

2. Install a new tappet guide gasket. Do not install any type of sealer on the gasket.

3. Hold the tappets with your fingers or use wire and install the tappet guide onto the gearcase. Do not allow the tappets to drop into the gearcase.

NOTE
The tappets can be installed into their guide facing in either direction.

4. Install the Tappet Guide Alignment Tool (part No. HD-33443) into the tappet screw hole closest to the tappet oil feed hole. Install the 3 tappet block mounting screws and tighten them securely. Remove the alignment tool and then install and tighten the remaining tappet block mounting screw.

5. Tighten the tappet guide retaining screws securely.

6. Have a dealer check pushrod length.

7. Install the pushrods as described in this chapter.

Tappet Oil Screen

The tappet oil screen should be cleaned at specified service intervals. See Chapter Three for complete information.

CAUTION
Failure to clean the tappet oil screen as described in Chapter Three will cause premature tappet wear.

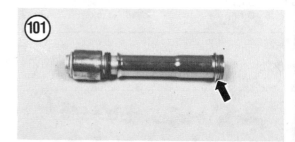

OIL PUMP

The oil pump is installed at the rear of the gear-case. The pump consists of 2 sections: a feed pump which supplies oil under pressure to the engine components, and a scavenger pump which returns oil to the oil tank from the engine.

Removal/Disassembly

Refer to **Figure 103** for this procedure.

NOTE
Label all gears and Woodruff keys during removal so that they can be installed in their original position.

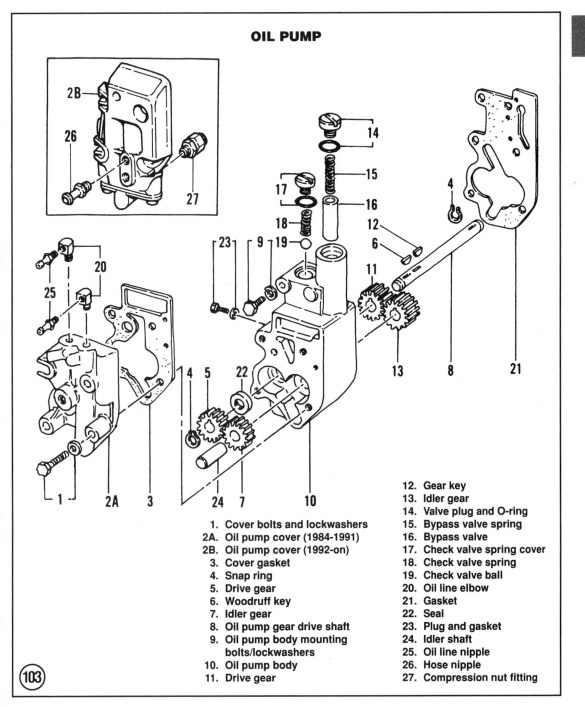

OIL PUMP

4

1. Cover bolts and lockwashers
2A. Oil pump cover (1984-1991)
2B. Oil pump cover (1992-on)
3. Cover gasket
4. Snap ring
5. Drive gear
6. Woodruff key
7. Idler gear
8. Oil pump gear drive shaft
9. Oil pump body mounting bolts/lockwashers
10. Oil pump body
11. Drive gear
12. Gear key
13. Idler gear
14. Valve plug and O-ring
15. Bypass valve spring
16. Bypass valve
17. Check valve spring cover
18. Check valve spring
19. Check valve ball
20. Oil line elbow
21. Gasket
22. Seal
23. Plug and gasket
24. Idler shaft
25. Oil line nipple
26. Hose nipple
27. Compression nut fitting

1. Drain the engine oil tank as described in Chapter Three.

NOTE
When disconnecting the oil lines in Step 2, make sure to tag each line so that it may be returned to its original position.

2A. On 1984-1991 models, disconnect the oil lines from the oil pump. Plug the oil lines to prevent oil leakage and contamination. On 1991 models, discard the one-piece band clamps as new clamps must be used during installation. Refer to the illustration for your model:

   a. **Figure 104**: 1984.

   b. **Figure 105**: 1985-1991.

2B. On 1992-on models (**Figure 106** or **Figure 107**), perform the following:

   a. Disconnect the oil tank vent line at the oil pump.

   b. Disconnect the main oil feed hose at the oil pump.

   c. Disconnect the oil filter-to-oil pump cover manifold oil hose as described under *Oil Filter Mount (1992-On)* in this chapter.

3. Remove the bolts securing the oil pump cover and remove the cover. See **Figure 108**.

4. Remove the snap ring, gear, Woodruff key and idler gear.

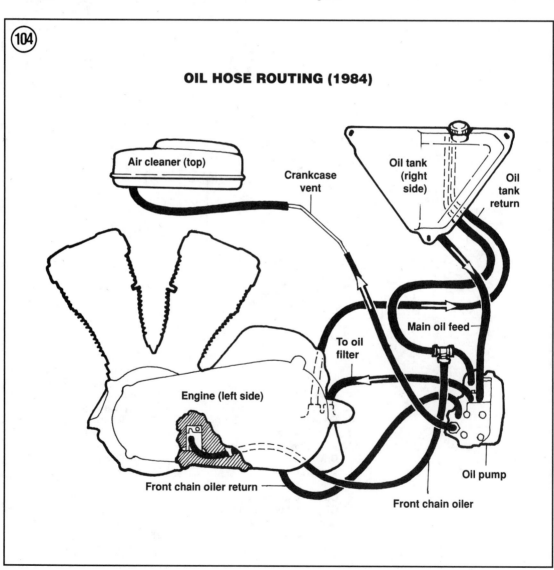

OIL HOSE ROUTING (1984)

CAUTION
When performing the following steps, make sure the drive gear shaft is not pushed into the gearcase; otherwise, the Woodruff key on the end of the shaft could fall into the gearcase.

5. Remove the oil pump body mounting bolts. Then slide the oil pump body off the drive gear shaft.

6. Remove the drive gear, Woodruff key and the idler gear.

7. Remove the check valve spring cover screw, check valve spring and the check valve ball.

8. Remove the bypass valve plug, bypass valve spring and the bypass valve.

9. Inspect the oil pump as described under *Inspection* in this chapter.

10. Assembly is the reverse of these steps. Note the following.

CAUTION
Never use "homemade" gaskets to check and reassemble the oil pump. Factory gaskets are made to a specified thickness with holes placed accurately to pass oil through the oil pump. Gaskets of the incorrect thickness can cause loss of oil pressure and severe engine damage.

4

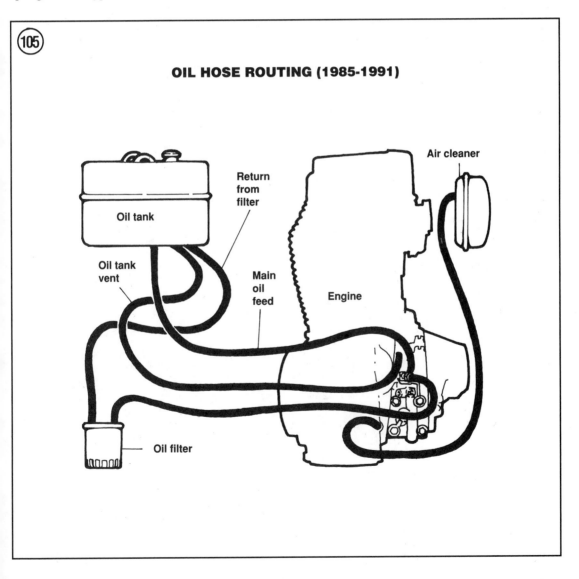

(105)

OIL HOSE ROUTING (1985-1991)

Air cleaner

Return from filter

Oil tank

Oil tank vent

Main oil feed

Engine

Oil filter

11. Coat all parts with fresh engine oil prior to installation, then place them on a clean lint-free cloth until their reassembly.

12. Install new circlips during assembly.

13. Tighten the valve plug (14, **Figure 103**) to 80-110 in.-lb. (9.2-12.6 N•m).

14. Tighten the oil pump body mounting bolts (9, **Figure 103**) to 60-85 in.-lb. (6.9-9.7 N•m).

> *CAUTION*
> *Do not overtighten the bolts in Step 15 as this will eliminate the pump gear side*

clearance and could cause the pump to seize, resulting in engine seizure.

15. Tighten the oil pump body and oil pump cover bolts to 90-120 in.-lb. (10.3-13.8 N•m).

16. Refill the engine oil tank as described in Chapter Three.

17A. On 1984-1991 models, reconnect the oil lines to the oil pump. On 1991 models, install new one-piece band clamps. Tighten hose clamp with Harley-Davidson hose clamp tool (part No. HD-97087-65A) or equivalent. On all other models,

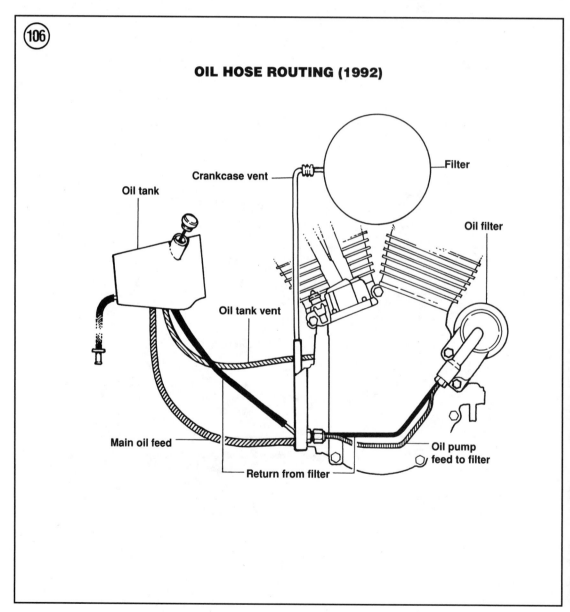

(106)

OIL HOSE ROUTING (1992)

Filter

Crankcase vent

Oil tank

Oil filter

Oil tank vent

Main oil feed

Oil pump feed to filter

Return from filter

replace damaged hose clamps as required and tighten securely. Refer to **Figure 104** (1984) or **Figure 105** (1985-1991).

17B. On 1992-on models (**Figure 106** or **Figure 107**), perform the following:

a. Reconnect the oil tank vent line at the oil pump.

b. Reconnect the main oil feed hose at the oil pump.

c. Reconnect the oil filter-to-oil pump cover manifold oil hose as described under *Oil Filter Mount (1992-On)* in this chapter.

Inspection

1. Clean all parts thoroughly in solvent.

2. Inspect the check valve ball and spring (**Figure 109**) for wear or damage. Replace the check valve spring cover screw O-ring if damaged. Replace parts as necessary.

3. Check the bypass valve spring plunger and spring (**Figure 110**) for wear and damage.

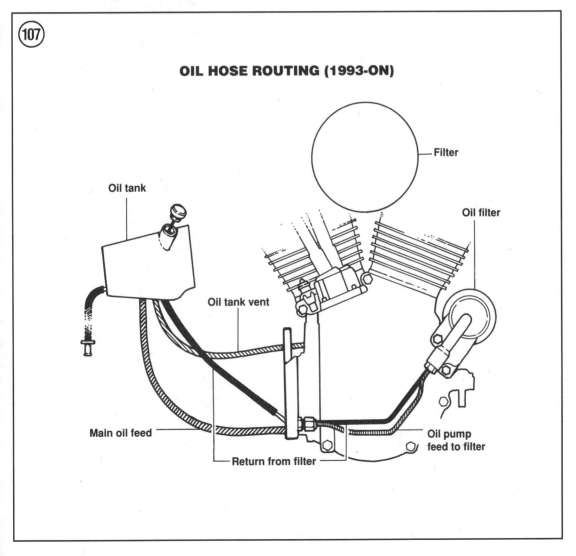

OIL HOSE ROUTING (1993-ON)

Filter

Oil filter

Oil tank

Oil tank vent

Main oil feed

Oil pump feed to filter

Return from filter

4. Check the drive shaft (A, **Figure 111**) for cracks, scoring or wear. Also check the drive shaft keyways (B, **Figure 111**) for cracking. Replace the drive shaft if necessary.

5. Check the oil pump gears (**Figure 112**) and the drive gear (**Figure 113**) for cracks, scoring or excessive wear.

6. Replace the oil seal (A, **Figure 114**) if it appears worn or damaged. The seal lip must face toward the feed gears.

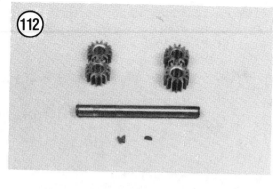

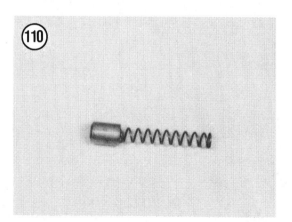

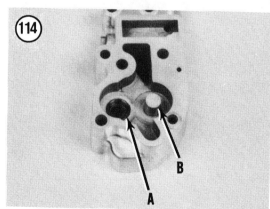

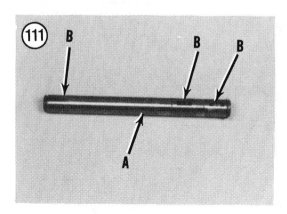

7. Check the oil pump idler gear shaft (B, **Figure 114**). If it is loose, replace the oil pump body as slippage will allow metal in the oil pump. A new shaft can be pressed in, but in most cases, the oil pin has wallowed the shaft bore in the housing.

8. Check the oil pump body machined surface (**Figure 115**) for nicks or gouging.

9. Assemble the feed and scavenger gears. See **Figure 116** and **Figure 117**. Lay a straight-edge across the gears and measure the height of the gears in relation to the gasket surface. The gear faces should extend above the pump body 0.003-0.004 in. (0.076-0.102 mm). Perform this check for both the feed and scavenger gears. If this clearance is incorrect, the oil pump must be replaced.

OIL FILTER MOUNT
(1992-ON)

Refer to **Figure 118** when performing procedures in this section. Refer to **Figure 106** (1992) or **Figure 107** (1993-on) when disconnecting and reconnecting the oil lines.

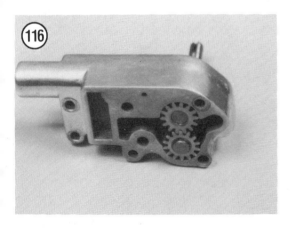

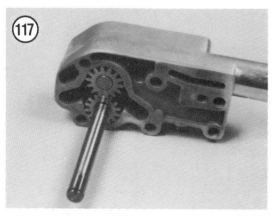

Removal

1. Park the bike on a level surface.

2. Drain the oil tank and remove the oil filter as described in Chapter Three.

3. Loosen the oil filter line compression nut at the oil pump cover manifold until it sets on the oil line.

4. Remove the oil pump cover manifold mounting bolts and washers and remove the manifold and O-rings from the oil pump cover.

5. Remove the oil line clamp nut, washer and spacer.

6. Loosen the oil line compression fittings at the oil filter mount. Then remove the oil lines from the oil filter mount.

7. Remove the oil filter mount screws and washers and remove the oil filter mount.

8. Remove the upper compression nut seals from the oil lines. If necessary, remove the upper compression nuts.

9. Loosen, then remove the compression nut fitting from the oil pump cover manifold.

10. Remove the lower seal and compression nut from the oil line.

11. If necessary, remove the oil filter adapter from the oil filter mount.

12. If necessary, remove the hose nipple from the oil pump cover.

Inspection

1. Inspect the oil lines for cracks or other damage.

2. If you replace the oil lines, make sure to remove the rubber sleeves from the oil lines and install them on the new lines in the same position.

3. Clean the compression nuts and compression nut fitting in solvent and dry thoroughly.

4. Replace worn or damaged parts as required.

Installation

1. Make sure all parts are clean and dry prior to installing them.

2. If removed, install the hose nipple (2, **Figure 118**) into the lower pump cover hole (1, **Figure 118**).

3. If removed, install the compression nut fitting (7, **Figure 118**) as follows:

    a. Apply Loctite 242 (blue) to the compression nut fitting threads prior to installation.

    b. Install the compression nut fitting and tighten to the torque specification in **Table 3**.

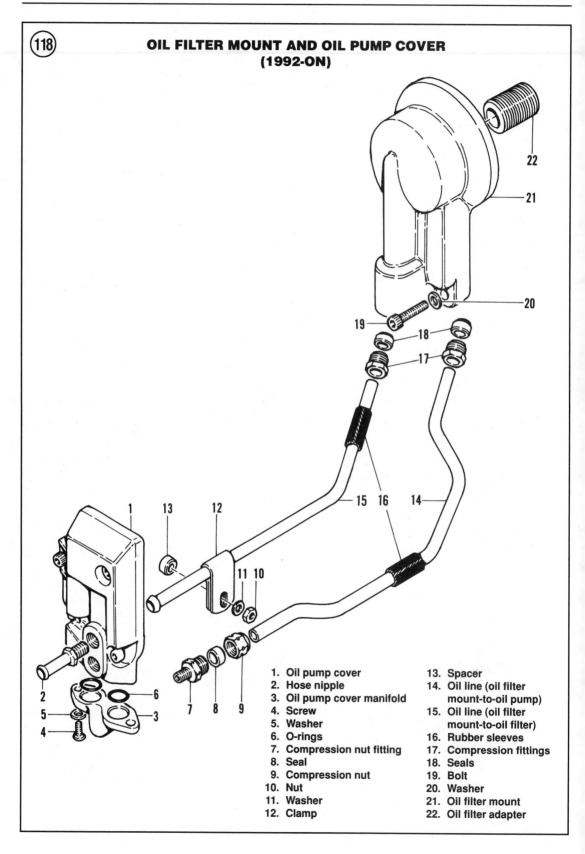

118

OIL FILTER MOUNT AND OIL PUMP COVER
(1992-ON)

1. Oil pump cover
2. Hose nipple
3. Oil pump cover manifold
4. Screw
5. Washer
6. O-rings
7. Compression nut fitting
8. Seal
9. Compression nut
10. Nut
11. Washer
12. Clamp
13. Spacer
14. Oil line (oil filter mount-to-oil pump)
15. Oil line (oil filter mount-to-oil filter)
16. Rubber sleeves
17. Compression fittings
18. Seals
19. Bolt
20. Washer
21. Oil filter mount
22. Oil filter adapter

4. If removed, install the oil filter adapter into the oil filter mount.

5. Install the oil filter mount and its mounting screws and washers. Tighten the oil filter mount screws to the torque specification in **Table 3**.

6. Slide the oil line compression nut (9, **Figure 118**) and seal (8, **Figure 118**) onto the oil line.

7. Install the 2 compression fitting oil seals (18, **Figure 118**) into the oil filter mount.

8. Install the upper oil line compression nut fittings (17, **Figure 118**) into the oil filter mount. Tighten the fittings finger-tight only.

9. Insert the oil lines (14 and 15, **Figure 118**) into their respective compression nut fittings until they bottom out.

10. Assemble the oil line clamp, spacer, washer and nut as shown in **Figure 118**; do not tighten the nut at this time.

11. Slide the oil pump manifold compression nut onto the oil line (14, **Figure 118**).

12. Install 2 new O-rings onto the oil pump cover manifold and place the manifold onto the bottom of the oil pump cover. Install the manifold screws and washers and tighten to the torque specification in **Table 3**.

13. Thread the compression nut (9, **Figure 118**) onto the compression nut fitting; tighten nut until it bottoms out on fitting.

14. Tighten the upper oil line compression fittings (17, **Figure 118**) until the hex portion on fittings seat against the oil filter mount.

15. Tighten the oil line securing nut (10, **Figure 118**) securely.

16. Install the oil filter and fill the oil tank as described in Chapter Three.

17. Start the engine and check for leaks.

GEARCASE COVER AND TIMING GEARS

Refer to **Figure 119** (1984-1992) or **Figure 120** (1993-on) when performing procedures in this section.

Removal

1. Remove the pushrods, valve tappets and guides as described in this chapter.

2. Remove the tappet oil screen cap and O-ring. Then remove the spring and screen. See **Figure 121**.

3. Remove the electronic ignition sensor plate and rotor as described in Chapter Nine.

4. Place an oil drain pan underneath the gearcase cover.

> *NOTE*
> *The gearcase cover screws are different lengths. To ease reassembly, draw an outline of the gearcase cover on cardboard, and then punch a hole along the outline to represent the position of each screw. Then, as you remove the screws from the gearcase, install them into the appropriate hole in the cardboard.*

5A. On 1984-1992 models, remove the gearcase cover as follows:

   a. Remove the gearcase cover screws.

   b. The gearcase cover is located by snug dowel pins and must be worked off carefully. Tap the cover lightly with a soft-faced hammer at the point where the cover projects beyond the crankcase and remove it (**Figure 122**).

   c. Remove the gasket.

5B. On 1993-on models, remove the gearcase cover as follows:

   a. Fabricate the puller shown in **Figure 123**.

   b. Mount the puller onto the gearcase cover and secure it with 2 bolts (**Figure 124**).

   c. Operate the puller pressure screw and remove the gearcase cover and gasket.

   d. Remove the puller from the gearcase cover.

6. Remove the cam gear (**Figure 125**).

7. Remove the cam gear spacer washer (1984-1987) and the cam gear thrust washer (**Figure 126**).

8. Remove the breather valve washer (**Figure 127**) and the breather gear (**Figure 128**).

9A. On 1984-1992 models, remove the pinion gear shaft nut and gear as follows:

> *NOTE*
> *The pinion gear shaft nut has left-hand threads. Turn the nut clockwise to remove it.*

   a. Remove the pinion gear shaft nut (**Figure 129**) using the Pinion Shaft Nut Socket (part No. HD-94-555-55A).

   b. Remove the pinion gear (**Figure 130**) using the pinion gear puller (part No. HD-96830-51A).

9B. On 1993-on models, remove the pinion gear shaft nut and gear as follows:

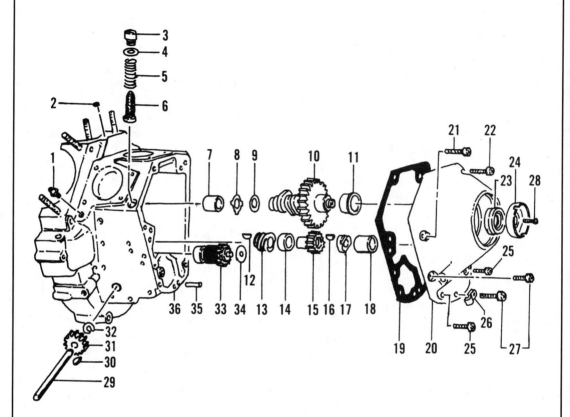

**GEARCASE ASSEMBLY
(1984-1992)**

1. Oil pressure switch
2. Plug
3. Oil screen cap
4. O-ring
5. Spring
6. Oil screen
7. Camshaft needle bearing
8. Cam gear thrust washer
9. Cam gear spacer washer (1984-1987)
10. Cam gear
11. Camshaft bushing
12. Woodruff key
13. Oil pump pinion shaft gear
14. Pinion gear spacer
15. Pinion gear
16. Woodruff key
17. Pinion shaft nut
18. Pinion shaft bushing
19. Gasket
20. Gearcase cover
21. Screw (1 3/4 in.)
22. Screw (1 1/4 in.)
23. Camshaft oil seal
24. Rotor
25. Screw (1 in.)
26. Clip
27. Screw (1 1/4 in.)
28. Rotor bolt
29. Oil pump shaft
30. Woodruff key
31. Oil pump drive gear
32. Oil pump drive lock ring
33. Breather gear
34. Breather gear spacer
35. Dowel
36. Gearcase

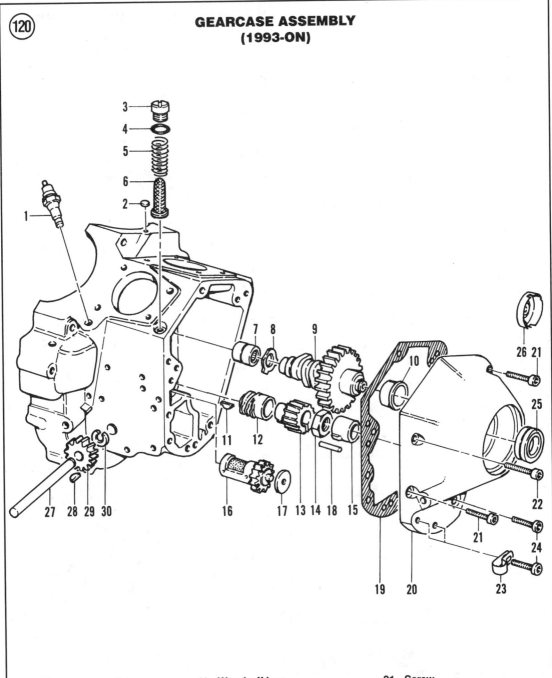

120

GEARCASE ASSEMBLY
(1993-ON)

4

1. Oil pressure switch
2. Plug
3. Oil screen cap
4. O-ring
5. Spring
6. Screen
7. Cam gear needle bearing
8. Cam gear thrust washer
9. Cam gear
10. Cam gear bushing
11. Woodruff key
12. Oil pump pinion shaft gear
13. Pinion gear
14. Pinion shaft nut
15. Pinion shaft bushing
16. Breather gear
17. Breather gear spacer
18. Dowel pin
19. Gasket
20. Gearcase cover
21. Screw
22. Screw
23. Clip
24. Screw
25. Cam gear oil seal
26. Rotor
27. Oil pump shaft
28. Woodruff key
29. Oil pump drive gear
30. Oil pump drive gear lock ring

NOTE
The pinion gear shaft nut has right-hand threads. Turn the nut counterclockwise to remove it.

a. Remove the pinion gear shaft nut (14, **Figure 120**) with a socket.

b. Remove the pinion gear (13, **Figure 120**).

10A. On 1984-1992 models, remove the following parts in order:

NOTE
1990-1992 models use a single Woodruff key for the pinion and oil pump gears.

a. *1984-1989*: Woodruff key (**Figure 131**).

b. Pinion gear spacer (**Figure 132**).

c. Oil pump pinion shaft gear (**Figure 133**).

d. Woodruff key (**Figure 134**).

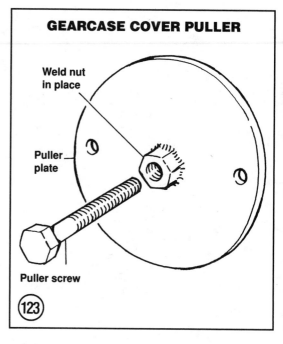

GEARCASE COVER PULLER

Weld nut in place

Puller plate

Puller screw

(123)

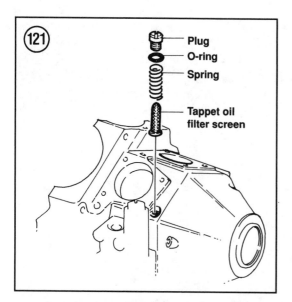

(121)

Plug

O-ring

Spring

Tappet oil filter screen

(122)

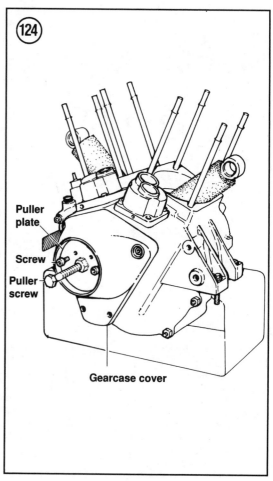

(124)

Puller plate

Screw

Puller screw

Gearcase cover

10B. On 1993-on models, remove the oil pump pinion shaft gear (12, **Figure 120**) and Woodruff key (11, **Figure 120**).

11. If required, remove the oil pump drive gear and oil pump as described in this chapter.

Inspection

1. Thoroughly clean gearcase compartment, cover and components with solvent. Blow out all oil passages with compressed air. Make sure that all traces of gasket compound are removed from the gasket mating surfaces.

2. Check the oil screen (**Figure 121**) to make sure it is not blocked or damaged. Test the screen by holding it upside down and filling it with engine oil. Watch the screen to see that the oil flows evenly through the screen. If not, replace the screen.

3. Check the pinion gear and cam gear bushings in the gearcase cover for grooving, pitting or other wear. If the bushings appear visibly worn, have them replaced by a Harley-Davidson dealer. If the bushings appear okay, perform Step 4.

4. Measure the cam gear (A, **Figure 135**) O.D. and its bushing I.D. to check cam gear shaft fit in bushing. See **Table 2** for specifications. If the clearance is excessive, have the bushings replaced by a Harley-Davidson dealer.

5. Measure the cam gear (A, **Figure 135**) small ends at the bearing surface and near the cam gear lobes with a micrometer. Compare the 2 different measuring points on the cam gear. If the camshaft is worn more than 0.003 in. (0.08 mm), replace the camshaft and its needle bearing. Have the needle bearing replaced by a Harley-Davidson dealer.

6. Measure the camshaft lobes (B, **Figure 135**) with a micrometer and compare to the lobes on a new Evolution cam. If the camshaft lobes are worn more than 0.006 in. (0.15 mm), replace the camshaft.

NOTE
Camshafts used in early V-twin models cannot be used in Evolution engines and vice versa. Do not use a non-Evolution cam when comparing lobe wear in Step 6.

7. Check the cam gear oil seal (**Figure 136**) in the gearcase cover. If worn, carefully pry it out of the case. Install a new seal by driving it into the gearcase cover using a suitable size drift or socket placed on the outside portion of the seal.

8. Inspect the breather gear (**Figure 137**) teeth for damage. Also check the screen for debris or damage and clean with solvent if necessary. Replace the breather gear if necessary.

9. Check all gears for signs of wear or damage; replace if necessary. If the cam gears appear okay, check the gear mesh as follows:

   a. Assemble the cam gear and pinion gears in the gearcase. Do not install the cam gear spacer.

NOTE
The cam gear spacer is not used on 1988 and later models.

   b. Install the gearcase cover (**Figure 122**) and secure it with a minimum of 3 screws. Tighten the screws securely.

   c. Check the gear mesh through the tappet guide hole (**Figure 138**) by hand. Gear mesh is correct when there is no play between the gears and the cam gear can be moved back and forth with slight drag.

   d. If gear mesh is incorrect, replace the cam and pinion gears.

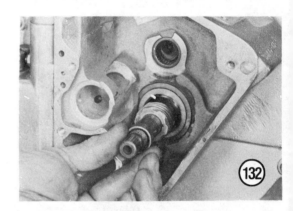

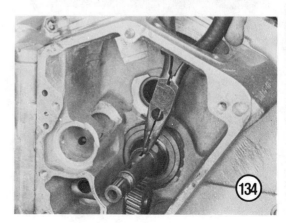

NOTE
Cam and pinion gears are color-coded by their pitch diameters. Replacement gears must be matched or abnormal gear noise will result. When replacing these gears, have gears matched by a Harley-Davidson dealer.

Assembly

Refer to **Figure 119** (1984-1992) or **Figure 120** (1993-on) when assembling the gearcase assembly.

1. Assembly is the reverse of disassembly, plus the following.

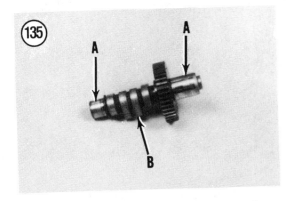

2. Before final assembly of gearcase components, check the breather gear end play as follows:

  a. Install the breather gear (**Figure 139**) and a new cover gasket to the gearcase.

  b. Install the spacer (**Figure 140**) on the breather gear.

  c. Lay a straightedge across the gearcase at the breather gear spacer. Then using a feeler gauge, measure the clearance between the straightedge and the spacer. See **Figure 141**.

  d. Subtract 0.006 in. (0.15 mm) from the clearance determined in sub-step c. This is the amount the gearcase gasket will compress.

  e. An end play clearance of 0.001-0.016 in. (0.02-0.41 mm) is correct. If the clearance exceeds this amount, install a thicker spacer (**Figure 142**). Spacers are available in various thicknesses from Harley-Davidson dealers.

3. Before final assembly of gearcase components, check the cam gear end play as follows:

  a. Install the cam gear thrust washer, cam gear spacer washer (1984-1987) (**Figure 143**) and the cam gear (**Figure 144**).

4

b. Install the gearcase cover (**Figure 122**) and a new gasket. Install a minimum of 4 gearcase cover screws. Tighten the screws securely.

c. Measure the cam gear end play between the gear shaft and the thrust washer with a feeler gauge inserted through the gear case tappet hole (**Figure 145**).

d. *1984-1987*: An end play clearance of 0.001-0.016 in. (0.02-0.41 mm) is correct. If the clearance exceeds this amount, install a suitable size spacer (**Figure 146**) to bring the clearance within specifications. Spacers in different thicknesses are available from Harley-Davidson dealers.

e. *1988-on*: An end play clearance of 0.001-0.050 in. (0.02-1.27 mm) is correct. If the clearance exceeds this amount, check for worn or damaged parts.

4. Slide the cam gear thrust washer, cam gear spacer washer (1984-1987) onto the end of the cam gear.

5. Install the oil pump pinion shaft gear Woodruff key (**Figure 134**) on 1984-1989 models. 1990 and later models use a single Woodruff key for the pinion and oil pump gears.

NOTE
*On 1984 and early 1985 models, install the oil pump pinion shaft gear (**Figure 133**) so that the chamfer on the gear faces toward the inside of the engine. On late 1985 and later models, the oil pump pinion shaft gears are chamfered on both sides and the gear can be installed either way.*

6. Slide the oil pump pinion shaft gear (**Figure 133**) onto the shaft, making sure to align the keyway in the gear with the Woodruff key.

7. On 1984-1992 models, install the pinion gear spacer (**Figure 132**) onto the end of the pinion gear.

8. Install the oil pump drive gear Woodruff key. Then install the oil pump drive gear and secure it with a new lock ring.

9. Install the breather gear spacer onto the end of the breather gear (**Figure 124**).

10. Install the cam, breather and pinion gears so that the timing marks on the gears align as shown in **Figure 144**.

11A. On 1984-1992 models, perform the following:

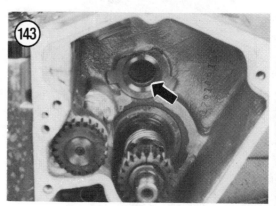

NOTE
The pinion shaft uses left-hand thread. Turn the nut counterclockwise to tighten it.

a. Put 2 drops of Loctite 262 (red) on the pinion shaft nut before installing and tightening it.

b. Install the pinion shaft nut and tighten it to 35-45 ft.-lb. (47-61 N•m). Ue the pinion shaft nut socket (HD-555-55A) to tighten the pinion shaft nut.

c. After tightening the pinion shaft nut, check that the pinion shaft spacer has noticeable end play. If not, remove the pinion shaft nut and

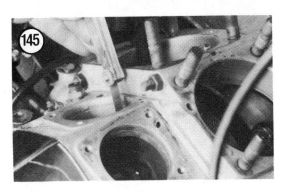

the pinion shaft gear and reinstall. Make sure the timing marks in Step 10 are correct.

11B. On 1993-on models, perform the following:

NOTE
The pinion shaft nut uses right-hand threads. Turn the nut clockwise to tighten it.

a. Put 2 drops of Loctite 262 (red) on the pinion shaft nut before installing and tightening it.

b. Install the pinion shaft nut and tighten to 35-45 ft.-lb. (47-61 N•m).

12. Turn the gear train to make sure all gears rotate freely. Any binding should be corrected before completing engine reassembly.

13. Coat a new gearcase gasket with a non-hardening gasket sealer and install it.

14. Install the gearcase and screws. Tighten the screws to 80-110 in.-lb. (9.2-12.6 N•m).

15. Pour approximately 1/4 pint (0.12 L) of engine oil through the tappet guide hold to provide initial gear train lubrication.

16. Install the ignition components as described in Chapter Nine.

CRANKCASE AND CRANKSHAFT

Crankcases must be disassembled to service the crankshaft, connecting rod bearings, pinion shaft bearings and sprocket shaft bearings. This section describes basic checks and procedures that can be performed in the home shop. Bearing and crankshaft service should be referred to a Harley-Davidson dealer equipped to handle such repairs.

Crankshaft End Play Check

It is recommended that crankshaft end play be measured before completely disassembling the crankcase. Crankshaft end play is a measure of sprocket shaft bearing wear.

1. Remove the engine from the frame as described in this chapter.

2. Mount the crankcase in a suitable fixture (**Figure 147**).

3. Install the bearing installation tool (part No. HD-97225-55) onto the sprocket shaft to preload the bearing races. See **Figure 147**.

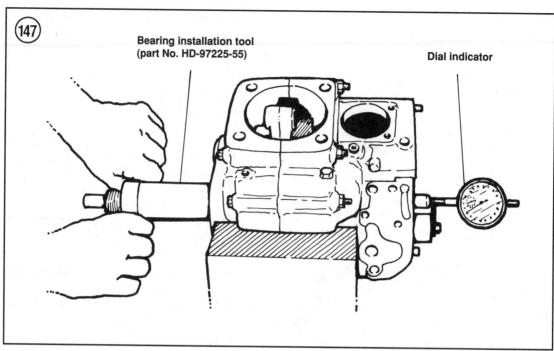

(147)

Bearing installation tool (part No. HD-97225-55)

Dial indicator

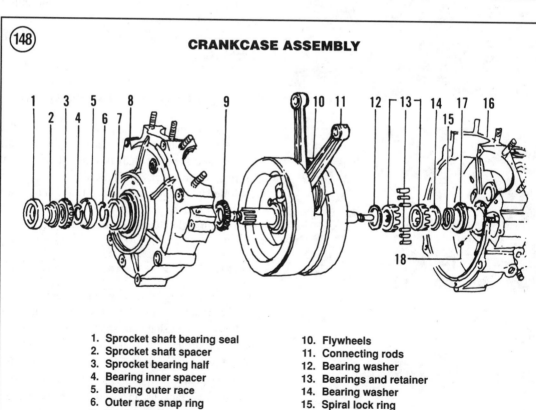

(148)

CRANKCASE ASSEMBLY

1. Sprocket shaft bearing seal
2. Sprocket shaft spacer
3. Sprocket bearing half
4. Bearing inner spacer
5. Bearing outer race
6. Outer race snap ring
7. Bearing outer race
8. Left crankcase half
9. Sprocket bearing half
10. Flywheels
11. Connecting rods
12. Bearing washer
13. Bearings and retainer
14. Bearing washer
15. Spiral lock ring
16. Right crankcase half
17. Pinion shaft bearing race
18. Lock screw

4. Attach a dial indicator so that the probe touches against the end of the crankshaft (**Figure 147**).

5. Turn and pull on the sprocket shaft while noting the end play registering on the dial indicator. If end play exceeds limit in **Table 2**, the inner bearing spacer (4, **Figure 148**) must be replaced by selecting a different spacer from the chart in **Table 4**.

Disassembly

Refer to **Figure 148** for this procedure.

1. Remove the engine from the frame as described in this chapter.

> *CAUTION*
> *After removing the cylinders, slip rubber hoses over the cylinder studs to prevent their damage during the following service procedures. In addition, do not lift the crankcase assembly by grabbing the cylinder studs. Bent or damaged cylinder studs may cause oil leakage.*

2. Disassemble and remove the gearcase assembly as described in this chapter.

3. Check the crankshaft end play as described in this chapter.

> *NOTE*
> *When removing the crankcase bolts and studs in Step 4, note that the top center stud (4, **Figure 149**) and the right bottom studs (5, **Figure 149**) are matched and fitted to the crankcase holes for correct crankcase alignment. During their removal, mark them so they can be reinstalled in their original position.*

4. See **Figure 149**. Remove the crankcase bolts and studs.

5. Lay the crankcase assembly on wood blocks so that right-hand side faces up.

6. Tap the crankcase with a plastic mallet and remove the right-hand crankcase half.

7. Remove the pinion shaft spiral lock ring (**Figure 150**).

8. Grasp the 2 bearing washers and remove the washers, bearings and retainers as an assembly (**Figure 151**). Store the complete assembly in a plastic bag.

> *NOTE*
> *Further disassembly of the crankcase/flywheel assembly is not recommended. A hydraulic press is required to*

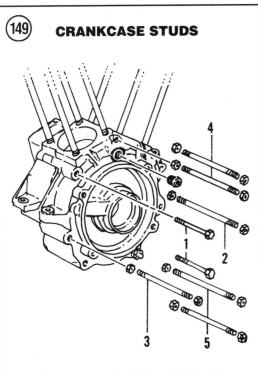

CRANKCASE STUDS

1. Crankcase stud bolt, 3/8 × 3-1/4 in. (2)
2. Crankcase stud, 5/16 × 5 in. (right center)
3. Crankcase stud, 5/16 × 6 in. (left center)
4. Crankcase stud, 5/16 × 5-7/16 in. (2) (top and top right)
5. Crankcase stud, 11/32 × 5-13/16 in. (2) (left and right bottom)

separate the crankshaft from the left-hand crankcase half. Furthermore, additional equipment is required to install and line ream new bearings properly.

9. Check connecting rod side play with a feeler gauge as shown in **Figure 152**. If the side play is not within the specifications in **Table 2**, refer service to a Harley-Davidson dealer.

10. Refer crankcases to a Harley-Davidson dealer for inspection and repair.

11. Installation is the reverse of these steps, noting the following.

12. If the crankcase was removed, have it pressed into the left-hand crankcase by a Harley-Davidson dealer.

13. Make sure rods are aligned as shown in **Figure 153** before assembling the right-hand crankcase.

14. Referring to **Figure 148**, install the bearing washer, bearings and retainer and the bearing washer. See **Figure 151**.

15. Install a new spiral lock ring (**Figure 150**) in the pinion shaft groove.

16. Coat the crankcase mating surfaces with Harley-Davidson Crankcase Sealant (part No. HD-99650-81) or 3M #800.

17. Align the crankcase halves and install the right-hand crankcase.

18. Referring to **Figure 149**, tap the No. 4 and No. 5 bolts into the crankcase. These bolts are used for alignment and must be installed first.

19. Install the remaining studs and bolts (**Figure 149**).

20A. On 1984-1992 models, install the stud nuts and tighten as follows:

    a. Install the stud nuts and tighten finger-tight.

    b. Tighten the stud nuts in the order shown in **Figure 154** until all are snug. Then tighten the bolts and nuts to the torque specification in **Table 3**.

20B. On 1993-on models, install the stud nuts and tighten as follows:

    a. Install the stud nuts and tighten finger-tight.

NOTE
The following torque procedure must be followed to ensure crankcase longevity.

    b. Tighten the crankcase nuts to 10 ft.-lb. (14 N•m) in the order shown in **Figure 154**.

    c. Install the cylinders and cylinder heads as described in this chapter, then perform sub-step d.

    d. Tighten the crankcase nuts to 15-17 ft.-lb. (20-35 N•m) in the order shown in **Figure 154**.

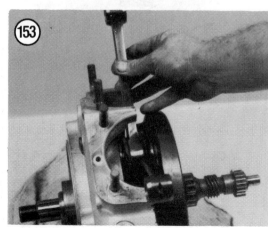

21. Install the sprocket shaft spacer (2, **Figure 148**). Then install a new sprocket shaft bearing seal (**Figure 155**). On dry clutch models, the seal lip must face toward the flywheels. On wet clutch models, the seal lip must face away from the flywheels. Press the seal into place with the Sprocket Shaft Seal Installation Tool (part No. HD-39361) (**Figure 156**) or equivalent.

22. Recheck flywheel end play as described in this chapter.

Cylinder Stud Replacement (1984-early 1985)

Bent or damaged cylinder studs must be replaced to prevent cylinder head and cylinder leakage. The following tools will be required to replace cylinder studs:

    a. Air or electric impact wrench.

    b. Harley-Davidson cylinder stud installer (part No. HD-34624).

1. If the engine is assembled, cover the crankcase opening to prevent abrasive particles from falling into the engine.

2. Remove the damaged stud with a stud remover.

3. Clean the crankcase threads and the new stud with solvent or contact cleaner. Blow dry.

NOTE
Cylinder studs are machined to have an interference fit with the crankcase threads. On worn engines, however, the engine crankcase threads may be a little looser. Check by hand-threading the stud into the case. If the stud fit is tight, apply engine oil to the stud threads prior to installation. If the stud fit is loose, apply Loctite Stud 'N' Bearing Mount to the stud theads.

4. Install the stud with the cylinder stud installer and an air or electric impact wrench. The Harley-Davidson cylinder stud installer will install the stud to its correct height. The correct stud installed height is 5.670-5.770 in. (144-146.56 mm).

CAUTION
Do not use a breaker bar or ratchet to install the studs. These tools will bend the stud and damage it.

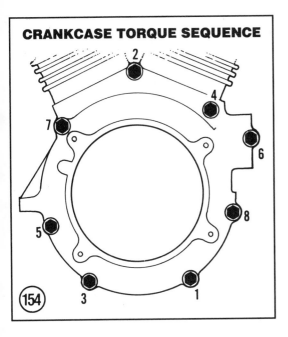

CRANKCASE TORQUE SEQUENCE

(154)

(155)

(156)

Sprocket shaft seal installation tool

5. Repeat for each stud.

Cylinder Stud Replacement (Late 1985-on)

Bent or damaged cylinder studs must be replaced to prevent cylinder head and cylinder leakage. The following tools will be required to replace the cylinder studs:

   a. Air or electric impact wrench.
   b. 0.313 in. diameter steel ball.

NOTE
For steel ball, use Harley-Davidson steel ball (part No. 8860).

1. If the engine is assembled, cover the crankcase opening to prevent abrasive particles from falling into the engine.

2. Remove the damaged stud with a stud remover.

3. Clean the crankcase threads and the new stud with solvent or contact cleaner. Blow dry.

NOTE
The cylinder studs have a shoulder on the upper end; see **Figure 157**.

4. Measuring from the top of the stud, paint a mark that is 5.750 in. (146.05 mm) down the stud; see **Figure 158**.

5. Drop the 0.313 in. diameter steel ball into a cylinder head bolt and thread the bolt onto the top of the new stud.

6. Hand-thread the new stud into the crankcase, then install it with an air gun until the paint mark on the stud aligns with the crankcase base gasket surface.

CAUTION
Do not use a breaker bar or ratchet to install the studs. These tools will bend the stud and damage it.

7. Remove the cylinder head bolt and steel ball from the cylinder stud.

8. Measure the stud's installed height with a vernier caliper. The stud's installed height should be 5.670-5.770 in. (144.02-146.56 mm).

9. Place a protective hose over the stud.

10. Repeat for each stud.

ENGINE BREAK-IN

Following cylinder servicing (new pistons, new rings, etc.) and major lower end work, the engine should be broken in just as though it were new. The performance and service life of the engine depends greatly on a careful and sensible break-in.

For the first 500 miles (800 km), no more than one-third throttle should be used and the speed should be varied as much as possible within the one-third throttle limit. Prolonged, steady running at one speed, no matter how moderate, is to be avoided as is hard acceleration.

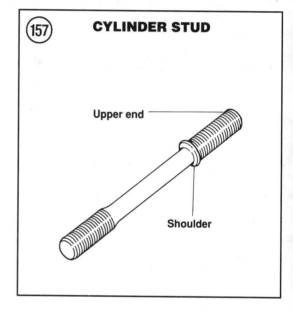

(157) **CYLINDER STUD**

Upper end

Shoulder

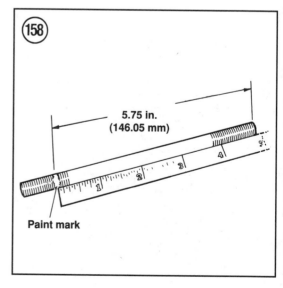

(158)

5.75 in. (146.05 mm)

Paint mark

Following the 500-mile (800 km) service, increasingly more throttle cam be used but full throttle should not be used until the motorcycle has covered at least 1,000 miles (1,600 km) and then it should be limited to short bursts until 1,500 miles (2,400 km) have been logged.

During engine break-in, oil consumption will be higher than normal. It is important to frequently check and correct the oil level in the tank, making sure to maintain a 1 in. (25.4 mm) air gap in the top of the tank.

500 Mile (800 km) Service

It is essential that the oil tank be drained, flushed and refilled and the oil filter serviced after the first 500 break-in miles (800 km). In addition, it is a good idea to repeat this service at the completion of break-in (about 1,500 miles [2,400 km]) to ensure that all of the particles produced during break-in are removed from the lubrication system. The small added expense may be considered a smart investment that will pay off in increased engine life.

Table 1 GENERAL ENGINE SPECIFICATIONS

Engine type	Air cooled, 4-stroke, OHV, V-twin
Number of cylinders	2
Bore and stroke	3.498 × 4.250 in. (88.85 × 107.95 mm)
Displacement	81.6 cu. in. (1,340 cc)
Compression ratio	8.5:1
Lubrication system	Forced feed oiling system

Table 2 ENGINE SERVICE SPECIFICATIONS

	Specification		Wear limit	
	in.	mm	in.[1]	mm[1]
Cylinder head				
Warpage	0-0.006	0-0.15	0.006	0.15
Valve seat in head	0.0045-0.0020	0.114-0.051	0.0020[2]	0.051[2]
Valve guide ID	0.0033-0.0020	0.084-0.051	0.0020[2]	0.051[2]
Valves				
Fit in guide				
Intake	0.0008-0.0026	0.020-0.066	0.0035	0.089
Exhaust	0.0015-0.0033	0.038-0.084	0.0040	0.102
Seat width				
1984	0.040-0.062	1.02-1.57	0.062	1.57
1985-on	0.040-0.062	1.02-1.57	0.090	2.29
Stem length from cylinder				
head boss	1.990-2.024	50.55-51.41	2.034	51.66
Valve springs				
Outer springs				
Free length	2.105-2.177	53.47-55.30	2.177	55.30
Compression				
Closed—1.751-1.848 in.				
(44.47-46.94 mm)	72-92 lbs.	33-42 kg	—	—
Open—1.282-1.378 in.				
(32.56-35.00 mm)	183-207 lbs.	83-94 kg	—	—
Inner springs				
Free length	1.926-1.996	48.92-50.70	1.996	50.70
Compression				
Closed—1.577-1.683 in.				
(40.06-42.75 mm)	38-49 lbs.	17.24-22.23 kg	—	—
Open—1.107-1.213 in.				
(28.12-30.81 mm)	98-112 lbs.	44.45-50.80 kg	—	—
Stem-to-face eccentricity	—	—	0.002	0.05
Rocker arm				
End clearance	0.003-0.013	0.08-0.33	0.025	0.63
Shaft clearance	0.0005-0.002	0.013-0.050	0.0035	0.089
Bushing fit in rocker arm	0.004-0.002	0.10-0.05	—	—
Rocker arm shaft				
Shaft fit in rocker cover	0.0007-0.0022	0.018-0.056	0.0035	0.089
Piston				
Clearance in cylinder				
1984-early 1985	0.0008-0.0023	0.020-0.058	0.0053	0.135
Late 1985-on[3]	0.00075-0.00175	0.019-0.044	0.0053	0.135
Piston pin				
Pin fit in piston				
1984	0.0002-0.0007	0.005-0.018	0.001	0.02
Early 1985	0.0002-0.0006	0.005-0.015	0.001	0.02
Late 1985-on[3]	0.0001-0.0004	0.002-0.010	0.001	0.02
Piston rings				
Compression ring end gap				
1984	0.008-0.015	0.20-0.38	0.030	0.76
1985-on	0.007-0.020	0.18-0.51	0.030	0.76
Oil control ring rail gap				
1984	0.015-0.055	0.38-1.40	0.065	1.65
1985-on	0.009-0.052	0.23-1.32	0.065	1.65
Compression ring side clearance				
1984				
Top	0.002-0.0047	0.05-0.12	0.006	0.15
2nd	0.0016-0.0043	0.041-0.109	0.006	0.15
1985-on				
Top	0.002-0.0045	0.05-0.11	0.006	0.15
2nd	0.0016-0.0041	0.041-0.104	0.006	0.15
	(continued)			

Table 2 ENGINE SERVICE SPECIFICATIONS (continued)

	Specification		Wear limit	
	in.	mm	in.[1]	mm[1]
Piston rings (continued)				
Oil control ring side clearance				
1984	0.001-0.006	0.02-0.15	0.008	0.20
1985-on	0.0016-0.0076	0.041-0.193	0.008	0.20
Cylinder bore sizes				
Taper			0.002	0.05
Out-of-round			0.003	0.08
Bore				
Standard	3.4980[4]	88.849[4]	3.501	88.925
0.005 in. (0.13 mm) oversize	3.5030[4]	88.976[4]	3.506	89.052
0.010 in. (0.25 mm) oversize	3.5080[4]	89.103[4]	3.511	89.179
0.020 in. (0.51 mm) oversize	3.5180[4]	89.357[4]	3.521	89.433
0.030 in. (0.76 mm) oversize	3.5280[4]	89.611[4]	3.531	89.687
Tappets				
Guide fit in crankcase				
1984	0.0025	0.063	—	—
1985-on	0.000-0.004	0.000-0.010	—	—
Fit in guide	0.0008-0.002	0.020-0.051	0.003	0.08
Roller fit				
1984	0.0006-0.001	0.015-0.025	0.0015	0.038
1985-on	—	—	—	—
Roller end clearance				
1984	0.010-0.014	0.25-0.35	0.015	0.38
1985-on	—	—	0.015	0.38
Connecting rods				
Piston pin fit				
1984	0.0008-0.002	0.020-0.051	0.001	0.03
1985	0.0003-0.0007	0.008-0.018	0.001	0.03
Side play @ crankshaft				
1984	0.005	0.13	0.030	0.76
1985-on	0.005-0.025	0.13-0.63	0.030	0.76
Fit on crankpin				
1984	0.0007	0.018	0.002	0.05
1985-on	0.0004-0.0017	0.010-0.043	0.002	0.05
Gearcase				
Breather gear end play	See text	—	—	—
Cam gear shaft fit in bushing				
1984	0.0008	0.020	0.003	0.08
1985-on	0.00075-0.00175	0.0190-0.0444	0.003	0.08
Cam gear shaft fit in bearing				
1984	0.0005	0.013	0.005	0.13
1985-on	0.0005-0.0025	0.013-0.063	0.005	0.13
Cam gear end play	See text	—	—	—
Oil pump drive shaft fit in crankcase bushing				
1984	0.0008	0.020	0.0025	0.063
1985-on	0.0004-0.0025	0.010-0.063	0.0035	0.089
Flywheels				
Runout (@ rim)				
1984	0.000-0.006	0.00-0.15	0.006	0.15
1985-on	0.000-0.010	0.00-0.25	0.015	0.38
Runout (@ shaft)				
1984	0.000-0.001	0.00-0.02	0.001	0.02
1985-on	0.000-0.002	0.00-0.05	0.003	0.08
End play				
1984	0.001	0.02	0.004	0.10
1985-on	0.001-0.005	0.02-0.13	0.006	0.15

(continued)

Table 2 ENGINE SERVICE SPECIFICATIONS (continued)

	Specification		Wear limit	
	in.	mm	in.[1]	mm[1]
Sprocket shaft bearing				
Cup fit in crankcase	0.0032-0.0012	0.081-0.030	—	—
Cone fit on shaft				
1984	0.0015-0.0002	0.038-0.005	—	—
1985-on	0.0015-0.0005	0.038-0.013	—	—
Pinion shaft bearing				
Roller bearing fit				
1984	0.0008	0.020	0.0020	0.051
1985-on	0.0002-0.0009	0.005-0.023	—	—
Cover bushing fit				
1984	0.0005	0.013	0.0025	0.063
1985-on	0.001-0.0025	0.025-0.063	0.0035	0.089

[1] Part should to be considered worn if measurement exceeds wear limit specification, unless otherwise noted; see below.
[2] Part should be considered worn if measurement is less than the wear limit specification.
[3] Specifies clearance of KSG pistons.
[4] ± 0.0002 in. (0.005 mm)

Table 3 ENGINE TIGHTENING TORQUES

	ft.-lb.	N·m
Cylinder head bolts	See text	—
Spark plug		
1984	18-28	24.8-38.6
1985-on	18-22	24.8-30.4
Rocker cover bolts		
1984		
1/4 in.	11-12	15.2-16.6
5/16 in.	22-25	30.4-34.5
1985-on		
1/4 in.	10-13	13.8-17.9
5/16 in.	15-18	20.7-24.8
Sprocket shaft nut		
1984-early 1985	290-320	400.2-441.6
Late 1985-on	—	—
Crankpin nut	180-210	248.4-289.8
Pinion shaft nut		
1984-1990	140-170	193.2-234.6
Pinion gear nut	35-45	48.3-62.1
Crankcase stud nut		
1984	12-15	16.6-20.7
1985-1992	15-19	20.7-26.2
1993-on	See text	
Crankcase bolt		
1984	22-26	30.4-35.9
1985-1992	15-19	20.7-26.2
1993-on	See text	
Rear engine mounting bolts	33-38	45.5-52.4
Front engine mounting bolts	33-38	45.5-52.4
Top center engine mounting bracket		
1984-1990	35-40	48.3-55.2
1991-1992	22-28	30.4-38.6
1993-on		
At cylinder heads	28-35	38.6-48.3
At frame	28-32	38.6-43

(continued)

Table 3 ENGINE TIGHTENING TORQUES (continued)

	ft.-lb.	N·m
Oil filter mount		
1993-on		
Compression nut fitting	8-12	11-16
Oil filter mount screws	13-17	18-23

	in.-lb.	N·m
Oil pump cover bolts	90-120	10.3-13.8
Oil pump cover manifold (1993-on)	70-80	7.9-9.0
Tappet guide bolts	90-120	10.3-13.8
Gearcase cover screws	90-120	10.3-13.8
Tappet screen plug		
1984	90-160	10.3-18.4
1985-on	90-120	10.3-13.8
Timer screws	15-30	1.7-3.4

4

Table 4 INNER BEARING SPACER SIZE

Part No.	Spacer size (in.)*
9120	0.0925-0.0915
9121	0.0945-0.0935
9122	0.0965-0.0955
9123	0.0985-0.0975
9124	0.1005-0.0995
9125	0.1025-0.1015
9126	0.1045-0.1035
9127	0.1065-0.1055
9128	0.1085-0.1075
9129	0.1101-0.1095
9130	0.1125-0.1115
9131	0.1145-0.1135
9132	0.1165-0.1155
9133	0.1185-0.1175
9134	0.1205-0.1195

*Multiply specification by 25.4 to find millimeter (mm) equivalent.

CHAPTER FIVE

CLUTCH, PRIMARY DRIVE AND STARTER DRIVE

The primary drive, clutch, transmission and final drive systems make up the power train assembly on your Harley-Davidson. This chapter describes service to the primary drive, clutch and starter drive assemblies. Transmission and final drive service are described in separate chapters.

The primary drive system uses sprockets and a primary drive chain to transmit power from the engine to the transmission. This system is designed to allow the engine sprocket to turn faster than the clutch sprocket (engine sprocket is smaller than clutch sprocket). This ratio difference increases engine torque and reduces the amount of power flowing into the transmission and final drive systems.

An external chain primary drive assembly is used on all Harley-Davidson V-twin engines. This system is used because the Harley engine is a non-unit engine; that is, the engine and transmission do not share a common case. The primary drive assembly is mounted inside the primary chain case, a sealed housing mounted on the left-hand side of the bike. The chain case contains the engine compensating sprocket, clutch and clutch sprocket, primary chain, chain adjuster, solenoid and starter drive mechanism. The engine and clutch turn in the same direction.

Abnormal gear noises are usually the first sign of trouble with the primary sprockets and chain. If you notice an increase in the primary chain case noise level, first check the oil level (wet clutch), then check the primary chain tension for looseness and for a damaged chain tensioner assembly. If necessary, remove the primary chain case cover and inspect the primary drive assembly. The primary chain and sprockets can be replaced without major engine disassembly.

The clutch is mounted in the primary housing between the engine sprocket and transmission. The clutch allows the rider to control power from the engine into the transmission by disengaging the clutch from the transmission when shifting from one gear to another. A dry clutch is used on early 1984 FXST models. All late 1984 and later models use a wet clutch. If the clutch should slip or drag, first perform the clutch adjustments described in Chapter Three. If adjustment does not solve the problem, service the clutch assembly as described in this chapter.

The starter drive mechanism is mounted in the chain case housing on 1984-1988 models. Starting with 1989 models, the starter drive mechanism was changed; a starter jackshaft assembly is mounted in the chain case housing. Refer to Chapter Nine for starter motor service.

Specifications are found in **Tables 1-5**. All tables are found at the end of the chapter.

DRY CLUTCH
(EARLY 1984 FXST)

The dry clutch is used on early 1984 FXST models. Refer to **Figure 1** when performing procedures in this section.

Removal

1. Disconnect the negative battery cable.
2. Remove the left footboard mounting bolts and move the footboard out of the way.

3. Remove the shift lever (**Figure 2**) and the left footpeg bracket, if necessary.

4. Remove the primary chain case cover screws. Then tap the cover (**Figure 3**) with a plastic-faced mallet to break the gasket seal. Pull the cover off of the engine and transmission housings.

5. The engine must be locked to prevent the crankshaft from turning when loosening the compensating sprocket nut (**Figure 4**). Lock the engine by shifting the transmission into gear. Then hold the compensating sprocket cover with a chain wrench. Wrap the compensating sprocket cover with shim stock to prevent damage from the chain wrench. If these tools are not available, an air gun and socket will be necessary.

5

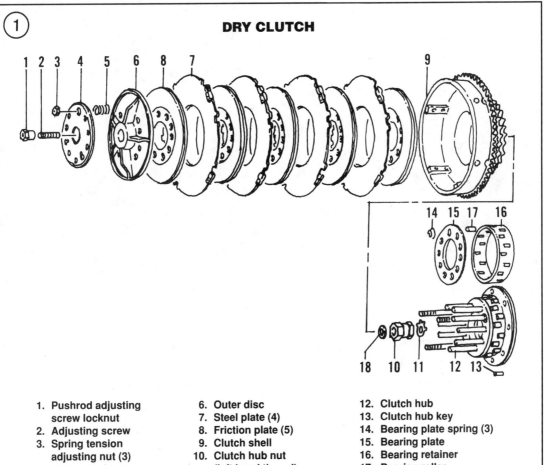

① DRY CLUTCH

1. Pushrod adjusting screw locknut	6. Outer disc
2. Adjusting screw	7. Steel plate (4)
3. Spring tension adjusting nut (3)	8. Friction plate (5)
4. Pressure plate	9. Clutch shell
5. Springs (10)	10. Clutch hub nut (left hand thread)
	11. Hub nut lockwasher
12. Clutch hub	
13. Clutch hub key	
14. Bearing plate spring (3)	
15. Bearing plate	
16. Bearing retainer	
17. Bearing roller	
18. Hub nut seal	

6. After locking the engine, use a large socket and breaker bar or air gun to loosen the compensating sprocket nut (**Figure 4**).

7. Refer to **Figure 5**. Remove the following parts in order:

   a. Nut (**Figure 4**).
   b. Cover (5, **Figure 5**).
   c. Sliding cam (**Figure 6**).

8. Remove the pushrod adjuster screw locknut (**Figure 7**).

9. Place a flat washer (1/8 in. thick, 1 3/4 in. O.D. and 3/8 in. I.D.) over the pushrod adjuster screw (**Figure 8**). Then reinstall the adjusting screw locknut removed in Step 8.

10. Refer to **Figure 8**. Tighten the pushrod adjuster screw locknut until the clutch spring adjusting nuts are loose. Then remove the clutch spring nuts.

NOTE
Do not disassemble the parts in Step 11 unless replacement is required. Disassembly is described under **Clutch Inspection** *in this chapter.*

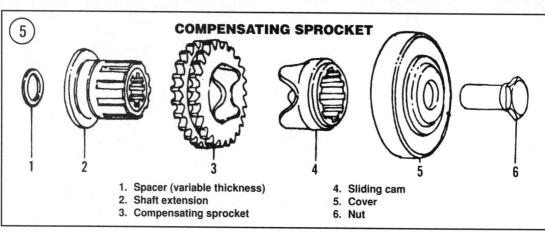

COMPENSATING SPROCKET

1. Spacer (variable thickness)
2. Shaft extension
3. Compensating sprocket
4. Sliding cam
5. Cover
6. Nut

11. Remove the pressure plate, clutch springs and the releasing disc as an assembly. See **Figure 1**.

12. Remove the friction (**Figure 9**) and steel (**Figure 10**) clutch plates in order.

13. Referring to **Figure 11**, remove the primary chain adjuster bolt and remove the chain adjuster assembly. See **Figure 12**.

14. Remove the oil hose from the primary chain adjuster fitting.

15. Remove the clutch shell, compensating sprocket and primary chain as one unit (**Figure 13**).

NOTE
The clutch nut uses left-hand threads. Turn the nut clockwise to loosen it.

16. Pry back the clutch hub lockwasher tab, then loosen the clutch nut (A, **Figure 14**) by turning it *clockwise*. Remove the nut and its lockwasher.

5

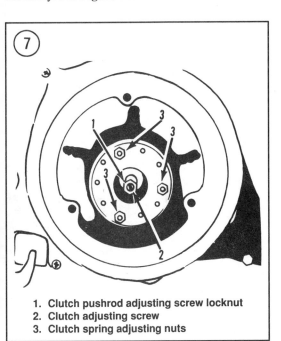

1. Clutch pushrod adjusting screw locknut
2. Clutch adjusting screw
3. Clutch spring adjusting nuts

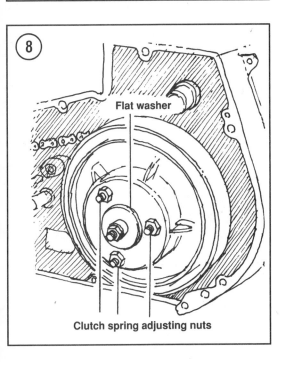

Flat washer

Clutch spring adjusting nuts

17. Attach the clutch hub puller (HD-95960-41) to the clutch hub (**Figure 15**). Then turn the puller's center bolt clockwise and remove the clutch hub (B, **Figure 14**).

18. Remove the clutch hub Woodruff key (**Figure 16**) from groove in mainshaft.

Inspection

1. Clean all clutch parts in a non-oil based solvent and thoroughly dry with compressed air.

2. To disassemble the pressure plate assembly:

  a. Install 3 bolts through the original pressure plate-to-clutch hub bolt holes. The bolts should be long enough to allow removal of the parts while under compression.

  b. Secure each nut with a flat washer and nut. Tighten all nuts in a crisscross pattern until the clutch springs compress slightly.

  c. Remove the adjuster locknut and remove the adjuster screw.

  d. Loosen the 3 nuts in a crisscross pattern. Loosen the nuts 1/2 to 1 turn at a time to release spring tension evenly.

  e. After loosening the nuts, remove the washers and 3 bolts. Then separate the pressure plate and remove the clutch springs.

3. Measure the free length of each clutch spring as shown in **Figure 17**. Replace any springs that are too short (**Table 1**).

4. Inspect steel clutch plates (A, **Figure 18**) for warping or wear grooves. Replace if necessary.

5. Inspect friction plates (B, **Figure 18**) for a shiny appearance or signs of oil soaking. Also check the plates for worn or grooved lining surfaces. Measure each plate (**Figure 19**) and compare thickness to the

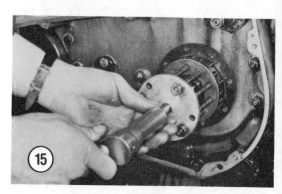

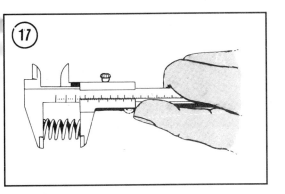

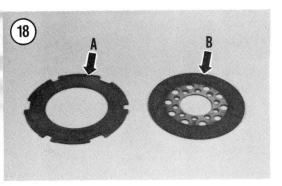

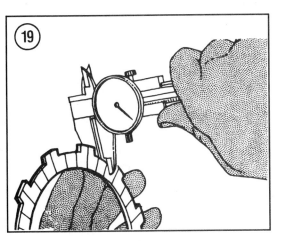

specifications in **Table 1**. Replace plates if thickness meets or exceeds minimum thickness.

6. Check for loose clutch plate rivets; replace if necessary.

7. Check the clutch shell inner bearing race (A, **Figure 20**) for grooves, wear or damage. Also check the clutch shell plate tabs (B, **Figure 20**) for looseness or damage. If found, replace the clutch shell.

8. Check the clutch shell gear teeth (**Figure 21**) for wear or damage. Replace the clutch shell if necessary.

9. Spin the clutch hub roller bearing assembly (A, **Figure 22**) by hand. If bearing assembly appears rough, disassemble it by removing the 3 bearing plate springs (B, **Figure 22**). Then slide the bearing plate off the hub pins and remove the bearing retainer. Check all parts for wear or damage; replace parts as required.

10. Pry the pushrod seal out of the hub nut. Install a new seal by tapping it into place.

5

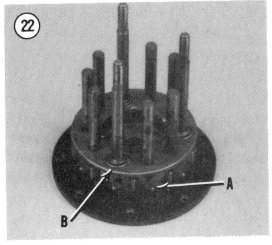

Installation

1. Install the Woodruff key (**Figure 16**) in the main-shaft keyway.

2. Install the pushrod, if removed.

3. Slide the clutch hub assembly (B, **Figure 14**) onto the mainshaft.

NOTE
The clutch nut uses left-hand threads.
Turn the nut counterclockwise to tighten
it.

4. Thread the clutch nut onto the mainshaft by turning the nut *counterclockwise*. Using a torque wrench, tighten the nut to the torque specification listed in **Table 4**. Use the same tools and procedures to prevent the mainshaft from turning as used during disassembly. Bend the lockwasher tab over the nut to lock it.

NOTE
Grease the clutch shell bearing before
installing the clutch shell in Step 5.

5. Install the clutch shell, primary chain and the compensating sprocket as an assembly. See **Figure 13**.

6. Refer to **Figure 5**. Install the following parts in order:

    a. Washer (if removed).

    b. Shaft extension (if removed).

    c. Sliding cam (**Figure 6**).

    d. Cover (**Figure 5**).

7. Install the compensating sprocket nut (**Figure 4**) and tighten it to 80-100 ft.-lb. (110.4-138 N•m).

8. Install the friction and steel clutch plates in the order shown in **Figure 1**. Install the steel clutch plates (**Figure 10**) with the side stamped *OUT* facing outward.

9. If the pressure plate unit was disassembled, assemble as follows:

    a. Place the clutch hub on the workbench so that the bolts face up (**Figure 22**).

    b. Install the retaining disc on the hub.

    c. Install the clutch springs on the hub pins and studs.

    d. Place the pressure plate over the clutch spring. Because of stud hole arrangement, plate collar in pressure plate will fit only one way.

    e. Screw the pushrod adjuster locknut onto the adjuster screw until the screw is flush with the

top of the nut. Install a 1 3/4 in. washer under the nut and thread the adjuster screw into the releasing disc.

    f. Tighten the nut to compress the clutch springs.

    g. Install the 3 clutch spring adjusting nuts.

    h. Remove the adjust screw locknut and remove the 1 3/4 in. washer. Then reinstall the locknut.

    i. Tighten the 3 adjusting nuts in a crisscross pattern until the distance from the releasing disc to the pressure plate is exactly 1 1/32 in. (26.19 mm). Tighten the adjusting locknut to maintain this distance.

10. Install the primary chain adjuster (**Figure 11**).

11. Adjust the primary drive chain as described in Chapter Three.

12. Check primary chain alignment as described in this chapter.

13. Install the primary chain cover dowel pin, if removed.

14. Install the primary chain cover using a new gasket.

15. Install all parts previously removed.

16. Perform the *Primary Housing Vacuum Check (Early 1984 Models With Dry Clutch)* as described in this chapter.

WET CLUTCH
(LATE 1984-1989)

This section describes service to the wet clutch installed on late 1984-1989 models. If you have a 1990 or later model, refer to *Wet Clutch (1990-On)* in this chapter. Refer to **Figure 23** when performing procedures in this section.

Removal/Installation

1. Disconnect the negative battery cable.

2. Clean the primary chain case cover thoroughly of all dirt, oil and road debris before removing it.

3. Refer to **Figure 24**. Remove the gearshift pedal (A) and the left-hand running board (B).

4. Place a drain pan under the primary cover and remove the drain plug (**Figure 25**). Allow the oil to drain.

5. Remove the primary chain case cover screws and cover (**Figure 26**). Remove the dowel pin.

6. Loosen and remove the 4 adjuster plate bolts (A, **Figure 27**) in a crisscross pattern.

**WET CLUTCH
(LATE 1984-1989)**

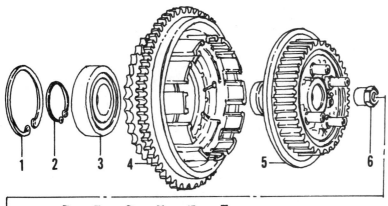

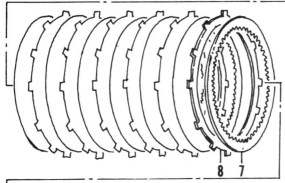

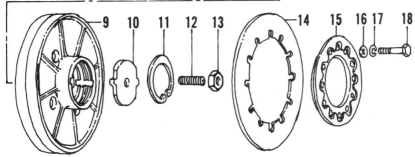

5

1. Circlip
2. Circlip
3. Pilot bearing
4. Clutch shell
5. Inner clutch hub
6. Nut
7. Steel clutch plate
8. Friction clutch plate
9. Pressure plate
10. Release plate
11. Circlip
12. Adjuster screw
13. Nut
14. Diaphragm spring
15. Adjuster plate
16. Washer
17. Lockwasher (late 1984-early 1985 only)
18. Bolt

7. Remove the adjuster plate (B, **Figure 27**) and the diaphragm spring (C, **Figure 27**).

8. Remove the circlip and the release plate from the pressure plate (**Figure 28**).

9. Remove the pressure plate (**Figure 29**).

10. Remove the steel (**Figure 30**) and friction (**Figure 31**) plates.

11. Remove the pushrod (**Figure 32**).

> *NOTE*
> *The clutch nut uses left-hand threads.*
> *Turn the nut clockwise to loosen it.*

> *NOTE*
> *Step 12 describes removal of the clutch*
> *nut. For additional information on loos-*
> *ening the clutch nut, refer to Step 7A and*
> *Step 7B under **Clutch Removal (Clutch***
> ***is not Disassembled)** for 1990 and later*
> *models in this chapter.*

12. Shift the transmission into first gear and apply the rear brake. Turn the clutch nut (**Figure 33**) *clockwise* and remove it.

13. Attach the puller (HD-95960-52B) to the clutch hub. See **Figure 34**.

14. Remove the primary chain adjuster bolt or nut. See **Figure 35**.

15. The engine must be locked to prevent the crankshaft from turning when loosening the compensating sprocket nut (**Figure 36**). Lock the engine by shifting the transmission into gear. Then hold the compensating sprocket cover with a chain wrench. Wrap the compensating sprocket cover with shim stock to prevent damage from the chain wrench. If these tools are not available, an air gun and socket will be necessary.

16. After locking the engine, use a large socket and breaker bar or air gun to loosen the compensating sprocket nut (**Figure 37**).

17. Refer to **Figure 36**. Remove the following parts in order:

    a. Nut (**Figure 37**).

    b. Cover (**Figure 36**).

    c. Sliding cam (**Figure 38**).

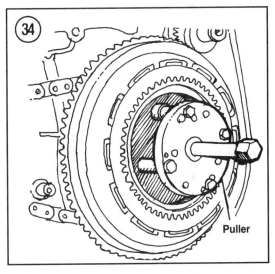

d. Turn the clutch hub puller pressure screw to pull the clutch hub and remove the clutch shell (with clutch hub attached), primary chain (with adjuster) and compensating sprocket at the same time. See **Figure 39**.

e. Remove the shaft extension and washer, if necessary.

18. Disassembly of the clutch shell and hub assembly is not required unless parts are damaged and require replacement.

19. Remove the Woodruff key.

Inspection

1. Clean all clutch parts in a non-oil based solvent and thoroughly dry with compressed air.

2. Inspect the friction plates (**Figure 40**) for worn or grooved lining surfaces. Measure each plate (**Figure 41**) and compare to the specifications in **Table 2**. Replace the friction plates as a set if one plate is found too thin.

3. Check each steel plate (**Figure 42**) for thickness with a vernier caliper (**Figure 43**). Also check each steel plate for flatness with a feeler gauge and straightedge in several places (**Figure 44**). Replace

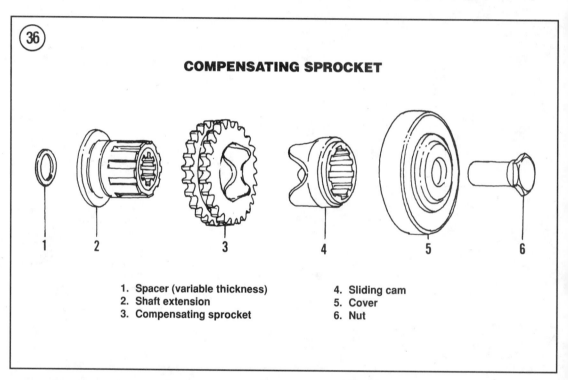

(36)

COMPENSATING SPROCKET

1   2   3   4   5   6

1. Spacer (variable thickness)   4. Sliding cam
2. Shaft extension   5. Cover
3. Compensating sprocket   6. Nut

(37)

(38)

any plate that is too thin or warped beyond specifications (**Table 2**).

4. Check the diaphragm spring (**Figure 45**) for wear or damage. Replace if necessary.

5. Check the pressure plate surfaces (**Figure 46** and **Figure 47**) for wear or cracking. Replace if necessary.

NOTE
The clutch shell assembly consists of the inner clutch hub, clutch shell and pilot bearing. Because of the possibility of

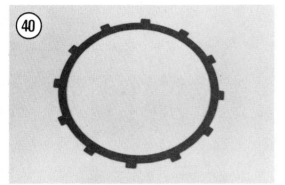

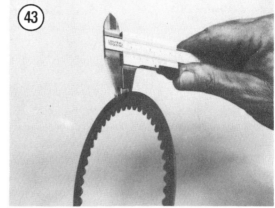

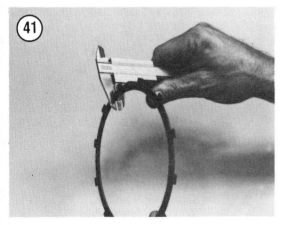

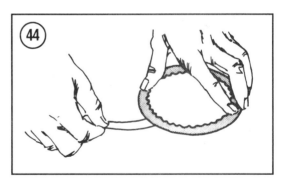

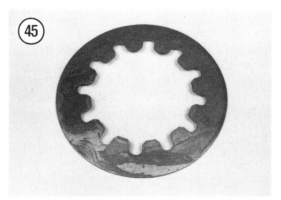

damaging the pilot bearing when re-moving it, do not disassemble these parts unless it is necessary to replace worn or damaged parts or to access the parts for closer inspection. A press is required for disassembly and reassembly.

6. Check the pilot bearing (A, **Figure 48**) for wear by holding the clutch hub and turning the clutch shell by hand. If the bearing appears worn, replace it as described in this chapter.

7. Check the clutch shell teeth (B and C, **Figure 48**) for wear or damage. Also check the inner clutch hub splines (**Figure 49**) for wear or damage. If worn or damaged parts are detected, disassemble the clutch shell assembly as described in this chapter.

Clutch Shell Disassembly/Reassembly

The clutch hub and shell should not be separated unless replacement of the hub, shell or bearing is required. Disassembly of the hub and shell may damage the pilot bearing; bearing replacement will be required during reassembly. A press is required for this procedure.

Read this procedure completely through before starting disassembly. Refer to **Figure 23**.

1. Remove the circlip from the clutch shell groove.

2. Remove the circlip from the clutch hub groove.

3. Support the clutch hub and shell in a press and press the clutch hub out of the bearing. Remove the clutch shell from the press.

4. Support the clutch shell in the press and press the bearing out of the shell. Discard the bearing if severely worn, damaged or if damaged during removal.

5. Discard worn or damaged parts. Clean reusable and new parts (except bearing) in solvent and dry thoroughly.

6. Place the clutch shell into the press. Then align the bearing with the clutch shell and press bearing into shell until bearing bottoms out against lower shoulder. When pressing the bearing into the clutch shell, press only on the outer bearing race. Installing the bearing by pressing on its inner race will damage the bearing. Refer to *Ball Bearing Replacement* in Chapter One for additional information.

7. Install the bearing circlip into the clutch shell groove. Make sure the circlip seats in the groove completely.

8. Press the clutch hub into the clutch shell as follows:

   a. Place the clutch shell in a press. Support the inner bearing race with a sleeve as shown in **Figure 50**.

CAUTION
*Failure to support the inner bearing race properly will cause bearing and clutch shell damage. Refer to **Figure 50** to make sure the inner bearing race is supported properly.*

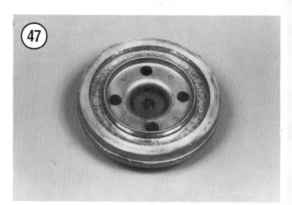

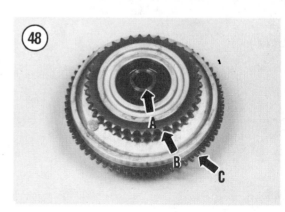

b. Align the clutch hub with the bearing and press the clutch hub into the bearing (**Figure 50**) until the clutch hub shoulder seats against the bearing.

c. Using circlip pliers, install the clutch hub circlip. Make sure the circlip seats in the clutch hub groove completely.

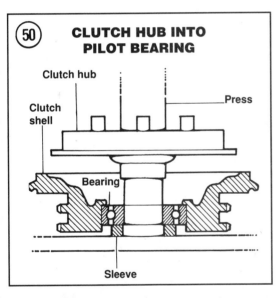

CLUTCH HUB INTO PILOT BEARING

Clutch hub

Clutch shell

Press

Bearing

Sleeve

9. After completing assembly, hold the clutch hub and rotate the clutch shell by hand. The shell should turn smoothly with no sign of roughness or binding. If the clutch shell binds or turns roughly, the bearing may have been damaged during reassembly.

Installation

Refer to **Figure 23** when installing the clutch assembly.

1. Install the Woodruff key (**Figure 51**) in the mainshaft.

NOTE
Check to make sure that the Woodruff key is parallel with the mainshaft taper.

2. Install the clutch shell and hub, primary chain and compensating sprocket and cam as an assembly. *Make sure* the Woodruff key is not knocked out of alignment during installation.

NOTE
The clutch nut uses left-hand threads. Turn the nut counterclockwise to tighten.

CAUTION
Overtightening the clutch nut can damage the clutch hub and pilot bearing.

3. Apply a few drops of Loctite 262 (red) to the clutch nut threads and thread the nut onto the mainshaft by turning the nut *counterclockwise*. Using a torque wrench, tighten the nut to the torque specification listed in **Table 4**. Use the same tools and procedures to prevent the mainshaft from turning as used during disassembly.

4. Refer to **Figure 36**. Install the following parts in order:

a. Washer (if removed).
b. Shaft extension (if removed).
c. Sliding cam.
d. Cover.

CAUTION
The compensating sprocket nut is tightened to a high torque specification. Make sure you hold the sprocket securely when tightening the nut in Step 5.

5. Apply a few drops of Loctite 262 (red) to the compensating sprocket nut and then install the nut and tighten to the torque specification listed in **Table 4**. Use the same tools and procedures to prevent the crankshaft from turning as used during disassembly.

6. Soak all friction plates in clean engine oil before reassembly.

7. Install the clutch plates in the order shown in **Figure 23**.

8. Thread the pushrod into the release plate, if removed.

NOTE
*If the release plate was removed from the pressure plate (**Figure 46**), reinstall it into the pressure plate and then secure*

it with the beveled circlip; install the circlip so that its beveled edge faces outward. Make sure the circlip seats in the pressure plate groove completely.

9. Install the pressure plate (**Figure 28**).

10. Install the spring diaphragm (C, **Figure 27**) with its convex side facing outward.

11. Install the adjuster plate (B, **Figure 27**).

12. Install the washer(s) onto each of the clutch hub bolts.

NOTE
Late 1984-Early 1985 models use a flat washer and a lockwasher on each of the clutch hub bolts. Late 1985 and later models do not use the lockwasher.

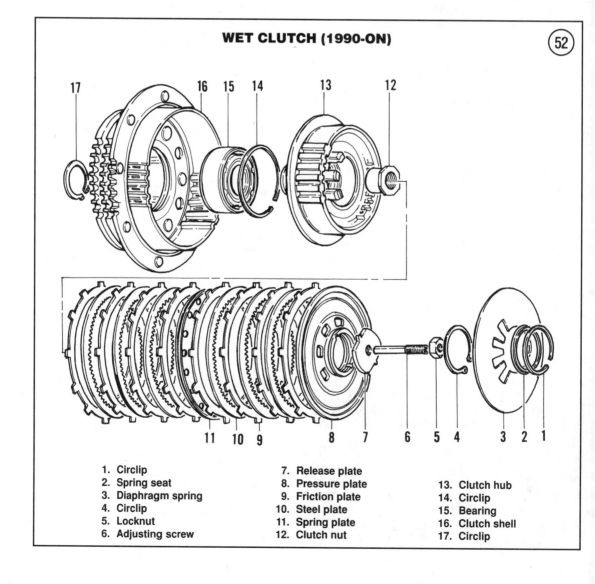

WET CLUTCH (1990-ON) 52

1. Circlip	7. Release plate	
2. Spring seat	8. Pressure plate	13. Clutch hub
3. Diaphragm spring	9. Friction plate	14. Circlip
4. Circlip	10. Steel plate	15. Bearing
5. Locknut	11. Spring plate	16. Clutch shell
6. Adjusting screw	12. Clutch nut	17. Circlip

13. Apply a few drops of Loctite 222 (purple) to threads on each of the clutch hub bolts. Then install the bolts through the adjuster and pressure plates and thread into the clutch hub. Tighten the bolts in a crisscross pattern to 6.5-8 ft.-lb. (9-11 N•m).

14. Adjust the clutch as described in Chapter Three.

NOTE
If new clutch components were installed, readjust the clutch at the first 500 mile interval.

15. Assemble and secure the primary chain adjust shoe assembly as described in this chapter.

16. Adjust the primary chain as described in Chapter Three.

17. Check primary chain alignment as described in this chapter.

18. Install the primary chain case cover dowel pin, if removed.

19. Install the primary chain case cover (**Figure 26**) together with a *new* gasket. Install the cover screws and washers and tighten each screw securely.

20. Refill the primary chain housing with the correct type and quantity oil as described in Chapter Three.

21. Check the clutch inspection cover O-ring and the primary chain inspection cover gasket for wear or damage; replace as required.

22. Install the clutch inspection cover with its O-ring. Install the primary chain inspection cover and its gasket. Tighten all of the cover screw securely.

23. Install all external parts previously removed.

24. Ride the bike a short distance and check the cover for oil leaks.

53

WET CLUTCH (1990-ON)

This section describes service to the wet clutch installed on 1990 and later models. If you are servicing a late 1984-1989 model, refer to *Wet Clutch (Late 1984-1989)* in this chapter. Refer to **Figure 52** when performing procedures in this section.

Preliminary Steps

Complete disassembly of the clutch will require the use of the Harley-Davidson Spring Compression Tool (part No. HD-38515) or equivalent. If you do not have access to the compression tool, you can remove the clutch intact from the bike and then take it to a Harley-Davidson dealer or independent repair shop for disassembly and service. Do not attempt to disassemble the clutch without the special tool. Observe the *WARNING* in the following procedures.

Clutch Removal (Clutch is Not Disassembled)

This procedure describes removal of the clutch unit only. If you wish to disassemble the clutch while it is installed on the bike, refer to *Clutch Disassembly on Bike* in this chapter.

1. Shift the transmission into 5th gear.

2. Disconnect the negative battery cable.

3. Clean the primary chain case cover thoroughly of all dirt, oil and road debris before removing it.

4. Place a drain pan under the primary cover and remove the drain plug (**Figure 25**). Allow the oil to drain completely.

5. Remove the primary case cover screws and cover (**Figure 53**). If the case appears to be stuck, make sure all of the cover screws have been removed. Then lightly tap the cover to break the gasket seal. Remove the 2 dowel pins.

6. Remove the circlip holding the adjust screw plate in position, then remove the adjust screw plate (**Figure 54**), adjust screw and nut.

NOTE
The 2 notches cast in the pressure plate can be used to help pry the circlip out when removing it.

5

NOTE
*An air gun is the simplest way to remove the clutch and compensating sprocket nuts. However, if you do not have an air gun, Step 7 describes 2 methods that can be used to remove the clutch nut (**Figure 55**).*

CAUTION
The clutch hub nut is secured with Loctite 262 (red) and tightened to a high torque reading. It will be tight. To loosen the clutch hub nut safely, make sure to read completely through the procedure first, and then perform the steps in order.

7A. *Method 1*: This method is recommended by Harley-Davidson. Remove the clutch hub nut (**Figure 55**) as follows:

 a. The transmission should be in 5th gear when loosening the clutch hub nut. See Step 1.

 b. Have an assistant apply the rear brake hard.

 c. Remove the clutch hub nut with a 1 3/16 in. socket. The clutch hub nut uses left-hand threads, so turn the nut *clockwise* to remove it.

7B. *Method 2*: This method of removing the clutch and compensating sprocket nuts uses a homemade clutch bar that fits between the compensating sprocket and clutch shell gear teeth. **Figure 56** shows the bar in use. The clutch bar can be made of steel or aluminum; the ends of the bar must be bent as shown in **Figure 57** to engage the teeth on both gears properly. Remove the clutch hub nut (**Figure 55**) as follows:

 a. Fit the clutch bar so that the ends of the bar engage the compensating sprocket and clutch shell gear teeth (**Figure 56**).

 b. Remove the clutch hub nut with a 1 3/16 in. socket. The clutch hub nut uses left-hand threads, so turn the nut *clockwise* to remove it.

8. Remove the nut and washer from the center bolt and remove the adjusting shoe (**Figure 58**).

NOTE
If you made the clutch bar in Step 7B, you can use it to hold the compensating sprocket and clutch shell while loosening the compensating sprocket nut.

9. Remove the compensating sprocket nut (**Figure 59**) as follows:

CAUTION
The compensating nut is secured with Loctite 262 (red) and torqued to 150-165 ft.-lb. (207-228 N•m). The nut is tight. To loosen the compensating nut safely, read the following procedure completely through first, and then perform the steps in order.

 a. The transmission should be in 5th gear when loosening the compensating sprocket nut. See Step 1.

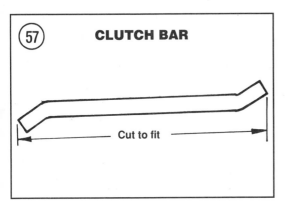

CLUTCH BAR

Cut to fit

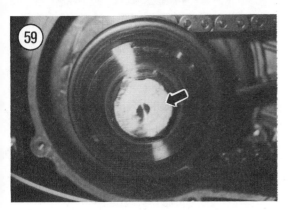

b. Hold the compensating sprocket cover with a chain wrench. Wrap the compensating sprocket cover with shim stock to prevent damage from the chain wrench. If these tools are not available, an air gun and socket will be required.

c. Loosen and remove the compensating sprocket nut (**Figure 59**), spacer, cover and sliding cam. See **Figure 36**.

10. Remove the clutch assembly, compensating sprocket, primary chain and adjuster bracket at the same time.

Clutch Disassembly on Bike

This procedure describes disassembly of the clutch while it is mounted on the bike. Compensating sprocket and primary chain removal is not required. Read this procedure completely through before starting disassembly.

1. Disconnect the negative battery cable.

2. Clean the primary chain case cover thoroughly of all dirt, oil and road debris before removing it.

3. Place a drain pan under the primary cover and remove the drain plug (**Figure 25**). Allow the oil to drain.

4. Remove the primary case cover screws and cover (**Figure 37**). If the case appears to be stuck, make sure all of the cover screws have been removed. Then lightly tap the cover to break the gasket seal. Remove the 2 dowel pins.

5. Loosen the clutch adjust screw locknut with a socket (**Figure 54**). Then remove the adjust screw and locknut.

WARNING
*The Harley-Davidson Spring Compression Tool (part No. HD-38515 [**Figure 60**]) or equivalent must be used when disassembling the clutch in the following steps. The clutch diaphragm spring is under considerable pressure and will fly off, possibly causing severe personal injury, if the tool is not used.*

6. Align the compression tool with the clutch assembly and thread the forcing screw on the tool into the release plate until the hex head on the forcing screw bottoms out against the release plate (**Figure 61**). Then turn the compression tool handle *clockwise* to compress the diaphragm tool while at the same time

moving the clutch spring seat inward and away from the large circlip. When the clutch spring seat has been moved away from the circlip, remove the circlip with circlip pliers or carefully pry it out with a small screwdriver (**Figure 62**).

7. After removing the circlip in Step 6, remove the spring compression tool from the clutch with the diaphragm spring and pressure plate still attached (**Figure 63**).

NOTE
Do not loosen the spring compression tool to remove the diaphragm spring or pressure plate unless these parts require close inspection or replacement. Loosening and removing the compression tool will require repositioning of the diaphragm spring during reassembly. This step will not be required as long as the compression tool is not removed from these parts.

8. Remove the friction and steel clutch plates (and the spring plate) from the clutch assembly in order (**Figure 64**). Note the spring plate installed between the 4th and 5th friction plate (**Figure 65**).

NOTE
*Further removal steps are not required unless it is necessary to remove the clutch hub and shell assembly. Remove these parts as described under **Clutch Removal (Clutch Is Not Disassembled)** in this chapter. See **Figure 66**.*

Inspection

Refer to **Figure 52** when performing the following.

1. Clean all parts (except friction plates and bearing) in a non-oil based solvent and thoroughly dry with compressed air. Place all cleaned parts on lint-free paper towels.

2. Check each steel plate (A, **Figure 67**) for visual damage such as cracks or wear grooves. Then place each plate on a surface plate and check for warpage with a feeler gauge. Replace the steel plates as a set if any one plate is warped more than 0.006 in. (0.15 mm).

NOTE
A piece of glass can be used as a surface plate when measuring warpage in Step 2.

3. Inspect the friction plates (B, **Figure 67**) for worn or grooved lining surfaces; replace the friction plates as a set if any 1 plate is damaged. If the friction plates do not show visual wear or damage, wipe each plate thoroughly with a lint-free cloth to remove as much

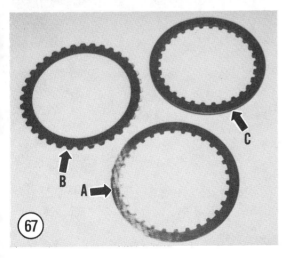

oil from the plates as possible. Then stack each of the 8 friction plates on top of each other and measure the thickness of the plate assembly with a vernier caliper or micrometer. Replace the friction plates as an assembly if the combined minimum thickness of the 8 plates is less than 0.661 in. (16.79 mm).

4. Check the spring plate (C, **Figure 67**) for cracks or damage. Check each of the rivets (**Figure 68**) for looseness or damage. Replace the spring plate if necessary.

5. Check the diaphragm spring for cracks or damage. Check also for bent or damaged tabs. Replace the diaphragm spring if necessary.

6. A double-row ball bearing is pressed into the clutch shell and the clutch hub is pressed into the bearing. Hold the clutch hub and rotate the clutch shell by hand. The shell should turn smoothly with no sign of roughness or tightness. If the clutch shell binds or turns roughly, the bearing is damaged and must be replaced. Refer to Step 10.

7. The steel clutch plate inner teeth mesh with the clutch hub splines (**Figure 69**). Check the splines for cracks or galling. They must be smooth for chatter-free clutch operation. If the clutch hub splines are damaged, the clutch hub must be replaced; refer to Step 10.

8. The friction plates (B, **Figure 67**) have tabs that slide in the clutch shell grooves. Inspect the shell grooves for cracks or wear grooves. The grooves must be smooth for chatter-free clutch operation. If the clutch shell grooves are damaged or worn severely, the clutch shell must be replaced; refer to Step 10.

9. Check the primary chain sprocket and the starter ring gear on the clutch shell for cracks, deep scoring, excessive wear or heat discoloration. If either the sprocket or ring gear are severely worn or damaged,

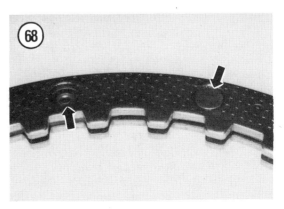

replace the clutch shell; refer to Step 10. If the sprocket is worn, also check the primary chain and the compensating sprocket as described in this chapter.

10. If the clutch hub, shell or bearing require replacement, refer to *Clutch Hub and Shell Disassembly/Reassembly* in this chapter.

Clutch Hub and Shell Disassembly/Reassembly

The clutch hub and shell should not be separated unless replacement of the hub, shell or bearing is required. Disassembly of the hub and shell will damage the double-row ball bearing; bearing replacement will be required during reassembly. A press is required for this procedure.

Read this procedure completely through before starting disassembly. Refer to **Figure 52** when performing this procedure.

1. Remove the clutch plates from the clutch hub and shell assembly, if they have not been previously removed. Refer to *Clutch Disassembly on Bike*.

2. Remove the circlip from the clutch hub groove with circlip pliers (**Figure 70**).

3. Support the clutch hub and shell in a press (**Figure 71**) and press the clutch hub out of the bearing. See **Figure 72**. Remove the clutch shell from the press.

> *WARNING*
> *The clutch hub is a sub-assembly held together with a circlip (**Figure 73**). The parts making up the clutch hub are not serviceable; if the clutch hub is damaged, replace it as a single unit. When handling and servicing the clutch hub, do **not** remove this circlip. The clutch hub is under considerable pressure and removal of the circlip would allow the clutch hub to fly apart under extreme force. This could result in severe personal injury.*

4. Locate the circlip (**Figure 74**) securing the bearing in the clutch shell. Carefully remove the circlip from the clutch shell groove.

> *NOTE*
> *When removing the bearing in Step 5, note that the bearing must be removed through the front side of the shell. The clutch shell is manufactured with a*

shoulder on the rear (primary chain) side.

5. Support the clutch shell in the press and press the bearing out of the shell. Discard the bearing.

6. Discard worn or damaged parts. Clean reusable and new parts (except bearing) in solvent and dry thoroughly.

7. Place the clutch shell into the press. Then align the bearing with the clutch shell and press bearing into shell until bearing bottoms out against lower shoulder (**Figure 75**). When pressing the bearing into the clutch shell, press only on the outer bearing race. Installing the bearing by pressing on its inner race will damage the bearing. Refer to *Ball Bearing Replacement* in Chapter One for additional information.

8. Install the bearing circlip into the clutch shell groove (**Figure 74**). Make sure the circlip seats in the groove completely. See **Figure 76**.

9. Press the clutch hub into the clutch shell as follows:

   a. Place the clutch shell in a press. Support the inner bearing race with a sleeve as shown in **Figure 77**.

CAUTION
*Failure to support the inner bearing race as described in sub-step a will cause bearing and clutch shell damage. Refer to **Figure 77** to make sure the inner bearing race is supported properly.*

   b. Align the clutch hub with the bearing and press the clutch hub into the bearing until the clutch hub shoulder seats against the bearing.

   c. Using circlip pliers, install the clutch hub circlip (**Figure 70**). Make sure the circlip seats in the clutch hub groove completely.

10. After completing assembly, hold the clutch hub and rotate the clutch shell by hand. The shell should turn smoothly with no sign of roughness or binding. If the clutch shell binds or turns roughly, the bearing may have been damaged during reassembly.

Clutch Assembly

This section describes clutch assembly. After assembly, the clutch will be installed back onto the bike. If you did not disassemble the clutch assembly, refer to *Clutch Installation*.

Refer to **Figure 52** when performing this procedure.

1. Soak all of the clutch plates in clean primary chain case oil for approximately 5 minutes before installing them.

> *NOTE*
> *Before installing the clutch plates, count the number of each plate. You should have 8 friction plates, 6 steel plates and 1 spring plate.*

2. Align the tabs on a friction plate with the clutch shell grooves and install the plate. Then align the inner teeth on a steel plate with the clutch hub grooves and install the plate. Repeat until all of the clutch plates have been installed. The spring plate (**Figure 65**) should be installed between the 4th and 5th friction plate. The last plate installed should be a friction plate.

> *NOTE*
> *During clutch removal, you had the option of whether or not to remove the spring compression tool from the diaphragm spring and pressure plate after removing the pressure plate assembly. If the spring compression tool was not removed from the diaphragm spring and pressure plate (**Figure 78**), proceed to Step 4. If the spring compression tool was removed and the diaphragm spring was separated from the pressure plate, proceed to Step 3.*

3. Assemble the pressure plate and diaphragm spring as follows:

a. If the release plate was removed from the pressure plate, install it onto the pressure plate by aligning its tabs with the slots in the pressure plate. Secure the release plate by installing the circlip into the pressure plate groove. Make sure the circlip seats in the groove completely. Do not thread the adjust screw and locknut into the release plate at this time.

b. Align the teeth on the pressure plate with the clutch hub, then insert the pressure plate into the clutch hub.

c. The diaphragm spring is not flat, but instead it has a convex side (side that curves outward). Install the diaphragm spring onto the pressure

plate so that the convex side faces *away* from the pressure plate—the convex side must face out. After installing the diaphragm spring, you will note that there is room for the diaphragm spring to move around within the pressure plate; this area within the pressure plate is called the spring pocket. For the diaphragm spring to be properly installed, it must be centered within the pressure plate spring pocket. Center the diaphragm spring by hand and hold it in position.

d. The clutch spring seat has a lip on one side. Install the spring seat onto the face of the diaphragm spring so that the lip faces out.

> *WARNING*
> *The following steps describe installation of the diaphragm spring circlip.*

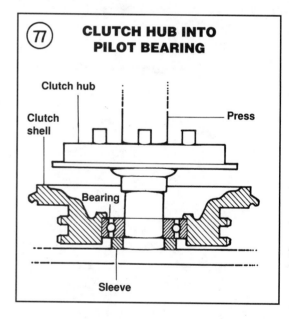

77 **CLUTCH HUB INTO PILOT BEARING**

Clutch hub

Clutch shell

Press

Bearing

Sleeve

78

Because of the force required to compress the diaphragm spring in order to install the circlip, the Harley-Davidson Spring Compression Tool (part No. HD-38515 [Figure 60]) or equivalent must be used. Severe personal injury could occur if the special tool is not used.

e. Align the compression tool with the clutch hub and thread the center screw on the tool into the release plate until the hex head on the forcing screw bottoms out against the release

plate (**Figure 79**). Then check that the diaphragm spring is still centered within the clutch hub spring pocket as described in sub-step c. If necessary, reposition the diaphragm spring. When the diaphragm spring position is correct, proceed to sub-step f.

f. Turn the compression tool handle *clockwise* to compress the diaphragm spring and move the clutch spring seat inward to access the clutch hub circlip groove. Then install the diaphragm spring circlip into the clutch hub groove, making sure the ends of the circlip do not overhang the bosses or posts on the end of the clutch hub.

g. After making sure the circlip is seated completely in the clutch hub groove and positioned as described in sub-step f, slowly turn the compression tool handle *counterclockwise* while checking that the clutch spring seat lip seats inside the circlip. After all tension has been removed from the compression tool, remove it from the release plate.

h. Thread the adjust screw and locknut into the release plate (**Figure 80**).

4. If the compression tool was not removed from the diaphragm spring, install the diaphragm spring as follows:

a. Align the teeth on the pressure plate (**Figure 81**) with the clutch hub, then insert the pressure plate into the clutch hub.

b. Turn the compression tool handle *clockwise* to compress the diaphragm spring and move the clutch spring seat inward to access the clutch hub circlip groove. Then install the diaphragm spring circlip into the clutch hub groove, making sure the ends of the circlip do not overhang the bosses or posts on the end of the clutch hub.

c. After making sure the circlip is seated completely in the clutch hub groove and positioned as described in sub-step b, slowly turn the compression tool handle *counterclockwise* while checking that the clutch spring seat lip seats inside the circlip. After all tension has been removed from the compression tool, remove it from the release plate.

d. Thread the adjust screw and locknut into the release plate (**Figure 80**).

Clutch Installation

1. Clean the primary chain case housing and the chain case cover gasket surfaces of all gasket residue. Wipe all oil residue out of the bottom of the chain case cover and housing.

2. Assemble the clutch assembly as described in the previous section.

3. Clean the crankshaft threads, compensating sprocket nut, clutch hub nut and mainshaft threads of all Loctite residue.

4. Install the sprocket shaft spacer (**Figure 82**) and the compensating sprocket shaft extension (**Figure 83**), if previously removed.

5. The compensating sprocket, primary chain, chain adjuster and clutch are installed as an assembly. Assemble the compensating sprocket and clutch shell sprocket with the primary chain. Likewise, engage the chain tensioner with the chain.

6. Lift the primary drive assembly as a unit and slide the compensating sprocket and clutch shell into the chain case. Make sure the chain tension assembly is still attached to the chain. See **Figure 84**.

> *NOTE*
> *The clutch hub nut uses left-hand threads. Turn the nut counterclockwise to tighten it.*

7. Apply 2 drops of Loctite 262 (red) to the clutch hub nut threads and thread the nut onto the mainshaft by turning the nut *counterclockwise*. Using a torque wrench, tighten the nut to the torque specifications listed in **Table 4**. Use the same tools and procedures to prevent the mainshaft from turning as used during disassembly.

> *CAUTION*
> *The compensating sprocket is tightened to a high torque specification. Make sure you hold the sprocket securely when tightening the nut in Step 8.*

8. Apply 2 drops of Loctite 262 (red) to the compensating sprocket nut threads and thread the nut onto the crankshaft threads. Using the same tools and procedures to prevent the compensating sprocket from turning, tighten the nut to the torque specification listed in **Table 4**.

9. Adjust the clutch as described in Chapter Three.

> *NOTE*
> *If new clutch components were installed, readjust the clutch at the first 500 mile interval.*

10. Assemble and secure the primary chain adjust shoe assembly as described in this chapter.

11. Adjust the primary chain as described in Chapter Three.

12. Check the primary chain alignment as described under *Primary Chain Alignment* in this chapter.

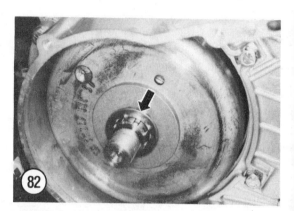

13. Install the 2 primary chain case cover dowel pins, if they have not been previously installed.

14. Install the primary chain case cover together with a *new* gasket. Install the cover screws and washers and tighten each screw securely.

15. Refill the primary chain housing with the correct type and quantity oil as described in Chapter Three.

16. Check the clutch inspection cover O-ring and the primary chain inspection gasket for wear or damage; replace as required.

17. Install the clutch inspection cover with its O-ring. Install the primary chain inspection cover with its gasket. Install the cover Allen screws and washers and tighten securely.

NOTE
The clutch inspection cover Allen head screws are longer than the primary chain inspection cover screws.

18. Ride the bike a short distance and check the cover for oil leaks.

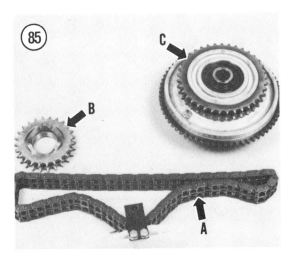

PRIMARY CHAIN

Removal/Installation

Remove the primary chain as described under the clutch removal procedure for your model in this chapter.

Inspection

Refer to the procedures in Chapter Three to lubricate and adjust the chain. If the chain cannot be adjusted within the specifications in Chapter Three, it must be replaced.

Always replace the primary drive chain (A, **Figure 85**) if it is worn or damaged. Attempting to repair a worn chain can cause expensive engine damage. If the primary drive chain is worn, also check the compensating sprocket (B, **Figure 85**) and the clutch shell driven sprocket (C, **Figure 85**) for wear or damage. Replace parts as necessary.

Adjustment Shoe Replacement

If the primary chain cannot be adjusted properly and the adjustment shoe (**Figure 86**) appears worn, replace it as follows.

1. Remove the primary chain case cover as described under clutch removal for your model in this chapter.

2. Remove the top shoe bracket bolt and remove the bracket.

3. Pry back the locking tabs and remove the adjusting shoe mounting bolts. Remove the old adjusting shoe and install a new one. Lock the new adjusting shoe in place by bending the lockwasher tabs over the mounting bolts.

4. Adjust the primary chain as described in Chapter Three.

5. Install the primary chain case cover as described under the clutch inspection procedure for your model in this chapter.

Alignment

The compensating sprocket is aligned with the clutch sprocket by a spacer placed between the alternator rotor and the shaft extension (**Figure 87**). The same spacer should be reinstalled any time the compensating sprocket is removed. However, if the primary chain is wearing on one side or if new clutch

5

components were installed that could affect alignment, perform the following.

Dry clutch

1. Disconnect the negative battery cable.

2. Remove the primary chain, compensating sprocket and clutch shell as described in this chapter.

3. Determine spacer thickness as follows:

  a. Install the clutch hub.

  b. Measure the distance from the alternator rotor hub to the primary drive housing gasket surface (A, **Figure 88**).

  c. Measure the distance from the clutch disc friction surface to the primary drive housing gasket surface (B, **Figure 88**).

  d. Subtract measurement B from A to obtain spacer thickness C.

  e. Select the proper spacer thickness from **Table 5**.

4. Reinstall all parts as described in this chapter.

Wet clutch

1. Remove the primary cover as described under the clutch removal procedure for your model in this chapter.

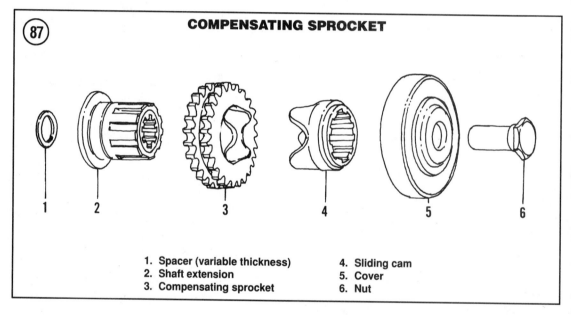

COMPENSATING SPROCKET

  1. Spacer (variable thickness)
  2. Shaft extension
  3. Compensating sprocket
  4. Sliding cam
  5. Cover
  6. Nut

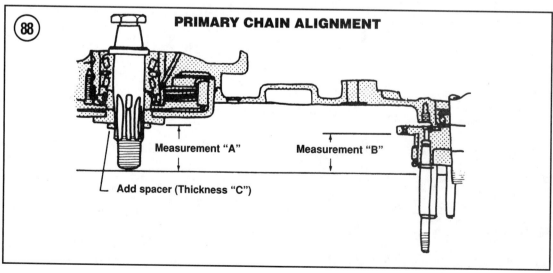

PRIMARY CHAIN ALIGNMENT

Measurement "A"

Measurement "B"

Add spacer (Thickness "C")

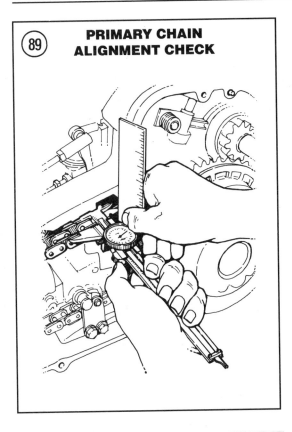

PRIMARY CHAIN ALIGNMENT CHECK

2. Check and adjust primary chain tension as described in Chapter Three.

3. Push the primary chain inward at the compensating sprocket. Then place a straightedge across the primary cover gasket surface near the compensating sprocket and measure the distance from the straightedge to the chain link sideplates. Measure as close to the sprocket as possible and record the measurement. See **Figure 89**.

4. Repeat Step 3 by measuring at the clutch sprocket. Record the measurement.

5. For proper primary chain alignment, the difference between Step 3 and Step 4 must be within 0.030 in. (0.76 mm). If the difference is greater than 0.030 in. (0.76 mm), a spacer (1, **Figure 87**) should be removed or installed on the engine sprocket, positioned between the shaft extension and alternator rotor. Spacers of different thicknesses are available from Harley-Davidson dealers.

COMPENSATING SPROCKET

Removal/Installation

Remove and install the compensating sprocket as described under *Clutch Removal/Installation*.

Inspection

Refer to **Figure 87** for this procedure.

1. Clean all parts in solvent, then blow dry.

2. Visually check the cam surfaces (A, **Figure 90**) for cracks, deep scoring or excessive wear.

3. Check the compensating sprocket gear teeth (B, **Figure 90**) for cracks or excessive wear.

> *NOTE*
> *If the compensating sprocket gear teeth are worn, also check the primary chain and clutch shell gear teeth for wear. See* ***Figure 85***.

4. Check the shaft extension splines (**Figure 91**) for wear or galling.

5. Inspect the cover (**Figure 92**) for damage.

6. Visually inspect the nut (**Figure 93**) for galling or wear and the threads for damage.

7. Replace any worn or damaged part.

8. If any component was replaced, check the primary chain alignment as described in this chapter.

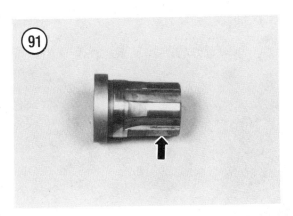

PRIMARY CHAIN CASE

The primary chain case houses the compensating sprocket assembly, primary chain, chain adjuster and clutch.

Removal
(1984-1988)

1. Remove the clutch, primary chain and compensating sprocket as described under the clutch removal procedure for your model in this chapter.

2. Remove the solenoid and plunger as described in Chapter Nine.

3. Remove the starter drive housing as described in this chapter.

4. Loosen the lower engine-to-frame mounting bolts and nuts.

5. Loosen the transmission-to-frame mounting bolts and nuts.

> *NOTE*
> *On early 1984 models, label the vent hoses before disconnecting them in Step 6 and Step 7.*

6. *Early 1984 models*: Disconnect the chain oil hose at the oil pump. Then find the T-fitting next to the oil pump that has the 2 attached vent hoses. Disconnect the crankcase and oil pump vent hoses from the T-fitting.

7. Perform the following:
   a. Cut any safety wire (**Figure 94**) used to lock the engine case bolts.
   b. Remove the primary-to-transmission case bolts. See **Figure 95** or **Figure 96**.

> *NOTE*
> *On models with 2 bolts (**Figure 96**) at the rear of the housing, also remove the 2 bolts from behind the case.*

   c. Remove the primary housing-to-engine case bolts. See **Figure 97** or **Figure 98**.
   d. On early 1984 models, pull the primary case out slightly and disconnect the remaining vent hose from the rear of the primary case. Then on all models, rotate the primary case clockwise on the mainshaft and remove it. On 1985-1988 models, pull the primary case away from the engine and remove it. See **Figure 99**.

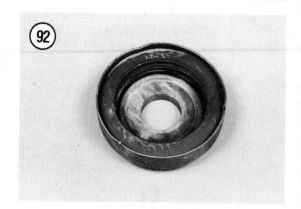

8. Inspect the primary chain case assembly as described in this chapter.

Installation
(1984-1988)

1. Replace the alternator O-ring (**Figure 100**) if worn or damaged.

> *NOTE*
> *Wipe the inner chain case oil seal lip with chain case oil before installing the chain case in Step 2. When installing the chain case, work the oil seal carefully along the mainshaft so that you don't damage it.*

2. Carefully align the chain case with the mainshaft and slide the chain case onto the mainshaft.

> *NOTE*
> *Use the ID marks made on the vent hoses prior to their disassembly when performing Step 3.*

3. *Early 1984 models*: Connect the oil return hose at its fitting on the bottom/rear of the primary housing. Then route the chain oiler and vent hoses between the engine and transmission housings. Reconnect the chain oil hose to its fitting on the oil pump. Connect the vent hoses from the oil tank and oil pump to the fitting on the primary vent hose.

> *CAUTION*
> *The following procedures should be followed in order to ensure that the transmission is properly aligned with the engine. Improper alignment could cause chain and transmission failure.*

4. Loosen the engine and transmission frame mounting fasteners if they were not loosened during removal.

5. Install the primary case-to-transmission mounting bolts finger-tight. See **Figure 95** or **Figure 96**, typical.

NOTE
*The 2 primary case-to-engine mounting bolts with the drilled head should be installed into the rear engine mounting holes. **Figure 94** shows these 2 bolts.*

6. Install the primary case-to-engine mounting bolts finger-tight. See **Figure 97** or **Figure 98**.

7. Tighten the primary case-to-engine mounting bolts to 18-22 ft.-lb. (24.8-30.4 N•m). See **Figure 97** or **Figure 98**.

8. Align the primary case with the transmission housing.

NOTE
*Before tightening the primary case-to-transmission bolts, check the bolts for binding by screwing them in and out by hand. Likewise, check the mainshaft (**Figure 101**) for binding by turning it by hand. If the bolts or mainshaft show any sign of binding, you must reposition the primary case where it mounts on the transmission. If necessary, loosen the primary case-to-engine mounting bolts and start over. When there is no apparent binding when the engine mounting bolts are tight (Step 7), proceed to Step 9.*

9. Tighten the primary case-to-transmission mounting bolts to 18-22 ft.-lb. (24.8-30.4 N•m). Bend the lockwasher tab over the bolt head to lock it.

10. Tighten the lower engine-to-frame mounting bolts and nuts to 33-38 ft.-lb. (45.5-52.4 N•m).

11. Tighten the transmission-to-frame mounting bolts to 33-38 ft.-lb. (45.5-52.4 N•m).

NOTE
*Recheck that the mainshaft (**Figure 101**) turns freely with no sign of binding.*

12. Safety wire the 2 rear primary case-to-engine bolts as shown in **Figure 102** and **Figure 103**.

CAUTION
*Always install safety wire so that it tightens the bolt. **Figure 104** shows the correct way to safety wire two bolts by the double twist method. Always use stainless steel wire approved for safety wiring.*

14. Install the starter and starter drive housing as described in this chapter.

15. Install the solenoid and plunger as described in Chapter Nine.

16. Install the clutch, engine compensating sprocket, chain adjuster, primary chain and primary case cover as described in this chapter.

17. On dry clutch models, perform the *Primary Housing Vacuum Check (Early 1984 with Dry Clutch)* in this chapter.

Primary Housing Vacuum Check
(Early 1984 with Dry Clutch)

The primary housing must be checked for air tightness after reassembly.

1. Remove one of the clutch inspection cover screws and thread the Vacuum Gauge (part No. HD 96950-68) into the screw hole.

2. Start the engine and allow it to idle. The vacuum gauge should read 9 inches of water vacuum (minimum).

3. Locate the 3/8 in. (9.5 mm) vent hose connected between the chain case and the tee connector. Pinch this hose closed and bring the engine idle speed up

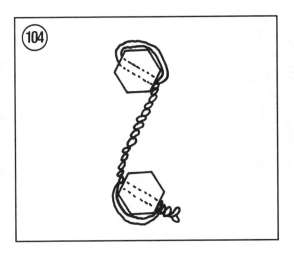

to 1,500 rpm. The vacuum gauge should now read 25 inches of water vacuum.

4. If the vacuum gauge shows a lower reading, there is an air leak into the primary housing. The primary housing should now be pressurized with compressed air (10 psi [0.7 kg/cm^2] maximum).

5. Pinch all of the oil lines running to the primary housing. Pinch the hoses as close to the housing as possible.

CAUTION
Do not apply more than 10 psi (0.7 kg/cm^2) of compressed air into the primary housing.

6. Pressurize the housing with 10 psi (0.7 kg/cm^2) of compressed air. Now listen for air leaks at the following locations:
    a. All O-ring and gasket surfaces.
    b. All hose and oil seal fittings.
    c. Starter drive and solenoid mounting areas.
    d. Timing inspection hole.
    e. Transmission filler hole.
    f. Along the primary chain case housing and cover (possible cracks or casting defects).

7. Leaking areas must be repaired before putting the bike back into service.

Removal
(1989-on)

1. Remove the clutch, primary chain and compensating sprocket as described under the clutch removal procedure for your model in this chapter.

2. Remove the starter jackshaft as described in this chapter.

3. Remove the starter motor as described in Chapter Nine.

4. Loosen the lower engine-to-frame mounting bolts and nuts.

5. Loosen the transmission-to-frame mounting bolts and nuts.

NOTE
*ID the primary housing mounting bolts that use folding lockwashers (**Figure 105**, typical). These bolts must be installed in their original position with the same type of lockwasher.*

6. Pry the lockwasher tab away from the chain case mounting bolts (**Figure 106**).

7. Remove the primary-to-transmission case bolts. See A, **Figure 106**.

8. Remove the primary housing-to-engine case bolts. See B, **Figure 106**.

NOTE
*The lower front engine mounting bolt is not shown in **Figure 106**.*

9. Remove the primary chain case from the engine and transmission assemblies.

10. Inspect the primary chain case assembly as described in this chapter.

Installation
(1989-on)

1. Replace the alternator O-ring (**Figure 100**) if worn or damaged.

NOTE
Wipe the inner chain case oil seal lip with chain case oil before installing the chain case in Step 2. When installing the chain case, work the oil seal carefully along the mainshaft so that you don't damage it. Wrap the mainshaft splines with tape to protect the inner chain case oil seal when installing it over the mainshaft.

2. Carefully align the chain case with the mainshaft and slide the chain case onto the mainshaft.

CAUTION
The following procedures should be followed in order to ensure that the transmission is properly aligned with the engine. Improper alignment could cause chain and transmission failure.

3. Loosen the engine and transmission frame mounting fasteners if they were not loosened during removal.

NOTE
Chain case mounting bolts should be installed in same position with the same type of lockwasher. Replace damaged lockwashers as required.

4. Install the primary case-to-transmission mounting bolts finger-tight. See A, **Figure 106**.

5. Install the primary case-to-engine mounting bolts finger-tight. See B, **Figure 106**.

NOTE
*The lower front engine mounting bolt is not shown in **Figure 106**.*

6. Tighten the primary case-to-engine mounting bolts to 18-22 ft.-lb. (24.8-30.4 N•m). See B, **Figure 106**.

7. Align the primary case with the transmission housing.

NOTE
*Before tightening the primary case-to-transmission bolts, check the bolts for binding by screwing them in and out by hand. Likewise, check the mainshaft (**Figure 106**) for binding by turning it by hand. If the bolts or mainshaft show any sign of binding, you must reposition the primary case where it mounts on the transmission. If necessary, loosen the primary case-to-engine mounting bolts and start over. When there is no apparent binding when engine mounting bolts are tight (Step 8), proceed to Step 10.*

8. Tighten the primary case-to-transmission mounting bolts to 18-22 ft.-lb. (24.8-30.4 N•m).

9. Tighten the lower engine-to-frame mounting bolts and nuts to 33-38 ft.-lb. (45.5-52.4 N•m).

10. Tighten the transmission-to-frame mounting bolts to 33-38 ft.-lb. (45.5-52.4 N•m).

NOTE
Recheck that the mainshaft turns freely with no sign of binding.

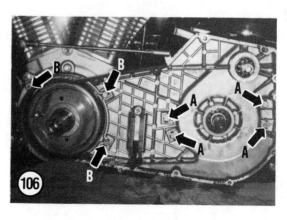

11. Where folding lockwashers are used, bend the lockwasher tab over the bolt head to lock it (**Figure 105**).

12. Install the starter as described in Chapter Nine.

13. Install the starter jackshaft as described in this chapter.

14. Install the clutch, engine compensating sprocket, chain adjuster, primary chain and primary case cover as described in this chapter.

Inspection
(All Models)

1. Clean the primary case in solvent and dry thoroughly.

2. Check the inner primary case oil seal (**Figure 107**) for wear or damage. If the seal is damaged, carefully pry it out of the primary case with a screwdriver. Place a rag underneath the screwdriver to avoid damaging the case.

3. See **Figure 107**. Check the primary case bearing. Turn the inner bearing race by hand and check for excessive play, roughness or noise; both conditions indicate a worn or damaged bearing. To replace the bearing:

   a. Remove the 2 bearing circlips.

   b. Support the primary case carefully and drive the bearing out with a suitable bearing driver or socket.

   c. Install the outer circlip.

   d. Install the new bearing by driving it into the primary case from the inside with a bearing driver or socket placed on the outer bearing race; drive bearing in until it seats against the outer circlip.

   e. Install the inner circlip.

   f. Make sure both circlips seat into their groove completely.

4. Install a new inner primary case oil seal with a bearing driver or socket; install oil seal so that it seats against the inner circlip.

NOTE
Before removing needle bearing or bushings in Step 5, note their position in the chain case or primary cover. If they are installed so that one end is flush with the case or cover, they must be reinstalled the same way.

5. Check the needle bearing or bushings installed in the primary cover for wear or damage. Replace if necessary.

6. *1989-on*: Check the jackshaft oil seal and metal scraper (1989) for wear or damage. Replace damaged parts as required. Note the following when replacing the oil seal or metal scraper (1989):

   a. On 1989 models, maintain a 0.060 in. (1.52 mm) clearance between the metal scraper and the oil seal.

   b. 1990 and later models do not use the metal scraper. If you are installing a 1990 or later jackshaft into a 1989 primary case, do not install the metal scraper.

   c. When installing the oil seal on 1990 and later models, make sure the oil seal seats against the shoulder in the primary case as shown in **Figure 108**.

   d. If you are installing a 1990 or later jackshaft assembly into a 1989 primary case, drive the oil seal into the case—from the inside of the case—to a depth of 0.110-0.120 in. (2.79-3.05 mm).

107 PRIMARY HOUSING BEARING ASSEMBLY

1. Oil seal
2. Circlip
3. Bearing
4. Circlip
5. Primary housing

ELECTRIC STARTER DRIVE
(1984-1988)

Removal (Type I)

The Type I electric drive (**Figure 109**) is used on all 1984-1988 chain drive models.

1. Disconnect the negative battery cable.

2. Remove the starter as described in Chapter Nine.

3. Remove the primary cover as described in this chapter.

4. Remove the drive gear housing bolts (**Figure 109**) and remove the drive gear housing.

5. Remove the oil deflector and gasket.

6. Working from the left-hand side, disengage the shifter lever fingers from the shifter collar. Then remove the pinion gear and shaft assembly.

7. To remove the shifter lever, perform the following:

    a. Remove the battery and battery carrier as described in Chapter Three.

    b. Remove the oil tank mounting brackets.

    c. Remove the solenoid as described in Chapter Nine.

    d. Remove the shifter lever screw and remove the shifter lever.

Inspection

1. Check the drive gear for worn, chipped or broken teeth. Replace the gear if necessary.

> *NOTE*
> *If the drive gear is worn, check the starter gear for wear or damage.*

2. Check the drive gear thrust washer for damage or cupping. Replace the washer if necessary.

3. Check the drive gear housing needle bearing for wear or damage. Rotate the bearing with your fingers and check for noise, roughness or looseness. If the bearing's condition is doubtful, replace it. Replace the bearing with a press.

4. Lubricate the needle bearing with a high temperature grease such as Lubriplate 110.

5. Install the drive gear and thrust washer in the drive housing.

6. Inspect the pinion gear needle bearing installed in the primary cover as described in Step 3. See **Figure 110**. Also check the pinion shaft collar bearing sur-

face. If the bearing or collar is worn, replace them both. Replace the bearing as described in Step 3.

7. Check the pinion gear for worn, chipped or broken teeth. Replace the gear if necessary.

> *NOTE*
> *If the pinion gear is worn, check the clutch ring gear as described in this chapter under Clutch Inspection.*

8. Check the shifter collar groove and the shifter lever fingers for wear. Replace both parts if either is worn.

9. To disassemble the pinion gear shaft assembly, perform the following:

    a. Secure the pinion shaft in a vise with soft jaws.

    b. Remove the pinion shaft nut.

    c. Remove the washer and pinion shaft collar.

    d. Remove the slide pinion gear and shifter collar as one unit.

    e. Remove the spacer.

    f. If necessary, remove the circlip and separate the pinion gear and shifter collar.

    g. Inspect components as described in this section.

10. Assemble the pinion gear and shaft assembly by reversing Step 9 while noting the following:

    a. Inspect all parts for wear and damage as described in this procedure. Replace parts as necessary.

    b. Install the circlip.

    c. Lubricate all parts with a high temperature grease.

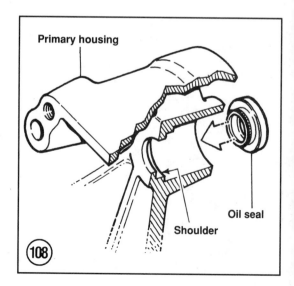

Primary housing

Oil seal

Shoulder

(108)

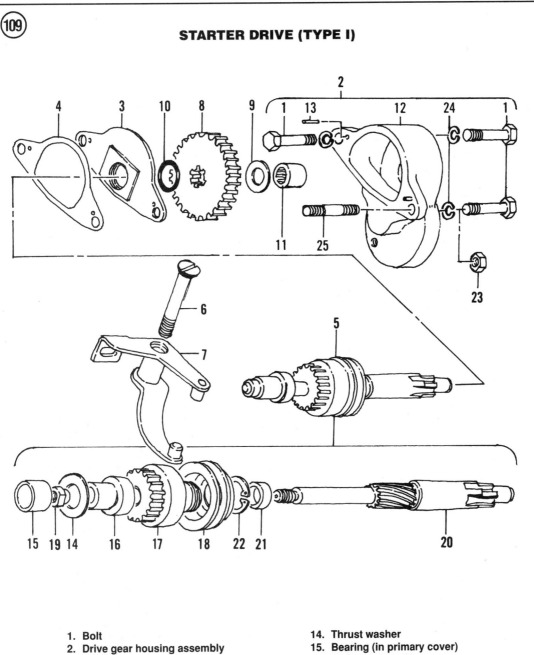

STARTER DRIVE (TYPE I)

1. Bolt
2. Drive gear housing assembly
3. Oil deflector
4. Gasket
5. Pinion gear and shaft assembly
6. Shifter lever screw
7. Shifter lever
8. Drive gear
9. Thrust washer
10. O-ring
11. Bearing (in drive gear housing)
12. Drive gear housing
13. Locating pin

14. Thrust washer
15. Bearing (in primary cover)
16. Pinion shaft collar
17. Pinion gear
18. Shifter collar
19. Pinion shaft nut
    (left hand thread)
20. Pinion shaft
21. Spacer
22. Circlip
23. Nut
24. Lockwasher
25. Stud

Installation

1. Assemble the pinion gear and shaft assembly as described under *Inspection.*

2. Install the pinion shaft assembly. Engage the shifter lever fingers (7, **Figure 109**) with the shifter collar drum (18).

3. Install the shifter lever assembly into the inner primary case. Lubricate the shifter lever screw with a high temperature grease and install it through the shifter lever. Tighten the screw securely.

4. Install the drive gear housing (with gear). See **Figure 111**.

5. Install a new O-ring in the oil deflector.

6. Install the oil deflector into the drive gear housing.

7. Install a new gasket on the oil deflector.

8. Install the primary cover as described in this chapter.

9. Install the solenoid and starter as described in Chapter Nine.

10. Reinstall the battery and the oil tank mounting brackets.

Removal (Type II)

The Type II electric starter drive (**Figure 112**) is used on all 1986-1988 belt drive models.

1. Disconnect the negative battery cable.

2. Remove the starter as described in Chapter Nine.

3. Remove the primary cover as described in this chapter.

4. Remove the outer drive gear housing bolts (**Figure 112**).

5. Remove the outer drive housing, gasket and drive gear.

6. Remove the inner drive housing bolts and remove the housing and gasket.

7. Working from the left-hand side, disengage the shifter lever fingers from the shifter collar. Then remove the pinion gear and shaft assembly.

Inspection

1. Check the drive gear for worn, chipped or broken teeth. Replace the gear if necessary.

> *NOTE*
> *If the drive gear is worn, check the starter gear.*

2. Inspect the inner drive gear housing seal for wear or damage. If necessary, remove the seal by prying it out of the housing with a screwdriver. Install the new seal with a large socket placed on the outside seal surface. Install the seal with the lip side facing toward the drive gear.

3. Grasp the locating pins on both sides of the inner drive gear housing. The pins should be tight. If not, check the pin locations to make sure the housing is not cracked.

4. Check the inner drive gear housing needle bearing for wear or damage. Rotate the bearing with your fingers and check for noise, roughness or looseness. If the bearing's condition is doubtful, replace it. Replace the bearing with a press.

5. Lubricate the needle bearings with a high temperature grease.

6. Inspect the pinion gear needle bearing installed in the outer drive gear housing as described in Step 4. Also check the pinion shaft collar bearing surface. If bearing or collar is worn, replace them both. Replace the bearing as described in Step 4.

7. Check the pinion gear for worn, chipped or broken teeth. Replace the gear if necessary.

(112)

STARTER DRIVE (TYPE II)

5

1. Bolt, lockwasher and washer
2. Allen head bolt
3. Outer drive gear housing half
4. Gasket
5. Drive gear
6. Bolt and lockwasher
7. Inner drive gear housing half
8. Gasket
9. Shifter lever screw
9A. Shifter lever plug and shaft
10. Shifter lever (1985)
10A. Shifter lever (1986-1988)
11. Bearing (in outer drive gear housing)
12. Seal (in inner drive gear housing)
13. Thrust washer
14. Bearing (in outer primary cover)
15. Pinion shaft collar
16. Pinion gear
17. Shifter collar
18. Pinion shaft nut (left hand thread)
19. Pinion shaft (1985)
19A. Pinion shaft (1986-1988)
20. Circlip
21. Locating pins

NOTE
If the pinion gear is worn, check the clutch ring gear as described in this chapter under **Clutch Inspection**.

8. Check the shifter collar groove and the shifter lever fingers for wear. Replace both parts if any one part is worn.

9. To disassemble the pinion gear shaft assembly, perform the following:

NOTE
The pinion shaft nut uses left-hand threads.

   a. Secure the pinion shaft in a vise with soft jaws.
   b. Turn the pinion shaft nut *clockwise* to loosen and remove it.
   c. Remove the washer and pinion shaft collar.
   d. Remove the slide pinion gear and shifter collar as one unit.
   e. If necessary, remove the circlip and separate the pinion gear and shifter collar.
   f. Inspect components as described in this section.

10. Assemble the pinion gear and shaft assembly by reversing Step 9 while noting the following:

   a. Inspect all parts for wear and damage as described in this procedure. Replace parts as necessary.
   b. Install a new circlip.
   c. Lubricate all parts with a high temperature grease.

Installation

1. Assemble the pinion gear and shaft assembly as described under *Inspection*.

2. Install the shifter lever assembly into the inner primary case. Lubricate the shifter lever screw with a high temperature grease and install it through the shifter lever. Tighten the screw securely.

3. Install the pinion shaft assembly. Engage the shifter lever fingers (10 or 10A, **Figure 112**) with the shifter collar (17).

4. Glue a new gasket onto the inner drive gear housing.

5. Install the inner drive gear housing over the pinion shaft assembly and install onto the primary case. Install the mounting bolts and tighten securely.

6. Lubricate the drive gear with high temperature grease and slide it onto the pinion shaft.

7. Cement a new gasket onto the outer drive gear housing. Then install the housing and tighten the mounting bolts securely.

8. Install the starter motor as described in Chapter Nine.

9. Install the primary cover as described in this chapter.

10. Install the solenoid as described in Chapter Nine.

STARTER JACKSHAFT (1989-ON)

The starter jackshaft is mounted in the primary chain case (**Figure 113**). The 1989 and the 1990 and later jackshaft assemblies are not interchangeable.

Removal/Disassembly (1989)

Refer to **Figure 114** for this procedure.

1. Disconnect the negative battery cable.

2. Remove the clutch as described in this chapter.

3. Remove the starter-to-jackshaft coupling if it did not come off with the starter.

4. Pry the lockplate tab away from the jackshaft bolt. Then hold the pinion gear and loosen the jackshaft bolt. Withdraw the jackshaft bolt, lockplate and O-ring from the jackshaft.

5. Slide the jackshaft assembly out of the primary housing.

6. Disassemble the jackshaft as follows:

   a. Slide the sleeve off of the jackshaft and remove the key from the jackshaft if it did not come off with the sleeve.
   b. Remove the pinion gear.

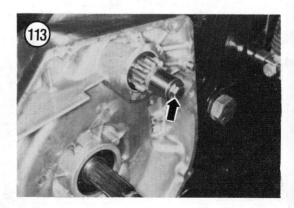

c. Slide the coupling off the jackshaft, then remove the spring from inside the coupling. If necessary, remove the circlip from inside the coupling.

d. If necessary, remove the circlip from the jackshaft.

7. Clean and inspect the starter jackshaft assembly as described in this chapter.

Assembly/Installation (1989)

Refer to **Figure 114** when performing this procedure.

1. Prior to assembly, perform the *Inspection* procedure to make sure all worn or defective parts have been replaced. All parts should be thoroughly cleaned before installation or assembly.

NOTE
Install new circlips during assembly.

2. Install the circlip onto the jackshaft, if previously removed.

3. Install the circlip into the coupling and slide the coupling onto the jackshaft. Place the spring inside the coupling.

4. Slide the pinion gear onto the jackshaft, with the small OD end facing inward.

5. Install the key in the jackshaft keyway.

5

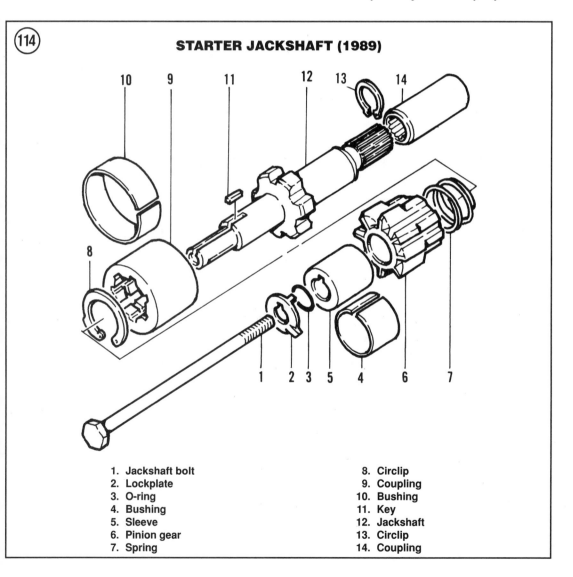

STARTER JACKSHAFT (1989)

1. Jackshaft bolt	8. Circlip
2. Lockplate	9. Coupling
3. O-ring	10. Bushing
4. Bushing	11. Key
5. Sleeve	12. Jackshaft
6. Pinion gear	13. Circlip
7. Spring	14. Coupling

6. Align the keyway in the sleeve with the key and slide the sleeve onto the jackshaft.

7. Slide the lockplate and O-ring onto the jackshaft bolt, then insert the bolt into the jackshaft.

8. Align the inner tab on the lockplate with the keyway in the jackshaft, then tighten the bolt finger-tight.

CAUTION
The inner lockplate tab must be installed in the jackshaft keyway. The lockplate serves 2 purposes; it prevents the key from sliding out of the sleeve and locks the jackshaft bolt to prevent it from backing out of the jackshaft. Install a new lockplate, if one of the tabs is cracked or broken.

9. Slide the jackshaft-to-starter coupling onto the end of the jackshaft.

10. Slide the jackshaft into the primary chain case, with the pinion gear facing outward. Make sure the coupling engages the starter shaft as the jackshaft assembly is installed.

11. Hold the pinion gear and tighten the jackshaft bolt to 7-9 ft.-lb. (9.6-12.4 N•m). Bend the lockplate tab against the jackshaft bolt head to lock it. If the lockplate tab does not align with one of the bolt head flats, tighten the bolt until the 2 parts align with each other; do not loosen the bolt to align the tab.

12. Install the clutch as described in this chapter.

13. Reconnect the negative battery cable.

**Removal/Disassembly
(1990-on)**

Refer to **Figure 115** for this procedure.

1. Disconnect the negative battery cable.

2. Remove the clutch as described in this chapter.

3. Pry the lockplate tab (2) away from the bolt (1).

4. Hold the pinion gear and loosen the bolt. Then remove the bolt, lockplate, thrust washer and O-ring (if used).

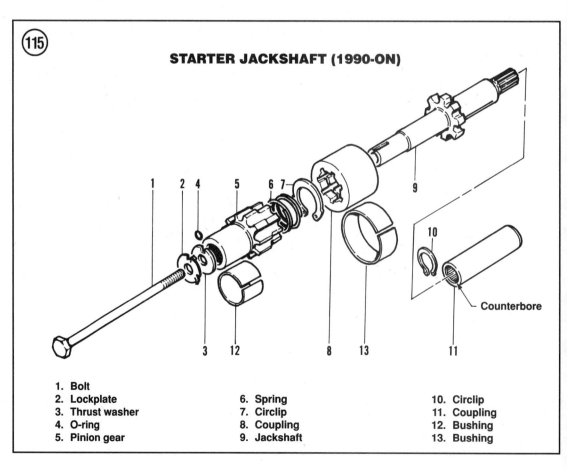

(115)

STARTER JACKSHAFT (1990-ON)

Counterbore

1. Bolt
2. Lockplate
3. Thrust washer
4. O-ring
5. Pinion gear
6. Spring
7. Circlip
8. Coupling
9. Jackshaft
10. Circlip
11. Coupling
12. Bushing
13. Bushing

5. Remove the pinion gear (5).

6. Remove the spring (6) and coupling (8).

7. Remove coupling circlip (7) if necessary.

8A. On 1990-1993 models, remove the coupling and circlip (11 and 10).

8B. On 1994 models, remove the coupling and circlip (11 and 10):

    a. Remove the starter motor as described in Chapter Nine.

    b. Remove the coupling and circlip.

CAUTION
If the starter motor is not removed prior to removing the coupling and circlip on 1994 models, the primary chain case oil seal will be damaged.

9. Clean and inspect the jackshaft assembly as described in this chapter.

Assembly/Installation (1990-on)

Refer to **Figure 115** when performing this procedure.

1. Prior to assembly, perform the **Inspection** procedure to make sure all worn or defective parts have been replaced. All parts should be thoroughly cleaned before installation or assembly.

NOTE
Install new circlips during assembly.

2. Install the circlip (7, **Figure 115**) inside the coupling (8).

3. Install the coupling (11) onto the starter output shaft with the coupling's counterbore facing toward the jackshaft.

CAUTION
On 1994 models, the coupling (11) must be installed before installing the jackshaft. Otherwise, the primary chain case oil seal will be damaged.

4. Install spring (6) inside coupling. Slide coupling onto jackshaft.

5. Install pinion gear (5) on jackshaft (9).

6. Install lockplate (2), thrust washer (3) and O-ring (4 [if used]) onto the bolt.

7. Insert the bolt into the jackshaft.

8. Install the circlip (10), if previously removed, onto the jackshaft groove.

9. Insert the jackshaft assembly onto the inner primary assembly.

10. Align the lockplate tab and thrust washer slot with the jackshaft keyway. Screw the bolt (1) into the starter shaft.

CAUTION
The lockplate tab must be installed in the jackshaft keyway to hold the lockplate and thrust washer in place.

11. Hold the pinion gear and tighten the bolt (1) to 7-9 ft.-lb. (9-12 N•m).

12. Bend the lockplate tab against the bolt head.

13. Install the clutch as described in this chapter.

14. Reconnect negative battery cable.

Inspection (All Models)

1. Clean all jackshaft components thoroughly in solvent. Dry with compressed air, if available.

2. Visually check the jackshaft surfaces for cracks, deep scoring, excessive wear or discoloration. Check the keyway slot and circlip grooves for damage.

3. Check the jackshaft and pinion gear teeth for cracks, severe wear or damage.

4. Check the O-ring for hardening or damage.

5. Check the spring for stretching or damage.

6. Check the jackshaft bolt and jackshaft threads for stripping, cross-threading or deposit buildup. If necessary, use a tap to true up jackshaft threads and remove any deposits. Replace the jackshaft bolt if threads or bolt head is damaged.

7. Check the large coupling for surface damage. Check the spline and the circlip groove inside the coupling for damage.

8. On 1989 models, inspect the small sleeve for surface damage. Check the keyway inside the sleeve for damage. Check the key for damage.

9. Inspect the lockplate closely for cracked, broken or weak alignment and lock tabs.

10. Replace worn or damaged parts as required.

Tables 1-5 are on the following pages.

Table 1 DRY CLUTCH SPECIFICATIONS

Item	Specification
Type	Dry, multiple disc
Spring adjustment	1 1/32-1 7/8 in. (26.2-47.6 mm) from spring collar edge
Spring free length	1 47/64-1 45/64 in. (44.04-43.26 mm)
Friction plates	
Minimum lining thickness	1/32 in. (0.8 mm)
Warpage limit	0.010 in. (0.25 mm)
Steel disc warpage limit	0.010 in. (0.25 mm)
Clutch screw adjustment	See text
Clutch hand lever free play	1/16 in. (1.59 mm)

Table 2 WET CLUTCH SPECIFICATIONS (1985-1989)

Type	Wet, multiple disc
Clutch hand lever free play	1/8-3/16 in. (3.17-4.76 mm)
Steel disc	
Minimum thickness	0.044 in. (1.12 mm)
Warpage limit	0.011 in. (0.30 mm)
Friction plate	
Minimum thickness	0.078 in. (1.98 mm)

Table 3 WET CLUTCH SPECIFICATIONS (1990-ON)

Type	Wet, multiple disc
Clutch hand lever free play	
1984-1990	1/8-3/16 in. (3.2-4.8 mm)
1991-on	1/16-1/8 in. (1.6-3.2 mm)
Steel disc	
Warpage limit	0.006 in. (0.15 mm)
Friction plate assembly	
Minimum lining thickness (assembly)	0.661 in.* (16.8 mm)

* See text for procedures on measuring friction plates.

Table 4 CLUTCH TIGHTENING TORQUES

	ft.-lb.	N•m
Compensating sprocket nut		
1984	80-100	110.4-138
1985-1990	90-100	124.2-138
1991	150-165	207-227.7
Clutch hub nut		
1984	50-60	69-82.8
1985-1990	50	69
1991	70-80	96.6-110.4
Primary cover screws		
1984	18-22	24.8-30.4
1985-on	9-10	12.4-13.8
Jackshaft bolt		
1989-on	7-9	9.6-12.4

Table 5 PRIMARY CHAIN ALIGNMENT (DRY CLUTCH)

Dimension C	Spacer thickness
0.2500-0.2812 in. (6.35-7.14 mm)	0.060 in. (1.52 mm)
0.2812-0.3125 in. (7.14-7.94 mm)	0.090 in. (2.29 mm)
0.3125-0.3427 in. (7.94-8.70 mm)	0.120 in. (3.05 mm)
0.3437-0.3750 in. (8.73-9.52 mm)	0.150 in. (3.81 mm)
0.3750-0.4063 in. (9.52-10.32 mm)	0.180 in. (4.57 mm)
0.4062-0.4375 in. (10.32-11.11 mm)	0.210 in. (5.33 mm)

5

CHAPTER SIX

4-SPEED TRANSMISSION

The 4-speed Harley-Davidson transmission and shifter assembly is mounted in a separate housing and can be completely disassembled and serviced without having to disassemble the engine. However, removal of the transmission housing will first require removal of the primary drive assembly; see Chapter Five. The 4-speed transmission was used on 1984-1985 FXST models.

The transmission service procedures in this chapter are arranged by sub-assembly—shifter assembly and transmission. Before servicing the transmission or shifter assembly, make sure the problem is not due to a faulty clutch adjustment or a problem with the primary drive system.

An external shift linkage assembly connects the gearshift lever to the transmission. The shift linkage assembly requires adjustment to compensate from normal wear to the linkage/shifter mechanism components or when the transmission housing was removed from the bike.

A ratchet-type kickstarter assembly is mounted in the transmission right-hand side cover. The kickstarter mechanism can be removed with the transmission mounted on the bike.

This chapter includes all service procedures for the 4-speed transmission and kickstarter. **Table 1** and **Table 2** are at the end of the chapter.

TRANSMISSION

Removal/Installation
(1984)

1. Disconnect the negative battery cable. Then remove the battery and battery carrier.
2. Drain the transmission oil as described in Chapter Three.
3. Remove the compensating sprocket, primary belt, clutch and primary housing as described in Chapter Five.
4. Remove the starter motor as described in Chapter Nine.
5. Remove the starter drive housing as described in Chapter Five.
6. Label and disconnect the wires at the starter solenoid.
7. Remove the master link from the drive chain. Then slide the drive chain along the front sprocket and remove it.
8. Disconnect the clutch cable from the clutch release lever.
9. Remove the left side oil tank mounting bolts.
10. Disconnect the neutral indicator switch wire at the transmission.

NOTE
The transmission can be removed with its mounting plate attached.

11. Remove the transmission mounting plate fasteners and the transmission-to-frame mounting bolt from underneath the right-hand side.

12. Remove the transmission from the left-hand side.

Installation
(1984)

1. Install the mounting plate onto the transmission and leave the plate-to-transmission mounting bolts loose. Then place the transmission into the frame and install the mounting plate bolts finger-tight.

2. Install and tighten the oil tank mounting nuts.

3. Install the shifter rod onto the shifter linkage.

4. Reinstall the drive chain and master link. Make sure the open end of the link faces in the opposite direction of chain travel.

5. Insert the clutch cable into the release rod end.

6. Install the primary housing as described in Chapter Five.

7. Tighten the following in order:
   a. Tighten the transmission mounting plate-to-frame mounting bolts to 21-27 ft.-lb. (28.9-37.3 N•m).
   b. Tighten the transmission-to-mounting plate bolts to 18-22 ft.-lb. (24.8-30.4 N•m).
   c. Install the right-hand transmission-to-frame mounting bolt and tighten to 18-22 ft.-lb. (24.8-30.4 N•m).

8. Install the starter housing and starter motor.

9. Reconnect the wires at the starter solenoid.

10. Install the compensating sprocket, primary chain and clutch as described in Chapter Five.

11. Refill the transmission with the recommended type and quantity oil as described in Chapter Three.

12. Adjust the primary chain as described in Chapter Three.

13. Check primary chain alignment as described in Chapter Five under *Primary Chain Alignment.*

14. Adjust the rear drive chain or drive belt as described in Chapter Three.

15. Adjust the clutch as described in Chapter Three.

Removal
(1985 FXST)

1. Drain the transmission oil as described in Chapter Three.

2. Remove the battery and battery carrier as described in Chapter Three.

3. Remove the passenger grab strap and seat.

4. Remove the rear cylinder exhaust pipe as described in Chapter Eight.

5. Remove the starter as described in Chapter Nine.

6. Remove the compensating sprocket, primary chain and clutch as described in Chapter Five.

7. Remove the primary housing as described in Chapter Five.

8. Remove the starter relay, battery circuit breaker and wiring from the oil tank.

9. Drain and remove the oil tank.

10. Disconnect the transmission shifter rod from the shifter linkage.

11. Disconnect the clutch cable from the release lever.

12. Disconnect the wiring at the solenoid.

13. Disconnect the neutral indicator switch wire at the transmission.

14. Remove the drive chain.

15. Perform the following:
   a. Support the motorcycle on a stand so that the rear wheel clears the ground.
   b. Loosen all of the shock absorber mounting bolts. Then remove the front bolt from each shock.
   c. Pivot each shock so that it faces down and away from the bike.
   d. Remove the transmission-to-mounting plate fasteners.
   e. Remove the mounting plate-to-frame fasteners.
   f. Remove the brake line tee bracket.
   g. Remove the shock hose securing clip.
   h. Remove the transmission-to-frame mounting bolt from the right-hand side.
   i. Remove the rear brake line clip from the transmission end cover stud.

16. Remove the transmission from the left-hand side.

Installation
(1985 FXST)

1. Install the mounting plate onto the transmission and leave the plate-to-transmission mounting bolts loose. Then place the transmission into the frame. Install the mounting plate bolts and tighten to 30-33 ft.-lb. (41.4-45.5 N•m).

2. Reinstall the drive chain and master link. Make sure the open end of the link faces in the opposite direction of chain travel.

3. Install the shifter rod onto the shifter linkage.

4. Install the primary housing as described in Chapter Five.

5. Install the starter housing, starter motor and starter motor mounting bracket.

6. Reconnect the wires at the starter solenoid.

7. Tighten the following bolts in order:

    a. Tighten the transmission-to-mounting plate bolts to 21-27 ft.-lb. (28.9-37.3 N•m).

    b. Install the right-hand side transmission-to-frame mounting bolt and washers and tighten to 21-27 ft.-lb. ((28.9-37.3 N•m).

8. Install the compensating sprocket, primary chain and clutch as described in Chapter Five.

9. Install and tighten the shock absorber mounting bolts as described in Chapter Thirteen.

10. Install the clutch cable.

11. Install the master cylinder reservoir mounting bracket onto the transmission end cover.

12. Reinstall the oil tank. Refill with the correct type of engine oil as described in Chapter Three.

13. Install the battery circuit breaker, starter relay and wiring onto the oil tank.

14. Reinstall the rear exhaust pipe as described in Chapter Eight.

15. Refill the transmission with the recommended type and quantity oil as described in Chapter Three.

16. Adjust the primary chain as described in Chapter Three.

17. Check primary chain alignment as described in Chapter Five under *Primary Chain Alignment*.

18. Adjust the rear drive chain or drive belt as described in Chapter Three.

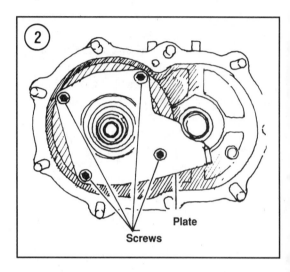

Plate

Screws

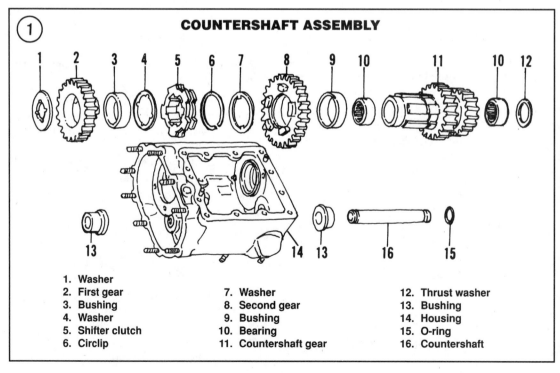

COUNTERSHAFT ASSEMBLY

1. Washer	
2. First gear	7. Washer
3. Bushing	8. Second gear
4. Washer	9. Bushing
5. Shifter clutch	10. Bearing
6. Circlip	11. Countershaft gear

12. Thrust washer
13. Bushing
14. Housing
15. O-ring
16. Countershaft

19. Adjust the clutch as described in Chapter Three.

Countershaft Disassembly

Refer to **Figure 1** for this procedure.

1. Remove the following assemblies as described in this chapter:

    a. Transmission.

    b. Shifter cover.

    c. Side cover.

    d. Shift forks.

2. Referring to **Figure 2**, remove the retaining plate screws and remove the retaining plate.

3. While holding the gear cluster (**Figure 3**) with one hand, withdraw the countershaft through the side cover (**Figure 4**).

4. Lift the gear cluster out of the housing (**Figure 5**).

5. Remove the thrust washer from the transmission case (B, **Figure 6**).

6. Remove the following parts in order:

    a. First gear (**Figure 7**).

    b. Bushing (if necessary).

    c. Washer (**Figure 8**).

    d. Shifter clutch (**Figure 9**).

7. Using a pointed tool, carefully pry the retaining ring from the gear cluster (**Figure 10**). Then remove the following parts in order:

    a. Washer (**Figure 11**).

    b. Second gear (**Figure 12**).

    c. Bushing (**Figure 13**).

8. Remove the thrust washer (12, **Figure 1**).

9. The countershaft bearings are single unit needle bearings. Replace the bearings as described under *Inspection*.

6

Inspection

1. Examine gears for worn or chipped teeth, pitting, scoring or other damage. See **Figure 14** and **Figure 15**.

2. Examine shifter clutch (**Figure 16**) for rounded edges or severe wear.

3. Check gear dogs for wear or rounded edges (**Figure 17**).

4. Examine gear and shaft splines (**Figure 18**) for wear or rounded edges.

5. Slip gears on shafts and check for free movement without appreciable play.

6. Replace worn or damaged thrust washers.

7. Check the countershaft gear needle bearings (**Figure 19**) for wear or roughness. If worn or damaged, they must be replaced as follows:

CAUTION
The Harley-Davidson countershaft gear bearing installer (part No. HD-34733) **must** *be used to install the countershaft gear bearings. The tool is*

shown in **Figure 20**. *The Harley-Davidson tool is designed so that all loading applied to the bearing during installation is placed on the outer edge of the bearing race. This prevents the type of damage that normally occurs to needle bearings when they are installed with a socket. Driving the bearings in with a socket will damage them.*

a. Support the countershaft and remove the old bearings with a bearing remover or drive them out with a long drift.

NOTE
Align both needle bearings with countershaft gear so that ID mark stamped on end of bearing faces out.

b. Install the new bearings with the Harley-Davidson tool (part No. HD-34733) and a press as shown in **Figure 20**.

8. Inspect the transmission housing bushings and oil seals as described in this chapter.

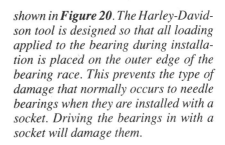

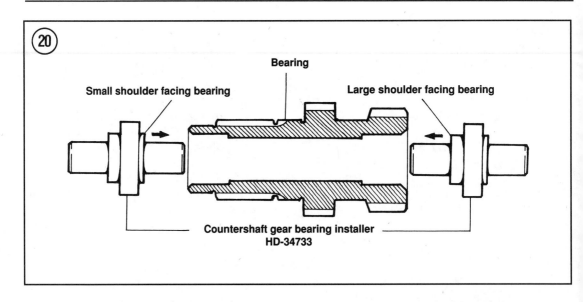

20

Small shoulder facing bearing

Bearing

Large shoulder facing bearing

Countershaft gear bearing installer
HD-34733

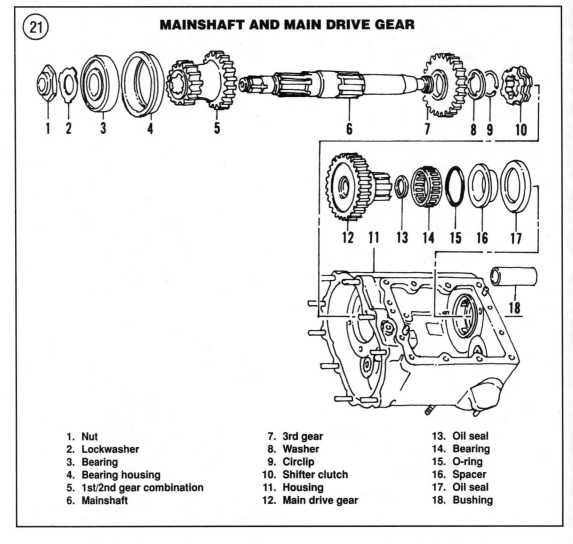

21

MAINSHAFT AND MAIN DRIVE GEAR

1. Nut	7. 3rd gear	13. Oil seal
2. Lockwasher	8. Washer	14. Bearing
3. Bearing	9. Circlip	15. O-ring
4. Bearing housing	10. Shifter clutch	16. Spacer
5. 1st/2nd gear combination	11. Housing	17. Oil seal
6. Mainshaft	12. Main drive gear	18. Bushing

Countershaft
Assembly/Installation

1. Coat all parts with engine oil prior to assembly.

2. Slide on the bushing and install second gear (**Figure 12**).

3. Install the washer (**Figure 11**).

4. Install a new circlip (**Figure 10**). Make sure the circlip seats completely in the gear cluster groove.

5. Install the shifter clutch (**Figure 9**), washer (**Figure 8**), bushing and first gear (**Figure 7**).

6. Install the thrust washer (A, **Figure 6**) into its recess.

7. Coat the countershaft end thrust washer (B, **Figure 6**) with grease and install it in the transmission case.

8. Install a new O-ring on the countershaft (15, **Figure 1**).

9. Install the gear cluster in the transmission case (**Figure 5**). Hold it in position with one hand.

10. Insert the countershaft through the gear cluster from the sprocket side of the transmission case. The O-ring should be on the sprocket side (**Figure 1**).

11. Measure the gear end play between the washer and the countershaft gear with a feeler gauge. Correct end play is listed in **Table 1**. If the end play is incorrect, replace the washer (1, **Figure 1**) with a suitable size washer. Washers are available in the following sizes: 0.074, 0.078, 0.082, 0.085, 0.090, 0.095 and 0.100 in. (1.88, 1.98, 2.08, 2.16, 2.29, 2.41 and 2.54 mm).

NOTE
If the mainshaft does not require removal, perform Step 12. If mainshaft removal is required, remove it now as described in this chapter.

12. Install the retaining plate (**Figure 2**). Tighten the screws to 7-9 ft.-lb. (9.7-12.4 N•m).

Mainshaft
Removal/Disassembly

Refer to **Figure 21** for this procedure.

1. Remove the transmission case as described in this chapter.

2. *Late 1984-1985*: Remove the bearing race from the end of the mainshaft with the Bearing Race Puller & Installation Tool (part No. HD-34902). See **Figure 22**.

3. Remove countershaft as described in this chapter.

NOTE
*The mainshaft retaining plate (**Figure 2**) was removed during countershaft removal.*

4. Using a brass or rawhide mallet, drive the mainshaft (**Figure 23**) out of the transmission case through the side cover end until second gear almost contacts the case.

6

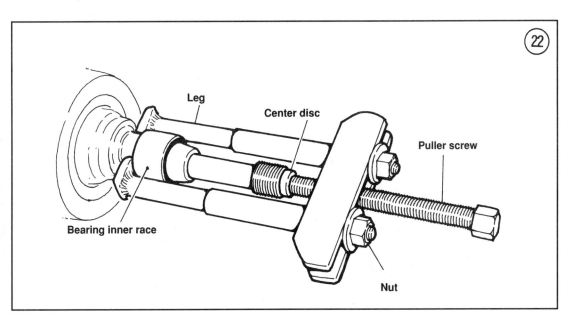

㉒

Leg

Center disc

Puller screw

Bearing inner race

Nut

5. Pry the circlip (**Figure 24**) between the washer and shifter clutch out of its groove and slide it on the mainshaft splines. See **Figure 25**.

6. Slide the mainshaft out of the case while at the same time sliding third gear (**Figure 26**), washer (**Figure 27**), circlip (**Figure 28**) and the shifter clutch (**Figure 29**) off the shaft. Then remove the parts through the case opening.

7. If necessary, remove the main drive gear from the transmission case as described in this chapter.

8. If removal of the bearing (A, **Figure 30**) and the first/second gear combination (B, **Figure 30**) is required, perform the following:

    a. Clamp the mainshaft in a vise with soft jaws (i.e., Harley-Davidson copper jaws [part No. HD-96798-43]).

    b. Bend the lockwasher tab away from the mainshaft nut, then remove the nut and lockwasher.

    c. Support first/second gear combination in a press. Then press off the bearing, bearing housing and first/second gear.

Mainshaft Inspection

1. Examine gears for worn or chipped teeth, pitting, scoring or other damage. See **Figure 31**.

2. Examine dog clutches (**Figure 32**) for rounded edges or severe wear.

3. Slip gears on shafts and check for free movement without appreciable play.

4. Replace worn or damaged thrust washers.

5. Inspect the main drive gear bushing for cracks or severe wear. If bushing is worn or damaged, have it replace by a Harley-Davidson dealer.

CAUTION
Improper bushing installation can cause bushing and mainshaft failure from improper lubrication. In addition,

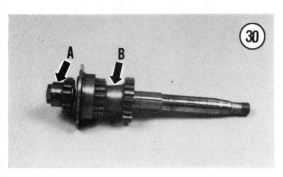

honing may be required to obtain correct main drive gear-to-mainshaft clearance after installing a new bushing. Refer bushing replacement to a Harley-Davidson dealer.

Mainshaft
Assembly/Installation

1. Coat all parts with transmission oil prior to assembly.

2. Install the main drive gear in the transmission case as described in this chapter.

3. Install the first/second combination and bearing onto the mainshaft, if previously removed, as follows:

    a. Align the lettered side on the bearing with the flange end on the bearing housing and press the bearing into the bearing housing.

    b. Slide the first/second combination gear and the bearing housing onto the mainshaft. The lettered side of the bearing must face out when installed on the mainshaft. See **Figure 21**.

NOTE
The support block described in sub-step c should have the following dimensions: 1 in. (25.4 mm)I.D. × 1 3/8 in. (34.9 mm) O.D. × 2 1/4 in. (57.1 mm) long.

    c. Install the support block over the end of the mainshaft so that it rests against the inner bearing race and place the assembly into a press. Press the bearing onto the mainshaft.

    d. Support the mainshaft in a vise with soft jaws. Install the lockwasher and nut onto the end of the mainshaft. Tighten the nut to 50-60 ft.-lb. (69-82.8 N•m), then bend the lockwasher tab over a flat on the nut to lock it.

NOTE
If the mainshaft nut was loosened only, tighten the mainshaft nut as described in Step 3, sub-step d.

4. Install the mainshaft into the transmission and slide it so that second gear barely contacts the case.

5. Slide the following parts on the mainshaft:
   a. Bushing.
   b. Third gear (**Figure 26**).
   c. Washer (**Figure 27**).
   d. New circlip (**Figure 28**).

NOTE
Make sure the circlip seats in the mainshaft groove completely.

   e. Shifter clutch (**Figure 29**).

NOTE
Install the shifter clutch so that the word HIGH on one side faces toward the main drive gear.

6. Lightly tap the mainshaft into the transmission case until the bearing housing flange seats against the case.

7. Install the countershaft as described in this chapter.

8. Install the retaining plate (**Figure 33**). Tighten the screws to 7-9 ft.-lb. (9.7-12.4 N•m).

9. *Late 1984-1985*: Install the bearing race as follows:

NOTE
The Harley-Davidson Bearing Race Puller & Installation Tool (part No. HD-34902) will be required to install the bearing race onto the mainshaft.

   a. Slide the bearing race (**Figure 34**) onto the mainshaft so that the chamfer edge on the race faces inward (toward transmission housing).

NOTE
The sleeve pilot installed in sub-step b uses left-hand threads. Turn the sleeve pilot counterclockwise to install it.

   b. Thread the sleeve pilot onto the end of the mainshaft (**Figure 34**).
   c. Slide the sleeve over the sleeve pilot and rest it against the bearing race (**Figure 35**). Then

secure the sleeve with the washer and nut (**Figure 35**).

   d. Place a wrench on the end of the sleeve pilot threads (flat portion) and tighten the nut to push the bearing race onto the mainshaft. Install the bearing race so that its inside edge is 0.200 in. (5.08 mm) from the main drive gear. Before measuring the bearing race to main drive gear clearance, pull the main drive gear towards the end of the mainshaft.

   e. When the bearing race is properly installed, remove the installation tool.

Main Drive Gear Removal/Installation

Refer to **Figure 21** for this procedure.

1. Remove the countershaft and mainshaft as described in this chapter.

2. If the countershaft sprocket was not removed during transmission case removal, remove it as follows:

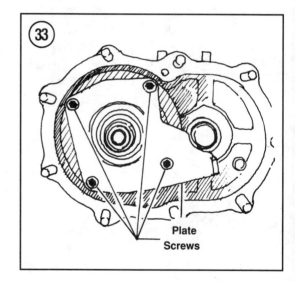

Plate
Screws

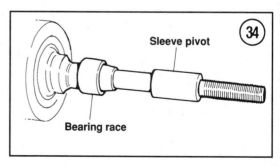

Sleeve pivot

Bearing race

a. Hold the sprocket with a chain wrench or a universal holding tool.

b. Remove the set screw that locks against the sprocket nut.

NOTE
The sprocket nut uses left-hand threads. Turn the nut counterclockwise to remove it.

c. Loosen the sprocket nut.

d. Remove the lockwasher, if used.

e. Remove the sprocket.

3. Measure the main drive gear end play with a dial indicator. Correct end play is listed in **Table 1**. If the end play is incorrect, replace the main drive gear.

4. Push the main drive gear (**Figure 36**) into the case, then remove it through the shifter cover opening.

5. Remove the main drive gear oil seal (**Figure 37**) by carefully prying it out of the transmission housing.

6. Remove the main drive gear spacer and bearing case.

7. Examine gears for worn or chipped teeth, pitting, scoring or other damage.

8. Examine gear and shaft splines for wear or rounded edges.

9. Remove the drive gear oil seal by prying it out with a sharp tool or a small screwdriver.

6

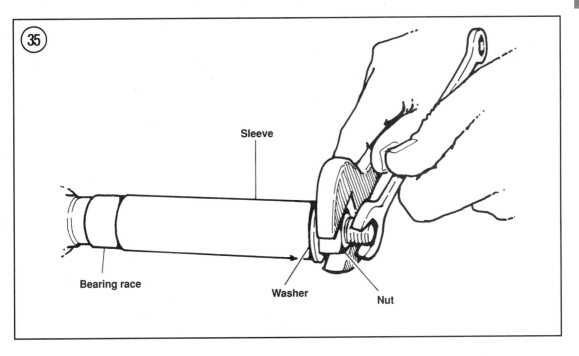

Sleeve

Bearing race

Washer

Nut

10. Check the needle bearing (14, **Figure 21**) for wear or roughness. If worn or damaged, replace as follows:

   a. Remove the spacer (16, **Figure 21**) if it was not previously removed.

   b. Press the bearing out of the transmission housing.

   c. Lubricate the new bearing's outer race with a light weight oil.

   d. Align the bearing with the bore in the housing so that the ID mark on the bearing faces toward the bearing installer.

CAUTION
The bearing installer tool described in sub-step e ensures correct bearing installation. Installing the bearing without the Harley-Davidson Main Drive Gear Bearing Installer (part No. HD-33428) can cause bearing damage.

   e. Install the bearing with a press and the Harley-Davidson tool (part No. HD-33428). The small diameter center guide on the bearing installer should fit into the bearing cavity when installing the bearing. Press the bearing in until the tool bottoms against the steel sleeve insert. When the tool bottoms out, the bearing is installed to its specified depth.

11. Install a new main drive gear oil seal and spacer as shown in **Figure 21**.

12. Carefully tap the main drive gear into the transmission housing (**Figure 38**) until the flange on the bearing housing seats against the transmission housing.

13. Lightly oil a new drive gear seal. Then install the seal into the end of the drive gear using a piece of pipe with a 1 in. (25.4 mm) I.D. and a 1 3/16 in. (30.2 mm) O.D.

Main Drive Gear Oil Seal Replacement (With Transmission Installed)

The main drive gear oil seal (**Figure 39**) can be replaced with the transmission installed in the frame.

1. Remove the countershaft sprocket.

2. Remove the primary chain case as described in Chapter Five.

3. Pry the oil seal from the transmission as shown in **Figure 40**.

4. Carefully install the new oil seal over the shaft (**Figure 41**) and align it with the seal bore in the transmission housing.

5. Install the new seal by driving it squarely into the transmission housing.

6. Install all parts previously removed.

Transmission Housing

Remove the transmission mounting plate bolts (**Figure 42**) and remove the plate. Reverse to install. Tighten the nuts securely.

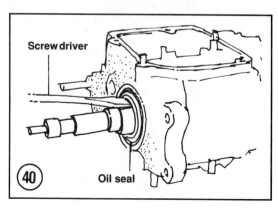

SHIFTER COVER

Removal

The shifter cover can be removed with the transmission installed on the motorcycle. If transmission repairs are also required, remove the transmission and shifter cover as one unit. This procedure describes removal of the shifter cover only.

Refer to **Figure 43** for this procedure.

1. Remove the battery and battery carrier.
2. Drain the oil tank as described in Chapter Three. Then remove the oil tank.
3. Remove the bolts and washers attaching the shift cover to the transmission; the bolt from the hole shown with an arrow in **Figure 43** can be loosened, but not removed. To remove the bolt, the shifter shaft cover must be removed first.
4. Lift the shifter cover off of the transmission housing. Discard the shifter cover gasket.
5. Installation is the reverse of these steps, noting the following.
6. Install a new shift cover gasket during installation.

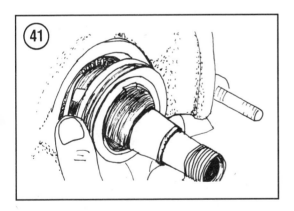

7. Lightly coat the shift cover mounting bolts with Loctite Lock N' Seal. Tighten the mounting bolt to 13-16 ft.-lb. (17.9-22.1 N•m).
8. Adjust the shift linkage as described in this chapter.

Disassembly

Refer to **Figure 43** for this procedure.

1. Remove the neutral indicator switch and washer.
2. Remove the shifter shaft cover bolts and washers.
3. Remove the shift lever bolt and washer.
4. Remove the shifter linkage assembly from the transmission cover.
5. Remove remaining shifter cover bolt.
6. If necessary, remove the top plug from the shift cover as follows:
   a. Drill a 1/4 in. hole through the top plug. Drill only far enough to penetrate completely through the top plug.
   b. Pry the top plug off of the shift cover with a punch inserted through the drilled hole.
   c. Discard the top plug; a new plug must be installed during reassembly.
7. Remove the shift cam retaining ring and washer through the top plug hole opening and remove the shifter cam and pawl assembly.
8. Disassemble the shifter cover (**Figure 44**) as follows:
   a. Remove the cam follower and spring from the cam follower body.
   b. Pry back the lockwasher tabs and remove the cam follower body bolts.
   c. Lift the cam follower body out of the shift cover.
   d. Remove the screws, pawl stops and remove the long springs.

Inspection

1. Thoroughly clean all parts (except neutral switch) in solvent, then blow dry.

NOTE
When parts have been disassembled and cleaned, visually inspect them for any signs of wear, cracks, breakage or other damage. If there is any doubt as to the condition of any part, replace it with a new one.

SHIFTER COVER

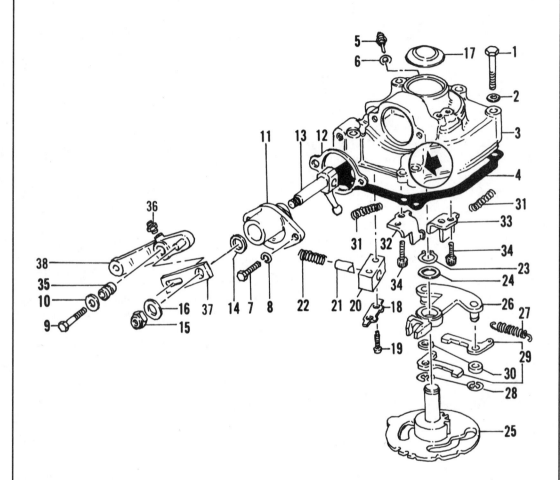

1. Bolt	14. Oil seal	
2. Washer	15. Nut	
3. Shift cover	16. Washer	27. Shifter pawl spring
4. Gasket	17. Plug	28. Retaining ring
5. Neutral indicator switch	18. Lockplate	29. Pawl
6. Washer	19. Bolt	30. Spacer
7. Bolt	20. Plunger body	31. Pawl carrier spring
8. Lockwasher	21. Plunger	32. Shift pawl stop, rear
9. Bolt	22. Spring	33. Shift pawl stop, front
10. Washer	23. Retaining ring	34. Socket head screw
11. Shifter shaft cover	24. Thrust washer	35. Bushing
12. Gasket	25. Shifter cam	36. Grease fitting
13. Shifter shaft	26. Pawl carrier	37. Shift lever arm (1985 FXST)
		38. Shift lever (1985 FXST)

2. Replace any circlips and retaining rings that were removed during disassembly as removal sometimes deforms and weakens them.

3. Check the shift cam slots for worn or grooved cam slots. Excessive wear will result in difficult shifting.

4. Check pawl stops for breakage or surface cracks.

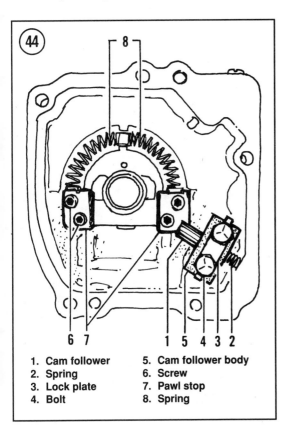

1.	Cam follower	5.	Cam follower body
2.	Spring	6.	Screw
3.	Lock plate	7.	Pawl stop
4.	Bolt	8.	Spring

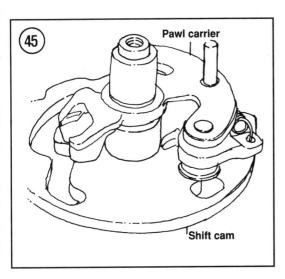

Pawl carrier

Shift cam

Assembly

1. Lubricate the pawl stop springs with multi-purpose grease.

2. Install the pawl stops and secure with the Allen bolts.

3. Install the pawl stop springs.

4. Install the cam follower body, lockwasher and bolts. Tighten the bolts and bend the lockwasher tabs over the bolts to lock them.

5. Install the spring and cam follower into the cam follower body.

6. Coat the neutral switch threads with Loctite Pipe Sealant With Teflon. Install the neutral switch and washer and tighten to 5-10 ft.-lb. (6.9-13.8 N•m).

7. Refer to **Figure 45**. Slide the pawl assembly on the shift cam. Engage the pawls with the shift cam gear teeth.

8. Install the shift cam and pawl assembly into the shift cover. Position the tab on the pawl assembly between the pawl stop springs.

9. Install the shift cam washer and a new circlip.

10. Coat a new top plug with Seal-All. Then place the top plug in the cover and seat it with a ball peen hammer.

11. Assemble the shift linkage using a new circlip. Tighten all linkage bolts securely.

SHIFT FORKS

Removal/Disassembly

Refer to **Figure 46** for this procedure.

1. Remove the shifter cover as described in this chapter.

2. Remove the shifter finger rollers (**Figure 47**) from each shifter finger.

3. Remove the circlip (**Figure 48**) from the end of the shifter fork shaft.

4. Tap the shifter fork shaft with a drift and remove it from the housing (**Figure 49**).

5. Remove the shift forks (**Figure 50**).

NOTE
Do not disassemble the forks unless replacement of a part or parts is necessary.

NOTE
When disassembling the shift fork assemblies, label each sub-assembly as

they are not interchangeable (Figure 51).

6. Loosen and remove the shift finger nuts (**Figure 52**) and remove them. Then disassemble the shift forks in the order shown in **Figure 46**.

7. Repeat Step 4 for the opposite shift finger assembly.

Inspection

1. Clean all parts in solvent.

2. Inspect each shift fork (**Figure 52**) for signs of wear or damage. Make sure the forks slide smoothly on the shifter fork shaft. Replace any worn forks.

3. Check for any arc-shaped wear or burn marks on the shift forks (**Figure 53**). If this is apparent, the shift fork has come in contact with the gear, indicating that the fingers are worn beyond use and the fork must be replaced.

4. Roll the shift fork shaft (**Figure 54**) on a flat surface and check for bending. If the shaft is bent, it must be replaced.

5. Install each shift finger on the shift shaft (**Figure 55**). The shift fingers should slide smoothly without any sign of binding.

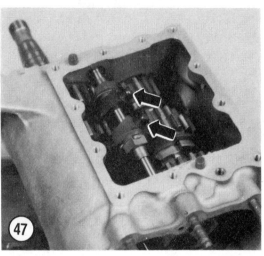

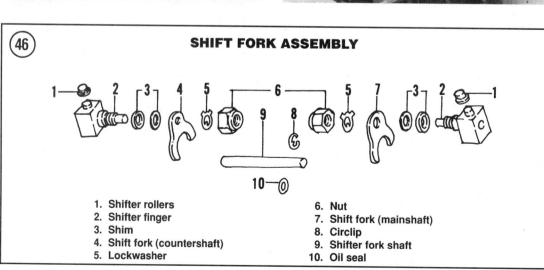

SHIFT FORK ASSEMBLY

1. Shifter rollers
2. Shifter finger
3. Shim
4. Shift fork (countershaft)
5. Lockwasher
6. Nut
7. Shift fork (mainshaft)
8. Circlip
9. Shifter fork shaft
10. Oil seal

Assembly

NOTE
If any part was replaced, the shifter clutch clearance must be checked and adjusted. Because this procedure requires special tools, refer clearance check to a Harley-Davidson dealer.

1. Coat all bearing and sliding surfaces with assembly oil.

2. Install the spacer(s), shift fork, lockwasher and nut on the shift finger. Tighten the nut to 10-12 ft.-lb. (13.8-16.5 N•m). Bend the lockwasher tab against the nut to lock it.

CAUTION
Do not exceed the torque specifications in Step 2 as this could cause the shift finger to bind on the shift shaft.

3. Position the shift fork assemblies (**Figure 56** and **Figure 57**) in the transmission case. See **Figure 50**. Engage the shift forks with their respective gears.

4. Slide the shift shaft through the transmission case (**Figure 58**) and through the shift fork assemblies (**Figure 49**). Secure the shaft with a new circlip (**Figure 59**). See **Figure 48**.

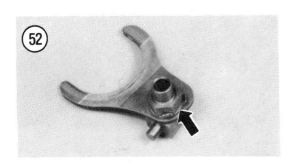

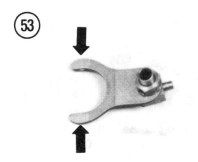

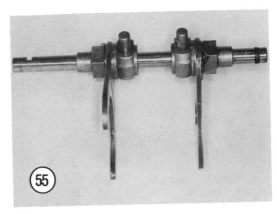

5. Install the shift rollers (**Figure 47**) onto the shift fingers.

6. If any part was replaced, have the shift fork adjustment checked by a Harley-Davidson dealer.

KICKSTARTER AND STARTER CLUTCH

Removal/Disassembly

Refer to **Figure 60** for this procedure.

1. Disconnect the negative battery cable.
2. Perform the following:
   a. Remove the exhaust pipes. See Chapter Eight.
   b. Remove the rear brake line support clip.
   c. Remove the starter motor bracket.
3. Drain the transmission oil as described in Chapter Three.
4. Remove the kickstarter pedal.
5. Remove the side cover mounting bolts and remove the side cover (**Figure 61**).
6. If necessary, disassemble the side cover as described in this chapter.
7. Installation is the reverse of these steps. Note the following.
8. Install a new side cover gasket.
9. Pull the pushrod assembly partway out as shown in **Figure 62**.
10. Position the release lever to the left of the cover as shown in A, **Figure 63**.
11. Align the pushrod oil slinger (**Figure 64**) with the release lever mechanism (B, **Figure 63**) and install the side cover. The lever should face as shown in **Figure 65**.
12. Install the side cover mounting bolts and tighten them to 13-16 ft.-lb. (17.9-22.1 N•m).
13. Refill the transmission with the correct type and quantity oil as described in Chapter Three.

14. Reinstall all parts previously removed. If a brake line was disconnected, bleed the rear brake as described in Chapter Fourteen.

Disassembly

Refer to **Figure 60** for this procedure.

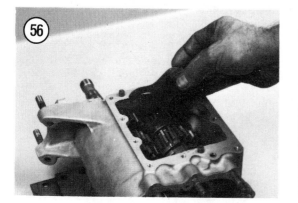

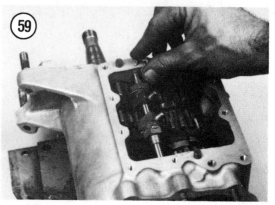

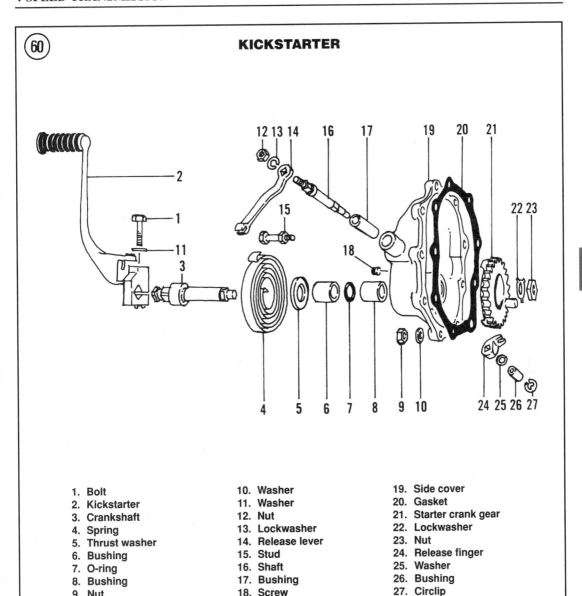

KICKSTARTER

1. Bolt
2. Kickstarter
3. Crankshaft
4. Spring
5. Thrust washer
6. Bushing
7. O-ring
8. Bushing
9. Nut

10. Washer
11. Washer
12. Nut
13. Lockwasher
14. Release lever
15. Stud
16. Shaft
17. Bushing
18. Screw

19. Side cover
20. Gasket
21. Starter crank gear
22. Lockwasher
23. Nut
24. Release finger
25. Washer
26. Bushing
27. Circlip

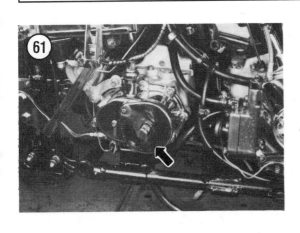

1. Clamp the end of the kickstarter shaft in a vise with soft jaws. Then from inside the cover, pry back the kickstarter shaft lockwasher and remove the nut (A, **Figure 66**).

2. Using a universal type claw puller (**Figure 67**), remove the kickstarter gear. See B, **Figure 66**.

3. Support the side cover in a vise or on wood blocks. Do not block the kickstarter shaft or spring. Drive the kickstarter shaft out of the cover using a plastic hammer. Remove the thrust washer (11, **Figure 57**).

4. Remove the release lever nut and washer.

5. Pull the release lever off of the shaft with a universal type claw puller.

6. Remove the clip. Then remove the shaft from the cover.

7. Remove the release finger and washer.

Inspection

1. Clean all components thoroughly with solvent. Remove any gasket residue from the cover-to-transmission machined surfaces. Check the threads in the transmission case to be sure they are clean. If dirty or damaged, use a tap to true up the threads and remove any deposits.

2. Visually check the shaft surfaces for cracks, deep scoring, excessive wear or heat discoloration.

3. Check the kickstarter gear for worn or damaged gear teeth.

4. If oil leaks out of the side cover along the kickstarter shaft, the oil seal must be replaced by removing the front bushing with a blind hole bearing

remover and slide hammer. Have the new bushings installed by a Harley-Davidson dealer or machine shop as a press is required.

5. Check the kickstarter spring. If it is damaged or broken, replace it by performing the following:

   a. Remove the kickstarter shaft as described in this chapter.

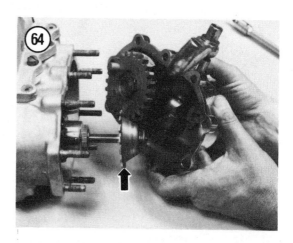

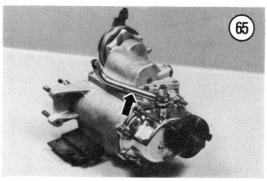

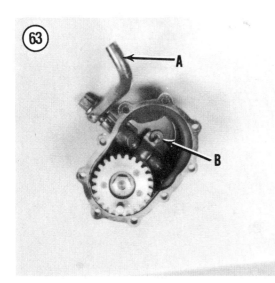

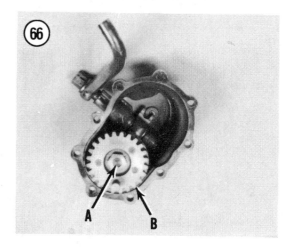

b. Lift the outer spring hook off of the shaft spring stop.

c. Tap the spring off the kickstarter shaft with a punch and hammer.

d. Install the new spring, so that the outer spring hook faces to the left-hand side when looking at the kickstarter crank end. See **Figure 68**.

STARTER CRANK GEAR

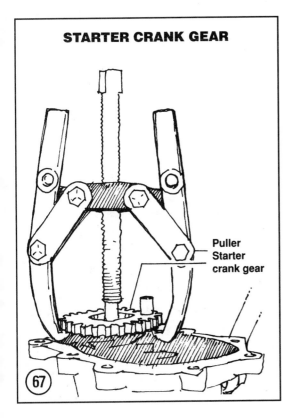

Puller
Starter
crank gear

67

68

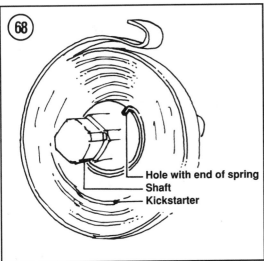

Hole with end of spring
Shaft
Kickstarter

Assembly

Refer to **Figure 60** for this procedure.

1. Assemble the release finger as follows:
   a. Install the washer and release finger into the side cover.
   b. Insert the release lever shaft into the side cover and through the release finger and washer. Secure the shaft with a new circlip.
   c. Install the release lever. Then install the lockwasher and the nut. Tighten the nut until the release lever bottoms on the shaft.

2. Install the washer on the kickstarter shaft so that the chamfered side of the washer faces the spring.

3. See **Figure 69**. Install the kickstarter gear as follows:
   a. Turn the kickstarter shaft so that the flat side is straight up (12 o'clock).
   b. Slide the kickstarter gear onto the shaft. When installed correctly, the kickstarter gear dowel pin is in the 7 o'clock position.

4. Hold the kickstarter shaft in a vise with soft jaws as during disassembly.

5. Engage the end of the kickstarter spring with the stud on the side cover.

6. Press the kickstarter gear onto the kickstarter shaft.

6

69

12 o'clock position

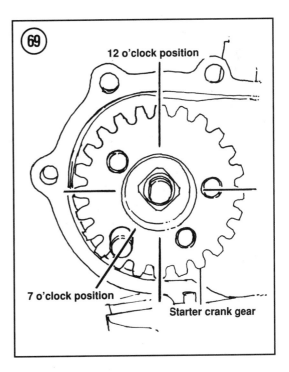

7 o'clock position

Starter crank gear

7. Install the kickstarter gear lockwasher and nut. Tighten the nut to 30-40 ft.-lb. (41.4-55.2 N•m). Bend the lockwasher tab over the nut to lock it.

Starter Clutch
Removal/Inspection/Installation

Refer to **Figure 70** for this procedure.

1. Remove the kickstarter side cover as described in this chapter.

2. Remove the pushrod (**Figure 62**).

3. Lock the transmission into 2 gears at once.

4. Bend the lockwasher tab away from the starter clutch nut (**Figure 71**).

5. Remove the starter clutch with the Harley-Davidson starter clutch puller (HD-95650-42). See **Figure 72**.

6. Remove the Woodruff key, starter clutch gear and spring.

7. Check the starter gear and starter clutch teeth. Teeth should be sharp and show no signs of cracking, scoring or excessive wear. Replace starter clutch and starter gear if teeth are rounded or if the kickstarter has been slipping.

8. Visually check the starter clutch for cracks, deep scoring and excessive wear.

9. Slide the starter gear on the mainshaft and check play by hand; the gear should just be loose enough to slide under spring pressure. If gear is loose, re-

place the bushing in the gear with a press. Do not attempt to drive a new bushing into the gear with a socket and hammer.

10. Installation is the reverse of these steps. Note the following:

   a. Lubricate the mainshaft with engine oil.

   b. Install the spring and starter gear onto the mainshaft.

   c. Push the starter gear towards the transmission and release it. The spring should be able to push the gear forward. If the gear is tight, the gear bushing should be reamed. Refer this service to a Harley-Davidson dealer.

   d. Press the starter clutch onto the mainshaft.

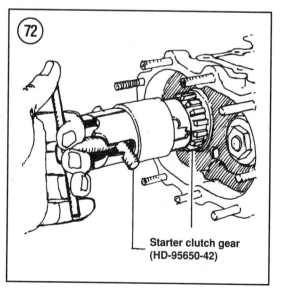

Starter clutch gear (HD-95650-42)

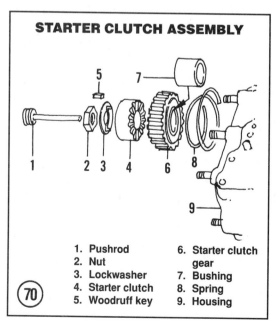

STARTER CLUTCH ASSEMBLY

1. Pushrod
2. Nut
3. Lockwasher
4. Starter clutch
5. Woodruff key
6. Starter clutch gear
7. Bushing
8. Spring
9. Housing

e. Tighten the starter clutch nut to 34-42 ft.-lb. (46.9-57.9 N•m). Bend the lockwasher tab over the nut to lock it.

SIDE COVER (ELECTRIC START)

Removal/Disassembly

Refer to **Figure 73** for this procedure.

1. Disconnect the negative battery cable.

2. Drain the transmission oil as described in Chapter Three.

3. Remove the exhaust system as described in Chapter Eight.

4. Remove the rear master cylinder reservoir. See Chapter Fourteen.

5. Remove the starter bracket.

6. Remove the side cover mounting bolts and remove the side cover and gasket.

7. If necessary, disassemble the side cover as described in this chapter.

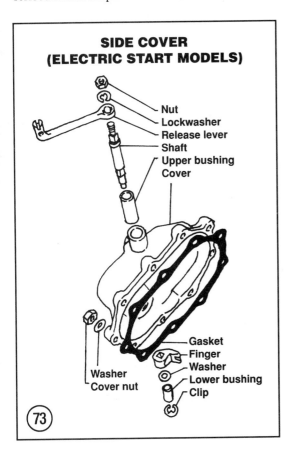

SIDE COVER (ELECTRIC START MODELS)

Nut
Lockwasher
Release lever
Shaft
Upper bushing
Cover
Gasket
Finger
Washer
Lower bushing
Clip
Washer
Cover nut

(73)

8. Installation is the reverse of these steps. Note the following.

9. Install a new side cover gasket.

10. Pull the pushrod assembly partway out as shown in **Figure 62**.

11. Position the release lever to the left of the cover as shown in A, **Figure 63**.

12. Align the pushrod oil slinger (**Figure 64**) with the release lever mechanism (B, **Figure 63**) and install the side cover. The lever should face as shown in **Figure 65**.

13. Install the side cover mounting bolts and tighten them to 13-16 ft.-lb. (17.9-22.1 N•m).

14. Refill the transmission with the correct type and quantity oil as described in Chapter Three.

Disassembly/Inspection/Reassembly

Refer to **Figure 73** for this procedure.

1. Remove the release lever nut and washer.

2. Pull the release lever off of the shaft with a universal type claw puller.

3. Remove the clip. Then remove the shaft from the cover.

4. Remove the release finger and washer.

5. Clean all components thoroughly with solvent. Remove any gasket residue from the cover-to-transmission machined surfaces. Check the threads in the transmission case to be sure they are clean. If dirty or damaged, use a tap to true up the threads and remove any deposits.

6. Visually check the shaft surfaces for cracks, deep scoring, excessive wear or heat discoloration.

7. Slide the shaft release lever shaft into the side cover. Check the shaft-to-bushing wear by moving the shaft back and forth. If there is excessive shaft wear, replace the upper and lower bushings with a blind hole bearing remover and slide hammer. Use a press to install the new bushing.

8. Assemble the release finger as follows:

a. Install the washer and release finger into the side cover.

b. Insert the release lever shaft into the side cover and through the release finger and washer. Secure the shaft with a new circlip.

c. Install the release lever. Then install the lockwasher and the nut. Tighten the nut until the release lever bottoms on the shaft.

6

SHIFTER ADJUSTMENT

Shifter adjustment is required to compensate for component wear or whenever the transmission has been removed.

Shift Linkage Adjustment

Shift linkage should operate so that the shift pedal can travel to its full limit without interference when making gear changes. If necessary, perform the following. See **Figure 74**.

1. Remove the retaining clip.
2. Slide the shift linkage rod off of the clevis pin.
3. Loosen the locknut and turn the shift linkage rod as required so that the shift linkage can travel its full limit without interference.
4. Tighten the locknut.
5. Reconnect the shift linkage rod and secure it with the retaining clip.

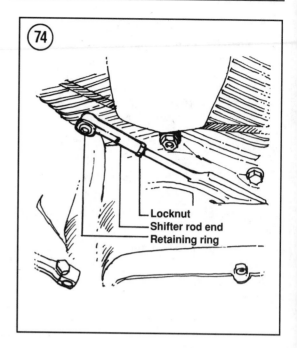

Locknut
Shifter rod end
Retaining ring

Table 1 TRANSMISSION SPECIFICATIONS

Item	Specification		Wear limit	
	in.	mm	in.	mm
Mainshaft main drive gear				
End play				
1984	0.010-0.025	0.25-0.63	0.025	0.63
1985	0.010-0.035	0.25-0.89	0.035	0.89
Mainshaft bushing	0.0018-0.0032	0.046-0.081	0.004	0.10
Mainshaft				
Third gear end play				
1984	0.000-0.0017	0.00-0.04	0.020	0.51
1985	0.005-0.021	0.13-0.53	0.021	0.53
Shift fork clutch gear spacing	0.100-0.110	2.54-2.79	0.110	2.79
Countershaft				
Gear end play	0.004-0.012	0.10-0.30	0.015	0.38
Second gear end play	0.003-0.017	0.08-0.43	0.020	0.51
Shift fork clutch gear spacing	0.080-0.090	2.03-2.29	0.090	2.29
Gear backlash	0.003-0.006	0.08-0.15	0.010	0.25

6

Table 2 TRANSMISSION TIGHTENING TORQUES

Item	ft.-lb.	N·m
Drain screw	12-15	16.5-20.7
Primary cover screws	18-22	24.8-30.4
Transmission sprocket	80-90	110.4-124.2
Mainshaft ball bearing nut	50-60	69-82.8
Retaining plate screws	7-9	9.7-12.4
Shift clutch nut*	34-42	46.9-57.9
Starter crankcase nut	18-22	24.8-30.4
Transmission end cover stud nut	13-16	17.9-22.1
Shift fork nut	10-12	13.8-16.5
Neutral switch	5-10	6.9-13.8
Top cover bolts	13-16	17.9-22.1
Frame to transmission bolt	21-27	28.9-37.3
Sprocket nut locking screw	50-60 in.-lb.	5.7-6.9
Countershaft nut (1984)	55-65	75.9-89.7
Transmission mounting fasteners	See text	—

* Kickstarter models only.

5-SPEED TRANSMISSION

The 5-speed Harley-Davidson transmission and shifter assembly is mounted in a separate housing and can be completely disassembled and serviced without having to disassemble the engine or remove the transmission housing. The 5-speed transmission is used on all 1986 and later Softail models.

The transmission service procedures in this chapter are arranged by sub-assembly—shifter assembly and transmission. Before servicing the transmission or shifter assembly, make sure the problem is not due to a faulty clutch adjustment or a problem with the primary drive system.

An external shift linkage assembly connects the gearshift lever to the transmission. The shift linkage assembly requires adjustment to compensate from normal wear to the linkage/shifter mechanism components or when the transmission housing was removed from the bike.

This chapter provides service procedures for the 5-speed transmission. **Tables 1-3** are found at the end of the chapter.

PRODUCTION GEARS
(1994 MODELS)

During the 1994 production year, two types of transmission gear sets were produced by Harley-Davidson—domestic ratios (U.S., Canada and Japan) and HDI ratios (Harley-Davidson International). Domestic ratio gears can be identified by a 0.03 in. (0.76 mm) radius groove machined in the center of each gear tooth. Motorcycles with HDI ratios are equipped with high contact ratio (HCR) gears installed on the mainshaft and countershaft 2nd through 5th gears. HDI ratio gears do not have grooved gear teeth.

> *CAUTION*
> *Domestic and HDI ratio gears should not be intermixed. Running both types of gears in a single transmission assembly will damage mating gears.*

SHIFT CAM ASSEMBLY

The shifter cam is mounted to the top of the transmission case, directly underneath the transmission top cover (**Figure 1**).

> *NOTE*
> *Late 1991 and later models are equipped with a new style shifter cam (8, **Figure 1**) that does not require the use of the inner thrust washer (11, **Figure 1**). Early and late style shifter cams can be identified by the neutral indicator actuator (**Figure 2**) mounted on the shifter cam. A cast neutral indicator actuator is used on early style shifter cams. Later style shifter cams use a pressed-in pin. In addition, on models with the late style shifter cam, 2 locating dowel pins are used to locate the left-hand support block (10, **Figure 1**) to the transmission case.*

Removal

1. Disconnect the negative battery cable.

2. Remove the battery.

3. Drain and remove the engine oil tank (Chapter Three).

4. Disconnect the clutch cable at the engine (**Figure 3**).

5. Disconnect the neutral switch wire at the switch (**Figure 4**).

6. Remove the transmission top cover mounting bolts and remove the cover and gasket. See **Figure 5**.

7. Remove the shift cam mounting bolts (**Figure 6**) and lift the shift cam assembly out of the transmission. See **Figure 7**.

8. Slide the left side support block (**Figure 8**) off the shift cam. On late 1991-on models, remove the 2 dowel pins.

NOTE
On 1986-early 1991 models, label all of the thrust washers removed in the fol-

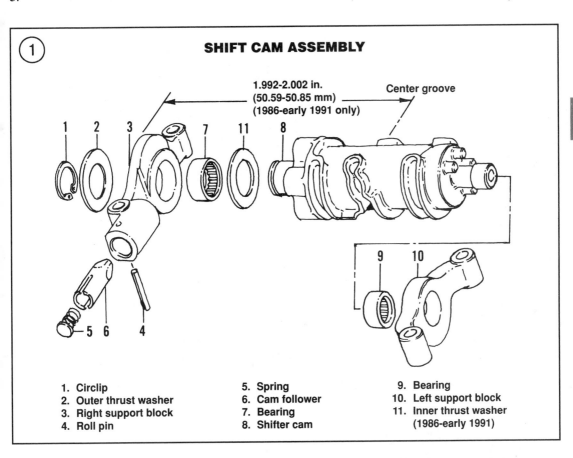

SHIFT CAM ASSEMBLY

1.992-2.002 in. (50.59-50.85 mm) (1986-early 1991 only)

Center groove

1. Circlip
2. Outer thrust washer
3. Right support block
4. Roll pin
5. Spring
6. Cam follower
7. Bearing
8. Shifter cam
9. Bearing
10. Left support block
11. Inner thrust washer (1986-early 1991)

7

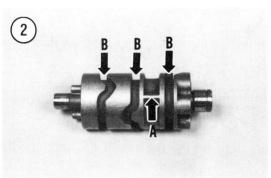

lowing steps so that you don't mix them up during reassembly.

9. Refer to **Figure 9**. Remove the shift cam circlip (A) and outer thrust washer (B).

10. Remove the right-hand support block (**Figure 10**).

11. On 1986-early 1991 models, remove the inner thrust washer (**Figure 11**) from the shift cam.

Inspection

1. Clean all parts (except support block bearings) in solvent.

2. Check the grooves in the shift cam (**Figure 2**) for wear or roughness. If any of the groove profiles have excessive wear or damage, replace the shift cam.

3. Check the support block bearings. See **Figure 12** and **Figure 13**. Make sure they operate smoothly with no signs of wear or damage.

4. Check the support blocks for wear or damage. Replace if necessary.

Installation

Refer to **Figure 1** when performing this procedure.

1. Coat all bearing and sliding surfaces with assembly oil.

2A. On 1986-early 1991 models, install the inner thrust washer (**Figure 11**) and right support block (**Figure 10**) on the shifter cam.

2B. On late 1991-on models, install the right support block (**Figure 10**) on the shifter cam.

3. On 1986-early 1991 models, check shift drum position as follows:

  a. Install the shifter drum/right support block onto the transmission case. Engage the right support block with its dowel pins.

  b. Turn the shifter drum to its neutral position. The neutral indicator ramp mounted on the shifter drum, as shown in **Figure 16**, can be used as a reference point.

  c. Push the shifter drum so that it fits snug against the right support block thrust washer.

  d. Measure from the outer bearing support machined surface to the nearest edge of the center shifter cam groove as shown in **Figure 16**. The correct distance is 1.992-2.002 in. (50.59-50.85 mm).

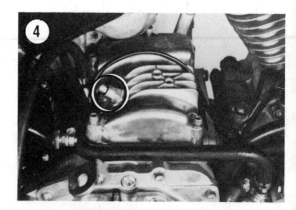

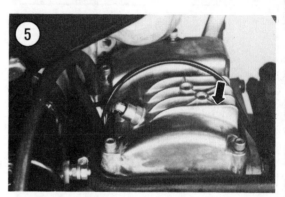

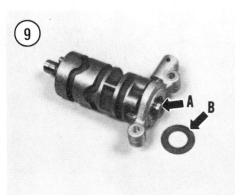

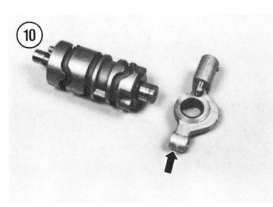

e. If the distance is incorrect, replace the inner thrust washer (11, **Figure 1**) with a different thickness thrust washer. Different thickness thrust washers are available from Harley-Davidson dealers.

f. Remove the shifter drum/right support block from the transmission case.

4. Install the outer thrust washer (B, **Figure 9**) and a new circlip (A, **Figure 9**).

NOTE
*After installing the circlip, make sure the outer thrust washer (2, **Figure 1**) can be rotated by hand.*

5. Measure shifter cam end play as follows:

a. Install the shifter drum/right support block onto the transmission case. Engage the right support block with its dowel pins.

b. Measure end play between the outer thrust washer and shifter cam (**Figure 17**). Correct end play measurement is 0.001-0.004 in. (0.025-0.10 mm).

c. If necessary, correct end play by replacing the outer thrust washer (2, **Figure 1**) with a suitable thickness thrust washer.

CAUTION
*On 1986-early 1991 models, do not correct shifter cam end play by changing the inner thrust washer (11, **Figure 1**) clearance. This washer is used to set shift cam position only. Late 1991-on models do not use the inner thrust washer.*

NOTE
Inner and outer thrust washers are available from Harley-Davidson dealers in the following thicknesses: 0.017 in. (0.43 mm), 0.020 in. (0.51 mm), 0.022 in. (0.56 mm), 0.025 in. (0.63 mm), 0.028 in. (0.71 mm), 0.031 in. (0.79 mm), 0.035 in. (0.89 mm) and 0.039 in (0.99 mm).

d. Remove the shifter drum/right support block from the transmission case.

6. Install the left support block (**Figure 8**) onto the shifter cam.

NOTE
The numbers on the left support block should face down (toward transmission) when shifter cam assembly is installed.

7. Align the shift fork pins (**Figure 14**) with the shifter cam slots and install the shifter cam into position. See **Figure 7**. On 1986-early 1991 models, engage the transmission case dowel pins with the right support block mounting holes. On late 1991-on models, engage the left and right support block mounting holes with the transmission case dowel pins.

8. Engage the shift lever with the shifter cam (**Figure 15**).

9. Install the shifter cam mounting bolts (**Figure 6**). Tighten bolts in a crisscross pattern to 7-9 ft.-lb. (9-12 N•m).

NOTE
On 1986-early 1991 models, check that the left support block is not cocked or binding on its bearing.

CAUTION
On all models, overtightening the shifter cam mounting bolts can distort

the cam follower and cause shifting problems.

10. Perform the *Gear Engagement Check/Adjustment* procedure in this chapter.

11. Install the top cover (**Figure 5**) using a new gasket.

12. Reconnect the neutral switch wire (**Figure 4**) at the switch.

13. Install all parts previously removed.

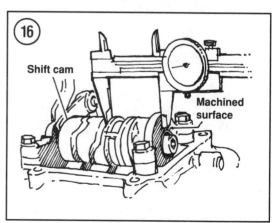

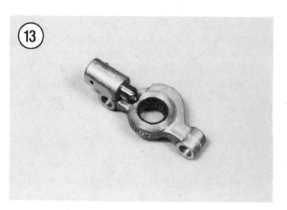

SHIFT FORKS

Removal

Refer to **Figure 18** when performing this procedure.

1. Remove the shift cam as described in this chapter.

Shifter cam

Outer
thrust
washer

17

2. Remove the right-hand side shift shaft case plug (**Figure 19**).

NOTE
Mark each shift fork during removal as they are different and must be reinstalled in their original position.

3. Slide the shift shaft (**Figure 20**) out of the transmission case and remove the shift forks (**Figure 21**) from the transmission.

Inspection

1. Inspect each shift fork (**Figure 22**) for signs of wear or damage. Replace worn or damaged shift forks as required.
2A. On 1986-1992 models, check the shift forks for wear and bending. Place the shift forks on a flat surface at the points where they contact the sliding gear grooves (A, **Figure 23**) and measure flatness with a feeler gauge. Replace any shift fork that is worn or bent more than 0.020 in. (0.51 mm).
2B. On 1993-on models, measure the width of each shift fork finger where it contacts the sliding gear groove (**Figure 18**). The finger width service limit

7

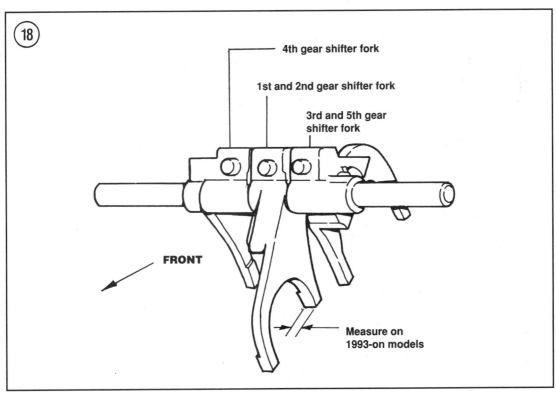

18

4th gear shifter fork

1st and 2nd gear shifter fork

3rd and 5th gear
shifter fork

FRONT

Measure on
1993-on models

is 0.165 in. (4.19 mm). Replace shift fork(s) if finger width is equal to or less than the service limit.

3. Check for any arc-shaped wear or burn marks on the shift forks (B, **Figure 23**). If this is apparent, the shift fork has come in contact with the gear, indicating that the fingers are worn beyond use and the forks must be replaced.

4. Roll the shift fork shaft on a flat surface and check for bending. If the shaft is bent, it must be replaced.

5. Install each shift fork on the shift shaft. The shift fingers should slide smoothly without any sign of binding.

Assembly

1. Coat all bearing and sliding surfaces with assembly oil.

2. Refer to **Figure 18** and **Figure 24**. Install the shift forks as follows:

    a. Insert the No. 1 shift fork into the mainshaft first gear.

    b. Install the No. 2 shift fork into the countershaft third gear.

    c. Install the No. 3 shift fork into the mainshaft second gear.

3. Insert the shift shaft through the transmission case (**Figure 20**), through each of the 3 shift forks and into the transmission case.

4. Apply a light coat of Loctite Pipe Sealant With Teflon on the shift shaft plug threads and install it (**Figure 19**). Tighten the plug securely.

5. Check that forks move smoothly when the gear position is changed by hand.

6. Install the shift cam as described in this chapter.

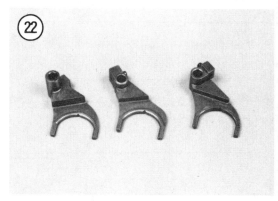

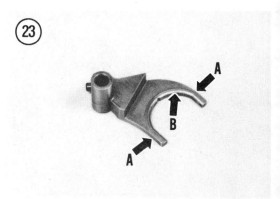

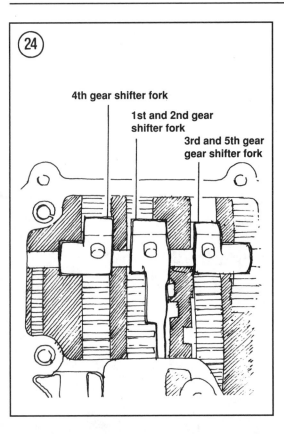

4th gear shifter fork

1st and 2nd gear
shifter fork

3rd and 5th gear
gear shifter fork

TRANSMISSION

The transmission assembly can be removed without removing the transmission case or the engine assembly from the frame.

Removal

1. Remove the exhaust pipes. See Chapter Eight.
2. Drain the transmission oil as described in Chapter Three.
3. Remove the clutch as described in Chapter Five.
4. Remove the shift forks as described in this chapter. See **Figure 24**.
5. Remove the clutch arm (**Figure 25**).
6A. *1986*: Remove the transmission side cover (**Figure 26**).
6B. *1987-on*: Remove the transmission side cover as described in this chapter.
7. Remove the roller (**Figure 27**) and pushrod (**Figure 28**).
8. Turn the transmission by hand and mesh the transmission into 2 gears at the same time so that the shafts cannot rotate.

7

9. Loosen the countershaft and mainshaft locknuts and spacers. See **Figure 29**.

NOTE
*On all models, the transmission can be removed without removing the main drive gear. However, if main drive gear removal is required, the Bearing Race Puller and Installation Tool (HD-34902) will be required. See **Figure 30** and **Figure 31**.*

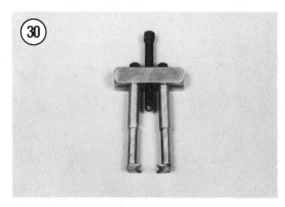

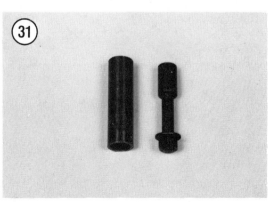

NOTE
The main drive gear bearing will have to be replaced if the main drive gear is removed. Removal of the main drive gear damages its bearing.

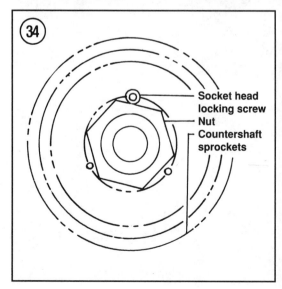

10. To remove the main drive gear:
  a. Remove the primary chain case as described in Chapter Five.
  b. Install the bearing race puller onto the bearing inner race as shown in **Figure 32**.

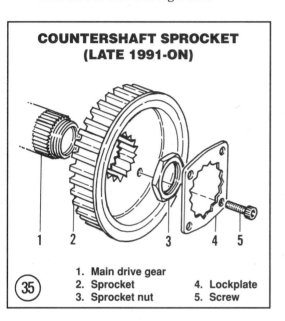

COUNTERSHAFT SPROCKET (LATE 1991-ON)

1 2 3 4 5

1. Main drive gear
2. Sprocket
3. Sprocket nut
4. Lockplate
5. Screw

(35)

(36)

A

B

(37)

  c. Remove the bearing inner race from the transmission mainshaft. See **Figure 33**.
  d. On 1986-early 1991 models, remove the sprocket nut locking screw (**Figure 34**). On late 1991-on models, remove the 2 locking scews and lockplate (**Figure 35**).
  e. Have an assistant apply the rear brake.

NOTE
The countershaft nut uses left-hand threads. Turn the nut clockwise to remove it.

  f. Using a deep socket, loosen and remove the countershaft nut (A, **Figure 36**).

NOTE
Harley-Davidson dealers sell a deep socket (HD-94660-37) that can be used to remove the countershaft nut.

  g. Loosen the rear axle adjuster to obtain as much drive belt slack as possible.
  h. Remove the countershaft sprocket (B, **Figure 36**).

CAUTION
Wrap the mainshaft clutch hub splines on 1990 and later models with tape to prevent the splines from damaging the inner primary housing oil seal.

11. Remove the transmission access cover mounting fasteners (**Figure 37**). Then remove the access cover (**Figure 38**) together with the countershaft and mainshaft as an assembly. See **Figure 39**.

Transmission Shafts
Removal/Installation

Refer to **Figure 40** for this procedure.
1. Remove the countershaft and mainshaft nuts (**Figure 41**) loosened during transmission removal. Then remove the washers and transmission shafts from the access cover. See **Figure 42**.
2. Remove the pushrod and clutch release bearing assembly from the mainshaft.
3. Assemble by reversing these steps. Tighten the countershaft and mainshaft nuts after installing the transmission assembly into the transmission housing.

7

Countershaft
Disassembly/Reassembly

Refer to **Figure 40** for this procedure.
1. Disassemble the countershaft as follows:
    a. Spacer (**Figure 43**).
    b. Countershaft 4th gear (**Figure 44**).
    c. Spacer (**Figure 45**).
    d. Countershaft 1st gear (**Figure 46**).
    e. Bearings (**Figure 47**).
    f. Thrust washer (**Figure 48**).
    g. Circlip (**Figure 49**).
    h. Countershaft 3rd gear (**Figure 50**).
    i. Circlip (**Figure 51**).
    j. Countershaft 5th gear (**Figure 52**).

NOTE
*The spacer (**Figure 53**) is used on 1986-early 1987 models only.*

    k. Spacer (**Figure 53**).
    l. Countershaft 2nd gear (**Figure 54**).
    m. Bearings (**Figure 55**).
    n. Thrust washer (**Figure 56**).
    o. Circlip (**Figure 57**).
2. Inspect the countershaft assembly as described under *Inspection* in this chapter.
3. Assemble the countershaft by reversing Step 1, noting the following:
    a. Make sure all circlips seat completely in their grooves.
    b. Make sure the bearing halves are installed correctly (**Figure 58**).
    c. Make sure all gears are correctly installed. See **Figure 59**.

NOTE
*If you have a 1986-early 1987 model and you replaced countershaft 5th gear, do not install the spacer (**Figure 53**). Confirm this with your dealer when purchasing the new 5th gear.*

Mainshaft
Disassembly/Reassembly

Refer to **Figure 40** for this procedure.
1. Disassemble the mainshaft as follows:
    a. Mainshaft spacer (**Figure 60**).
    b. Mainshaft 4th gear (**Figure 61**).
    c. Bearings (**Figure 62**).
    d. Thrust washer (**Figure 63**).

    e. Mainshaft 2nd gear (**Figure 64**).
    f. Circlip (**Figure 65**).
    g. Mainshaft 1st gear (**Figure 66**).
    h. Circlip (**Figure 67**).
    i. Thrust washer (**Figure 68**).
    j. Mainshaft 3rd gear (**Figure 69**).
    k. Bearings (**Figure 70**).
    l. Thrust washer (**Figure 71**).
    m. Circlip (**Figure 72**).
2. Inspect the mainshaft assembly as described under *Inspection* in this chapter.
3. Assemble the mainshaft by reversing Step 1 while noting the following:
    a. Make sure all circlips seat completely in their grooves.
    b. Make sure the bearing halves are installed correctly (**Figure 58**).
    c. Make sure all gears are correctly installed. See **Figure 73**.

Main Drive Gear
Removal/Inspection/Installation

Refer to **Figure 74** for this procedure.

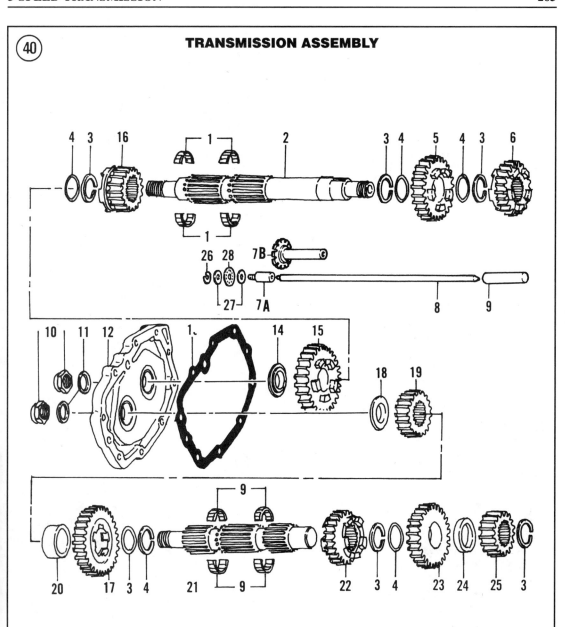

TRANSMISSION ASSEMBLY

1. Bearings	9. Left-hand pushrod end
2. Mainshaft	(early models)
3. Circlip	10. Nuts
4. Thrust washer	11. Spacer
5. Mainshaft 3rd gear	12. Access cover
6. Mainshaft 2nd gear	13. Gasket
7A. Right-hand pushrod end	14. Spacer
(1984-early 1991)	15. Mainshaft 4th gear
7B. Pushrod end with oil slinger	16. Mainshaft 1st gear
(late 1991-on)	17. Countershaft 1st gear
8. Pushrod	18. Spacer

19. Countershaft 4th gear
20. Spacer
21. Countershaft
22. Countershaft 3rd gear
23. Countershaft 2nd gear
24. Spacer (1984-early 1987)
25. Countershaft 5th gear
26. Circlip
27. Thrust washers
28. Clutch release bearing

7

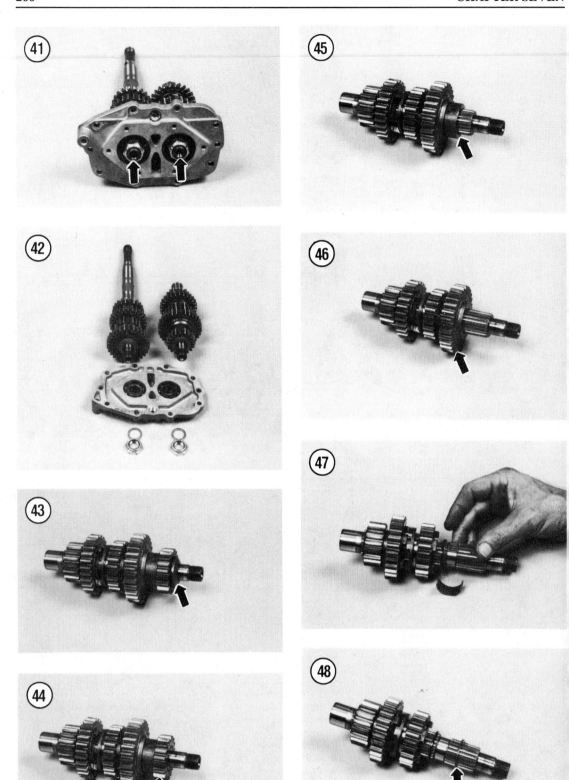

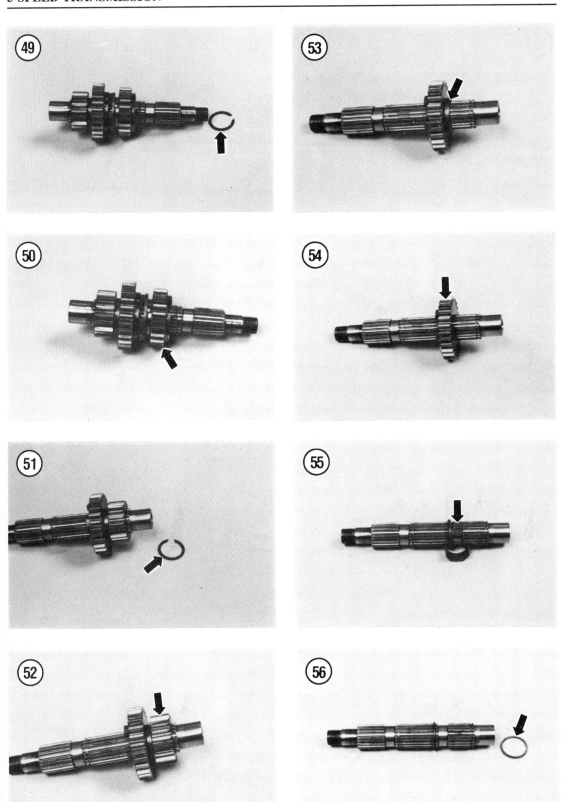

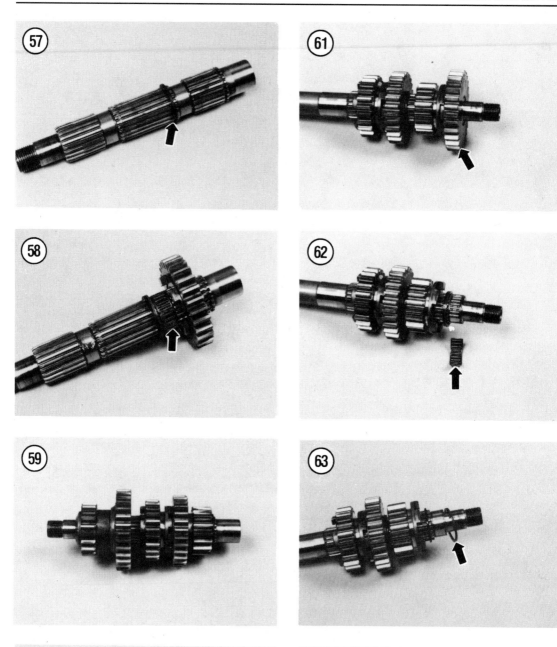

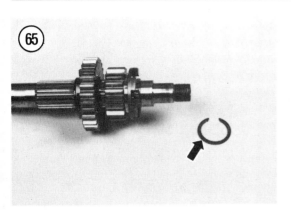

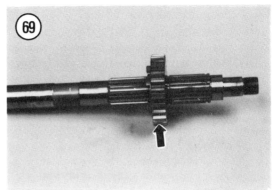

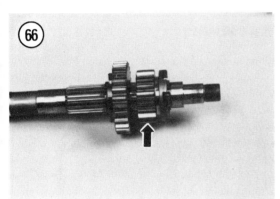

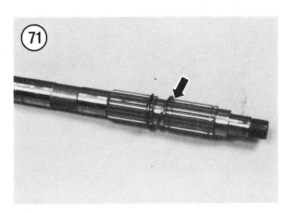

7

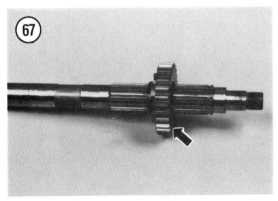

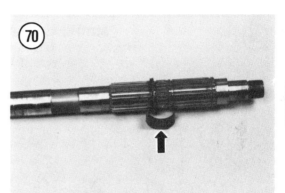

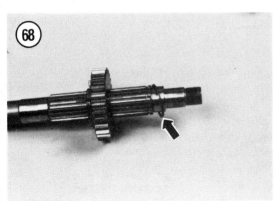

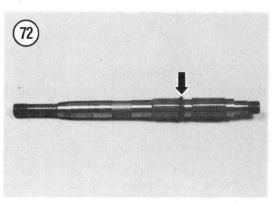

1. Place the transmission case in a press.

2. Using the Main Drive Gear Remover and Installer (HD-35316), remove the main drive gear (**Figure 75**). Remove the gear through the access cover opening (**Figure 76**).

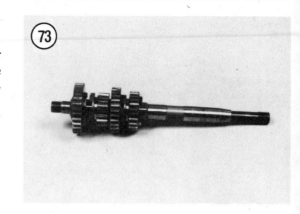

NOTE
If the main drive gear remover/installer is not used to remove the main drive gear, check the housing bearing for damage.

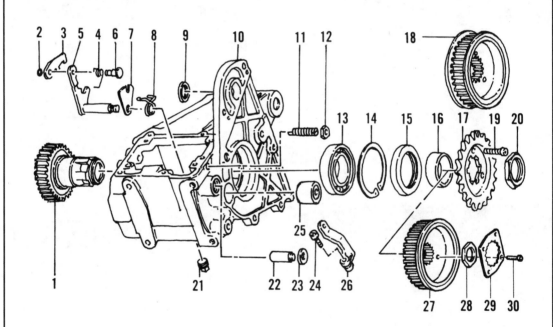

MAIN DRIVE GEAR ASSEMBLY

1. Main drive gear
2. Circlip
3. Pawl
4. Spring
5. Shift arm
6. Pin
7. Centering plate
8. Spring
9. Oil seal
10. Transmission case
11. Spring
12. Nut
13. Bearing
14. Circlip
15. Oil seal
16. Spacer
17. Sprocket
18. Sprocket
19. Screw
20. Nut
21. Drain plug
22. Spacer
23. Oil seal
24. Screw
25. Bearing
26. Shifter lever
27. Sprocket (1992-on)
28. Nut (1992-on)
29. Lockplate (1992-on)
30. Screw (1992-on)

3. Check the main drive gear (**Figure 77**) and shaft splines (**Figure 78**) for wear or damage. Replace if necessary.

4. Check the needle bearings (**Figure 79**) on the inside of the main drive gear. If these bearings are questionable, check the transmission mainshaft bearing race surface for pitting or wear grooves. If such wear is found, have a Harley-Davidson dealer replace the main drive gear needle bearings and seal.

5. Place the main drive gear into the transmission and align with the bearing.

6. Install the main drive gear using the main drive gear installation tool (HD-34723).

Transmission Inspection

1. Examine gears for worn or chipped teeth, pitting, scoring or other damage. See **Figure 80**.

2. Examine dog clutches (**Figure 81**) for chips and rounded edges or wear.

3. Check the shafts for worn or damaged splines or damaged circlip grooves. See **Figure 82**.

4. Slip gears on shafts and check for free movement without appreciable play.

7

5. Replace worn or damaged thrust washers.

6. Check the needle bearings (**Figure 83**) for wear or roughness.

7. Check the access cover bearings (**Figure 84**) for wear or roughness. If replacement is required, perform the following:

    a. Remove the circlips from the access cover grooves.

    b. Remove the bearings with a press.

    c. Clean the access cover in solvent and dry thoroughly.

    d. Align the new bearings with the access cover so that the ID number on each bearing faces toward the outside of the access cover.

    e. When pressing in the new bearings, support the opposite side of the access cover at the bearing bores with a flat plate; otherwise you may damage the access cover when pressing the bearings in.

    f. Install the bearing circlips into the access cover grooves. Make sure each circlip seats in its groove completely.

Transmission Installation

1. If the main drive gear was removed, install it as described in this chapter.

> *CAUTION*
> *Wrap the mainshaft clutch hub splines on 1990 and later models with tape to prevent the splines from damaging the inner primary housing oil seal.*

2. Install the transmission assembly (**Figure 85**) into the transmission case, using a new access cover gasket. Install and tighten the access cover bolts and screws as follows:

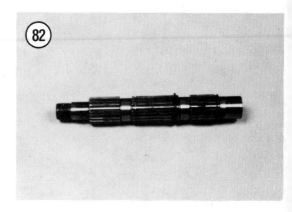

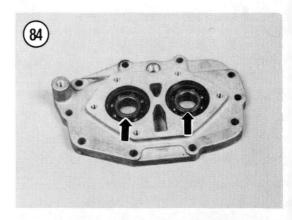

a. 5/16 in. bolts: 13-16 ft.-lb. (17.9-22.1 N•m).

b. 1/4 in. screws: 7-9 ft.-lb. (9.7-12.4 N•m).

3. Lock the transmission into two different gears.

4. Tighten the countershaft and mainshaft locknuts to 27-33 ft.-lb. (37.3-45.5 N•m). See **Figure 86**.

5. Install the spacer and countershaft sprocket on the main drive gear (**Figure 87**). Apply a drop of Loctite 262 (red) to the countershaft sprocket nut threads and install the nut hand-tight.

NOTE
The sprocket nut uses left-hand threads.
Turn the sprocket nut counterclockwise
to tighten it.

6. Using the same socket as during removal, tighten the countershaft sprocket nut to the torque specification in **Table 3**.

7A. On 1986-early 1991 models, locate a lockscrew hole in the sprocket that most closely matches the alignment shown in **Figure 88**. If none of the tapped holes align, turn the sprocket counterclockwise to obtain correct alignment. Coat the lockscrew threads with Loctite 242 (blue) and screw it into the sprocket and main drive gear tapped threads. Tighten the lockscrew to 50-60 in.-lb. (5.7-6.9 N•m).

WARNING
Do not exceed 150 ft.-lb. (203 N•m) or
loosen the sprocket nut when trying to
align the screw hole.

7B. On late 1991-on models, install the lockplate (**Figure 89**) and align 2 of the lockplate holes with the 2 tapped holes in the sprocket (**Figure 90**). If you cannot get the holes to align, turn the sprocket counterclockwise to obtain correct alignment. Coat the lockscrew threads with Loctite 242 (blue). Then install the screws and tighten to 7-9 ft.-lb.

7

Socket head locking screw
Nut
Countershaft sprockets

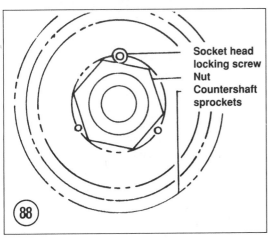

COUNTERSHAFT SPROCKET (LATE 1991-ON)

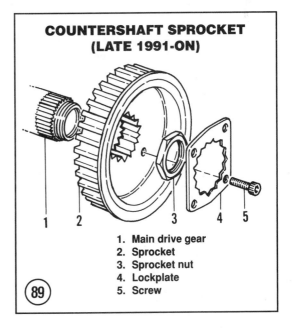

1. Main drive gear
2. Sprocket
3. Sprocket nut
4. Lockplate
5. Screw

WARNING
Do not exceed 150 ft.-lb. (203 N•m) or loosen the sprocket nut when trying to align the screw holes.

8. Install the main drive gear bearing race as follows, using the puller and installation tool HD-34902 (**Figure 91**).

   a. Measure the length of the bearing inner race. Early 1985 models had a race 0.8975-0.8125 in. (22.796-20.637 mm) long. Late 1985 and later models have a race that is 0.9950-1.000 in. (25.273-25.4 mm) long. Length of race will determine its final installation position.

   b. Slide the bearing inner race on the mainshaft (**Figure 92**). The bearing's chamfer edge should face toward the transmission.

   c. Thread the tool's sleeve pilot onto the mainshaft (the mainshaft uses left-hand threads).

   d. Slide the sleeve over the sleeve pilot and rest it against the bearing race (**Figure 93**).

   e. Place a suitable size washer over the adapter screw and install the nut.

NOTE
The installation specification described in sub-step f must be maintained to align the bearing inner race properly with the bearing outer race in the primary chain case.

   f. Place a wrench on the end of the sleeve pilot screw flats. Then tighten the large nut until the bearing inner race inside edge is 0.200 in. (5.08 mm) (early 1985 models with the 0.8975-0.8125 in. [22.796-20.637 mm] long race) or 0.100 in. (2.54 mm) (late 1985 and later models with the 0.9950-1.000 in. [25.273-25.4 mm] long race) from the drive gear. See **Figure 94**.

9. Install the shift forks as described in this chapter.

10. Install all parts previously removed.

TRANSMISSION CASE

Transmission case removal is only necessary if it requires replacement or when performing extensive frame repair or replacing a frame.

Removal/Installation

1. Remove the main drive gear and transmission shafts as described in this chapter.
2. Remove the primary chain case as described in Chapter Five.
3. Disconnect the oil hoses at the transmission case.
4. Remove the oil tank.
5. Support the engine with a block of wood and a hydraulic jack.
6. Remove the bolts securing the transmission case to the frame and remove the case.
7. Installation is the reverse of these steps while noting the following.
8. Tighten the transmission case bolts to 33-38 ft.-lb. (45.5-52.4 N•m).

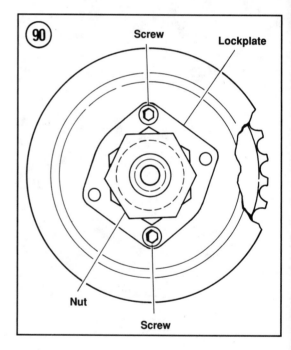

(90) Screw — Lockplate — Nut — Screw

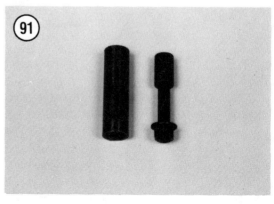

(91)

9. Perform the shifter adjustment in this chapter.

10. Refill with transmission oil as described in Chapter Three.

Shift Arm
Disassembly/Inspection/Assembly

Refer to **Figure 74** for this procedure.

1. Loosen the shift lever screw at the bottom of the transmission case and slide the shift lever off of the shift arm.

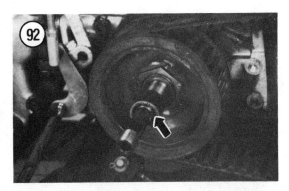

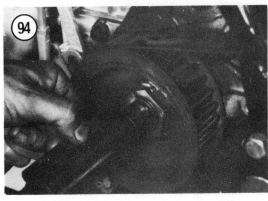

2. Loosen the shift lever adjusting screw and turn it counterclockwise until it clears the centering plate. Then pull the shift arm assembly out of the transmission case.

3. Remove the circlip and remove the pawl and spring.

4. Slide the spring and centering plate off of the shift arm.

5. The pawl pin is a press fit. If removal is necessary, drive it out with a suitable size punch.

6. Check the shift pawl and centering plate for wear. Replace the pawl if its ends are damaged. Replace the centering plate if its adjustment slot is elongated.

7. Check the springs for wear or damage. Assemble the pawl and spring on the shift arm pin. If the spring will not hold the pawl on the cam, replace it.

8. Place the centering plate on the shift lever.

9. Assemble the springs, pin and pawl. Secure with a new circlip.

10. Install the shift arm assembly into the transmission case.

11. Align the adjusting screw with the centering plate slot.

12. Slide the shift lever on the shift arm. Install the screw and tighten it to 18-22 ft.-lb. (24.8-30.4 N•m).

TRANSMISSION SIDE COVER
(1987-ON)

Removal

1. Remove the exhaust system.

2. Drain the transmission oil as described under *Transmission Oil Change* in Chapter Three.

3. Remove the transmission fill plug/dipstick assembly.

4. Loosen the clutch cable adjuster locknut (**Figure 95**) and turn the adjuster to provide as much slack in the cable as possible.

5. Remove the side cover bolts and remove the side cover (**Figure 96**).

6. Refer to **Figure 97**. Perform the following:
   a. Remove the circlip (A, **Figure 98**).
   b. Remove the inner ramp and coupling (B) from the side cover.
   c. Disconnect the clutch cable (C) from the ball and ramp coupling (D).
   d. If necessary, remove the cable fitting from the side cover.

7

Inspection

1. Wash the side cover and all components thoroughly in solvent and dry thoroughly.

2. Check the release mechanism balls and the ramp ball socket surfaces for cracks, deep scoring or excessive wear (**Figure 98**).

3. Check the hub ramp for looseness.

4. Check the side cover (**Figure 99**) for cracks or damage. Check the clutch cable threads and the coupling circlip groove for damage. Check the ramp bore in the side cover for severe wear, lips or grooves that could catch the ramps and bind them sideways, causing improper clutch adjustment.

5. Replace worn or damaged parts.

Assembly/Installation

1. If removed, screw the clutch cable guide into the side cover. Do not tighten it at this point.

2. Refer to **Figure 97**. Perform the following:

   a. Align the tang on the outer ramp with the slot in the side cover and install the outer ramp (**Figure 100**). B, **Figure 97** shows the outer ramp installed.

   b. Place a steel ball in each of the outer ramp slots. There are a total of 3 balls used in this assembly. **Figure 101** shows the outer ramp with the 3 balls installed.

   c. Attach the clutch cable (C, **Figure 97**) coupling onto the end of the inner ramp (D, **Figure 97**).

   d. Install the inner ramp into the side cover.

   e. Secure the inner and outer ramp assembly with the large circlip (A, **Figure 97**).

NOTE
The circlip opening must be installed so that it faces to the right of the outer ramp tang slot.

   f. Attach the clutch cable to the side cover.

3. Install the side cover using a new gasket. Install the side cover bolts and tighten to 10-12 ft.-lb. (13.8-16.6 N•m).

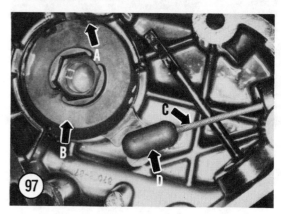

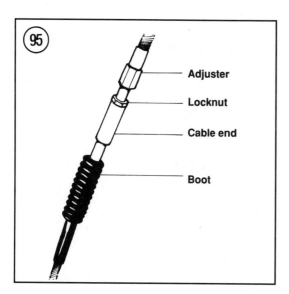

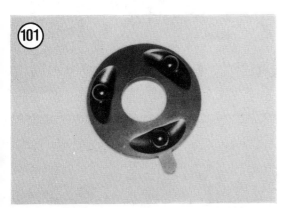

4. Refill the transmission oil as described in Chapter Three.

5. Install the exhaust system.

6. Adjust the clutch as described in Chapter Three.

TRANSMISSION ADJUSTMENTS

Shift Linkage Adjustment

Shift linkage adjustment should only be required if the linkage rod is damaged or if the gears do not engage properly.

1. Disconnect one end of the shifter rod. See **Figure 102** (front) or **Figure 103** (rear).

2. Loosen the locknuts on the end of the shifter rod disconnected in Step 1. Then turn the shifter rod until the gears engage properly.

3. Reconnect the shifter rod and tighten the locknuts securely.

Gear Engagement Check/Adjustment

When the transmission gears do not engage properly, perform the following checks (sub-steps a-d) before proceeding to Step 1.

   a. Check clutch adjustment and operation. See Chapter Three.

   b. Check the shift linkage adjustment as described in this chapter. If the shift linkage appears to be correct, check the shift linkage rod for damage or interference.

   c. Check the shift forks for wear or damage as described in this chapter.

   d. If these checks do not solve the shifting problem, perform the following procedures.

1. Disconnect the negative battery cable.

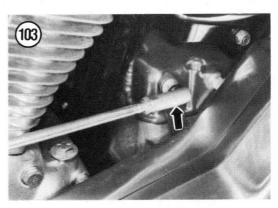

7

2. *1986*: Disconnect the clutch cable at the engine (**Figure 104**).

3. Disconnect the neutral switch wire at the switch (**Figure 105**).

4. Remove the transmission top cover mounting bolts and remove the top cover and gasket. See **Figure 106**.

5. Shift the transmission into third gear.

NOTE
Third gear can be easily found by pushing the motorcycle forward and shifting the transmission until third gear is reached. Then set the jiffy stand and continue the procedure.

6. Move the shifter lever (**Figure 107**) to check for free play and spring pressure in both directions.

7. The gear engagement is correct if the spring pressure is the same in both directions and there is approximately 0.010 in. (0.25 mm) clearance between the shifter pawl arms and the shift cam pins as shown in **Figure 108**. If necessary, adjust the gear engagement as described in Step 8.

8. Refer to **Figure 109**. Loosen the adjusting screw locknut and turn the bolt in 1/4 turn increments or

less (clockwise or counterclockwise) until the shifter lever travel spring pressure is equal on both sides and the 0.010 in. (0.25 mm) clearance is maintained. Tighten the locknut and recheck the adjustment.

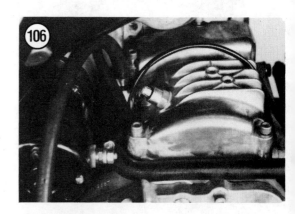

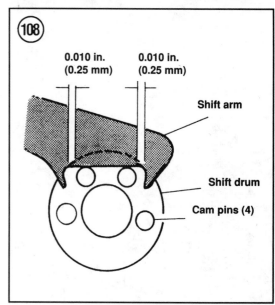

108

0.010 in.
(0.25 mm)　　0.010 in.
(0.25 mm)

Shift arm

Shift drum

Cam pins (4)

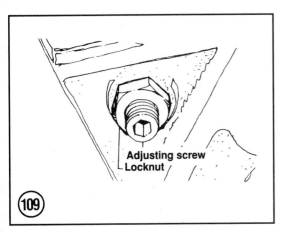

Adjusting screw
Locknut

(109)

NOTE
If you cannot adjust the adjusting screw because of interference with the primary case, Harley-Davidson recommends grinding away a small portion of the case with a die grinder. Only grind enough material to gain access to the adjust screw. This should affect earlier production models only.

9. Reinstall all previously removed parts as described in this chapter.

10. *1986*: Adjust the clutch after reconnecting the clutch cable (**Figure 104**). Refer to Chapter Three.

7

Table 1 5-SPEED TRANSMISSION SPECIFICATIONS

	Specification	
	in.	mm
Mainshaft		
Runout	0.000-0.003	0.00-0.08
End play	0.000	0.00
1st gear clearance	0.0000-0.0080	0.00-0.20
2nd gear clearance	0.0000-0.0080	0.00-0.20
3rd gear		
Clearance	0.0003-0.0019	0.008-0.048
End play	0.0050-0.0420	0.127-1.067
4th gear		
Clearance	0.0003-0.0019	0.008-0.048
End play	0.0050-0.0310	0.127-0.787
Mainshaft drive gear (5th)		
End play	0.000	0.00
Fit on mainshaft	0.00001-0.0009	0.0002-0.0229
Fit in bearing		
Loose	0.0001	0.002
Tight	0.0009	0.023
Countershaft		
Runout	0.000-0.003	0.00-0.08
End play	0.000	0.00
1st gear		
Clearance	0.0003-0.0019	0.008-0.048
End play	0.0050-0.0390	0.127-0.990
2nd gear		
Clearance	0.0003-0.0019	0.008-0.048
End play	0.0050-0.0440	0.127-1.118
3rd gear clearance	0.0000-0.0080	0.000-0.200
4th gear		
Clearance	0.0000-0.0080	0.000-0.200
End play	0.0050-0.0390	0.127-0.991
5th gear		
Clearance	0.0000-0.0080	0.000-0.200
End play	0.0050-0.0440	0.127-0.102
(continued)		

Table 1 TRANSMISSION SPECIFICATIONS (continued)

	Specification	
	in.	mm
Shifter cam assembly		
Shifter cam end play	0.0001-0.004	0.002-0.102
Right edge of middle cam groove		
to right support block	See text	—
Shift forks		
Shift fork taper (1986-1992)	0.000-0.020	0.00-0.51
Shift fork to cam groove end play	0.0017-0.0019	0.043-0.048
Shift fork to gear groove end play	0.0010-0.0110	0.025-0.279
Side door bearing		
Fit on mainshaft		
Loose	0.0001	0.002
Tight	0.0007	0.018
Fit on countershaft		
Loose	0.00001	0.0002
Tight	0.0008	0.018
Fit on side door (tight)	0.0014-0.0001	0.035-0.002

Table 2 SHIFT DOG CLEARANCE

	Min.		Max.	
Gears	in.	mm	in.	mm
2nd-5th	0.035	0.89	0.139	3.53
2nd-3rd	0.035	0.89	0.164	4.16
1st-4th	0.035	0.89	0.152	3.86
1st-3rd	0.035	0.89	0.157	3.99

Table 3 TRANSMISSION TIGHTENING TORQUES

	ft.-lb.	N•m
All 1/4 in. fasteners	7-9	9.7-12.4
Front bracket mounting bolts		
1986-1991	33-38	45.5-52.4
1992-on	30-33	41-30
Rear mounting bracket bolts		
1986-1991	13-16	17.9-22.1
1992-on	15-20	20-27
Support block bolts	7-9	9.7-12.4
Side door mounting screws		
5/16 in.	13-16	17.9-22.1
1/4 in.	7-9	9.7-12.4
Neutral indicator switch	3-5	4.1-6.9
Top cover mounting bolts	7-9	9.7-12.4
Side cover mounting bolts	7-9	9.7-12.4
Mainshaft/countershaft side door nuts	27-33	37.3-45.5
Shifter arm screw	18-22	24.8-30.4
Shifter arm adjusting screw locknut	20-24	27.6-33.1
Countershaft sprocket nut	110-120	151.8-165.6
Countershaft sprocket		
Lockscrew (1986-1991)	50-60 in.-lb.	5.7-6.9
Allen bolts (1992-on)	7-9	9-12
Clutch cable bracket screws	6-8	8.3-11
Clutch release arm nut		
1985-1986	8-10	11-13.8

CHAPTER EIGHT

FUEL, EXHAUST AND EMISSION CONTROL SYSTEMS

This chapter includes service procedures for all parts of the fuel, exhaust and emission control systems.

Carburetor specifications are listed in **Table 1**. **Table 1** and **Table 2** are found at the end of the chapter.

AIR CLEANER

The air cleaner must be cleaned or replaced at the intervals specified in Chapter Three (or more frequently in dusty areas).

Service to the air cleaner element is described in Chapter Three.

CARBURETOR
(1984-1989)

Service

Major carburetor service (removal and cleaning) should be performed when poor engine performance and/or hesitation is observed. Alterations in jet size should be attempted only if you're experienced in this type of "tuning" work; a bad guess could result in costly engine damage or, at best, poor performance.

If after servicing the carburetors and making adjustments as described in this chapter, the motorcycle does not perform correctly (and assuming that other factors affecting performance are correct, such as ignition timing and condition, valve adjustment, etc.), the motorcycle should be checked by a dealer or a qualified performance tuning specialist.

Removal/Installation

1. Remove the air cleaner as described in Chapter Three.

2. Turn the fuel valve off.

3. Disconnect the throttle (**Figure 1**) and choke (**Figure 2**) cables at the carburetor.

4. Disconnect the fuel hose at the fuel valve (**Figure 3**).

5. Label and disconnect all hoses at the carburetor.

6. Remove the carburetor mounting screws and remove the carburetor (**Figure 4**) and insulator block.

NOTE
Drain most of the gasoline from the carburetor assembly and place it in a clean heavy-duty plastic bag to keep it clean until it is worked on or reinstalled.

7. While the carburetor is removed, examine the intake manifold on the cylinder head for any cracks or damage that would allow unfiltered air to enter the engine. Any damaged parts should be replaced.

8. Install by reversing these removal steps. Tighten the carburetor mounting screws to the specifications in **Table 2**.

9. Adjust the throttle and choke cables as described in Chapter Three.

Disassembly

Refer to **Figure 5** for this procedure.

1. Remove the float bowl (**Figure 6**).

2. Remove the accelerating pump housing at the bottom of the float bowl (**Figure 7**). Then remove the spring (**Figure 8**) and diaphragm (**Figure 9**).

3. Remove the O-ring (**Figure 10**) from the accelerating pump housing.

4. Remove the following from the float bowl:
   a. Overflow hose (**Figure 11**).
   b. Rubber boot (**Figure 12**).
   c. O-ring (**Figure 13**).

5. Remove the float pin screw (**Figure 14**) and withdraw the float pin and float (**Figure 15**).

6. Detach the fuel valve (**Figure 16**) from the float and remove the clip (**Figure 17**).

7. Remove the accelerator pump rod from the float bowl.

8. Remove the main jet (**Figure 18**).

9. Remove the pilot jet plug (**Figure 19**) and remove the pilot jet (**Figure 20**).

10. If necessary, remove the cable guide (**Figure 21**) at the top of the carburetor housing.

11. The throttle (**Figure 22**) and choke (**Figure 23**) valve assemblies are matched to the individual carburetor during manufacturing. If these parts are damaged, the carburetor must be replaced.

Inspection

CAUTION
Before cleaning plastic or rubber components, make sure that the cleaning agent is compatible with these materials. Some types of solvents can cause permanent damage. Carburetor cleaner use is described in Step 1.

1. Clean all metal parts that were removed from the carburetor body in a good grade of carburetor

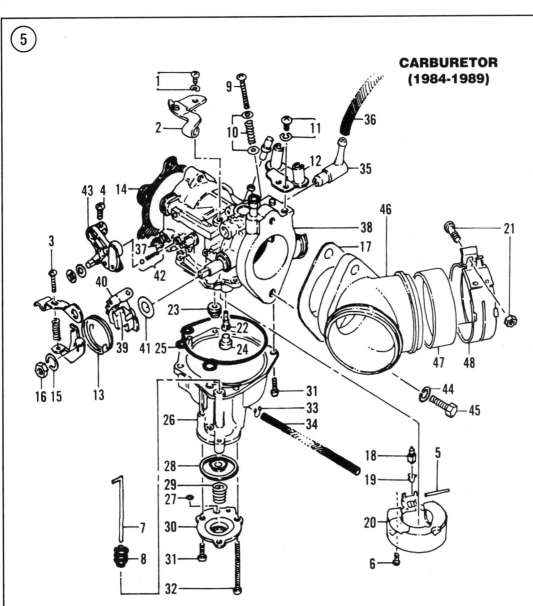

**CARBURETOR
(1984-1989)**

1. Screw and washer
2. Choke cable bracket
3. Fast idle adjusting screw
4. Choke cable screw
5. Float pin
6. Float retaining screw
7. Accelerating pump rod
8. Rubber boot
9. Throttle stop screw
10. Washers
11. Screw and washer
12. Throttle cable bracket
13. Spring
14. Gasket
15. Lockwasher
16. Nut

17. Gasket
18. Inlet valve with clip
19. Clip
20. Float assembly
21. Screw and nut
22. Pilot jet
23. Main jet
24. Plug
25. Rubber gasket
26. Float bowl
27. O-ring (accelerating pump)
28. Accelerating pump diaphragm
29. Accelerating pump spring
30. Accelerating pump housing
31. Screw and washer
32. Screw and washer

33. Overflow line clip
34. Overflow line
35. Fuel inlet fitting
36. Fuel inlet hose
37. Choke lever shaft
38. Housing
39. Spring
40. Rocker arm
41. Washer
42. Choke detent ball and spring
43. Fast idle cam
44. Lockwasher
45. Bolt
46. Intake manifold
47. Intake seal
48. Intake clamp

8

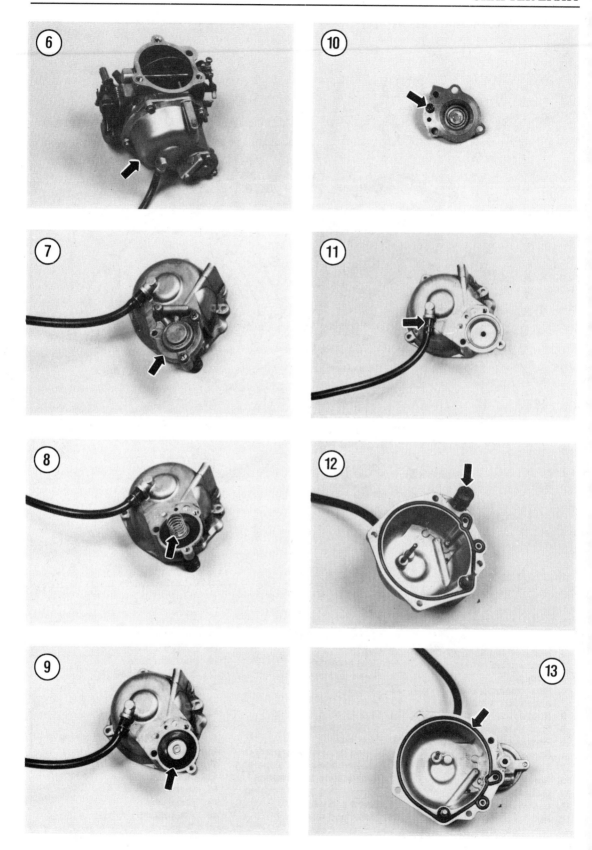

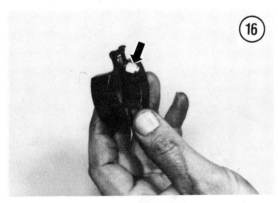

8

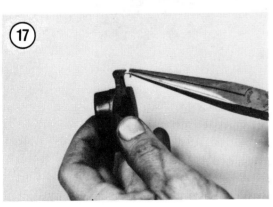

cleaner. This solution is available at most automotive supply stores, in a small, resealable tank with a dip basket. If it is tightly sealed when not in use, the solution will last for several cleanings. Follow the manufacturer's instructions for correct soaking time.

CAUTION
Do not soak the carburetor body in a tank of carburetor cleaner. The cleaner can damage the non-removable rubber seals used at the throttle plate shaft assembly.

2. Remove all parts from the cleaner and blow dry with compressed air. Blow out the jets with compressed air. *Do not* use a piece of wire to clean them as minor gouges in a jet can alter the flow rate and upset the air/fuel mixture.

3. Make sure all fuel and air openings are clear. Blow out with compressed air if necessary.

4. Check the float assembly for leaks. Place the float in a container of water and push it down. There should be no bubbles. Replace the float assembly if it leaks.

5. Check the float needle and seat contact areas closely. Both contact surfaces should appear smooth without any gouging or other apparent damage. Replace both needle and seat as a set if any one part is worn or damaged.

6. A damaged accelerating pump diaphragm will cause poor acceleration. Hold the diaphragm up to a strong light and check the diaphragm for pin holes, cracks or other damage (**Figure 24**). Replace if necessary.

7. Replace the pump rod if bent or worn.

8. O-rings tend to become hardened after prolonged use and heat and therefore lose their ability to seal properly. Inspect all O-rings and replace if necessary.

9. Inspect the pilot jet for wear or damage that may have occurred during removal. Check the slot in the top of the jet for cracks or breakage. Do not install a damaged pilot jet as you may not be able to remove it.

Assembly

Refer to **Figure 5** when performing this procedure.

1. Prior to assembly, perform the *Inspection* procedure to make sure all worn or damaged parts have been repaired or replaced. All parts should be thoroughly cleaned before assembly.

NOTE
Before installing new jets, double check the jet size and compare it to the old jet. If you are not rejetting the carburetor, make sure to install the same size jet(s).

2. Drop the pilot jet (**Figure 20**) into the passage and tighten it with the same screwdriver used during removal.

3. Install the pilot jet plug (**Figure 19**).

4. Install the main jet (**Figure 18**).

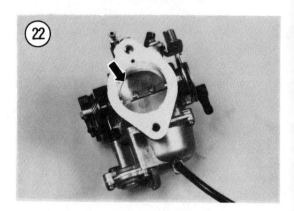

5. Install the fuel valve (**Figure 17**) onto the float and position the float onto the carburetor so that the valve drops into its seat. Align the float pivot arm with the 2 carburetor mounting posts and slip the pin through the float pivot arm and mounting posts. See **Figure 15**.

6. Check float level as described in this chapter.

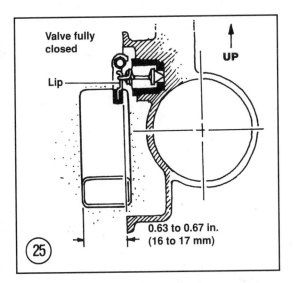

Valve fully closed
UP
Lip
0.63 to 0.67 in.
(16 to 17 mm)

㉕

㉖

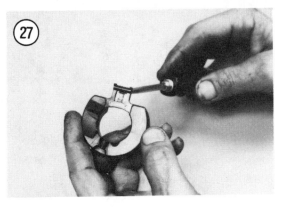

㉗

7. Assemble and install the float bowl as follows:

  a. Install the O-ring into the cover passageway hole (**Figure 10**).

  b. Insert the accelerator pump diaphragm into the accelerator pump housing in the bottom of the float bowl. Make sure the diaphragm seats around the bowl groove evenly. See **Figure 9**.

  c. Install the spring into the accelerator pump cover (**Figure 8**).

  d. Align the cover assembly with the diaphragm and bowl and install the cover assembly. Install the screws and lockwashers and tighten securely.

  e. Insert the accelerator pump nozzle into the float bowl, if removed.

  f. Install the boot onto the float bowl (**Figure 12**).

  g. Install a new float bowl O-ring. Then align the float bowl with the carburetor and install the float bowl. Install the float bowl screws and lockwasher and tighten them in a crisscross pattern to prevent warpage.

  h. Insert the pump rod through the boot on the float bowl and engage the rod with the diaphragm. Then connect the pump rod with the lever assembly.

  i. If the drain hose was removed from the float bowl, install it now.

Float Level Measurement

1. Remove the carburetor as described in this chapter.

2. Remove the float bowl as described in this chapter.

3. Turn the carburetor to position the float bowl as shown in **Figure 25**. Measure the float height from the face of the bowl mounting flange surface to the bottom float surface (**Figure 26**). Bend the float tang with a screwdriver to adjust. See **Figure 27**.

4. Reinstall the float bowl and install the carburetor as described in this chapter.

CARBURETOR
(1990-ON)

Service

Major carburetor service (removal and cleaning) should be performed when poor engine performance and/or hesitation is observed. Alterations in jet size

8

should be attempted only if you're experienced in this type of "tuning" work; a bad guess could result in costly engine damage or, at best, poor performance.

If after servicing the carburetors and making adjustments as described in this chapter, the motorcycle does not perform correctly (and assuming that other factors affecting performance are correct, such as ignition timing and condition, valve adjustment, etc.), the motorcycle should be checked by a dealer or a qualified performance tuning specialist.

Vacuum Piston Inspection

If you suspect that the vacuum piston is not operating properly (failing to rise or close properly), perform the following procedures before removing the carburetor.

1. Check vacuum piston rise as follows:
   a. Remove the air cleaner assembly so that you can see the vacuum piston.

NOTE
Figure 28 shows the vacuum piston with the carburetor removed for clarity. The carburetor must be installed on the bike when performing the following.

WARNING
When you are checking vacuum piston operation with the engine running as described in sub-step b, protect your eyes from a possible back-fire by wearing safety glasses and standing a safe distance away from the carburetor. Have an assistant operate the throttle; do not operate the throttle and watch the vacuum piston at the same time. You will be too close to the bike.

   b. With the engine running and properly warmed up, have an assistant open and close the throttle several times while you watch vacuum piston operation. The vacuum piston should rise and lower when the throttle is opened and closed. Turn the engine off.
   c. With the engine off, lift the vacuum piston all the way in the carburetor bore with your finger and release it. Note how the piston traveled upward in the bore. The piston should move smoothly with no sign of roughness or binding.

2. Check piston closing as follows:
   a. With the engine off, lift the vacuum piston all the way in the carburetor bore with your finger and release it. Note how the piston drops in the bore. It should drop smoothly and come to a stop at the bottom of the bore.
   b. Without touching the piston after releasing it in sub-step a, observe the bottom of the piston in relation to the piston bore. The lower edge of the piston should align or rest with the horizontal groove at the bottom end of the piston track.

3. If the vacuum piston failed to operate properly as described in these steps, refer to Chapter Two for carburetor troubleshooting.

Removal/Installation

1. Remove the air cleaner and backplate as described in Chapter Three.
2. Turn the fuel valve off.
3. Label and disconnect the throttle and choke cables at the carburetor.
4. Disconnect the fuel hose at the fuel valve.
5. Label and disconnect all hoses at the carburetor.
6. Pull the carburetor off of its seal ring and manifold.

NOTE
The front and rear intake manifold flanges (Figure 29) have different part numbers. ID the flanges during removal so that you don't mix them up during reassembly.

7. Remove the manifold Allen bolts and nuts and remove the manifold, the 2 flanges and 2 intake manifold seals (**Figure 29**).

Drain the gasoline from the carburetor assembly and place it in a clean heavy-duty plastic bag to keep it clean until it is worked on or reinstalled.

8. Check the intake manifold seals (**Figure 29**) for wear, deterioration or other damage. Replace the seals if necessary.

9. Inspect the carburetor seal ring (**Figure 29**) and replace it if it is worn or damaged.

10. Install by reversing these removal steps, plus the following.

11. Install the intake manifold as follows:

  a. Install the front and rear flanges onto the intake manifold so that the slot in each flange can align with the cylinder head stud (**Figure 29**).

CAUTION
Do not tighten the manifold nuts and bolts until the manifold, flanges and carburetor has been aligned with each other. Attempting to align the assembly after tightening the bolts will damage the manifold seals.

  b. Install an intake manifold seal into the front and rear manifold-to-cylinder head openings.

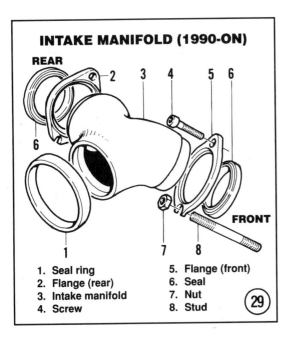

INTAKE MANIFOLD (1990-ON)

REAR

FRONT

1. Seal ring	5. Flange (front)
2. Flange (rear)	6. Seal
3. Intake manifold	7. Nut
4. Screw	8. Stud

㉙

  c. Install the intake manifold onto the cylinder heads, then install the washer and nut on each stud. Tighten finger-tight.

  d. Install the intake manifold Allen bolts and its washers (if used). Tighten finger-tight.

  e. Install the carburetor seal ring onto the intake manifold, then insert the carburetor into the seal ring.

  f. Align the manifold, flanges and carburetors as an assembly. When the assembly is properly aligned, remove the carburetor.

  g. Tighten the mounting screws and nuts to the torque specification listed in **Table 2**.

  h. Install the carburetor into the seal ring in the manifold so that it is in a vertical position.

NOTE
The float bowl overflow hose should be routed between the rear cylinder pushrods and then down between the engine oil pump cover and crankcase.

12. Adjust the throttle and choke cables as described in Chapter Three.

Disassembly

When servicing the carburetor, you will be working with a number of small parts that can easily become lost. As the carburetor is disassembled, store the parts in a metal pan or tray.

Refer to **Figure 30** for this procedure.

1. Disconnect the overflow hose from the float bowl (**Figure 31**).

2. Unscrew and remove the enrichener cable (**Figure 32**).

3. Remove the screws and washers securing the throttle cable bracket to the carburetor. Remove the bracket (**Figure 33**).

4. Remove the remaining cover screws and washers and remove the cover (**Figure 34**) and spring (**Figure 35**).

5. Remove the vacuum piston (**Figure 36**) from the carburetor housing. Do not damage the jet needle sticking out of the bottom of the vacuum piston.

NOTE
An accelerator pump diaphragm is installed in a separate chamber on the bottom side of the float bowl. The accelerator pump reduces engine hesitation by injecting a fine spray of fuel into the

8

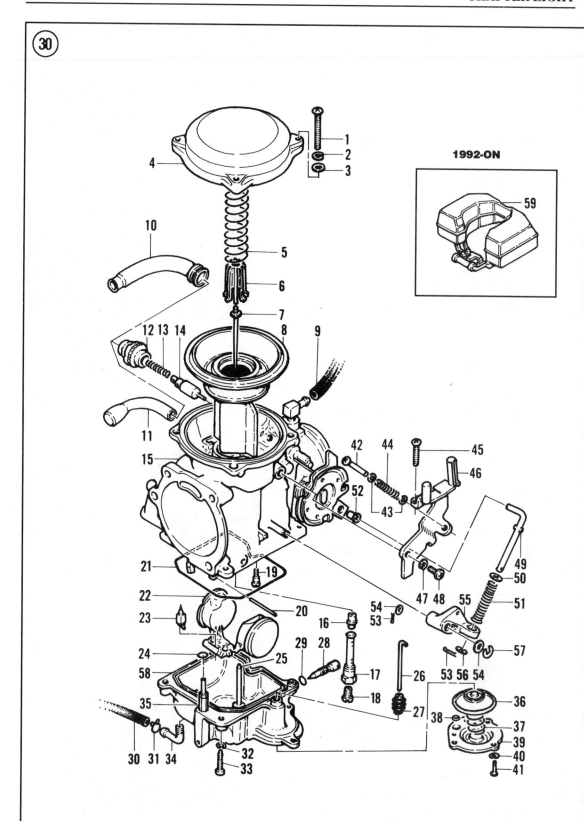

1992-ON

CARBURETOR (1990-ON)

1. Screw
2. Lockwasher
3. Flat washer
4. Cover
5. Spring
6. Spring seat
7. Jet needle
8. Vacuum piston
9. Vacuum hose
10. Cable guide
11. Starter cap
12. Cable sealing cap
13. Spring
14. Enrichener valve
15. Body
16. Needle jet
17. Needle jet holder
18. Main jet
19. Pilot jet
20. Float pin
21. O-ring
22. Floats
23. Fuel valve and clip
24. O-ring
25. Overflow pipe
26. Rod
27. Boot
28. Drain screw
29. O-ring
30. Hose
31. Clamp
32. Lockwasher
33. Screw
34. Fitting
35. Accelerator pump nozzle
36. Diaphragm
37. Spring
38. O-ring
39. Cover
40. Lockwasher
41. Screw
42. Idle adjust screw
43. Washer
44. Spring
45. Screw
46. Throttle cable bracket
47. Washer
48. Screw
49. Rod
50. Washer
51. Spring
52. Collar
53. Cotter pin
54. Washer
55. Lever
56. Washer
57. E-clip
58. Float bowl
59. Float

8

carburetor intake passage during sudden acceleration. Because the pump is synchronized with the throttle plate, note the position of the throttle and pump rods when removing the float bowl in the following steps.

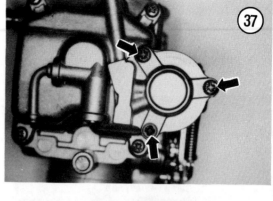

6. Remove the accelerator pump diaphragm as follows:

    a. Remove the screws and lockwashers holding the pump cover (**Figure 37**) to the float bowl and remove the cover.

    b. Remove the small pump cover O-ring (**Figure 38**).

    c. Remove the spring (A, **Figure 39**) and diaphragm (B, **Figure 39**).

7. Remove the float bowl as follows:

    a. Remove the screws and washers securing the float bowl (C, **Figure 39**) to the carburetor. Remove the float bowl from the carburetor while allowing the pump rod (**Figure 40**) to withdraw from the boot on the bowl.

    b. Disconnect the pump rod from the lever assembly on the carburetor (**Figure 41**).

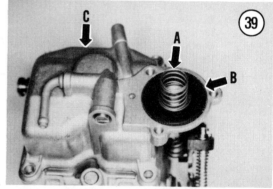

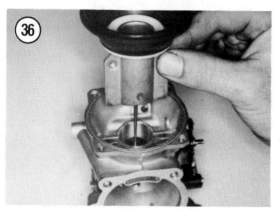

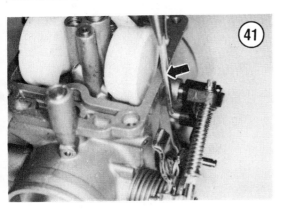

c. Carefully pull the boot (**Figure 42**) off of the float bowl.

8A. On 1984-1991 models, remove the float pin (**Figure 43**) and lift off the float and needle valve assembly (**Figure 44**).

8B. On 1992-on models, remove the float pin (**Figure 45**) and lift off the float and needle valve assembly (**Figure 46**).

9. The main jet is screwed into the top of the needle jet holder. Either remove the main jet (**Figure 47**) and then the needle jet (**Figure 48**) or remove the needle jet with the main jet attached.

10. Remove the needle jet from the needle jet bore in the carburetor (**Figure 49**).

11. Using a flat-tipped screwdriver that fits the pilot jet slot, loosen and remove the pilot jet (**Figure 50**).

> *CAUTION*
> *If the screwdriver used to remove the pilot jet is too small, you may break the slots at the top of the jet and damage it. If necessary, grind a screwdriver tip to fit.*

8

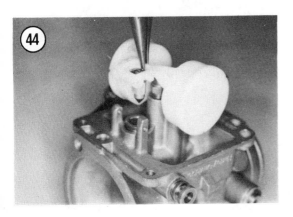

NOTE
*Replacement parts are not available for the throttle plate (**Figure 51**) assembly. Do not remove it.*

Inspection

CAUTION
Before cleaning plastic or rubber components, make sure that the cleaning agent is compatible with these materials. Some types of solvents can cause

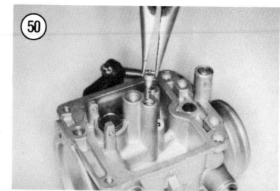

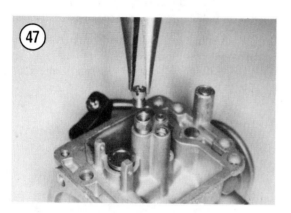

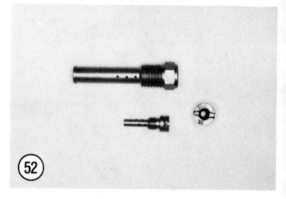

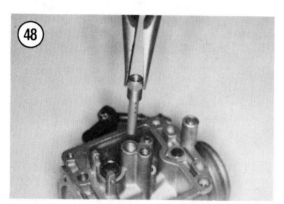

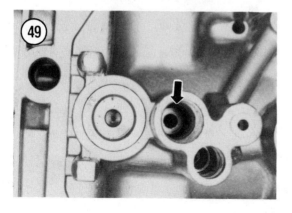

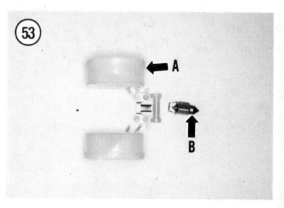

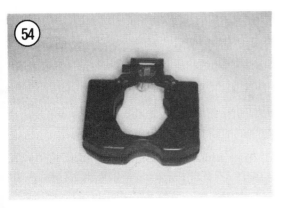

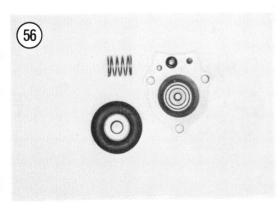

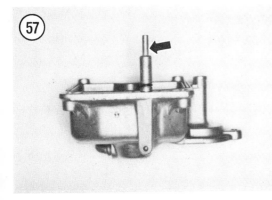

permanent damage. Carburetor cleaner use is described in Step 1.

1. Clean all metal parts that were removed from the carburetor body in a good grade of carburetor cleaner. This solution is available at most automotive supply stores, in a small, resealable tank with a dip basket. If it is tightly sealed when not in use, the solution will last for several cleanings. Follow the manufacturer's instructions for correct soaking time.

CAUTION
Do not soak the carburetor body in a tank of carburetor cleaner. The cleaner can damage the non-removable rubber seals used at the throttle plate shaft assembly.

2. Remove all parts from the cleaner and blow dry with compressed air. Blow out the jets (**Figure 52**) with compressed air. *Do not* use a piece of wire to clean them as minor gouges in a jet can alter the flow rate and upset the air/fuel mixture.

3. Make sure that the needle jet holder (**Figure 52**) bleed tube orifices are clear.

4. Make sure all fuel and air openings are clear. Blow out with compressed air if necessary.

5. Check the float assembly for leaks; see A, **Figure 53** (1984-1991) or **Figure 54** (1992-on). Place the float in a container and push it down. There should be no bubbles. Replace the float if it leaks.

6. Check the float needle (B, **Figure 49**) and seat (**Figure 55**) contact areas closely. Both contact surfaces should appear smooth without any gouging or other apparent damage. Replace the needle if damaged. The seat is a permanent part of the carburetor housing; if damaged the housing must be replaced.

7. A damaged accelerating pump diaphragm (**Figure 56**) will cause poor acceleration. Hold the diaphragm up to a strong light and check the diaphragm for pin holes, cracks or other damage. Replace if necessary.

8. Remove the accelerator pump nozzle and its O-ring (**Figure 57**) from the float bowl. Clean the nozzle with compressed air.

9. Replace the pump rod if bent or worn.

10. O-rings tend to become hardened after prolonged use and heat and therefore lose their ability to seal properly. Inspect all O-rings and replace if necessary. When replacing an O-ring, make sure the

8

new O-ring fits in its groove properly. See **Figure 58**, typical.

11. Inspect the pilot jet (**Figure 52**) for wear or damage that may have occurred during removal. Check the slot in the top of the jet for cracks or breakage. Do not install a damaged pilot jet as you may not be able to remove it.

NOTE
Step 12 describes bench checks that should be performed on the vacuum piston. Operational checks with the vacuum installed in the carburetor and with the engine running are described in this chapter.

12. Bench check the vacuum piston as follows:
   a. Check the spring (**Figure 59**) for fatigue, stretching, distortion or other damage.
   b. Check the vacuum passage through the bottom of the piston (**Figure 60**) for contamination. Clean passage if blocked.
   c. The sides of the piston ride in grooves machined in the carburetor bore. Check these sides for roughness, nicks, cracks or distortion. If the piston sides are damaged, check the mating grooves in the carburetor for damage. Minor roughness can be removed with emery cloth or by buffing. If the sides are severely damaged, the vacuum piston will have to be replaced.
   d. Hold the vacuum piston up to a light and check the diaphragm for pin holes, tearing, cracks, age deterioration or other damage. Check the diaphragm where it is mounted against the piston. If the diaphragm is damaged, the vacuum piston must be replaced.
   e. Check jet needle for bending or damage.

13. A plugged, improperly seating or contaminated enrichener system will cause hard starting as well as poor low and high speed performance. Check the following:
   a. Check for a rough or damaged enrichener valve. Check the needle (**Figure 61**) on the end of the enrichener valve for bending or contamination.
   b. Check the enrichener valve spring for fatigue, stretching or distortion.
   c. The enrichener valve chamber (A, **Figure 62**) in the carburetor must be clean. Clean the chamber carefully, making sure the enrichener

valve air inlet and the air/fuel passages are clear.

   d. Check the enrichener valve cable (**Figure 63**) for kinks or other damage.

14. Check the throttle rod (**Figure 61**) and all external carburetor components for missing or damaged parts.

15. Check that the throttle valve shaft E-clip (B, **Figure 59**) is properly secured in the groove on the end of the shaft.

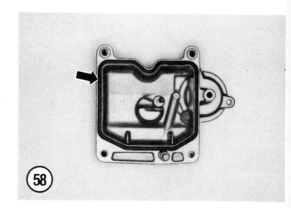

58

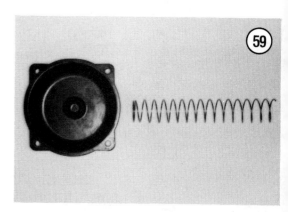

59

60

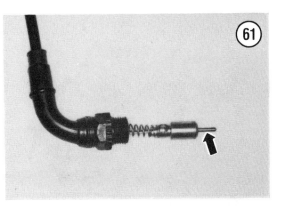

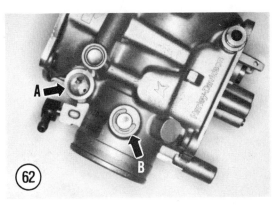

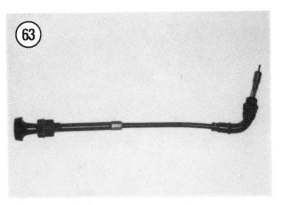

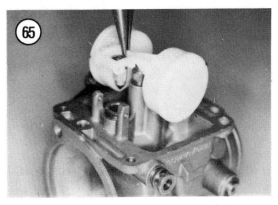

Assembly

Refer to **Figure 30** when performing this procedure.

1. Prior to assembly, perform the *Inspection* procedure to make sure all worn or damaged parts have been repaired or replaced. All parts should be thoroughly cleaned before assembly.

NOTE
Before installing new jets, double check the jet size and compare it to the old jet. If you are not rejetting the carburetor, make sure to install the same size jet(s).

2. Drop the pilot jet (**Figure 50**) into the passage and tighten with the same screwdriver used during removal.

3. The needle jet has 2 different sides and can be installed incorrectly. Install the needle jet into its passage (**Figure 49**) so that the end with the larger opening faces up toward the vacuum piston chamber.

4. Install the needle jet holder (**Figure 48**) into the main jet passage and tighten it securely.

5. Install the main jet (**Figure 47**) onto the end of the needle jet holder and tighten securely.

6A. On 1984-1991 models, install the float as follows:

   a. Install the fuel valve onto the float (**Figure 65**) and position the float onto the carburetor so that the valve drops into its seat.

   b. Align the float pivot arm with the 2 carburetor mounting posts and slip the pin through the float pivot arm and mounting posts (**Figure 66**).

6B. On 1992-on models, install the float as follows:

8

a. Install the fuel valve onto the float (**Figure 67**) and position the float onto the carburetor so that the valve drops into its seat.

b. Align the float pivot arm with the 2 carburetor mounting posts and slip the pin through the float pivot arm and mounting posts (**Figure 68**).

7. Check float level as described in this chapter.

8. Assemble and install the float bowl as follows:

a. Insert the accelerator pump nozzle into the float bowl. Install the O-ring onto the nozzle. See **Figure 57**.

b. Install the rubber boot (A, **Figure 69**) and O-ring (B, **Figure 69**) onto the float bowl.

c. Connect the pump rod onto the lever assembly on the carburetor (**Figure 70**).

d. Insert the pump rod through the boot on the float bowl and engage the rod with the diaphragm while installing the float bowl (**Figure 71**). Then check that the pump rod is still attached to the lever assembly as shown in **Figure 72**. Check also to see if the pump rod is visible through the hole in the pump chamber in the float bowl (**Figure 73**). If not, re-

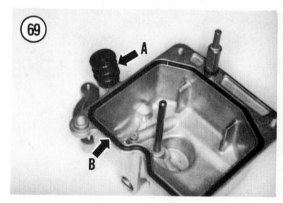

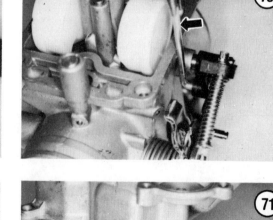

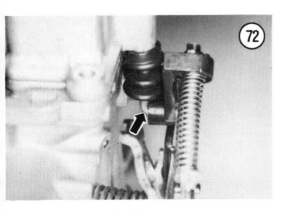

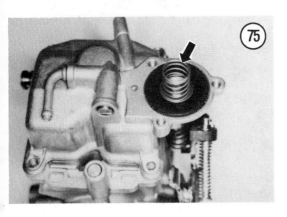

move and reinstall the float bowl and pump rod.

e. Install the float bowl screws and washers and tighten securely in a crisscross pattern.

9. Install the accelerator pump diaphragm assembly as follows:

a. Insert the accelerator pump diaphragm into the bottom of the float bowl. Make sure the diaphragm seats around the bowl groove evenly (**Figure 74**).

b. Install the spring into the center of accelerator pump diaphragm (**Figure 75**).

c. Install the O-ring into the cover passageway hole (**Figure 76**).

d. Align the cover assembly with the diaphragm and bowl and install the cover assembly. Install the screws and lockwashers and tighten securely. See **Figure 77**.

10. Drop the jet needle through the center hole in the vacuum piston. Insert the spring seat over the top of the needle to secure it.

11. Align the slides on the vacuum piston with the grooves in the carburetor bore and install the vacuum piston (**Figure 78**). The slides on the piston are

8

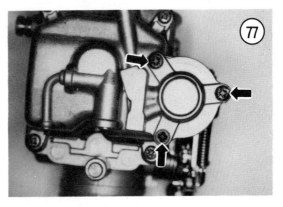

offset, so the piston can only be installed one way. When installing the vacuum piston, make sure the jet needle drops through the needle jet.

12. Seat the outer edge of the vacuum piston into the groove at the top of the carburetor piston chamber.

13. Insert the spring (**Figure 77**) into the vacuum piston so that the end of the spring fits over the spring seat.

14. Align the free end of the spring with the carburetor top and install the top onto the carburetor, compressing the spring.

15. Hold the carburetor top in place and lift the vacuum piston with your finger. The piston should move smoothly. If the piston movement is rough or sluggish, the spring may be improperly installed. Remove the top and reinstall the spring.

16. Install the 3 carburetor top screws, lockwashers and flat washers finger-tight (**Figure 80**).

17. Install the throttle cable bracket (A, **Figure 81**) onto the carburetor so that the end of the idle speed screw engages the top of the throttle cam stop (B, **Figure 81**). Hold the bracket in place and install the bracket's side mounting screw and washer; tighten screw securely. Then install the upper bracket mounting screw (**Figure 82**), lockwasher and flat washer finger-tight.

18. Tighten the 4 carburetor cap screws securely in a crisscross pattern.

19. Align the enrichener valve needle with the needle passage in the carburetor (**Figure 83**) and install the enrichener valve. Tighten the valve nut securely.

20. Install the float bowl overflow hose and secure it with its clamp.

Float Level Adjustment
(1984-1991)

An incorrect float level can cause flooding as well as poor fuel economy and acceleration.

> *NOTE*
> *If you have a 1990-1991 model and the engine is flooding, replace the 3-sided fuel valve with a 4-sided fuel valve and perform the **Float Level Adjustment (1992-on)** procedure in this chapter.*

The carburetor must be removed and partially disassembled for this adjustment.

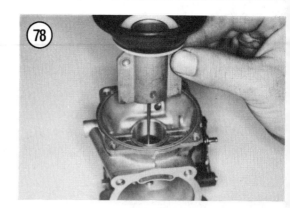

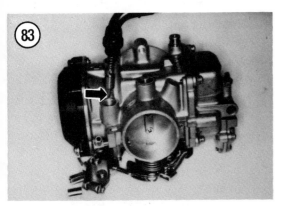

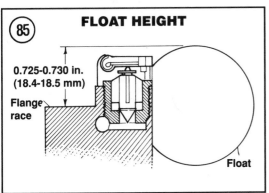

FLOAT HEIGHT

0.725-0.730 in.
(18.4-18.5 mm)

Flange
race

Float

NOTE
*1990-1991 model carburetors are equipped with a 3-sided fuel valve. Starting with 1992 models, carburetors are equipped with a 4-sided fuel valve. The 3-sided fuel valves are no longer available as replacement items. If you have a 1990-1991 model and it is equipped with a 3-sided fuel valve, service the float level as described in the following steps. If you have replaced the fuel valve on your model (you now have a 4-sided valve), refer to **Float Level Adjustment (1992-on)** in this chapter.*

1. Remove the carburetor as described in this chapter.
2. Remove the float bowl as described in this chapter.
3. One-piece floats are used in the CVH carburetor. Before checking the float level, check that the 2 float halves (**Figure 84**) are aligned at an equal height with each other. If the float halves are not in alignment, remove the float and check it for damage.
4. Turn the carburetor to position the float bowl as shown in **Figure 85**. Measure the float level from the face of the bowl mounting flange surface to the bottom float surface (**Figure 85**). Do not apply pressure to the float when measuring. The correct float level is 0.725-0.730 in. (18.4-18.5 mm).
5. If the float level is incorrect, remove the float pin and float.
6. Bend the float tang with a screwdriver to adjust.
7. Reinstall the float and the float pin and recheck the float level. Repeat until the float level is correct.
8. Reinstall the float bowl and carburetor as described in this chapter.

Float Adjustment (1992-on)

NOTE
This procedure should be followed if you have a 1990-1991 model carburetor that has had the fuel valve replaced with a 4-sided fuel valve.

An incorrect float level can cause flooding as well as poor fuel economy and acceleration.

The carburetor must be removed and partially disassembled for this adjustment.

1. Remove the carburetor as described in this chapter.

2. Remove the float bowl as described in this chapter.

3. One-piece floats are used in the carburetor. Before checking the float level, check that the 2 float halves (**Figure 86**) are aligned at an equal height with each other. If the float halves are not in alignment, remove the float and check for damage.

4. Place the carburetor intake spigot on a flat surface as shown in **Figure 87**. This is the base position.

5. Tilt the carburetor counterclockwise 15-20 degrees as shown in **Figure 88**. At this position, the float will come to rest as the float pin compresses without compressing the pin return spring.

> *NOTE*
> *If the carburetor is tilted less than 15 degrees or more than 20 degrees, the following carburetor measurements will be incorrect.*

6. Measure from the carburetor flange surface to the top of the float with a caliper or float gauge as shown in **Figure 88**. When measuring float level, mske sure you do not compress the float. The correct float level measurement is:

   a. 1990-1991 models with replacement 4-sided fuel vales: 0.725-0.730 in. (18.41-18.54 mm).

   b. 1992-on models: 0.413-0.453 in. (10.49-11.51 mm).

7. If the float level is incorrect, remove the float pin and float. With a screwdriver, bend the tab on the float hinge that contacts the fuel valve.

8. Reinstall the float and the float pin and recheck the float level. Repeat until the float level is correct.

9. Reinstall the float bowl and carburetor as described in this chapter.

CARBURETOR REJETTING

Do not try to solve a poor running engine problem by rejetting the carburetor if all of the following conditions hold true.

1. The engine has held a good tune in the past with the standard jetting.

2. The engine has not been modified (this includes the addition of accessory exhaust systems).

3. The motorcycle is being operated in the same geographical region under the same general climatic conditions as in the past.

(86)

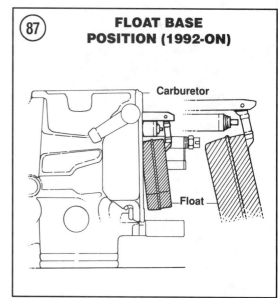

(87) **FLOAT BASE POSITION (1992-ON)**

Carburetor

Float

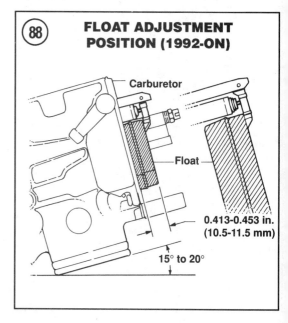

(88) **FLOAT ADJUSTMENT POSITION (1992-ON)**

Carburetor

Float

0.413-0.453 in. (10.5-11.5 mm)

15° to 20°

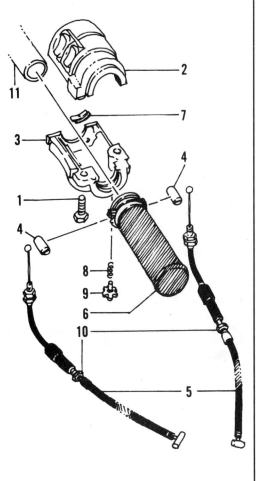

(89)

HANDLEBAR THROTTLE CONTROL ASSEMBLY

1. Screw
2. Upper housing
3. Lower housing
4. Ferrule
5. Control cable
6. Throttle grip
7. Friction spring
8. Spring
9. Adjusting screw
10. Adjusting nut
11. Handlebar

4. The motorcycle was and is being ridden at average highway speeds.

If those conditions all hold true, the chances are that the problem is due to a malfunction in the carburetor or in another component that needs to be adjusted or repaired. Changing carburetion jet size probably won't solve the problem. Rejetting the carburetor may be necessary if any of the following conditions hold true.

1. A non-standard type of air filter element is being used.

2. A non-standard exhaust system is installed on the motorcycle.

3. Any of the following engine components have been modified: pistons, cam, valves, compression ration, etc.

NOTE
When installing accessory engine equipment, manufacturers often enclose guidelines on rejetting the carburetor.

4. The motorcycle is in use at considerably higher or lower altitudes or in a considerably hotter or colder climate than in the past.

5. The motorcycle is being operated at considerably higher speeds than before and changing to colder spark plugs does not solve the problem.

6. Someone has previously changed the carburetor jetting.

7. The motorcycle has never held a satisfactory engine tune.

NOTE
If it is necessary to rejet the carburetor, check with a dealer or motorcycle per-formance tuner for recommendations as to the size of jets to install for your specific situation.

THROTTLE AND IDLE CABLE REPLACEMENT

All models use a dual cable arrangement. The throttle cable is installed into the right-hand anchor slot at the top of the throttle housing. The idle cable is installed into the left-hand anchor slot at the top of the throttle housing. See **Figure 89**, typical.

NOTE
You can identify the throttle and idle cables by checking the size of the

8

threads used on each cable's threaded adjuster. The throttle cable uses a 5/16-18 threaded adjuster. The threaded adjuster on the idle cable uses 1/4-20 threads.

1. Remove the fuel tank as described in this chapter.
2. Remove the air filter. See Chapter Three.

NOTE
Make a diagram of each cable's routing path before removing the cables from the bike. Also ID the cable guides or plastic ties on the diagram where used.

3. Loosen the friction adjusting screw.
4. Loosen the cable adjust nuts and turn the cable adjuster to obtain as much cable slack as possible.
5. Remove the screws securing the upper and lower right-hand switch/throttle housing together and separate the housing from the handlebar (**Figure 82**).
6. Loosen the cable locknuts at the lower switch housing.
7. Unhook the cables from the throttle grip and remove the ferrule from the end of each cable.
8. Unscrew each cable and remove it from the lower housing assembly.
9. At the carburetor, hold the lever up with one hand and disengage the cable end. Slip the cable out through the carburetor bracket. Repeat for the other cable.
10. Cut any plastic ties used to route the cables.
11. Remove the cables from the bike.
12. Clean the throttle in solvent and dry thoroughly. Check the throttle slots for cracks or other damage. Replace the throttle if necessary.
13. The friction adjust screw is secured to the lower switch housing with a circlip. If necessary, remove the friction spring, circlip, spring and friction adjust screw. Check these parts for wear or damage. Replace damaged parts and reverse to install. Make sure the circlip seats in the friction screw completely.
14. Clean the right-hand handlebar with solvent or electrical contact cleaner.
15. Wipe the right-hand handlebar and the inside of the throttle grip with graphite.

NOTE
The throttle cable uses a 5/16-18 threaded cable adjuster.

16. Screw the throttle cable into the lower switch housing and fit the ferrule onto the end of the cable.

Then insert the ferrule into the right-hand anchor slot at the top of the throttle.

NOTE
The idle cable uses a 1/4-20 threaded cable adjuster.

17. Screw the idle cable into the lower switch housing and fit the ferrule onto the end of the cable. Then insert the ferrule into the left-hand anchor slot at the top of the throttle.

18. Assemble the upper and lower switch housings and slide the throttle grip onto the handlebar. Install the housing screws and tighten securely. Operate the throttle and make sure both cables move in and out properly.

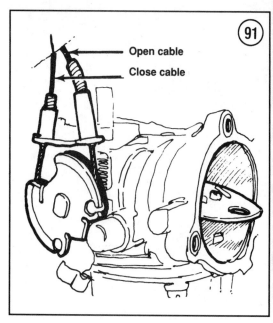

Open cable
Close cable

NOTE
Use your routing diagram along with
Step 18 when routing the new cables.

19A. *1984-1989 models except FLST/C*: Pass both cables so that they are positioned between the brake hose and the steering head and then route the cables along the frame to the carburetor.

19B. *1989 and earlier FLST/C*: With the throttle and idle cables hanging down from the throttle housing, position them next to the brake hose and then secure

them to the brake hose with a plastic tie. Then route the cables along the frame to the carburetor.

19C. *1990-on models except Springer*: Route both cables so that they are positioned between the brake hose and the right-hand handlebar. Then route then under the top frame tube, between the wiring harness connectors and their bracket and to the carburetor.

19D. *1990-on Springer*: Pass both cables through the vinyl covered clamp mounted under the bottom frame bracket and then route them under the frame bracket and to the carburetor. Secure both cables with a plastic tie where they pass under the frame bracket.

20. Locate the 2 cable support sleeves on the carburetor; one cable sleeve is longer than the other. See **Figure 91**, typical. Install the idle cable onto the *longer* support sleeve; attach the end of the cable onto the cable spool. Install the throttle cable onto the *shorter* support sleeve; attach the end of the cable onto the cable spool.

21. Operate the throttle grip and make sure the carburetor throttle linkage is operating correctly and with no binding. If operation is incorrect or there is binding, carefully check that the cables are attached correctly and there are no tight bends in the cables.

22. Adjust the throttle and idle cables as described in Chapter Three.

23. Install the fuel tank and seat.

24. Start the engine and turn the handlebar from side-to-side. Do not operate the throttle. If the engine speed increases as the handlebar assembly is turned, the throttle cables are routed incorrectly. Remove the seat and fuel tank and recheck the cable routing.

CHOKE/ENRICHENER CABLE REPLACEMENT

A choke cable is used on 1984-1989 models. An enrichener cable is used on 1990 and later models.

1. Remove the air cleaner assembly, if necessary to access the cable at the carburetor.

2. The pull knob can be found either between the fuel tanks (**Figure 92**) or on the left-hand side of the bike (**Figure 93**). If the pull knob is located between the fuel tanks, remove the trim panel and instruments as described under *Fuel Tank Removal* in this chapter.

3A. *1984-1989*: Perform the following:

   a. Disconnect the choke cable at the carburetor (**Figure 94**).

b. Disconnect the choke cable at the opposite end. See **Figure 95** or **Figure 96**.

c. Remove the choke cable.

3B. *1990-on*: Perform the following:

a. Disconnect the enrichener cable at the pull end (**Figure 93**).

b. Remove the carburetor and unscrew the enrichener from the carburetor.

c. Remove the enrichener cable.

4. Installation is the reverse of these steps. On 1990 and later models, align the enrichener valve needle with the needle passage in the carburetor (**Figure 83**) and install the enrichener valve. Tighten the valve nut securely.

5. Adjust the choke or enrichener cable as described in Chapter Three.

FUEL TANKS

Two steel fuel tanks are bolted to the upper frame tube and to each other; see **Figure 97** (1984-1991) or **Figure 98** (1992-on). Rubber grommets are used at almost all tank mounting points. A 3-way fuel shutoff valve is mounted onto the left-hand fuel tank; the tanks are connected by a crossover fuel line.

Fuel Tank Venting (1984-1991)

On 1984-1991 models, the fuel tanks are vented through the right-hand vuel cap.

Fuel Tank Venting (1992-on)

All 1992-on fuel tanks are vented through a vapor valve. The vent tube is connected to a standpipe mounted in the top of the right-hand fuel tank.

The vapor valve prevents fuel from flowing through the vent opening when the motorcycle is dropped or positioned at a low angle.

When replacing the vapor valve, note the following:

a. The vapor valve must be installed in a vertical position.

b. The vapor valve has 2 different end fittings. The long fitting must be installed at the top.

> *CAUTION*
> *If the vapor valve is installed correctly, excessive pressure may build in the fuel tank.*

Removal/Installation

When removing the fuel tanks, keep track of all fasteners and grommets so that you don't mix them up during installation.

Refer to **Figure 97** (1984-1991) or **Figure 98** (1992-on).

> *WARNING*
> *Gasoline is very volatile and presents an extreme fire hazard. Be sure to work in a well-ventilated area away from any open flames (including pilot lights on household appliances). Do not allow anyone to smoke in the area. Have a fire extinguisher rated for gasoline fires handy.*

1. Disconnect the battery negative lead.

2. Remove the odometer knob and screw from the instrument panel (**Figure 99**).

3. Remove the choke knob and nuts (**Figure 92**), if so equipped.

4. Remove the trim panel at the bottom of the tanks (**Figure 100**).

5. Remove the instrument panel mounting fasteners and lift it off of the fuel tanks.

6. Disconnect the fuel line at the fuel shutoff valve (**Figure 101**). Connect a longer hose to the shutoff valve fitting and place the open end of the hose in a gasoline fuel tank. Turn the shutoff valve to RE-

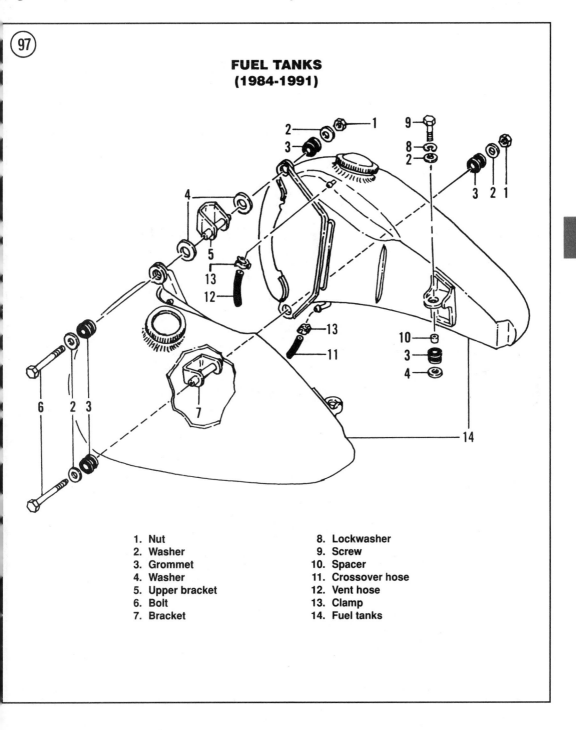

(97)

**FUEL TANKS
(1984-1991)**

1. Nut
2. Washer
3. Grommet
4. Washer
5. Upper bracket
6. Bolt
7. Bracket
8. Lockwasher
9. Screw
10. Spacer
11. Crossover hose
12. Vent hose
13. Clamp
14. Fuel tanks

8

SERVE and drain the fuel into the tank. Don't lose the fuel line insulator.

NOTE
Before disconnecting the crossover fuel line in Step 4, you should be prepared to plug both tank fittings after the hose is disconnected. The crossover tube can be plugged with a bolt or golf tee. The other

fuel tank can be plugged by installing a separate piece of hose, plugged in one end, onto the crossover tank fitting.

7. Disconnect the crossover fuel line (**Figure 102**). Plug the crossover fuel line and plug the other tank's fuel fitting.

8. On 1992-on models, disconnect the vent hose from the right-hand fuel tank; see **Figure 98**.

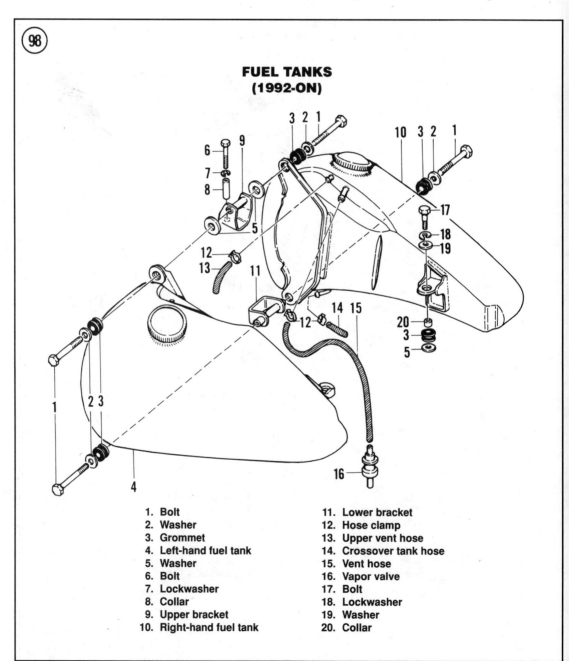

FUEL TANKS (1992-ON)

1. Bolt
2. Washer
3. Grommet
4. Left-hand fuel tank
5. Washer
6. Bolt
7. Lockwasher
8. Collar
9. Upper bracket
10. Right-hand fuel tank
11. Lower bracket
12. Hose clamp
13. Upper vent hose
14. Crossover tank hose
15. Vent hose
16. Vapor valve
17. Bolt
18. Lockwasher
19. Washer
20. Collar

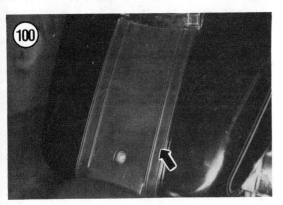

9. Remove the front upper and lower mounting bolts, washers and nuts.

NOTE
Note that 2 different size washers are used at the rear tank mounting bolts.

10. Remove the rear bolts, washers and spacers securing the tanks to the frame.

11. Disconnect the upper vent line (**Figure 103**) from the fuel tanks.

12. Check the fuel tanks for any remaining fasteners and remove the tanks from the frame.

NOTE
After removing the tanks, store them in a safe place—away from open flame or objects that could fall and damage them.

13. Drain any remaining fuel left in the tanks into the storage tank.

14. Installation is the reverse of these steps. Note the following.

15. Position the fuel tanks onto the frame tubes and install the washers, bolts and nuts in their original mounting positions. The large I.D. washers fit over the left- and right-hand ends on the upper bracket spacer tube and over the tapped anchor insert at the rear tank brackets. See **Figure 104**, typical.

16. Tighten the front and rear bolts to the tightening torque listed in **Table 2**.

17. Route the crossover tube over the lower front tank bracket and reconnect it at the other tank. Secure the line with new clamps. See **Figure 105**.

18. Remove the drain tube from the fuel tank and reconnect the fuel line. Secure the fuel line with a new hose clamp. Make sure the insulator is placed over the fuel line before reconnecting it.

8

19. Refill the tanks and check for leaks.

Inspection

Refer to **Figure 97** or **Figure 98** for this procedure.

1. Inspect all of the fuel and vent lines for cracks, age deterioration or damage. Replace damaged lines with the same type and size materials. The fuel line must be flexible and strong enough to withstand engine heat and vibration.

2. Check the fuel line insulator for damage.

3. Check for damaged or missing rubber dampers.

4. Remove the fuel tank caps and inspect the inside of the tank for rust or contamination. If there is a rust buildup inside the tank, clean and flush the tank as described in this chapter.

5. Inspect the fuel tank for leaks. If fuel was noted on the outside of the tank, and it was not spilled during refilling, the tank is leaking. If the leakage point is small, repair the leak as described in this chapter. If the leak is large, or if it cannot be repaired with a tank sealant, replace the fuel tank.

Fuel Tank Flushing

While the fuel tanks require very little in the way of service, moisture can build in the tanks. From this moisture, rust will form on the interior of the tank. If allowed to go unchecked, it will build and then mix with the gas in the tank, causing fuel supply and carburetion problems as it works it way through the fuel line and into the carburetor. If rust has formed in the tanks, perform the following.

1. Remove and drain the fuel tanks as described in this chapter.

2. Remove the fuel shutoff valve as described in this chapter. While the valve is off the tank, you should clean it as described in this chapter.

3. Plug all of the tank openings.

NOTE
The following steps describe the use of soap and water to clean the tank. If you plan to use a commercial fuel tank cleaning agent, follow the manufacturer's instructions.

4. To help break up the rust buildup, add a number of non-ferrous balls or pellets into the tank. Count the number of balls put into the tank so that you can be sure all of the balls are removed after cleaning.

WARNING
Do not use metal balls to loosen fuel tank deposits. Metal balls can produce a spark that could ignite fumes trapped in the tank, causing a serious explosion and possible personal injury.

5. Prepare a soap and water solution and pour it into the tank. Install the fuel cap and shake the tank to move the balls around and break up the rust deposits.

6. After cleaning the inside of the tank, pour the tank's contents into a container so that you can count the balls added previously.

7. If necessary, repeat Steps 5 and 6 until all of the rust has been removed. If the rust buildup is difficult to remove, you may have to use a commercial cleaning agent.

NOTE
If you are going to put the tank into storage, pour an equal amount of fuel and oil into each tank. This will prevent rust buildup during storage. Drain and

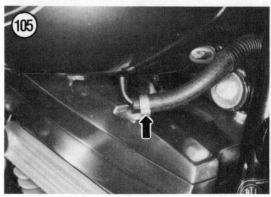

flush the tanks before starting the engine.

8. After all of the rust has been removed and the tank has been thoroughly flushed, allow it to air dry before installing it.

Repairing Minor Tank Leaks (Pin Hole Size)

Small pin hole size leaks can be repaired with a commercial fuel tank sealant. Follow the manufacturer's instructions. If the leak cannot be repaired with the sealant, refer further service to your dealer.

> *WARNING*
> *Welding a metal tank is serious business, as any trace of fuel left in the tank can cause it to explode. If the tank must be welded, refer service to your dealer. Do not attempt this repair at home. A tank explosion can cause severe personal injury.*

FUEL SHUTOFF VALVE

A 3-way fuel shutoff valve is mounted onto the left-hand fuel tank. A replaceable fuel strainer is mounted at the top of the shutoff valve.

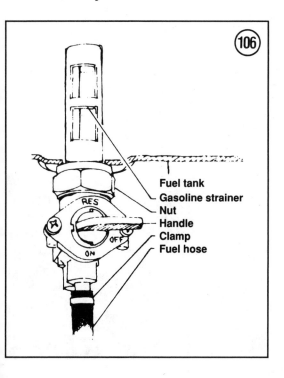

- Fuel tank
- Gasoline strainer
- Nut
- Handle
- Clamp
- Fuel hose

> *CAUTION*
> *Because the carburetor overflow fitting on California models is plugged closed, the fuel valve should always be turned off when the engine is not running. Otherwise, if fuel drains into the engine from a stuck carburetor fuel valve, the fuel will dilute the engine oil and cause engine damage. The carburetor overflow fitting is plugged because of the evaporative emission control system.*

Removal/Installation and Filter Cleaning

The fuel filter removes particles which might otherwise enter into the carburetor and possibly cause the float needle to remain in the open position. Refer to **Figure 106** for this procedure.

> *WARNING*
> *Gasoline is very volatile and presents an extreme fire hazard. Be sure to work in a well-ventilated area away from any open flames (including pilot lights on household appliances). Do not allow anyone to smoke in the area and have a fire extinguisher rated for gasoline fires handy.*

1. Disconnect the battery negative lead.
2. Turn the fuel valve to OFF.
3. Disconnect the fuel line at the fuel shutoff valve. Connect a longer hose to the shutoff valve fitting and place the open end of the hose in a gasoline fuel tank. Turn the shutoff valve to RESERVE and drain the fuel into the tank. Don't lose the fuel line insulator.
4. Loosen the shutoff valve fitting and remove the shutoff valve from the fuel tank. Catch any gas that may leak from the tank after the valve is removed.
5. Check the fuel strainer for contamination or damage. If the strainer cannot be thoroughly cleaned, replace it. Install a new gasket when installing a new strainer.

> *NOTE*
> *If the strainer is contaminated, the fuel tank may require cleaning and flushing. Refer to **Fuel Tank Flushing** in this chapter.*

6. Inspect the condition of the gasket; replace if necessary.

8

7. Clean the fuel tank threads of all sealant.

8. Coat the shutoff valve threads with Loctite Pipe Sealant With Teflon and insert the valve into the tank. Tighten the valve fitting to secure the valve.

9. Remove the drain tube from the fuel tank and reconnect the fuel line. Secure the fuel line with a new hose clamp. Make sure the insulator is placed over the fuel line before reconnecting it.

10. Refill the fuel tanks.

11. Check the area around the valve carefully to make sure no fuel is leaking.

EXHAUST SYSTEM

Removal/Installation

A number of exhaust systems have been used on the Harley-Davidson models covered in this manual. This procedure presents a general guideline for exhaust system removal and installation.

The O.E.M. exhaust system consists of exhaust pipes, mufflers, chrome covers, hose clamps, pipe gaskets, studs, washers and nuts. See **Figure 107**, typical.

Each exhaust pipe clamps to its respective cylinder head exhaust port with a flange plate and 2 nuts. Knitted steel gaskets (**Figure 108**) are placed between the cylinder exhaust pipe and cylinder head to prevent exhaust leakage. The 5/16 in. (7.9 mm) O.D. exhaust pipe studs are threaded with a fine thread (5/16-24) on one end and a coarse thread (5/16-18) on the opposite end. The coarse thread end threads into the cylinder head. The fine thread end is used to secure the 2 exhaust pipe flange mounting nuts.

1. Secure the bike on a suitable stand.

2. The exhaust pipe covers are held to the pipes with hose clamps. These clamps rust easily, so before removing them, spray each clamp with WD-40 or a similar lubricant to help prevent thread strippage when loosening them. You can hold a rag behind the clamp when spraying it to prevent the lubricant from contacting the engine or other components. Turn the hose clamp screws until the clamp is disconnected from around the pipe, then remove the covers.

3. Remove the bolts and washers securing the muffler to the support tube.

4. Loosen the muffler clamp bolts at the exhaust pipe and remove the muffler by twisting it off the exhaust pipe.

NOTE
Rust that forms between the muffler and exhaust pipe mating surfaces can make muffler removal difficult.

5. Loosen the hose clamp connecting the front and rear exhaust pipes.

6. Remove the nuts and washers securing the exhaust pipe flange at the cylinder head (**Figure 109**).

7. Slide the rear cylinder exhaust flange off of the cylinder head studs and remove the rear exhaust pipe. Repeat to remove the front cylinder exhaust

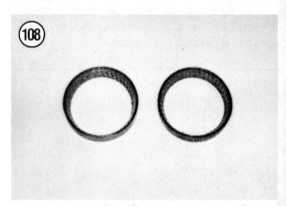

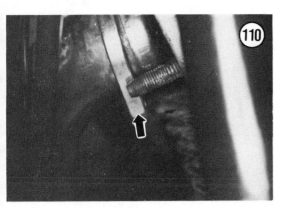

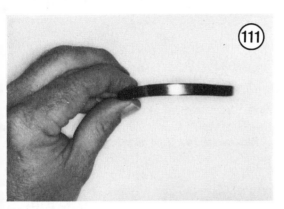

pipe. Stuff the exhaust port openings with a clean rag until reassembly. Note the gasket and exhaust washer, if used, as it is installed where the 2 exhaust pipes join. Discard the gasket.

CAUTION
If the exhaust flanges (Figure 110) do not slide off of the cylinder head studs easily in Step 7, the flange plate has distorted, a condition usually caused by overtightened flange nuts. Figure 111 shows a distorted or bowed flange. If a flange is severely distorted, the distance between the flange holes is reduced, causing the flange to wedge against the stud.

The edge of the flange will tend to dig into the stud threads as you try to slide it off, damaging the threads in the process. If a flange is tight, remove one of the cylinder head studs using the 2 nut technique (see Chapter One) before the stud threads are damaged, or if necessary, with a pair of Vise-grip pliers. The stud can be reinstalled before installing the exhaust pipe. The flange can either be removed from the exhaust pipe and flattened, or replaced as described later in this chapter.

8. Remove and discard the exhaust port gaskets (**Figure 112**).

9. Inspect the exhaust system as described in this chapter.

10. Install by reversing these removal steps while noting the following.

11. Before installing the new exhaust port gasket, scrape the gasket and the pipe fitting surfaces in the port (**Figure 113**) with a knife blade or similar tool to remove all carbon residue—removing the carbon will assure a good gasket fit. Wipe the port out with a rag, then align the new gasket with the port and push it into place. The new gasket should fit snugly in the port (**Figure 112**). Repeat for the other exhaust port and gasket.

12. If an exhaust flange was removed from its pipe, check that the retaining ring holding the flange to the exhaust pipe fits on the pipe tightly.

NOTE
If you had to remove or discard an exhaust stud, install the stud now. Refer to Stud Replacement in Chapter One.

8

13. Install the front cylinder exhaust pipe by inserting the end of the pipe into the exhaust port and sliding the flange over the studs. Install the washer and nut onto each stud. Tighten the nuts finger-tight only.

14. Repeat Step 13 to install the rear cylinder exhaust pipe, while inserting the crossover tube into the mating tube on the front exhaust pipe. If a gasket and exhaust washer were used where the 2 exhaust pipes mate, install a new gasket and the exhaust washer.

15. Install the mufflers onto the exhaust pipes, twisting them back and forth if necessary. Install the muffler bolts, lockwashers and flat washers and tighten the bolts finger-tight.

NOTE
Harley-Davidson does not list a torque specification for the exhaust pipe flange nuts. The nuts used are 5/16-24, grade 2 steel. Cross-referencing this information with the General Torque Specifications torque table in Chapter One, the nuts should not be tightened more than 12 ft.-lb. (16.5 N•m).

16. Starting at the exhaust pipe flange, tighten the exhaust pipe nuts to 12 ft.-lb. (16.5 N•m) with a torque wrench. Then work your way rearward and tighten the exhaust pipe and then the muffler mounting bolts securely. Do not overtighten the flange nuts or you may distort the flange.

NOTE
By tightening the exhaust pipe fasteners as described in Step 16 (front to rear), you can minimize exhaust leaks at the cylinder heads.

17. Wipe the exhaust pipes and mufflers with a clean rag to remove all traces of oil and grease, then polish the exhaust pipes.

18. Install the exhaust pipe covers and tighten securely with their hose clamps. Then clean and polish the covers.

NOTE
If you are installing new pipes, check with the pipe manufacturer and your dealer for information regarding tuning changes that may be required with the new pipes. You want the carburetor jetting and ignition timing to be as spot-on

as possible before starting the engine to prevent exhaust pipe bluing. If the pipes are new (have not been installed on a running engine), you may want to consider coating the inside of the exhaust pipes with a special sealer, such as DYNO-KOTE Pipe Bluing Preventative before installing them. See your dealer for additional information.

19. Start the engine and check for leaks. Some smoke will be evident after starting, especially if WD-40 was used on the hose clamps (prior to removal) or if oil and grease residue was not wiped off of the exhaust pipes and mufflers.

Inspection

1. Check the exhaust pipe for cracks or spots that have rusted through. A damaged or leaking pipe should be replaced.

2. Remove all rust from all pipe and muffler mating surfaces.

3. Check all of the hoses for damage or severe rusting. Clean or repair clamps as required.

4. If the exhaust flange is distorted, you should repair or replace it before reinstalling it. Perform the following:

   a. Each exhaust flange is secured to its exhaust pipe with a retaining ring. Pry the ring out of its groove and remove the flange. Discard the ring. See **Figure 114**.

   b. Examine the flange for distortion or other damage; the flange must be flat to fit properly onto the exhaust studs. If the flange is not severely distorted, you may be able to hammer or press it flat. If not, install a new flange. Make sure you do not damage the edges or holes in the flange when straightening it.

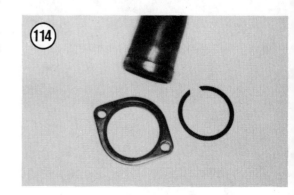

c. If you straightened a flange, check its fit on the exhaust studs before installing it onto the pipe.

NOTE
Chrome replacement flanges are available from accessory manufacturers.

d. Clean the end of the pipe to remove all rust and other debris. If you are reinstalling a used flange, clean the inside of the flange thoroughly.

e. Slide the flange on the exhaust pipe so that the shoulder on the flange faces toward the retaining ring groove. Install a new retaining ring and check its fit; it must be secure in its groove.

f. Repeat for the other exhaust pipe and flange, if required.

5. Replace worn or damaged exhaust pipe cover hose clamps as required (**Figure 115**).

6. Store the exhaust pipes in a safe place until they are reinstalled.

Exhaust System Care

The exhaust system greatly enhances the appearance of any motorcycle. And more importantly, the exhaust system is a vital key to the motorcycle's operation and performance. As the owner, you should periodically inspect, clean and polish the exhaust system. Special chemical cleaners and preservatives compounded for exhaust systems are available at most motorcycle shops.

Severe dents which cause gas flow restrictions require the replacement of the damaged part.

Problems occurring within the exhaust pipes are normally caused by rust from the collection of water

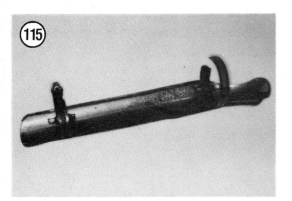

in the pipe. Periodically, or whenever the exhaust pipes are removed, turn the pipes to remove any trapped water.

EMISSION CONTROL
(1985-1991 CALIFORNIA MODELS)

All 1985 and later models sold in California are equipped with an evaporative emission control system. This system is used to prevent gasoline vapors from escaping into the atmosphere.

When the engine is not running, fuel vapor from the fuel tank is routed through the vapor valve and stored in a carbon canister. When the engine is running, these vapors are drawn through a purge hose and into the carburetor where they are to be burned in the combustion chambers. The vapor valve also prevents gasoline vapors from escaping from the carbon canister if the bike should fall onto its side.

During the 1988 model year, a set of reed valves and a vacuum operated valve (VOV) were added to the system. The reed valves are installed in the carburetor backplate to prevent vapors from the carbon canister from escaping into the atmosphere when the engine is not running. The VOV vents fuel vapors from the carburetor float bowl to the atmosphere when the engine is not running; when the engine is turned off, the VOV closes off the carburetor vent tube, preventing vapors from escaping into the atmosphere. A damaged VOV can cause the engine to run lean at high speeds. If you have a 1988 or later model and the engine is running lean at high speeds, test the VOV as described in this section.

Inspection/Replacement
(All Models)

Refer to **Figure 116** (1985-1987) or **Figure 117** (1988-on) for the components and the hose routing to the various parts. Before removing the hoses from any of the parts, mark the hose and the fitting with a piece of masking tape and identify where the hose goes. There are so many hoses on some of these models, it can be very confusing where each one is supposed to be attached.

1. Check all emission control lines or hoses to make sure they are correctly routed and properly connected.

2. Make sure that there are no kinks in the lines or hoses and that there are no signs of excessive wear or burning on lines that are routed near engine hot spots.

3. Check the physical condition of all lines and hoses in the system for cuts, tears or loose connections. These lines and hoses are subjected to various temperature and operating conditions and eventually become brittle and crack. Damaged lines or hoses should be replaced.

4. Check all components in the emission control system for visible signs of damage, such as broken fittings or broken nipples on the component.

5. When replacing one or more lines or hoses, refer to the diagram for your model. Disconnect one end of the line from the component, then connect one end of the new line to the component fitting. Disconnect the other end of the line and connect the other end of the new line. In this way, you will not make any mistakes and will be able to follow the routing of the old line, correcting any improper placement that

carries the line near components where it might rub and wear or be burned by hot components.

NOTE
Emission control hoses with different inside diameters come in bulk lengths and are cut to order by Harley-Davidson dealers or automotive parts stores. To assure that you get the right sizes, you should take a sample of each line with a different inside diameter, along with an estimate of the amount of each size that you will need.

Vapor Valve Replacement

Refer to **Figure 118**, typical.

1. Label the hoses at the vapor valve and then disconnect them.

2. Note that one end of the vapor valve is longer than the other end. The longer end must face up. Remove and replace the vapor valve.

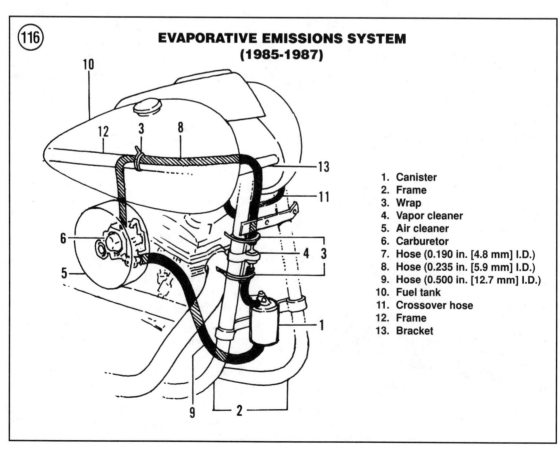

EVAPORATIVE EMISSIONS SYSTEM (1985-1987)

1. Canister
2. Frame
3. Wrap
4. Vapor cleaner
5. Air cleaner
6. Carburetor
7. Hose (0.190 in. [4.8 mm] I.D.)
8. Hose (0.235 in. [5.9 mm] I.D.)
9. Hose (0.500 in. [12.7 mm] I.D.)
10. Fuel tank
11. Crossover hose
12. Frame
13. Bracket

CAUTION
*The vapor valve must be installed in a vertical position with the **longer end** facing upward or excessive pressure will build in the fuel tank.*

Carbon Canister Replacement

1. Label and then disconnect the hoses at the canister.

2. Remove the canister mounting brackets, clamps, etc., and remove the canister.

3. Install by reversing these steps.

CAUTION
*Do not alter the carbon canister position. The canister must be mounted **below** the carburetor to work correctly.*

Reed Valves
(1988-1991)

Whenever the air filter assembly is removed from the bike, check the reed valve assembly for broken reed valves. To replace damaged reed valves, perform the following.

1. Remove the air filter (Chapter Three).

2. Remove the screw and lockwasher securing the reed stop to the backplate. Remove the top and bottom reeds (**Figure 119**).

3. Install the reed in the order shown in **Figure 119**. Install the screws and lockwashers and tighten securely.

Vacuum Operated Valve
(1988-1991)

During engine operation, the vacuum operated valve (VOV) vents fuel vapors from the carburetor

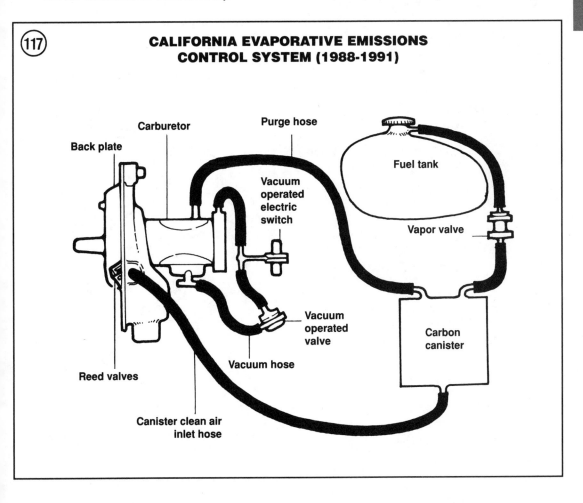

CALIFORNIA EVAPORATIVE EMISSIONS CONTROL SYSTEM (1988-1991)

(117)

float bowl to the atmosphere. When the engine is turned off, the VOV closes off the carburetor vent tube, preventing vapors from escaping into the atmosphere. If the diaphragm in the VOV should become damaged and leak, a vacuum leak would occur and cause the engine to run lean at high speeds. The vapor operated valves can be tested with a hand vacuum pump (Harley-Davidson part No. HD-23738 or equivalent).

1. Disconnect the VOV from the emission control system.

2. Attach a vacuum pump to port A in **Figure 120**.

3. Apply 1-2 in. HG vacuum to the valve while watching the pump gauge. The vacuum should remain steady. If vacuum reading decreases rapidly, the diaphragm is damaged.

4. If vacuum remains constant (Step 3), blow into port C; air should pass through the VOV. If air cannot pass through, the VOV is damaged.

5. Remove the vacuum pump and blow into port B; air should not pass through the VOV. If air can pass through, the VOV is damaged.

6. If the VOV failed to react as described in Steps 3-5, replace it with a new one.

EVAPORATIVE EMISSION CONTROL SYSTEM (1992-ON CALIFORNIA MODELS)

All of the California models covered by this manual are equipped with an evaporative emission control system (**Figure 121**). This system is used to prevent gasoline vapors from escaping into the atmosphere. When the engine is not running, fuel vapor from the fuel tank is routed through the vapor valve and stored in a carbon canister. When the engine is running, these vapors are drawn through a purge hose and into the carburetor where they are to be burned in the combustion chambers. The vapor valve also prevents gasoline vapors from escaping from the carbon canister if the bike should fall onto its side.

Solenoid-Operated Butterfly Valve Troubleshooting (1992-on)

On 1992-on California models, a solenoid-operated butterfly valve (**Figure 122**) is installed in the air filter backplate to seal off the backplate when the

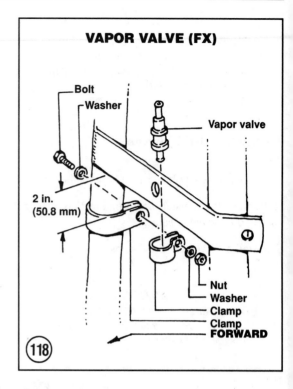

VAPOR VALVE (FX)

Bolt
Washer
Vapor valve
2 in. (50.8 mm)
Nut
Washer
Clamp
Clamp
FORWARD
(118)

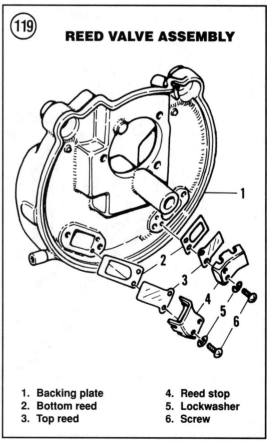

(119)

REED VALVE ASSEMBLY

1
2
3
4
5
6

1. Backing plate
2. Bottom reed
3. Top reed
4. Reed stop
5. Lockwasher
6. Screw

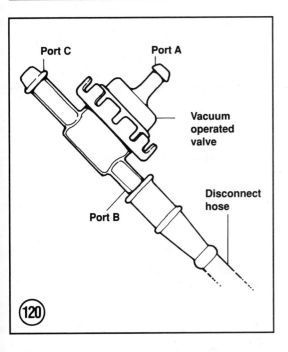

Port C

Port A

Vacuum operated valve

Port B

Disconnect hose

(120)

ignition switch is turned off to prevent fuel vapors from escaping into the atmosphere. Turning the ignition switch to the ON or IGNITION position energizes the solenoid hold-in windings. When the start switch is operated, the solenoid pull-in windings are energized. The hold-in windings will keep the butterfly valve open until the ignition switch is turned off.

Test the solenoid-operated butterfly valve if the engine suffers from sluggish acceleration and the engine's top speed tops out at 40 mph.

1. First check that all of the hoses are properly connected (see **Figure 121**). If the hoses are okay, proceed with Step 2.

2. Butterfly valve is not opening due to an electrical malfunction:

  a. Check that the solenoid valve electrical connector (**Figure 122**) is properly connected. If the connection is okay, disconnect the connec-

8

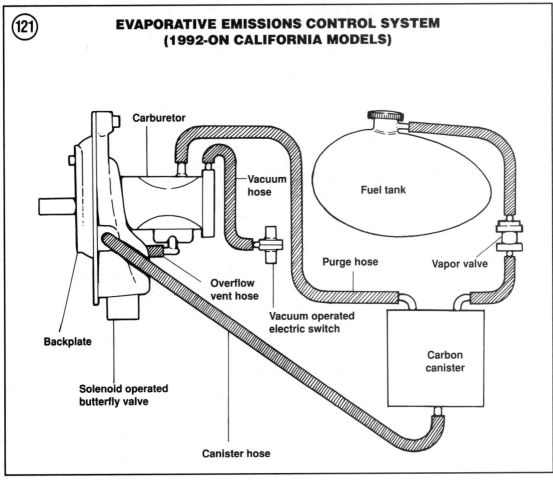

(121) **EVAPORATIVE EMISSIONS CONTROL SYSTEM (1992-ON CALIFORNIA MODELS)**

Carburetor

Vacuum hose

Fuel tank

Purge hose

Vapor valve

Overflow vent hose

Vacuum operated electric switch

Backplate

Carbon canister

Solenoid operated butterfly valve

Canister hose

tor and check for dirty or loose-fitting terminals; clean and repair as required. If okay, continue with sub-step b.

b. Test the solenoid as described under *Solenoid Testing* in this chapter.

3. Butterfly valve not opening and closing properly due to mechanical problem:

a. Check the mechanical linkage assembly (**Figure 122**) for corroded, loose, broken or missing components. The butterfly valve linkage and plunger should be cleaned every 5,000 miles as described in this chapter.

b. Check for a broken solenoid spring (**Figure 122**). If the spring is broken, replace the solenoid assembly. The spring cannot be replaced separately. Replace as described in this chapter.

Solenoid Valve Electrical Testing (1992-on)

Prior to testing the solenoid valve, fabricate the test harness shown in **Figure 123**.

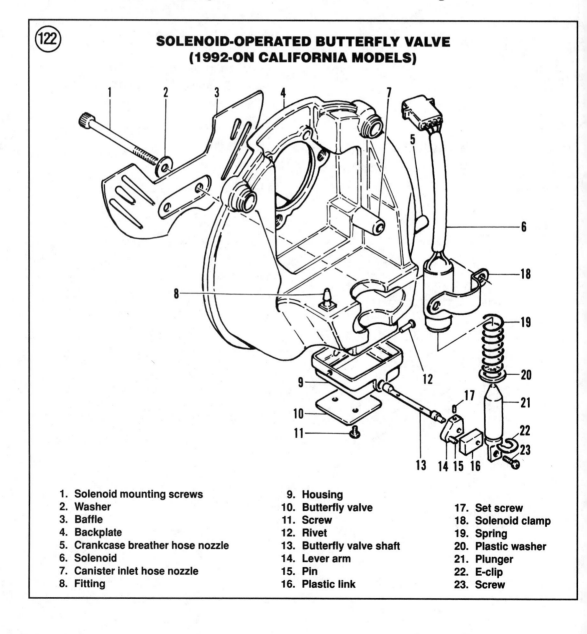

SOLENOID-OPERATED BUTTERFLY VALVE (1992-ON CALIFORNIA MODELS)

1. Solenoid mounting screws
2. Washer
3. Baffle
4. Backplate
5. Crankcase breather hose nozzle
6. Solenoid
7. Canister inlet hose nozzle
8. Fitting
9. Housing
10. Butterfly valve
11. Screw
12. Rivet
13. Butterfly valve shaft
14. Lever arm
15. Pin
16. Plastic link
17. Set screw
18. Solenoid clamp
19. Spring
20. Plastic washer
21. Plunger
22. E-clip
23. Screw

Solenoid winding resistance test

1. Remove the air filter and backplate as described under *Butterfly Valve Solenoid Removal/Installation/Adjustment (1992-on)* in this chapter.

2. Disconnect the solenoid valve 4 prong electrical connector (**Figure 122**).

3. Check for dirty or loose-fitting terminals and connectors.

4. Connect the solenoid test connector to the solenoid connector (**Figure 124**).

5. Refer to **Figure 125** for test connections and values and compare your meter readings to the stated values. If any of the meter readings differ from the stated values, replace the solenoid as described in this chapter.

6. If the resistance readings are correct, proceed with the following dynamic tests.

Pull-in coil test

A fully charged 12-volt battery is required for this test.

1. Remove the air filter and backplate as described under *Butterfly Valve Solenoid Removal/Installation/Adjustment (1992-on)* in this chapter.

2. Disconnect the solenoid valve 4-prong electrical connector (**Figure 122**).

3. Check for dirty or loose-fitting terminals and connectors.

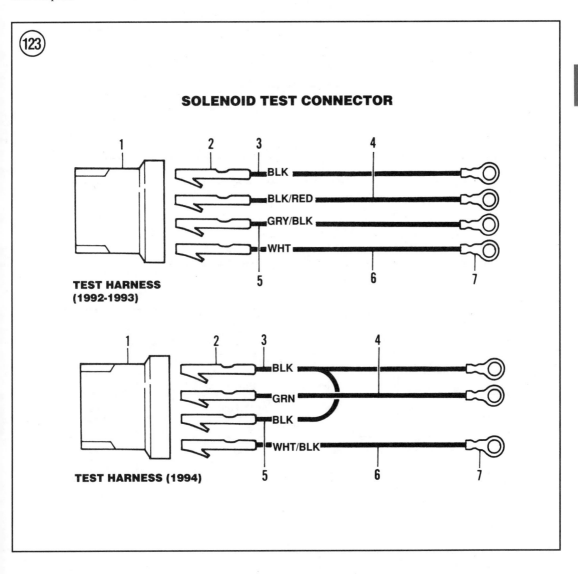

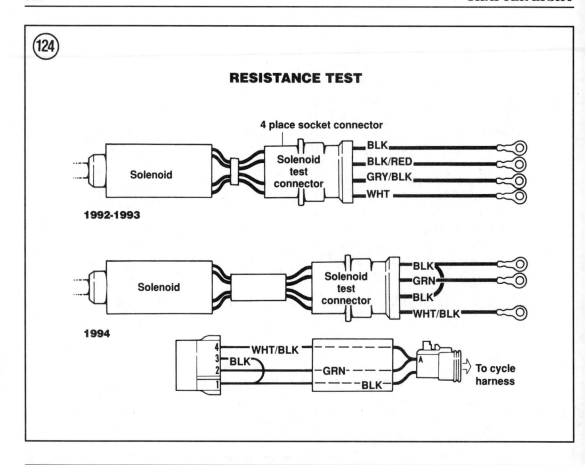

RESISTANCE TEST

4 place socket connector

Solenoid

Solenoid test connector

BLK
BLK/RED
GRY/BLK
WHT

1992-1993

Solenoid

Solenoid test connector

BLK
GRN
BLK
WHT/BLK

1994

4 WHT/BLK
3 BLK
2 GRN
1 BLK

To cycle harness

SOLENOID WINDING RESISTANCE

TEST	POSITIVE PROBE (+)	NEGATIVE PROBE (–)	RESISTANCE
1992-1993			
Pull-in	Back/Red	Gray/Black	4-6 Ohms
Hold-in	White	Black	21-27 Ohms
1994			
Pull-in	Green	Black	4-6 Ohms
Hold-in	White/Black	Black	21-27 Ohms

4. Connect the solenoid test connector to the solenoid connector (**Figure 124**).

5. Connect a 12-volt battery to the 2 solenoid test connector wires shown in **Figure 126**. The butterfly valve should open when battery voltage is applied. Disconnect the battery connections and note the following:

  a. If the butterfly valve now opens but did not open when originially connected to the wiring harness, perform Step 6.

  b. If the butterfly valve did not open, check the linkage for corroded, missing or damaged

parts. If the linkage assembly appears okay, retest with a new solenoid.

6. Perform the following:

  a. Switch an ohmmeter to R × 1 and cross the test leads. Then check for ground at the grey/black connector pin in the solenoid 4-prong connector. The ohmmeter should read 1 ohm or less.

  b. Reconnect the solenoid 4-prong connector.

  c. Switch a voltmeter to the 12 VDC scale.

  d. Connect the positive voltmeter lead to the black/red lead in the 4-prong connector and the negative probe to a good engine ground.

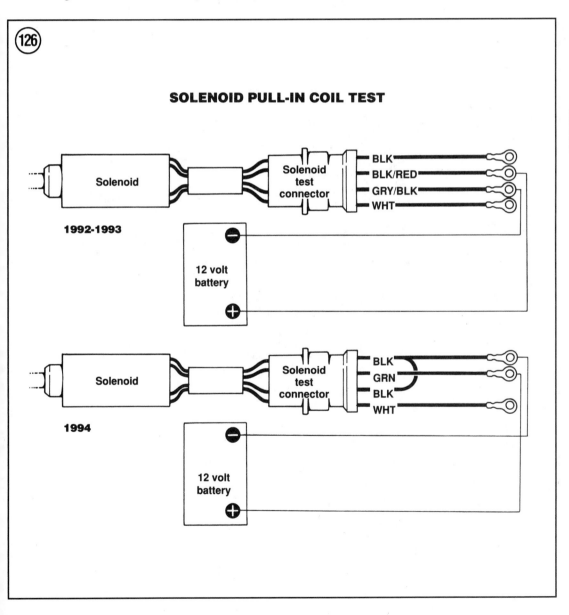

Press the start button while reading the voltage indicated on the voltmeter. It should be 12 volts.

7. If any of the meter readings differ from those specified in Step 6, there is a problem in the solenoid wiring harness. Use voltage and resistance checks to locate the damaged wire(s). After repairing the wire(s), repeat the above checks.

8. If the meter readings were correct as performed in Step 7, perform the following test.

Hold-in coil test

A fully charged 12-volt battery is required for this test.

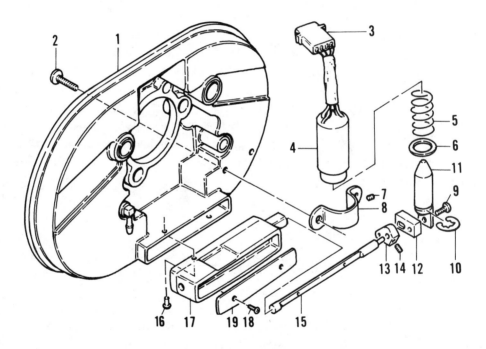

**SOLENOID/BUTTERFLY VALVE ASSEMBLY
(1992-ON CALIFORNIA MODELS)**

1. Backplate
2. Screw
3. Connector
4. Solenoid
5. Spring
6. Plastic washer
7. Set screw
8. Clamp
9. Screw
10. E-clip
11. Plunger
12. Plastic link
13. Lever arm
14. Set screw
15. Shaft
16. Rivet
17. Housing
18. Screw
19. Butterfly plate

1. Remove the air filter and backplate as described under *Butterfly Valve Solenoid Removal/Installation/Adjustment (1992-on)* in this chapter.

2. Disconnect the solenoid valve 4-prong electrical connector (**Figure 127**).

3. Check for dirty or loose-fitting terminals and connectors.

4. Connect the solenoid test connector to the solenoid connector (**Figure 124**).

5. Connect a 12-volt battery to the 2 solenoid test connector wires shown in **Figure 128** and perform the following:

    a. Open the butterfly valve carefully with a screwdriver by pushing inward on the left-hand side of the butterfly valve.

    b. Remove the screwdriver. The butterfly valve should remain open as long as the solenoid hold-in windings are energized.

    c. Disconnect the negative battery cable from the solenoid test connector. The butterfly valve should close.

    d. If the butterfly valve operated as described in sub-steps b and c, the solenoid hold-in windings are operating correctly.

    e. If the butterfly valve failed to operate properly, perform Step 6.

    f. Disconnect the positive battery cable from the solenoid test connector.

6. If the butterfly valve did not remain open in Step 5, sub-step b, perform the following:

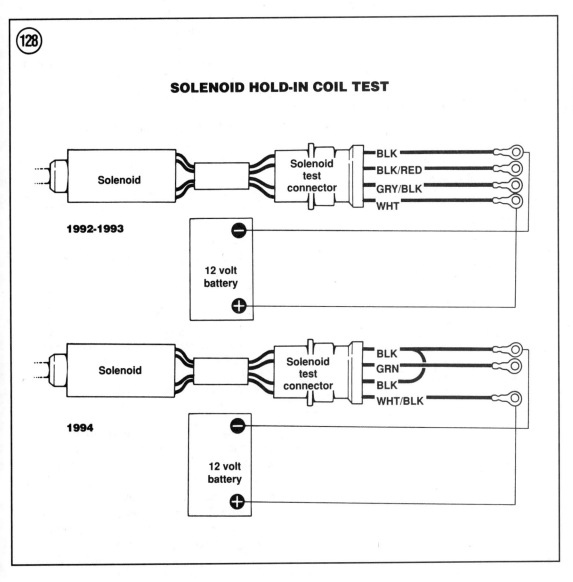

SOLENOID HOLD-IN COIL TEST

a. Switch an ohmmeter to R × 1 and cross the test leads. Then check for ground at the black connector pin in the solenoid 4-prong connector. The ohmmeter should read 1 ohm or less.

b. Reconnect the solenoid 4-prong connector.

c. Switch a voltmeter to the 12 VDC scale.

d. Connect the positive voltmeter lead to the white lead in the 4-prong connector and the negative probe to a good engine ground. Turn the ignition switch to the ON or IGNITION position and read the voltage indicated on the voltmeter. It should be 12 volts.

7. If any of the meter readings differ from those specified in Step 6, there is a problem in the solenoid wiring harness. Use voltage and resistance checks to locate the damaged wire(s). After repairing the wire(s), repeat the above checks.

8. If the solenoid test readings were correct but the butterfly valve does not work properly, perform Step 3 under *Solenoid-Operated Butterfly Valve Troubleshooting (1992-on)*.

9. Remove all test equipment and reconnect the solenoid 4-prong connector.

**Butterfly Valve and Solenoid
Cleaning and Lubrication
(1992-on)**

Refer to **Figure 122**.

1. Remove the air filter and backplate as described under *Butterfly Valve Solenoid Removal/Installation/Adjustment (1992-on)* in this chapter.

2. At every 2,500 mile (4,022 km) interval, inspect the butterfly valve and solenoid for proper operation.

3. At every 5,000 mile (8,045 km) interval, spray the butterfly valve and plunger with carburetor cleaner. Then, after the carburetor cleaner evaporates, lubricate the linkage and plunger with a dry film spray lubricant.

4. Reinstall the air filter and backplate as described in Chapter Three.

**Butterfly Valve Solenoid
Removal/Installation/Adjustment
(1992-on)**

Refer to **Figure 122**.

1. Remove the air filter as described in Chapter Three.

2. Disconnect the solenoid harness connector.

3. Disconnect the overflow hose from the backplate fitting.

4. Disconnect the canister inlet hose from the backplate fitting.

5. Remove the backplate mounting screws and backplate as follows (**Figure 122**):

a. Remove the backplate mounting screws.

b. Loosen the backplate-to-carburetor mounting screws in small amounts in a crisscross pattern. Continue until all of the screws are loosened, then remove the backplate and gasket.

6. To remove the solenoid:

a. Remove the small screw securing the plunger to the plastic link.

b. Remove the 2 long screws and washers securing the solenoid clamp to the backplate.

c. Remove the solenoid assembly.

7. Clean the backplate and lubricate the butterfly valve linkage as described under *Butterfly Valve and Solenoid Cleaning and Lubrication (1992-on)* in this chapter.

8. Assemble the plastic link to the plunger screw as follows:

a. Apply Loctite 222 (purple) to the plunger screw.

b. Then secure the plastic link to the plunger's deep side with the plunger screw. When doing so, the link slot must face toward the pin on the lever arm.

c. Tighten the plunger screw securely.

9. Install the solenoid into the backplate groove and install the lever arm pin into the plastic link.

NOTE
*Prior to installing the solenoid mounting screws, make sure the bottom of the baffle (3, **Figure 122**) is mounted behind the rib in the backplate. Otherwise, the solenoid plunger may bind when its mounting screws are tightened.*

10. Apply Loctite 222 (purple) to the solenoid mounting screws prior to installation. Install the screws, washers and clamp as shown in **Figure 122**. Do not tighten the screws at this time.

11. Adjust the solenoid plunger as follows:

a. Push the solenoid plunger into the solenoid until it bottoms out. Hold it in this position.

b. Check that the butterfly valve plate (10, **Figure 122**) is in its full-open position. Tighten the solenoid mounting screws to 20-22 in.-lbs (2.3-2.5 N•m).

CAUTION
Do not overtighten the solenoid mount-
ing screws; otherwise, the plunger may
bind in the solenoid.

c. Release the solenoid plunger and check that the butterfly valve plate is closed.

12. Reverse Steps 1-6 to complete installation.

Vapor Valve Replacement

1. Label the hoses at the vapor valve and then disconnect them.

2. Note that one end of the vapor valve is longer than the other end. The longer end must face *up*. Remove and replace the vapor valve.

CAUTION
The vapor valve must be installed in a
*vertical position with the **longer end***
facing upward or excessive pressure
will build in the fuel tank.

Emission/Carburetor Hose Routing (All Models)

Refer to **Figure 119** for emission hose routing.

Tables 1 and 2 are on the following page.

8

Table 1 CARBURETOR SPECIFICATIONS

	Main jet	Pilot jet
1984	160	50
1985	165	50
1986	170	50
1987	165	50
1988-1989		
49-state models	165	52
California	140	42
1990-1991		
49-state models	185	45
California	165	42
1992		
49-state models	165	40
California	160	40
1993		
49-state models	175	42
California	160	42
HDI*	165	40
1994		
49-state models	165	42
California	165	42
HDI*	165	42
* Harley-Davidson international models.		

Table 2 TIGHTENING TORQUES

	ft.-lb.	N·m
Carburetor mounting screws		
1984	6-8	8.3-11
1985-on	15-17	20-23.4
Carburetor Allen head mounting bolt	10-12	14-16
Captive carburetor bolt		
1984	—	—
1985-on	3-5	4-7
Fuel tank bolts	15-19	20-26

CHAPTER NINE

ELECTRICAL SYSTEM

All models covered in this manual are equipped with a 12-volt, negative-ground electrical system. Many electrical problems can be traced to a simple cause such as a loose or corroded connection or frayed wire. While these are easily corrected problems which may not appear important, they can quickly lead to serious difficulty if allowed to go uncorrected.

This chapter provides service procedures for the battery, charging system, ignition system, starter, lights, switches and circuit breakers. Tune-up procedures involving the ignition system are described in Chapter Three.

Tables 1-4 are found at the end of chapter.

BATTERY

The battery is the single most important component in the motorcycle electrical system. Yet most electrical system troubles can be traced to battery neglect. In addition to checking and correcting the battery electrolyte level on a weekly basis, the battery should be cleaned and inspected at periodic intervals. Battery capacity is listed in **Table 1**.

Safety Precautions

When working with batteries, use extreme care to avoid spilling or splashing the electrolyte. This solution contains sulfuric acid, which can ruin clothing and cause serious chemical burns. If any electrolyte is spilled or splashed on clothing or skin, immediately neutralize with a solution of baking soda and water, then flush with an abundance of clean water.

> *WARNING*
> *Electrolyte splashed into the eyes is extremely harmful. Safety glasses should always be worn while working with batteries. If electrolyte is splashed into the eyes, call a physician immediately, force the eyes open and flood with cool, clean water for approximately 15 minutes.*

If electrolyte is spilled or splashed onto any surface, it should be immediately neutralized with baking soda and water solution and then rinsed with clean water.

While batteries are being charged, highly explosive hydrogen gas forms in each cell. Some of this gas escapes through filler cap openings and may form an explosive atmosphere in and around the battery. This condition can persist for several hours. Sparks, an open flame or a lighted cigarette can ignite the gas, causing an internal battery explosion and possible serious personal injury.

Take the following precautions to prevent an explosion:

1. Do not smoke or permit any open flame near any battery being charged or which has been recently charged.

9

2. Do not disconnect live circuits at battery terminals since a spark usually occurs when a live circuit is broken.

3. Take care when connecting or disconnecting any battery charger. Be sure its power switch is off before making or breaking connections. Poor connections are a common cause of electrical arcs which cause explosions.

4. Keep all children and pets away from charging equipment and batteries.

Care and Inspection

For maximum battery life, it should be checked periodically for electrolyte level, state of charge and corrosion. During hot weather periods, frequent checks are recommended. If the electrolyte level is below the bottom of the vent well in one or more cells, add distilled water as required. To assure proper mixing of the water and acid, operate the engine immediately after adding water. *Never* add battery acid instead of water—this will shorten the battery's life.

On all models covered in this manual, the negative side is grounded. When removing the battery, disconnect the negative (–) ground cable first, then the positive (+) cable. This minimizes the chance of a tool shorting to ground when disconnecting the "hot" positive cable.

> *WARNING*
> *When performing the following procedures, protect your eyes, skin and clothing. If electrolyte gets into your eyes, flush your eyes thoroughly with clean water and get prompt medical attention.*

1. Remove the seat.

2. Disconnect the negative battery cable from the battery (**Figure 1**).

3. Disconnect the positive battery cable from the battery.

4. Remove the battery hold-down strap and disconnect the battery vent tube at the battery.

5. Remove the battery from the motorcycle.

> *CAUTION*
> *Be careful not to spill battery electrolyte on painted or polished surfaces. The liquid is highly corrosive and will damage the finish. If it is spilled, wash it off*

immediately with soapy water and thoroughly rinse with clean water.

6. Check the entire battery case for cracks or other damage.

7. Inspect the battery tray and cushion for contamination or damage. Clean with a solution of baking soda and water.

8. Check the battery hold-down strap for age deterioration, cracks or other signs of damage. Replace strap if required.

9. Check the battery terminal parts—bolts, spacers and nuts—for corrosion or damage. Clean parts thoroughly with a solution of baking soda and water. Replace severely corroded or damaged parts.

10. Cover the vent holes in each cap with small pieces of masking tape.

> *NOTE*
> *Keep cleaning solution out of the battery cells or the electrolyte level will be seriously weakened.*

11. Clean the top of the battery with a stiff bristle brush using the baking soda and water solution.

Rinse the battery case with clean water and wipe dry with a clean cloth or paper towel.

12. Check the battery cable clamps for corrosion and damage. If corrosion is minor, clean the battery cable clamps with a stiff wire brush. Replace severely worn or damaged cables.

NOTE
Do not overfill the battery cells in Step 13. The electrolyte expands due to heat from charging and will overflow if the level is above the upper level line.

13. Remove the caps (**Figure 2**) from the battery cells and check the electrolyte level. Add distilled water, if necessary, to bring the level within the upper and lower level lines on the battery case (**Figure 3**).

14. Reposition the battery in the battery tray. Make sure the rubber cushion is installed in the bottom of the tray before installing the battery. Install the battery strap to secure the battery.

15. Reinstall the positive battery cable, then the negative battery cable. See **Figure 1**.

CAUTION
Be sure the battery cables are connected to their proper terminals. Connecting the battery backwards will reverse the polarity and damage the rectifier.

WARNING
After installing the battery, make sure the vent tube is not pinched. A pinched or kinked tube would allow high pressure to accumulate in the battery and cause the battery to explode. If the vent tube is damaged, replace it.

16. Coat the battery connections with a petroleum jelly such as Vaseline or a water resistant grease.

③

Testing

Hydrometer testing is the best way to check battery condition. Use a hydrometer with numbered graduations from 1.100 to 1.300 rather than one with just color-coded bands. To use the hydrometer, squeeze the rubber ball, insert the tip into the cell and release the ball (**Figure 4**).

NOTE
Do not attempt to test a battery with a hydrometer immediately after adding water to the cells. Charge the battery for 15-20 minutes at a rate high enough to cause vigorous gassing and allow the water and electrolyte to mix thoroughly.

Draw enough electrolyte to float the weighted float inside the hydrometer. When using a temperature-compensated hydrometer, release the electrolyte and repeat this process several times to make sure the thermometer has adjusted to the electrolyte temperature before taking the reading.

Hold the hydrometer vertically and note the number in line with the surface of the electrolyte (**Figure 5**). This is the specific gravity for this cell. Return the electrolyte to the cell from which it came.

The specific gravity of the electrolyte in each battery cell is an excellent indication of that cell's condition (**Table 2**). A fully charged cell will read 1.275-1.280 while a cell in good condition reads from 1.225-1.250 and anything below 1.225 is dead. Charging is also necessary if the specific gravity varies more than 0.050 from cell to cell.

NOTE
If a temperature-compensated hydrometer is not used, add 0.004 to the specific gravity reading for every 10° above 80° F (25° C). For every 10° below 80° F (25° C), subtract 0.004.

Charging

A good state of charge should be maintained in batteries used for starting. When charging the battery, note the following:

a. During charging, the cells will show signs of gas bubbling. If one cell has no gas bubbles or if its specific gravity is low, the cell is probably shorted.

9

b. If a battery not in use loses its charge within a week after charging or if the specific gravity drops quickly, the battery is defective. A good battery should only self-discharge approximately 1% each day.

> *CAUTION*
> *Always remove the battery from the bike before connecting charging equipment.*

> *WARNING*
> *During charging, highly explosive hydrogen gas is released from the battery. The battery should be charged only in a well-ventilated area, and open flames and cigarettes should be kept away. Never check the charge of the battery by arcing across the terminals; the resulting spark can ignite the hydrogen gas.*

1. Remove the battery from the bike as described in this chapter.
2. Connect the positive (+) charger lead to the positive battery terminal and the negative (–) charger lead to the negative battery terminal.
3. Remove all vent caps (**Figure 2**) from the battery, set the charger at 12 volts, and switch it on. Normally, a battery should be charged at a slow charge rate of 1/10 its given capacity. See **Table 1** for battery capacity.

> *CAUTION*
> *The electrolyte level must be maintained at the upper level during the charging cycle; check and refill with distilled water as necessary.*

4. The charging time depends on the discharged condition of the battery. The chart in **Figure 6** can be used to determine approximate charging times at different specific gravity readings. For example, if the specific gravity of your battery is 1.180, the approximate charging time would be 6 hours.
5. After the battery has been charged for about 8 hours, turn the charger off, disconnect the leads and check the specific gravity. It should be within the limits specified in **Table 2**. If it is, and remains stable for one hour, the battery is charged.

New Battery Installation

When replacing the old battery with a new one, be sure to charge it completely (specific gravity,

1.260-1.280) before installing it. Failure to do so, or using the battery with a low electrolyte level will permanently damage the battery.

Jump Starting

If the battery becomes severely discharged, it is possible to start and run an engine by jump starting

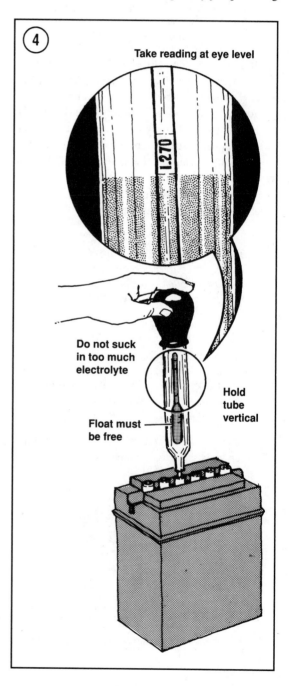

4

Take reading at eye level

1.270

Do not suck in too much electrolyte

Float must be free

Hold tube vertical

it from another battery. If the proper procedure is not followed, however, jump starting can be dangerous. Check the electrolyte level before jump starting any battery. If it is not visible or if it appears to be frozen, do not attempt to jump start the battery, as the battery may explode or rupture.

The booster battery must be a fully charged 12 volt battery.

WARNING
Use extreme caution when connecting a booster battery to one that is discharged to avoid personal injury or damage to the system. Do not lean over the batteries when making the connections. Safety glasses should be worn when performing the following procedure.

1. Position the 2 vehicles so that the jumper cables will reach between batteries, but the vehicles do not touch.
2. Remove the seat to gain access to the dead battery. Remove parts as required to access the booster battery.
3. Make sure all electrical accessories are turned off.
4. Connect the jumper cables in the following order (**Figure 7**):

    a. Connect the positive (+) jumper cable between the 2 battery positive terminals.

    b. Connect one end of the negative (–) jumper cable to the booster battery negative terminal. Connect the opposite end to an unpainted engine case bolt on the bike with the dead battery. *Do not* connect the jumper cable to the negative battery terminal on the dead battery.

WARNING
*An electrical arc may occur when the final connection is made. This could cause an explosion if it occurs near the battery. For this reason, the final connection should be made to a good ground **away** from the battery and not to*

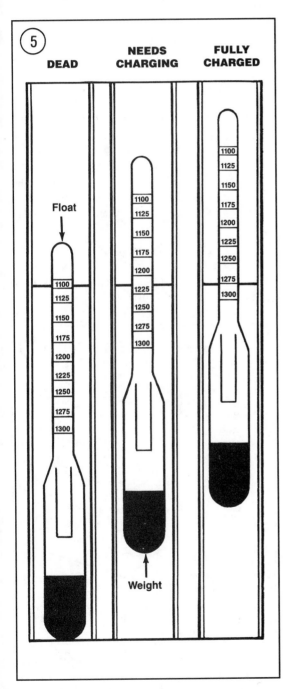

⑤

DEAD	NEEDS CHARGING	FULLY CHARGED

Float

Weight

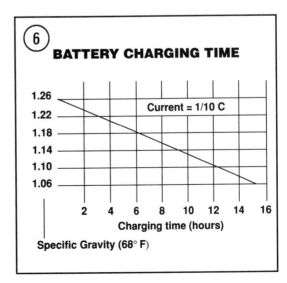

⑥

BATTERY CHARGING TIME

Current = 1/10 C

Specific Gravity (68° F)

Charging time (hours)

9

the battery itself. This includes keeping the connection away from the battery vent tube.

NOTE
Do not connect the negative jumper cable to a chrome or painted part as the connection may discolor it.

5. Check that all jumper cables are out of the way.

NOTE
When attempting to start the engine in Step 6, do not operate the starter longer than 6 seconds. Excessive starter operation will overheat the starter and cause damage. Allow 15 seconds between starting attempts.

6. Start the engine. Once it starts, run it at a moderate speed.

CAUTION
Racing the engine may cause damage to the electrical system.

7. Remove the jumper cables in the exact reverse order.

CHARGING SYSTEM

The charging system consists of the battery, alternator, regulator, ignition switch, circuit breaker and connecting wiring.

The alternator generates an alternating current (AC) which the rectifier converts to direct current (DC). The regulator maintains the voltage to the battery and load (lights, ignition, etc.) at a constant voltage regardless of variations in engine speed and load.

Service Precautions

Before servicing the charging system, observe the following precautions to prevent damage to any charging system component.
1. Never reverse battery connections. Instantaneous damage may occur.
2. Do not short across any connection.
3. Never attempt to polarize an alternator.
4. Never start the engine with the alternator disconnected from the voltage regulator/rectifier, unless instructed to do so in testing.

5. Never start or run the engine with the battery disconnected.

6. Never attempt to use a high-output battery charger to assist in engine starting.

7. Before charging battery, disconnect the negative battery lead.

8. Never disconnect the voltage regulator connector with the engine running.

9. Do not mount the voltage regulator/rectifier unit at another location.

10. Make sure the battery negative terminal is connected to both engine and frame.

Testing

A malfunction in the charging system generally causes the battery to remain undercharged. Perform the following visual inspection to determine the cause of the problem. If the visual inspection proves satisfactory, test the charging system as described in Chapter Two.

1. Make sure the battery cables are connected properly (**Figure 1**). The red cable must be connected to the positive battery terminal. If polarity is reversed, check for a damaged rectifier.

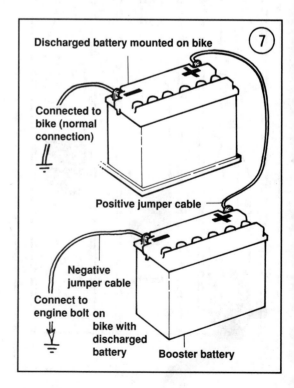

Discharged battery mounted on bike ⑦

Connected to bike (normal connection)

Positive jumper cable

Negative jumper cable

Connect to engine bolt on bike with discharged battery

Booster battery

2. Inspect the terminals for loose or corroded connections. Tighten or clean as required.

3. Inspect the physical condition of the battery. Look for bulges or cracks in the case, leaking electrolyte or corrosion build-up.

4. Carefully check all connections at the alternator to make sure they are clean and tight.

5. Check the circuit wiring for corroded or loose connections. Clean, tighten or connect as required.

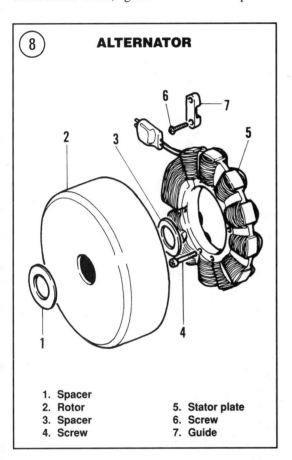

ALTERNATOR

1. Spacer	5. Stator plate
2. Rotor	6. Screw
3. Spacer	7. Guide
4. Screw	

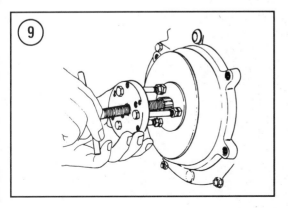

Rotor
Removal/Installation

Refer to **Figure 8**, typical for this procedure.

1. Disconnect the negative battery cable at the battery.

2. Remove the primary cover, compensating sprocket, primary drive, clutch and primary case (1984-1988 models only) as described in Chapter Five.

3A. *1984 models*: Screw the rotor puller into the rotor as shown in **Figure 9**. Use the Harley-Davidson rotor puller (part No. HD-95-960-52B) or equivalent. Turn the rotor puller center bolt with a wrench until the rotor is free. Remove the rotor and puller.

3B. *1985-on*: The rotor installed on these models can either be slip fit or machined with splines. Spacers are installed on both sides of the rotor. These spacers are different, so follow the installation procedure later in this chapter so you don't mix them up. To remove the rotor, first remove the large O.D. spacer (**Figure 10**). Use 2 bolts as shown in **Figure 11** or slip 3 pieces of wire and hook it behind the rotor and remove the rotor from the end of the crankshaft. Remove the small O.D. spacer from behind the rotor (**Figure 12**).

Inspection

1. Check the rotor (**Figure 13**) carefully for cracks or breaks.

> *WARNING*
> *A cracked or chipped rotor must be replaced. A damaged rotor may fly apart at high rpm, throwing metal fragments over a large area. Do not attempt to repair a damaged rotor.*

2. Check the rotor bore or taper for signs of scoring, cracks or other damage.

3. Replace damaged parts as required.

Installation

> *CAUTION*
> *Carefully inspect the inside of the rotor (**Figure 13**) for small bolts, washers or other metal "debris" that may have been picked up by the magnets. These small metal bits can cause severe damage to the alternator stator assembly.*

9

1. Install the stator assembly, if previously removed, as described in this chapter.

2A. *1984*: Slide the rotor onto the crankshaft.

2B. *1985-on*: Install the rotor assembly as follows:

   a. Install the smaller O.D. spacer onto the crankshaft (**Figure 12**).

   b. Slide the rotor (**Figure 13**) onto the crankshaft.

   c. Install the larger O.D. spacer onto the crankshaft (**Figure 10**).

> *NOTE*
> *The small washer (A, **Figure 14**) shown next to the large O.D. rotor spacer (B, **Figure 14**) is used for primary chain alignment. This washer will be installed when you install the primary drive assembly in Chapter Five. Do not confuse it with a spacer used with the rotor assembly.*

3. Install the primary drive components as described in Chapter Five. Make sure to torque the compensating sprocket nut as described in Chapter Five.

Stator
Removal/Installation

The stator (**Figure 8**) is mounted behind the rotor and bolted to the left-hand crankcase half. Early models used a lockplate and screw combination to secure the stator to the crankcase. Later models use Torx screws with a locking adhesive applied to the screw. Torx screws must be replaced after removal.

1. Remove the rotor as described in this chapter.

2. Disconnect the electrical connector at the stator (**Figure 15**).

3. Push the connector through the engine crankcase as shown in **Figure 16**.

4A. *Early models*: Bend the lockplates away from the stator screws. Then remove the screws and lockplates.

4B. *Later models*: Remove and discard the stator plate Torx screws (**Figure 17**).

5. Remove the stator assembly (**Figure 18**).

6. Inspect the stator wires (**Figure 19**) for fraying or damage. Check the stator connector pins for looseness or damage. Replace the stator if necessary.

7. Installation is the reverse of these steps. Note the following.

8. On early models, replace the lockplates if they cannot be reused. On late models, secure the stator plate with *new* Torx screws.

9. Install the rotor as described in this chapter.

Voltage Regulator
Removal/Installation

The regulator cannot be rebuilt; if damaged it must be replaced.

1. Disconnect the voltage regulator electrical connectors.

2. Remove the voltage regulator mounting fasteners and remove the voltage regulator (**Figure 20**).

3. Install by reversing these removal steps.

IGNITION SYSTEM

The ignition system consists of a single ignition coil, 2 spark plugs, an inductive pickup unit, an ignition module and a vacuum operated electric switch (VOES). This system has a full electronic advance. The inductive pickup unit is driven by the engine and generates pulses which are routed to the solid-state ignition control module. This control module computes the ignition timing advance and ignition coil dwell time, eliminating the need for mechanical advance and routine ignition service.

9

The vacuum operated electric switch (VOES) senses intake manifold vacuum through a carburetor body opening. The switch is open when the engine is in low vacuum situations such as acceleration and high load. The switch is closed when engine vacuum is high as during a low engine load condition. The VOES allows the ignition system to follow 2 spark advance curves. A maximum spark curve can be used during a high-vacuum condition to provide improved fuel economy and performance. During heavy engine load and acceleration (low vacuum) conditions, the spark can be retarded to minimize ignition knock and still maintain performance.

The timing sensor is triggered by the leading and trailing edges of the 2 rotor slots. As rpm increases, the control module "steps" the timing in 3 stages of advance.

Refer to **Figure 21** or **Figure 22** for a diagram of the ignition circuit.

Ignition Component Replacement

Refer to **Figure 23** for this procedure.

1. Disconnect the negative battery lead.

2. Drill out the outer cover rivets with a 3/8 in. (9.5 mm) drill bit (**Figure 24**).

3. Using a punch, tap the rivets through the outer cover (**Figure 25**) and remove the outer cover. See **Figure 26**.

4. Using a punch, tap the rivets through the inner cover (**Figure 27**). Then remove the inner cover Phillips screws and remove the cover (**Figure 28**).

5. Remove the gasket (**Figure 29**).

6. Remove the screws (**Figure 30**) securing the sensor plate to the crankcase.

7A. On 1984-1992 models, disconnect the sensor wire connector at the crankcase. Then remove the

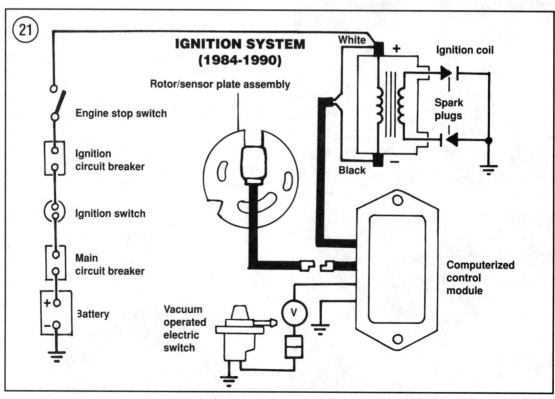

IGNITION SYSTEM (1984-1990)

Engine stop switch
Ignition circuit breaker
Ignition switch
Main circuit breaker
Battery
Vacuum operated electric switch
Rotor/sensor plate assembly
White
Black
Ignition coil
Spark plugs
Computerized control module

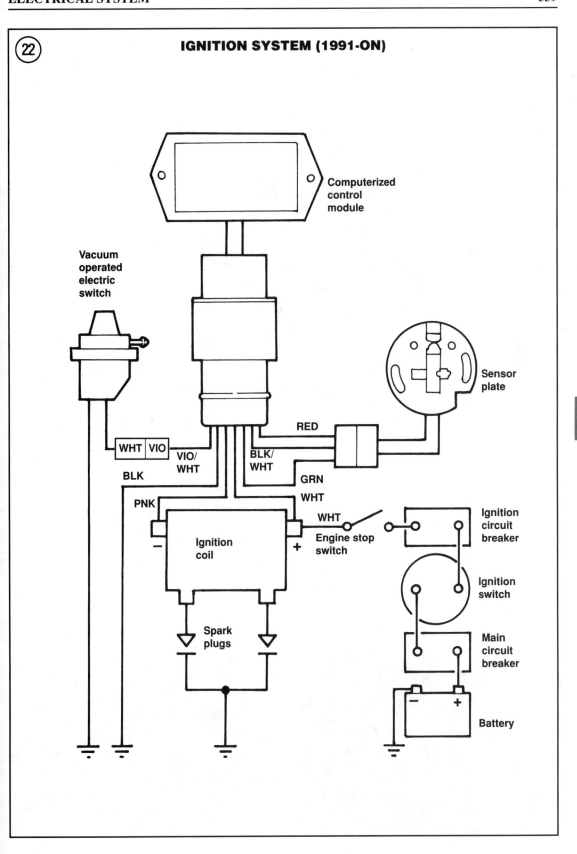

IGNITION SYSTEM (1991-ON)

22

Computerized
control
module

Vacuum
operated
electric
switch

Sensor
plate

9

RED

WHT | VIO

VIO/
WHT

BLK/
WHT

BLK

GRN

PNK

WHT

WHT

Engine stop
switch

Ignition
circuit
breaker

Ignition
coil

−

+

Ignition
switch

Spark
plugs

Main
circuit
breaker

−   +

Battery

IGNITION SYSTEM

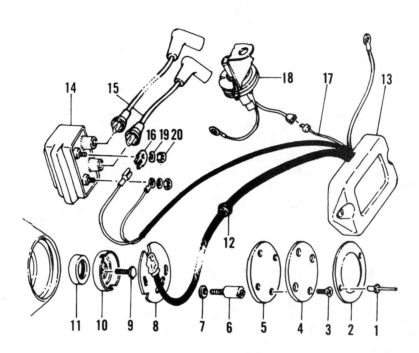

1. Outer cover rivet (2)
2. Outer cover
3. Inner cover screw (2)
4. Inner cover
5. Gasket
6. Sensor plate screw (2)
7. Washer (2)
8. Sensor plate
9. Rotor screw and
   star washer
10. Rotor
11. Camshaft oil seal
12. Connector
13. Ignition coil module
14. Ignition coil
15. Spark plug cable (2)
16. Ignition coil terminal
17. VOES wire
18. Vacuum operated
    electric switch
19. Washer
20. Nut

connector from the wires. Withdraw the wires through the crankcase hole one wire at a time. Remove the sensor plate and wires. See **Figure 31**.

NOTE
On 1993 and later models, the Cannon Connector Tool (part No. 201051) will be required to remove the wire terminals from the plug end of connector in Step 7B. The tool can be ordered through Pico Corp., 444 Constitution Ave., Camarillo, CA, 93012.

7B. On 1993-on models, disconnect the sensor wire at the crankcase. Make a drawing of the wire terminals in the plug end of the connector so that they can be installed in their original positions. Then remove the wire terminals from the plug end of the connector with the Cannon Connector Tool. Withdraw the wires through the crankcase hole one wire at a time. Remove the sensor plate and wires. See **Figure 31**.

8. Remove the rotor bolt and rotor (**Figure 32**).

9. To remove the sensor plate, disconnect the sensor-to-ignition module wire connector. Then pull the sensor plate wire harness through the chain case hole.

10. Remove the ignition module as follows:

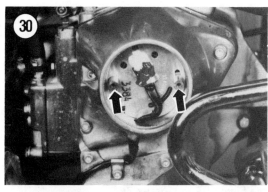

9

a. Disconnect the ignition module wires at the ignition coil.

b. Loosen and remove the ground wire connection at the frame.

c. Remove the module mounting bolts and remove the module assembly.

11. Installation is the reverse of these steps. Note the following.

12. Align the tab on the back of the rotor (**Figure 33**) with the notch in the end of the crankshaft (A, **Figure 34**).

13. Apply Loctite 222 (purple) to the rotor bolt and install it. Tighten the bolt to 75-80 in.-lb. (8.6-9.2 N•m).

14. On 1993-on models, reconnect the wiring terminals as follows:

a. Refer to your disassembly drawing or notes when reinstalling the wire terminals.

b. Install the wire terminals into their correct position using the Cannon Connector Tool (described during removal). The wire colors must match up in both connector halves.

NOTE
If all of the wire terminals were removed, it may be necessary to install new wire pins, sockets and connector body.

15. Before riveting the cover in place, check the ignition timing as described in Chapter Three.

CAUTION
Make sure to use the correct rivets in Step 15. These are special timing cover rivets which do not have ends that will fall into the timing compartment and damage the ignition components.

16. Rivet the outer cover to the inner cover. Use only rivets (part number 8699) to secure the outer cover. See **Figure 35** and **Figure 36**.

Inspection

1. If necessary, follow the procedures in Chapter Two to troubleshoot the ignition system.

2. Check the ignition compartment for oil leakage. If present, remove the crankcase seal (B, **Figure 34**) by prying it out with a screwdriver or seal remover. Install a new seal by tapping it in place with a suitable size socket placed on the outside of the seal. Drive the seal in until it seats in the crankcase.

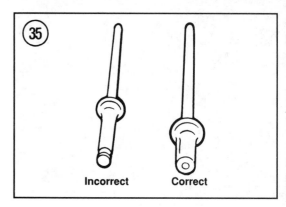

Incorrect   Correct

NOTE
If the crankcase seal is not installed all the way, it will leak.

IGNITION COIL

The ignition coil is a form of transformer which develops the high voltage required to jump the spark plug gap. The only maintenance required is that of keeping the electrical connections clean and tight and occasionally checking to see that the coils are mounted securely.

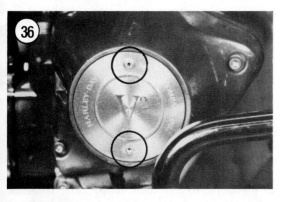

Removal/Installation

1. Disconnect all ignition coil wiring.
2. Remove the coil cover, if so equipped.
3. Remove the coil mounting bolts and remove the coil (**Figure 37**).
4. Remove the coil cover (if so equipped).
5. Installation is the reverse of these steps.

CAUTION
*When replacing an ignition coil, make sure the coil is marked **ELECTRONIC ADVANCE**. Installing an older type ignition coil could damage electronic ignition components.*

STARTER

The starting system consists of the starter motor, starter gears, solenoid and the starter button.

When the starter button is pressed, it engages the starter solenoid switch that completes the circuit allowing electricity to flow from the battery to the starter motor.

CAUTION
Never attempt to operate the starter by pushing the starter button for more than 5 seconds at a time. If the engine fails to start, wait a minimum of 30 seconds to allow the starter to cool. Overheating the starter may result in damage.

Removal
(1984-1988)

Refer to **Figure 38** for this procedure.

1. Disconnect the negative battery cable.

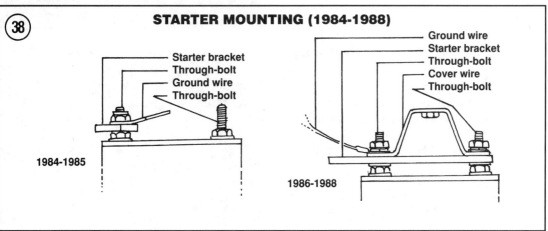

STARTER MOUNTING (1984-1988)

Starter bracket
Through-bolt
Ground wire
Through-bolt

1984-1985

Ground wire
Starter bracket
Through-bolt
Cover wire
Through-bolt

1986-1988

2. Disconnect the solenoid cable at the starter.

3. Remove the starter bracket bolts at the transmission case.

4. Remove the chrome end cover and cover bracket.

5. Remove the relay-to-starter ground wire at the starter.

6. Remove the starter housing bolts.

7. Hold the front and rear starter covers to prevent the starter from coming apart and remove it from the bike.

Installation
(1984-1988)

Refer to **Figure 38** for this procedure.

1. Insert the through-bolts through the rear cover holes and through the starter frame and front cover.

2. Place the starter into the bike and turn it so that the terminal stud on the starter faces to the front of the bike.

3. Install the solenoid wire over the terminal and secure it with the flat washer, lockwasher and nut. Tighten the nut securely.

4. Place the starter bracket over the transmission studs and through-bolts (**Figure 38**).

5. Install a washer and a new nut onto each of the through-bolts and tighten nuts securely.

6. Install the washers and nuts onto the transmission studs and tighten nuts to 13-16 ft.-lb. (17.9-22.1 N•m).

7. Place the relay-to-starter ground wire to the end of the through-bolt. Then install the chrome end cover bracket and secure it with its washer and a new nut. Tighten nut securely.

8. Install the chrome end cover.

Removal
(1989-on)

1. Disconnect the negative battery cable.

2. Remove the primary chain case cover as described in Chapter Five.

3. Remove the rear exhaust pipe.

4. Pry the lockplate tab away from the jackshaft bolt. Then hold the pinion gear to keep it from turning and loosen the jackshaft bolt (**Figure 39**). Remove the jackshaft bolt and lockplate from the jackshaft.

NOTE
On some models, it may be necessary to loosen the oil tank mounts to access the starter motor.

5. Remove the fasteners securing the chrome cover to the end of the starter motor and remove the cover.

6. Remove the starter motor Allen bolts and washers and lift the starter out of the frame. Then disconnect the battery (**Figure 40**) and solenoid wires at the starter and remove the starter from the right-hand side.

NOTE
The jackshaft-to-starter coupling may come off with the starter or it may stay attached to the jackshaft. If the coupling comes off with the starter, put it back onto the jackshaft. The coupling on 1989 models is symmetrical; either coupling end can be installed over the jackshaft. The coupling on 1990 and later models is asymmetrical; install the coupling so that the end with the couterbore is installed over the jackshaft.

Installation
(1989-on)

1. Install the solenoid and battery cable over the solenoid stud and secure with the washer and nut.

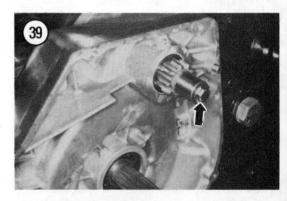

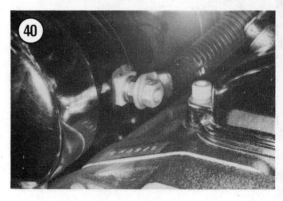

2. Install the starter from the right-hand side, engaging the starter shaft with the jackshaft-to-starter coupling. If the coupling came off with the starter during removal and you didn't reinstall it, refer to the *NOTE* under *Starter Removal* when installing the coupling. On 1990 and later models, you can install the coupling incorrectly.

3. Install the starter mounting bolts and washers and tighten to 13-20 ft.-lb. (17.9-27.6 N•m).

NOTE
Install a new lockplate if the lock tab is cracked or broken.

4. Slide the lockplate onto the jackshaft bolt and insert the bolt through the jackshaft assembly. Turn the lockplate so that tab on the lockplate fits into the jackshaft keyway groove. Hold the pinion gear by hand and tighten the jackshaft bolt (**Figure 39**) to 7-9 ft.-lb. (9.6-12.4 N•m). Bend the lockplate tab over the bolt to lock it.

5. Install the primary chain case cover and fill the primary chain case as described in Chapter Five.

6. Install the chrome starter cover and secure it with its fasteners.

NOTE
If you had to loosen the oil tank mounts, tighten them now.

7. Install the rear exhaust pipe.
8. Reconnect the negative battery cable.

**Disassembly
(1984-1988)**

Refer to **Figure 41** for this procedure.
1. Clean all grease, dirt and carbon from the case and end covers.
2. Remove the starter housing bolts (if they were reinstalled after removing the starter from the bike).
3. Remove the rear cover screws and remove the rear cover. The rear cover screws secure the brush holder to the rear cover.
4. Using a piece of wire, lift the brush springs and pull the brushes out of the holder.

NOTE
Write down the number of thrust washers on the shaft next to the commutator. Be sure to install the same number when reassembling the starter.

9

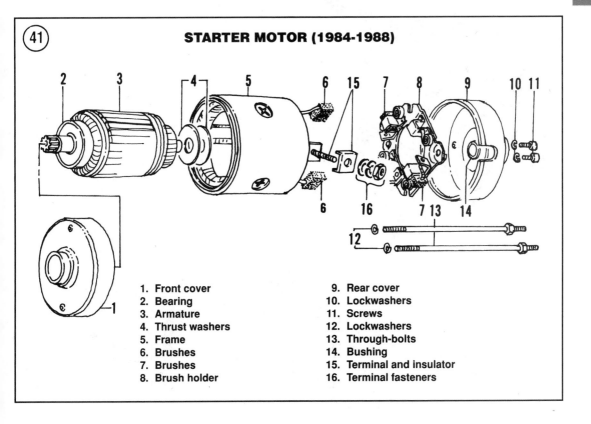

STARTER MOTOR (1984-1988)

1. Front cover
2. Bearing
3. Armature
4. Thrust washers
5. Frame
6. Brushes
7. Brushes
8. Brush holder
9. Rear cover
10. Lockwashers
11. Screws
12. Lockwashers
13. Through-bolts
14. Bushing
15. Terminal and insulator
16. Terminal fasteners

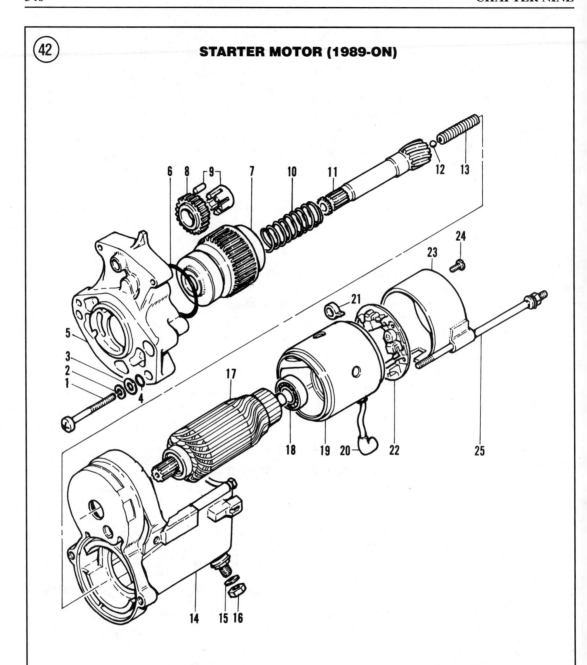

STARTER MOTOR (1989-ON)

1. Bolt
2. Lockwasher
3. Washer
4. O-ring
5. Drive housing
6. O-ring
7. Drive assembly/
   overrunning clutch
8. Idler gear
9. Idler gear bearing
   assembly
10. Spring
11. Shaft
12. Ball
13. Spring
14. Solenoid housing
15. Washer
16. Nut
17. Armature
18. Bearing
19. Field coil assembly
20. Starter cable
21. Brush spring
22. Brush plate
23. End cap
24. Screw
25. Bolt

5. Remove the armature and field frame.

6. Inspect the starter assembly as described in this chapter.

Reassembly
(1984-1988)

Refer to **Figure 41** for this procedure.

1. Prior to assembly, perform the *Inspection* procedure to make sure all worn or defective parts have been repaired or replaced. All parts should be thoroughly cleaned before assembly.

2. Install the armature into the frame so that the commutator side faces toward the brush holder side.

3. Install the front cover over the armature shaft and engage it with the frame.

4. Install the brush holder into the frame.

5. Install the 2 positive brushes as follows:

   a. The positive brushes are soldered to the field coil assembly.

   b. Pull a positive brush out of its brush holder. A piece of wire bent to form a small hook on one end can be used to access the brushes.

   c. Insert the positive brush into its brush holder.

   d. Release the spring so that tension is applied against the brush.

   e. Repeat for the other positive brush.

6. Install the 2 negative brushes as follows:

   a. The negative brushes are mounted onto the brush holder.

   b. Pull a negative brush out of its brush holder. A piece of wire bent to form a small hook on one end can be used to access the brushes.

   c. Insert the negative brush into its brush holder.

   d. Release the spring so that tension is applied against the brush.

   e. Repeat for the other negative brush.

7. Install the thrust washers onto the armature shaft.

8. Align the slot in the rear cover with the terminal in the frame and install the rear cover. Install the through-bolts through the starter assembly.

9. Secure the brush holder to the rear cover with the 2 screws and washers. Tighten the screws securely.

Disassembly
(1989-on)

Refer to **Figure 42** for this procedure.

1. Clean all grease, dirt and carbon from the case and end covers.

2. Disconnect the solenoid wire.

3. Loosen and remove the 2 starter housing through-bolts.

4. Remove the 2 screws securing the end cover to the brush holder. Remove the end cover.

5. Lift the field coil brush springs out of their holders with a small hook and remove the brushes from their holders.

6. Slide the brush holder off of the commutator.

7. Remove the armature and field frame assembly. Slide the armature out of the field frame.

8. If necessary, remove and disassemble the drive housing (**Figure 43**) as follows:

   a. Remove the 2 screws and washers securing the drive housing to the solenoid housing. O-rings are installed on the screws used on 1989-1990 models.

   b. Remove the drive housing from the solenoid housing.

   c. Remove the ball and spring from the end of the shaft to prevent their loss.

   d. Remove the drive, idler gear and idler gear bearing assembly from the drive housing.

   e. Carefully pry the O-ring out of the groove in the bottom of the drive housing.

   f. Remove the spring and shaft from the drive assembly.

9

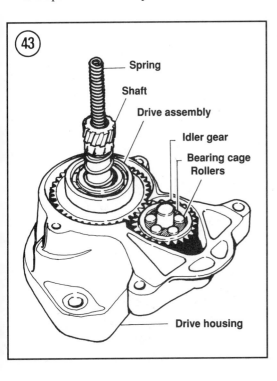

43

Spring

Shaft

Drive assembly

Idler gear

Bearing cage
Rollers

Drive housing

9. Inspect the starter assembly as described in this chapter.

Assembly
(1989-on)

Refer to **Figure 42** for this procedure.

1. Prior to assembly, perform the *Inspection* procedure to make sure all worn or defective parts have been repaired or replaced. All parts should be thoroughly cleaned before assembly.

2. Smear a thin film of Lubriplate 110 onto the drive housing O-ring and insert the O-ring into the groove in the bottom of the housing. Make sure that the O-ring seats squarely in the groove.

3. After the drive assembly components have been cleaned and dried, lubricate all components with Lubriplate 110.

4. Place the idler gear over the shaft in the drive housing. Then place the idler bearing cage in the gear so that the open cage end faces toward the solenoid. Install the bearing pins in the cage.

5. Insert the drive assembly into the drive housing, then slide the spring over the shaft and insert the shaft into the drive assembly (**Figure 43**).

6. Drop the ball into the shaft and slide the spring over the solenoid plunger shaft.

7. Align the drive housing with the solenoid housings and assemble both housings. On 1989-1990 models, secure the drive housing with the screws, lockwashers, flat washers and O-rings. On 1991 models, install the screws and lockwashers.

8. Pack the armature bearings with Lubriplate 110. Then insert the armature into the field frame housing and install the field frame housing onto the solenoid housing.

9. Install the brush plate into the end of the field frame and install the 4 brushes so that they ride over the commutator.

10. Install the 2 positive brushes as follows:
    a. The positive brushes are soldered to the field coil assembly.
    b. Pull a positive brush out of its brush holder. A piece of wire bent to form a small hook on one end can be used to access the brushes.
    c. Insert the positive brush into its brush holder.
    d. Release the spring so that tension is applied against the brush.
    e. Repeat for the other positive brush.

11. Install the 2 negative brushes as follows:

    a. The negative brushes are mounted onto the brush holder.
    b. Pull a negative brush out of its brush holder. A piece of wire bent to form a small hook on one end can be used to access the brushes.
    c. Insert the negative brush into its brush holder.
    d. Release the spring so that tension is applied against the brush.
    e. Repeat for the other negative brush.

12. Align the slot in the rear cover with the terminal in the frame and install the rear cover. Install the through-bolts through the starter assembly.

13. Secure the brush holder to the rear cover with the 2 screws and washers. Tighten the screws securely.

14. Reconnect the solenoid wire.

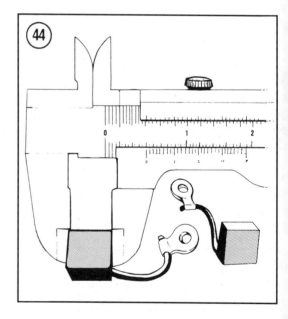

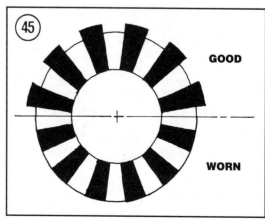

Inspection
(All Models)

1. The starter components should be cleaned thoroughly. Do not clean the field coils or armature in any cleaning solution that could damage the insulation. Wipe these parts off with a clean rag. Likewise, do not soak the overrunning clutch in any cleaning solution as the chemicals could dissolve the lubrication within the clutch and ruin it.

2. Measure the length of each brush with a vernier caliper (**Figure 44**). If the length is less than specified in **Table 3**, it must be replaced. Replace the brushes in sets of four, even though only one may be worn to this dimension.

NOTE
The field coil brushes are soldered in position. To replace, first apply heat to the brushes' soldered joint to unsolder. Remove the old brushes. Solder the new brushes in place with rosin core solder—do not use acid core solder.

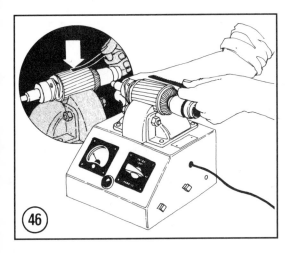

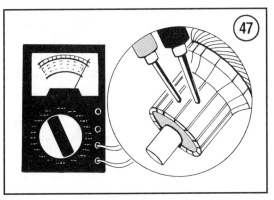

3. Inspect the condition of the commutator. The mica in the commutator should be at least 0.008 in. (0.20 mm) undercut. If the mica undercut is less than this amount, undercut the mica with a piece of hacksaw blade to a depth of 1/32 in. (0.79 mm). This procedure can also be performed by a dealer or automotive specialist with a undercutting machine. When undercutting mica, each groove must form a right angle. Do not cut the mica so that a thin edge is left next to the commutator segment. **Figure 45** shows the proper angle. After undercutting the mica, remove burrs by sanding commutator lightly with crocus cloth.

4. Inspect the commutator copper bars for discoloration. If a pair of bars are discolored, grounded armature coils are indicated.

5. The armature can be checked for winding shorts with a growler. To do this, the mechanic inserts the armature into a growler (**Figure 46**). The growler is then turned on while a hacksaw blade is held close to but not touching the armature. The armature is then rotated slowly by hand; if the blade vibrates and is attracted to the armature, an armature winding is shorted. If this is the case, the armature must be replaced. Refer this test to a Harley-Davidson dealer or automotive electrical specialist.

6. Place the armature in a lathe or between crankshaft centers and check commutator runout with a dial indicator. If runout exceeds 0.002 in. (0.05 mm), commutator should be trued on a lathe. When truing the commutator to eliminate the out-of-round condition, make the cuts as light as possible. Replace the armature if the commutator OD meets or is less than the wear limit listed in **Table 3**.

7. Use an ohmmeter and check for continuity between the commutator bars (**Figure 47**); there should be continuity between pairs of bars. If there is no continuity between pairs of bars, the armature is open. Replace the armature.

8. Connect an ohmmeter between any commutator bar and the armature core (**Figure 48**); there should be no continuity. If there is continuity, the armature is grounded. Replace the armature.

9. Connect an ohmmeter between the starter cable terminal and each field frame brush (**Figure 49**); there should be continuity. If there is no continuity at either brush, the field windings are open. Replace the field frame assembly.

10. Connect an ohmmeter between the field frame housing and each field frame brush (**Figure 50**);

9

there should be no continuity. If there is continuity at either brush, the field windings are grounded. Replace the field frame assembly.

11. Connect an ohmmeter between the brush holder plate and each brush holder (**Figure 51**); there should be no continuity. If there is continuity at either brush holder, the brush holder or plate is damaged. Replace the brush holder plate.

12A. *1984-1988*: Service the armature bearing and rear cover bushing as follows:

    a. Check the bearing on the armature shaft. If worn or damaged, remove and install new bearing with a bearing splitter and a press.

    b. Inspect the bushing installed in the rear cover. If the bushing is severely worn or damaged, replace the rear cover; replacement bushings are not sold separately.

    c. Inspect the bushing surface on the armature shaft. If this surface is severely worn or damaged, replace the armature.

    d. Check the bearing bore in the front cover. Replace the cover if this area is severely worn or damaged.

12B. *1989-on*: Service the armature bearings as follows:

    a. Check the bearings on the armature shaft. If worn or damaged, remove and install new bearings with a bearing splitter and a press.

NOTE
Note that the 2 bearings installed on the armature shaft have different part numbers. When replacing the bearings, ID the old bearings before their removal in relationship to their position on the armature. This information can then be used to make sure the new bearings are installed correctly.

    b. Check the bearing bores in the end cover and solenoid housing. Replace the cover or housing if this area is severely worn or cracked.

13. *1989-on*: The drive assembly is bolted onto the end of the solenoid housing. Inspect it as follows:

    a. Check the teeth on the idler gear and drive assembly for wear or damage.

    b. Check for chipped or worn bearing rollers. Damaged rollers would cause the pinion to turn roughly in the overrunning direction.

    c. Replace worn or damaged parts as required.

STARTER SOLENOID
(1984-1988)

The solenoid installed on 1984-1988 models is separate from the starter motor.

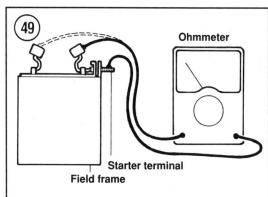

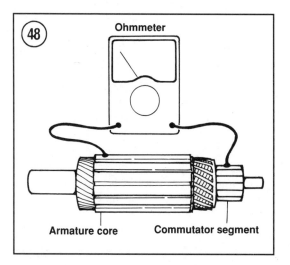

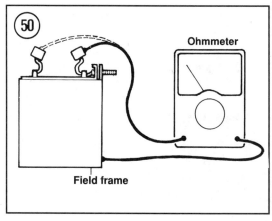

Removal/Installation

1. Disconnect the negative battery cable.

2. Label and disconnect the cables at the solenoid. See **Figure 52** (1984), **Figure 53** (early 1985) or **Figure 54** (late 1985-1988).

3. Remove the solenoid mounting bolts and remove the solenoid, spacer, spring and gasket.

4. Installation is the reverse of these steps. Tighten the mounting bolts to 12 ft.-lb. (16.5 N•m).

Disassembly/Reassembly

Refer to **Figure 55** for this procedure.

1. Clean the solenoid housing of all dirt and residue before disassembling it.

2. Remove the nut and lockwasher from the short large terminal.

3. Remove the nut and lockwasher from the small O.D. terminal.

4. Remove the 2 screws and washers securing the solenoid cover to the solenoid and remove the cover.

NOTE
When disassembling the inner plunger assembly in Step 5, note the position and condition of the copper washer as it is installed on the plunger between the plastic washer and seat. If one side of

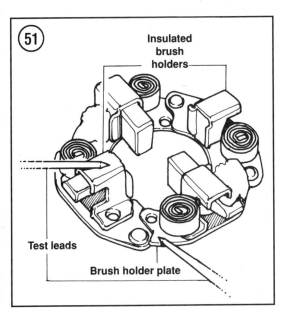

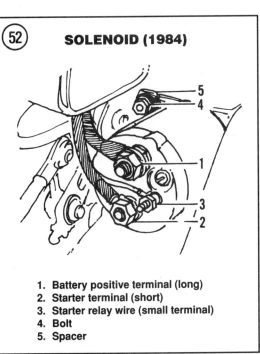

SOLENOID (1984)

1. Battery positive terminal (long)
2. Starter terminal (short)
3. Starter relay wire (small terminal)
4. Bolt
5. Spacer

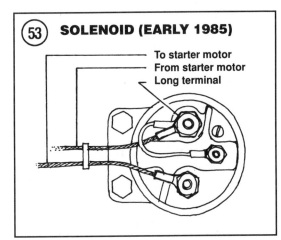

SOLENOID (EARLY 1985)

To starter motor
From starter motor
Long terminal

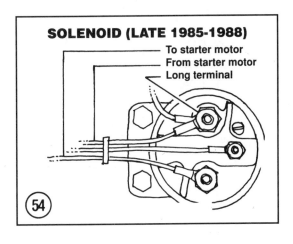

SOLENOID (LATE 1985-1988)

To starter motor
From starter motor
Long terminal

the copper washer is grooved or burnt, label the washer as to how it is positioned on the plunger, and then turn it around during reassembly so that the worn side is facing in the opposite direction. Because inner plunger assembly components are not available separately, this will extend the life of the copper washer.

5. Referring to **Figure 55**, disassemble the solenoid assembly, keeping the outer and inner plunger parts separate.

6. Clean and inspect the solenoid components as described in this chapter.

7. Assembly is the reverse of these steps. Note the following.

8. Lightly wipe the plunger and the plunger bore with Lubriplate 110.

9. Assemble the inner plunger assembly as follows:

    a. Lay out the inner plunger components in the order shown in **Figure 55**. Note that the plunger has 2 grooves; these are identified as groove No. 1 and groove No. 2 in **Figure 55**. Note also that the 2 collars are identical.

    b. Install a collar into the No. 2 plunger groove so that the collar spring seat faces toward the No. 1 plunger groove.

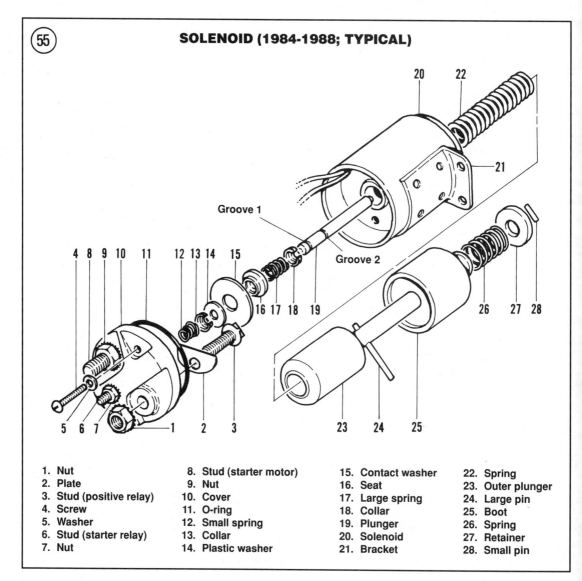

SOLENOID (1984-1988; TYPICAL)

1. Nut	15. Contact washer
2. Plate	16. Seat
3. Stud (positive relay)	17. Large spring
4. Screw	18. Collar
5. Washer	19. Plunger
6. Stud (starter relay)	20. Solenoid
7. Nut	21. Bracket
8. Stud (starter motor)	22. Spring
9. Nut	23. Outer plunger
10. Cover	24. Large pin
11. O-ring	25. Boot
12. Small spring	26. Spring
13. Collar	27. Retainer
14. Plastic washer	28. Small pin

c. Slide the large spring over the plunger and seat it against the collar.

d. Slide the seat over the plunger with the seat shoulder facing the No. 1 plunger groove.

e. Slide the copper washer over the plunger and center it onto the seat shoulder installed in sub-step d.

f. Slide the plastic washer over the plunger and seat it against the copper washer.

g. Install the remaining collar into the No. 1 plunger groove so that the collar spring seat faces away from the assembled parts installed in sub-steps a-f.

10. Insert the plunger assembly into the plunger bore in the solenoid housing.

11. Stand the solenoid housing upright and slide the small spring over the plunger and seat it against the collar.

12. Install the gasket onto the solenoid housing.

CAUTION
When installing the solenoid cover in Step 13, route the internal solenoid wires so that they cannot contact the copper washer as it travels with the

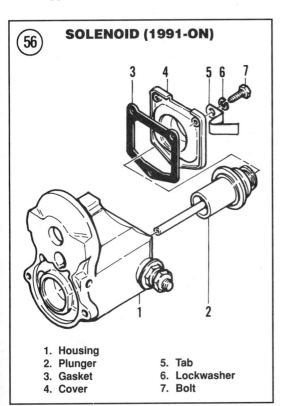

SOLENOID (1991-ON)

56

3 4   5 6 7

1. Housing
2. Plunger
3. Gasket   5. Tab
4. Cover   6. Lockwasher
                  7. Bolt

plunger during solenoid operation. Contact of these parts will eventually wear away the wire insulation and cause the circuit to remain closed.

13. Align the solenoid cover with the solenoid housing and place it into position, making sure the small plunger spring, plunger and terminal enter the cover bore properly.

14. Slide a washer onto each of the screws and install the screw through the cover and into the solenoid housing. Tighten the screws securely. Install the terminal nuts and washers previously removed.

Cleaning and Inspection

1. Clean all parts thoroughly.

2. Visually check all parts for severe wear, cracks or other damage. The contact washer can be turned around during reassembly as described in the *NOTE* prior to Step 5 under *Disassembly/Reassembly*.

3. Replace all worn or damaged parts, if available, as required.

STARTER SOLENOID (1989-1990)

Service procedures are not specified for these models.

STARTER SOLENOID (1991-ON)

The starter solenoid, starter motor and drive assembly are assembled as one unit.

Disassembly/Reassembly

Refer to **Figure 56** for this procedure.

1. Remove the starter motor as described in this chapter.

2. Three screws secure the cover to the solenoid housing. Mark the wire clip position on the cover, then remove the 3 screws, washers and clip.

3. Remove the cover and gasket.

4. Remove the solenoid plunger from the solenoid housing.

5. Inspect the parts for severe wear or damage. Replace parts as required.

6. Installation is the reverse of these steps. Note the following.

7. Make sure the solenoid plunger shaft engages the spring in the drive assembly shaft.

9

STARTER RELAY

Replacement

On 1992 and earlier models, the starter relay is mounted between the fuel tanks. On 1993 and later models, the starter relay is mounted underneath the seat, adjacent to the ignition module and battery.

LIGHTING SYSTEM

The lighting system consists of a headlight, taillight/brake light combination, turn signals, indicator lights, speedometer illumination lights, running lights and fender tip lights.

Always use the correct wattage bulb. Harley-Davidson lists bulb sizes by part number. The use of a larger wattage bulb will give a dim light and a smaller wattage bulb will burn out prematurely. Replacement bulbs can be purchased through Harley-Davidson dealers by part number or by reading the number of the defective bulb and cross-referencing it with another supplier.

Headlight Replacement

Refer to **Figure 57**, typical for this procedure.

1. Remove the outer headlight clamp screw and remove the clamp.

2. Carefully remove the headlight from the rubber mounting ring.

3. Disconnect the connector from the headlight and remove the headlight.

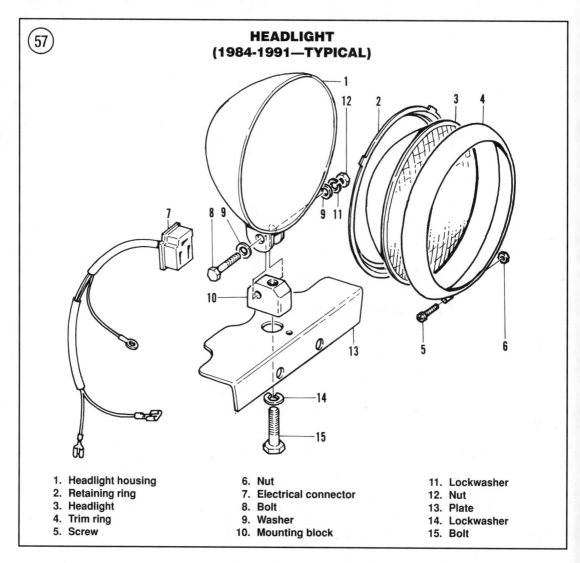

**HEADLIGHT
(1984-1991—TYPICAL)**

57

1. Headlight housing	6. Nut	11. Lockwasher
2. Retaining ring	7. Electrical connector	12. Nut
3. Headlight	8. Bolt	13. Plate
4. Trim ring	9. Washer	14. Lockwasher
5. Screw	10. Mounting block	15. Bolt

4. Remove the retaining ring from the sealed beam unit and remove the sealed beam.

5. Install by reversing these removal steps. Note the following.

6. Clean the headlight electrical block with electrical contact cleaner.

7. Adjust the headlight as described in this chapter.

Headlight Bulb Replacement (1992-on)

FXSTC/S models are equipped with a quartz Halogen bulb. FLSTC/F/N models are equipped with a sealed beam headlight assembly. See **Figure 58**.

CAUTION
Carefully read all instructions shipped with the replacement quartz Halogen bulb. Do not touch the glass with your fingers because any traces of skin oil on the quartz Halogen bulb will create hot spots that will drastically reduce bulb life. Clean any traces of oil from the bulb with a cloth moistened in alcohol.

WARNING
The quartz bulb contains Halogen gas that is under pressure. Wear safety glasses when handling the bulb to prevent possible injury from a damaged bulb.

1. Loosen the screw securing the outer molding clamp to the headlight housing. Then remove the molding clamp and its gasket.

2. Pull the lens out and disconnect the electrical connector from the back of it.

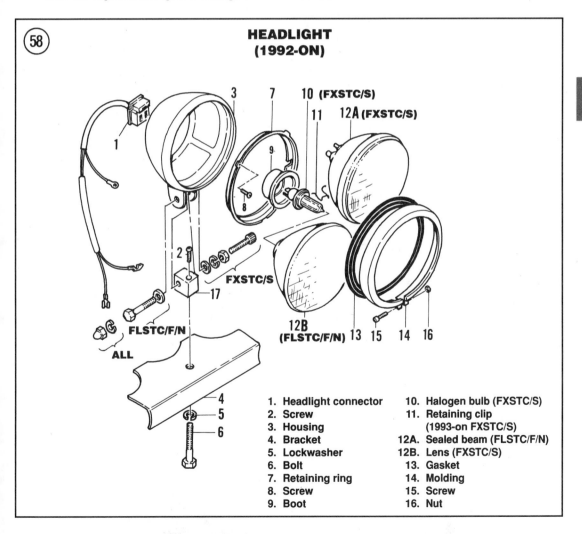

58

HEADLIGHT (1992-ON)

10 (FXSTC/S)
11   12A (FXSTC/S)

FXSTC/S

17

FLSTC/F/N

ALL

12B
(FLSTC/F/N) 13 15 14 16

1. Headlight connector
2. Screw
3. Housing
4. Bracket
5. Lockwasher
6. Bolt
7. Retaining ring
8. Screw
9. Boot
10. Halogen bulb (FXSTC/S)
11. Retaining clip
    (1993-on FXSTC/S)
12A. Sealed beam (FLSTC/F/N)
12B. Lens (FXSTC/S)
13. Gasket
14. Molding
15. Screw
16. Nut

9

3. Remove the lens from the headlight housing.

4A. On FLSTC/F/N models, replace the lens assembly.

4B. On 1992 FXSTC/S models, remove the boot and bulb from the lens.

4C. On 1993-on FXSTC/S models, remove the boot. Then remove the wire retaining clip and withdraw the bulb.

5. Install by reversing these steps. Make sure the bulb contacts are clean prior to reconnecting them.

Headlight Adjustment

Adjust the headlight horizontally and vertically according to Department of Motor Vehicle Regulations in your area.

1. Park the motorcycle on a level surface 25 feet (7.6 m) from a wall (test pattern). Have a rider (with same approximate weight as the vehicle's owner) sit on the seat and make sure the tires are inflated to the corect pressure when performing this adjustment. Make sure bike is facing straight ahead.

2A. *FXSTC/S models*: Draw a horizontal line on a wall which is 35 in. (889 mm) above the floor (**Figure 59**).

2B. *All others*: Draw a horizontal line on the wall the same height as the center of the headlight (**Figure 60**).

3. Turn on the headlight. Switch headlight to high beam.

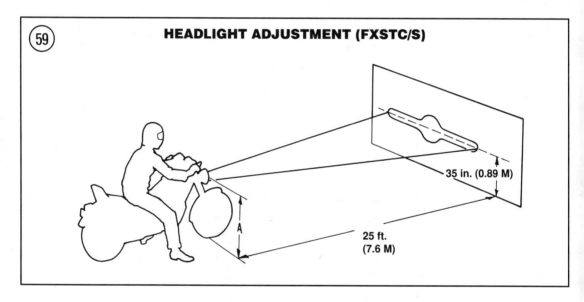

HEADLIGHT ADJUSTMENT (FXSTC/S)

59

35 in. (0.89 M)

A

25 ft. (7.6 M)

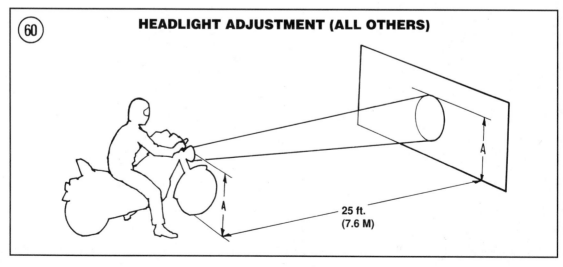

HEADLIGHT ADJUSTMENT (ALL OTHERS)

60

A

25 ft. (7.6 M)

HEADLAMP ADJUSTMENT (FXSTS)

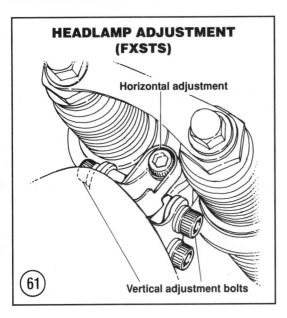

Horizontal adjustment

Vertical adjustment bolts

61

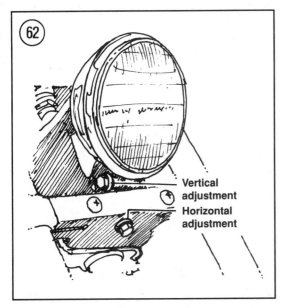

62

Vertical adjustment

Horizontal adjustment

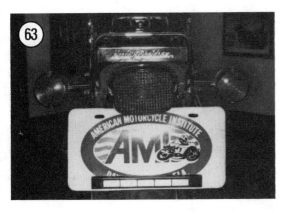

63

4A. *FXSTC/S models*: Main beam should be centered on the horizontal line with equal areas of light above and below line as shown in **Figure 59**. There should also be equal areas of light to th eleft and right of center.

4B. *All others*: The top of the main beam should be even with, but not higher than, the horizontal line drawn in **Figure 60**. There should also be equal areas of light to the left and right of center.

5. If the beam is incorrect, adjust as follows for your model.

6A. To adjust headlight on FXSTS models:

    a. Loosen the 2 vertical adjust bolts (**Figure 61**) to move the headlight beam up and down. Tighten adjust bolts to 30 ft.-lb. (41N•m).

    b. Loosen the horizontal adjust bolt (**Figure 62**) to move the headlight beam from side to side. Then move the headlight adjustment mechanism forward to the end of the bracket slot. Tighten adjust bolt to 30 ft.-lb. (41 N•m).

CAUTION
The headlight must be moved as far forward as possible (see sub-step b) to prevent the headlight from contacting the front springs. Check before riding the motorcycle.

6B. To adjust headlight on all other models:

    a. Loosen the bottom adjust bolt to move the headlight beam from side to side (**Figure 62**). Tighten adjust bolt securely.

    b. Loosen the upper adjust bolt to move the headlight beam up and down. Tighten adjust bolt securely.

7. Recheck headlight aim.

Taillight/Brake Light Replacement

1. Remove the rear lens (**Figure 63**).
2. Push in on the bulb and remove it.
3. Replace the bulb and install the lens.

Turn Signal Light Replacement

1. Remove the turn signal lens.
2. Push in on the bulb and remove it.
3. Replace the bulb and install the lens.

Passing Light Replacement/Adjustment

Refer to **Figure 64**, typical, for this procedure.

9

1. Remove the sealed beam retaining ring screw and remove the retaining ring.

2. Pull the bulb partway out and disconnect the electrical connector.

3. Installation is the reverse of these steps.

4. Adjust the passing light as follows:

    a. Remove the 2 turn signal bracket screws and lift the turn signal off of the bracket.

    b. Loosen the nut on the inside of the turn signal bracket and turn the light so that it shines straight ahead and the top of the light is just below a line on a wall 25 feet (7.62 m) away.

    c. Hold the light in position and tighten the nut securely.

    d. Reinstall the turn signal assembly.

Indicator Lights
Replacement

Indicator lights (**Figure 65**) are used to monitor the headlight high beam, oil pressure, neutral position, turn signals and speedometer assemblies.

1. Remove the instrument panel cover as follows:

    a. Remove the odometer screw and knob (**Figure 66**).

    b. Unscrew the choke knob and locknut on 1984-1989 models (**Figure 67**).

    c. Remove the instrument panel Acorn nut on 1990 and later models.

    d. Remove the instrument panel cover (**Figure 68**).

2. Locate the defective bulb and remove it from its socket and replace with a new one. See **Figure 69**.

3. Install the instrument panel cover.

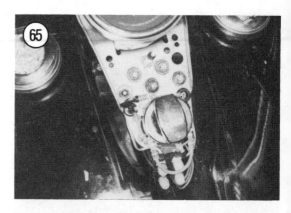

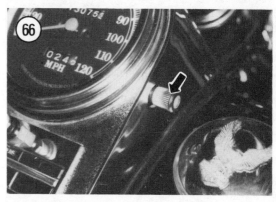

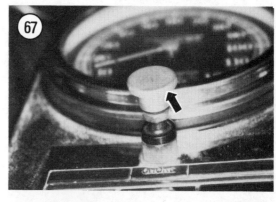

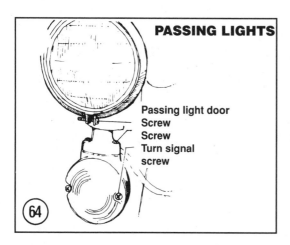

PASSING LIGHTS

Passing light door
Screw
Screw
Turn signal
screw

SWITCHES

Switches can be tested for continuity with an ohmmeter (see Chapter One) at the switch connector plug by operating the switch in each of its operating positions and comparing results with the switch operation. When testing switches, consider the following:

a. First check the circuit breaker.

b. Check the battery as described in this chapter and bring the battery to the correct state of charge, if required.

c. When separating 2 connectors, pull on the connector housings and not the wires.

d. After locating a defective circuit, check the connectors to make sure they are clean and properly connected. Check all wires going into a connector housing to make sure each wire is properly positioned and that the wire end is not loose.

e. To connect connectors properly, push them together until they click into place.

Handlebar Switch Replacement

Refer to **Figure 70** for this procedure.

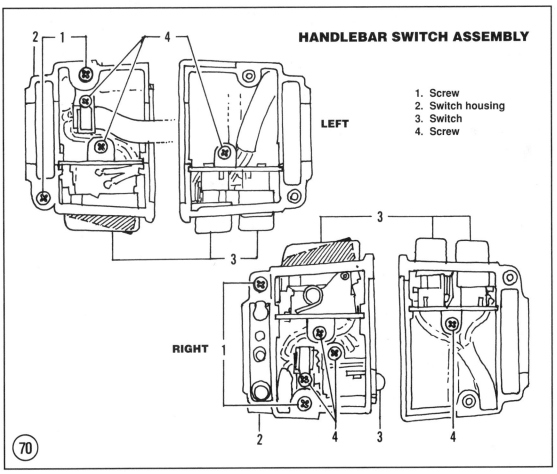

HANDLEBAR SWITCH ASSEMBLY

1. Screw
2. Switch housing
3. Switch
4. Screw

LEFT

RIGHT

9

1. Remove the screws securing the switch housing to the handlebar. See **Figure 71** or **Figure 72**. Then carefully separate the switch housing to gain access to the defective switch.

2. Disconnect the switch wire at the electrical connection.

3. Replace the defective switch by removing the holding screw. Then pull the switch out of the housing.

4. Installation is the reverse of these steps. Make sure to route the wires to prevent damaging them when tightening the switch housing.

Ignition/Lighting Switch
Removal/Installation

1. Disconnect the negative battery cable.

2. Remove the instrument panel cover.

3. Label and disconnect the electrical connectors at the switch.

4. Remove the switch screws and washers and remove the switch.

5. Installation is the reverse of these steps.

Ignition/Lighting Switch
Disassembly/Reassembly
(Early 1984)

The ignition/lighting switch on early 1984 models is non-repairable. If the switch is damaged, replace it.

Ignition/Lighting Switch
Disassembly/Reassembly
(Late 1984-on)

Refer to **Figure 73** (early models) or **Figure 74** (late models) for this procedure.

1. Remove the ignition switch as described in this chapter.

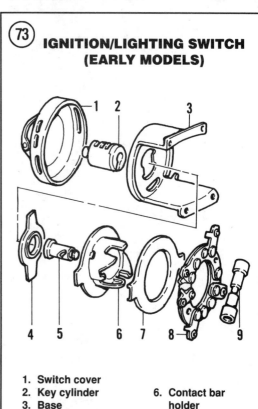

**IGNITION/LIGHTING SWITCH
(EARLY MODELS)**

1. Switch cover
2. Key cylinder
3. Base
4. Lock plate
5. Roller contact retainer
6. Contact bar holder
7. Plate
8. Switch plate
9. Roller contact

2. Insert the key into the switch and turn the switch to its OFF and unlocked position.

3. Hold the roller contact retainer with pliers, then move the retainer up and away from the roller contact.

NOTE
Before performing Step 4, note how the switch mounting plate is mounted in the switch housing; the switch terminals face away from the lock cover hinge.

4. Remove the roller contact and switch mounting plate from the switch assembly.

5A. *Early model switch*: Refer to **Figure 73** and perform the following:

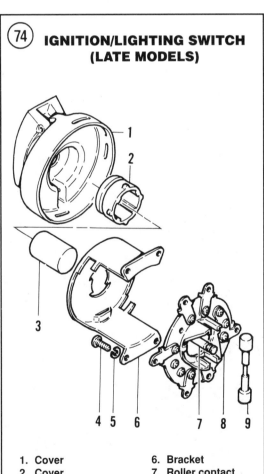

(74) IGNITION/LIGHTING SWITCH (LATE MODELS)

1. Cover
2. Cover
3. Key cylinder
4. Screw
5. Lockwasher
6. Bracket
7. Roller contact retainer
8. Switch plate
9. Roller contact

a. The reinforcing plate, contact bar holder and roller contact retainer are removed at the same time.
b. Slip the plate, holder and retainer sideways to uncover one tab from the slot in the switch cover. Then lift and slide the assembly in the opposite direction to uncover the other tab.
c. Remove the assembly.
d. Remove the ignition switch cylinder from the switch cover.

5B. *Late model switch*: Refer to **Figure 74** and perform the following:

a. Remove the switch base from the switch cover.
b. Remove the ignition switch cylinder from the switch cover.

6. Clean and inspect switch components as described in this chapter.

7. Assembly is the reverse of these steps. Note the following.

8. Lightly wipe the following parts with grease:
a. Roller contact retainer head.
b. Lock plate.
c. Roller contact and contact buttons on the switch mounting plate.

9. Install the ignition cylinder as follows:
a. Insert the ignition cylinder into the switch base so that any 1 of the 4 tumblers in the ignition cylinder register with the switch base.
b. Press the ignition cylinder into the switch base and turn with ignition key clockwise as far as possible. Remove the key and complete assembly.

Inspection

1. Wash all of the switch components with a nonflammable cleaning solvent and dry with compressed air.

2. Inspect the brass buttons and roller surfaces for excessive wear.

3. Check for damaged or loose switch mounting plate terminals.

NOTE
Excessive wear or looseness of contact parts may allow slippage of parts and cause the switch to short out.

4. Replace worn or damaged parts.

Oil Pressure Switch
Testing/Replacement

The oil pressure indicator light should come on when the ignition is turned on prior to starting the engine. When the engine is running, the oil pressure indicator light should go off when engine speed rises above idle. This procedure tests the electrical part of the oil pressure switch assembly. If the oil pressure switch, indicator bulb and related wiring are okay, inspect the lubrication system as described in Chapter Two.

The oil pressure switch is located on the right-hand crankcase next to the rear tappet guide (**Figure 75**). The electrical wire is connected to the switch with a lockwasher and nut.

1. Remove the rubber boot and disconnect the electrical connector at the switch.
2. Turn the ignition switch ON.
3. Ground the switch wire to the engine.
4. The oil pressure indicator light on the instrument panel should light.
5. If the signal indicator light does not light, check for a burned-out indicator light and inspect all wiring between the switch and the indicator light. If necessary, replace the light as described in this chapter.
6A. If the problem was solved in Steps 3-5, attach the electrical connector to the pressure switch. Make sure the connection is tight and free from oil. Slide the rubber boot back into position.
6B. If the problem was not solved in Steps 3-5 and the warning light remains ON when the engine is running, shut the engine off. Check the engine lubrication system as described in Chapter Two.
7. To replace the switch, unscrew it from the engine and install a new one. Test the new switch as described in Steps 1-4.

Neutral Indicator Switch
Testing/Replacement

The neutral indicator switch is mounted in the shifter cover on 4-speed models and on top of the transmission cover on 5-speed models (**Figure 76**). The neutral indicator light on the instrument panel should light when the ignition is turned ON and the transmission is in NEUTRAL.

1. Slide the rubber boot up the neutral switch wire and disconnect the electrical connector to the switch.
2. Turn the ignition switch ON.

3. Ground the switch wire to the transmission housing.
4. The neutral indicator light on the instrument panel should light.
5. If the signal indicator light does not light, check for a burned-out indicator light and inspect all wiring between the switch and the indicator light. If necessary, replace the light as described in this chapter.
6A. If the problem was solved in Steps 3-5, attach the electrical connector to the neutral switch. Make sure the connection is tight and free from oil. Slide the rubber boot back into position.
6B. If the problem was not solved in Steps 3-5, remove the neutral switch and its gasket and depress its plunger by hand. If the plunger does not return when depressed or if it moves roughly, replace the neutral switch.
7. When installing a neutral switch, check the neutral switch gasket for wear. Install the neutral switch gasket over the neutral switch threads then thread the switch into the cover and tighten securely. Reconnect the electrical connector, making sure the

rubber boot on the end of the connector is positioned over the connector.

Front Brake Light Switch Testing/Replacement

A mechanical, plunger-type switch is mounted in the front master cylinder. When the front brake lever is applied, the switch closes the brake light circuit and the rear brake light comes on. If the brake light does not come on when the front brake lever is applied and the ignition switch is turned ON, first check for a blown taillight bulb. If the bulb is okay, test the switch as follows.

1. Disconnect the electrical wires to the brake light switch.
2. Use an ohmmeter and check for continuity between the 2 terminals on the brake light switch connector. There should be no continuity (infinite resistance) with the brake lever released. With the brake lever applied there should be continuity (low resistance). If the switch fails either of these tests, the switch must be replaced.
3. Refer to *Front Master Cylinder Disassembly and Reassembly* in Chapter Fourteen to replace the switch.

Rear Brake Light Switch Testing/Replacement

A hydraulic, normally-open rear brake light switch is used on all models; see **Figure 77**, typical. The rear brake light switch threads into a hole intersecting a brake fluid passageway in the rear brake line tee fitting that connects the rear master cylinder and brake caliper hoses. When the ignition switch is turned ON and the brake pedal is released, the brake

switch contacts are open and the rear brake light is off. When the rear brake pedal is applied, hydraulic pressure closes the switch contacts, providing a ground path for the rear brake light to come on.

If the rear brake light does not come on when the ignition is turned ON and the rear brake pedal is applied (with sufficient hydraulic pressure to lock the brake), perform the following.

1. Turn the ignition switch OFF.
2. Use an ohmmeter and check for continuity between the 2 terminals on the brake light switch connector. There should be no continuity (infinite resistance) with the rear brake pedal released. With the rear brake pedal applied there should be continuity (low resistance). If the rear brake switch fails either of these tests, the switch must be replaced.
3. Purchase the new switch before removing the old switch.
4. Disconnect the wires at the switch.

NOTE
There will be some brake fluid leakage after removing the old switch.

5. Loosen and remove the old switch. Then cover the hole opening with your finger to prevent excessive brake fluid from spilling out.
6. Remove your finger from the hole opening and install the new switch. Tighten the switch securely.
7. Reconnect the switch wires.
8. Bleed the rear brake as described in Chapter Thirteen.

WARNING
Do not ride the motorcycle until the rear brake is operating properly.

HORN

The horn is an important safety device and should be kept in working order. If the horn is damaged, it should be replaced immediately.

Removal/Installation

1. If the horn fails to blow properly, check for broken or frayed horn wires. Also check the battery as described in this chapter.
2. Remove all components as necessary to gain access to the horn.
3. Disconnect the horn electrical connector.

9

4. Remove the horn mounting attachments and remove the horn.

5. Installation is the reverse of these steps.

TURN SIGNAL MODULE
(1991-ON)

All 1991-on models are equipped with a turn signal module, an electronic microprocessor that controls the turn signals and the 4-way hazard flasher. The turn signal module receives its information from the speedometer and turn signal switches.

The turn signal module is mounted on the upper frame tubes between the fuel tanks (**Figure 78**).

Troubleshooting

The following basic troubleshooting procedures will help isolate some specific problems to the module. If it is necessary to access the turn signal module, remove the fuel tanks as described in Chapter Eight.

One or both turn signals do not flash. Light on front or rear side is lit, but does not flash

1. Remove the lens and check for a burned out bulb. Replace bulb if necessary.

2. If the bulb is okay, check for one of the following problems:

    a. Check the bulb socket contacts for corrosion. Clean contacts and recheck. If you have a problem with corrosion building on the contacts, wipe the contacts with a dielectric grease before installing the bulb.

    b. Check for a broken bulb wire. Repair wire or connector.

    c. Check for a loose bulb socket where it is staked to the housing. If the bulb socket is loose, replace the light assembly.

    d. Check for a poor ground connection. If the ground is poor, scrape the ground mounting area or replace damaged ground wire(s), as required.

Turn signals do not operate on one side

1. Perform the checks listed under *One or both turn signals do not flash. Light on front or rear side is lit,*

but does not flash. If these checks do not locate the problem, proceed to Step 2.

2. Inoperative handlebar directional switch. Perform the following:

    a. Turn the ignition switch ON.

    b. Disconnect the turn signal module electrical connector.

    c. Referring to **Figure 79**, locate pin 8 or pin 10 on the module pin connector.

    d. With a voltmeter set on the DC scale, connect the negative lead to a good ground and the positive lead to pin 8 or pin 10 and press the turn signal switch. The voltmeter should read 12 volts when the switch is pressed in.

    e. If there is 12 volts, proceed to Step 3.

    f. If there is no voltage reading, proceed to Step 4.

3. Inoperative module. If 12 volts were recorded in Step 2, and the lights and connecting wires are in good condition, the module may be damaged. Replace the module and retest.

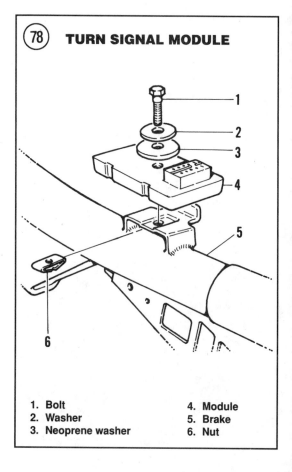

(78) TURN SIGNAL MODULE

1. Bolt	4. Module
2. Washer	5. Brake
3. Neoprene washer	6. Nut

4. Damaged directional switch wire circuit. If no voltage was recorded in Step 2, check the handlebar switch and related wiring for damage. Tests can be made by performing continuity and voltage checks.

5. Reconnect the turn signal module electrical connector.

Turn signals/hazard lights do not operate on both sides

1. If none of the turn signals or hazard flashers operate, check the module for proper ground with an ohmmeter. Using the wiring diagram at the end of this book for your model, trace the ground connection from the module to the frame tab. If a ground is not present, remove the ground wire at the frame and scrape the frame and clean the connector. Check the ground wire for breaks. Repair as required. If a ground is present, perform Step 2.

2. Refer to the wiring diagram for your model and locate the accessory circuit breaker. Turn the ignition switch ON and check for voltage on the hot or load side of the circuit breaker with a voltmeter. If there is no voltage, check the following components:

a. Accessory circuit breaker.

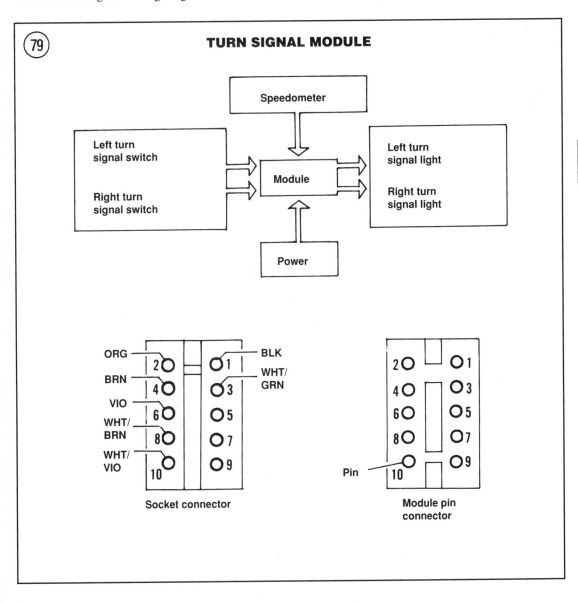

TURN SIGNAL MODULE

b. Main circuit breaker.
c. Starter relay.
d. Ignition switch.
e. Circuit wiring.

Turn signals do not cancel

1. Support the bike so that the front wheel clears the ground.
2. Connect an ohmmeter to the speedometer switch white/green wire and ground. Spin the front wheel and watch the ohmmeter scale. The ohmmeter should alternate between 0 ohms and infinity.
  a. If ohmmeter reading is correct, disconnect the module pin connector. With a voltmeter set on the DC scale, connect the negative lead to a good ground and the positive lead to the No. 3 pin socket connector. The voltmeter should read 12 volts. If ohm and volt readings are correct, the module is damaged.
  b. If ohmmeter reading is incorrect, check for damaged wiring from the speedometer switch white/green wire to the module. If wiring is okay, the reed switch in the speedometer may be damaged.

Removal/Installation

1. Remove the fuel tank console.
2. Disconnect the harness plug from the module.
3. See **Figure 78**. Remove the bolt, steel washer and neoprene washer securing the module to the frame tube. Remove the module.
4. Install by reversing these steps. Make sure to place the neoprene washer so that is it against the module. Tighten the bolt securely.

CIRCUIT BREAKERS

All models use circuit breakers (**Figure 80**, typical) to protect the electrical circuit. Circuit breaker ratings for the different circuits are listed in **Table 4**.

Whenever a failure occurs in any part of the electrical system, each circuit breaker is self-resetting and will automatically return power to the circuit when the electrical fault is found and corrected.

> *CAUTION*
> *If the electrical fault on circuit breaker-equipped models is not found and corrected, the breakers will cycle on and off continuously. This will cause the motorcycle to run erratically and eventually the battery will lose its charge.*

Usually the trouble can be traced to a short circuit in the wiring connected to the circuit breaker. This may be caused by worn-through insulation or by a wire which has worked loose and shorted to ground. Occasionally, the electrical overload may occur in a switch or motor. By following the wiring diagrams at the end of the book, the circuits protected by each circuit breaker can be determined.

A tripped circuit breaker should be treated as more than a minor annoyance; it should serve also as a warning that something is wrong in the electrical system.

Replace a defective circuit breaker by disconnecting the wire and pulling it out of its holder. Reverse to install.

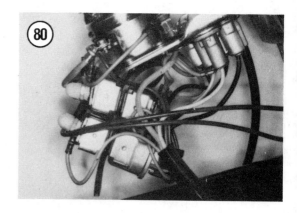

Table 1 BATTERY CAPACITY

All models	12 volt, 19 amp hr.

Table 2 BATTERY STATE OF CHARGE

1.110-1.130	Discharged
1.140-1.160	Almost discharged
1.170-1.190	One-quarter charged
1.200-1.220	One-half charged
1.230-1.250	Three-quarters charged
1.260-1.280	Fully charged

Table 3 STARTER SPECIFICATIONS

	in.	mm
Starter brush length		
1984-1988	0.438	11.1
1989-1990	0.354	8.9
1991-1992	0.413	10.5
1993-on	0.354	8.9
Commutator diameter wear limit (minimum OD)		
1984-1988	—	—
1989-on	1.141	28.9

9

Table 4 CIRCUIT BREAKER RATINGS

Circuit	Rating (amps)
Main (battery)	30
Ignition	15
Lights	15
Accessory	15

CHAPTER TEN

WHEELS, HUBS AND TIRES

This chapter describes disassembly and repair of the front and rear wheels, hubs and tire service. For routine maintenance, see Chapter Three.

Softail models are equipped with either wire spoke, cast or disc wheels. Make sure you use the procedure and illustrations applicable to your bike.

Tire service is a critical aspect to the overall operation and safety of your motorcycle. Tires should be properly mounted, balanced and maintained while in service.

Tables 1-4 are found at the end of the chapter.

FRONT WHEEL

Proper front wheel maintenance and inspection is critical to the safe operation of your Harley. The following section describes complete service to the front wheel. Service to the front hub and bearings is described later in this chapter.

Removal
(Non-Springer Models)

1. Support the bike so that the front wheel clears the ground.

2. Remove the brake caliper mounting bolts (**Figure 1**) and lift the caliper away from the brake disc. Support the caliper with a cord so that the weight of the caliper is not supported by the brake line.

NOTE
Insert a piece of wood or vinyl in the caliper between the brake pads. That way, if the brake lever is inadvertently squeezed, the piston will not be forced out of the cylinder. If this does happen, the caliper might have to be disassembled to reseat the piston and the system will have to be bled.

3. Remove the axle nut, lockwasher and flat washer.

4. Loosen the fork slider cap nuts (A, **Figure 2**). Do not remove the nuts and slider cap.

5. Tap the end of the axle with a soft-faced mallet and remove it from the wheel (B, **Figure 2**). If the axle is tight, tap the end of the axle with a brass or aluminum drift.

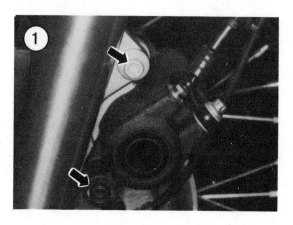

6. Pull the wheel away from the fork sliders slightly and remove the speedometer drive gear from the wheel.

NOTE
The shoulder on the right-hand axle spacer is inserted through the oil seal. The spacer should not fall out when the wheel is removed.

CAUTION
Do not set the wheel down on the disc surface, as it may be scratched or warped. Either lean the wheel against a wall or place it on a couple of wood blocks.

7. When servicing the wheel assembly, install the washer and nut on the axle to prevent their loss.

8. Inspect the front wheel assembly as described in this chapter.

Installation
(Non-Springer Models)

1. Clean the axle in solvent and dry thoroughly. Make sure the axle bearing surfaces on both fork sliders and the axle are free from burrs and nicks.

2. Apply an anti-seize lubricant to the axle shaft prior to installation.

3. Make sure that the right-hand spacer is inserted through the oil seal as shown in C, **Figure 2**. If necessary, reinstall the spacer as described under *Front Hub* in this chapter.

4. Install the wheel as follows:

    a. Install the speedometer drive onto the wheel gear case by aligning the speedometer drive dogs with the gear case notches.

b. Hold the speedometer drive in position and install the wheel between the fork tubes.

c. Insert the axle through the front forks and wheel from the right-hand side (B, **Figure 2**) and install the flat washer, lockwasher and axle nut finger-tight. Check that the right-hand axle spacer (C, **Figure 2**) is positioned properly.

d. Tighten the slider cap nuts securely to prevent the axle from turning and then tighten the axle nut to the torque specification listed in **Table 2**. Loosen the slider cap nuts and then retighten to the torque specification listed in **Table 2**.

e. Make sure gap between the slider cap and fork slider is equal on both sides.

5. Perform the *Front Axle End Play Check* in this chapter.

6. Remove the vinyl tubing or pieces of wood from the brake caliper. Then *carefully* insert the pads between the disc when installing the brake caliper. Be careful not to damage the leading edge of the brake pads when installing the brake disc. Tighten the brake caliper bolts to the specifications in **Table 2**.

7. After the wheel and brake are completely installed, rotate it several times and apply the front brake a couple of times to make sure the wheel rotates freely and that the brake pads are against the disc correctly.

Removal
(Springer Models)

1. Support the bike so that the front wheel clears the ground.

2. Remove the brake caliper as follows:

    a. Remove the lower brake caliper mounting bolt (**Figure 3**).

    b. Remove the upper brake caliper mounting bolt cotter pin and washer (**Figure 4**). Then unscrew and remove the bolt and its outer washer (**Figure 5**).

    c. Lift the caliper away from the brake disc. Support the caliper with a cord so that the weight of the caliper is not supported by the brake line.

10

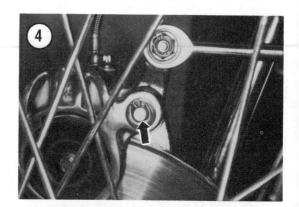

NOTE
Insert a piece of wood or vinyl in the caliper between the brake pads. That way, if the brake lever is inadvertently squeezed, the piston will not be forced out of the cylinder. If this does happen, the caliper might have to be disassembled to reseat the piston and the system will have to be bled.

3. Remove the axle locknut and washer (**Figure 6**). Discard the locknut.

4. Tap the end of the axle with a soft-faced mallet and remove it from the wheel (A, **Figure 7**). If the axle is tight, tap the end of the axle with a brass or aluminum drift. Remove the washer (B, **Figure 7**) installed between the caliper bracket and the right-hand rocker

5. See **Figure 8**. Remove the bushing, wave washer and Teflon washer from the brake bracket (**Figure 9**) and install them onto the axle along with the axle washer so as not to lose them.

6. Pull the wheel away from the rockers and remove the speedometer drive gear (**Figure 10**) from the wheel.

CAUTION
Do not set the wheel down on the disc surface, as it may be scratched or warped. Either lean the wheel against a wall or place it on a couple of wood blocks.

7. Inspect the front wheel assembly as described in this chapter.

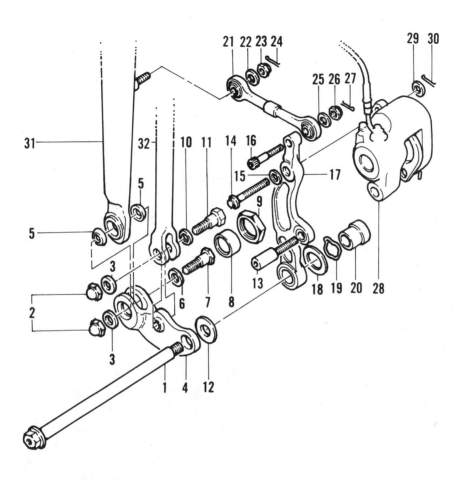

⑧ ROCKER AND FRONT BRAKE (SPRINGER)

1. Front axle	16. Bolt
2. Acorn nut	17. Brake bracket
3. Washer	18. Thrust washer (large I.D.)
4. Rocker	19. Wave washer
5. Spherical bearings	20. Spacer
6. Thin washer (mid 1989 and earlier; see text for application)	21. Brake reaction link
	22. Washer
7. Pivot stud	23. Nut
8. Bearing retainer	24. Cotter pin
9. Locknut	25. Washer
10. Thin washer (mid 1989 and earlier; see text for application)	26. Nut
	27. Cotter pin
11. Pivot stud	28. Brake caliper
12. Thrust washer (small I.D.)	29. Washer
13. Lower mounting bolt	30. Cotter pin
14. Upper mounting bolt	31. Rigid fork
15. Washer	32. Spring fork

10

Installation
(Springer Models)

> *NOTE*
> *The 2 Teflon washers should be in-spected for wear before installation. Note that one side of each washer is coated with Teflon. If a washer is worn enough so that the brass shows through the Teflon coating, replace the washer(s).*

1. Clean the axle in solvent and dry thoroughly. Make sure the axle bearing surfaces on the axle are free from burrs and nicks.

2. Wipe the axle with an anti-seize lubricant prior to installation.

> *NOTE*
> *To make installation of the wheel easier, insert a dummy axle partway through the left-hand rocker and wheel hub when installing the axle and assembling the brake bracket components in the following steps.*

> *NOTE*
> *Note that the 2 Teflon thrust washers have different inside diameters (I.D.). The washer installed between the wave washer and brake bracket has a larger I.D. than the washer installed between the brake bracket and right-hand rocker.*

3. Assemble and install the brake bracket bushing assembly as follows:
   a. Slide the wave washer onto the bushing so that it seats against the bushing's shoulder (**Figure 8**).
   b. Install the Teflon washer (with larger I.D.) onto the bushing so that it seats against the wave washer. The Teflon side of the washer must be installed so that it will face *against* the brake bracket when the wheel is installed (**Figure 8**).
   c. Insert the bushing assembly into the brake bracket in the direction shown in **Figure 9**.

4. Insert the wheel through the rockers so that the brake disc is on the right-hand side and the brake bracket is positioned between the right-hand rocker and the wheel hub.

5. Insert the axle (A, **Figure 7**) from the right-hand side so that it enters the rocker only. Then insert the Teflon washer (with smaller I.D.) between the rocker and the brake bracket (B, **Figure 7**) and push the axle through the washer, brake bracket and wheel hub.

6. When the axle is almost all the way through the hub, remove the dummy axle, if used. Then install the seal onto the speedometer drive (if removed) and insert the drive into the left-hand side of the hub so that the drive engages the notch in the wheel hub; see **Figure 10**. Then push the axle through the seal and speedometer drive and the left-hand rocker.

7. Install the flat washer and a *new* locknut (**Figure 6**). Tighten the locknut to the torque specification listed in **Table 3**.

> *NOTE*
> *Check that the speedometer drive is still properly indexed with the wheel notch (**Figure 11**).*

8. Perform the *Front Axle End Play Check* in this chapter.

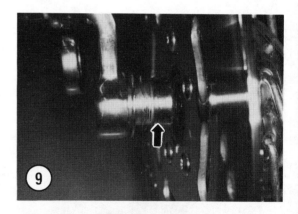

9. Remove the vinyl tubing or pieces of wood from the brake caliper. Then *carefully* insert the pads between the disc when installing the brake caliper. Be careful not to damage the leading edge of the brake pads when installing the brake disc. Install and tighten the caliper bolts as follows:

   a. Install the lower caliper mounting bolt finger-tight.

   b. Install the upper caliper mounting bolt and washer finger-tight.

   c. Tighten the brake caliper bolts to the specifications in **Table 3**.

   d. Install the upper caliper mounting bolt washer and a new cotter pin at the back of the caliper as shown in **Figure 4**. Bend the cotter pin arms over to lock it.

10. After the wheel and brake are completely installed, rotate it several times and apply the front brake a couple of times to make sure the wheel rotates freely and that the brake pads are against the disc correctly.

Inspection (All Models)

1. Remove any corrosion on the front axle with a piece of fine emery cloth.

2. Install the wheel in a wheel truing stand and spin the wheel. Visually check the wheel for excessive wobble or runout. If it appears that the wheel is not running true, remove the tire from the rim as described later in this chapter. Then remount the wheel into the truing stand and measure axial and lateral runout (**Figure 12**) with a pointer or dial indicator. Compare actual runout readings with service limit specifications listed in **Table 1**. Note the following:

   a. Cast or disc wheels: If the runout meets or exceeds the service limit (**Table 1**), check the wheel bearings as described under *Front Hub* in this chapter. If the wheel bearings are okay, cast and disc wheels will have to be replaced as they cannot be serviced. Inspect the wheel for signs of cracks, fractures, dents or bends. If it is damaged in any way, it must be replaced.

   b. Laced wheels: If the wheel bearings, spokes, hub and rim assembly are not damaged, the runout can be removed by accurately truing the wheel. Refer to *Spoke Adjustment* in this chapter. If the rim is dented or damaged in any way, the rim should be replaced and the wheel respoked and trued by a Harley-Davidson dealer or a qualified repair shop familiar with rebuilding Harley wheels.

WARNING
Do not try to repair any damage to cast or disc wheels as it will result in an unsafe riding condition.

10

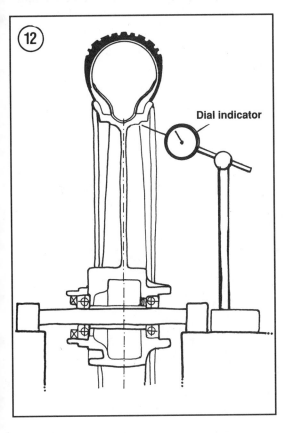

Dial indicator

3. While the wheel is off, check the tightness of the brake disc bolts. Refer to the tightening torques listed at the end of Chapter Fifteen.

4. *Springer models*: Perform the following inspection procedures:

   a. The 2 Teflon washers installed on the brake bracket (**Figure 8**) should be inspected for wear. Note that one side of each washer is coated with Teflon. If a washer is worn enough so that the brass shows through the Teflon coating, replace the washer(s).

   b. Inspect the brake bracket wave washer for cracks or other damage.

   c. Inspect the bushing surface for cracks, deep scoring or excessive wear.

   d. Replace worn or damaged parts before reinstalling the front wheel.

Front Wheel Bearing End Play Check/Adjustment (1984-1991 Models)

Proper wheel bearing end play is important to your Harley's steering and handling performance. Incorrect wheel bearing end play can cause poor handling or excessive bearing side loading and premature bearing wear.

On these models, wheel bearing end play is controlled by the length of the center hub spacer; see **Figures 14-16** for your model. End play should be checked each time the front wheel is reinstalled or whenever unstable handling is felt.

1. Support the bike so that the front wheel is off the ground.

2. Tighten the front axle nut to the torque specification in **Table** 2 or **Table 3**.

3. Tighten the slider cap nuts to the torque specification in **Table 2**.

4. Mount a dial indicator so that the plunger contacts the end of the axle (**Figure 5**). Grasp the wheel and move it back and forth by pushing and pulling it along the axle center line. Read axle end play by observing the dial indicator needle. Compare with end play specification for your model in **Table 1**.

5. If the end play is incorrect, replace the center hub spacer; see **Figures 14-16** for your model. Install a longer spacer for less end play and a shorter spacer for more end play. Different length spacers can be purchased through Harley-Davidson dealers. To install a new spacer, remove the wheel and disassemble the front hub as described under *Front Hub* in this chapter. Reverse to install. Recheck end play after reinstalling the front wheel.

Front Wheel Bearing End Play Check/Adjustment (1992-on)

Proper wheel bearing end play is important to your Harley's steering and handling performance. Incorrect wheel bearing end play can cause poor handling or excessive bearing side loading and premature bearing wear.

On these models, wheel bearing end play is controlled by the thickness of the bearing spacer installed between the spacer washer and the center hub spacer; see **Figures 17-19** for your model. End play should be checked each time the front wheel is reinstalled or whenever unstable handling is felt.

1. Support the bike so that the front wheel is off the ground.

2. Tighten the front axle nut to the torque specification in **Table 2** or **Table 3**.

3. Tighten the slider cap nuts to the torque specification in **Table 2** or **Table 3**.

4. Mount a dial indicator so that the plunger contacts the end of the axle (**Figure 5**). Grasp the wheel and move it back and forth by pushing and pulling it along the axle center line. Read axle end play by observing the dial indicator needle. Compare with end play specification for your model in **Table 1**.

5. If the end play is incorrect, replace the bearing spacer; see **Figures 17-19** for your model. Install a

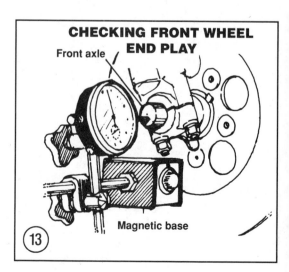

CHECKING FRONT WHEEL END PLAY

Front axle

Magnetic base

13

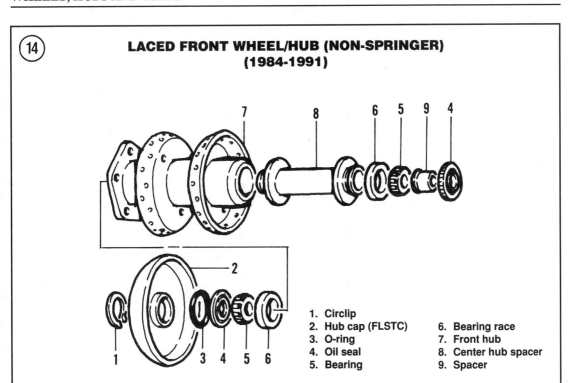

LACED FRONT WHEEL/HUB (NON-SPRINGER)
(1984-1991)

1. Circlip
2. Hub cap (FLSTC)
3. O-ring
4. Oil seal
5. Bearing
6. Bearing race
7. Front hub
8. Center hub spacer
9. Spacer

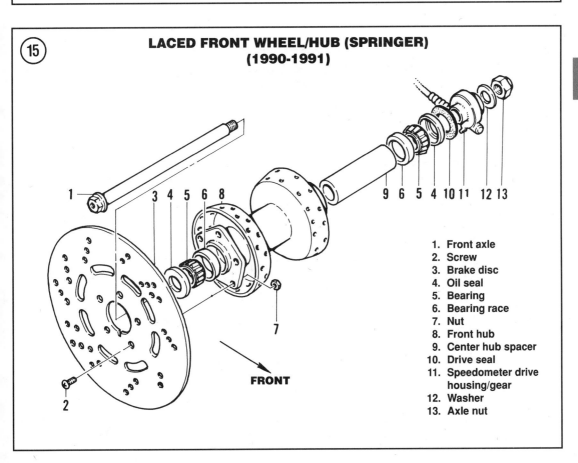

LACED FRONT WHEEL/HUB (SPRINGER)
(1990-1991)

10

1. Front axle
2. Screw
3. Brake disc
4. Oil seal
5. Bearing
6. Bearing race
7. Nut
8. Front hub
9. Center hub spacer
10. Drive seal
11. Speedometer drive housing/gear
12. Washer
13. Axle nut

FRONT

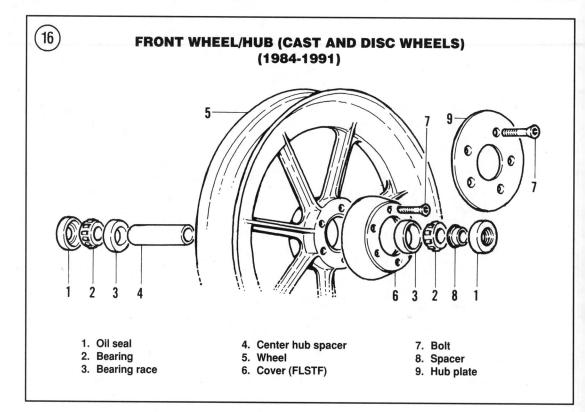

**FRONT WHEEL/HUB (CAST AND DISC WHEELS)
(1984-1991)**

1. Oil seal
2. Bearing
3. Bearing race
4. Center hub spacer
5. Wheel
6. Cover (FLSTF)
7. Bolt
8. Spacer
9. Hub plate

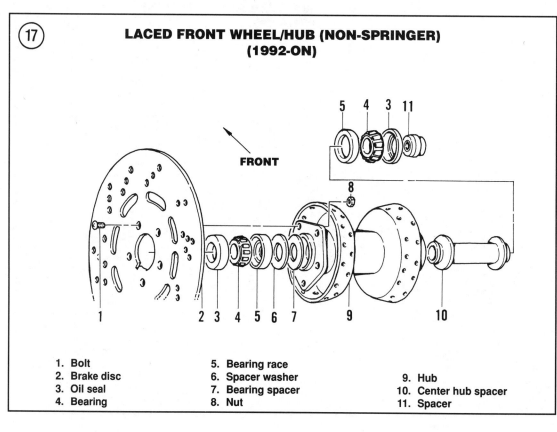

**LACED FRONT WHEEL/HUB (NON-SPRINGER)
(1992-ON)**

FRONT

1. Bolt
2. Brake disc
3. Oil seal
4. Bearing
5. Bearing race
6. Spacer washer
7. Bearing spacer
8. Nut
9. Hub
10. Center hub spacer
11. Spacer

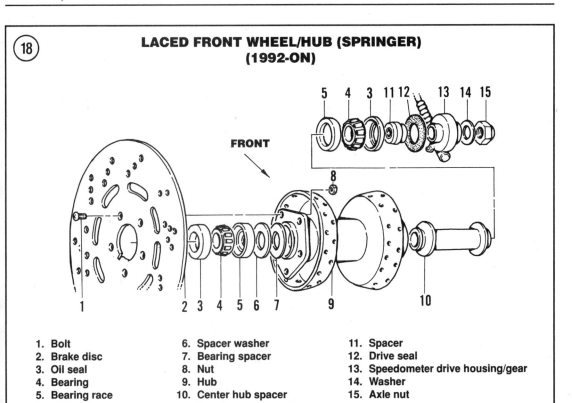

**LACED FRONT WHEEL/HUB (SPRINGER)
(1992-ON)**

FRONT

1. Bolt
2. Brake disc
3. Oil seal
4. Bearing
5. Bearing race
6. Spacer washer
7. Bearing spacer
8. Nut
9. Hub
10. Center hub spacer
11. Spacer
12. Drive seal
13. Speedometer drive housing/gear
14. Washer
15. Axle nut

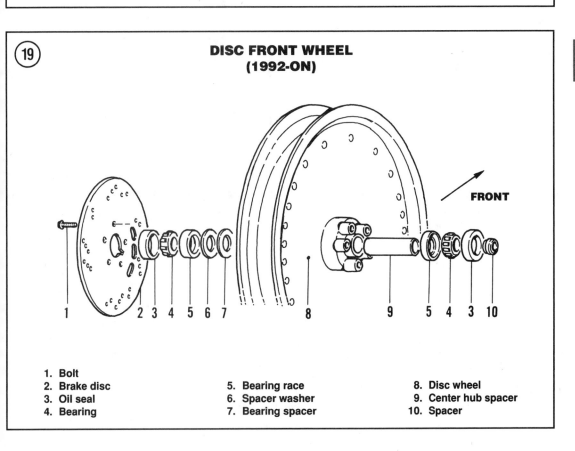

**DISC FRONT WHEEL
(1992-ON)**

FRONT

10

1. Bolt
2. Brake disc
3. Oil seal
4. Bearing
5. Bearing race
6. Spacer washer
7. Bearing spacer
8. Disc wheel
9. Center hub spacer
10. Spacer

thinner spacer for less end play and a thicker spacer for more end play. Do not replace the center hub spacer as this spacer is not used for end play adjustment. Different thickness bearing spacers can be purchased through Harley-Davidson dealers. To install a new bearing spacer, remove the wheel and disassemble the front hub as described under *Front Hub* in this chapter. Reverse to install. Recheck end play after reinstalling the front wheel.

FRONT HUB

Tapered roller bearings are installed on each side of the hub. Oil seals are installed on the outside of each bearing to protect them from dirt and other contaminants. The bearings can be removed from the hub after removing the outer oil seals. The bearing races are pressed into the hub and should not be removed unless they require replacement.

Disassembly/Inspection/Reassembly

Refer to the exploded view drawing for your model when servicing the front hub bearings:

a. *1984-1991 laced wheel (non-Springer):* **Figure 14**.

b. *1992-on laced wheel (non-Springer):* **Figure 17**.

c. *1990-1991 laced wheel (Springer):* **Figure 15**.

d. *1992-on laced wheel (Springer):* **Figure 18**.

e. *1984-1991 cast and disc wheels:* **Figure 16**.

f. *1992-on disc wheels:* **Figure 19**.

Prior to servicing the hub, note the following:

a. The bearings and races are matched pairs. Label the bearings so that they may be returned to their original positions.

b. Remove the bearing races only if the bearings are being replaced. Do not remove the races for inspection.

c. Remove the oil seals by prying them out of the hub with a wide-blade screwdriver or seal remover (**Figure 20**). If you are using a screwdriver, pad the screwdriver to prevent from damaging the hub.

d. Pack the lip of each oil seal with a waterproof bearing grease prior to installation.

e. Install all oil seals with their closed side facing out.

1. Remove the front wheel as described in this chapter.

2. If necessary, remove the brake disc as described in Chapter Fifteen.

3. On models with hubcap, remove the circlip, hubcap and O-ring.

4A. On 1990-1991 models (**Figure 14**, **Figure 15** or **Figure 16**), perform the following:

a. Remove the oil seals.

b. Remove the bearings.

c. Remove the center hub spacer.

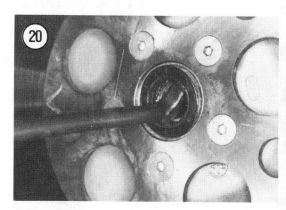

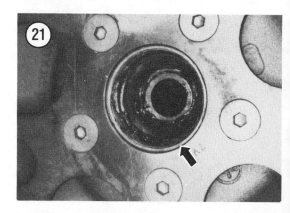

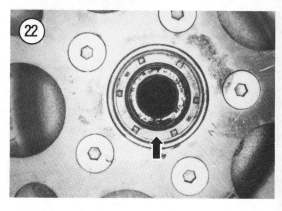

4B. On 1992-on models (**Figure 17**, **Figure 18** or **Figure 19**), perform the following:

    a. Remove the oil seals.

    b. Remove the bearings.

    c. Remove the spacer washer and bearing spacer from the brake disc side.

    d. Remove the center hub spacer.

5. Wash the bearings thoroughly in clean solvent and dry with compressed air. Wipe the bearing races off with a clean rag dipped in solvent. Then check the roller bearings and races for wear, pitting or excessive heat (bluish tint). Replace the bearing and races as a complete set. Replace the bearing races as described in Step 6. If the bearing and its race do not require replacement, proceed to Step 7. If you are going to reinstall the original bearing(s), pack the bearing thoroughly with grease and wrap it in a clean, lint-free cloth or wax paper. Wipe a film of grease across the bearing race (**Figure 20**). If the bearings and races are not lubricated after cleaning them, they may begin to rust.

6. Replace the bearing races (**Figure 21**) as follows:

    a. A universal bearing remover should be used to remove the races from the hub. If this tool is unavailable, insert a drift punch through the hub and tap the race out of the hub with a hammer. Move the punch around the race to make sure the race is driven squarely out of the hub. Do not allow the race to bind in the hub as this can damage the race bore in the hub. Severe damage to the race bore will require replacement of the hub.

    b. Clean the inside and outside of the hub with solvent. Dry with compressed air.

    c. Wipe the outside of the new race with oil and align it with the hub. Using a bearing driver or socket with an outside diameter slightly smaller than the bearing race, drive the race into the hub until it bottoms out on the hub shoulder. As you begin to drive the race into the hub, stop and check your work often to make sure the race is square with the hub bore. Do not allow the race to bind during installation.

NOTE
If you do not have the proper size tool to drive the race into the hub, have a Harley-Davidson dealer or independent repair shop install the race. Do not attempt to install the race by driving it into the hub with a small diameter punch or rod.

7. Blow any dirt or foreign matter out of the hub prior to installing the bearings.

8. Apply bearing grease to each race.

9. Pack the bearings with grease and set them aside for assembly.

10A. On 1990-1991 Springer models (**Figure 15**), perform the following:

    a. Install the center hub spacer into the hub.

    b. Install a bearing into its race.

    c. Align the oil seal with the hub so that its closed side faces out (away from hub). Then, using a bearing driver or socket with an O.D. slightly smaller than the oil seal, carefully drive the oil seal into the hub until it is flush with the hub or no more than 0.015 in. (0.38 mm) below the bearing bore surface.

    d. Turn the hub over and repeat to install the opposite bearing and oil seal.

10B. On 1992-on Springer models (**Figure 18**), perform the following:

    a. Place the wheel on the workbench so that the left-hand side faces up.

    b. Install the left-hand bearing into its race.

    c. Pack the area between the bearing and oil seal with grease.

    d. Drive the left-hand oil seal into the hub until it is flush with or no more than 0.020 in. (0.51 mm) below the hub surface.

    e. Turn the wheel over so that the right-hand side (disc side) faces up.

    f. Install the center hub spacer into the hub.

    g. Install the bearing spacer into the hub.

    h. Install the spacer washer—shoulder side first—into the hub.

10

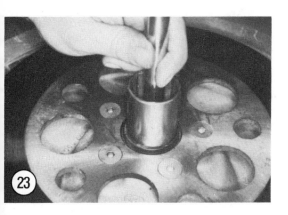

23

i. Install the right-hand bearing into its race.

j. Pack the area between the bearing and oil seal with grease.

k. Install the right-hand oil seal as described in sub-step d.

10C. On 1984-1991 models with laced wheels (non-Springer) (**Figure 14**), perform the following:

a. Place the wheel on the workbench so that the right-hand side faces up.

b. Install the right-hand bearing into its race.

c. Insert the right-hand wheel spacer into one of the new oil seals so that the spacer shoulder faces toward the outside (closed end) of the seal.

d. Install the oil seal and spacer into the right-hand side of the hub. Drive the oil seal into the hub until it is flush with or no more than 0.015 in. (0.38 mm) below the hub surface.

e. Turn the wheel over so that the left-hand side faces up.

f. Install the center hub spacer into the hub.

g. Install the left-hand bearing into the hub.

h. Install the left-hand oil seal as described in sub-step d.

10D. On 1992-on models with laced wheels (non-Springer) (**Figure 17**), perform the following:

a. Place the wheel on the workbench so that the right-hand side faces up.

b. Install the right-hand bearing into its race.

c. Pack the area between the bearing and oil seal with grease.

d. Drive the right-hand oil seal into the hub until it is flush with or no more than 0.020 in. (0.51 mm) below the hub surface.

e. Turn the wheel over so that the left-hand side faces up.

f. Install the center hub spacer into the hub.

g. Install the bearing spacer into the hub.

h. Install the spacer washer—shoulder side first—into the hub.

i. Install the left-hand bearing into its race.

j. Pack the area between the bearing and oil seal with grease.

k. Install the left-oil seal as described in sub-step d.

l. Install the spacer into the right-hand oil seal.

10E. On 1992-on models with disc wheels (**Figure 19**), perform the following:

a. Place the wheel on the workbench so that the right-hand side faces up.

b. Install the right-hand bearing into its race.

c. Pack the area between the bearing and oil seal with grease.

d. Drive the right-hand oil seal into the hub until it is flush with or no more than 0.040 in. (1.01 mm) below the hub surface.

e. Turn the wheel over so that the left-hand side faces up.

f. Install the center hub spacer into the hub.

g. Install the bearing spacer into the hub.

h. Install the spacer washer—shoulder side first—into the hub.

i. Install the left-hand bearing into its race.

j. Pack the area between the bearing and oil seal with grease.

k. Install the left-oil seal as described in sub-step d.

l. Install the spacer into the right-hand oil seal.

11. If the brake disc was removed, refer to Chapter Fifteen for correct procedures and tightening torques.

12. Install the hub cap, if removed.

13. After the wheel is installed on the bike and the front axle tightened to the specified torque specifi-

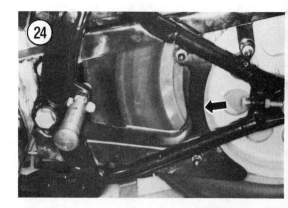

cation, the bearing end play should be checked as described in this chapter.

14. If the hub on spoke wheels is damaged, the hub can be replaced by removing the spokes and having a dealer assemble a new hub. If the hub on disc or cast wheels is damaged, the wheel assembly must be replaced; it cannot be repaired.

REAR WHEEL

Proper rear wheel maintenance and inspection is critical to the safe operation of your Harley. The following section describes complete service to the rear wheel. Service to the rear hub and bearings is described later in this chapter.

Removal

1. Support the bike so that the rear wheel clears the ground.

2. Remove the belt or chain guard (**Figure 24**).

3. Remove the saddlebags, if necessary.

NOTE
On all models except the 1990 FLSTF, the axle nut is installed on the right-hand side. If you have a 1990 FLSTF, note the position of the axle and axle nut so that you will reinstall them in their original mounting position.

4. Remove and discard the rear axle cotter pin, if so equipped.

5. Loosen the drive chain or belt adjusting locknuts and adjuster bolts. See **Figure 25**, typical.

6. Loosen and remove the axle nut and washers. See **Figure 25**, typical.

7. Slide the axle out of the wheel (**Figure 26**) and allow the wheel to drop to the ground.

8. Remove the left-hand axle spacer (**Figure 27**).

NOTE
The shoulder on the right-hand axle spacer is inserted through the oil seal. The spacer should not fall out when the wheel is removed.

9. Lift the drive chain or belt off of the sprocket and remove the rear wheel.

NOTE
Insert a piece of wood or vinyl tubing in the caliper between the brake pads in place of the disc. That way, if the brake pedal is inadvertently depressed, the piston will not be forced out of the cylinder. If this does happen, the caliper might have to be disassembled to reseat the piston and the system will have to be bled. By using the wood or vinyl tubing, bleeding the brake should not be necessary when installing the wheel.

10. If the wheel is going to be off for any length of time, or if it is to be taken to a shop for repair, install the chain adjusters and axle spacers on the axle along with the axle nut to prevent losing any parts.

CAUTION
Do not set the wheel down on the disc surface, as it may be scratched or warped. Either lean the wheel against a wall or place it on a couple of wood blocks.

11. Inspect the rear wheel assembly as described in this chapter.

10

Installation

1. Clean the axle in solvent and dry thoroughly. Make sure the axle bearing surfaces on the axle are free from burrs and nicks.

2. Apply an anti-seize lubricant to the axle shaft prior to installation.

NOTE
On 1992-on models, install the left- and right-hand axle spacers with their large chamfered ends facing toward their respective bearings.

3. Install the axle spacer onto the axle (**Figure 28**).

4. Make sure the right-hand wheel spacer is inserted through the oil seal as shown in **Figure 29**. If necessary, install the spacer and oil seal as described under *Rear Hub* in this chapter.

5. Remove the vinyl tubing from the brake caliper. Then position the rear wheel into the swing arm, through the drive chain or belt, and install the left-hand wheel spacer (**Figure 27**). **Figure 30** shows the right-hand axle spacer. Carefully insert the disc between the pads when installing the wheel.

6A. *All models except the 1990 FLSTF*: Insert the axle through the wheel from the left-hand side (**Figure 26**).

6B. *1990 FLSTF models*: Insert the axle through the wheel from the right-hand side.

NOTE
If the axle is installed opposite from that described in Step 6B for 1990 FLSTF models, the axle nut may rub against the muffler when you are riding the bike.

7. Install the washer, lockwasher and nut. If your model does not use a cotter pin, install a *new* axle locknut.

8. Adjust the drive chain or belt as described in Chapter Three.

9. Tighten the axle nut to the torque specification listed in **Table 4**.

NOTE
*If it is necessary to tighten the axle nut a bit more to line up the axle nut slot with the cotter pin hole in the axle, make sure you do not exceed the maximum torque specification listed in **Table 4**.*

10. Perform the *Rear Axle End Play Check* in this chapter.

11. Install a new cotter pin (if used), and bend its arms over to lock it.

12. Rotate the wheel several times to make sure it rotates freely and that the brakes work properly.

13. Install the drive chain or belt guard.

14. Reinstall the saddlebags, if necessary.

Inspection (All Models)

1. Remove any corrosion on the rear axle with a piece of fine emery cloth.

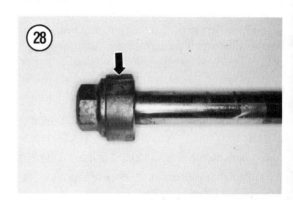

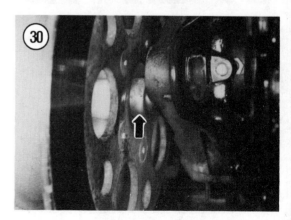

2. Install the wheel in a wheel truing stand and spin the wheel. Visually check the wheel for excessive wobble or runout. If it appears that the wheel is not running true, remove the tire from the rim as described later in this chapter. Then remount the wheel into the truing stand and measure axial and lateral runout (**Figure 31**) with a pointer or dial indicator. Compare actual runout readings with service limit specifications listed in **Table 1**. Note the following:

a. *Cast or disc wheels:* If the runout meets or exceeds the service limit (**Table 1**), check the wheel bearings as described under *Front Hub* in this chapter. If the wheel bearings are okay, cast and disc wheels will have to be replaced as they cannot be serviced. Inspect the wheel for signs of cracks, fractures, dents or bends. If it is damaged in any way, it must be replaced.

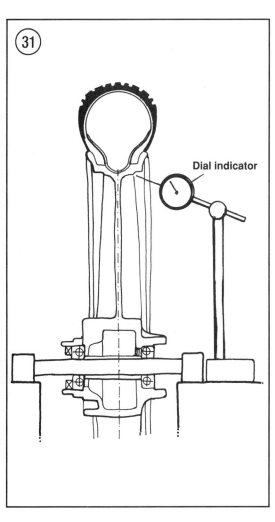

Dial indicator

b. *Laced wheel:* If the wheel bearings, spokes, hub and rim assembly are not damaged, the runout can be removed by accurately truing the wheel. Refer to *Spoke Adjustment* in this chapter. If the rim is dented or damaged in any way, the rim should be replaced and the wheel respoked and trued by a Harley-Davidson dealer or a qualified repair shop familiar with rebuilding Harley wheels.

WARNING
Do not try to repair any damage to cast or disc wheels as it will result in an unsafe riding condition.

3. While the wheel is off, check the tightness of the brake disc bolts. Refer to the tightening torque listed at the end of Chapter Fourteen.

Rear Wheel Bearing End Play Check/Adjustment (1984-1991)

Proper wheel bearing end play is important to your Harley's steering and handling performance. Incorrect wheel bearing end play can cause poor handling or excessive bearing side loading and premature bearing wear.

On these models, wheel bearing end play is controlled by the length of the center hub spacer; see **Figure 32** or **Figure 33**. End play should be checked each time the rear wheel is removed or whenever unstable handling is felt.

1. Support the bike so that the rear wheel is off the ground.

2. Tighten the rear axle nut to the torque specification in **Table 3**.

3. Mount a dial indicator so that the plunger contacts the end of the axle (**Figure 5**). Grasp the wheel and move it back and forth by pushing and pulling it along the axle center line. Read axle end play by observing the dial indicator needle and compare to specification in **Table 1**.

4. If the end play is incorrect, replace the center hub spacer; see **Figure 32** or **Figure 33** for your model. Install a longer spacer for less end play and a shorter spacer for more end play. Different length spacers can be purchased through Harley-Davidson dealers. To install a new spacer, remove the wheel and disassemble the rear hub as described under *Rear Hub*

10

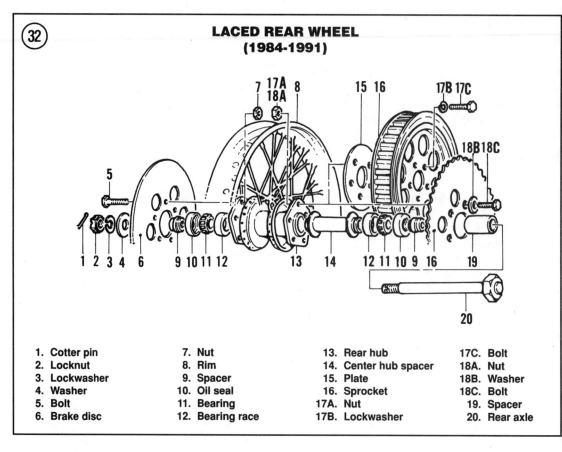

LACED REAR WHEEL
(1984-1991)

1. Cotter pin
2. Locknut
3. Lockwasher
4. Washer
5. Bolt
6. Brake disc
7. Nut
8. Rim
9. Spacer
10. Oil seal
11. Bearing
12. Bearing race
13. Rear hub
14. Center hub spacer
15. Plate
16. Sprocket
17A. Nut
17B. Lockwasher
17C. Bolt
18A. Nut
18B. Washer
18C. Bolt
19. Spacer
20. Rear axle

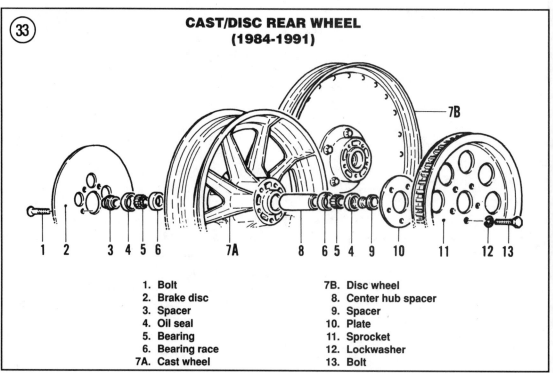

CAST/DISC REAR WHEEL
(1984-1991)

1. Bolt
2. Brake disc
3. Spacer
4. Oil seal
5. Bearing
6. Bearing race
7A. Cast wheel
7B. Disc wheel
8. Center hub spacer
9. Spacer
10. Plate
11. Sprocket
12. Lockwasher
13. Bolt

in this chapter. Reverse to install. Recheck end play after reinstalling rear wheel.

Rear Wheel Bearing End Play Check/Adjustment (1992-on)

Proper wheel bearing end play is important to your Harley's steering and handling performance. Incorrect wheel bearing end play can cause poor handling or excessive bearing side loading and premature bearing wear.

On these models, wheel bearing end play is controlled by the thickness of the bearing spacer installed between the spacer washer and the center hub spacer; see **Figure 34**. End play should be checked each time the rear wheel is removed or whenever unstable handling is felt.

1. Support the bike so that the rear wheel is off the ground.

2. Tighten the rear axle nut to the torque specification in **Table 3**.

3. Mount a dial indicator so that the plunger contacts the end of the axle (**Figure 5**). Grasp the wheel and move it back and forth by pushing and pulling it along the axle center line. Read axle end play by observing the dial indicator needle and compare to specification in **Table 1**.

4. If the end play is incorrect, replace the bearing spacer (**Figure 35**). Install a thinner spacer for less end play and a thicker spacer for more end play. Do not replace the center hub spacer as this spacer is not used to adjust end play. Different thickness bearing

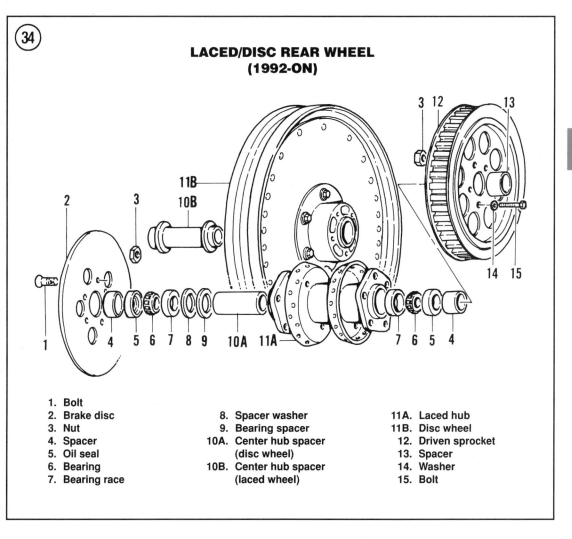

LACED/DISC REAR WHEEL (1992-ON)

1. Bolt
2. Brake disc
3. Nut
4. Spacer
5. Oil seal
6. Bearing
7. Bearing race
8. Spacer washer
9. Bearing spacer
10A. Center hub spacer (disc wheel)
10B. Center hub spacer (laced wheel)
11A. Laced hub
11B. Disc wheel
12. Driven sprocket
13. Spacer
14. Washer
15. Bolt

spacers can be purchased through Harley-Davidson dealers. To install a new bearing spacer, remove the wheel and disassemble the rear hub as described under *Rear Hub* in this chapter. Reverse to install. Recheck end play after reinstalling the rear wheel.

REAR HUB

Tapered roller bearings are installed on each side of the hub. Oil seals are installed on the outside of each bearing to protect them from dirt and other contaminants. The bearings can be removed from the hub after removing the outer oil seals. The bearing races are pressed into the hub and should not be removed unless they require replacement.

Disassembly/Inspection/Reassembly

Refer to the exploded view drawing for your model when servicing the rear hub bearings:

a. *1984-1991 laced rear wheel:* **Figure 32**.
b. *1984-1991 cast/disc rear wheel:* **Figure 33**.
c. *1992-on rear wheel (all):* **Figure 34**.

Prior to servicing the hub, note the following:

a. The bearings and races are matched pairs. Label the bearings so that they may be returned to their original positions.
b. Remove the bearing races only if the bearings are being replaced. Do not remove the races for inspection.
c. Remove the oil seals by prying them out of the hub with a wide-blade screwdriver or seal remover (**Figure 35**). If you are using a screwdriver, pad the screwdriver to prevent from damaging the hub.
d. Pack the lip of each oil seal with a waterproof bearing grease prior to installation.
e. Install all oil seals with their closed side facing out.

1. Remove the rear wheel as described in this chapter.

2. If necessary, remove the brake disc as described in Chapter Fifteen.

3A. On 1990-1991 models (**Figure 32** or **Figure 33**), perform the following:

a. Remove the oil seals and outer spacer.
b. Remove the bearings.
c. Remove the center hub spacer.

3B. On 1992-on models (**Figure 34**), perform the following:

a. Remove the oil seals.
b. Remove the bearings.
c. Remove the spacer washer and bearing spacer from the brake disc side.
d. Remove the center hub spacer.

4. Wash the bearings thoroughly in clean solvent and dry with compressed air. Wipe the bearing races off with a clean rag dipped in solvent. Then check the roller bearings and races for wear, pitting or excessive heat (bluish tint). Replace the bearing and races as a complete set. Replace the bearing races as described in Step 5. If the bearing and its race do not require replacement, proceed to Step 6. If you are going to reinstall the original bearing(s), pack the bearing thoroughly with grease and wrap it in a clean, lint-free cloth or wax paper. Wipe a film of grease across the bearing race (**Figure 21**). If the bearings and races are not lubricated after cleaning them, they may begin to rust.

5. Replace the bearing races (**Figure 21**) as follows:

a. A universal bearing remover should be used to remove the races from the hub. If this tool is unavailable, insert a drift punch through the hub and tap the race out of the hub with a hammer. Move the punch around the race to make sure the race is driven squarely out of the hub. Do not allow the race to bind in the hub as this can damage the race bore in the hub. Severe damage to the race bore will require replacement of the hub.
b. Clean the inside and outside of the hub with solvent. Dry with compressed air.
c. Wipe the outside of the new race with oil and align it with the hub. Using a bearing driver or socket with an outside diameter slightly smaller than the bearing race, drive the race into the hub until it bottoms out on the hub shoulder. As you begin to drive the race into

the hub, stop and check your work often to make sure the race is square with the hub bore. Do not allow the race to bind during installation.

NOTE
If you do not have the proper size tool to drive the race into the hub, have a Harley-Davidson dealer or independent repair shop install the race. Do not attempt to install the race by driving it into the hub with a small diameter punch or rod.

6. Blow any dirt or foreign matter out of the hub prior to installing the bearings.

7. Apply bearing grease to each race.

8. Pack the bearings with grease and set them aside for assembly.

9A. On 1984-1991 models (**Figure 32** or **Figure 33**), perform the following:

a. Place the wheel on the workbench so that the right-hand side faces up.

b. Install the right-hand bearing into its race.

c. Insert the right-hand wheel spacer into one of the new oil seals so that the spacer shoulder faces toward the outside (closed end) of the seal.

d. Install the oil seal and spacer into the right-hand side of the hub. Drive the oil seal into the hub so that the height distance, measured from the top of the hub to the top of the oil seal, is set as follows:
1984 FXST: 0.22-0.20 in. (5.60-5.1 mm)
1985-1990 laced wheels: 0.203-0.219 in. (5.2-5.5 mm)
1991 laced wheels: 0.260-0.280 in. (6.6-7.1 mm)
1991 disc wheels: 0.312 in. (7.9 mm)

e. Turn the wheel over so that the left-hand side faces up.

f. Install the center hub spacer into the hub.

g. Install the left-hand bearing into the hub.

h. Install the left-hand oil seal as described in sub-step d.

9B. On 1992-on models (**Figure 34**), perform the following:

a. Place the wheel on the workbench so that the right-hand side faces up.

b. Install the right-hand bearing into its race.

c. Pack the area between the bearing and oil seal with grease.

d. On laced wheels, drive the right-hand oil seal into the hub until it is 0.260-0.280 in. (6.60-7.11 mm) below the hub surface. On disc wheels, install the right-hand oil seal so that its outer surface is flush with the hub.

e. Turn the wheel over so that the left-hand side faces up.

f. Install the center hub spacer into the hub.

g. Install the bearing spacer into the hub.

h. Install the spacer washer—shoulder side first—into the hub.

CAUTION
The smaller spacer washer outer diameter must face against the bearing. Otherwise, the larger spacer washer outer diameter will contact the bearing rollers and damage the bearing.

i. Install the left-hand bearing into its race.

j. Pack the area between the bearing and oil seal with grease.

k. On all models, drive the left-hand oil seal into the hub until it is 0.31 in. (7.9 mm) below the hub surface.

10. If the brake disc was removed, refer to Chapter Fifteen for service procedures and tightening torques.

11. If the driven sprocket was removed, install it as described in this chapter.

12. After the wheel is installed on the bike and the rear axle tightened to the specified torque specification, the bearing end play should be checked as described in this chapter.

13. If the hub on spoke wheels is damaged, the hub can be replaced by removing the spokes and having a dealer assemble a new hub. If the hub on disc or cast wheels is damaged, the wheel assembly must be replaced; it cannot be repaired.

DRIVEN SPROCKET ASSEMBLY

The driven sprocket is bolted to the rear wheel. On chain drive models, the sprocket is bolted to the hub using bolts, lockwashers and nuts. On belt drive models, the sprocket is bolted into the hub using threaded holes in the hub. A spacer is used between the sprocket and wheel hub on cast and disc wheel models.

10

Refer to **Figure 32** or **Figure 33** when performing the following procedures.

Removal/Installation

1. Remove the rear wheel as described in this chapter.
2. Remove the bolts and nuts securing the sprocket to the hub and remove the sprocket. See **Figure 36**, typical.
3. Remove any sprocket spacer as required.
4. Install the sprocket by reversing these removal steps, plus the following.
5. Apply 2 drops of Loctite 271 (red) to each sprocket bolt. Install the nuts and tighten the sprocket bolts to the torque specification in **Table 4**.

Inspection

Inspect the teeth of the sprocket. If the teeth are visibly worn, replace both sprockets and the drive chain or drive belt. **Figure 37** shows sprocket comparison for chain drive models. Never replace any one sprocket or chain as a separate item; worn parts will cause rapid wear of the new component.

DRIVE CHAIN

Removal/Installation

1. Loosen the rear axle nut, chain adjuster nuts and the anchor bolt (if so equipped).
2. Push the rear wheel as far forward in the swing arm as possible.
3. Turn the rear wheel and locate the drive chain master link on the rear sprocket.
4. Remove the master link spring clip and separate the chain.

NOTE
It may be necessary to use a chain breaking tool to press the connecting link from the side plate. Chain breakers can be purchased at most motorcycle dealerships.

5. If installing a new drive chain, connect the new chain to the old chain with the old master link. Pull

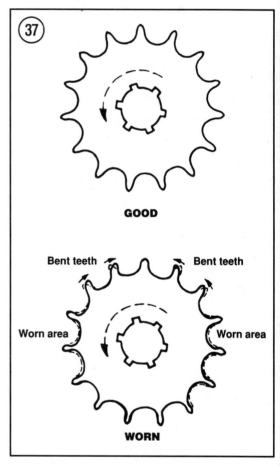

GOOD

Bent teeth   Bent teeth

Worn area   Worn area

WORN

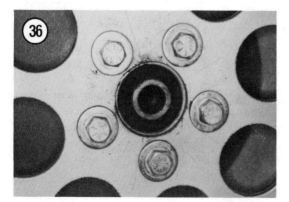

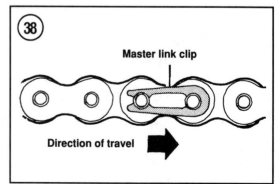

Master link clip

Direction of travel

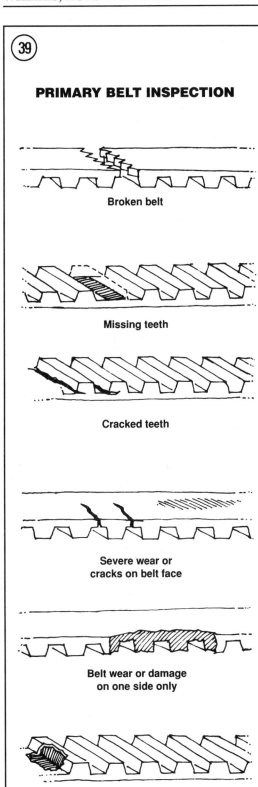

(39)

PRIMARY BELT INSPECTION

Broken belt

Missing teeth

Cracked teeth

Severe wear or cracks on belt face

Belt wear or damage on one side only

Tooth wear

the new chain through the front sprocket. If the original chain is to be reinstalled, tie a piece of wire approximately 20 inches long to the drive chain. Pull the chain so that the wire is routed around the front sprocket. Disconnect the wire from the chain so that it can be used to route the chain during installation.

6. Install by reversing these removal steps while noting the following:

    a. Install a new drive chain master link spring clip with the closed end facing in the direction of chain travel (**Figure 38**).

    b. Adjust the drive chain as described in Chapter Three.

    c. Tighten the axle nut to the torque specification listed in **Table 4**.

    d. Rotate the wheel several times to make sure it rotates smoothly. Apply the brake several times to make sure it operates correctly.

    e. Adjust the rear brake as described in Chapter Three.

Lubrication

For lubrication of the drive chain, refer to Chapter Three.

DRIVE BELT

Removal/Installation

1. Remove the rear wheel as described in this chapter.

2. Remove the compensating sprocket and clutch as described in Chapter Five.

3. Remove the primary housing as described in Chapter Five.

4. Remove the swing arm as described in Chapter Thirteen.

5. Remove the drive belt from the sprocket.

6. Installation is the reverse of these steps. Adjust the drive belt tension as described in Chapter Three.

Inspection

The drive belt has a built-in polyethylene lubricant coating that burnishes off during break-in. Do not apply lubricants. Inspect the drive belt for wear or damage. Replace any belt that appears questionable. See **Figure 39**.

10

When handling a drive belt, never bend the belt sharply as this will weaken the belt and cause premature failure.

LACED WHEELS

Laced or wire wheels consist of a rim, spokes and nipples and a hub (containing the bearings and axle spacer). The spokes are inserted through the hub and attached to the rim in a specific crossover pattern. Spoke nipples secure the spokes to the rim. A rubber rim strip is inserted into the rim well.

Loose or improperly tightened spokes can cause handling problems, hub damage and overall handling problems. Both wheels should be checked for looseness, missing or damaged spokes, rim damage, runout and balance at the maintenance intervals listed in Chapter Three. Wheel bearing service is described under front or rear hub service in this chapter.

Inspection and Replacement

1. To inspect the wheels, the wheel should be raised off of the ground so that it can spin freely. If you have access to a wheel truing stand, remove the wheel and mount it securely on the stand. If you do not have a stand, you can raise the front or rear of the bike off the ground and spin the wheel to access all areas on the wheel for complete inspection.

NOTE
Wheel truing stands are expensive, but if you plan on servicing your Harley's wheels, you should either invest in a good truing stand or fabricate one. Another route you can take is to purchase a discarded swing arm from a motorcycle wrecking yard. The swing arm can be clamped securely in a vise and the wheel placed into position on the swing arm for servicing. When choosing a swing arm to be used as a truing stand, check the size of the swing arm to make sure that both of your Harley's wheels can fit into it with enough clearance for checking runout; measure the inside swing arm distance on your bike as a starting point. The rear wheel will be the wider of the two, though you may have to remove the tire from the front

wheel for the wheel to fit into the swing arm.

2. Check the rim for dents, cracks or other damage. Severe rim damage is easily detected, though most small dents are discovered while the rim is spinning on a stand.

3. Check the hub for cracks or damage. Check closely where the spokes seat into the hub.

4. Check for bending, loose or broken spokes. Damaged spokes should be replaced as soon as they are detected, as they can destroy the hub. Replace a damaged spoke as follows:

CAUTION
*When replacing a broken spoke, do **not** bend the new spoke when installing it. If you cannot install a new spoke without bending it, you will have to loosen all of the spokes and then remove some of the spokes to provide clearance to install the new spoke. Because Harley wheels are laced to a specific offset dimension, wheel disassembly and retruing should be referred to a Harley-Davidson dealer or independent Harley repair shop.*

a. Remove the brake disc or rear sprocket as required.
b. Unscrew the nipple from the spoke and depress the nipple into the rim far enough to free the end of the spoke; take care not to push the nipple all the way in. Remove the damaged spoke from the hub and use it to match a new spoke of identical length.

NOTE
Replacement spokes are generally sold through Harley-Davidson dealers in complete sets only, though you may find a dealer who stocks individual spokes, removed from damaged or discarded wheels, for sale in small quantities. If you purchase spokes in this manner, compare the replacement spoke with the corresponding spoke on the wheel. Spokes differ in length, size, head angle and length of spoke throat. Compare these differences closely.

c. If necessary, trim the new spoke to match the original and dress the end of the thread with a thread die. Install the new spoke in the hub and screw on the nipple; tighten it until the spoke's tone is similar to the tone of the other spokes in the wheel. After installing the spoke, seat its head into the hub as described in this chapter. Periodically check the new spoke; it will stretch and must be retightened several times before it takes a final set.

NOTE
If a replacement spoke requires more than 2 turns to tighten it properly, the end of the spoke may protrude through the end of the nipple and puncture the tube. If necessary, remove the spoke and grind the end to a suitable length. To make sure that the spoke is not too long, remove the tube from the tire and check the end of the spoke.

5. Spokes loosen with use and should be checked periodically. The "tuning fork" method for checking spoke tightness is simple and works well. Tap the center of each spoke with a spoke wrench or screwdriver (**Figure 40**) and listen for a tone. A tightened spoke will emit a clear, ringing tone and a loose spoke will sound flat or dull. All the spokes in a correctly tightened wheel will emit tones of similar pitch but not necessarily the same precise tone. The tension of the spokes does not determine wheel balance.

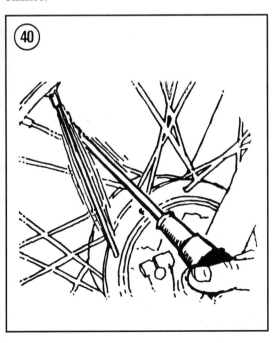

Spoke Adjustment

This section describes minor spoke adjustment. If a few spokes are loose, you can tighten the spokes with a spoke wrench. If there are many spokes loose, retruing will also be required. Wheels in which a large number of spokes were replaced or if the wheel is severely out of true should be serviced by a qualified Harley-Davidson mechanic as Harley wheels are laced to a specific offset dimension.

One way to check rim runout is to mount a dial indicator on the front fork or swing arm, so that it bears against the rim.

If you don't have a dial indicator, improvise one as shown in **Figure 41**. Adjust the position of the bolt until it just clears the rim. Rotate the rim and note whether the clearance increases or decreases. Mark the tire with chalk or light crayon at areas that produce significantly large or small clearances. Clearance must not change by more than 1/32 in. (0.8 mm).

To pull the rim out, tighten spokes which terminate on the same side of the hub and loosen spokes which terminate on the opposite side of the hub (**Figure 42**). In most cases, only a slight amount of adjustment is necessary to true a rim. After adjustment, rotate the rim and make sure another area has not been pulled out of true. Continue adjustment and checking until runout is less than 1/32 in. (0.8 mm)

CAUTION
Overtightening the spokes can cause spoke and nipple damage.

Seating Spokes

When spokes loosen or when installing new spokes, the head of the spoke should be checked for proper seating in the hub. If it is not seated correctly, it can loosen further and may cause severe damage to the hub. If one or more spokes require reseating, hit the head of the spoke with a punch. True the wheel as described under *Spoke Adjustment* in this chapter.

Rim Replacement

If the rim becomes bent or damaged, it should be replaced. A bent or dented rim can cause serious handling problems. If the spokes are not bent or

10

damaged, they may be reused. Refer all service to a Harley-Davidson dealer or qualified Harley mechanic.

CAST OR DISC WHEELS

The stock cast and disc wheels (**Figure 43**) consist of a single assembly equipped with bearings, oil seals and a hub spacer.

While these wheels are virtually maintenance free, they should be checked for damage at the maintenance intervals listed in Chapter Three. Wheel bearing service is described under front and rear hub service in this chapter.

Inspection and Replacement

1. Remove the wheel and mount it on a wheel truing stand.
2. Mount a dial indicator or pointer near the rim bead as shown in **Figure 41**. Spin the wheel and measure lateral and radial runout. The maximum lateral and radial runout dimension is listed in **Table 1**. If the runout exceeds this dimension, check the wheel bearings as described in this chapter.
3. If the wheel's bearings are okay, the wheel will have to be replaced as the wheel cannot be serviced. Inspect the wheel for signs of cracks, fractures, dents

or bends. If it is damaged in any way, it must be replaced.

WARNING
Do not try to repair any damage to a cast or disc wheel as it will result in an unsafe riding condition.

WHEEL BALANCE

An unbalanced wheel results in unsafe riding conditions. Depending on the degree of unbalance and the speed of the motorcycle, the rider may experience anything from a mild vibration to a violent shimmy which may result in loss of control.

Before you attempt to balance the wheel, check to be sure that the wheel bearings are in good condition and properly lubricated and that the brakes do not drag. The wheel must rotate freely.

On alloy wheels, weights are attached to the flat surface on the rim (**Figure 44**). On laced wheels, the weights are attached to the spoke nipples (**Figure 45**).

This procedure describes static wheel balancing using a truing or wheel balancing stand. If you do much high-speed or touring riding, you may want to have the wheels machined balanced by a Harley-Davidson dealer.

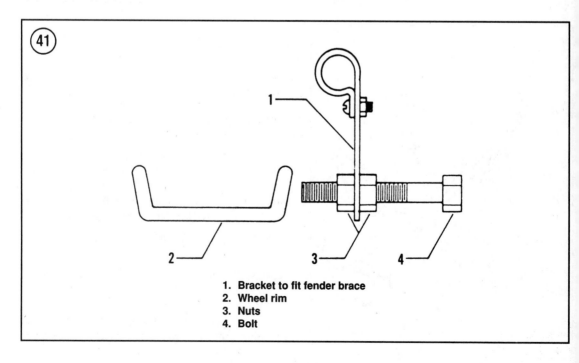

41

1. **Bracket to fit fender brace**
2. **Wheel rim**
3. **Nuts**
4. **Bolt**

Before attempting to balance the wheels, check to be sure that the wheel bearings are in good condition and properly lubricated. The wheel must rotate freely.

1. Remove the wheel to be balanced.

2. Mount the wheel on a fixture such as the one in **Figure 46** so it can rotate freely.

3. Give the wheel a spin and let it coast to a stop. Mark the tire at the lowest point.

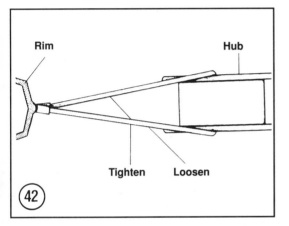

Rim   Hub

Tighten   Loosen

42

43

44

4. Spin the wheel several more times. If the wheel keeps coming to rest at the same point, it is out of balance.

5. Tape a test weight to the upper (or light) side of the wheel.

6. Experiment with different weights until the wheel, when spun, comes to rest at a different position each time.

7. Remove the test weight and install the correct size weight.

8. When applying weights to cast or disc wheels, note the following:

   a. Self-adhesive weights can be purchased through Harley-Davidson dealers in black, silver and gold colors.

   b. Weights are attached to the flat surface on the rim (**Figure 44**). Clean the rim to remove all

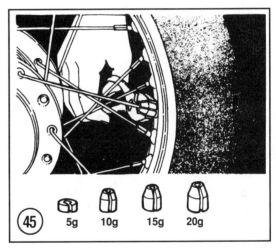

45   5g   10g   15g   20g

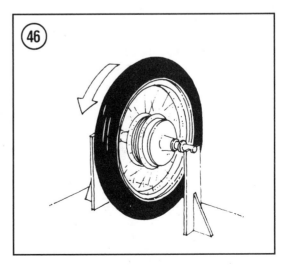

46

10

road residue before installing the weights; otherwise, the weights may fall off.

c. Weights should be added in 1/4 oz. (5 g) increments. If 1 oz. (10 g) or more must be added to one location on the wheel, apply half the amount to each side of the rim.

d. Harley-Davidson recommends that the wheel should not be used for 48 hours after installing weights to allow the weight adhesive to cure properly.

TIRES

Proper tire service includes frequent inflation checks and adjustment as well as tire inspection, removal, repair and installation practices. By maintaining a routine tire maintenance schedule, tire damage or other abnormal conditions can be detected and repaired before they affect the operation and handling of your motorcycle. Refer to Chapter Three for general tire inspection and inflation procedures.

Inspection

Visually inspect the tires for tread wear, cracks, cuts, aging and other damage. Check the tire for areas where the tread has broken or torn out. Stones imbedded between the tread rows can be carefully pried out with a key or screwdriver. Check the tread closely for secondary damage after removing the stone or other foreign objects. Uneven tread wear can be caused by improper inflation pressure, vehicle overloading or an unbalanced tire.

Run your hand along the sidewall and check for bulges or knots. If a bulge is noted, mark the area with chalk and then remove the tire from the rim; check the inside and outside of the tire carefully, looking for broken or separated piles. This type of damage can cause the tire to blow out. Likewise, if a tire is damaged on the outside, the tire should be removed from the rim and the inside checked carefully for broken or separated plies or other damage.

WARNING
If you suspect tire damage, the tire should be removed from the rim and examined closely inside and out. Tires exhibiting bulges or other questionable damage should be inspected by a motor-

cycle technician before the tire is put back into use. A damaged or deformed tire can fail and cause loss of control and personal injury.

Service Notes

Before changing tires, note the following:
1. Tire changing should only be undertaken when you have access to the proper tools:
   a. At least 2 motorcycle tire irons.
   b. Rim protectors (part No. HD-01289 or equivalent) or scrap pieces of leather.
   c. A bead breaker will be required when breaking tires from alloy rims and may be required on laced wheels.
   d. Accurate tire gauge.
   e. Water and liquid soap solution or a special tire mounting lubricant.
   f. Talcum power for tube tires.
2. The stock cast wheel is aluminum and the exterior appearance can easily be damaged. Special care must be taken with tire irons when changing a tire to avoid scratches and gouges to the outer rim surface. Insert scraps of leather between the tire iron and the rim to protect the rim from damage.
3. When removing a tubeless tire, take care not to damage the tire beads, inner liner of the tire or the wheel rim flange. Use tire levers or flat-handled tire irons with rounded ends—do not use screwdrivers or similar tools to remove tires.
4. Note that DUNLOP front and rear tires designed for use on FLSTC/F models are not the same. Do not install a front tire on the rear wheel or a rear tire on the front wheel. See your dealer for additional information.
5. When installing a new tube type tire, install a new tube.

WARNING
Proper tire changing is critical to the overall handling and safety of your motorcycle. Improper tire installation or tire repair will adversely affect handling. When changing tires, the following WARNINGS, as specified by Harley-Davidson, must be observed:

a. Rim strips that are in good condition must be used on all laced wheels.
b. Tires must be installed with their directional arrow facing in the proper di-

rection. Some tires that can be used on both front and rear wheels require a different tire rotation, depending on which wheel the tire is installed on. Confirm this prior to installing the tire.
c. Do not mix tire brands.
d. Tubeless tires should not be installed on tube type rims unless an inner tube is also installed.

Removal

> *NOTE*
> *If you do not have access to a motorcycle tire changer, you will probably be servicing the tire with the wheel placed on*

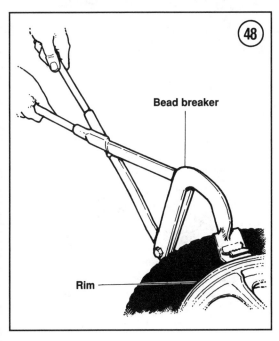

Bead breaker

Rim

the ground. To avoid scratching or damaging the brake disc or wheel, place the wheel on a piece of plywood or other soft surface. If you do a lot of tire changing, you may want to construct a small wooden frame that, along with getting the wheel off the ground, will make it easier to work the tire during changing.

1. Remove the wheel from the motorcycle and place it on a suitable stand or surface.

2. Place a chalk mark on the tire aligning the tire with the valve stem (**Figure 47**). This helps to maintain tire and wheel balance during reassembly.

3. Remove the valve cap and unscrew the valve core to deflate the tire or tube. Block the valve core with your hand or the core removal tool to keep it from flying out. Remove the valve core and store it with the valve cap.

4. Press the entire bead on both sides of the tire into the center of the rim. If the bead is tight, a bead breaker (**Figure 48**) will be required.

> *CAUTION*
> *Do **not** attempt to insert the tire irons between the tire bead and rim flange to break the bead. This can permanently damage both the tire and rim.*

5. Lubricate the beads with a tire lubricant or soapy water.

6. Place rim strips (**Figure 49**) along the rim near the valve stem and insert the tire iron under the bead next to the valve, making sure the tire iron contacts the rim strip and not the rim. Step on the side of the tire opposite the valve stem with your knee and pry the bead over the rim with the tire iron.

> *CAUTION*
> *Do not use excessive force when prying the tire over the rim or you may stretch or break the bead wires in the tire.*

7. Insert a second tire iron next to the first to hold the bead over the rim. Then work around the tire with the first tool prying the bead over the rim (**Figure 50**). On tube-type tires, be careful not to pinch the inner tube with the tools.

8. On tube-type tires, use your thumb and push the valve from its hole in the rim to the inside of the tire. Carefully pull the tube out of the tire and lay it aside.

10

NOTE
Step 9 is required only if it is necessary to remove the tire from the rim completely, such as for tire replacement or tubeless tire repair.

9A. *Tube-type tires*: Stand the wheel upright. Insert a tire tool between the second bead and the same side of the rim that the first bead was pried over. Force the bead on the opposite side from the tool into the center of the rim. Pry the second bead off the rim, working around the wheel with 2 tire irons as with the first. Remove the rim band.

9B. *Tubeless tires*: The second bead can generally be removed from the rim without having to use tire irons. Relubricate the second bead thoroughly and stand the wheel upright. Grasp the wheel at the top with one hand to steady it and then lift and pull the second bead over the top of the rim at the top of the wheel and remove the tire.

Inspection

1. *Tubeless tires*: All disc wheels use a bolt-in type valve stem. Inspect the rubber grommet (**Figure 51**) where the valve stem seats against the inner surface of the wheel. If it's starting to deteriorate or has lost its resiliency, replace the valve stem as this is a common location of air loss. To replace the valve stem:

   a. Loosen and remove the 2 valve stem nuts.

   b. Remove the valve stem from the wheel, together with its washer and rubber grommet.

   c. Remove all rubber residue from the wheel left by the previous rubber grommet.

   d. Before installing the new valve stem, remove the valve cap, 2 nuts and washer from the stem.

   e. Slide the rubber grommet down onto the valve stem so that the shoulder on the grommet seats into the valve stem head recess.

   f. Insert the valve stem into the rim and hold it in position, making sure the rubber grommet seats against the wheel. Then slide the washer onto the valve stem so that the side of the washer with the raised center faces away from the rim.

   g. Install the first valve stem nut and tighten to 20-25 in.-lb. (2.3-2.8 N•m).

   h. Hold the first valve stem nut with a wrench, then install and tighten the second nut to 40-60 in.-lb. (4.6-6.9 N•m).

WARNING
Because of weight and design configurations, valve stems and valve caps should be replaced with O.E.M. Harley-Davidson parts. Valve stem and valve cap combinations that are too long or heavier than stock parts may contact a component when the vehicle is under way. Damage to the valve will cause rapid tire deflation and loss of control.

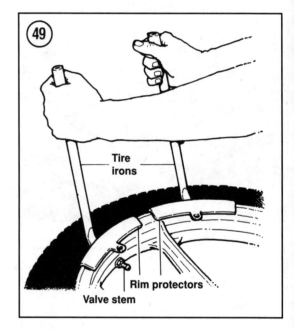

Tire irons
Rim protectors
Valve stem

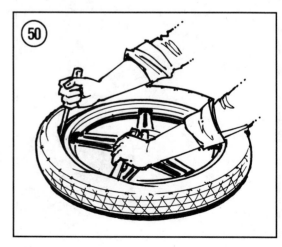

2. Clean the rim thoroughly to remove all dust and dirt residue. Use steel wool, a stiff wire brush or sandpaper to remove rust from wire wheels.

> *CAUTION*
> *Work carefully when removing burrs or other rough spots from the rim flange on disc wheels; otherwise, you may damage the air-sealing surfaces, requiring replacement of the wheel.*

3. Mount the wheel on a truing stand (if available) and check the rim-to-tire mating surface for dents, burrs or other rough spots. Emery cloth can be used

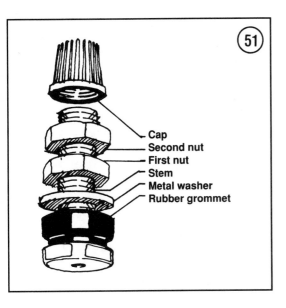

- Cap
- Second nut
- First nut
- Stem
- Metal washer
- Rubber grommet

to remove burrs on disc wheels. A file or sandpaper can be used to remove burrs on wire wheels.

4. Check the wheel for dents or other damage. If the wheel has been dented by an accident or from running into a curb or other hard object, it should be replaced. On wire wheels, the rim can be replaced by a qualified mechanic. On cast and disc wheels, the entire wheel assembly must be replaced.

> *WARNING*
> *Never operate your motorcycle with a bent wheel that has been straightened. The wheel may fail while under use and cause you to lose control.*

5. Check wheel runout as described in this chapter. Check for protruding spokes on wire wheels. File or grind the end of the spokes as required.

6. If you have access to compressed air, blow out the inside of the tire casing to remove all dust and dirt. Run your hand along the tire casing and check for small nails, cracks or other damage.

7. If a tire has been punctured, refer to *Tire Repairs* in this chapter.

8. *Tube-type tires*: Inspect the rim band for tearing or excessive wear. Replace the rim band if necessary. Install the valve core into the tube and then fill the tube with air. Check the tube for leaks. If the tube holds air, check the base of the valve stem for tearing or other signs of wear that may cause the tube to fail later. If the tube is damaged, replace it. Do not attempt to repair a tube unless you are in an emergency situation (i.e., you find yourself in the middle of Death Valley, a flat tire, no spare tube and vultures circling overhead). If you patch a tube, replace it with a new tube as soon as possible. Refer to *Tube Repairs* in this chapter.

10

Installation

1. A new tire may have balancing rubber weights inside. These are not patches and should not be disturbed. A colored spot near the bead indicates a lighter point on the tire. This spot should be placed next to the valve stem (**Figure 52**).

2. Install the rim band over the wheel (wire wheels) and align the hole in the rim band with the hole in the rim. If you replaced the rim band, make sure it is the correct diameter and width for your wheel.

3. Align the tire with the rim so that the directional arrows molded in the tire's side wall face in the normal rotation position.

NOTE
On some tires, the rotation arrow may have to be reversed, depending on whether the tire is mounted on the front or rear wheel. Follow the directions on the tire side wall or the tire manufacturer's instructions.

4. Lubricate both beads of the tire with soapy water.
5. With the tire properly aligned with the wheel, press the first bead over the rim, working around the tire in both directions with your hands only (**Figure 53**). If necessary, use a tire iron (with rim protectors) for the last few inches of bead (**Figure 54**).

NOTE
Dust the tube with talcum powder before installing it in the tire. The talcum powder will prevent the tube from sticking to the tire.

6. On tube-type tires, inflate the tube just enough to round it out. Too much air will make installation difficult. Wipe the outside of the tube with talcum powder to help reduce friction between the tire and tube during operation. Place the tube on top of the tire, aligning the valve stem with the matching hole in the rim. Then insert the tube into the tire. Lift the upper tire bead away from the rim with your hand and insert the tube's valve stem through the rim hole. Check the tube to make sure that the valve stem is straight up (90°), not cocked to one side. If necessary, reposition the tube in the tire. If the valve stem wants to slide out of the hole and back into the tire, install the valve stem nut at the top of the valve; do not tighten the nut yet.
7. Relubricate the upper bead with soapy water if necessary.
8. Starting 180° away from the valve stem, press the upper bead into the rim. Using tire tools and rim protectors, work around the rim to the valve. On tube-type tires, the last few inches will offer you the most difficulty and the greatest chance of pinching the tube. Work the tire tools carefully to avoid pinching the tube.
9. On tube-type tires, the valve stem should be straight up (90°). If the valve is cocked to one side, align the tube by sliding the tire along the rim one

way or the other while holding the rim securely. When the valve stem is straight up, screw the valve nut onto the valve, but do not tighten it against the rim. After aligning the tube with the rim, check that the tube was not forced outward so that it rests between the tire bead and the rim. If so, push the tube back into the tire; otherwise, the rim will pinch the tube when the tube is filled with air.
10. Check the bead on both sides of the tire for an even fit around the rim.
11. Relubricate both tire beads.

WARNING
When seating the tire beads in Step 12, never inflate the tire beyond the tire manufacturer's maximum pressure specification listed on the tire's side wall. Exceeding this pressure could cause the tire or rim to burst, causing severe personal injury. If the beads fail to seat properly, deflate the tire and relubricate the beads. Never stand directly over a tire while inflating it.

12A. *Tube-type tires*: Inflate the tube to its maximum tire pressure to seat the beads in the rim. If the beads do not seat properly, release all air pressure from the tire and relubricate the tire beads. The tire is properly seated when the wheel rim and tire side wall lines are parallel (**Figure 55**). When the tire has seated properly on both sides, remove the valve core to deflate the tube; this allows the tube to straighten out, then reinstall the valve core and inflate the tire to the pressure reading listed in Chapter Three. Tighten the valve stem nuts and screw on the valve cap.
12B. *Tubeless tires*: Place an inflatable band around the circumference of the tire. Slowly inflate the band

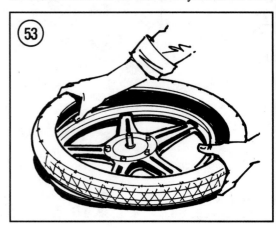

until the tire beads are pressed against the rim. Inflate the tire enough to seat it, deflate the band and remove it. The tire is properly seated when the wheel rim and tire side wall lines are parallel (**Figure 55**). Inflate the tire to the pressure reading listed in Chapter Three. Screw on the valve cap.

13. Check tire runout as described in this chapter.

14. Balance the wheel assembly as described in this chapter.

Tire Runout

The tires should be checked for excessive lateral and radial runout after wheel mounting or if the motorcycle developed a wobble that cannot be traced to another component. The wheels should be mounted on their axles when making the following checks.

1. *Lateral runout*: This procedure will check the tire for excessive side-to-side play. Perform the following:

a. Position a fixed pointer next to the tire side wall as shown in **Figure 56**. The pointer tip should be located so that it is not directly in line with the molded tire logo or any other raised surfaces.

b. Rotate the tire and measure the amount of lateral runout.

c. The lateral runout should not exceed 0.080 in. (2 mm). If runout is excessive, remove the tire from the wheel and recheck the wheel's lateral runout as described in this chapter. If the runout is excessive, the wheel must be retrued (laced wheels) or replaced (disc wheels). If wheel runout is correct, the tire runout is excessive and the tire must be replaced.

2. *Radial runout*: This procedure will check the tire for excessive up-and-down play. Perform the following:

a. Position a fixed pointer at the center bottom of the tire tread as shown in **Figure 57**.

b. Rotate the tire and measure the amount of radial runout.

c. The radial runout should not exceed 0.090 in. (2.3 mm). If runout is excessive, remove the tire from the wheel and recheck the wheels radial runout as described in this chapter. If the runout is excessive, the wheel must be retrued (laced wheels) or replaced (disc wheels). If

10

(54)

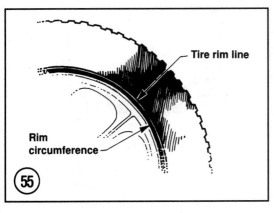

(55)

Tire rim line

Rim circumference

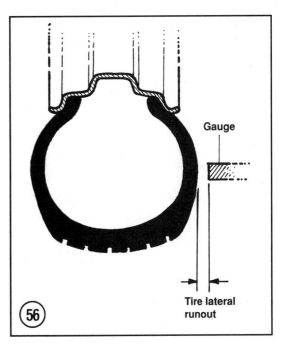

(56)

Gauge

Tire lateral runout

wheel runout is correct, the tire runout is excessive and the tire must be replaced.

TIRE REPAIRS
(TUBE-TYPE TIRES)

Every rider will eventually experience trouble with a tire or tube. Repairs and replacement are fairly simple and every rider should know the techniques.

Patching a motorcycle tube is only a temporary fix. A motorcycle tire flexes too much and the patch could rub right off. However, a patched tube should get you far enough to buy a new tube.

Tube Repair Kits

The repair kits can be purchased from motorcycle dealers and some auto supply stores. When buying, specify that the kit you want is for motorcycles.

There are 2 types of tube repair kits:

a. Hot patch.
b. Cold patch.

Hot patches are stronger because they actually vulcanize to the tube, becoming part of it. However, they are far too bulky to carry for roadside repairs and the strength is unnecessary for a temporary repair.

Cold patches are not vulcanized to the tube; they are simply glued to it. Though not as strong as hot patches, cold patches are still very durable. Cold patch kits are less bulky than hot and more easily applied under adverse conditions. A cold patch kit contains everything necessary and tucks easily in with your emergency tool kit.

Tube Inspection

1. Remove the inner tube as described in this chapter.

2. Install the valve core into the valve stem and inflate the tube slightly. Do not overinflate.

3. Immerse the tube in water a section at a time. Look carefully for bubbles indicating a hole. Mark each hole and continue checking until you are certain that all holes are discovered and marked. Also make sure that the valve core is not leaking; tighten it if necessary.

NOTE
If you do not have enough water to immerse sections of the tube, try running your hand over the tube slowly and very close to the surface. If your hand is damp, it works even better. If you suspect a hole anywhere, apply some water to the area to verify it.

4. Apply a cold patch according to the manufacturer's instructions.

5. Dust the patch area with talcum powder to prevent it from sticking to the tire.

6. Carefully check the inside of the tire casing for small rocks or sand which may have damaged the tube. If the inside of the tire is split, apply a patch to the area to prevent it from pinching and damaging the tube again.

7. Check the inside of the rim.

8. Deflate the tube prior to installation in the tire.

TIRE REPAIRS
(TUBELESS TYPE)

Patching a tubeless tire on the road is very difficult. If both beads are still in place against the rim, a can of pressurized tire sealant may inflate the tire and seal the hole. The beads must be against the wheel for this method to work. Because an incor-

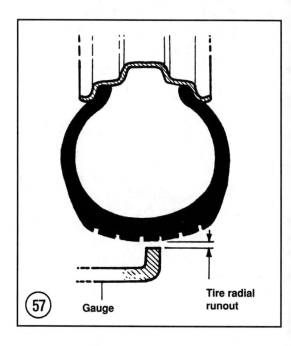

(57) Gauge   Tire radial runout

rectly patched tire might blow out and cause an accident, note the following:

a. Due to the variations of material supplied with different tubeless tire repair kits, follow the instructions and recommendations supplied with the repair kit.

b. The tire industry recommends that tubeless tires be patched from the inside. Therefore, do not patch the tire with an external type plug. If you find an external patch on a tire, it is recommended that it be patch-reinforced from the inside or discarded.

c. Do not patch tires which have less than 1/16 in. (1.6 mm) of tread left.

d. Do not patch a tire in which the puncture hole is larger than 1/4 in. (6.35 mm).

e. Patches should only be applied to puncture holes in the tread area. Do not apply patches to holes in the tire's side wall.

f. When in doubt about whether or not to patch a tire, seek advice from a motorcycle technician.

Table 1 WHEEL AND WHEEL BEARING SERVICE SPECIFICATIONS

	in.	mm
Wheel bearing end play		
1984-1991		
Front and rear	0.004-0.018	0.10-0.45
1992-on		
Front and rear	0.002-0.006	0.05-0.15
Wheel runout		
Laced wheels		
Lateral and radial	0.031	0.79
Disc and cast wheels		
Lateral	0.040	1.02
Radial	0.030	0.76

Table 2 FRONT WHEEL TIGHTENING TORQUES (NON-SPRINGER)

	ft.-lb.	N·m
Front axle		
1984	50	69
1985-on	45-50	62-69
Slider cap nuts	45-50	62-69
Front brake caliper		
1984	115-120 in.-lb.	13.2-13.8
1985-on	25-30	34.5-41.4

10

Table 3 FRONT WHEEL TIGHTENING TORQUES (SPRINGER)

	ft.-lb.	N·m
Front axle	60-65	81-88
Front brake caliper		
Top bolt	42-46	57-62
Bottom bolt	25-30	34-41

Table 4 REAR WHEEL TIGHTENING TORQUES

	ft.-lb.	N·m
Rear axle		
1984	65-70	88-96.6
1985-on	60-65	82.8-88
Sprocket bolts		
1984	35	48.3
1985-1991	65-70	88-96.6
1992-on	55-65	75-88

FRONT SUSPENSION AND STEERING (MODELS WITH TELESCOPIC FRONT FORKS)

This chapter covers the handlebar, steering head and the telescopic front fork assemblies.

Table 1 is at the end of the chapter.

HANDLEBAR

The handlebars are clamped to the upper triple clamp with 2 caps and holders. Allen bolts are inserted through the caps and holders and secured with nuts to keep the assembly tight. Rubber bushings are mounted between the handlebar holders and the upper triple clamp to help reduce vibration. The handlebars are knurled where they fit between the clamps and holders; this machining process is used to provide additional holding power to help prevent the handlebars from slipping.

Handlebars are an important part in the overall comfort and safety of your motorcycle. The handlebars should be inspected at regular intervals for loose mounting bolts or damage. The controls, master cylinder and turn signals, mounted on the handlebars, should be checked frequently for loose or missing fasteners.

The handlebars should be replaced when they become bent or damaged. Never try to heat, bend or weld handlebars. These efforts will seriously weaken the bar and may cause it to break.

When replacing a handlebar, you can order an exact replacement through Harley-Davidson dealers using their part numbers, or you can order bars through an accessory manufacturer. When ordering accessory bars, you will have to know the handlebars' outside diameter, width, bar height and sweep (**Figure 1**). When changing handlebars, make sure that the new bar has enough room to mount the controls, brake master cylinder, etc., without excessive crowding and that the controls feel comfortable when the front end is turned from side to side. In addition, if the new handlebars are higher, make sure the stock cables and switch wiring harnesses are long enough. If not, you will have to purchase longer cables and extend the wiring harnesses.

11

Removal

1. Place the bike on its jiffy stand.
2. Unscrew and remove the mirrors.

NOTE
Cover the fuel tank with a heavy cloth or plastic tarp to protect it from accidental spilling of brake fluid. Wash any spilled brake fluid off any painted or plated surface immediately. Use soapy water and rinse thoroughly.

NOTE
Make a drawing of the clutch and throttle cable routing before removing them.

3. Remove the bolts securing the master cylinder and support it with a Bungee cord. It is not necessary to disconnect the hydraulic brake line.

4. Refer to **Figure 2**. Separate the 2 halves of the start switch assembly. Disconnect the throttle cable from the twist grip.

5. Slacken the clutch cable and disconnect it at the hand lever.

6. Disconnect the clutch cable. Then separate the 2 halves of the directional signal switch assembly (**Figure 3**).

7. Remove the turn signals if mounted on the handlebar.

8. Remove the clamps securing the electrical cables to the handlebar.

9. Remove the handlebar cap bolts and nuts (**Figure 4**) and remove the cap and handlebar.

10. Install by reversing these steps. Note the following.

11. Check the knurled rings on the handlebar for galling and bits of aluminum blocking up the rings. Clean the knurled section with a wire brush.

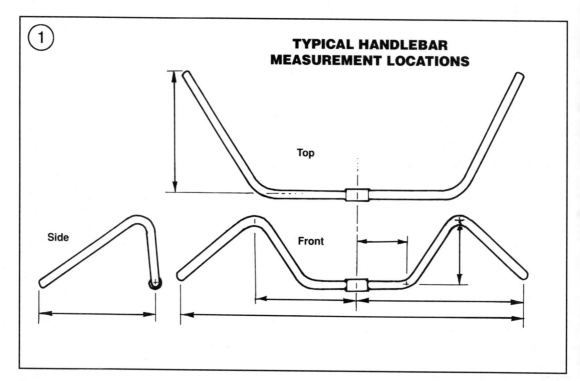

TYPICAL HANDLEBAR MEASUREMENT LOCATIONS

Top

Side

Front

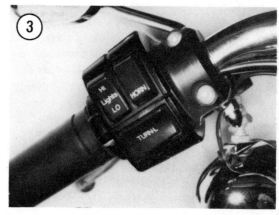

12. Check the handlebar for cracks, bends or other damage. Replace the handlebar if necessary. Do not attempt to repair it.

13. Clean the clamps and holders thoroughly of all residue before installing the handlebar.

14. After installing the handlebar, cap, bolts and nuts, reposition the handlebar while straddling the bike. Push it forward and backward to best suit your riding style. Make sure, before tightening the cap bolts, that the knurled sections at the base of the handlebar are aligned with the cap and holder. Hold the Allen bolts with a wrench and tighten the nuts securely.

STEERING HEAD
AND STEM

The fork stem is mounted onto the lower triple clamp. A dust shield and a tapered bearing are installed onto the bottom of the fork stem. The fork stem is inserted through the steering head where another bearing is installed at the top of the steering head. Both bearings seat against races pressed into the steering head. Dust covers are used at both bearing areas to protect bearings from dust and other contaminants.

Disassembly/Reassembly
(FXST and FXSTC)

Refer to **Figure 5** for this procedure.

1. Remove the front wheel as described in Chapter Ten.

2. Remove the fuel tank as described in Chapter Eight.

3. Remove the front forks as described in this chapter.

4. Remove the headlight and headlight bracket.

5. Remove the brake hose bracket at the bottom of the fork stem bracket (**Figure 6**). Do not disconnect the brake hose connection.

6. Disconnect the ground wire at the fork stem bracket (**Figure 7**).

7. Remove the fork stem cap from the fork stem nut.

8. The fork stem nut is secured with a tab lockwasher (**Figure 8**); the tab is bent up so that it seats against one flat on the nut. Bend the tab away from the nut.

9. Loosen and remove the fork stem nut and the tab lockwasher. Discard the tab lockwasher.

10. Remove the upper bracket together with the handlebar assembly from the fork stem. Position the handlebar so that the control cables are not kinked.

11. Remove the bearing seat (1984-1986) or the adjusting nut (1987-on) and lower the fork stem out of the steering head.

12. Remove the upper dust shield.

13. Remove the bearing from the upper bearing race in the steering head cup.

14. Inspect the fork stem assembly as described later in this chapter.

15. After the fork stem assembly has been inspected and worn or damaged parts replaced, proceed to Step 16 to assemble the fork stem. If the bearing races were damaged, install them now as described under *Steering Head Bearing Race* in this chapter. Likewise, the lower bearing and dust shield must be installed onto the fork stem before installing the fork stem into the steering head. Refer to the same section to install these parts, if necessary.

16. Wipe the bearing races in the steering head with a clean lint-free cloth. Then wipe the face of each race with bearing grease.

17. Pack the bearings thoroughly with bearing grease. The lower bearing and lower dust shield should be installed on the fork stem prior to installing the fork stem in the steering head. If necessary, install the lower bearing as described under *Steering Head Bearing Race* in this chapter. Cover the upper bearing with a sheet of wax paper or other lint-free material until it can be installed.

18. With the lower bearing and its dust shield properly installed on the fork stem, insert the fork stem up through the steering head until the bearing contacts the lower race and hold the assembly in position.

19. Install the upper bearing over the fork stem and seat it next to the upper race. Then install the upper dust shield.

11

20. Thread the bearing seat (1984-1986) or the adjusting nut (1987-on) onto the fork stem until fork stem can pivot smoothly from side to side with no noticeable axial or lateral play.

> *CAUTION*
> *Do not overtighten the bearing seat or adjusting nut in Step 20 or you may damage the bearings and races. Final adjustment of the fork stem will take place after the front forks and front wheel have been installed on the bike.*

21. Install the fork bracket over the fork stem. Install a *new* tab lockwasher over the fork stem. Insert the pin on the lockwasher into the hole in the fork bracket. Then install the fork stem nut (**Figure 8**) until it is finger-tight. Check again that the pin on the lockwasher engages the hole in the fork bracket.

> *NOTE*
> *Final tightening of the fork stem nut will take place after the front wheel has been installed and you are adjusting front steering play.*

22. Install the brake hose bracket to the lower fork stem bracket (**Figure 6**) and tighten to 11 ft.-lb. (15 N•m).

23. Install the headlight bracket and headlight. Adjust the headlight as described in Chapter Nine.

24. Reinstall the front forks as described in this chapter.

25. Install the front wheel as described in Chapter Ten.

26. Adjust the front steering as described in this chapter. After tightening the fork stem nut when adjusting the steering play, install the fork stem cap over the nut.

Disassembly/Reassembly (All FLSTC/F)

Refer to **Figure 9** for this procedure.

1. Remove the front wheel as described in Chapter Ten.

2. Remove the fuel tank as described in Chapter Eight.

3. Remove the front forks as described in this chapter.

4. Remove the headlight and headlight bracket.

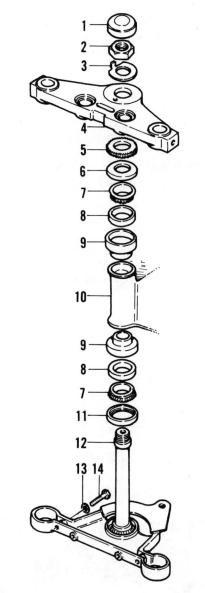

(5) FORK STEM AND BRACKET (ALL FXST/C)

1. Cap
2. Fork stem nut
3. Lockwasher
4. Upper bracket
5. Adjust nut
6. Upper dust shield
7. Bearing
8. Bearing race
9. Bearing cup
10. Frame
11. Lower dust shield
12. Fork stem and bracket
13. Washer
14. Bolt

5. Remove the brake hose bracket at the bottom of the fork stem bracket (**Figure 6**). Do not disconnect the brake hose connection.

6. Remove the front and rear panel assemblies.

7. Remove the screws and lockwashers securing the slider covers to the lower fork bracket and remove the covers.

8. Remove the fork stem cap from the fork stem nut.

9. Loosen and remove the fork stem bolt and washer.

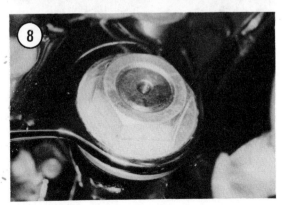

NOTE
Hold onto the lower fork bracket after loosening the upper bracket pinch bolt (Step 10) to prevent the fork stem from falling to the floor.

10. Loosen the upper bracket pinch bolt. Then remove the upper bracket together with the handlebar assembly from the fork stem. Position the handlebar so that the control cables are not kinked.

11. Lower the fork stem assembly out of the steering head assembly and remove it.

12. Remove the upper dust shield and bearing.

13. Inspect the fork stem assembly as described later in this chapter.

14. After the fork stem assembly has been inspected and worn or damaged parts replaced, proceed to Step 15 to assemble the fork stem. If the bearing races were damaged, install them now as described under *Steering Head Bearing Race* in this chapter. Likewise, the lower bearing and dust shield must be installed onto the fork stem before installing the fork stem into the steering head. Refer to the same section to install these parts, if necessary.

15. Wipe the bearing races in the steering head with a clean lint-free cloth. Then wipe the face of each race with bearing grease.

16. Pack the bearings thoroughly with bearing grease. The lower bearing and lower dust shield should be installed on the fork stem prior to installing the fork stem in the steering head. If necessary, install the lower bearing as described under *Steering Head Bearing Race* in this chapter. Cover the upper bearing with a sheet of wax paper or other lint-free material until it can be installed.

17. With the lower bearing and its dust shield installed on the fork stem, insert the fork stem up through the steering head until the bearing contacts the lower race and hold the assembly in position.

18. Install the upper bearing over the fork stem and seat it next to the upper race. Then install the upper dust shield.

19. Position the fork bracket over the fork stem, then install a *new* washer over the fork stem. Install and tighten the front fork stem bolt until the fork stem assembly can be turned from side to side with no noticeable axial or lateral play. When play is correct, tighten the pinch bolt securely.

11

CAUTION
Do not overtighten the fork stem bolt in Step 19 or you may damage the bearings and races. Final adjustment of the fork stem will take place after the front forks and front wheel have been installed on the bike.

20. Install the brake hose bracket to the lower fork stem bracket and tighten to 11 ft.-lb. (15 N•m).

21. Install the headlight bracket and headlight. Adjust the headlight as described in Chapter Eight.

22. Install the slider covers and the front and rear panel assemblies.

23. Reinstall the front forks as described in this chapter.

24. Install the front wheel as described in Chapter Ten.

25. Adjust the front steering as described in this chapter.

Inspection
(All Models)

The bearing races are pressed into a steering head cup which is pressed into the frame's steering head. The bearing races should not be removed unless they are damaged and require replacement.

Wheel bearing grease should be used to pack bearings and races when performing the following steps.

1. Wipe the bearing races with a solvent-soaked rag and then dry with compressed air or a lint-free cloth. Check the races in the steering head cups for pitting, scratches, galling or severe wear. If any of these conditions exist, replace the races and steering head cups as described in this chapter. If the races are okay, wipe the face of each race with grease.

2. Clean the bearings in solvent to remove all of the old grease. Blow the bearing dry with compressed air, making sure you do not allow the air jet to spin the bearing. Do not remove the lower bearing from the fork stem unless its replacement is required; clean the bearing together with the steering stem.

3. After the bearings are dry, hold the inner race with one hand and turn the outer race with your other hand. Turn the bearing slowly, checking for roughness, looseness, trapped dirt or grit. Visually check the bearing for pitting, scratches or visible damage. If the bearings are worn, check the dust shields for wear or damage or for improper bearing lubrication.

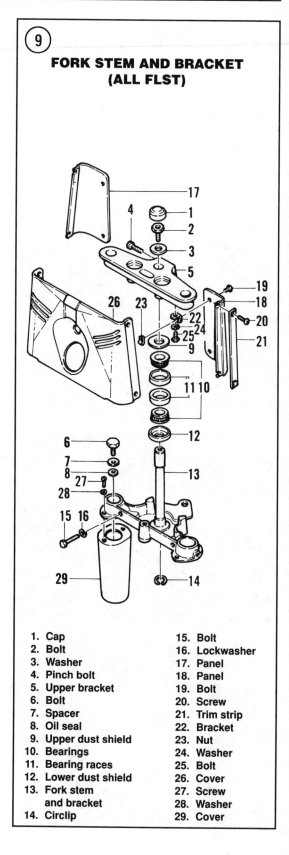

⑨

FORK STEM AND BRACKET (ALL FLST)

1. Cap	15. Bolt
2. Bolt	16. Lockwasher
3. Washer	17. Panel
4. Pinch bolt	18. Panel
5. Upper bracket	19. Bolt
6. Bolt	20. Screw
7. Spacer	21. Trim strip
8. Oil seal	22. Bracket
9. Upper dust shield	23. Nut
10. Bearings	24. Washer
11. Bearing races	25. Bolt
12. Lower dust shield	26. Cover
13. Fork stem	27. Screw
and bracket	28. Washer
14. Circlip	29. Cover

Replace the bearing if necessary. If the bearing can be reused, pack it with grease and wrap it with wax paper or some other type of lint-free material until it can be reinstalled. Do not store the bearings for any length of time without lubricating them or they will begin to rust.

NOTE
Because a trace of dirt can quickly damage a bearing, your hands should be clean when handling bearings, especially when packing the bearing with grease.

4. Check the fork stem for cracks or damage. Check the threads at the top of the stem for strippage or damage. Check the mating fastener by installing it on the stem; make sure they screw on easily with no roughness. If necessary, clean the threads carefully with a brush and solvent or use a tap or die of the correct thread type and size.

5. Worn or damaged parts should be replaced. When discarding a bearing, both bearings and their races should be replaced. Replace bearing races as described in this chapter.

6. Check for broken welds on the frame around the steering head. If any are found, have them repaired by a competent frame shop or welding service familiar with motorcycle frame repair.

STEERING HEAD BEARING RACE

Whenever the steering stem and bearings are removed from the steering head, cover the steering head with a cloth to protect the bearing races from accidental damage. If a race is damaged, the bearing and race must be replaced as a set. Because the bearing races are pressed into place, do not remove them unless they are worn and require replacement.

Fork Stem Bearing, Outer Bearing Race and Steering Head Cup Replacement

Each individual bearing assembly consists of a tapered roller bearing, bearing race, dust shield and steering head cup (early models). When replacing a bearing, all of these parts must be replaced as a set. On early models, the bearing races are first pressed into the steering head cups and then the cups are pressed in the frame steering head. On late models,

the bearing races are pressed into the frame. The lower bearing is installed over the fork stem. The upper bearing is placed in the upper bearing race after the fork stem has been inserted through the frame steering head.

Outer bearing race and steering head cup

1A. *Models with steering head cups*: To remove the steering head cup, insert a drift or similar tool into the frame steering head and carefully tap the cup out from the inside. After it is started, tap around the cup so that it does not bind in the frame head. When the cup is removed, discard the cup and the race installed in the cup. Repeat to remove the opposite cup.

1B. *Models without steering head cups*: To remove the steering head race on these models, a bead must be welded around the inside of the race. Then, when the weld cools, the bead will shrink the race and it can then be removed from the steering head. Refer this service to a Harley-Davidson dealer.

2. Clean the frame steering head of all old grease with solvent and dry thoroughly.

3A. *Models with steering head cups*: Assemble the steering head cups and races and install the cups as follows:

    a. After purchasing new bearings and 2 new steering head cups, match a new bearing with one cup. Then align the new bearing race with the cup and tap it squarely into the cup until it bottoms out. Repeat to assemble the opposite cup and bearing race.

    b. Align the upper steering head cup with the steering head and tap the cup into the frame, using a wood block and hammer, until the cup bottoms out. Make sure to drive the cup squarely into the frame.

    c. Repeat to install the lower steering head cup.

3B. *Models without steering head cups*: Install the bearing races as follows:

    a. Clean the race thoroughly before installing it.

    b. Align the upper race with the frame steering head and tap it slowly in place with a block of wood, a suitable socket or bearing driver, making sure you do *not* contact the bearing race tapered surface. See **Figure 10**. If you saved an old race, grind its outside rim so that it is a slip fit in the steering head, then use it to drive the new race into place. Drive the race into the

11

steering head until it bottoms out on the bore shoulder.

   c. Repeat to install the lower race into the steering head.

4. Wipe the bearing races with bearing grease.

Fork stem lower bearing assembly

> *NOTE*
> *Do **not** remove the fork stem lower bearing (**Figure 11**) unless it is going to be replaced with a new bearing. Do **not** reinstall a bearing that has been removed as it is no longer true to alignment.*

> *WARNING*
> *Use insulated gloves to hold onto the fork stem when removing the inner race in Step 1.*

1. Using a chisel, break the bearing cage and rollers from the inner race. When the bearing cage and rollers are free, all you will be left with is the inner race on the fork stem. To remove the inner race, heat the race with a torch until it expands enough to slide or drop off the fork stem. Remove and discard the dust shield after removing the bearing.

2. Clean the fork stem with solvent and dry thoroughly.

3. Pack the new bearing with grease before installing it.

4. Slide a new dust shield over the fork stem until it bottoms out on the lower bracket.

5. Align the new bearing with the fork stem and press or drive it onto the fork stem until it bottoms out. When installing the bearing onto the fork stem, a bearing driver must be used against the inner bearing race (**Figure 12**). Do *not* install the bearing by driving against the outer bearing race.

STEERING ADJUSTMENT

1. Support the bike so that the front wheel clears the ground.

2. Remove the windshield (if used) and all other accessory weight from the handlebar and front forks that could affect this adjustment.

> *NOTE*
> *If any control cable affects handlebar movement, disconnect it.*

3. Loosen the lower fork bracket pinch bolts (**Figure 13**).

4. Apply a strip of masking tape across the end of the fender.

5. Swing the handlebar so that the front wheel faces straight ahead.

6. Place a pointer on a stand so that its tip points to the center of the fender when the wheel is facing straight ahead.

7. Lightly push the fender towards the right-hand side until the front end starts to turn by itself. Mark this point on the tape.

8. Repeat Step 7 for the left-hand side.

9. Measure the distance between the 2 marks on the tape. For proper bearing adjustment, the distance should be 1-2 in. (25.4-50.8 mm) If the distance is incorrect, perform Step 10.

10. Adjust the steering bearings as follows:

   a. If the adjustment is less than 1 in. (25.4 mm), tighten the adjustment nut slightly.

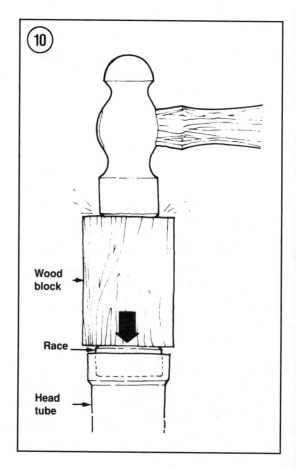

b. If the adjustment is more than 2 in. (50.8 mm), loosen the adjustment nut slightly.

c. Repeat Steps 7 and 8. Continue until the adjustment is within 1-2 in. (25.4-50.8 mm).

d. Tighten the lower fork bracket pinch bolts to the torque specification listed in **Table 1**.

11. Reinstall all parts previously removed.

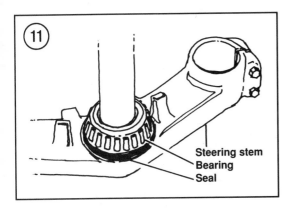

Steering stem
Bearing
Seal

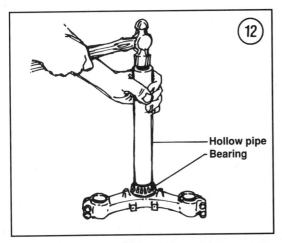

Hollow pipe
Bearing

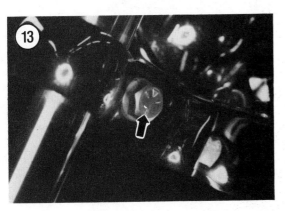

FRONT FORKS

The front suspension consists of a spring-controlled, hydraulically dampened telescopic fork.

Before suspecting major trouble, drain the front fork oil and refill with the proper type and quantity; refer to Chapter Three. If you still have trouble, such as poor damping, a tendency to bottom or top out or leakage around the rubber seals, follow the service procedures in this section.

To simplify fork service and to prevent the mixing of parts, the legs should be removed, serviced and installed individually.

Removal

1. Support the bike so that the front wheel clears the ground. Double check to make sure that the bike is stable before removing the front wheel and forks.

2. Remove the front wheel as described in Chapter Ten.

3. Remove the front fender as described in Chapter Fifteen.

4. Loosen the fork tube cap at the top of the upper fork bracket. Then remove the cap, washer and oil seal.

> *NOTE*
> *Label the left- and right-hand fork tubes so they can be reinstalled in their original position.*

5. Loosen the fork bracket pinch bolts (**Figure 13**) and slide the fork tube out of the fork brackets. It may be necessary to rotate the fork tube slightly while removing it (**Figure 14**).

6. If fork service is required, refer to *Disassembly* in this chapter.

11

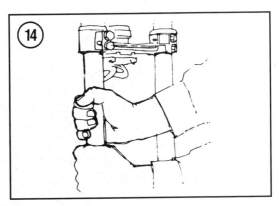

Installation

1. Clean off any corrosion or dirt on the upper and lower fork bracket receptacles.

2. Make sure the fork tube plug screwed into the top of each fork tube is tight. Check also that the threads in the plug are not contaminated or damaged.

> *NOTE*
> *The fork assemblies must be reinstalled on the correct side of the bike so the brake caliper and front fender can be properly installed. If the fork assemblies are installed on the wrong side, the bolt holes on these components will not line up properly.*

3. Slide the fork tube up through the lower and upper fork brackets. Push the fork tube up until the fork tube plug bottoms out on the upper fork bracket. Then turn the fork tube so that one flat on the fork tube plug faces toward the inside of the fork tube.

4. Slide a flat washer and oil seal onto the fork stem cap threads, then thread the cap into the fork tube plug and tighten securely. After tightening the fork tube plug, check that one flat on the fork tube plug still faces toward the inside of the fork tube.

5. Tighten the fork bracket pinch bolt to the torque specification listed in **Table 1**.

6. Install the front fender as described in Chapter Fifteen.

7. Install the front wheel and front master cylinder as described in Chapter Ten.

8. Apply the front brake and pump the front forks several times to seat the forks and front wheel.

Disassembly/Reassembly

To simplify fork service and to prevent the mixing of parts, the legs should be disassembled and assembled individually.

Refer to **Figure 15** for this procedure.

1. Using the front axle boss at the bottom of the fork tube, clamp the slider in a vise with soft jaws. Do *not* clamp the slider at any point above the fork axle boss in a vise.

> *NOTE*
> *The Allen screw inserted through the bottom of the slider may be difficult to remove because the damper rod will turn inside the slider when the Allen bolt*

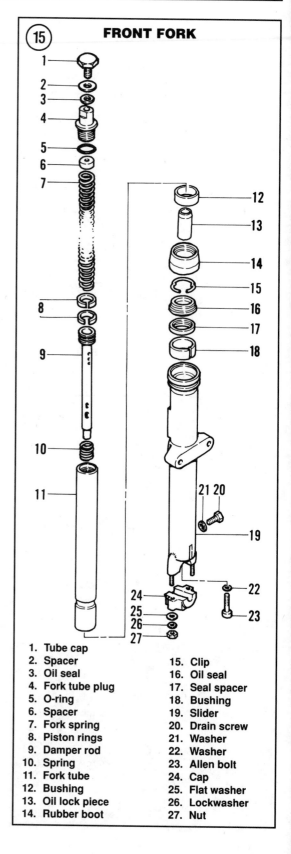

FRONT FORK

1. Tube cap	15. Clip
2. Spacer	16. Oil seal
3. Oil seal	17. Seal spacer
4. Fork tube plug	18. Bushing
5. O-ring	19. Slider
6. Spacer	20. Drain screw
7. Fork spring	21. Washer
8. Piston rings	22. Washer
9. Damper rod	23. Allen bolt
10. Spring	24. Cap
11. Fork tube	25. Flat washer
12. Bushing	26. Lockwasher
13. Oil lock piece	27. Nut
14. Rubber boot	

is turned. *If you have access to an air impact driver, you can remove the Allen screw after removing the fork spring in the following steps. If, however, you do not have access to air tools, you may want to loosen the Allen bolt before removing the fork spring. If you are unable to remove it, take the fork tubes to a dealer and have the screws removed.*

2. If you do not have access to air tools, loosen but do not remove the Allen screw at the bottom of the slider.

WARNING
The fork tube plug is under spring pressure. When removing the plug, note that it may fly off. Keep your face away from the plug when removing it. In addition, make sure the fork tube is fully extended from the slider. If the forks are damaged and stuck in a compressed state, the fork should be disassembled by a dealer or qualified mechanic, as the plug and spring will fly out from the fork tube under considerable pressure when the plug is removed.

3. Loosen and remove the fork tube plug at the top of the fork tube. Remove the fork tube plug, spacer (if so equipped) and the fork spring.

NOTE
The spacer installed between the fork tube plug and spring was used on early FLST models only. Later models use longer fork springs without the spacers.

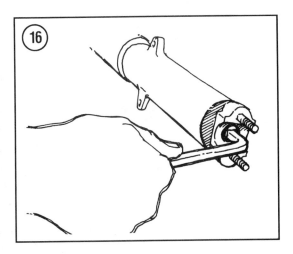

The spacers on some models have holes drilled through them to simplify fork oil changes. If you are servicing an FLST model with a spacer that does not have a hole through it, drill a 3/8 in. (9.5 mm) hole through the center of each spacer before reassembling the fork tubes.

4. Remove the fork tube from the vise and pour the oil out of the fork into a clean container. Pump the fork several times by hand to expel most of the remaining oil. Check the oil for contamination, indicating worn or damaged parts. Discard the oil after examining it.

5. *FXST:* Slip the dust seal out of the lower fork tube and remove it.

6. Remove the retaining ring securing the oil seal in the slider.

7. Remove the Allen screw and washer (**Figure 16**) at the bottom of the slider.

NOTE
The bushing installed in the slider is an interference fit. When separating the fork tube and slider, the bushing, spacer seal and oil seal will be removed together.

8. While grasping the slider in one hand, work the fork tube in an up-and-down motion to hit the upper bushing installed on the fork tube against the lower bushing in the slider. As the lower bushing works its way free, it will push the oil seal and seal spacer out of the slider. Continue this action until the components are separated.

9. Remove the rebound sleeve from the damper rod.

10. Insert a small rod into the end of the damper rod and push it out of the fork tube.

Inspection

CAUTION
Before cleaning rubber components, make sure the cleaning agent is compatible with rubber. Some types of solvent can cause permanent damage.

1. Thoroughly clean all parts in solvent and dry them. Place cleaned parts on newspaper or other types of lint-free material until reassembly. Ordinary paper towels should not be used to dry parts because of the lint left on the parts.

11

2. Check upper fork tube exterior for bending, scratches or other damage. The fork tubes can be checked for bending with a set of V-blocks and a dial indicator. If you do not have these tools, you can roll the fork tube on a large plate of glass and check for any runout. Harley-Davidson does not provide service limit specifications for runout. If a fork tube is slightly bent, it can be straightened with a press and special blocks; see your Harley-Davidson dealer or repair shop. If a fork tube is bent so much that the metal has cracked or wrinkled, the fork tube should be replaced.

3. Check the slider for dents or exterior damage that may cause the fork tube to hang up during riding conditions. Check the circlip groove in the top of the slider for cracks or corrosion. Clean out the groove if necessary so that the circlip can seat correctly during assembly. Replace the slider if the groove is cracked or damaged.

4. Check the axle bearing surfaces on the slider for wear or gouges. Check the cap for cracks or damage. Clean up the surfaces or replace the slider and/or cap if necessary.

5. Check the axle cap studs in the bottom of the slider(s) for thread damage or looseness. If necessary, replace the studs as described in Chapter One.

6. Replace worn or damaged washers as required.

7. Check the damper rod rebound sleeve and piston rings for wear or damage. Replace the piston rings by removing them from the damper rod and installing new ones.

8. Check the damper rod for straightness with a set of V-blocks and a dial indicator (**Figure 17**) or by rolling it on a piece of plate glass. Harley-Davidson does not provide service limit specifications for runout.

9. Make sure the oil passage holes in the damper rod and fork tube are clean. If clogged, clean out with solvent and dry with compressed air.

10. Check the treads in the damper rod for stripping, cross-threading or deposit buildup. The hole should be blown out with compressed air as dirt buildup in the bottom of the hole may prevent the Allen screw from being properly torqued. Use a tap to true up the threads and remove any deposits.

11. Check the damper rod rebound spring and the fork spring for wear or damage. Harley-Davidson does not provide service limit specifications for spring free length.

NOTE
When replacing fork springs on early FLST models that use a spacer at the top of each fork spring, discard the spacers when purchasing new fork springs. The new fork springs are longer than the original springs and do not require spacers for preload. To keep the left- and right-hand fork tubes balanced, always replace both fork springs at the same time. Compare the length of the new and old springs to make sure the new springs are longer.

12. Check the upper bushing mounted in the slider and the lower bushing mounted on the fork tube for severe wear, cracks or damage. The upper bushing was removed together with the oil seal. The lower bushing installed on the fork tube should not be removed unless worn or damaged. To replace it, perform the following:

    a. Wedge a screwdriver into the bushing split to expand the bushing slightly and slide it off of the fork tube.

    b. Install a new bushing by expanding the split as during removal. Expand the new split bushing only enough to fit it over the fork tube.

    c. Seat the new bushing into the groove in the fork tube.

13. *FXST*: Inspect the outer dust seals for cracks, age deterioration or other damage.

14. The oil seals should be replaced. If you plan to install the original seals, inspect them closely for wear or deterioration. When in doubt, replace the seals as a set.

15. Any parts that are worn or damaged should be replaced. When replacing springs, replace both springs as a set; do not replace only 1 spring. Simply cleaning and reinstalling unserviceable components will not improve performance of the front suspension.

Assembly

Refer to **Figure 15** for this procedure.

1. Prior to assembly, perform the *Inspection* procedure to make sure all worn or defective parts have been repaired or replaced. All parts should be thoroughly cleaned before assembly.

2. Coat all parts with Harley-Davidson Type E Fork Oil or equivalent before assembly.

3. If removed, install a new fork tube bushing as described under *Inspection*.

4. If removed, install 2 new damper rod friction rings as described under *Inspection*.

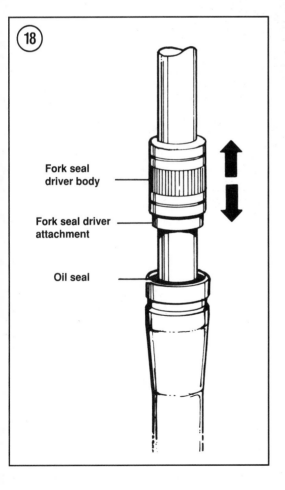

Fork seal driver body

Fork seal driver attachment

Oil seal

5. Slide the rebound spring onto the damper rod and insert this assembly into the fork tube.

6. Place the rebound sleeve onto the end of the damper rod.

7. Insert the fork spring into the fork tube so that the tapered side of the spring faces down (toward damper rod). Tension the spring to hold the damper rod in place and insert the fork tube into the slider. Make sure the rebound sleeve stays on the end of the damper rod.

8. Temporarily install the spacer (early FLST with original fork springs) and the fork tube plug into the top of the fork tube. Tighten the fork tube plug.

9. Make sure the gasket is on the damper rod Allen screw.

10. Apply Loctite 271 (red) to the threads of the Allen head screw prior to installing it. Install it through the slider and thread it into the end of the damper rod. Tighten the screw securely.

11. Remove the fork tube plug, spacer (early FLST with original fork springs) and the fork spring.

NOTE
The bushing, seal spacer and oil seal are installed into the slider at the same time with a suitable driver placed over the fork tube and against the oil seal. The Harley-Davidson fork seal driver (part No. HD-34634) can be used. A piece of pipe can also work as a tool when installing the parts into the slider. If you plan to use a piece of pipe or similar tool, care must be taken to prevent damage to the slider, oil seal or fork tube. If both ends of the pipe or tool are threaded, wrap one end with duct tape to prevent the threads from damaging the slider, oil seal or fork tube.

12. Install the upper bushing, seal spacer and oil seal at the same time. Perform the following:

　　a. Coat the upper bushing with fork oil and slide the bushing down the fork tube and rest it short of the slider cavity.

　　b. Install the seal spacer over the fork tube (flange surface facing up). Rest the seal spacer on the upper bushing.

　　c. Slide a new oil seal over the fork tube (lettered side facing up). Rest the oil seal on the seal spacer.

　　d. Slide the fork seal driver down the fork tube (**Figure 18**).

e. Drive the bushing, seal spacer and oil seal into the slider until the groove in the slider can be seen above the top surface of the oil seal.

f. Remove the installation tool.

13. Install the circlip into the slider groove. Make sure the circlip is completely seated in the groove.

14. *FXST*: Slide the dust seal down the fork tube and seat it in the slider groove.

15. Fill the fork tube with the correct quantity of Harley-Davidson Type E Fork Oil. Refer to Chapter Three for fork oil quantity.

16. The fork spring is tapered at one end. Install the spring so that the tapered end faces toward the bottom of the fork.

17. *Early FLST*: Install the spacer, if so equipped.

18. Align the fork tube plug with the spring and push down on the plug to compress the spring. Start the plug slowly, don't cross thread it.

19. Place the slider in a vise with soft jaws and tighten the fork tube plug securely.

20. Install the fork tube as described in this chapter.

Table 1 FRONT SUSPENSION TIGHTENING TORQUES

	ft.-lb.	N·m
Brake hose bracket	11	15
Fork bracket pinch bolts	30-35	41-47

CHAPTER TWELVE

SPRINGER FRONT FORK

The Harley-Davidson Springer front fork consists of a single shock absorber, 2 top mounted rebound springs, 2 outer compression springs, 4 inner compression springs, a rigid fork assembly and a spring fork. A rocker assembly is mounted at the bottom of the rigid fork and spring fork assemblies. The Springer front fork offers 4 inches (101.6 mm) of travel.

Table 1 is at the end of the chapter.

Service Note

When servicing the Springer front end, note the following:

1. Read the applicable service procedure through before performing any service work. In some instances, it will be necessary to fabricate special tools or to have various types of supplies on hand. Acquire these items before starting work.

2. The front wheel will have to be raised off of the ground when servicing many of the Springer components. Make sure that the bike is secured in a safe manner.

3. Make sure all Springer parts and fasteners are replaced with the same type and grade. Do not assemble the Springer front fork with inferior parts or fasteners.

4. In most cases, each bolt should have a washer under its head and every nut should have a washer under it. The washers will prevent galling to the part when tightening the fastener and will provide you with the best chance of obtaining a correct torque reading. If you are putting something back that you didn't take apart, refer to the exploded view drawing representing the components you are servicing so that you will know if washers are required.

5. Fasteners should be tightened to their respective torque specifications listed in **Table 1**. When tightening a bolt and nut assembly, hold the bolt head with a wrench and tighten the nut with a torque wrench and socket.

6. If you are unsure about your ability to service the Springer front end, refer service to a Harley-Davidson dealer or a qualified Harley repair shop.

> *WARNING*
> *All of the components that make up the Springer front end (forks, tire, front fender, etc.) are designed to work together to offer optimum handling, steering and braking performance. Changing or modifying these components can alter the handling and steering characteristics of the Springer front end and may cause you to lose control. If you are going to modify or add accessory components to the Springer front end, you should consult with your Harley-Davidson dealer first. Specifically, Harley-Davidson recommends that you should **not** do the following:*
> *a. Do not install a tire with a higher-aspect ratio. During hard stops, the front tire could bind against the fender.*
> *b. Do not lower the fender from its stock position. During hard stops or when hitting big road bumps, the front tire could bind against the fender.*
> *c. 21 in. front tires are installed on all Springer models. Do not replace this tire with a 16 in. front wheel, tire and front fender combination. A 16 in. tire would change the motorcycle's steering*

and handling characteristics as well as bind against the front fender.

Rocker Bearing Adjustment

The rocker pivots on the rigid fork leg through a split ball bearing assembly. The rocker bearings should be adjusted every 10,000 miles (16,000 km).

Refer to **Figure 1** when performing this procedure.

1. Raise and secure the bike so that the front wheel is off the ground.

2. Remove the front brake caliper and brake line as described in Chapter Fourteen.

NOTE
Insert a piece of vinyl tubing or wood in the caliper in place of the brake disc. That way if the brake lever is inadvertently squeezed, the piston will not be forced out of the cylinder. If this does happen, the caliper may have to be disassembled to reseat the piston and the system will have to be bled.

3. Remove the front wheel as described in Chapter Ten.

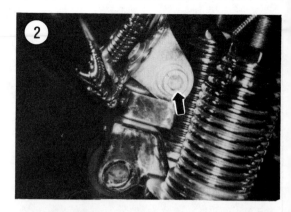

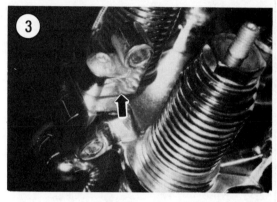

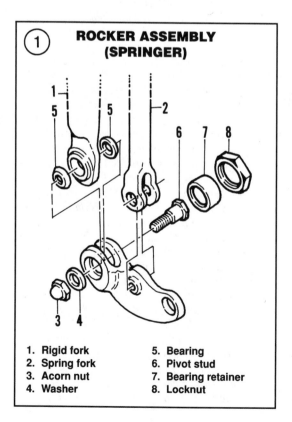

ROCKER ASSEMBLY (SPRINGER)

1. **Rigid fork**
2. **Spring fork**
3. **Acorn nut**
4. **Washer**
5. **Bearing**
6. **Pivot stud**
7. **Bearing retainer**
8. **Locknut**

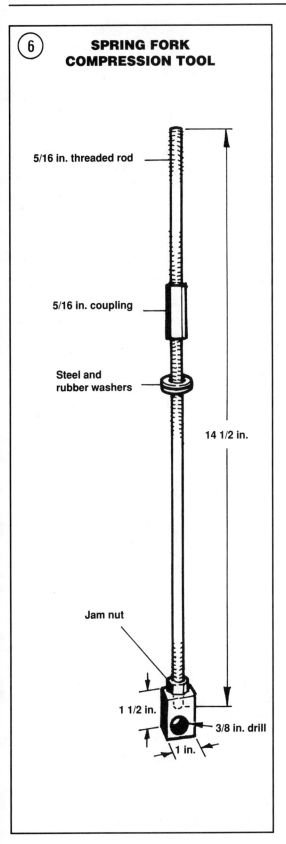

⑥ **SPRING FORK COMPRESSION TOOL**

5/16 in. threaded rod

5/16 in. coupling

Steel and rubber washers

14 1/2 in.

Jam nut

1 1/2 in.

3/8 in. drill

1 in.

4. Remove the front fender as described in Chapter Fifteen.

5. Remove the bolt, washer and nut securing the headlight housing to its mounting block (**Figure 2**). Then carefully remove the headlight housing and position it aside and out of the way. You may want to cover the headlight with a towel to prevent it from being damaged. Remove the headlight mounting block bolt and remove the block (**Figure 3**).

6. Remove the fork shock absorber as described in this chapter.

WARNING
Plastic ties are installed around the spring fork and rigid fork legs (Step 7) to prevent the spring fork from flying forward when compressing the fork springs in the following steps; otherwise, you could suffer serious personal injury if the spring fork should fly up and hit you.

7. Install a heavy-duty plastic tie around the spring fork and rigid fork legs on both sides of the fork as shown in **Figure 4**. Double-check to make sure the plastic ties are secured properly.

8. Compress the lower compression springs (**Figure 5**) as follows:

   a. Fabricate the Springer fork spring compression tool shown in **Figure 6**. The 5/16 in. threaded rod and 5/16 in. coupling can be purchased at most hardware stores (**Figure 7**). The block mounted at the bottom of the threaded rod should be made of cold-roll steel. The width of the block should be cut so that the block can fit between the lower shock absorber mounting eye in the spring fork. The hole drilled horizontally through the block

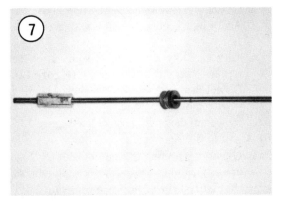

⑦

12

should be made with a 3/8 in. drill bit. See
Figure 6.

NOTE
After making the block, round off each
of the block corners with a file. Likewise
remove all burrs from the side of the
block that were made when the hole was
drilled through the block. This step will
prevent the block from damaging any of
the front fork components.

b. Insert the steel block between the lower shock
absorber mount arms in the spring fork. Secure the block with the shock absorber bolt,
washers and Acorn nut (**Figure 8**). Insert the
threaded rod (without the coupling, washers
or jam nut) through the headlight mount.
Thread the jam nut onto the bottom of the
threaded rod and then thread the threaded rod
into the block until it bottoms out; tighten the
jam nut securely against the steel block with a
wrench. Slide a rubber and then a steel washer
down the threaded rod until they seat against
the headlight mount. Then thread the coupling
onto the threaded rod and tighten the coupling
against the washers with a wrench (**Figure 9**).
Continue to tighten the coupling until the
compression springs bottom out on their travel
bumpers.

NOTE
The travel bumpers are installed be-
tween the rigid fork assembly and the
spring cup at the top of the compression
spring. The compression springs are the
2 lower springs. The 2 upper springs are
the rebound springs.

9. Disconnect the rocker from the spring fork leg as
follows:

a. Loosen and remove the spring fork pivot stud
Acorn nut (**Figure 10**) and washer (**Figure
11**).

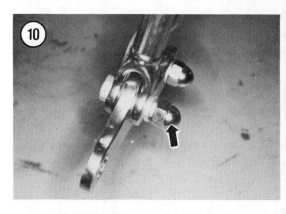

b. Then carefully tap the pivot stud out of the
fork leg assembly and remove it (**Figure 12**).
Do not damage the spherical rocker bearing
when removing the stud.

c. Repeat for the opposite side. See **Figure 13**.

10. Adjust the bearing retainer as follows:

a. Loosen the bearing retainer locknut (A, **Figure 14**) and then loosen the bearing retainer
(B, **Figure 14**) with an Allen wrench.

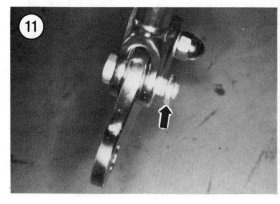

b. Pivot the right-hand rocker up against its rigid fork leg; pivot the left-hand rocker down and back against its rigid fork leg. This helps to hold the rocker in position when tightening the bearing retainer.

c. Tighten bearing retainer until you feel it contacting its spherical bearing, then stop. Next, tighten bearing retainer an additional 1/6 of a turn only. You can gage 1/6 of a turn by marking one flat on the bearing retainer and then turning the bearing retainer until the next flat aligns with the mark.

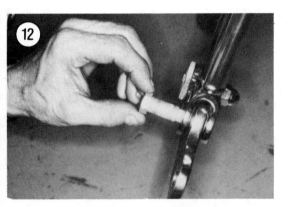

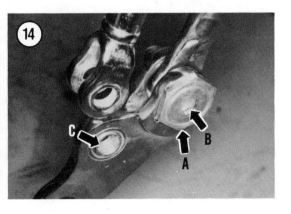

NOTE
Because a high torque reading will be required when tightening the bearing retainer locknut, and because it is critical that the bearing retainer is not allowed to turn, you may want to hold the bearing retainer while an assistant tightens the locknut.

d. Hold the bearing retainer (B, **Figure 14**) with the Allen wrench and tighten the locknut (A, **Figure 14**) to the torque specification listed in **Table 1**. Remember, do *not* allow the bearing retainer to turn when tightening the locknut.

NOTE
When the bearing retainer is properly adjusted, the end of the retainer will extend out of the locknut approximately 1/16 in. (1.6 mm).

e. Repeat for the opposite side.

11. Pivot both rockers (**Figure 13**) by hand. The rockers should move snugly with no sign of grinding or excessive noise. You may notice that the left- and right-hand rockers do not have the same degree of tightness. Disregard this difference as it is temporary; the bearings will equalize after the bike is ridden for a few miles.

CAUTION
If you notice a grinding sound when pivoting a rocker in Step 11, the bearings are either severely worn or damaged. Replace the spherical bearing assembly as described in this chapter.

12. Pivot a rocker around and insert it between its spring fork leg, aligning the bearing in the rocker with the 2 stud holes in the spring fork leg. Wipe the pivot stud with bearing grease. Insert the pivot stud through the spring fork leg from the inside of the leg (**Figure 12**). Install the thick washer (**Figure 11**) and Acorn nut (**Figure 10**) and tighten to the torque specification listed in **Table 1**.

13. Repeat Step 12 for the opposite side.

14. After reinstalling the left- and right-hand rockers, loosen and remove the spring compression tool. Then cut the plastic ties at fork legs and discard them.

15. Reinstall the shock absorber as described in this chapter.

16. Reinstall the headlight mounting block (**Figure 3**) and the headlight (**Figure 2**). Check that the

⑮ ROCKER AND FRONT BRAKE (SPRINGER)

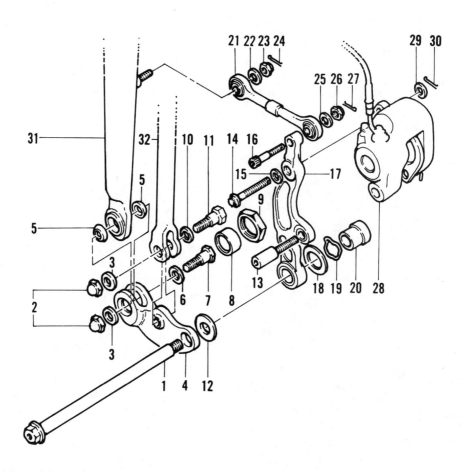

1. Front axle
2. Acorn nut
3. Washer
4. Rocker
5. Spherical bearings
6. Thin washer (mid 1989 and earlier; see text for application)
7. Pivot stud
8. Bearing retainer
9. Locknut
10. Thin washer (mid 1989 and earlier; see text for application)
11. Pivot stud
12. Thrust washer (small I.D.)
13. Lower mounting bolt
14. Upper mounting bolt
15. Washer
16. Bolt
17. Brake bracket
18. Thrust washer (large I.D.)
19. Wave washer
20. Spacer
21. Brake reaction link
22. Washer
23. Nut
24. Cotter pin
25. Washer
26. Nut
27. Cotter pin
28. Brake caliper
29. Washer
30. Cotter pin
31. Rigid fork
32. Spring fork

headlight wiring harness is routed properly. Secure the headlight housing with its bolt and washer; install the bolt and washer through the mounting plate and thread it into the mounting block. Tighten bolt securely. Adjust headlight as described in Chapter Nine.

17. Reinstall the front fender as described in Chapter Fifteen.

18. Reinstall the front wheel as described in Chapter Ten.

19. Remove the wood or vinyl wedge from the front brake caliper and install the caliper as described in Chapter Fourteen.

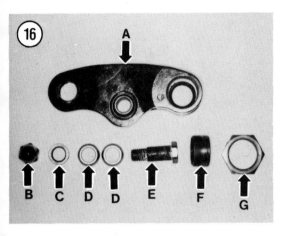

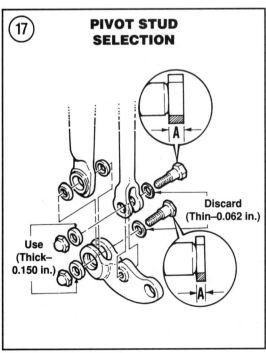

PIVOT STUD SELECTION

Discard (Thin–0.062 in.)

Use (Thick–0.150 in.)

20. Lower the bike from its support so that the front wheel is back onto the ground. Support the bike with its jiffy stand.

> *WARNING*
> *Do not ride the motorcycle until you are sure the front brake is operating correctly with full hydraulic advantage. Check brake operation by straddling the bike (engine off) and operating the front brake lever while pushing forward on the handlebars.*

Rocker Bearing Inspection (50,000 Mile [80,500 km] Intervals)

The spherical bearings in each rocker assembly (**Figure 15**) should be visually inspected at 50,000 mile (80,500 km) intervals. A teflon lining covers the outside of each spherical bearing. If the teflon lining is worn completely through at any point, showing the metal underneath, the bearing must be replaced. Inspect and service the rockers as described in this chapter.

Rocker Removal

Refer to **Figure 15** and **Figure 16** when performing this procedure.

1. Disconnect the rocker from the spring fork as described under *Rocker Bearing Adjustment*, Steps 1-9 in this chapter.

> *WARNING*
> *Make sure to observe the **WARNING** when disconnecting the rocker under **Rocker Bearing Adjustment** in this chapter.*

2. Loosen and remove the bearing retainer locknut (A, **Figure 14**), then loosen and remove the bearing retainer (B, **Figure 14**) from the rocker.

3. See **Figure 16**. Remove the pivot stud Acorn nut (B) and washer (C) from the pivot stud. Then slide the pivot stud (E) out of the rocker fork leg and remove the rocker (A) and the bearings (D).

> *NOTE*
> *1988 and early 1989 models have a thin washer installed on the rocker pivot studs (**Figure 17**). Late 1989 and later models use rocker pivot studs with thicker bolt heads and no washer. If you have an earlier model, remove the washer with the rocker pivot stud.*

12

4. Repeat to remove the opposite rocker.

Inspection

1. Clean all of the parts in solvent and dry thoroughly.

2. Check the rocker pivot studs (A, **Figure 18**) for wear or damage.

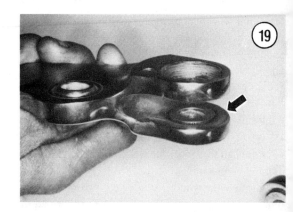

> *NOTE*
> *If you have a 1988 or early 1989 model that uses thin head rocker pivot studs and thin washers, the replacement studs will have a thicker bolt head. When installing the thicker head pivot studs, discard the thin washer. See **Figure 17**. Confirm this with your dealer's parts manager when purchasing the replacement parts.*

3. Check the spherical bearing ball surfaces (B, **Figure 18**) for cracks, deep scoring or excessive wear. Check the spherical bearing race in the rocker (**Figure 19**) and in the bearing retainer (F, **Figure 16**) for the same conditions. Replace the bearings as a set, if required. Replace the bearing races with a press.

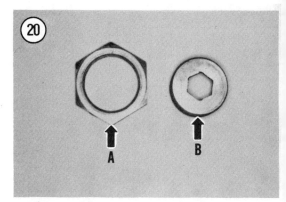

4. Check the bearing locknut (A, **Figure 20**) for hex or thread damage (**Figure 21**).

5. Check the bearing retainer (B, **Figure 20**) for hex or thread damage.

6. Check the spherical bearing in the rocker (**Figure 22**). A teflon lining covers the outside of each spherical bearing. If the teflon lining is worn completely through at any point, showing the metal underneath, the bearing must be replaced as described in this chapter.

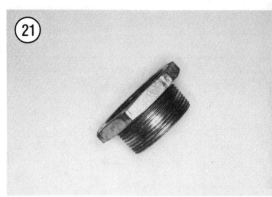

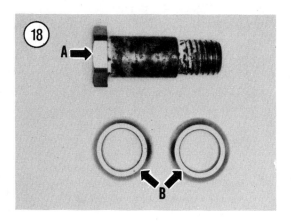

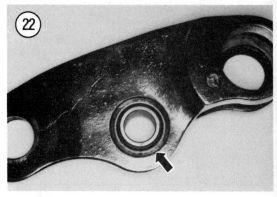

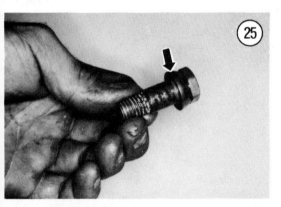

Rocker Installation

Refer to **Figure 15** and **Figure 16** when performing this procedure.

NOTE
*Before installing the rockers, make sure the bearing race in the rocker and bearing retainer (F, **Figure 16**) is properly seated.*

1. Wipe the rocker (**Figure 23**) and bearing retainer (**Figure 24**) bearing races with wheel bearing grease. Then install each spherical ball bearing into the rocker so that the spherical surface on each bearing faces toward their respective rocker race. See **Figure 19** or **Figure 25**.

NOTE
*The rockers are identified with a "L" (left-hand) or "R" (right-hand). See **Figure 26**. When installing the rockers, the threaded side of each rocker must face inward.*

2. Align a rocker with its rigid fork leg so that it faces in its normal operating position, then insert the rocker into the fork leg, making sure the outer bearing does not fall out.

3. Insert the pivot stud and the inner bearing through the rigid fork leg, rocker and outer bearing from the inside out as shown in **Figure 27**. Check that the spherical bearings are properly installed and seated in their races.

4. Wipe the bearing retainer threads with anti-seize and thread the retainer into the rocker partway (**Figure 28**); do not seat the retainer against the bearing. Then install the locknut onto the bearing retainer (**Figure 29**).

12

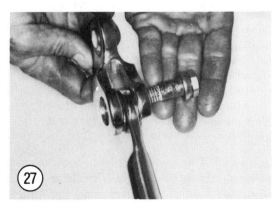

5. With the bearing retainer installed into the rocker, the next step is to adjust the rocker bearing. For this step, refer to *Rocker Bearing Adjustment* and perform Step 10 and Step 11.

6. Repeat for the opposite rocker.

7. Install the thick washer (**Figure 30**) onto the pivot stud and apply Loctite 242 (blue) to the stud threads. Install and tighten the pivot stud Acorn nut (**Figure 31**) to the torque specification listed in **Table 1**.

8. After both rockers have been adjusted, complete reassembly by performing Steps 12-20 under *Rocker Bearing Adjustment*.

> *WARNING*
> *Do not ride the motorcycle until you are sure the front brake is operating correctly with full hydraulic advantage. Check brake operation by straddling the bike (engine off) and operating the front brake lever while pushing forward on the handlebars.*

Rocker Bearing Replacement

The rocker bearings play an important part in the operation of the Springer front fork assembly. Because of the special skills required to replace the rocker bearings, refer all bearing replacement to a Harley-Davidson dealer.

Handlebar and Handlebar Riser Removal/Installation

Refer to **Figure 32** for this procedure.

1. Support the bike securely on a stand so that the front wheel clears the ground.

2. Remove the fuel tank as described in Chapter Eight.

> *NOTE*
> *Handlebar removal will not require removal of the brake master cylinder or any of the control cables. However, to avoid damaging or kinking a cable, set the handlebar assembly aside carefully. Check the master cylinder reservoir for tightness before removing the handlebar. Drape a blanket over the bike to prevent the accidental spilling of brake fluid, should an accident occur.*

3. Loosen 2 of the handlebar Allen bolts on the same side and remove the bolts and handlebar holder. Then hold onto the handlebar (to prevent it from dropping) and loosen the remaining 2 holder bolts; remove the bolts and holder, then carefully place the handlebar back and away from the front fork.

> *NOTE*
> *Remove the springs on 1991 models.*

4. Hold the rigid fork leg stud with a wrench, then loosen and remove the locknut with a socket. Lift the riser off of the rigid fork leg stud by twisting and pulling it upward, then turn the riser over to remove the locknut and washer. Repeat for the opposite side. Discard the locknut(s) after removing them.

5. Each riser is equipped with 2 rubber bushings that ride against the rigid fork leg stud. Eventually these rubber bushings will wear so inspect them each time the riser is removed or if you notice more vibration or abnormal movement in the handlebars. If the rubber bushings are worn or damaged, remove them by driving them out of the riser with a punch. Note that removing the rubber bushings will usually destroy them, so don't remove them unless replacement is required. After removing the bushings, clean the inside of the riser of all rubber residue, then allow to dry thoroughly. Install the new bushings by first

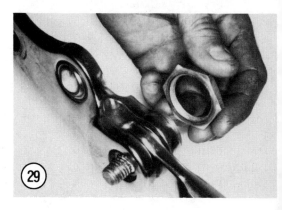

lubricating them with a soap and water solution, then drive them separately into the riser with a suitable socket or driver. Drive each bushing in so that the bottom of the bushing seats into the riser recess completely. Repeat for the opposite side.

6. When installing the risers, first align the handlebar slot in the riser so that it will face correctly for handlebar installation, then install the riser over the rigid fork leg stud.

7. Note the 2 slots cut into each riser washer. Install the washer by aligning these slots with the riser bosses, then drop them into the riser and install a *new* riser locknut. Hold the rigid fork leg stud with a wrench and tighten the riser locknut with a torque wrench to the torque specification listed in **Table 1**.

8. Before installing the handlebar, check the knurled section on the handlebar for dirt or bits of aluminum. Clean the knurled section completely so that it will offer a good "bite" when the clamps are tightened.

9. Place the handlebar onto the risers and install the 2 handlebar clamps and their 2 screws. Straddle the bike and position the handlebar to best suit your riding position, then tighten the clamp screws to the tightening torque listed in **Table 1**. While tightening

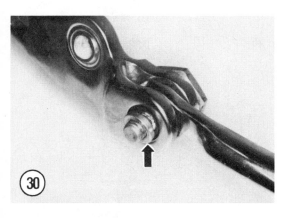

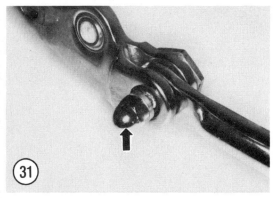

the clamp screws, maintain an even gap at the front and rear of the clamp.

10. Reinstall all assemblies on the handlebar if removed. Make sure all cable routing is correct and check front brake operation.

> *WARNING*
> *Keeping the riser assembly tight is critical to the steering and safe operation of your Harley. Make sure to install a **new** riser locknut whenever the old nut has been removed from the rigid fork leg stud and to tighten the new nut to the torque specification listed in **Table 1**. Failure to observe this information may allow the riser(s) to loosen and to cause you to lose control of the bike.*

Shock Absorber
Removal/Installation

Refer to **Figure 33** for this procedure.

1. Support the bike so that the front wheel clears the ground.

2. Remove the Acorn nuts, washers and bolts (**Figure 34**), then remove the shock absorber from the bike.

3. The shock absorber (**Figure 35**) is non-rebuildable. Check the shock for oil leakage or loss of damping. Replace shock if damaged.

4. Replace the shock bushings (**Figure 36**) if worn or damaged.

5. Clean all Loctite residue from the shock absorber mounting bolts and nuts.

> *NOTE*
> *When installing the shock mounting bolts in Step 6, a washer must be installed under each bolt head and one between the mounting bracket and each nut.*

6. Insert the shock absorber into the upper and lower mounting brackets so that decal on shock faces forward. Install a washer on each bolt and insert the bolts through the mounting brackets and shock. Install the second washer and then apply Loctite 242 (blue) to the end of the bolt. Install the Acorn nuts and tighten to the torque specification listed in **Table 1**.

> *WARNING*
> *After tightening the shock absorber bolts and nuts, there should be zero*

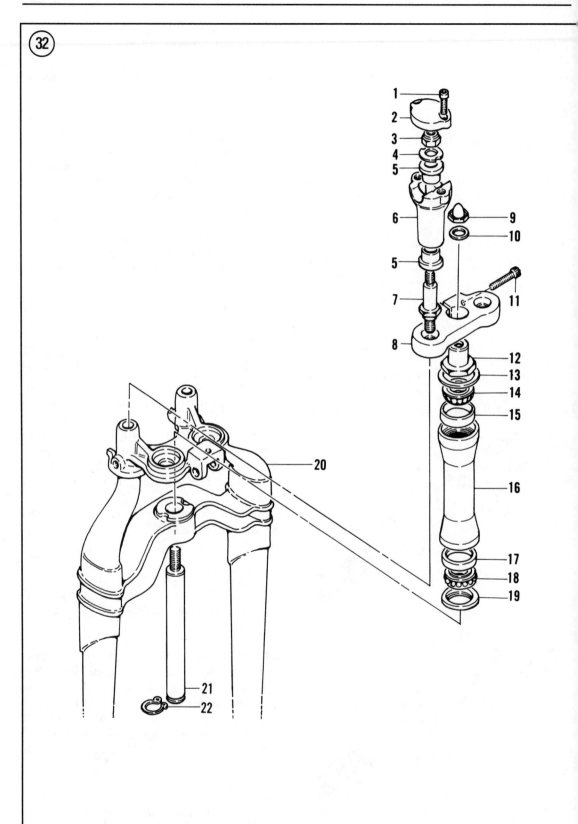

SPRINGER FRONT FORK
PART I

1. Bolt
2. Riser cap
3. Nut
4. Washer
5. Rubber bushing
6. Riser
7. Rigid fork leg stud
8. Upper triple clamp
9. Acorn nut
10. Washer
11. Pinch bolt
12. Bearing retainer
13. Dust shield
14. Bearing
15. Bearing seat
16. Frame tube
17. Bearing seat
18. Bearing
19. Dust shield
20. Rigid fork
21. Steering stem
22. Circlip

clearance between the shock absorber and the shock mounting brackets. If there is measurable clearance between the shock eye and the mounting bracket, first check for loose or damaged bolts. If the bolts are torqued properly, check the mounting brackets for cracks or other damage. Do not ride the bike until the shock is properly installed and tightened.

Spring Fork
Removal/Disassembly

The spring fork assembly can be removed from the rigid fork with the rigid fork installed on the bike. If you wish to remove the front fork assembly with the rigid and spring fork assemblies intact, refer to *Front Fork Removal* in this chapter. If you are going to service the rigid fork assembly, remove the spring fork assembly as described in this section and then remove the rigid fork as described later in this chapter.

Refer to **Figure 33** when performing this procedure.

NOTE
Because Harley does not list service specifications for the springs used on the spring fork assembly, you may want to label the springs in regards to their mounting position (left- or right-hand side) so that you don't mix them up. You can then compare the 2 sets of springs during inspection for spring sag or other visual differences.

1. Perform Steps 1-9 under *Rocker Bearing Adjustment* in this chapter.

2. With the special fork tool in place and the fork legs secured (**Figure 37**), tighten the coupling (A, **Figure 38**) until the compression springs bottom out on their travel bumpers. The rebound springs should now be free of all tension.

NOTE
The travel bumpers are installed between the rigid fork assembly and the spring cup at the top of the compression spring. The compression springs are the 2 lower springs. The 2 upper springs are the rebound springs. See ***Figure 33***.

12

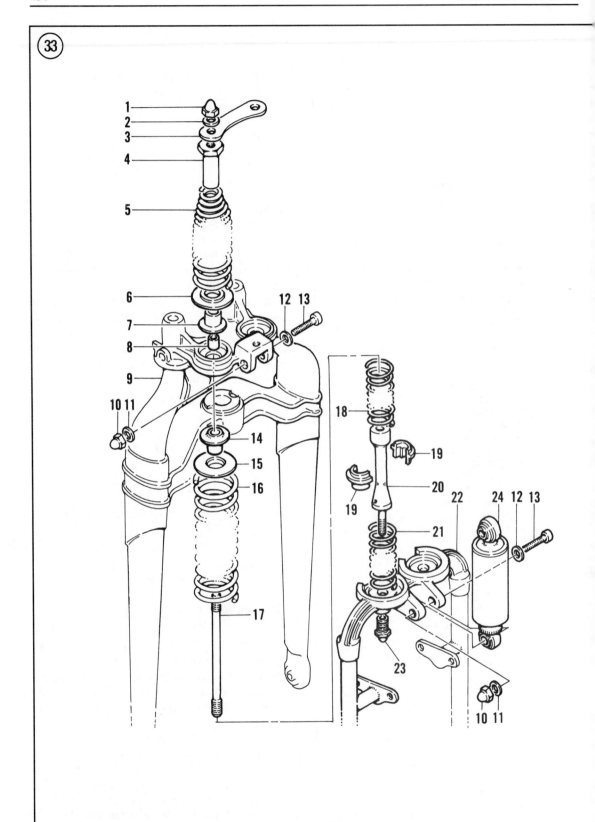

SPRINGER FRONT FORK
PART II

1. Acorn nut
2. Washer
3. Spring bridge
4. Upper spring restraint
5. Upper rebound spring
6. Rebound spring cups
7. Rubber bushing
8. Bushing
9. Rigid fork assembly
10. Acorn nut
11. Washer
12. Washer
13. Bolt
14. Rubber bushing
15. Spring cup
16. Outer compression spring
17. Upper spring rod
18. Inner compression spring (upper)
19. Spring seat
20. Lower spring rod
21. Inner compression spring (lower)
22. Spring fork assembly
23. Acorn nut
24. Front shock absorber

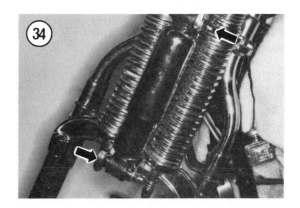

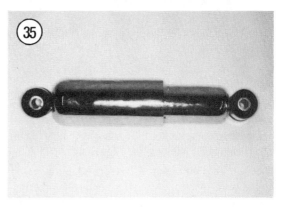

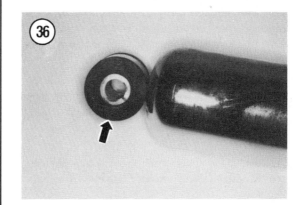

12

3. Check that there is *no* tension on the 2 upper rebound springs. If the springs are still under tension, recheck your work in Step 2.

4. With no tension on the rebound springs (B, **Figure 38**), loosen and remove the 2 Acorn nuts, washers and the spring bridge. See **Figure 33**.

NOTE
*Before removing the spring restraints in Step 5, measure the distance from the top of the spring restraint to the upper spring rod (**Figure 39**). Record the distance for reassembly.*

5. Loosen and remove the upper spring restraints (A, **Figure 40**).

6. Remove the rebound springs (B, **Figure 40**) and their spring cups (**Figure 41**).

7. Remove the rubber travel bumpers (**Figure 42**) and the bushing (**Figure 43**).

8. Disconnect the rocker from the spring fork leg as described in this chapter. See **Figure 44**.

9. Slowly turn the compression tool coupling *counterclockwise* to release tension from the compression springs (**Figure 45**). Hold the spring fork assembly when loosening the compression tool. Then, when all tension has been removed from the springs, lift the spring fork out of the plastic ties and away from the rigid fork.

10. Remove the compression spring cups and the lower rubber travel bumpers from the spring (**Figure 46**). Then remove the outer compression spring (A, **Figure 47**) and the inner compression spring (B, **Figure 47**).

11. Remove the lower compression spring (A, **Figure 48**) and the spring rod (B, **Figure 48**) assembly as follows:

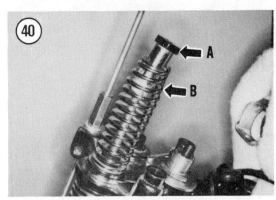

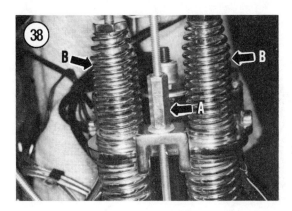

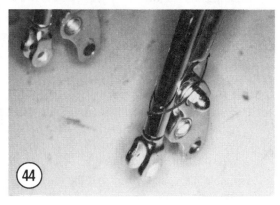

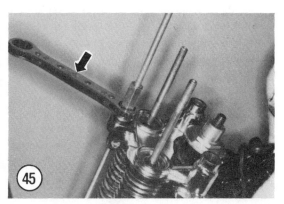

a. Locate the cross-hole drilled in the lower spring rod and insert the end of a #2 Phillips screwdriver into the hole. This will prevent the spring rod assembly from turning when loosening the lower Acorn nut.

b. Loosen and remove the lower Acorn nut (C, **Figure 48**) holding the spring rod to the spring fork assembly. Separate and remove the lower compression spring, spring seat and spring rod assembly.

NOTE
The 2 inner compression springs (both sides) are identical.

CAUTION
The spring rod assembly (B, Figure 48) is comprised of an upper and lower rod assembly. Harley-Davidson recommends that these rods should not be separated.

Inspection

The following steps describe inspection of the spring fork assembly. Because Harley-Davidson

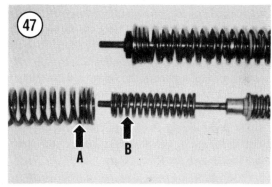

does not list service specifications for the fork spring assembly (except rocker bearings), inspection is performed by close visual inspection of the components. If the front end was involved in a crash, you should have the front fork assembly inspected by a Harley-Davidson dealer.

CAUTION
Before cleaning rubber travel bumpers, make sure the cleaning agent is compatible with rubber. Some types of solvents can cause permanent damage.

1. Clean all components thoroughly in solvent and dry with compressed air. Make sure to remove all anti-seize residue from the upper spring rod and spring restraint threads.

2. Check the spring fork assembly for cracks, bending or other damage. Check the rocker assembly mounting area on each spring fork leg for damage. If the spring fork assembly is damaged, replace it with a new unit.

3. If you separated the left- and right-hand spring sets during disassembly, compare the springs for sag. A difference in length would indicate spring sag. Also inspect the springs for cracks or other visual damage.

4. Check the spring rod assembly for thread damage, bending or other damage. Check the threaded portion on the lower spring rod for bending. You can check the upper spring rod for bending by holding it next to a small square. If the spring rod assembly is damaged, have the new spring rods assembled by a Harley-Davidson dealer.

5. Check the spring seat halves for cracks or severe wear at the spring contact areas. Replace the spring seat halves as a set, if necessary.

6. Check the rubber travel bumpers (**Figure 49**) for cracks, splitting or wear caused from age deterioration.

Assembly/Installation

The lower compression spring assembly should be assembled one side at a time. Refer to **Figure 33** for this procedure.

1. Prior to assembly, perform the *Inspection* procedure to make sure all worn or defective parts have been repaired or replaced. All parts should be thoroughly cleaned before assembly.

2. Assemble the lower compression spring and spring rod assembly as follows:

   a. The upper and lower spring rod assemblies should be assembled before installing the lower compression spring. If you have to replace the spring rod assembly, have the new parts assembled by a Harley-Davidson dealer.

   b. Place the 2 spring seats onto the lower spring rod.

   c. Slide the lower compression spring over the lower spring rod and engage the spring with spring seat (**Figure 50**). Then place the end of the lower spring rod through the spring fork mounting hole and thread the Acorn nut (C, **Figure 48**) onto the end of the spring rod.

   d. Locate the cross-hole drilled in the lower spring rod and insert the end of a #2 Phillips screwdriver into the hole. This will prevent the spring rod assembly from turning when tightening the lower Acorn nut. Then tighten the Acorn nut (C, **Figure 48**) to the torque specification listed in **Table 1**.

3. Assemble the upper (inner) and the outer compression springs as follows:

   a. Slide the upper (inner) compression spring (B, **Figure 47**) over the upper spring rod and seat the spring onto the spring seat.

   b. Slide the outer compression spring (A, **Figure 47**) over the upper spring rod and seat it onto the spring fork assembly.

   c. Place the compression spring cup onto the outer compression spring and insert the lower rubber travel bumper into the compression spring cup. See **Figure 46**.

4. Repeat Steps 2 and 3 to assemble the opposite side.

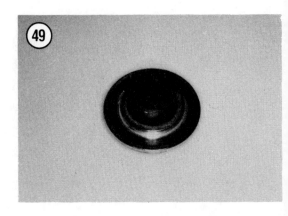

NOTE
It would be helpful to have an assistant on hand when assembling the spring fork and rigid fork assemblies. If you find yourself tackling the job alone, read Steps 5 and 6 completely through to give you an idea of the necessary steps and so that you can have all of the tools and parts close by.

5. To assemble the spring fork onto the rigid fork, grasp the spring fork assembly and place it into position next to the rigid fork so that the lower rubber travel bumpers, compression spring cups and compression springs engage the bottom rigid fork spring brace. Check that the lower rubber travel bumpers seat in the rigid fork spring brace properly.

NOTE
Check that both sides of the spring fork are properly installed in the rigid fork.

6. Install the spring compression tool used during reassembly (**Figure 45**). Insert the steel block between the lower shock absorber mount arms in the spring fork. Secure the block with the shock absorber bolt, washers and Acorn nut. Insert the threaded rod (without the coupling, washers or jam nut) through the headlight mount. Thread the jam nut onto the bottom of the threaded rod and then thread the threaded rod into the block until it bottoms out; tighten the jam nut securely against the steel block with a wrench. Slide a rubber and then a steel washer down the threaded rod until they seat against the headlight mount. Then thread the coupling onto the threaded rod and tighten the coupling against the washers with a wrench. Continue to tighten the coupling until the 2 outer compression springs are

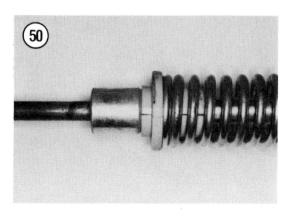

compressed enough to hold the spring fork assembly in position.

WARNING
Plastic ties are installed around the spring fork and rigid fork legs (Step 7) to prevent the spring fork from flying forward when performing the following steps; otherwise, you could suffer serious personal injury if the spring fork should fly up and hit you.

7. Install a large plastic tie around the spring fork and rigid fork legs on both sides of the fork as shown in **Figure 44**. Double-check to make sure the plastic ties are secured properly.

8. With the fork legs secured with the 2 plastic ties, tighten the compression tool coupling (**Figure 45**) to compress the lower compression springs until the rocker mounting holes in the bottom of the spring fork legs are approximately even with the rigid fork leg rocker holes.

9. If the rockers were removed from the rigid fork legs, install and adjust the rockers as described in this chapter. The rocker(s) must be installed onto the rigid fork leg *before* installing them onto the spring fork leg. When the rockers have been installed and adjusted on the rigid fork legs, proceed to Step 10.

10. Install both rockers onto their spring fork leg as described in this chapter.

11. Install the rebound springs as follows:

   a. Oil the spring rod bushing and slide it onto the end of the upper spring rod. Push the bushing down the rod until it bottoms out against the lower rubber travel bumper. See **Figure 43**.

   b. Install the rubber travel bumper over the spring rod and spring rod bushing. See **Figure 42**.

   c. Place the rebound spring cup over the rubber travel bumper so that its shoulder faces up (**Figure 41**), then place the rebound spring onto the spring cup so that the small diameter spring end faces up. See B, **Figure 40**.

   d. Repeat sub-steps a, b and c for the opposite side. When both rebound springs have been installed, proceed to Step 12.

12. Secure and tighten the rebound springs as follows:

   a. Wipe the top 1/2 in. (12.7 mm) of the upper spring rods with an anti-seize lubricant.

12

NOTE

Because of the long thread engagement between the upper spring rod and spring restraint, galling and seizure of these parts is possible due to their exposure to weather and other conditions. If these parts should seize together, the upper spring rod could turn and unthread from the lower spring rod when attempting to loosen the spring restraint at a later date. This would make disassembly extremely difficult. To prevent this from happening, make sure to apply anti-seize as described in sub-step a.

b. Install a spring restraint (A, **Figure 40**) onto an upper spring rod and tighten it until the spring rod protrudes 5/8-3/4 in. (15.8-19.0 mm) from the top of the restraint (**Figure 39**). Repeat for the opposite side. Compare this distance to the distance recorded during reassembly.

c. Place the spring bridge over the upper spring rods so that its curved portion faces *forward*.

d. Install a washer and Acorn nut onto each spring rod. Tighten the spring bridge Acorn nuts to the torque specification listed in **Table 1**.

13. Loosen and remove the spring compression tool. Then cut the plastic ties at fork legs and discard them.

14. Reinstall the shock absorber as described in this chapter.

15. Reposition the headlight housing and its mounting block onto its mounting plate. Check that the headlight wiring harness is routed properly. Secure the headlight housing with its bolt and washer; install the bolt and washer through the mounting plate and thread it into the mounting block. Tighten bolt securely.

16. Reinstall the front fender as described in Chapter Fifteen.

17. Reinstall the front wheel as described in this Chapter Ten.

18. Remove the wood or vinyl wedge from the front brake caliper and install the caliper as described in Chapter Fourteen.

19. Lower the bike from its support so that the front wheel is back onto the ground. Support the bike with its jiffy stand.

WARNING

Do not ride the motorcycle until you are sure the front brake is operating correctly with full hydraulic advantage. Check brake operation by straddling the bike (engine off) and operating the front brake lever while pushing forward on the handlebars.

Rigid Fork
Removal

The front fork assembly consists of the rigid and spring fork assemblies. This procedure describes removal of the rigid fork assembly. If you wish to remove only the spring fork assembly, refer to the spring fork service information in this chapter. This procedure can also be used to remove the spring and rigid fork assembly together. Refer to **Figure 33** when performing procedures in this section.

1. Raise and secure the bike so that the front wheel is off the ground.

2. Remove the front brake caliper and brake line as described in Chapter Fourteen.

NOTE
Insert a piece of vinyl tubing or wood in the caliper in place of the brake disc. That way if the brake lever is inadvertently squeezed, the piston will not be forced out of the cylinder. If this does happen, the caliper may have to be disassembled to reseat the piston and the system will have to be bled.

3. Remove the front wheel as described in Chapter Ten.

4. Remove the front fender as described in Chapter Fifteen.

5. Remove the bolt and washer securing the headlight housing and its mounting block to the mounting plate. Then carefully remove the headlight housing and position it aside and out of the way. You may want to cover the headlight with a towel to prevent it from being damaged.

6. *Spring fork removal*: If it is going to be necessary to remove the spring fork assembly to service the rigid fork assembly, remove the spring fork assembly while the rigid fork is mounted on the bike. Remove the spring fork as described in this chapter.

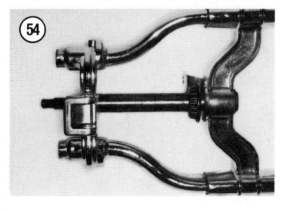

It is easier to remove the spring fork now, than when the rigid fork has been removed from the bike.

7. Remove the handlebar and handlebar risers as described in this chapter.

8. Remove the fork shock absorber as described in this chapter.

9. Loosen and remove the fork stem Acorn nut and washer.

10. Loosen the upper triple clamp pinch bolt.

11. Loosen and remove the rigid fork leg studs from the top of the upper triple clamp.

12. Remove the upper triple clamp assembly.

NOTE
The rigid fork assembly can fall once the bearing retainer is removed in Step 13. Secure the rigid fork before removing the bearing retainer.

13. Loosen and remove the bearing retainer (**Figure 51**) from the fork stem.

14. Remove the dust shield (**Figure 52**) installed under the bearing retainer.

15. Slide the fork assembly out of the steering head and remove it. See A, **Figure 53**.

16. Remove the upper steering bearing (B, **Figure 53**).

Inspection

The following steps describe inspection of the rigid fork assembly. If the front end was involved in a crash, you should have the front fork assembly inspected by a Harley-Davidson dealer.

1. Clean all components thoroughly in solvent and dry with compressed air.

2. Check the rigid fork assembly (**Figure 54**) for cracks, bending or other damage. If you suspect that the rigid fork is bent, have it checked by a Harley-Davidson dealer or by a qualified motorcycle frame alignment shop.

3. Check the rigid fork leg stud threads for stripping or cross-threading. Check the threaded portion on both ends of the stud for bending or other damage. Replace the studs if necessary.

4. Check the fork leg stud threaded holes in the rigid fork for stripping, cross-threading or deposit buildup. The threaded holes should be blown out with compressed air as dirt buildup in the bottom of the hole may prevent the stud from being torqued properly. If necessary, use a tap to true up the threads and to remove any deposits.

12

5. Check the upper triple clamp for cracks or damage. Check the pinch bolt for thread damage. Also check the threads in the triple clamp for damage; use a tap as described in Step 4.

6. Repeat Step 5 to check the bearing retainer. If the hex on the bearing retainer has started to round out, replace the retainer.

7. Inspect the steering stem and the steering head bearings as described in the following procedure.

Steering Stem and Bearing Inspection/Replacement

1. Clean the bearing races in the steering head with solvent. See **Figure 55** (upper) and **Figure 56** (lower).

2. Clean the bearings with solvent and blow dry with compressed air. Hold the bearings to prevent the air jet from spinning them.

> *NOTE*
> *The upper bearing (B, **Figure 53**) has been removed. The lower bearing (**Figure 57**) is mounted on the steering stem in the rigid fork.*

3. Check the races (**Figure 55** and **Figure 56**) for pitting, galling and corrosion. If any of these conditions exist, replace the races and bearings as a set as described in this chapter.

4. Check the bearings for pitting, scratches or discoloration indicating wear or corrosion. Check for damaged or loose bearing rollers. Replace the bearings and races as a set.

5. Replace the lower bearing (**Figure 57**) as follows:

   a. The fork stem bracket has 2 notches that can be used to remove the bearing and the lower dust shield.

   b. Place 2 large wide-blade screwdrivers into the fork stem bracket notches as shown in **Figure 58**. Then work the bearing and the lower dust shield off the steering stem bearing surface. When the bearing and dust shield are free, remove them (**Figure 59**).

   c. Clean the fork stem with solvent before installing the new bearing and dust shield.

   d. Install the new bearing and dust shield by driving the bearing onto the fork stem with a driver that fits against the inner bearing race. Drive the bearing onto the fork stem until the dust shield and bearing bottoms out.

6. The fork stem (**Figure 60**) should be replaced by a Harley-Davidson dealer.

Bearing Race Replacement

1. To replace the races (**Figure 55** and **Figure 56**), Harley-Davidson recommends to weld a bead around the inside of the race. When the weld and race cool, the bead will shrink the race and you can then remove it. This procedure should be referred to a Harley-Davidson dealer or repair shop familiar with Harley repair.

> *NOTE*
> *Save the old race so that it can be used to install the new race.*

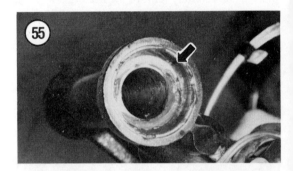

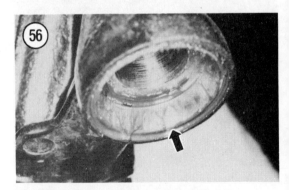

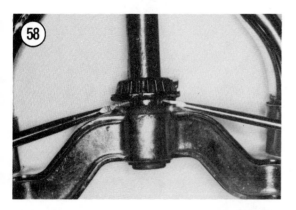

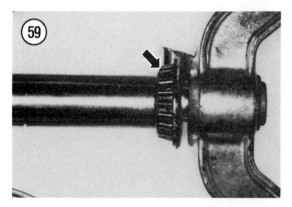

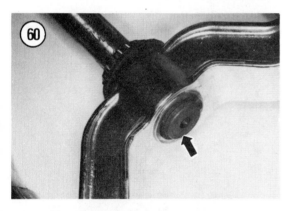

2. Install the new race as follows:

   a. Grind the outer circumference of the old race so that it can slide into the frame steering head.

   b. Align the new race with steering head and drive it squarely into the steering head using the old race as a driver. Drive the new race into the steering head until it bottoms out against the shoulder in the head.

   NOTE
   Make sure the race is seated firmly in the steering head. An incorrectly installed race will affect the bike's handling.

Rigid Fork
Installation

This section describes installation of the rigid fork (and the spring fork if attached to the rigid fork). If the spring fork is removed from the rigid fork, first install the rigid fork as described in this section. Then install the spring fork as described in this chapter. Refer to **Figure 33** when performing this procedure.

1. Make sure the upper and lower outer bearing races are properly seated in the steering head tube. Wipe the face of each bearing race with bearing grease. See **Figure 56** and **Figure 57**.

2. Pack the bearings with bearing grease before installation.

   NOTE
   Before installing the fork assembly, check once more that the steering bearings are properly lubricated and correctly installed.

3. With an assistant's help, insert the fork stem up through the frame's steering head (**Figure 61**) and hold it firmly in place, then install the upper bearing (B, **Figure 53**).

4. Install the upper dust shield (**Figure 52**) over the fork stem and install the bearing retainer onto the stem so that its hex head faces down. See **Figure 51**.

5A. On 1989-1992 models, tighten the bearing retainer (**Figure 51**) until there is no appreciable play in the steering bearings. Then turn the fork assembly from side-to-side; the fork should pivot smoothly with no sign of roughness or tightness. If the fork does not pivot smoothly, remove the bearing retainer and recheck the bearings and fork stem.

12

5B. On 1993-on models, tighten the bearing retainer (**Figure 51**) to 45-50 ft.-lb. (61-68 N•m) and let set for 1 minute to seat bearings. Then loosen the bearing retainer and then tighten until there is no appreciable play in the steering bearings. Turn the fork assembly from side to side; the fork should pivot smoothly with no sign of roughness or tightness. If the fork does not pivot smoothly, remove the bearing retainer and recheck the bearings and fork stem.

6. Place the upper triple clamp over the fork stem and onto the rigid fork legs (**Figure 33**).

7. Install and tighten the rigid fork leg studs as follows:

    a. Thread both studs into the rigid fork legs, then tighten them both hand-tight.

    b. Using a torque wrench, tighten the rigid fork leg studs to the torque specification listed in **Table 1**.

8. Wipe the upper triple clamp pinch bolt with anti-seize and install the bolt into the triple clamp. Tighten the pinch bolt to the torque specification listed in **Table 1**.

9. Adjust the steering as described under *Steering Adjustment* in this chapter.

10. Install the fork stem washer over the fork stem and install the Acorn nut. Tighten the Acorn nut to the torque specification listed in **Table 1**.

11. Turn the fork from side-to-side once again (Step 5). If the fork does not pivot smoothly, readjust the steering as described in this chapter.

12. Reinstall the handlebar risers and handlebar as described in this chapter.

13. *Spring fork assembly*: If the spring fork was originally removed from the rigid fork, install it now as described in this chapter.

14. Install the shock absorber as described in this chapter.

15. Reposition the headlight housing and its mounting block onto its mounting plate. Check that the headlight wiring harness is routed properly. Secure the headlight housing with its bolt and washer; install the bolt and washer through the mounting plate and thread it into the mounting block. Tighten the bolt securely.

16. Reinstall the front fender as described in Chapter Fifteen.

17. Reinstall the front wheel as described in Chapter Ten.

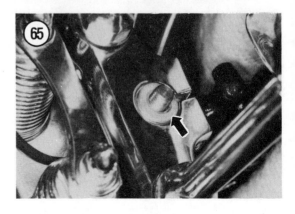

18. Remove the wood or vinyl wedge from the front brake caliper and install the caliper as described in Chapter Fourteen.

19. Lower the bike from its support so that the front wheel is back onto the ground. Support the bike with its jiffy stand.

WARNING
Do not ride the motorcycle until you are sure the front brake is operating correctly with full hydraulic advantage. Check brake operation by straddling the

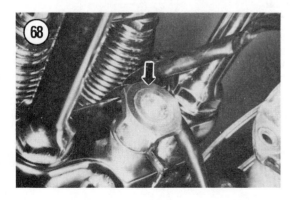

bike (engine off) and operating the front brake lever while pushing forward on the handlebars.

STEERING ADJUSTMENT

Steering Tool Fabrication

To adjust the steering, you will have to make a steering adjust tool. Purchase a bearing retainer (part No. 48306-88) and 2 roll pins (part No. 614) from your Harley-Davidson dealer. See **Figure 62**. Cut the roll pins in half with a hacksaw, then select 3 pin halves which are approximately the same length. Coat one end of each pin with Loctite 242 (blue) and tap the pins into the pre-drilled holes located in the bearing retainer. See **Figure 63**. Allow the Loctite to set up before using the tool.

Adjustment

1. Fabricate the steering tool as previously described.
2. Support the bike so that the front wheel clears the ground.
3. Remove the windshield (if used) and all other accessory weight from the handlebar and front forks that could affect this adjustment.

NOTE
If any control cable affects handlebar movement, disconnect it.

4. Remove the steering stem Acorn nut (**Figure 64**) and washer (**Figure 65**).
5. Loosen the upper triple clamp pinch bolts (**Figure 66**).
6. Hang a plumb bob from the hole in the rear of the front fender (**Figure 67**).
7A. On 1989-1992 models, tighten the bearing adjuster (**Figure 68**) until there is no appreciable play in the steering bearings.
7B. On 1993-on models, tighten the bearing adjuster (**Figure 68**) to 45-50 ft.-lbs. (61-68 N•m).

NOTE
*Align the pins in the bearing adjuster (**Figure 69**) with the holes in the bearing retainer (**Figure 70**).*

8. Turn the front end all the way to the left (full lock).
9. Place a ruler directly underneath the plum bob so that the point on the plum bob aligns with zero (**Figure 71**).

12

10. Lightly bring the front wheel to its balance point, then tap it until it falls-away to the right. Measure the distance from zero to fall-away. Steering adjustment is correct when the zero to fall-away distance is 4-6 in. (10.2-15.2 cm). If necessary, adjust steering with the bearing adjuster (**Figure 68**). Repeat until adjustment is correct.

11. Remove the plumb bob and ruler when adjustment is correct.

12. Tighten the triple clamp pinch bolts (**Figure 66**) to the torque specification listed in **Table 1**.

13. Install the washer (**Figure 65**) and the fork stem Acorn nut (**Figure 64**). Tighten the Acorn nut to the torque specification listed in **Table 1**.

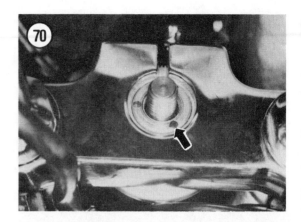

Table 1 FRONT SUSPENSION TIGHTENING TORQUES

	ft.-lb.	N•m
Handlebar screws	12-15	17-21
Bearing retainer locknut	95-105	129-142
Lower spring rod Acorn nut	20-25	27-34
Spring bridge Acorn nuts	30-35	41-47
Rigid fork leg studs	60-65	83-90
Upper triple clamp pinch bolts		
1992 and earlier models	45-50	61-68
1993-on	20-25	27-34
Fork stem Acorn nut	20-25	27-34
Shock absorber Acorn nuts	45-50	61-68
Riser locknuts	25-35	34-47
Rocker pivot stud Acorn nut	45-50	61-68

CHAPTER THIRTEEN

REAR SUSPENSION

The twin shock absorbers are mounted horizontally underneath the transmission and between the lower frame rails.

This chapter includes repair and replacement procedures for rear shocks and rear swing arm.

Tightening torques are listed in **Table 1** at the end of the chapter.

REAR SHOCK ABSORBERS

The 2 rear shock absorbers are mounted horizontally below the transmission and within the lower frame rails.

The shock absorbers used on 1984-1988 models use separate reservoirs, each with a single pressure hose connecting the reservoir to the main shock housing (**Figure 1**). The reservoirs store additional shock oil and are nitrogen charged (approximately 15 psi [1.05 kg/cm^2]) to help prevent cavitation problems from the horizontal shock mounting position. No external adjustment is provided for on reservoir-equipped shock absorbers.

The shock absorbers used on 1989 and later models do not use reservoirs (**Figure 2**). These shock absorbers are adjustable, however, by turning an adjuster plate at the rear of the shock housing with a special spanner wrench.

Removal

Refer to **Figure 1** or **Figure 2** for this procedure.
1. Support the bike in such a way as to allow you access to the shock absorbers. Make sure the bike is stable and secure; you will be working underneath it to remove the shock absorbers.

> *CAUTION*
> *The shocks are under pressure. Do not attempt to loosen or disconnect the hose connection at the reservoir or shock body (**Figure 1**). Do not attempt to disassemble the shock absorbers (**Figure 1** or **Figure 2**). These shocks cannot be recharged. If you loosen a hose connection, the charge will be lost and you must replace the shock.*

2. Remove the rear wheel as described in Chapter Ten.
3. If the muffler interferes with removal of the right-hand shock bolts, remove the muffler or exhaust pipe assembly as described in Chapter Eight.
4A. *Reservoir models*: Remove the shock assembly as follows:

> *NOTE*
> *The left- and right-hand shock absorbers have different part numbers. This is due to the different hose angles on the shock body that are required for proper*

13

shock mounting and hose routing. Label the shock absorbers so you don't mix them up during installation.

a. Locate the reservoirs between the swing arm and frame. Before removing the reservoirs from their mounting position, compare the hose routing of both reservoirs with the routing diagram in **Figure 3** (1984-1985) or **Figure 4** (1986-1988) for your model. Make any notes on the diagram to help with the routing of hoses during reassembly.

NOTE
Circuit breakers are mounted onto the front of the inner rear wheel cover. Make sure to remove them or to disconnect all

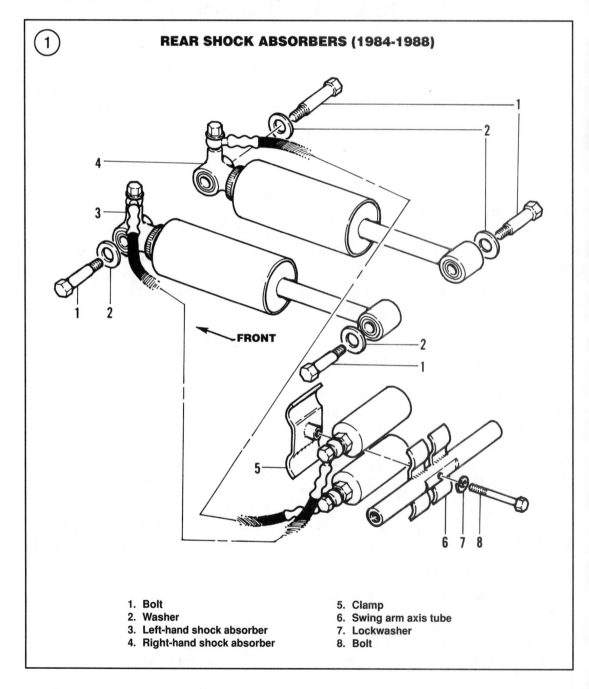

REAR SHOCK ABSORBERS (1984-1988)

FRONT

1. **Bolt**
2. **Washer**
3. **Left-hand shock absorber**
4. **Right-hand shock absorber**
5. **Clamp**
6. **Swing arm axis tube**
7. **Lockwasher**
8. **Bolt**

electrical connectors as required before removing the cover.

b. Remove the inner rear wheel cover (**Figure 5**).

c. Remove the bolt and washer (**Figure 6**) holding the reservoir brackets in place and allow the reservoirs to hang down from their mounting position. Do *not* disconnect the hoses. See **Figure 6**.

d. Before removing a shock absorber, identify its reservoir so that you can trace the reservoir hose and reservoir removal path.

e. Remove the front (**Figure 7**) and rear (**Figure 8**) bolts and washers holding the shock body to the frame, and remove the shock together with the reservoir and attaching hose. Handle the reservoir carefully to avoid damaging the reservoir housing or hose.

f. Remove the opposite shock absorber and reservoir.

4B. *Non-reservoir models*: Remove the front (**Figure 7**) and rear (**Figure 8**) bolts and washers holding the shock body to the frame and remove the shock absorber. Repeat for the opposite shock absorber.

Inspection

1. Clean the shock absorbers (and reservoirs) in solvent and dry thoroughly (**Figure 9**). Check the shock absorbers for leakage or shaft damage. On reservoir shocks, check the hose fittings (**Figure 10**) carefully for leakage or damage. Check the shock shaft for cracks, bending or other damage (**Figure 11**). The shock absorbers on all models are not rebuildable. If a shock absorber is damaged or leaking, it must be discarded and a new shock installed.

2. *1989-on*: Check the adjuster plate locknut (**Figure 2**) for tightness.

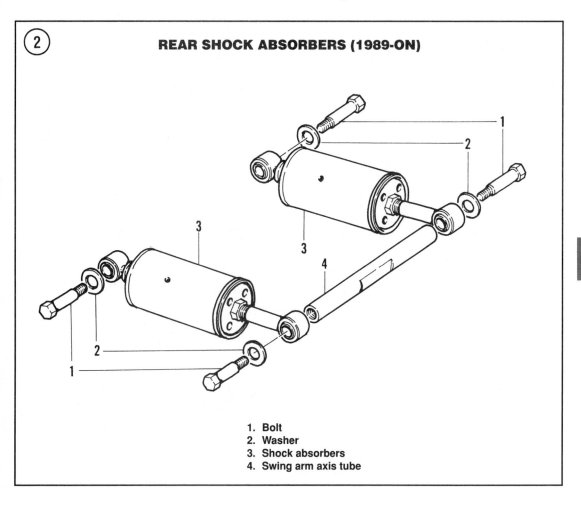

(2) **REAR SHOCK ABSORBERS (1989-ON)**

13

1. **Bolt**
2. **Washer**
3. **Shock absorbers**
4. **Swing arm axis tube**

3. Check the shock bolt threads for stripping, cross-threading or deposit buildup. The mating thread holes in the frame should be checked for the same conditions. If necessary, use a tap or die to true up the threads and to remove any deposits.

NOTE
Grade 8 bolts are used to secure the shock absorbers to the frame rails. If you are replacing these bolts, make sure to purchase Grade 8 bolts. In addition, make sure the grip length on the replacement bolt—the length of the unthreaded portion of the bolt shank—matches the grip length on the discarded bolt.

4. Check the washers for cupping, deformation, cracks or other damage. If necessary, replace the washers with the same size and thickness washers.

CAUTION
Because of the high shock absorber torque reading, it is critical that the bolts and washers used to secure the shocks are replaced with exact replacement parts. Do not install an inferior bolt or washer or you may cause secondary damage from fastener failure.

5. On reservoir models, check the reservoir mounting brackets and bolt for damage.

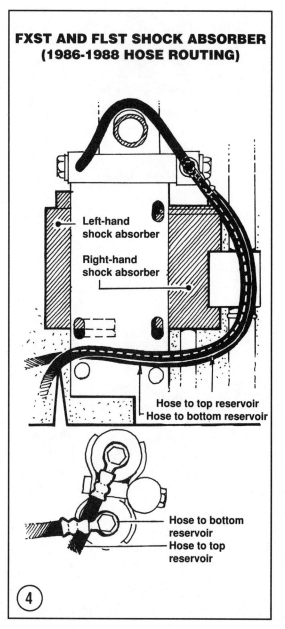

FXST AND FLST SHOCK ABSORBER (1986-1988 HOSE ROUTING)

Left-hand shock absorber

Right-hand shock absorber

Hose to top reservoir
Hose to bottom reservoir

Hose to bottom reservoir
Hose to top reservoir

④

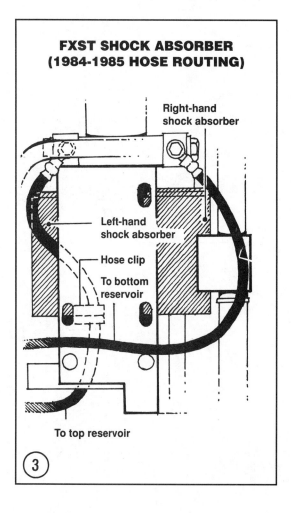

FXST SHOCK ABSORBER (1984-1985 HOSE ROUTING)

Right-hand shock absorber

Left-hand shock absorber

Hose clip

To bottom reservoir

To top reservoir

③

Installation

Refer to **Figure 1** (1984-1988) or **Figure 2** (1989-on) when performing this procedure.

1. Prior to assembly, perform the *Inspection* procedure to make sure all worn or defective parts have been repaired or replaced.

2. Install a washer onto each shock mounting bolt and coat the bolt threads with Loctite 242 (blue). Then install the rear mounting bolt and washer into the rear shock mounting eye so that the bolt head faces out. Repeat for the other shock bolt.

3A. *Reservoir models*: Install the shock absorbers as follows:

> *NOTE*
> *When installing the shock absorbers, follow the left- and right-hand identification marks made prior to removal. The shock absorbers must be installed on their original side.*

> *WARNING*
> *Do **not** attempt to loosen the reservoir hose mounting bolt at the shock absorber to change the hose angle.*

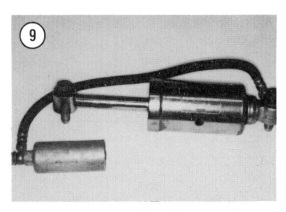

13

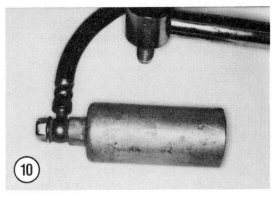

a. Align one of the shock absorbers with the frame (housing end faces forward) and install it. Repeat for the other shock absorber.

b. Thread the rear bolts into the frame bracket (**Figure 7**). Tighten bolts finger-tight.

c. Install the front shock mounting bolts so that the bolt head faces out (**Figure 8**). Tighten bolts finger-tight.

d. Route the reservoir hoses for your model as shown in **Figure 3** or **Figure 4**. On 1984-1985 models, install the left-hand reservoir hose in the clamp at the bottom of the transmission mounting plate; otherwise, the hose may become damaged.

e. After identifying the shock absorbers, place the reservoirs in the front reservoir clamp (**Figure 6**) and place the clamp (with the reservoirs) against the swing axis tube clamp. Align the holes in both clamps and insert the screw (with its lockwasher) through the rear clamp, between the reservoirs' bodies and thread into the front clamp.

f. Double-check to make sure the reservoir hoses are properly routed. Then tighten the reservoir mounting screw securely.

g. Install the inner rear wheel cover (**Figure 5**). Reconnect all electrical connectors as required.

3B. *Non-reservoir models*: Install the shock absorbers into the frame. Thread the 2 rear shock bolts into the frame bracket mounting holes. Install the 2 front bolts and washers so that the bolt head on each bolt faces out. Tighten all 4 mounting bolts finger-tight.

NOTE
*The Snap-On Torque Adaptor SRES24 (**Figure 12**) or equivalent will be required to tighten the bolts. Because the torque adapter is a horizontal adapter, it will effectively lengthen the torque wrench—the torque valve indicated on the torque wrench will not be the same amount of torque actually applied to the fastener. When using a torque wrench with a horizontal adapter, it will be necessary to compute the torque reading. In computing the torque reading, you will need to know the lever length of your torque wrench, the center-to-center length of your torque adaptor and the*

*actual bolt tightening torque. **Figure 13** shows how to do this.*

4. Mount the torque adaptor onto the torque wrench (**Figure 14**). Then install the torque adaptor/torque wrench assembly onto one of the shock bolts (**Figure 15**). Using the example in **Figure 13** to compute the torque reading, tighten the shock mounting bolts to 115-130 ft.-lb. (158.7-179.4 N•m). Repeat for each shock mounting bolt.

5. Install the rear wheel as described in Chapter Ten.

6. Lower the bike to the ground.

Rear Shock Adjustment (1989-on)

The spring preload on these shock absorbers can be varied to best suit the vehicle load and riding conditions. Refer to **Figure 16** when making this adjustment.

1. Support the bike in such a way as to allow you access to the shock absorbers. Make sure the bike is

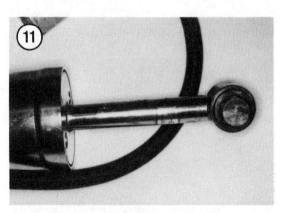

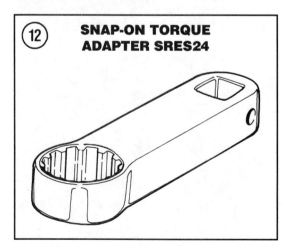

SNAP-ON TORQUE
ADAPTER SRES24

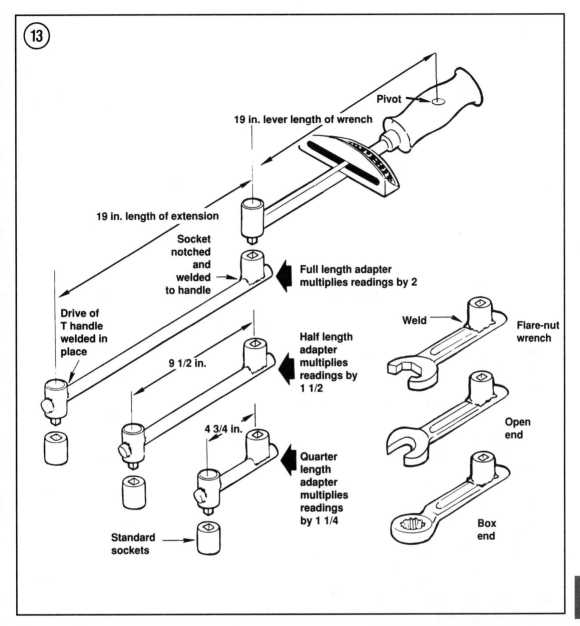

⑬

Pivot

19 in. lever length of wrench

19 in. length of extension

Socket notched and welded to handle

Full length adapter multiplies readings by 2

Drive of T handle welded in place

Weld

Flare-nut wrench

9 1/2 in.

Half length adapter multiplies readings by 1 1/2

4 3/4 in.

Open end

Quarter length adapter multiplies readings by 1 1/4

Standard sockets

Box end

13

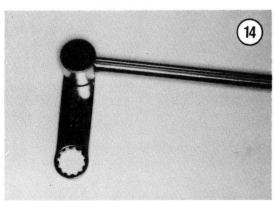

⑭

⑮

stable and secure; you will be working underneath it to adjust the shock absorbers.

> *NOTE*
> *Mark the adjuster plate hole on each shock absorber before adjusting them.*

> *WARNING*
> *Both shock absorbers must be adjusted to the same setting. Having the shock absorbers adjusted to different settings may cause difficult handling and loss of control.*

2. Loosen the locknut on each shock absorber.

3. Using the spanner wrench found in your bike's tool kit, turn the adjuster plate counterclockwise (outward) to increase spring preload or clockwise to decrease it.

4. Tighten the locknuts against their adjuster plate.

REAR SWING ARM

The triangulated swing arm pivots on 2 spherical bearings. A pivot bolt is inserted through each bearing from the outside of the swing arm and is threaded into an axis tube placed horizontally across the front of the swing arm. The axis tube is also used to help secure the remote shock reservoirs used on 1984-1988 models.

The spherical bearings are sealed and permanently lubricated. They may last the life of the bike if they are not damaged. The only maintenance required to the bearings is to wipe their outer surface off with a rag periodically and to check them for damage.

Damage to the bearings or swing arm can greatly affect handling performance and if worn parts are not replaced they can produce erratic and dangerous handling. Common symptoms are wheel hop, pulling to one side during acceleration and pulling to the other side during braking.

Minor changes were made to the rear frame section and to the swing arm starting with 1986 models.

Refer to **Figure 17** (1984-1988) or **Figure 18** (1989-on) when performing procedures in this section.

Removal

1. Support the bike in such a way as to allow you access to the rear shock absorber bolts and swing arm. Make sure the bike is stable and secure; you will be working underneath it to disconnect the rear shock mounting bolts.

2. Remove the mufflers as described in Chapter Eight.

3. Remove the rear wheel as described in Chapter Ten.

> *NOTE*
> *It is not necessary to disconnect the brake hydraulic lines. Instead, hang the brake caliper from the frame with wire or Bunjee cords.*

4. Cut the brake hose clamp at the swing arm (**Figure 19**), then remove the rear brake caliper from the swing arm as described in Chapter Fourteen.

> *NOTE*
> *Circuit breakers are mounted onto the front of the inner rear wheel cover. Make sure to remove them or to disconnect all electrical connectors as required before removing the cover.*

5. Remove the inner rear wheel cover (**Figure 5**).

6. *Reservoir models*: If your model uses reservoir-type shock absorbers, remove the reservoirs from the swing arm axis tube as described under *Shock Absorber Removal* in this chapter.

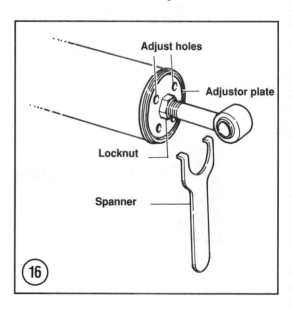

Adjust holes

Adjustor plate

Locknut

Spanner

(16)

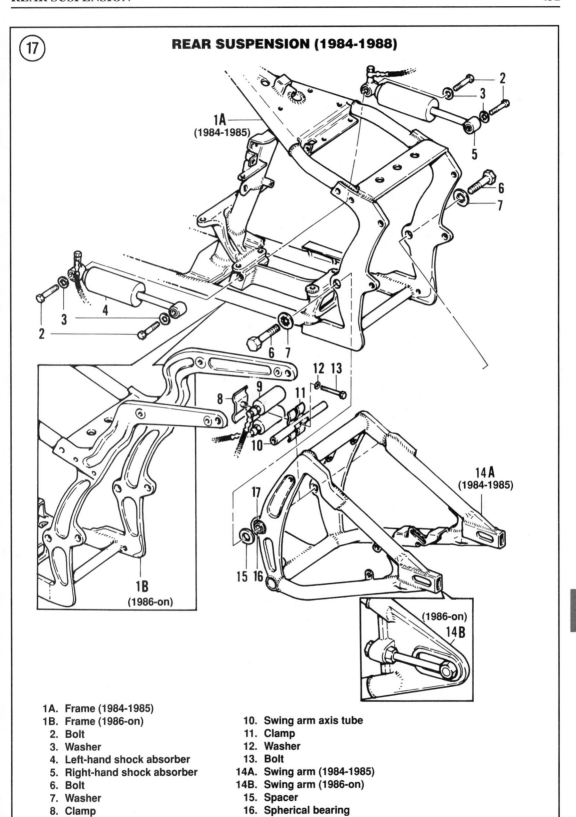

REAR SUSPENSION (1984-1988)

1A. (1984-1985)
1B. (1986-on)
14A. (1984-1985)
14B. (1986-on)

13

1A. Frame (1984-1985)
1B. Frame (1986-on)
2. Bolt
3. Washer
4. Left-hand shock absorber
5. Right-hand shock absorber
6. Bolt
7. Washer
8. Clamp
9. Reservoir
10. Swing arm axis tube
11. Clamp
12. Washer
13. Bolt
14A. Swing arm (1984-1985)
14B. Swing arm (1986-on)
15. Spacer
16. Spherical bearing
17. Circlip

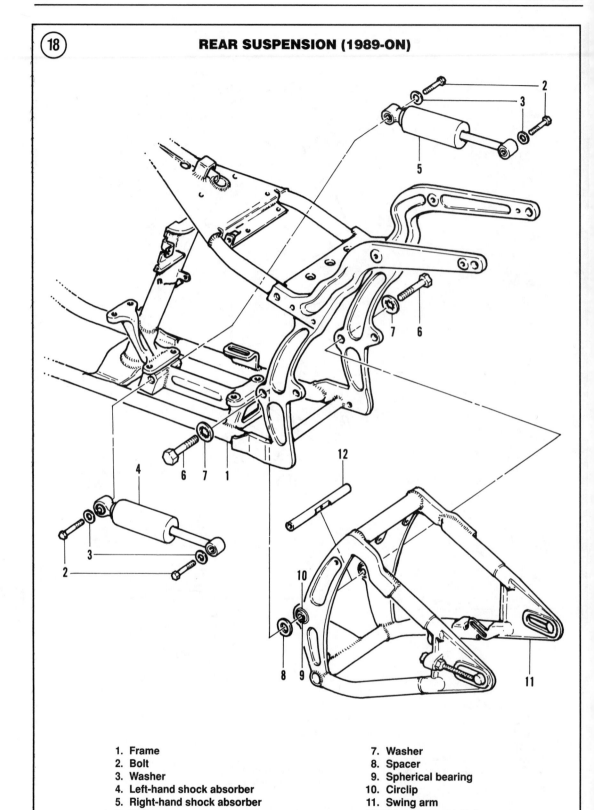

REAR SUSPENSION (1989-ON)

1. Frame
2. Bolt
3. Washer
4. Left-hand shock absorber
5. Right-hand shock absorber
6. Bolt
7. Washer
8. Spacer
9. Spherical bearing
10. Circlip
11. Swing arm
12. Swing arm axis tube

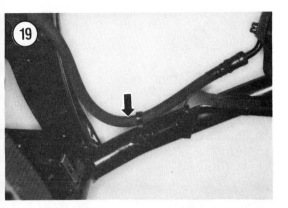

CAUTION
The reservoir shocks are under pressure. Do not attempt to loosen or disconnect the hose connection at the reservoir or shock body. These shocks cannot be recharged. If you loosen a hose connection, the charge will be lost and you must replace the shock.

7. Remove the bolts and washers securing the shock absorbers to the swing arm (**Figure 20**). Do not remove the front shock absorber mounting bolts.

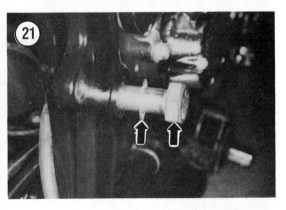

NOTE
Prior to completing swing arm removal, check its condition by grasping the swing arm on both sides and trying to move it from side to side. If the free play is excessive (approximately 1/32 in. [0.8 mm] of movement), first check for damaged or missing spacers installed between the swing arm and frame on both sides. If the spacers are correctly installed and the pivot bolts properly tightened, the swing arm bearings may be damaged.

NOTE
To prevent the swing arm axis tube from turning when loosening the pivot bolts in Step 8, hold the axis tube with a wrench across the flats machined in the middle of the axis tube.

8. Loosen and remove the swing arm pivot bolts and washers (**Figure 21**) from both sides of the swing arm. Then pull the swing arm (**Figure 22**) away from the frame, accounting for the left- and right-hand spacers installed between the swing arm and frame. See **Figure 23**.

13

NOTE
Because swing arm removal is required to replace the drive belt, inspect it now, so that you can purchase and install a new belt if required. Refer to Chapter Ten for belt inspection.

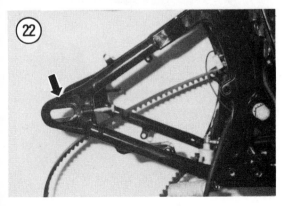

Inspection

1. Clean the swing arm thoroughly in solvent. Do not scrub or clean the bearings vigorously.

2. Inspect the swing arm (**Figure 24**) for wear, cracks or damage. Replace the swing arm if necessary.

3. Wipe the bearing bore with a clean rag to remove all dirt and residue from the bearing. Then visually check the bearing (**Figure 25**) for damage. If a bearing is damaged, replace both bearings as described in this chapter.

4. Make sure that the bearing circlips (**Figure 26**) are seated completely in the swing arm circlip grooves.

5. Check the shock pivot bolt threads (**Figure 27**) for stripping, cross-threading or deposit buildup. If necessary, use a tap to true up the threads and to remove any deposits.

6. Check the swing arm axis shaft (**Figure 28**) for cracks, bending or other damage. Check the swing arm axis shaft threads (**Figure 29**) for the same conditions described in Step 5.

7. Check the swing arm spacers for cracks or damage. If necessary, replace with the same size and thickness spacer.

8. Replace the swing arm pivot bolts (**Figure 30**) if they show any sign of thread damage. Make sure to replace with the same grade bolt.

Installation

Refer to **Figure 17** or **Figure 18** when performing this procedure.

1. Prior to assembly, perform the *Inspection* procedure to make sure all worn or defective parts have

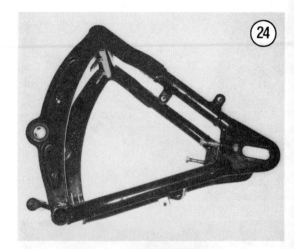

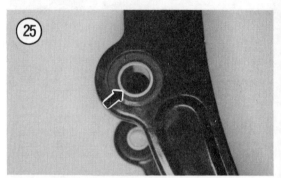

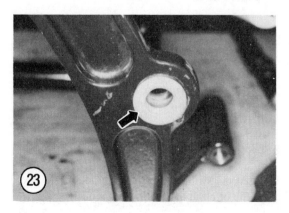

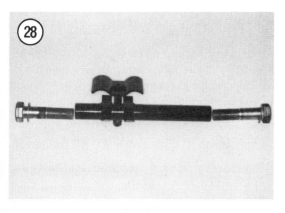

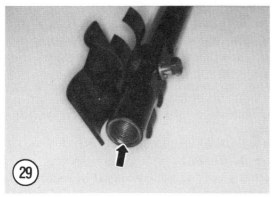

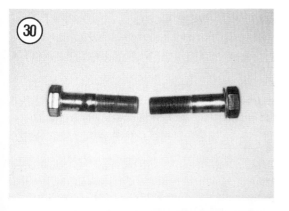

been replaced. All parts should be thoroughly cleaned before installation.

2. Install a washer on each swing arm pivot bolt, then coat the bolt threads with an anti-seize compound.

NOTE
Install the rear shock absorber bolts and washers through the shock absorbers (Figure 31) before installing the swing arm into the frame.

NOTE
Be sure to slide the swing arm through the drive chain or drive belt before installing the swing arm in Step 3—the chain or belt must be on the inside of the swing arm.

3. Position the swing arm in the frame so that the pivot bolt holes in the frame line up with the bearings in the swing arm. Place the swing arm axis tube between the swing arm bearing bores. Insert a pivot bolt and washer (**Figure 21**) through the frame hole and then place a spacer between the frame and swing arm (**Figure 23**). Continue installing the pivot bolt by inserting it through the spacer and then threading it into the end of the axis tube. Tighten the bolt finger-tight.

NOTE
Make sure the drive belt is routed around the swing arm as shown in Figure 32.

NOTE
Make sure the brake hose is routed over the swing arm axis tube as shown in Figure 33.

13

4. Repeat Step 3 to install the opposite pivot bolt. Make sure to install the spacer between frame and swing arm.

5. Pivot the swing arm up and down. It should pivot smoothly.

6. Hold the axis tube with a wrench across its 2 flats and tighten the swing arm pivot bolts to the torque specification listed in **Table 1**.

> *CAUTION*
> *Make sure the swing arm pivot bolts are torqued to the correct specifications. An incorrect torque reading may cause swing arm misalignment.*

7. Pivot the swing arm once again. It should move smoothly with no sign of roughness or tightness. Stand behind the swing arm and visually check swing arm alignment in relation to the frame. There should be no apparent distortion or bending. If there is a problem, check for a cracked or damaged frame or swing arm member.

8. Remount the shock absorbers to the swing arm brackets and install the shock reservoirs (if used) as described in this chapter.

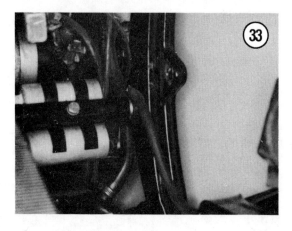

9. Reinstall the rear brake caliper (Chapter Fourteen).

10. Reinstall the inner rear wheel cover (**Figure 5**). Reconnect all electrical connectors as required.

11. Reinstall the rear wheel (Chapter Ten).

12. Install the muffler (Chapter Eight).

Rear Swing Arm Bearing Replacement

The spherical bearings are pressed into the swing arm and secured with a circlip.

> *CAUTION*
> *Do not remove the bearings for inspection purposes. Never reinstall a bearing that has been removed. During removal it becomes slightly damaged and is no longer true to alignment. If installed, it may create an unsafe riding condition.*

1. Remove the swing arm as described in this chapter.

2. Remove the circlip from the groove in the swing arm (**Figure 26**).

3. Using a drift, drive the bearing (**Figure 25**) out of the swing arm bore.

4. Thoroughly clean out the inside surfaces of the pivot portions of the swing arm with solvent and dry with compressed air.

5. Check the circlip grooves in the swing arm for cracks or damage.

6. Install a new bearing into the swing arm. Use a suitable size socket that matches the outer race of the bearing. Tap the bearing in slowly and squarely until it seats completely. Make sure it is properly seated.

7. Install the bearing circlip into the swing arm groove. Make sure the circlip seats in the groove completely. See **Figure 26**.

8. Repeat for the bearing on the other side.

9. Install the swing arm as described in this chapter.

Table 1 REAR SUSPENSION TIGHTENING TORQUES		
	ft.-lb.	**N•m**
Shock absorber mounting bolts	See text	
Swing arm pivot bolts	120-150	165.6-207

CHAPTER FOURTEEN

BRAKES

The brake system consists of disc brakes on the front and rear. This chapter describes repair and replacement procedure for all brake components.

The disc brakes are actuated by hydraulic fluid from the master cylinder. The master cylinder is controlled by the hand or foot lever. As the brake pads wear, the brake fluid level drops in the master cylinder reservoir and automatically adjusts for pad wear.

When working on hydraulic brake systems, it is necessary that the work area and all tools be absolutely clean. Any tiny particles of foreign matter or grit on the caliper assembly or the master cylinder can damage the components. Also, sharp tools must not be used inside the caliper or on the caliper piston. If there is any doubt about your ability to correctly and safely carry out major service on the brake components, take the job to a Harley-Davidson dealer or qualified Harley repair shop.

Table 1 and **Table 2** are at the end of the chapter.

Disc Brake System Service Hints

Consider the following when servicing the front and rear disc brake systems.

1. Disc brake components rarely require disassembly, so do not disassemble them unless necessary.

2. When adding brake fluid use only a type clearly marked DOT 5 and use it from a sealed container.

3. Always keep the master cylinder's reservoir cover closed to prevent dust or moisture from entering.

4. Use only DOT 5 brake fluid to wash parts. Never clean any internal brake component with solvent.

Solvents will cause the seals to swell and distort and require replacement.

5. Whenever *any* brake line has been removed from the brake system the system is considered "opened" and must be bled to remove air bubbles. Also, if the brake feels "spongy," this usually means there are air bubbles in the system and it must be bled. For safe brake operation, refer to *Bleeding the System* in this chapter for complete details.

FRONT BRAKE PADS

There is no recommended mileage interval for changing the friction pads in the disc brake. Pad wear depends greatly on riding habits and conditions. The pads should be checked for wear initially at 500 miles (800 km), then every 2,500 miles (4,000 km) and replaced when the lining thickness reaches 1/16 in. (1.6 mm) from the brake pad backing plate. To maintain an even brake pressure on the disc always replace both pads in the caliper at the same time.

Replacement

Refer to **Figure 1** for this procedure.

1. To prevent accidental application of the front brake lever, place a spacer between the front brake lever and the hand grip. Hold the spacer in place with a large rubber band, a tie wrap or piece of tape.

2A. *Springer models*: Remove the brake caliper as follows:

    a. Remove the lower brake caliper mounting bolt (**Figure 2**).

①

FRONT BRAKE CALIPER

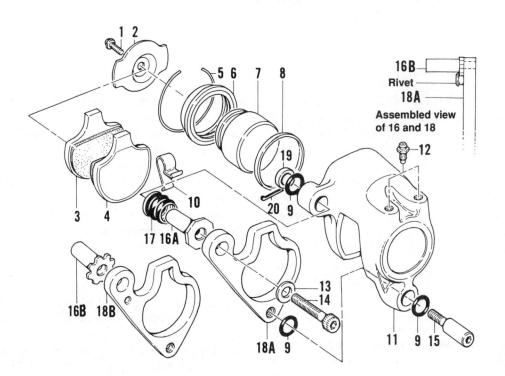

16B
Rivet
18A

Assembled view
of 16 and 18

1. Screw
2. Pad retainer
3. Brake pads
4. Retaining wire
5. Dust boot
6. Piston
7. Piston seal
8. Cotter pin (Springer)
9. Washer (Springer)
10. O-ring
11. Spring clip
12. Caliper bracket
   (non-springer models shown)
13. O-ring
14. Bleed screw
15. Housing
16. Mounting bolt
17. Threaded bushing
18. Washer
19. Bolt
20. Bolt (Springer)
21. Boot

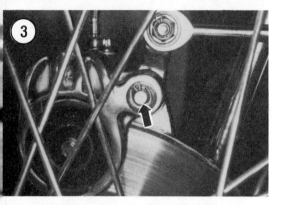

b. Remove the upper brake caliper mounting bolt cotter pin and washer (**Figure 3**); discard the cotter pin. Then unscrew and remove the bolt and its outer washer (**Figure 4**).

2B. *All other models*: The front brake caliper is mounted on the front fork slider with 2 mounting bolts (**Figure 5**). Remove both bolts.

3. Lift the brake caliper off of the brake disc.

4. Remove the outer pad, pad holder and spring clip as an assembly (**Figure 6**).

5. Remove the screw (**Figure 7**) and remove the inner brake pad (**Figure 8**).

6. Push the outer pad free of the spring clip and remove it. See **Figure 9**.

7. Check the brake pads (**Figure 10**) for wear or damage. Replace the brake pads if they are worn to 1/16 in. (1.6 mm) or less (**Figure 11**). Replace both pads as a set.

8. Replace the caliper bolts (**Figure 12**) if necessary.

9. Check the pad retainer (**Figure 13**) for damage, replace if necessary.

10. When new pads are installed in the caliper the master cylinder brake fluid level will rise as the caliper piston is repositioned. Clean the top of the

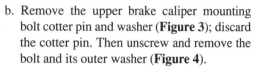

14

master cylinder of all dirt and foreign matter. Remove the cap and diaphragm from the master cylinder and slowly push the caliper piston (**Figure 14**) into the caliper. Constantly check the reservoir to make sure brake fluid does not overflow. Remove fluid, if necessary, prior to it overflowing. The piston should move freely. If not and if there is evidence of it sticking in the cylinder, the caliper should be removed and serviced as described in this chapter.

11. Install the spring clip at the top of the pad holder as shown in **Figure 15** (Non-Springer models) or A, **Figure 16** (Springer models).

12. Place the brake pad with the insulator backing on top of the spring clip with the lower end of the pad slightly entering the pad holder opening. With the brake pad insulator backing facing toward the pad holder, push the brake pad down until it is held firmly in the pad holder by the spring clip.

13. Insert the outer brake pad/pad holder assembly into the caliper so that the brake pad insulator backing faces against the piston. See **Figure 6**.

> *WARNING*
> *The spring clip loop and the brake pad friction material must face away from the piston. Brake failure will occur if the brakes are assembled incorrectly.*

14. Install the inner brake pad (without the insulator backing) in the caliper recessed seat (**Figure 8**).

15. Insert the pad retainer within the counterbore inside the caliper. Install the self-tapping screw through the pad retainer and thread into the brake pad (**Figure 7**). Tighten the screw to 55-70 in.-lb. (6.3-8 N•m).

16. Coat the lower mounting bolt with Dow Corning Moly 44 grease.

17A. *Springer models*: Install the brake caliper as follows:

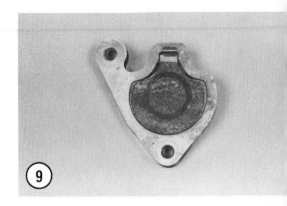

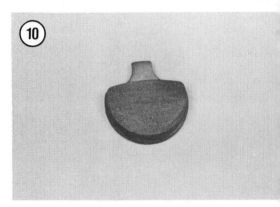

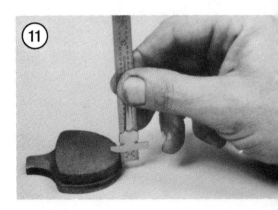

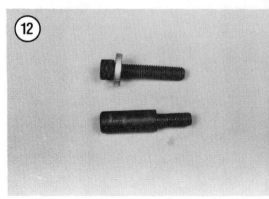

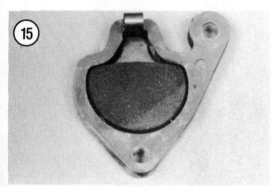

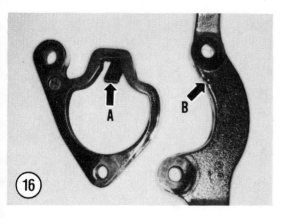

a. Install the caliper over the brake disc, making sure the friction surface on each pad faces against the disc.

b. Align the 2 mounting holes in the caliper with the 2 brake bracket mounting holes while at the same time aligning the blind hole in the brake pad mounting plate with the nub cast in the brake bracket (B, **Figure 16**).

c. Install a washer onto the upper mounting bolt (**Figure 4**) and insert the bolt through the brake bracket and then thread into the caliper bushing. Install the bolt finger-tight.

d. Insert the lower mounting bolt (**Figure 2**) through the caliper and then thread into the brake bracket. Tighten mounting bolt finger-tight.

e. Tighten the lower mounting bolt to the torque specification listed in **Table 2**.

f. Tighten the upper mounting bolt to the torque specification listed in **Table 2**. Then slide the washer onto the end of the upper mounting bolt and secure with a *new* cotter pin. Bend the ends of the cotter pin over to lock it. See **Figure 3**.

17B. *All other models*: Install the brake caliper as follows:

a. Install the caliper over the brake disc, making sure the friction surface on each pad faces against the disc.

CAUTION
*On 1992-on models, the splined head on the threaded bushing (16B, **Figure 1**) must be installed between the rivet head and the pad holder as shown in the assembled view drawing in **Figure 1**. In addition, one of the bushing head splined notches must engage the rivet head as shown in **Figure 1**. If the bushing is installed incorrectly, the rivet will be damaged when the caliper mounting bolts are tightened.*

b. Align the 2 mounting holes in the caliper with the slider mounting lugs.

c. Install a washer onto the upper mounting bolt (**Figure 1**) and insert the bolt through the slider lug and then thread into the caliper bushing. Install the bolt finger-tight.

d. Insert the lower mounting bolt through the caliper and then thread into the slider lug. Tighten mounting bolt finger-tight.

14

e. Tighten the lower mounting bolt to the torque specification listed in **Table 2**.

f. Tighten the upper mounting bolt to the torque specification listed in **Table 2**.

18. Refill the master cylinder reservoir, if necessary, to maintain the correct fluid level. Install the diaphragm and top cap.

> *WARNING*
> *Use brake fluid clearly marked DOT 5 from a sealed container. Other types may vaporize and cause brake failure. Always use the same brand name; do not intermix, as many brands are not compatible.*

> *WARNING*
> *Do not ride the motorcycle until you are sure the brakes are operating correctly with full hydraulic advantage. If necessary, bleed the brake system as described in this chapter.*

FRONT BRAKE CALIPER

It is unnecessary to remove the front wheel in order to remove the front brake caliper.

Removal/Installation
(Non-Springer Models)

1. Loosen and remove the banjo bolt holding the brake line to the caliper (A, **Figure 17**). Remove the bolt and the 2 washers. Place the end of the brake line in a plastic bag and secure the bag against the brake line with a plastic tie to prevent brake fluid from dripping onto the front wheel.

2. Remove the upper mounting bolt (and washer) and the lower mounting bolt and remove the brake caliper.

3. Remove the brake caliper from the disc.

4. Disassemble the brake caliper, if necessary, as described in this chapter.

Installation
(Non-Springer Models)

1. If removed, install the brake pads into the caliper as described in this chapter.

2. Coat the lower mounting bolt with Dow Corning Moly 44 grease.

3. Install the caliper over the brake disc, making sure the friction surface on each pad faces against the disc (**Figure 18**).

4. Align the 2 mounting holes in the caliper with the slider mounting lugs.

5. Install a washer onto the upper mounting bolt (**Figure 1**) and insert the bolt through the slider lug and then thread into the caliper bushing. Install the bolt finger-tight.

6. Insert the lower mounting bolt through the caliper and then thread into the slider lug. Tighten mounting bolt finger-tight.

7. Tighten the lower mounting bolt to the torque specification listed in **Table 2**.

8. Tighten the upper mounting bolt to the torque specification listed in **Table 2**.

9. Tighten the bleed screw if it was previously loosened.

> *WARNING*
> *When installing replacement banjo bolts and washers used to connect the brake hose to the brake caliper, note that 2 different types of banjo bolt washers have been used. Washers used on early models were made of copper with a zinc coating (A, Figure 19). Late models use steel washers equipped with a*

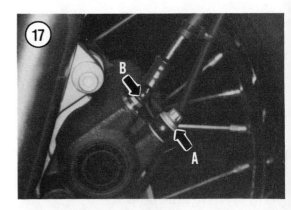

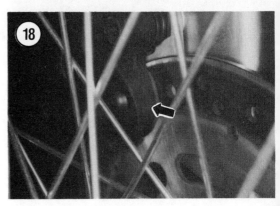

*rubber O-ring (B, **Figure 19**). Because the banjo bolts are designed to be used with a specific type of washer, make sure that replacement banjo washers or bolts match the original parts used. Using an incorrect washer or bolt may allow the brake hose to leak and result in loss of complete brake pressure. If necessary, ask your dealer's parts or service manager to identify the correct washers and banjo bolts used on your model.*

NOTE
*Install **new** banjo bolt washers when performing Step 10.*

10. Assemble the brake line onto the caliper by placing a washer on both sides of the brake line fitting, then secure the fitting to the caliper with the banjo bolt. Tighten the banjo bolt to the torque specification listed in **Table 2**. Make sure the fitting seats against the caliper as shown in A, **Figure 17**.

NOTE
*Note that the tightening torques for the copper and steel/rubber banjo bolts are different. Make sure to use the tightening torque for the type of washer installed on your bike (**Table 2**).*

11. Refill the system and bleed the brake as described in this chapter.

WARNING
Do not ride the motorcycle until you are sure the brakes are operating properly.

Removal
(Springer Models)

Refer to **Figure 20** for this procedure.

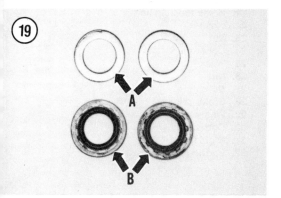

1. Loosen and remove the banjo bolt holding the brake line to the caliper (A, **Figure 21**). Remove the bolt and the 2 washers. Place the end of the brake line in a plastic bag and secure the bag against the brake line with a plastic tie to prevent brake fluid from dripping onto the front wheel.
2. Remove the lower brake caliper mounting bolt (**Figure 2**).
3. Remove the upper brake caliper mounting bolt cotter pin and washer (**Figure 3**); discard the cotter pin. Then unscrew and remove the bolt and its outer washer (**Figure 4**).
4. Remove the brake caliper from the disc.
5. Disassemble the brake caliper, if necessary, as described in this chapter.

Installation
(Springer Models)

1. If removed, install the brake pads into the caliper as described in this chapter.
2. Coat the lower mounting bolt with Dow Corning Moly 44 grease.
3. Install the caliper over the brake disc, making sure the friction surface on each pad faces against the disc (**Figure 22**).
4. Align the 2 mounting holes in the caliper with the 2 brake bracket mounting holes while at the same time aligning the blind hole in the brake pad mounting plate with the nub cast in the brake bracket (B, **Figure 16**).
5. Install a washer onto the upper mounting bolt (**Figure 4**) and insert the bolt through the brake bracket and then thread into the caliper bushing. Install the bolt finger-tight.
6. Insert the lower mounting bolt through the caliper and then thread into the brake bracket. Tighten mounting bolt finger-tight.
7. Tighten the lower mounting bolt to the torque specification listed in **Table 2**.
8. Tighten the upper mounting bolt to the torque specification listed in **Table 2**. Then slide the washer onto the end of the upper mounting bolt and secure with a *new* cotter pin. Bend the ends of the cotter pin over to lock it (**Figure 3**).
9. Tighten the bleed screw (B, **Figure 21**) if it was previously loosened.

WARNING
When installing replacement banjo bolts and washers used to connect the

14

ROCKER AND FRONT BRAKE (SPRINGER)

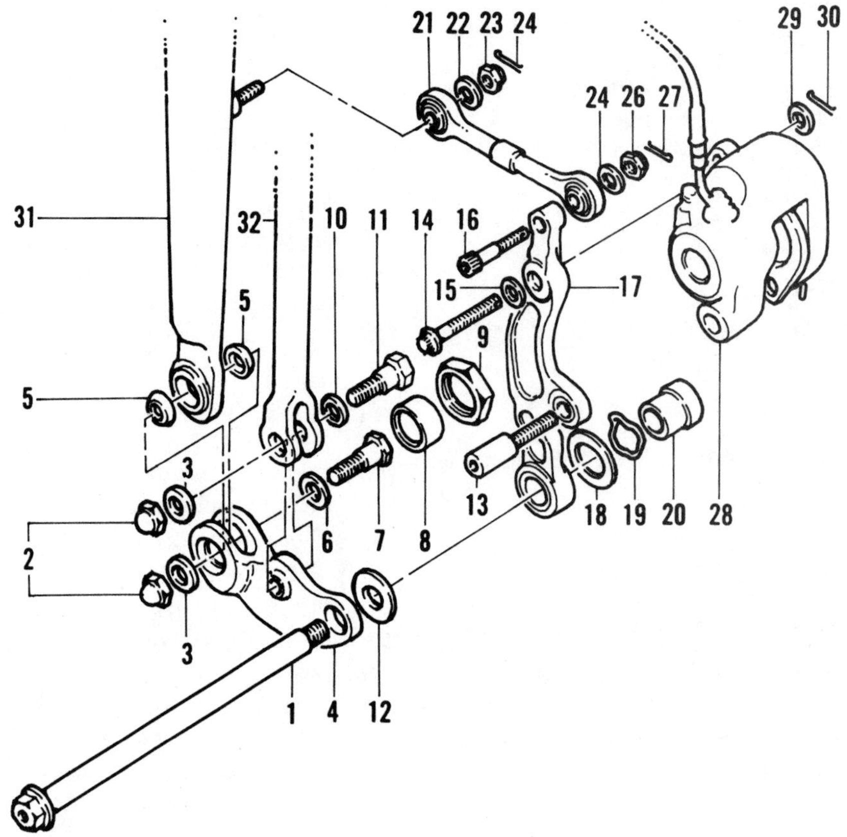

1. Front axle
2. Acorn nut
3. Washer
4. Rocker
5. Spherical bearings
6. Thin washer (mid 1989 and earlier; see text for application)
7. Pivot stud
8. Bearing retainer
9. Locknut
10. Thin washer (mid 1989 and earlier; see text for application)
11. Pivot stud
12. Thrust washer (small I.D.)
13. Lower mounting bolt
14. Upper mounting bolt
15. Washer
16. Bolt
17. Brake bracket
18. Thrust washer (large I.D.)
19. Wave washer
20. Spacer
21. Brake reaction link
22. Washer
23. Nut
24. Cotter pin
25. Washer
26. Nut
27. Cotter pin
28. Brake caliper
29. Washer
30. Cotter pin
31. Rigid fork
32. Spring fork

brake hose to the brake caliper, note that 2 different types of banjo bolt washers have been used. Washers used on early models were made of copper with a zinc coating (A, Figure 19). Late models use steel washers equipped with a rubber O-ring (B, Figure 19). Because the banjo bolts are designed to be used with a specific type of washer, make sure that replacement banjo washers or bolts match the original parts used. Using an incorrect washer or bolt may allow the brake hose to leak and result in loss of complete brake pressure. If necessary, ask your dealer's parts or service manager to identify the correct washers and banjo bolts used on your model.

NOTE
Install new banjo bolt washers when performing Step 10.

10. Assemble the brake line onto the caliper by placing a washer on both sides of the brake line

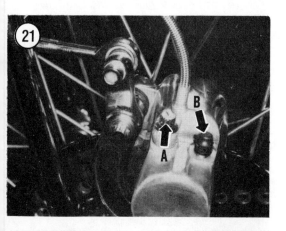

fitting, then secure the fitting to the caliper with the banjo bolt (A, **Figure 21**). Tighten the banjo bolt to the torque specification listed in **Table 2**.

NOTE
Note that the tightening torques for the copper and steel/rubber banjo bolts are different. Make sure to use the tightening torque for the type of washer installed on your bike (Table 2).

11. Refill the system and bleed the brake as described in this chapter.

WARNING
Do not ride the motorcycle until you are sure the brakes are operating properly.

Caliper Overhaul

Harley-Davidson does not provide any specifications for wear limits on any of the front caliper components (except brake pads). Replace any parts that appear to be worn or damaged.

Refer to **Figure 1** for this procedure.

1. Remove the brake pads as described in this chapter.

2. Carefully pry the retaining ring out of the caliper body with a small screwdriver inserted in the notched groove machined in the bottom of the piston bore. Do not pry elsewhere in the caliber bore or you may damage the caliper.

3. Remove the piston dust boot from the groove at the top of the piston.

WARNING
When performing Step 4, the piston may shoot out like a bullet. Keep your fingers out of the way. Wear shop gloves and apply compressed air gradually.

4. Place a rag or piece of wood in the path of the piston (**Figure 23**). Blow the piston out with compressed air directed through the hydraulic hole fitting. Use a service station air hose if you don't have a compressor.

5. Remove the piston seal from the groove in the caliper body.

6. Pull the threaded bushing out of the caliper, then remove the pin boot.

7. Remove the 3 O-rings from the caliper body.

8. Inspect the caliper body for damage; replace the caliper body if necessary.

14

9. Inspect the hydraulic fluid passageway in the cylinder bore. Apply compressed air to the opening and make sure it is clear. Clean out, if necessary, with fresh brake fluid.

10. Inspect the cylinder wall and the piston for scratches, scoring or other damage. Replace worn, corroded or damaged parts.

11. Inspect the banjo bolt and bleed valve threads in the caliper body. If the threads are slightly damaged, clean them up with the proper size thread tap. If the threads are worn or damaged beyond repair, replace the caliper body.

12. Make sure the hole in the bleed valve screw is clean and open. Apply compressed air to the opening if necessary.

13. Check the mounting plate for cracks or damage. Check the threads in the plate for damage. If the threads are slightly damaged, clean them up with the proper size thread tap. If the threads are worn or damaged beyond repair, replace the mounting plate.

14. Check the threaded bushing, upper mounting bolt and the lower mounting pin for thread damage. Repair threads or replace damaged parts as required. Check the mounting pin shoulder for deep scoring or excessive wear; replace if necessary.

15. Check the pad retainer for cracks or damage.

16. Check the brake pads (**Figure 10**) for wear or damage. Replace the brake pads if they are worn to 1/16 in. (1.6 mm) or less (**Figure 11**). Replace both pads as a set.

17. Check all of the rubber parts (dust boot, O-rings, piston seal, etc.) for cracks, wear or age deterioration. Because very minor damage or age deterioration can make these parts useless, questionable parts should be replaced. If you plan to reuse a rubber part, clean the part thoroughly in new brake fluid and place on a lint-free cloth until reassembly.

18. If serviceable, clean all metal parts with rubbing alcohol.

19. After replacing all worn or damaged parts, coat the following parts with new DOT 5 brake fluid. Place the parts on a clean lint-free cloth to prevent contamination before assembly.
 a. Piston.
 b. Piston seal.

20. Make sure the retaining wire, piston and caliper bore are thoroughly clean. If necessary, reclean and allow to air dry before reassembly.

21. Install the piston seal into the caliper body groove.

22. Install the 3 O-rings into the caliper grooves.

23. Wipe the inside of the pin boot with Dow Corning MOLY 44 grease. Then insert the boot into the bushing bore so that the flange end on the boot seats in the bushing bore internal groove.

24. The piston dust boot is installed on the piston *before* the piston is installed in the caliper bore. Perform the following:
 a. Place the piston on your workbench so that the open side faces up.
 b. Align the piston dust boot with the piston so that the shoulder on the dust boot faces up.
 c. Slide the piston dust boot onto the piston until the inner lip on the dust boot seats in the piston groove.

25. Coat the piston and the caliper bore with DOT 5 brake fluid.

26. Align the piston with the caliper bore so that its open end faces out. Then push the piston in until it bottoms out.

NOTE
If you are installing new brake pads, you will have to push the piston all the way into the bore. If necessary, use a C-clamp to push the piston into the bore.

27. Locate the retaining wire groove in the end of the caliper bore. Then align the retaining wire so that the gap in the wire (**Figure 24**) is at the top of the caliper bore and install the wire into the wire groove. Make sure that the retaining wire is seated completely in the groove and that it is pushing against the piston dust boot.

28. Wipe the caliper mounting lug bores with Dow Corning MOLY 44 grease.

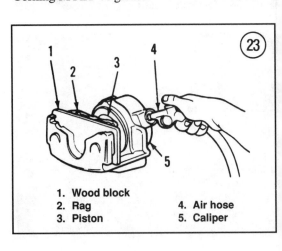

1. Wood block
2. Rag
3. Piston
4. Air hose
5. Caliper

29. Insert the threaded bushing into the pin boot until the end of the pin boot seats in the groove adjacent to the threaded bushing hexagonal head.

30. Install the brake pads as described in this chapter.

FRONT MASTER CYLINDER

The front master cylinder is mounted onto the right-hand handlebar.

Removal/Installation

Refer to **Figure 25** for this procedure.

> *CAUTION*
> *Cover the fuel tank, instrument cluster and front fairing with a heavy cloth or plastic tarp to protect them from accidental brake fluid spills. Wash brake fluid off any painted or plated surfaces immediately. Use soapy water and rinse completely.*

1. Flip the rubber cover off of the front caliper bleeder valve (B, **Figure 17**, typical) and insert a hose onto the end of the valve. Insert the open end of the hose into a container. Open the front bleeder valve and drain the brake fluid from the front brake assembly by operating the hand lever. Remove the hose and close the bleeder valve after draining the assembly. Discard the brake fluid.

2. Place a couple of shop cloths under the banjo bolt and remove the banjo bolt and washers securing the brake hose to the master cylinder (**Figure 26**).

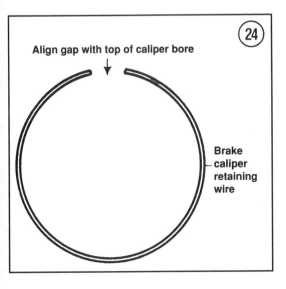

Align gap with top of caliper bore

Brake caliper retaining wire

24

3. Remove the screws securing the clamp to the master cylinder and remove the clamp and master cylinder housing.

4. Install by reversing these removal steps while noting the following.

5. Clean the handlebar of all brake fluid residue.

6. Clean the banjo bolt (**Figure 27**) fluid passage thoroughly. Use air to dry the bolt or allow it to air dry thoroughly before installation into the master cylinder.

7. Check the clamp for cracks or damage. Replace if necessary.

8. Position the master cylinder onto the handlebar and install the clamp and its 2 attaching screws. Tighten the screws to the torque specification listed in **Table 2**.

> *WARNING*
> *When installing replacement banjo bolts and washers used to connect the brake hose to the brake caliper, note that 2 different types of banjo bolt washers have been used. Washers used on early models were made of copper with a zinc coating (A, **Figure 19**). Late models use steel washers equipped with a rubber O-ring (B, **Figure 19**). Because the banjo bolts are designed to be used with a specific type of washer, make sure that replacement banjo washers or bolts match the original parts used. Using an incorrect washer or bolt may allow the brake hose to leak and result in loss of complete brake pressure. If necessary, ask your dealer's parts or service manager to identify the correct washers and banjo bolts used on your model.*

> *NOTE*
> *Install **new** banjo bolt washers when performing Step 9.*

9. Install the brake hose onto the cylinder. Be sure to place a new washer on each side of the hose fitting (**Figure 26**) when installing the banjo bolt. Tighten the banjo bolt to the torque specification listed in **Table 2**.

> *NOTE*
> *Note that the tightening torques for the copper and steel/rubber banjo bolts are different. Make sure to use the tightening torque for the type of washer installed on your bike (**Table 2**).*

14

10. Fill the master cylinder with new DOT 5 brake fluid. Bleed the brake system as described in this chapter.

master cylinder components are working properly.

NOTE
When actuating the brake lever in Step 10, a small spurt of fluid should break through the fluid surface in the master cylinder to indicate that all internal

11. Install the master cylinder diphragm and cover after bleeding the brakes. Sit on the motorcycle and check that the brake lever position is suitable to your riding position. If necessary, loosen the clamp screws and reposition the master cylinder; retighten the clamp screws to the torque specification listed in **Table 2**.

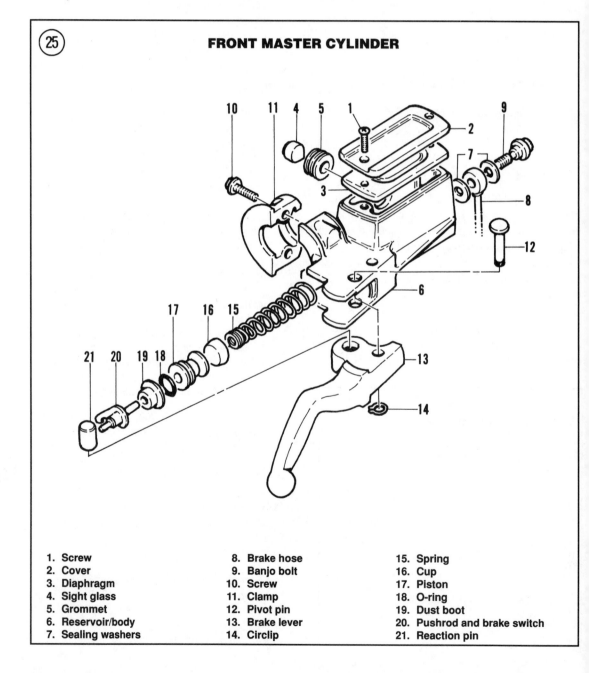

FRONT MASTER CYLINDER

1. Screw	8. Brake hose	15. Spring
2. Cover	9. Banjo bolt	16. Cup
3. Diaphragm	10. Screw	17. Piston
4. Sight glass	11. Clamp	18. O-ring
5. Grommet	12. Pivot pin	19. Dust boot
6. Reservoir/body	13. Brake lever	20. Pushrod and brake switch
7. Sealing washers	14. Circlip	21. Reaction pin

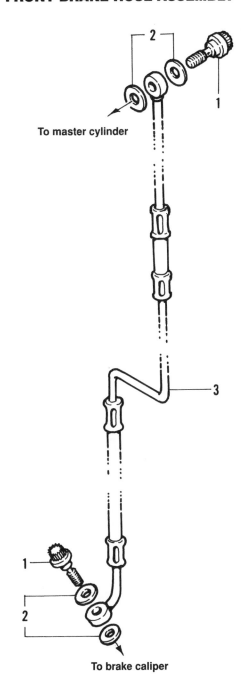

FRONT BRAKE HOSE ASSEMBLY

To master cylinder

To brake caliper

1. Banjo bolt
2. Washer
3. Hose

WARNING
Do not ride the motorcycle until you are sure the brakes are working properly.

Disassembly

Refer to **Figure 25** when performing this procedure.

1. Drain and remove the master cylinder as described in this chapter.

2. Remove the screws securing the top cover and remove the cover and diaphragm.

3. The brake lever pivot pin is secured with a circlip. Remove the circlip and remove the pivot pin and brake lever (**Figure 28**).

4. Remove the reaction pin from the hand lever (**Figure 28**).

5. Referring to **Figure 25**, remove the following in order:

    a. Push rod and brake switch actuator.
    b. Dust boot.
    c. Piston and O-ring.
    d. Cup.
    e. Spring.

6. If damaged, remove the grommet and sight glass from the rear side of the master cylinder housing.

Inspection

Harley-Davidson does not provide any specifications for wear limits on any of the master cylinder components. Replace any parts that appear to be damaged or worn.

1. Clean all parts in denatured alcohol or fresh DOT 5 brake fluid. Cleaned parts should be placed on a clean lint-free cloth until reassembly.

2. The piston assembly consists of the dust boot, O-ring, piston, cup and spring. Inspect the rubber

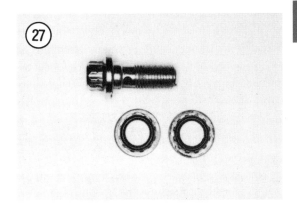

14

parts for wear, cracks, swelling or other damage. Check the piston for severe wear or damage. Check the spring for fatigue or breakage. If any one part of the piston assembly is damaged, the entire piston assembly must be replaced; individual parts are not available from Harley-Davidson.

NOTE
Do not remove the O-ring from the piston if you plan on reusing the piston and O-ring.

3. Inspect the master cylinder walls for scratches or wear grooves. The master cylinder housing should be replaced if the cylinder walls are damaged.
4. Check to see that the vent hole in the cover is not plugged.
5. Check the banjo bolt threads in the master cylinder. If the threads are slightly damaged, clean them up with the proper size thread tap. If the threads are severely worn or damaged, replace the master cylinder body.

NOTE
If you use a tap to clean the threads in the master cylinder, flush the master cylinder thoroughly and blow dry.

6. Inspect the piston bore in the master cylinder for wear, corrosion or damage. Replace the master cylinder if necessary.
7. Make sure the fluid passage hole through the banjo bolt is clear. Flush bolt if necessary.
8. Check the reaction pin and pivot pin holes in the brake lever for cracks, spreading or other damage. Check the lever for cracks or damage.
9. Check the reaction and pivot pins for severe wear or damage. Check the fit of each pin in the brake lever. Replace worn or damaged parts as required.

Assembly

1. Soak the piston O-ring and cup in fresh DOT 5 brake fluid for at least 15 minutes to make the cups pliable. Apply a thin coat of brake fluid to the cylinder bore before assembly.
2. Install the grommet and sight glass if removed.
3. Insert the cup onto the small end of the spring. The O-ring should be installed onto the piston before installing it.
4. Insert the spring and cup into the master cylinder as shown in **Figure 25**.

5. Install the O-ring onto the piston and insert the piston into the master cylinder.
6. Install the dust boot and reaction pin/switch.
7. Lightly coat the reaction pin with Loctite Anti-seize.
8. Referring to **Figure 28**, assemble the brake lever as follows:
   a. Install the reaction pin into the large hole in the brake lever.
   b. Position the brake lever into the master cylinder, making sure the end of the pushrod fits into the hole in the reaction pin.

NOTE
Make sure the pushrod and switch are fully seated in the reaction pin hole. If the hand lever binds or is not smooth in action, disassemble the parts and reassemble them correctly.

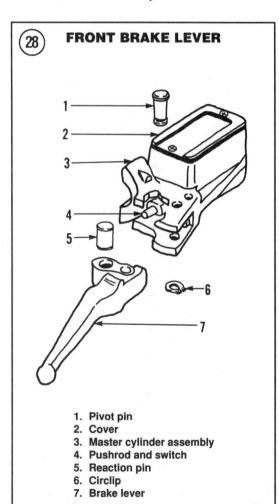

28 **FRONT BRAKE LEVER**

1. **Pivot pin**
2. **Cover**
3. **Master cylinder assembly**
4. **Pushrod and switch**
5. **Reaction pin**
6. **Circlip**
7. **Brake lever**

c. Insert the pivot pin through the master cylinder and engage the brake lever. Secure the pivot pin with the circlip.

REAR DISC BRAKE

The rear disc brake is actuated by hydraulic fluid and is controlled by the right-hand foot-operated pedal that is linked to the master cylinder. As the brake pads wear, the brake fluid level drops in the reservoir and automatically adjusts for wear.

REAR BRAKE PAD REPLACEMENT

There is no recommended mileage interval for changing the friction pads in the disc brake. Pad wear depends greatly on riding habits and conditions. The pads should be checked for wear initially at 500 miles (800 km), then every 2,500 miles (4,000 km) and replaced when the lining thickness reaches 1/16 in. (1.6 mm) from the brake pad backing plate. To maintain an even brake pressure on the disc, always replace both pads in the caliper at the same time.

1984-early 1987 models

Refer to **Figure 29** for this procedure.

1. To prevent accidental application of the rear brake lever, tie the pedal up to the frame so it cannot be depressed.
2. Remove the 2 brake caliper Allen bolts and lift the caliper off of the brake disc. Do not disconnect the brake hose at the caliper.
3. Remove the brake pads from the caliper body.
4. Remove the pad spring from inside the caliper.
5. Check the abutment shim in the caliper frame (**Figure 30**). If it is worn or damaged, replace it as follows:
   a. Pry the abutment shim away from the caliper.
   b. Remove all adhesive from the caliper surface where the abutment shim is located.
   c. Clean the abutment shim surface with denatured alcohol.
   d. Apply silicone sealant to the abutment shim surface on the caliper and install the abutment shim. Hold the shim in position by installing the brake pads in the bracket.
   e. Allow the silicone sealant to dry thoroughly before completing brake pad installation.
   f. Check that the brake pads slide freely in the bracket.

6. Check the brake pads for wear or damage. Replace the brake pads if they are worn to 1/16 in. (1.6 mm) or less. Replace both pads as a set.
7. When new pads are installed in the caliper the master cylinder brake fluid level will rise as the caliper piston is repositioned. Clean the top of the master cylinder of all dirt and foreign matter. Remove the cap and diaphragm from the master cylinder and slowly push the caliper piston into the caliper. Constantly check the reservoir to make sure brake fluid does not overflow. Remove fluid, if necessary, prior to it overflowing. The piston should move freely. If not, and there is evidence of it sticking in the cylinder, the caliper should be removed and serviced as described in this chapter.
8. Push the caliper piston in all the way to allow room for the new pads.
9. Refer to **Figure 31**. Install the pad spring into the top of the caliper so that the spring's long tab extends above the piston. Hook the spring's short tab above the ridge on the caliper casting opposite the piston.

NOTE
The upper and lower pins should be positioned so that the flats on each pin are parallel with the bracket opening.

10. Install the brake pads on the bracket. Then install the caliper body over the brake pads and onto the bracket. Make sure the upper and lower pins do not move when installing the caliper body.
11. Install the caliper screws and tighten to the torque specification listed in **Table 2**. Make sure the upper and lower pin flats are properly positioned. See *NOTE* prior to Step 10.

CAUTION
*If the reaction pin is loosened or removed, tighten the pin and nut to the torque specification listed in **Table 2**.*

12. If you tied the rear brake pedal to the frame, disconnect the wire so that the pedal can be operated.
13. Refill the master cylinder reservoir, if necessary, to maintain the correct fluid level. Install the diaphragm and top cap.

WARNING
Use brake fluid clearly marked DOT 5 from a sealed container. Other types may vaporize and cause brake failure. Always use the same brand name; do

14

not intermix, as many brands are not compatible.

> **WARNING**
> *Do not ride the motorcycle until you are sure the brakes are operating correctly with full hydraulic advantage. If necessary, bleed the brake system as described in this chapter.*

Late 1987 and later models

> **NOTE**
> *There was a design change between early 1991 and late 1991-on brake pads and shims. When servicing the rear brakes on one of these models, refer to* **Brake Pad/Pad Shim Identification** *under* **Rear Brake Caliper (Late 1986-ON** *in this chapter.*

Refer to **Figure 32** for this procedure.

1. To prevent accidental application of the rear brake lever, tie the pedal up to the frame so it cannot be depressed.

2. Remove the muffler as described in Chapter Eight.

3. Remove the 2 caliper pin bolts (A, **Figure 33**) and lift the caliper (B, **Figure 33**) off of the mounting bracket. Do not disconnect the brake hose at the caliper.

4. Pull the retainer clip (**Figure 34**) over the mounting bracket and remove it.

5. Slide the outer brake pad off the mounting bracket (**Figure 34**).

6. Slide the inner brake pad toward the wheel and off the mounting bracket.

7. Remove the 2 pad shims from the mounting bracket.

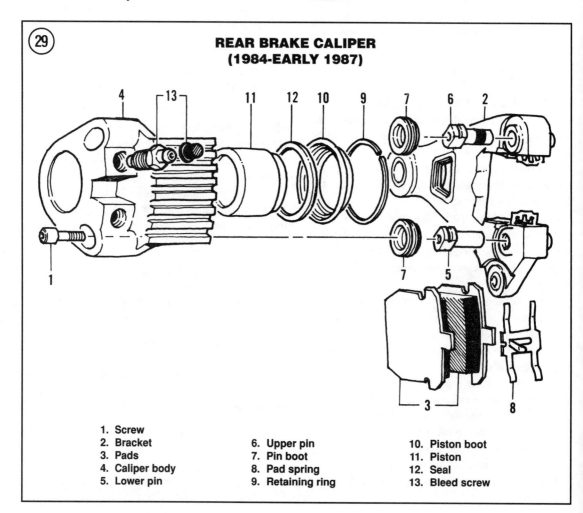

29

**REAR BRAKE CALIPER
(1984-EARLY 1987)**

1. Screw
2. Bracket
3. Pads
4. Caliper body
5. Lower pin
6. Upper pin
7. Pin boot
8. Pad spring
9. Retaining ring
10. Piston boot
11. Piston
12. Seal
13. Bleed screw

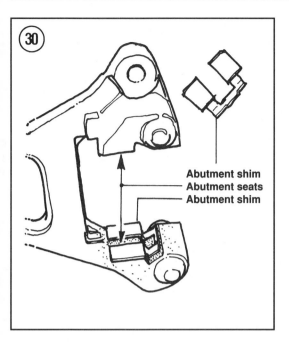

Abutment shim
Abutment seats
Abutment shim

8. Check the brake pads (**Figure 35**) for wear or damage. Replace the brake pads if they are worn to 1/16 in. (1.6 mm) or less. Replace both pads as a set.

9. Clean the pad shims thoroughly and check for cracks or damage. Replace if necessary.

10. Clean the shim mounting area on the mounting bracket thoroughly.

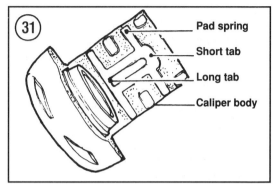

Pad spring
Short tab
Long tab
Caliper body

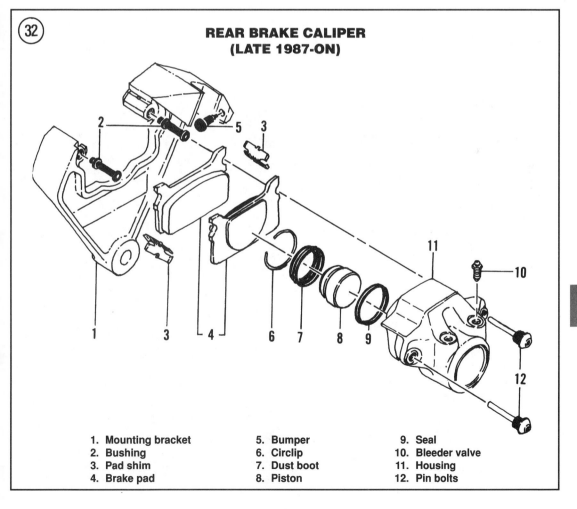

REAR BRAKE CALIPER (LATE 1987-ON)

1. Mounting bracket
2. Bushing
3. Pad shim
4. Brake pad
5. Bumper
6. Circlip
7. Dust boot
8. Piston
9. Seal
10. Bleeder valve
11. Housing
12. Pin bolts

14

11. Check the pad clip for damage; replace if necessary.

12. When new pads are installed in the caliper the master cylinder brake fluid level will rise as the caliper piston is repositioned. Clean the top of the master cylinder of all dirt and foreign matter. Remove the cap and diaphragm from the master cylinder and slowly push the caliper piston into the caliper. Constantly check the reservoir to make sure brake fluid does not overflow. Remove fluid, if necessary, prior to it overflowing. The piston should move freely. If not, and there is evidence of it sticking in the cylinder, the caliper should be removed and serviced as described in this chapter.

13. Push the caliper piston in all the way to allow room for the new pads.

14. Install the pad shims onto the caliper mounting bracket rails as follows:

    a. On early 1991 and earlier models, insert the pad shim tabs (**Figure 36**) into the caliper bracket shim holes (3, **Figure 32**).

    b. On late 1991-on models, install the pad shims (**Figure 37**) so that their retaining loops face against the outer caliper mounting bracket rails as shown in B, **Figure 38** and **Figure 39**.

    c. On all models, hold the pad shims in place when installing the inner brake pad in Step 15.

15. Install the inner brake pad by sliding it over the pad shims so that it contacts the inside brake disc surface.

16. Install the outer brake pad by sliding it over the pad shims so that it contacts the outside brake disc surface.

17. Working on the inside of the mounting bracket, insert the ends of the pad clip into the 2 holes in the mounting bracket. Then pivot the clip over the top of the brake pads until it seats against the outer brake pad as shown in **Figure 34**.

CAUTION
After installing the pad clip, check that the outer brake pad is still contacting the 2 pad shims. Failure of the outer pad to contact both pad shims can result in irregular pad wear, brake drag or mounting bracket damage.

NOTE
The caliper should be installed carefully over the brake pads so it does not knock against the brake pads and dislodge the pad shims.

18. Align the caliper with the brake pads and install it over the pads (B, **Figure 33**). Align the holes in the caliper with the threaded holes in the mounting bracket and install the 2 pin bolts (A, **Figure 33**). Start the bolts by hand, then tighten with a torque wrench to the tightening torque listed in **Table 2**.

19. If you tied the rear brake pedal to the frame, disconnect the wire so that the pedal can be operated.

20. Refill the master cylinder reservoir, if necessary, to maintain the correct fluid level. Install the diaphragm and top cap.

WARNING
Use brake fluid clearly marked DOT 5 from a sealed container. Other types may vaporize and cause brake failure. Always use the same brand name; do not intermix, as many brands are not compatible.

WARNING
Do not ride the motorcycle until you are sure the brakes are operating correctly with full hydraulic advantage. If necessary, bleed the brake system as described in this chapter.

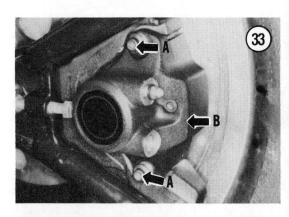

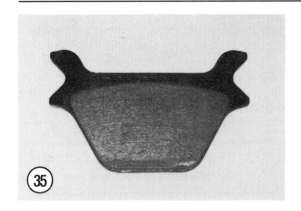

③⑤

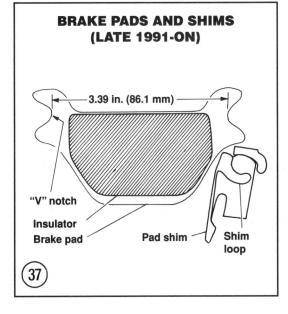

BRAKE PADS AND SHIMS (LATE 1987-EARLY 1991)

3.44 in. (87.4 mm)

"V" notch

Insulator

Brake pad

Pad shim

Shim tabs

③⑥

BRAKE PADS AND SHIMS (LATE 1991-ON)

3.39 in. (86.1 mm)

"V" notch

Insulator

Brake pad

Pad shim

Shim loop

③⑦

REAR BRAKE CALIPER (1984-EARLY 1987 MODELS)

Refer to **Figure 29** when performing procedures in this section.

Removal

1. Loosen and remove the banjo bolt holding the brake line to the caliper. Remove the bolt and the 2 washers. Place the end of the brake line in a plastic bag and secure the bag against the brake line with a plastic tie to prevent brake fluid from dripping onto the front wheel.

2. Remove the 2 brake caliper Allen bolts and lift the caliper off of the brake disc.

3. Disassemble the brake caliper, if necessary, as described in this chapter.

Installation

1. If removed, install the brake pads as described in this chapter.

③⑧

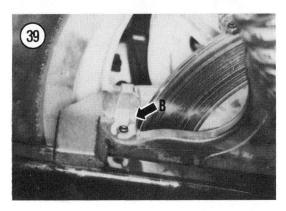

③⑨

14

NOTE
The upper and lower pins should be positioned so that the flats on each pin are parallel with the bracket opening.

2. Install the caliper body over the brake pads and onto the bracket. Make sure the upper and lower pins do not move when installing the caliper body.

3. Install the caliper screws and tighten to the torque specification listed in **Table 2**. Make sure the upper and lower pin flats are properly positioned. See *NOTE* prior to Step 2.

CAUTION
*If the reaction pin is loosened or removed, tighten the pin and nut to the torque specification listed in **Table 2**.*

WARNING
*When installing replacement banjo bolts and washers used to connect the brake hose to the brake caliper, note that 2 different types of banjo bolt washers have been used. Washers used on early models were made of copper with a zinc coating (A, **Figure 19**). Late models use steel washers equipped with a rubber O-ring (B, **Figure 19**). Because the banjo bolts are designed to be used with a specific type of washer, make sure that replacement banjo washers or bolts match the original parts used. Using an incorrect washer or bolt may allow the brake hose to leak and result in loss of complete brake pressure. If necessary, ask your dealer's parts or service manager to identify the correct washers and banjo bolts used on your model.*

NOTE
*Install **new** banjo bolt washers when performing Step 4.*

4. Install the brake hose onto the cylinder. Be sure to place a new washer on each side of the hose fitting when installing the banjo bolt. Tighten the banjo bolt to the torque specification listed in **Table 2**.

NOTE
*Note that the tightening torques for the copper and steel/rubber banjo bolts are different. Make sure to use the tightening torque for the type of washer installed on your bike (**Table 2**).*

Caliper Overhaul

Harley-Davidson does not provide any specifications for wear limits on any of the front caliper components (except brake pads). Replace any parts that appear to be worn or damaged.

Refer to **Figure 29** for this procedure.

1. Remove the brake pads as described in this chapter.

2. Carefully pry the retaining ring out of the caliper body with a small screwdriver.

3. Remove the piston dust boot from the groove at the top of the piston.

WARNING
When performing Step 4, the piston may shoot out like a bullet. Keep your fingers out of the way. Wear shop gloves and apply compressed air gradually.

4. Place a rag or piece of wood in the path of the piston (**Figure 23**). Blow the piston out with compressed air directed through the hydraulic hole fitting. Use a service station air hose if you don't have a compressor.

5. Remove the piston seal from the groove in the caliper body.

6. Carefully pry the piston seal out of the caliper bore groove.

7. Remove the upper and lower pins and their rubber boots.

8. Inspect the caliper body for damage; replace the caliper body if necessary.

9. Inspect the hydraulic fluid passageway in the cylinder bore. Make sure it is clean and open. Apply compressed air to the opening and make sure it is clear. Clean out, if necessary, with fresh brake fluid.

10. Inspect the cylinder wall and the piston for scratches, scoring or other damage. Replace worn, corroded or damaged parts.

11. Inspect the banjo bolt and bleed valve threads in the caliper body. If the threads are slightly damaged, clean them up with a proper size thread tap. If the threads are worn or damaged beyond repair, replace the caliper body.

12. Make sure the hole in the bleed valve screw is clean and open. Apply compressed air to the opening and make sure it is clear. Clean out, if necessary, with fresh brake fluid.

13. Check the mounting bracket for cracks or damage. Check the threads in the plate for damage. If the threads are slightly damaged, clean them up with a proper size thread tap. If the threads are worn or damaged beyond repair, replace the mounting bracket.

14. Check the mounting pin shoulder for deep scoring or excessive wear; replace if necessary.

15. Check the pad retainer for cracks or damage.

16. Check the brake pads for wear or damage. Replace the brake pads if they are worn to 1/16 in. (1.6 mm) or less. Replace both pads as a set.

17. Check all of the rubber parts for cracks, wear or age deterioration. Because very minor damage or age deterioration can make these parts useless, questionable parts should be replaced. If you plan to reuse a rubber part, clean the part thoroughly in new brake fluid and place on a lint-free cloth until reassembly.

18. If serviceable, clean all metal parts with denatured alcohol.

19. After replacing all worn or damaged parts, coat the following parts with new DOT 5 brake fluid. Place the parts on a clean lint-free cloth to prevent contamination before assembly.

    a. Piston.

    b. Piston dust boot.

    c. Piston seal.

20. Make sure the retaining wire, piston and caliper bore are thoroughly clean. If necessary, reclean in rubbing alcohol and allow to air dry before reassembly.

21. Install the piston seal into the caliper body groove.

22. Coat the piston and the caliper bore with DOT 5 brake fluid.

23. Align the piston with the caliper bore so that its open end faces out. Then push the piston in until it bottoms out.

24. Install the piston dust boot onto the end of the piston.

25. Locate the retaining wire groove in the end of the caliper bore and install the wire into the wire groove. Make sure that the retaining wire is seated completely in the groove and that it is pushing against the piston dust boot.

NOTE
If you are installing new brake pads, you will have to push the piston all the way into the bore. If necessary, use a C-clamp to push the piston into the bore.

26. Install the boot onto the upper and lower pins. Then wipe the pin shafts and the pin bores in the mounting bracket with silicone grease. Insert the pins into the pin bores. Install the pin with the nylon sleeve into the top mounting bracket hole.

27. Each pin hole has a boss around the hole. Fit the boot shoulder on each boot onto their respective boss. Rotate the pins so that flat on both pins are parallel with the bracket opening.

28. Install the brake pads and abutment shims as described in this chapter.

REAR BRAKE CALIPER (LATE 1987-ON)

Refer to **Figure 32** when performing procedures in this section.

Brake Pad/Pad Shim Identification

There was a design change between early 1991 and late 1991-on models regarding the brake pads and pad shims (**Figure 32**). When purchasing replacement parts, note the following while referring to **Figure 36** (late 1987-early 1991) or **Figure 37** (late 1991-on):

    a. Late 1987-early 1991 pad shim thickness is 0.015 in. (0.38 mm).

    b. Late 1991-on pad shim thickness is 0.030 in. (0.76 mm).

    c. Late 1987-early 1991 pad shims have a tab in the middle of each long side.

    d. Late 1991-on pad shims have an open loop at one end of the shim.

    e. Late 1987-early 1991 brake pads measure approximately 3.44 in. (87.4 mm) between the

14

"V" notches as shown in **Figure 36**. Late 1991-on brake pads measure approximately 3.39 in. (86.1 mm) as shown in **Figure 37**.

f. Late 1987-early 1991 outboard brake pads have an angle-cut, half-size insulator mounted on the back of the pad. The inboard brake pad has a full-size insulator.

g. Late 1991-on brake pads have full-size insulators mounted on the back of each pad.

> *WARNING*
> *When replacing brake pads, do not intermix late 1987-early 1991 and late 1991-on brake pads and pad shims. Otherwise, improper rear brake operation will occur. This may cause brake failure and loss of control, resulting in personal injury. When purchasing new brake pads, take your frame's serial number to the dealer and have them verify your model as an early or late model.*

Removal

1. Loosen and remove the banjo bolt holding the brake line to the caliper (**Figure 40**). Remove the bolt and the 2 washers. Place the end of the brake line in a plastic bag and secure the bag against the brake line with a plastic tie to prevent brake fluid from dripping onto the front wheel.

2. Remove the 2 brake caliper pin bolts (A, **Figure 33**) and lift the caliper off of the brake disc.

3. Disassemble the brake caliper, if necessary, as described in this chapter.

Installation

1. If removed, install the brake pads as described in this chapter.

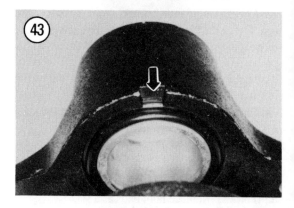

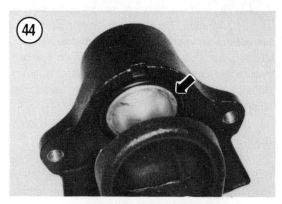

2. Install the caliper body over the brake pads and onto the bracket.

3. Install the caliper pin bolts (A, **Figure 33**) and tighten to the torque specification listed in **Table 2**.

WARNING
When installing replacement banjo bolts and washers used to connect the brake hose to the brake caliper, note that 2 different types of banjo bolt washers have been used. Washers used on early models were made of copper with a zinc coating (A, Figure 19). Late models use steel washers equipped with a rubber O-ring (B, Figure 19). Because the banjo bolts are designed to be used with a specific type of washer, make sure that replacement banjo washers or bolts match the original parts used. Using an incorrect washer or bolt may allow the brake hose to leak and result in loss of complete brake pressure. If necessary, ask your dealer's parts or service manager to identify the correct washers and banjo bolts used on your model.

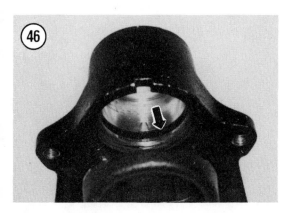

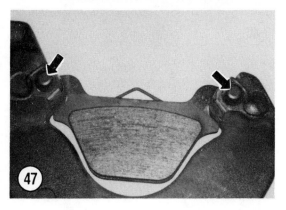

NOTE
*Install **new** banjo bolt washers when performing Step 4.*

4. Install the brake hose onto the cylinder. Be sure to place a new washer on each side of the hose fitting (**Figure 41**) when installing the banjo bolt. Tighten the banjo bolt to the torque specification listed in **Table 2**.

NOTE
Note that the tightening torques for the copper and steel/rubber banjo bolts are different. Make sure to use the tightening torque for the type of washer installed on your bike (Table 2).

Caliper Overhaul

Harley-Davidson does not provide any specifications for wear limits on any of the front caliper components (except brake pads). Replace any parts that appear to be worn or damaged.

Refer to **Figure 32** for this procedure.

1. Remove the brake pads as described in this chapter.

2. Carefully pry the retaining ring (**Figure 42**) out of the caliper body with a small screwdriver.

NOTE
Pry the circlip by inserting the screwdriver into the notch shown in Figure 43.

3. Remove the piston dust boot from the groove at the top of the piston (**Figure 44**).

WARNING
When performing Step 4, the piston may shoot out like a bullet. Keep your fingers out of the way. Wear shop gloves and apply compressed air gradually.

4. Place a rag or piece of wood in the path of the piston (**Figure 23**). Blow the piston out with compressed air directed through the hydraulic hole fitting. Use a service station air hose if you don't have a compressor. See **Figure 45**.

5. Remove the piston seal from the groove in the caliper body and discard it (**Figure 46**).

6. Replace the rubber bushings (**Figure 47**) in the mounting bracket if worn or damaged.

14

7. Inspect the caliper body for damage; replace the caliper body if necessary.

8. Inspect the hydraulic fluid passageway throughout the caliper body (**Figure 48**). Make sure they are clean and open. Apply compressed air to the openings and make sure it is clear. Clean out, if necessary, with fresh brake fluid.

9. Inspect the cylinder wall (**Figure 46**) and the piston (**Figure 49**) for scratches, scoring or other damage. Replace worn, corroded or damaged parts. Do not bore or hone the caliper bore cylinder.

10. Inspect the banjo bolt and bleed valve threads in the caliper body (**Figure 48**). If the threads are slightly damaged, clean them up with a proper size thread tap. If the threads are worn or damaged beyond repair, replace the caliper body.

11. Make sure the hole in the bleed valve screw (**Figure 50**) is clean and open. Apply compressed air to the opening and make sure it is clear. Clean out, if necessary, with fresh brake fluid.

12. Check the mounting bracket for cracks or damage. Check the threads in the plate for damage. If the threads are slightly damaged, clean them up with a proper size thread tap. If the threads are worn or damaged beyond repair, replace the mounting bracket.

13. Check the pin bolt shoulder for deep scoring or excessive wear; replace if necessary.

14. Check the pad retainer for cracks or damage.

15. Check the brake pads (**Figure 35**) for wear or damage. Replace the brake pads if they are worn to 1/16 in. (1.6 mm) or less. Replace both pads as a set.

16. Check all of the rubber parts for cracks, wear or age deterioration. Because very minor damage or age deterioration can make these parts useless, questionable parts should be replaced. If you plan to reuse a rubber part, clean the part thoroughly in new brake fluid and place on a lint-free cloth until reassembly.

17. If serviceable, clean all metal parts with denatured alcohol.

18. After replacing the piston seal and dust boot, as well as all worn or damaged parts, coat the following parts with new DOT 5 brake fluid. Place the parts on a clean lint-free cloth to prevent contamination before assembly.

    a. Piston (**Figure 49**).

    b. Piston dust boot (A, **Figure 51**).

    c. Piston seal.

19. Make sure the retaining wire (B, **Figure 51**), piston and caliper bore are thoroughly clean. If necessary, reclean in rubbing alcohol and allow to air dry before reassembly.

20. Install the piston seal (**Figure 46**) into the caliper body groove.

21. Coat the piston and the caliper bore with DOT 5 brake fluid.

22. Align the piston with the caliper bore so that its open end faces out (**Figure 45**). Then push the piston in until it bottoms out.

23. Install the piston dust boot onto the end of the piston. See **Figure 44**.

24. Locate the retaining wire groove in the end of the caliper bore and install the wire into the wire groove (**Figure 42**). Make sure that the retaining wire is seated completely in the groove and that it is pushing against the piston dust boot.

NOTE
If you are installing new brake pads, you will have to push the piston all the way into the bore. If necessary, use a C-clamp to push the piston into the bore.

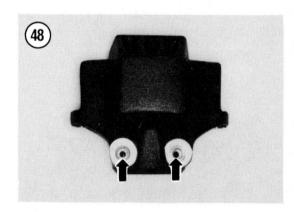

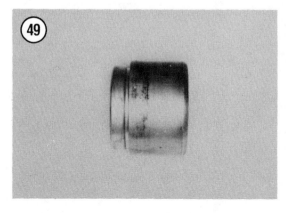

25. Install 2 new rubber bushings into the mounting bracket, if necessary.

26. Install the brake pads and pad shims as described in this chapter.

REAR MASTER CYLINDER AND RESERVOIR (1984-EARLY 1987 FXST)

Removal/Disassembly

Refer to **Figure 52** for this procedure.

> *CAUTION*
> *Cover the surrounding area of the frame and wheel with a heavy cloth or plastic covering to protect them from accidental brake fluid spills. Wash brake fluid off any painted or plated surfaces immediately. Use soapy water and rinse completely.*

> *NOTE*
> *Drain the brake fluid from the hose and discard it—never reuse brake fluid. Contaminated brake fluid may cause brake failure.*

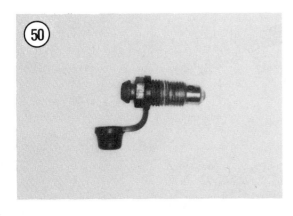

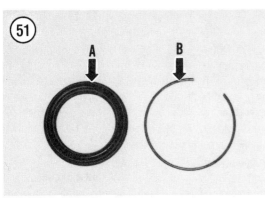

1. To drain the hydraulic fluid from the rear brake system, perform the following:
   a. Attach a hose to the bleed valve on the caliper assembly.
   b. Place the loose end of the hose in a container to catch the brake fluid.
   c. Open the bleed valve and continue to apply the rear brake pedal until the brake fluid is pumped out of the system.
   d. Disconnect the hose and tighten the bleed valve.
   e. Dispose of this brake fluid—*never* reuse brake fluid. Contaminated brake fluid may cause brake failure.

> *NOTE*
> *If you only want to drain the master cylinder reservoir, disconnect the reservoir supply hose from the fitting on the master cylinder and drain the brake fluid into a container. Plug the hose opening.*

2. Disconnect the brake supply hose at the master cylinder.

3. Disconnect the reservoir supply hose at the master cylinder. Plug the hose opening.

4. Remove the master cylinder mounting bolts. Then move the master cylinder to the rear slightly and the pushrod will disengage from the master cylinder piston assembly. Remove the master cylinder.

5. After removing the master cylinder, remove the brake spring washer, brake return spring and the rubber boot from the pushrod to prevent their loss.

6. To remove the master cylinder reservoir, perform the following:
   a. Remove the bolt and washer securing the master cylinder to the frame or bracket.
   b. Remove the reservoir.

7. Install by reversing these steps. Note the following.

8. Assemble the brake return spring and the spring washer over the end of the pushrod's small diameter end in the order shown in **Figure 52**. Hold in this position and slide the boot over the spring, washer and pushrod. Then bring the master cylinder up along its mounting position and insert the pushrod through the master cylinder and into the end of the piston assembly. Hold the master cylinder/pushrod assembly in position and install the master cylinder bolts and washers finger-tight. Then check that the

14

REAR MASTER CYLINDER
(1984-EARLY 1987 FXST)

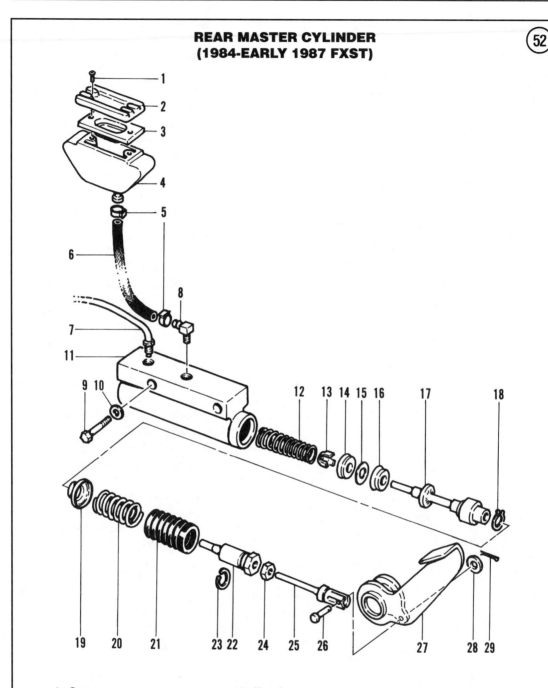

1. Screw
2. Cover
3. Diaphragm
4. Reservoir
5. Clamp
6. Hose
7. Hose
8. Connector
9. Bolt
10. Washer

11. Housing
12. Spring
13. Spring retainer
14. Piston cup
15. Piston cup washer
16. Seal
17. Piston
18. Circlip
19. Brake spring washer
20. Spring

21. Boot
22. Pushrod
23. Circlip
24. Nut
25. Clevis
26. Pin
27. Pedal
28. Washer
29. Cotter pin

pushrod boot seats against the master cylinder correctly. Tighten the bolts securely.

9. Connect the brake and reservoir supply hoses at the master cylinder.

10. Fill the master cylinder with new DOT 5 hydraulic brake fluid. Bleed brake system as described under *Bleeding Hydraulic System* in this chapter.

11. Install the master cylinder gasket and cover after bleeding the brakes.

12. Perform the *Rear Brake Adjustment* in Chapter Three.

> *WARNING*
> *Do not ride the motorcycle until you are sure the brakes are working properly.*

Disassembly

Refer to **Figure 52** for this procedure.

1. Remove the master cylinder as described in this chapter.

2. Remove the cover and gasket. Drain and discard the brake fluid from the master cylinder.

3. Depress the piston assembly slightly and remove the circlip from the end of the master cylinder.

4. Withdraw the piston assembly from the master cylinder.

Inspection

Harley-Davidson does not provide any specifications for wear limits on any of the master cylinder components. Replace any parts that appear to be damaged or worn.

1. Clean all parts in denatured alcohol or fresh DOT 5 brake fluid. Cleaned parts should be placed on a clean lint-free cloth until reassembly.

2. The piston assembly consists of the circlip, piston, seal, piston cup washer, piston cup, spring retainer and spring. Inspect the rubber parts for wear, cracks, swelling or other damage. Check the piston for severe wear or damage. Check the spring for fatigue or breakage. If any one part of the piston assembly is damaged, the entire piston assembly must be replaced; individual parts are not available from Harley-Davidson (except the piston cup washer).

> *NOTE*
> *Do not remove the seal from the piston if you plan on reusing the piston/seal assembly.*

3. Inspect the master cylinder walls for scratches or wear grooves. The master cylinder housing should be replaced if the cylinder walls are damaged.

4. Check to see that the vent hole in the cover is not plugged.

5. Check the threads in the master cylinder. If the threads are slightly damaged, clean them up with a proper size thread tap. If the threads are severely worn or damaged, replace the master cylinder body.

> *NOTE*
> *If you use a tap to clean the threads in the master cylinder, flush the master cylinder thoroughly with solvent and blow dry.*

6. Inspect the piston bore in the master cylinder for wear, corrosion or damage. Replace the master cylinder if necessary.

Assembly

Refer to **Figure 52** when performing this procedure.

1. Soak the piston O-ring and cup in fresh DOT 5 brake fluid for at least 15 minutes to make the cups pliable. Apply a thin coat of brake fluid to the cylinder bore before assembly.

2. Place the master cylinder in a vise with soft jaws. Do not tighten the jaws too much or the master cylinder may be damaged.

3. If you are installing a new piston assembly, install the new seal onto the new piston.

4. Install the piston cup washer, piston cup, spring retainer and spring onto the end of the piston.

> *CAUTION*
> *When installing the piston assembly, do not allow the piston cup to turn inside out as it will be damaged and allow brake fluid leakage within the cylinder bore.*

5. Install the piston assembly into the master cylinder.

6. Press the piston assembly into the master cylinder body and install the circlip into the groove in the end of the master cylinder. The piston assembly must be pressed in far enough so that the circlip can be installed in the groove. Make sure that the circlip seats in the groove completely.

7. After installing the circlip, push the piston assembly in and let the spring push it back out. Repeat this

14

step several times to make sure it is seated correctly and moves freely in the cylinder bore.

8. Install the master cylinder as described in this chapter.

REAR MASTER CYLINDER (EARLY 1987 FLST)

Removal/Disassembly

Refer to **Figure 53** for this procedure.

CAUTION
Cover the surrounding area of the frame and wheel with a heavy cloth or plastic covering to protect them from accidental brake fluid spills. Wash brake fluid off any painted or plated surfaces immediately. Use soapy water and rinse completely.

1. Remove the chrome master cylinder cover.

NOTE
Drain the brake fluid from the hose and discard it—never reuse brake fluid. Contaminated brake fluid may cause brake failure.

2. To drain the hydraulic fluid from the rear brake system, perform the following:
   a. Attach a hose to the bleed valve on the caliper assembly.
   b. Place the loose end of the hose in a container to catch the brake fluid.
   c. Open the bleed valve and continue to apply the rear brake pedal until the brake fluid is pumped out of the system.
   d. Disconnect the hose and tighten the bleed valve.
   e. Dispose of this brake fluid—*never* reuse brake fluid. Contaminated brake fluid may cause brake failure.

3. Disconnect the brake supply hose at the master cylinder.

4. Remove the master cylinder mounting bolts. Then move the master cylinder to the rear slightly and the push rod will disengage from the master cylinder piston assembly. Remove the master cylinder.

5. After removing the master cylinder, remove the brake spring washer, brake return spring and the rubber boot from the pushrod to prevent their loss.

6. Install by reversing these steps. Note the following.

7. Assemble the brake return spring and the spring washer over the end of the pushrod's small diameter end in the order shown in **Figure 53**. Hold in this position and slide the boot over the spring, washer and pushrod. Then bring the master cylinder up along its mounting position and insert the pushrod through the master cylinder and into the end of the piston assembly. Hold the master cylinder/pushrod assembly in position and install the master cylinder bolts and washers finger-tight. Then check that the pushrod boot seats against the master cylinder correctly. Tighten the bolts securely. Position the boot so that the hole in the boot faces down.

8. Connect the brake supply hose at the master cylinder.

9. Fill the master cylinder with new DOT 5 hydraulic brake fluid. Bleed brake system as described under *Bleeding Hydraulic System* in this chapter.

10. Install the master cylinder gasket and cover after bleeding the brakes.

11. Perform the *Rear Brake Adjustment* in Chapter Three.

WARNING
Do not ride the motorcycle until you are sure the brakes are working properly.

Disassembly

Refer to **Figure 53** for this procedure.

1. Remove the master cylinder as described in this chapter.

2. Remove the cover and gasket. Drain and discard the brake fluid from the master cylinder.

3. Depress the piston assembly slightly and remove the circlip from the end of the master cylinder.

4. Withdraw the piston assembly from the master cylinder.

Inspection

Harley-Davidson does not provide any specifications for wear limits on any of the master cylinder components. Replace any parts that appear to be damaged or worn.

1. Clean all parts in denatured alcohol or fresh DOT 5 brake fluid. Cleaned parts should be placed on a clean lint-free cloth until reassembly.

2. The piston assembly consists of the circlip, piston, seal, piston cup and spring seat and spring. Harley-Davidson recommends to replace the piston assembly whenever the master cylinder assembly is

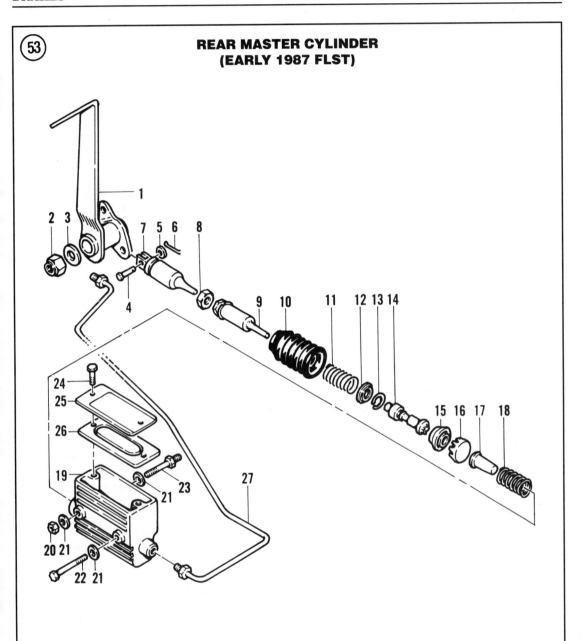

**REAR MASTER CYLINDER
(EARLY 1987 FLST)**

53

1. Pedal	10. Boot	
2. Nut	11. Spring	19. Reservoir
3. Washer	12. Cupped washer	20. Nut
4. Pin	13. Circlip	21. Washer
5. Washer	14. Piston	22. Bolt
6. Cotter pin	15. Seal	23. Bolt
7. Rod end	16. Piston cup	24. Bolt
8. Nut	17. Spring seat	25. Cover
9. Pushrod	18. Spring	26. Diaphragm

14

disassembled. Individual parts are not available from Harley-Davidson.

3. Inspect the master cylinder walls for scratches or wear grooves. The master cylinder housing should be replaced if the cylinder walls are damaged.

4. Check to see that the vent hole in the cover is not plugged.

5. Check the threads in the master cylinder. If the threads are slightly damaged, clean them up with a proper size thread tap. If the threads are severely worn or damaged, replace the master cylinder body.

NOTE
If you use a tap to clean the threads in the master cylinder, flush the master cylinder thoroughly with solvent and blow dry.

6. Inspect the piston bore in the master cylinder for wear, corrosion or damage. Replace the master cylinder if necessary.

Assembly

Refer to **Figure 53** for this procedure.

1. Soak the piston seal and cup in fresh DOT 5 brake fluid for at least 15 minutes to make the cups pliable. Dip all the remaining piston assembly components in brake fluid. Apply a thin coat of brake fluid to the cylinder bore before assembly.

2. Place the master cylinder in a vise with soft jaws. Do not tighten the jaws too much or the master cylinder may be damaged.

3. If you are installing a new piston assembly, install the new seal onto the new piston.

4. Insert the spring seat into the spring and insert the spring into the master cylinder bore.

CAUTION
When installing the piston cup and the piston in the following steps, do not allow the piston cup to turn inside out as it will be damaged and allow brake fluid leakage within the cylinder bore.

5. Insert the piston cup into the cylinder bore and place over the spring seat.

6. Install the new piston seal onto the piston.

7. Install the piston assembly into the master cylinder.

8. Press the piston assembly into the master cylinder body and install the circlip into the groove in the end of the master cylinder. The piston assembly must be

pressed in far enough so that the circlip can be installed in the groove. Make sure that the circlip seats in the groove completely.

9. After installing the circlip, push the piston assembly in and let the spring push it back out. Repeat this step several times to make sure it is seated correctly and moves freely in the cylinder bore.

10. Install the master cylinder as described in this chapter.

REAR MASTER CYLINDER (LATE 1987-ON FXST)

Removal

Refer to **Figure 54** for this procedure.

CAUTION
Cover the surrounding area of the frame and wheel with a heavy cloth or plastic covering to protect it from accidental brake fluid spills. Wash brake fluid off any painted or plated surfaces immediately. Use soapy water and rinse completely.

1. Remove the exhaust system as described in Chapter Eight.

2. Disconnect the clevis pin (**Figure 55**) at the brake pedal.

NOTE
Drain the brake fluid from the hose and discard it—never reuse brake fluid. Contaminated brake fluid may cause brake failure.

3. To drain the hydraulic fluid from the rear brake system, perform the following:

    a. Attach a hose to the bleed valve on the caliper assembly.

    b. Place the loose end of the hose in a container to catch the brake fluid.

    c. Open the bleed valve and continue to apply the rear brake pedal until the brake fluid is pumped out of the system.

    d. Disconnect the hose and tighten the bleed valve.

    e. Dispose of this brake fluid—*never* reuse brake fluid. Contaminated brake fluid may cause brake failure.

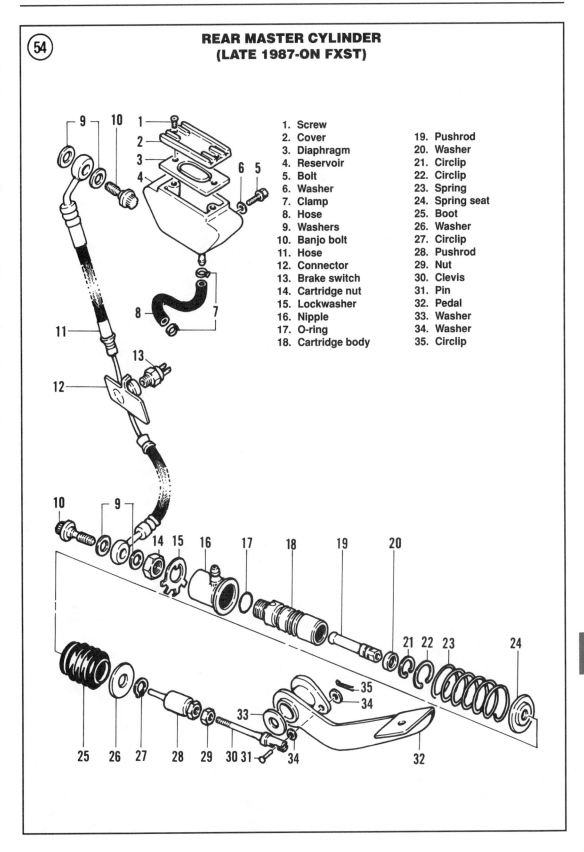

**REAR MASTER CYLINDER
(LATE 1987-ON FXST)**

1. Screw
2. Cover
3. Diaphragm
4. Reservoir
5. Bolt
6. Washer
7. Clamp
8. Hose
9. Washers
10. Banjo bolt
11. Hose
12. Connector
13. Brake switch
14. Cartridge nut
15. Lockwasher
16. Nipple
17. O-ring
18. Cartridge body
19. Pushrod
20. Washer
21. Circlip
22. Circlip
23. Spring
24. Spring seat
25. Boot
26. Washer
27. Circlip
28. Pushrod
29. Nut
30. Clevis
31. Pin
32. Pedal
33. Washer
34. Washer
35. Circlip

14

NOTE
If you only want to drain the master cylinder reservoir, disconnect the reservoir supply hose from the fitting on the master cylinder and drain the brake fluid into a container. Plug the hose opening.

4. Cut the supply hose clamp at the cartridge body (**Figure 56**) and disconnect the hose. Do not twist the hose back and forth sharply or you may break the hose nipple on the cartridge body.

CAUTION
*The banjo bolt (**Figure 57**) holding the metal brake line to the cartridge body is tight. When loosening the bolt, you don't want to twist the bolt as this may cause bolt or cartridge body damage. However, because the bolt is tight, it will want to twist as you attempt to loosen it. Furthermore, the metal brake line will want to turn with the bolt, a condition that could damage or break the line. To keep the bolt from twisting, shock it loose with a hand impact driver or hit the wrench carefully with a hammer.*

5. Loosen the banjo bolt at the cartridge body and remove the bolt and the 2 sealing washers. Place the open end of the hose in a plastic bag to prevent brake fluid leakage.
6. Bend the lockplate tab away from the cartridge body. Then remove the nut (**Figure 58**) and lockplate and remove the cartridge body.

Disassembly

Refer to **Figure 54** for this procedure.

CAUTION
Keep all dirt and grease away from the cartridge body in the following steps. After cleaning the cartridge body in Step 2, all work on the cartridge body should be performed on a clean lint-free cloth.

1. Remove the master cylinder as described in this chapter.
2. Clean the master cylinder cartridge body with denatured alcohol.
3. Screw the banjo bolt into the end of the cartridge body.

CAUTION
The banjo bolt installed into the cartridge body in Step 3 will protect the end of the cartridge while removing it. Failure to install the banjo bolt may cause the cartridge to be damaged before it is removed from the cartridge body.

4. Press down on the large washer (A, **Figure 59**) to compress the spring and put a wrench across the flat on the pushrod. Then use another wrench to loosen the pushrod jam nut (B, **Figure 59**) on the clevis and

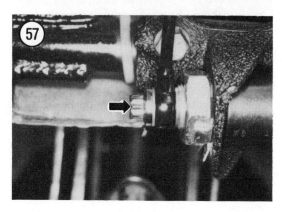

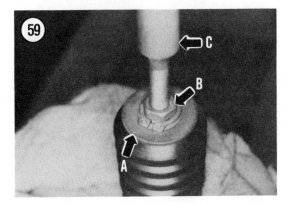

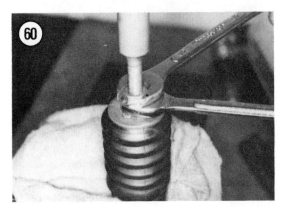

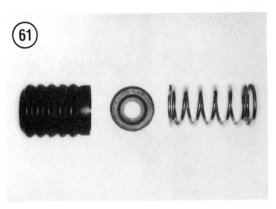

unscrew the clevis (C, **Figure 59**) from the end of the pushrod. See **Figure 60**.

5. Set the cartridge body upright so that it rests on the banjo bolt. Then compress the large washer (A, **Figure 59**) in the end of the cartridge body and remove the circlip from the groove in the pushrod. Release the washer and remove the washer, boot and spring.

6. Locate and remove the spring return retainer from inside the boot. See **Figure 61**.

7. Remove the circlip (**Figure 62**) from the cartridge body groove and remove the pushrod and its washer (**Figure 63**).

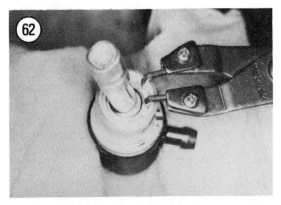

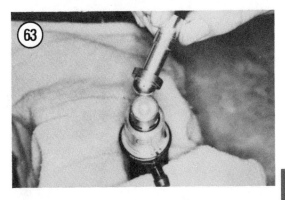

14

8. To replace the hose adaptor (**Figure 64**) on the cartridge body:

   a. Stand the cartridge body upright so that it rests on the banjo bolt.

   b. Push down on the hose adaptor and slide it off of the cartridge body. Protect the cartridge body from dirt or other damage.

   c. The O-rings (**Figure 65**) should not be removed unless replacement is required.

   d. Remove the outer cartridge body circlip.

NOTE
*Do not remove the piston assembly from the cartridge body (**Figure 66**). Replacement parts for the piston assembly are not available. If the piston and its seals are damaged, the cartridge body must be replaced as a set.*

Inspection

Harley-Davidson does not provide any specifications for wear limits on any of the master cylinder components. Because some of the parts that make up the piston assembly are only available in kits, not all of the parts will be available individually. See your dealer when ordering parts. Replace any parts that appear to be damaged or worn.

1. Clean all parts in denatured alcohol or fresh DOT 5 brake fluid. Cleaned parts should be placed on a clean lint-free cloth until reassembly.

2. Inspect the cartridge body (**Figure 65**) for cracks or damage.

3. Check the hose reservoir for damage (**Figure 66**).

4. Inspect the O-rings on the cartridge body (**Figure 65**) for wear or damage. If the O-rings are worn, they must be replaced together with the hose reservoir.

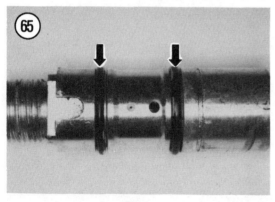

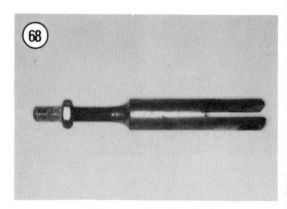

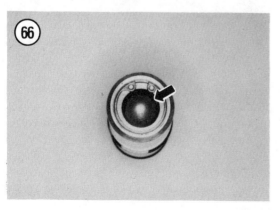

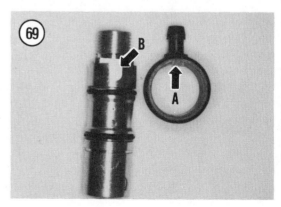

5. Check the threads on the cartridge body, banjo bolt and pushrod. Replace damaged parts as required.

6. Check the clevis (**Figure 68**) for cracks, bending or thread damage. Replace the clevis, if required.

7. Check the dust boot (**Figure 61**) for tears, age deterioration or other damage. Replace if necessary.

Assembly

Refer to **Figure 54** for this procedure.

1. Assemble the hose reservoir, if removed, as follows:

  a. Install the outer cartridge body circlip.

  b. Soak the new cartridge body O-rings in DOT 5 brake fluid. Then install the O-rings into the cartridge body grooves (**Figure 65**).

  c. The hose reservoir has a tab (A, **Figure 69**) that must align with a notch on the cartridge body (B, **Figure 69**).

  d. Using hand pressure only, insert the cartridge into the cartridge body. See **Figure 70**.

CAUTION
Do not force the cartridge into the cartridge body. If the parts do not assemble

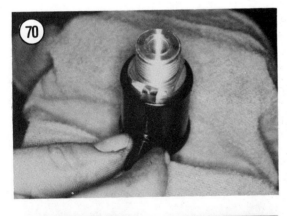

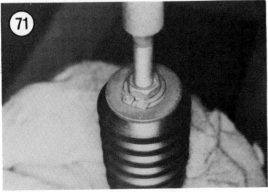

easily, the cartridge notch and cartridge body lug are not properly aligned. Forcing these parts together can damage them.

2. When the cartridge is properly installed in the cartridge body, thread the banjo bolt into the end of the cartridge body. Then stand the assembly up so that it is resting on the banjo bolt.

3. Install the washer onto the pushrod (opposite ball-end). See **Figure 63**.

4. Insert the pushrod (ball-end first) into the cartridge until the pushrod washer is seated in the cartridge bore. Then install the circlip into the cartridge groove to secure the pushrod (**Figure 62**). Make sure the circlip seats in the groove completely. After installing the circlip, rotate the pushrod by hand; it should turn freely. If the pushrod is tight, disassemble the cartridge to locate the damaged or improperly installed part.

5. Install the return spring, spring retainer, dust boot (**Figure 61**) and washer onto the pushrod. Rotate the dust boot so that the drain hole in the boot faces down.

6. Push the washer down to compress the return spring and install the circlip onto the end of the pushrod. Make sure the circlip seats in the groove completely.

7. Reinstall the clevis and its jam nut. Do not tighten the jam nut; adjustment will be made after installing the master cylinder. See **Figure 71** and **Figure 72**.

8. Seat the boot into the cartridge body.

Installation

Refer to **Figure 54** for this procedure.

1. If the reservoir was removed, place it into position and secure it with its screws and washers. Install the hose onto the reservoir nipple and secure the hose with a hose clamp.

CAUTION
Handle the cartridge body carefully when installing it as the hose reservoir can be easily cracked or broken off.

2. Align the tab on the lockwasher with the notch in the master cylinder mounting bracket and install the lockwasher (**Figure 73**).

3. Pivot the brake pedal as required to provide room when installing the cartridge body assembly into the frame mounting bracket. Then carefully insert the

14

threaded end of the cartridge body through the frame mounting bracket, making sure the hose nipple is facing up. The square portion on the cartridge body must engage the square hole in the mounting bracket.

4. Screw the cartridge body nut (**Figure 74**) onto the cartridge body and tighten to the torque specification listed in **Table 2**. Then bend the lockwasher arm over the nut to lock it.

> *WARNING*
> *When installing replacement banjo bolts and washers used to connect the brake hose to the cartridge body, note that 2 different types of banjo bolt washers have been used. Washers used on early models were made of copper with a zinc coating (A, **Figure 75**). Late models use steel washers equipped with a rubber O-ring (B, **Figure 75**). Because the banjo bolts are designed to be used with a specific type of washer, make sure that replacement banjo washers or bolts match the original parts used. Using an incorrect washer or bolt may allow the brake hose to leak and result*

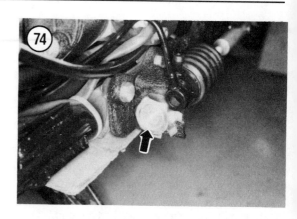

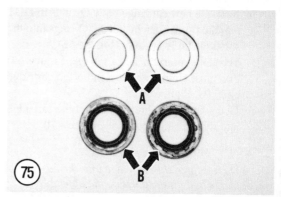

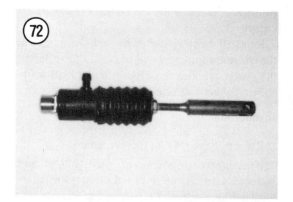

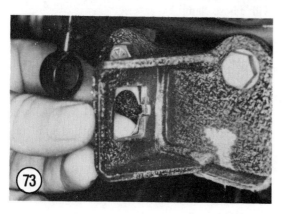

in loss of complete brake pressure. If necessary, ask your dealer's parts or service manager to identify the correct washers and banjo bolts used on your model.

NOTE
*Install **new** banjo bolt washers when performing Step 5.*

5. Assemble the brake line onto the cartridge body by placing a washer on both sides of the brake line fitting (**Figure 76**), then secure the fitting to the cartridge body with the banjo bolt. Adjust the brake line so that it is at a 45-50° angle from horizontal. When the brake line is angled properly, tighten the banjo bolt to the torque specification listed in **Table 2**.

NOTE
*Note that the tightening torques for the copper and steel/rubber banjo bolts are different. Make sure to use the tightening torque for the type of washer installed on your bike (**Table 2**).*

6. Slide a new hose clamp onto the hose and fit the hose onto the hose reservoir nipple (**Figure 77**).

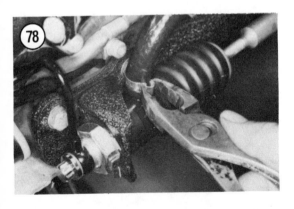

Slide the clamp down so that it is against the hose where the hose fits onto the nipple. Close the hose clamp so that it is tight against the hose (**Figure 78**).

NOTE
***Figure 79** shows the type of pliers that will be required to close the hose clamp.*

7. Pivot the brake pedal into position and attach the clevis to the brake pedal (**Figure 80**). Secure with a new spring pin or cotter pin, whichever one is used.
8. Adjust the brake pedal height as described in Chapter Three.
9. Fill the reservoir with new DOT 5 hydraulic brake fluid. Bleed brake system as described under *Bleeding Hydraulic System* in this chapter.
10. Install the reservoir gasket and cover after bleeding the brakes.

WARNING
Do not ride the motorcycle until you are sure the brakes are working properly.

REAR MASTER CYLINDER (LATE 1987-ON FLST)

Removal

Refer to **Figure 81** for this procedure.

CAUTION
Cover the surrounding area of the frame and wheel with a heavy cloth or plastic covering to protect it from accidental brake fluid spills. Wash brake fluid off any painted or plated surfaces immediately. Use soapy water and rinse completely.

1. Remove the exhaust system as described in Chapter Eight.

14

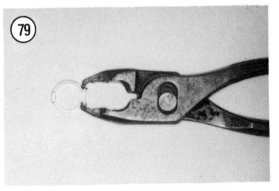

2. Disconnect the clevis pin at the brake pedal by removing the cotter pin, washer and pin. Discard the cotter pin.

NOTE
Drain the brake fluid from the hose and discard it—never reuse brake fluid. Contaminated brake fluid may cause brake failure.

3. To drain the hydraulic fluid from the rear brake system, perform the following:

a. Attach a hose to the bleed valve on the caliper assembly.

b. Place the loose end of the hose in a container to catch the brake fluid.

c. Open the bleed valve and continue to apply the rear brake pedal until the brake fluid is pumped out of the system.

d. Disconnect the hose and tighten the bleed valve.

e. Dispose of this brake fluid—*never* reuse brake fluid. Contaminated brake fluid may cause brake failure.

4. Loosen the banjo bolt at the master cylinder and remove the bolt and the 2 sealing washers. Place the

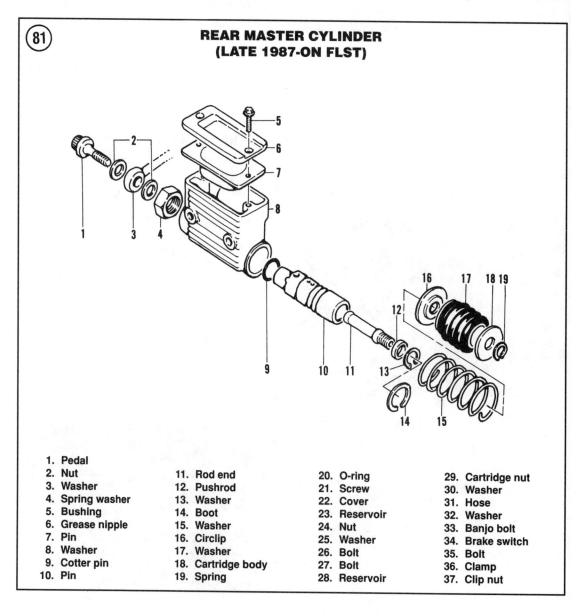

**REAR MASTER CYLINDER
(LATE 1987-ON FLST)**

1. Pedal	11. Rod end	20. O-ring	29. Cartridge nut
2. Nut	12. Pushrod	21. Screw	30. Washer
3. Washer	13. Washer	22. Cover	31. Hose
4. Spring washer	14. Boot	23. Reservoir	32. Washer
5. Bushing	15. Washer	24. Nut	33. Banjo bolt
6. Grease nipple	16. Circlip	25. Washer	34. Brake switch
7. Pin	17. Washer	26. Bolt	35. Bolt
8. Washer	18. Cartridge body	27. Bolt	36. Clamp
9. Cotter pin	19. Spring	28. Reservoir	37. Clip nut
10. Pin			

open end of the hose in a plastic bag to prevent brake fluid leakage.

5. Remove the nuts and washers securing the chrome cover to the master cylinder and remove the cover. Then remove the master cylinder nuts and washer and remove the master cylinder.

Disassembly

Refer to **Figure 81** for this procedure.

> *CAUTION*
> *Keep all dirt and grease away from the cartridge body in the following steps. After cleaning the master cylinder in Step 2, all work on the master cylinder and cartridge body should be performed on a clean lint-free cloth.*

1. Remove the master cylinder housing as described in this chapter.
2. Clean the master cylinder housing with denatured alcohol.
3. Screw the banjo bolt into the end of the cartridge.

> *CAUTION*
> *The banjo bolt installed into the cartridge body in Step 3 will protect the end of the cartridge before removing it. Failure to install the banjo bolt may cause cartridge damage before it is removed from the cartridge cylinder.*

4. Remove the dust boot from the end of the cartridge.
5. Drive the spring pin out of the clevis and pushrod. Then unscrew the clevis from the pushrod and remove the clevis.
6. Set the master cylinder upright so that it rests on the banjo bolt. Then compress the large washer in the end of the cartridge and remove the circlip from the groove in the pushrod. Release the washer and remove the washer, boot and spring.
7. Locate and remove the spring return retainer from inside the boot.
8. Remove the pushrod from the cartridge.
9. Remove the banjo bolt from the end of the cartridge.
10. Remove the 3/4-18 nut from the opposite end of the master cylinder and pull the cartridge out of the reservoir. Do not allow the cartridge to become dirty while it is removed from the reservoir.

Inspection

Harley-Davidson does not provide any specifications for wear limits on any of the master cylinder components. Because some of the parts that make up the piston assembly are only available in kits, not all of the parts will be available individually. See your dealer when ordering parts. Replace any parts that appear to be damaged or worn.

1. Clean all parts in denatured alcohol or fresh DOT 5 brake fluid. Cleaned parts should be placed on a clean lint-free cloth until reassembly.
2. Inspect the master cylinder for cracks or damage. Inspect the cartridge cylinder walls for scratches or wear grooves. The master cylinder should be replaced if the cartridge walls are damaged.
3. Remove the O-rings from inside the cartridge walls and check them for wear or damage. If the O-rings are worn, replace them.
4. Clean the O-ring grooves in the cartridge body with a cotton cloth soaked in alcohol. Allow to dry thoroughly.
5. Check the threads on the master cylinder, cartridge, banjo bolt and pushrod. Replace damaged parts as required.
6. Check the dust boot for age deterioration or other damage. Replace if necessary.
7. Inspect the cartridge, pushrod washer and pushrod for damage. Replace damaged parts as required.

Assembly

Refer to **Figure 81** for this procedure.
1. Soak the cartridge cylinder O-rings in DOT 5 brake fluid. Then install the O-rings into the cartridge cylinder grooves.
2. Install the cartridge into the cartridge cylinder as follows:
   a. Coat the cartridge cylinder walls with DOT 5 brake fluid.
   b. Using hand pressure only, insert the cartridge into the cartridge cylinder. The notch on the cartridge should engage the lug inside the cartridge cylinder.

> *CAUTION*
> *Do not force the cartridge into the cartridge cylinder. If the parts do not assemble easily, the cartridge notch and cartridge cylinder lug are not properly aligned. Forcing these parts together can damage them.*

14

3. When the cartridge is properly installed in the cartridge cylinder, thread the banjo bolt into the end of the cartridge. Then stand the master cylinder up so that it is resting on the banjo bolt.

4. Install the washer onto the pushrod (opposite ball-end). Then secure the washer by installing the circlip into the pushrod groove. Check that the circlip seats in the pushrod groove completely.

5. Insert the pushrod (ball-end first) into the cartridge until the pushrod washer is seated in the cartridge bore. Then install the circlip into the cartridge groove to secure the pushrod. Make sure the circlip seats in the groove completely. After installing the circlip, rotate the pushrod by hand; it should turn freely. If the pushrod is tight, disassemble the cartridge to locate the damaged or improperly installed part.

6. Insert the adapter into the end of the cartridge cylinder.

7. Install the return spring, spring retainer, dust boot and washer onto the pushrod. Rotate the dust boot so that the drain hole in the boot faces down.

8. Push the washer down to compress the return spring and install the circlip onto the end of the pushrod. Make sure the circlip seats in the groove completely.

9. Slide the dust boot onto the master cylinder and engage the dust boot lip with the groove on the master cylinder.

Installation

Refer to **Figure 81** for this procedure.

1. Thread the clevis onto the pushrod by rotating the master cylinder until the clevis and pushrod are tight. Then secure the clevis and pushrod with a new spring pin.

2. Thread the locknut onto the cartridge threads at the rear of the master cylinder. Do not tighten the locknut at this time.

WARNING
When installing replacement banjo bolts and washers used to connect the brake hose to the cartridge body, note that 2 different types of banjo bolt washers have been used. Washers used on early models were made of copper with a zinc coating (A, Figure 75). Late models use steel washers equipped with a rubber O-ring (B, Figure 75). Because the banjo bolts are designed to be used

with a specific type of washer, make sure that replacement banjo washers or bolts match the original parts used. Using an incorrect washer or bolt may allow the brake hose to leak and result in loss of complete brake pressure. If necessary, ask your dealer's parts or service manager to identify the correct washers and banjo bolts used on your model.

NOTE
Install new banjo bolt washers when performing Step 3.

3. Assemble the brake line onto the cartridge by placing a washer on both sides of the brake line fitting, then secure the fitting to the cartridge with the banjo bolt; tighten the banjo bolt to the torque specification listed in **Table 2**.

NOTE
Note that the tightening torques for the copper and steel/rubber banjo bolts are different. Make sure to use the tightening torque for the type of washer installed on your bike (Table 2).

4. Tighten the cartridge locknut to the torque specification listed in **Table 2**.

5. Install the master cylinder into position and secure it with its washers and nuts; do not tighten the nuts at this time.

6. Pivot the brake pedal into position and attach the clevis to the brake pedal using the pin, washer and a new cotter pin. Assemble the parts in the order shown in **Figure 81**.

7. Fill the reservoir with new DOT 5 hydraulic brake fluid. Bleed brake system as described under *Bleeding Hydraulic System* in this chapter.

8. Install the reservoir gasket and cover after bleeding the brakes.

9. Adjust the brake pedal height position as described in Chapter Three.

10. Reinstall the exhaust system.

WARNING
Do not ride the motorcycle until you are sure the brakes are working properly.

**BRAKE HOSE
AND LINE REPLACEMENT**

A combination of steel and flexible brake lines are used to connect the master cylinder to its brake

FRONT BRAKE HOSE ASSEMBLY

To master cylinder

To brake caliper

1. Banjo bolt
2. Washer
3. Hose

82

caliper. Where banjo bolts are used to connect a hose to a master cylinder or caliper, special sealing washers are used on both sides of the hose fitting. Where metal brake hoses are used, they screw directly into the brake caliper.

> *WARNING*
> *When purchasing new banjo bolts or washers, note that 2 different types of banjo bolts and washers have been used. The washers used on early models were made of copper with a zinc coating (A, **Figure 75**). Late models use steel washers equipped with a rubber O-ring (B, **Figure 75**). Because the washers are designed to be used with a specific style of banjo bolt, make sure that replacement banjo bolts or washers match each other. Using an incorrect washer or bolt may allow the brake hose to leak and result in loss of complete brake pressure. To ensure that you purchase the correct replacement part, take the old parts to your dealer and have them match the parts.*

There is no factory-recommended replacement interval, but it is a good idea to replace all flexible brake hoses every four years or when they show signs of swelling, cracking or damage.

Some brake hose assemblies will be made of steel and flexible lines permanently attached together. This assembly should be replaced every 4 years as the flexible portion of the assembly will eventually swell, fatigue and crack.

All metal brake lines do not require routine replacement unless they are damaged or the end fittings are leaking. When replacing the flexible brake hoses, inspect the metal brake lines for damage. If they have been hit, the lines may be restricted, thus decreasing braking effectiveness.

14

> *CAUTION*
> *Cover the wheels, fenders, fuel tank and swing arm with a heavy cloth or plastic tarp to protect them from the accidental spilling of brake fluid. Wash any spilled brake fluid off of any painted or plated surface immediately. Use soapy water and rinse completely.*

Front Hoses and Lines
Removal/Installation

A combination steel/flexible brake hose (**Figure 82**) is used to connect the front master cylinder to the front brake caliper. When purchasing a new hose, compare it to the old hose to make sure that the length and angle of the steel hose portion is correct. New banjo bolt washers should be installed.

1. Drain the hydraulic brake fluid from the front brake system as follows:

    a. Flip the rubber cap off the caliper bleed valve and connect a hose over the bleed valve.

    b. Insert the loose end of the hose in a container to catch the brake fluid.

    c. Open the bleed valve on the caliper and apply the front brake lever to pump the fluid out of the master cylinder and brake line. Continue until all of the fluid has been removed.

    d. Close the bleed valve and disconnect the hose.

    e. Dispose of this brake fluid—*never* reuse brake fluid. Contaminated brake fluid may cause brake failure.

2. Before removing the brake line, note how the brake line is routed from the master cylinder to the caliper. In addition, note the number and position of the metal hose clamps and plastic ties used to hold the brake line in place. The brake hose should be reinstalled following the same path and secured at the same position. The metal clamps can be reused. New plastic ties, however, will have to be installed.

3. Cut the plastic ties and discard them.

4. Remove the screw or nut holding the metal clamps around the brake line. Spread the clamp and remove it from the brake line.

NOTE
After disconnecting the brake hose in Step 5 and Step 6, place the hose end in a plastic resealable bag and zip it closed around the hose. This will prevent brake fluid from dripping onto parts of the motorcycle while it is being removed.

5. Remove the banjo bolt and washers securing the hose at the brake caliper.

6. Remove the banjo bolt and washers securing the hose at the master cylinder.

7. Remove the brake hose from the motorcycle.

8. If you plan on reusing the brake hose assembly, inspect it as follows:

    a. Check the metal pipe portion for cracks or fractures. Check the junction where the metal pipe enters and exits the flexible hose. Check the crimped clamp for looseness or damage.

    b. Check the flexible hose portion for swelling, cracks or other damage.

    c. Replace the hose assembly, if necessary.

9. Install a new brake hose, sealing washers and banjo bolt in the reverse order of removal. Be sure to install new sealing washers on both sides of the hose fitting.

10. Tighten all banjo bolts to the torque specification listed in **Table 2**.

NOTE
Note that the tightening torques for the copper and steel/rubber banjo bolts are different. Make sure to use the tightening torque for the type of washer installed on your bike (Table 2).

11. Refill the master cylinder with fresh brake fluid clearly marked DOT 5. Bleed the front brake system as described in this chapter.

WARNING
Do not ride the motorcycle until you are sure that the brakes are operating properly.

Rear Brake Hose
Removal/Installation

On 1984-early 1987 models, the brake line assembly consists of a steel brake line, a combination steel/flexible hose and a tee fitting. The steel brake line is connected from the master cylinder to the tee fitting. The combination steel/flexible brake hose is connected from the tee fitting to the brake caliper.

On late 1987 and later models, a single combination steel/flexible brake hose is used to connect the rear master cylinder to the rear brake caliper.

When purchasing a new hose, compare it to the old hose to make sure that the length and angle of the steel hose portion is correct. New banjo bolt washers should be installed, if used.

1. Remove the saddlebags, if so equipped.
2. Drain the hydraulic brake fluid from the front brake system as follows:
   a. Flip the rubber cap off the caliper bleed valve and connect a hose over the bleed valve.
   b. Insert the loose end of the hose in a container to catch the brake fluid.
   c. Open the bleed valve on the caliper and apply the front brake lever to pump the fluid out of the master cylinder and brake line. Continue until all of the fluid has been removed.
   d. Close the bleed valve and disconnect the hose.
   e. Dispose of this brake fluid—*never* reuse brake fluid. Contaminated brake fluid may case brake failure.
3. Before removing a brake line, note how the brake line is routed from the master cylinder to the caliper. In addition, note the number and position of the metal hose clamps and plastic ties used to hold the brake line in place. The brake hose should be reinstalled following the same path and secured at the same position. The metal clamps can be reused. New plastic ties, however, will have to be installed.
4. Cut the plastic ties and discard them.
5. Remove the screw or nut holding the metal clamps around the brake line. Spread the clamp and remove it from the brake line.

NOTE
After disconnecting the brake hose in Step 5 and Step 6, place the hose end in a plastic resealable bag and zip it closed around the hose. This will prevent brake fluid from dripping onto parts of the motorcycle while it is being removed.

6A. *1984-early 1987 models*: Perform the following:
   a. Loosen and then unscrew the metal brake line fitting at the master cylinder and at the tee fitting. Remove the brake line.
   b. Loosen and then unscrew the brake hose fitting at the tee fitting and at the brake caliper. Remove the brake line.

c. The tee fitting is mounted onto a bracket. If the brake fluid was contaminated, disconnect the brake light switch connector and remove the brake light switch at the tee fitting. Then unbolt the tee fitting and remove it from its mounting bracket. Clean the tee fitting with denatured alcohol and dry thoroughly with compressed air. Reinstall the tee fitting and the brake light switch.

6B. *Late 1987-on*: Perform the following:
   a. Remove the banjo bolt and washers securing the hose at the brake caliper (A, **Figure 83**).
   b. Remove the banjo bolt and washers securing the hose at the master cylinder.
   c. Remove the brake hose from the motorcycle.

7. If you plan on reusing the brake hose assembly, inspect it as follows:
   a. Check the metal pipe portion for cracks or fractures. Check the junction where the metal pipe enters and exits the flexible hose. Check the crimped clamp for looseness or damage.
   b. Check the flexible hose portion for swelling, cracks or other damage.
   c. Replace the hose assembly, if necessary.

8A. *1984-early 1987*: Install new brake lines in the reverse order of removal. Tighten all brake line fittings securely.

8B. *Later 1987-on*: Install a new brake hose, sealing washers and banjo bolts in the reverse order of removal. Be sure to install new sealing washers on both sides of the hose fitting (**Figure 84**).

NOTE
*Note that the tightening torques for the copper and steel/rubber banjo bolts are different. Make sure to use the tightening torque for the type of washer installed on your bike (**Table 2**).*

9. Refill the master cylinder with fresh brake fluid clearly marked DOT 5. Bleed the rear brake system as described in this chapter.

WARNING
Do not ride the motorcycle until you are sure that the brakes are operating properly.

14

BRAKE DISC (FRONT AND REAR)

A single brake disc is bolted to the front and rear wheels. Brake discs should be checked for runout and thickness. The minimum disc thickness is stamped on Harley-Davidson O.E.M. brake discs (**Figure 85**). **Table 1** lists disc brake specifications.

Removal/Installation

1. Remove the front or rear wheel as described in Chapter Ten.

> *NOTE*
> *Place a piece of wood or vinyl tube in the caliper in place of the disc. This way, if the brake lever is inadvertently squeezed, or the brake pedal depressed, the piston will not be forced out of the cylinder. If this does happen, the caliper may have to be disassembled to reseat the piston and the system will have to be bled.*

> *CAUTION*
> *Do not set the wheel down on the disc surface, as it may get scratched or warped. Set the wheel on 2 blocks of wood.*

2. Remove the bolts (and nuts) securing the brake disc to the hub and remove the disc. See **Figure 86**, typical.
3. Install by reversing these removal steps. Note the following.
4. Check the brake disc bolts (and nuts) for thread damage. Replace worn or damaged fasteners.
5. Clean the disc and the disc mounting surface thoroughly with brake cleaner or contact cleaner. Allow surfaces to dry before installation.
6. Coat the disc mounting bolts with Loctite Stud 'N Bearing mount. Tighten the bolts to the torque specification listed in **Table 2**.

Inspection

It is not necessary to remove the disc from the wheel to inspect it. Small marks on the disc are not important, but radial scratches deep enough to snag a fingernail reduce braking effectiveness and increase brake pad wear. If these grooves are found, the disc should be resurfaced or replaced.

1. Measure the thickness around the disc at several locations with vernier calipers or a micrometer (**Figure 87**). The disc must be replaced if the thickness at any point is less than the minimum stamped on each disc.

> *NOTE*
> *Use the disc specifications listed in **Table 1** if the stamping on the disc is unclear.*

2. Clean the disc of any rust or corrosion and wipe clean with lacquer thinner. Never use an oil-based solvent that may leave an oil residue on the disc.

BLEEDING THE SYSTEM

When air enters the brake system, the brake will feel soft or spongy, greatly reducing braking pressure. When this happens, the system must be bled to remove the air. Air can enter the system if there is a leak in the hydraulic system, a component has been replaced or the brake fluid has been replaced.

When bleeding the brakes, you can use one of two methods—manually or a brake bleeder.

Bleeding the Brake with a Brake Bleeder

This procedure uses a commercial brake bleeder that is available from motorcycle or automotive supply stores.

NOTE
Before bleeding the brake, check that all
brake hoses and lines are tight.

1. Remove the dust cap from the bleed valve on the caliper assembly.

2. Connect the brake bleeder to the bleed valve on the caliper assembly. See B, **Figure 83**, typical.

3. Clean the top of the master cylinder of all dirt and foreign matter.

4. Remove the screws securing the master cylinder top cover and remove the cover and rubber diaphragm.

5. Fill the reservoir almost to the top with DOT 5 brake fluid and reinstall the diaphragm and cover. Leave the cover in place during this procedure to prevent the entry of dirt.

WARNING
Do not intermix brake fluid. DOT 5
brake fluid was originally installed at
the time of manufacturer. Do not install
DOT 3 or DOT 4 brake fluid as it can
lead to brake system failure.

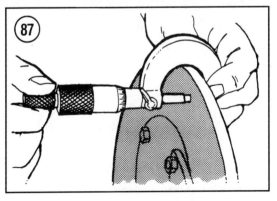

6. Pump the pump handle 10-15 times to create a vacuum and then open the bleed valve until brake fluid begins to enter the jar. Allow approximately 1 inch of fluid to enter the jar and then close the bleed valve. As the fluid enters the system and exits into the jar, the level will drop in the reservoir. Maintain the level to just about the top of the reservoir to prevent air from being drawn into the system.

NOTE
Do not allow the master cylinder reser-
voir to empty during the bleeding opera-
tion or more air will enter the system. If
this occurs, the entire procedure must be
repeated.

NOTE
If air is entering the brake bleeder hose
from around the bleed valve, apply sev-
eral layers of Teflon tape to the bleed
valve. This should make a good seal
between the bleed valve and the brake
bleeder hose. Teflon tape can be pur-
chased at hardware and plumbing sup-
ply stores.

7. If the fluid emerging from the hose into the jar is completely free of bubbles, the system should be properly bled. If there are signs of bubbles being withdrawn with the brake fluid, air is still trapped in the line. Repeat Step 6, making sure to refill the master cylinder to prevent air from being drawn into the system.

8. When the brake fluid is free of bubbles, tighten the bleed valve and remove the brake bleeder assembly. Reinstall the bleed valve dust cap.

NOTE
Do not reuse the brake fluid that was
forced into the brake bleeder jar. It
could be contaminated or dirty.

9. If necessary, add fluid to correct the level in the master cylinder reservoir. When topping off the front master cylinder, turn the handlebar until the reservoir is level; add fluid until it is level with the reservoir gasket surface. The rear master cylinder should be filled until the level is 1/8 in. (3.2 mm) below the gasket surface.

10. Reinstall the reservoir diaphragm and cap. Secure the cap with its 2 screws.

11. Test the feel of the brake lever or pedal. It should be firm and should offer the same resistance each

14

time it's operated. If it feels spongy, it is likely that there is still air in the system and it must be bled again. When all air has been bled from the system and the fluid level is correct in the reservoir, double-check for leaks and tighten all fittings and connections.

> **WARNING**
> *Before riding the bike, make certain that the brake is operating correctly by operating the lever or pedal several times.*

12. Test ride the bike slowly at first to make sure that the brakes are operating properly.

Bleeding the Brake Manually

When bleeding the brake manually, a clean jar, a suitable length of clear hose and a wrench will be required.

> **NOTE**
> *Before bleeding the brake, check that all brake hoses and lines are tight.*

1. Flip off the dust cap from the brake bleeder valve.
2. Connect a length of clear tubing to the bleeder valve on the caliper. Place the other end of the tube into a clean container. Fill the container with enough fresh DOT 5 brake fluid to keep the end submerged. The tube should be long enough so that a loop can be made higher than the bleeder valve to prevent air from being drawn into the caliper during bleeding. See **Figure 88**, typical.
3. Clean the top of the master cylinder of all dirt and foreign matter.
4. Remove the screws securing the master cylinder top cover and remove the cover and rubber diaphragm.
5. Fill the reservoir almost to the top with DOT 5 brake fluid and reinstall the diaphragm and cover. Leave the cover in place during this procedure to prevent the entry of dirt.

> **WARNING**
> *Do not intermix brake fluid. DOT 5 brake fluid was originally installed at the time of manufacturer. Do not install DOT 3 or DOT 4 brake fluid as it can lead to brake system failure.*

> **NOTE**
> *During this procedure, it is important to check the fluid level in the master cylinder reservoir often. If the reservoir runs*

dry, you'll introduce more air into the system which will require starting over.

6. Slowly apply the brake lever several times. Hold the lever in the applied position and open the bleeder valve about 1/2 turn. Allow the lever to travel to its limit. When this limit is reached, tighten the bleeder screw. As the brake fluid enters the system, the level will drop in the master cylinder reservoir. Maintain the level at about 3/8 in. (9.5 mm) from the top of the reservoir to prevent air from being drawn into the system.
7. Continue to pump the lever and fill the reservoir until the fluid emerging from the hose is completely free of air bubbles. If you are replacing the fluid, continue until the fluid emerging from the hose is clean.

> **NOTE**
> *If bleeding is difficult, it may be necessary to allow the fluid to stabilize for a few hours. Repeat the bleeding procedure when the tiny bubbles in the system settle out.*

8. Hold the lever in the applied position and tighten the bleeder valve. Remove the bleeder tube and install the bleeder valve dust cap.

> **NOTE**
> *Do not reuse the brake fluid that was forced into the jar. It could be contaminated or dirty.*

9. If necessary, add fluid to correct the level in the master cylinder reservoir. When topping off the

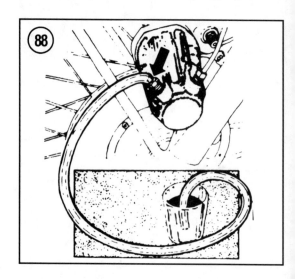

front master cylinder, turn the handlebar until the reservoir is level; add fluid until it is level with the reservoir gasket surface. The rear master cylinder should be filled until the level is 1/8 in. (3.2 mm) below the gasket surface.

10. Install the cap and diaphragm and tighten the screws securely.

11. Test the feel of the brake lever or pedal. It should be firm and should offer the same resistance each time it's operated. If it feels spongy, it is likely that there is still air in the system and it must be bled again. When all air has been bled from the system and the fluid level is correct in the reservoir, double-check for leaks and tighten all fittings and connections.

> *WARNING*
> *Before riding the bike, make certain that the brake is operating correctly by operating the lever or pedal several times.*

12. Test ride the bike slowly at first to make sure that the brakes are operating properly.

Table 1 BRAKE SPECIFICATIONS

	in.	mm
Brake pad minimum thickness		
Front and rear	0.062	1.57
Brake disc (front and rear)		
Minimum thickness	0.205	5.21
Outside diameter	11.50	292.1

Table 2 BRAKE TIGHTENING TORQUES

	ft.-lb.	N·m
Brake disc screws		
Front		
1984	23-27	31.7-37.2
1985-1991	16-18	22-25
1992-on	16-24	22-33
Rear		
1984	16-19	22-26
1985-1991	23-27	32-37
1992-on	30-45	41-61
Banjo bolts		
1984	—	—
1985-on		
FXSTC and FLSTC/F/N	25-30	34-41
FXSTS		
Top bolt	42-46	57-62
Bottom bolt	25-30	34-41
Rear brake caliper screws		
1985-on	12-15	—
Rear brake caliper reaction pin		
1984-on (FXSTC)	20	27

	in.-lb.	N·m
Brake bleeder nipple	32-40	3.7-4.6

14

FRAME, BODY AND FRAME REPAINTING

This chapter includes replacement procedures for components attached to the frame that are not covered in the rest of the manual.

This chapter describes procedures for completely stripping the frame. Recommendations are provided for repainting the stripped frame.

JIFFY STAND (SIDESTAND)

Removal/Installation

Refer to **Figure 1** for this procedure.

1. Support the bike so that it is secure.

2. Raise the jiffy stand and disconnect the return spring with a spring tool or vise-grip pliers.

3. Remove the nut, lockwasher, flat washer and leg stop at the top of the jiffy stand and remove the jiffy stand from the leg bracket.

4. To remove the leg bracket, remove the bolts and washers and remove the bracket.

5. Visually check the jiffy stand for cracks or damage. Check the pivot area at the top of the jiffy stand for deep scoring, excessive wear or damage.

6. Check the return spring for fatigue, stretching, cracks or other types of damage. If the spring has not been holding the jiffy stand securely in its retracted position, replace it.

7. Check the spring supports for cracks, hole elongation or other damage.

8. Check the leg bracket for damage.

9. Check jiffy stand and bolt threads for stripping, cross-threading or deposit buildup. Threaded holes in the frame should be cleaned to ensure proper bolt installation and tightening. If necessary, use a tap or die to true up the threads and to remove any deposits. Replace bolts, washers and nuts as required.

10. All worn or defective parts should be replaced.

11. Installation is the reverse of these steps while noting the following.

12. Apply a light coat of multipurpose grease to the pivot surfaces on the jiffy stand and leg bracket.

13. Apply Loctite 242 (blue) to all threaded fasteners and tighten securely. If the leg stop bolt (1, **Figure 1**) was removed, tighten to 19 ft.-lb. (26 N.m).

14. Check jiffy stand operation. The jiffy stand is designed to lock when it is placed in its full down (or forward) position *with* the weight of the bike resting on it. If the bike is raised momentarily while the jiffy stand is in place, the jiffy stand may retract slightly from its full down position. Before resting the weight of the bike on the jiffy stand, make sure the jiffy stand is in its full down position. Likewise,

make sure the jiffy stand retracts fully. Work the jiffy stand up and down to make sure it is fully operational in both positions.

FOOTPEGS

Rider and passenger pivot type footpegs are used. See **Figure 2**, typical. Replacement is fairly straightforward. When removing or replacing footpegs, check the bolts for cracks, deep scoring, excessive wear or thread damage. Check bolt holes for elongation or other damage. Rubber footpeg covers should be replaced when they become severely worn. When installing new covers, cut the old covers and remove them. Spray the inside of the new rubber cover with electrical contact cleaner and quickly install it over the metal footpeg. Push the rubber cover all the way onto the footpeg until it bottoms out. Loctite 242 (blue) should be used on all threaded fasteners. After tightening footpeg bolts, make sure footpegs pivot properly. The footpeg mounting brackets should be checked for damage and replaced if they do not offer adequate support.

FRONT FENDER
(1993-ON FXSTS)

Refer to **Figure 3** when removing and installing the front fender.

Removal

1. Support the bike with a suitable bike stand.
2. Slide the speedometer cable out of the speedometer cable fender bracket.
3. Remove the cotter pin, jam nut and shaft nut that secure the brake reaction link to the fender. Then remove the Allen bolt that is installed through the brake reaction link.

NOTE
Note the position of the nylon washer and rubber spacer installed inside the fender bushing. The washer and spacer may stay in the fender bracket bushing or come off with the shaft nut.

4. Repeat Step 3 for the opposite side.
5. Carefully lift the fender away from the front tire. Then install the Harley-Davidson fender link tool

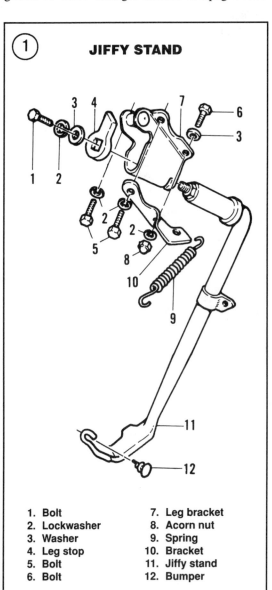

① JIFFY STAND

1. Bolt
2. Lockwasher
3. Washer
4. Leg stop
5. Bolt
6. Bolt
7. Leg bracket
8. Acorn nut
9. Spring
10. Bracket
11. Jiffy stand
12. Bumper

15

(part No. HD-39754 [**Figure 4**]) between the fender
links and tighten securely.

NOTE
*The fender link tool (**Figure 4**) is designed to spread and hold the fender
links in position when removing and
installing the front fender.*

6. Remove the flange nuts and shoulder bolts securing the fender link to the fender.

NOTE
*The fender insert is now a loose fit in the
fender. Do not lose it when removing the
fender.*

CAUTION
*It is easy to scratch the fender when
removing it in Step 7. Cover the fender
with a heavy cloth prior to removing it.*

7. Lift the fender and remove it from between the
forks and fender links.

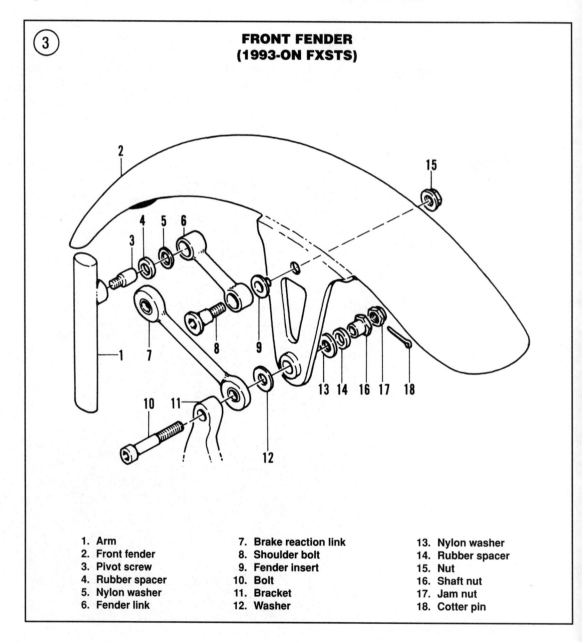

③

**FRONT FENDER
(1993-ON FXSTS)**

1. Arm	7. Brake reaction link
2. Front fender	8. Shoulder bolt
3. Pivot screw	9. Fender insert
4. Rubber spacer	10. Bolt
5. Nylon washer	11. Bracket
6. Fender link	12. Washer

13. Nylon washer
14. Rubber spacer
15. Nut
16. Shaft nut
17. Jam nut
18. Cotter pin

8. Remove the Harley-Davidson fender link tool.

9. If necessary, remove the fender links and pivot screws as follows:

    a. Remove the fender link from the pivot screw.

    b. Remove the nylon washer and rubber spacer.

    c. Loosen and remove the pivot screw.

    d. Repeat for the other side.

CAUTION
To help prevent from scratching the fender with installing it, cover the fender with a heavy cloth.

3. Install the front fender between the fork tubes and both fender links.

NOTE
Check that the fender insert is installed in the fender.

4. Install the shoulder bolts through the fender links and fender. Then install the flange nut.

5. Remove the fender link tool.

6. Tighten the shoulder bolts to 10-20 ft.-lb. (14-27 N.m).

7. Insert the nylon washer and rubber spacer into the fender bushing. Repeat for the other side.

8. Place a washer between the fender bushing and brake reaction link. Then install the Allen bolt through the assembly as shown in **Figure 3**.

9. Install the shaft nut onto the Allen bolt and tighten to 20-25 ft.-lb. (27-34 N.m).

10. Install the jam nut and tighten securely. Then install a new cotter pin and bend its ends over to lock it.

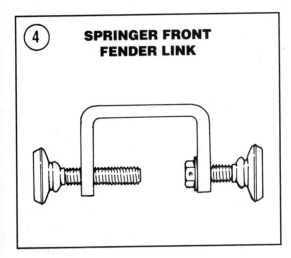

SPRINGER FRONT FENDER LINK

11. Insert the speedometer cable through the cable bracket.

Installation

1. If removed, install the fender links as follows:

    a. Apply Loctite 272 (red) to the pivot screw prior to installation.

    b. Install and tighten the pivot screw to 10-20 ft.-lb. (14-27 N.m).

    c. Install the rubber spacer and nylon washer onto the pivot screw.

    d. Install the fender link onto the pivot screw.

    e. Repeat for the other side.

2. Position the Harley-Davidson fender link tool (part No. HD-39754) between the fender links and tighten securely.

FRONT FENDER
(ALL OTHER MODELS)

Removal/Installation

1. Support the bike on the jiffy stand.

2. Disconnect the speedometer cable and remove it from the front fender guide, if necessary.

3. Disconnect the front fender lamp electrical connector, if so equipped.

4. Remove the bolts, washers and/or nuts securing the front fender to the front sliders. Remove the front fender.

5. Installation is the reverse of these steps. Make sure the front fender lamp, if so equipped, works properly.

REAR FENDER

Removal/Installation

1. Disconnect the negative battery cable.

2. Remove the seat.

3. Disconnect the wiring harness connector(s) interfering with rear fender removal.

4. Remove the taillamp and license plate bracket from the rear fender.

5. Remove the rear fender mounting hardware and remove the rear fender. Pull the wiring harness connectors through the fender as required to remove the fender.

15

6. Installation is the reverse of these steps. Note the following.

7. After pulling the wiring harness through the fender, secure the wiring harness with the fender clips.

8. After connecting the negative battery cable, turn the ignition switch ON and check the operation of the turn signals and taillight. Do not ride the motorcycle until these lights are operating properly.

SADDLEBAGS
(1993-ON)

Refer to **Figure 5** when removing and installing the saddlebags.

Removal/Installation

1. Remove the screws and washers securing the saddlebags to the brackets.

2. Remove the saddlebags.

3. To remove the saddlebag brackets:
    a. Remove the bolts and flat washers.
    b. Remove the acorn nut and washer at the bottom of the bracket.
    c. Remove the saddlebag brackets.

4. Replace worn or damaged grommets.

5. Install by reversing these steps.

FRAME

The frame is the "skeleton" of your motorcycle. It has been designed to support the engine, transmission and suspension systems and all other components in their proper relationship so that the motorcycle can operate as a unit. In addition, the frame is a determining factor in the overall styling of the motorcycle. Because of its importance in the overall operation of the motorcycle, proper frame care should include frequent cleaning and inspection. In addition, the frame should be inspected immediately after any accident or spill. If necessary, the frame should be mounted on a jig and checked for damage. Frame repair, which usually includes welding, should be performed by a dealer or frame specialist.

CAUTION
Do not refer frame repair to an inexperienced repair shop or welder.

Frame Inspection

Certain areas on the frame are more susceptible to stress and wear damage. The following areas should be inspected on a yearly schedule or whenever the bike has been involved in an accident or spill.

1. Closely examine the paint on the frame. Flaking or chipping paint can be an early sign of frame bending or damage. Investigate these areas closely before repainting.

NOTE
A bent frame tube can usually be straightened by heating and bending it back into shape. However, because this section may now be weaker than it was originally, the area may require additional repair in the form of tube sleeving, additional bracing or gusseting. Unless you are experienced in frame repair, do not attempt to straighten or weld a frame to repair it. Refer all frame repair to a frame specialist.

2. All motorcycles vibrate to some degree. However, if you notice an increase in vibration, park the bike and go over it thoroughly. Abnormal vibration can be caused by loose or worn parts or from a broken or damaged frame member.

3. Loose or damaged engine mount bolts can cause frame breakage or engine mount damage. Check for loose or missing fasteners. Refer to the respective chapters for engine, transmission and primary drive bolt tightening torques. Replace worn or damaged engine mount fasteners.

4. The steering head is designed and constructed to withstand stress from braking and steering while supporting the weight of the front end. However, this area is very suspectable to damage from accidents. Inspect the steering head carefully for cracks, bending and other damage. The steering head bearings should be serviced as described in Chapter Eleven or Chapter Twelve. Steering adjustment should be checked on a routine maintenance schedule and adjusted to remove all excessive bearing play. Worn bearings and races should be replaced as soon as they are detected.

5. The swing arm pivot area and the rear shock absorber mounting brackets are subjected to stress from acceleration, braking and turning. The swing arm and its bearings should be serviced as described in Chapter Thirteen. Check the swing arm and the

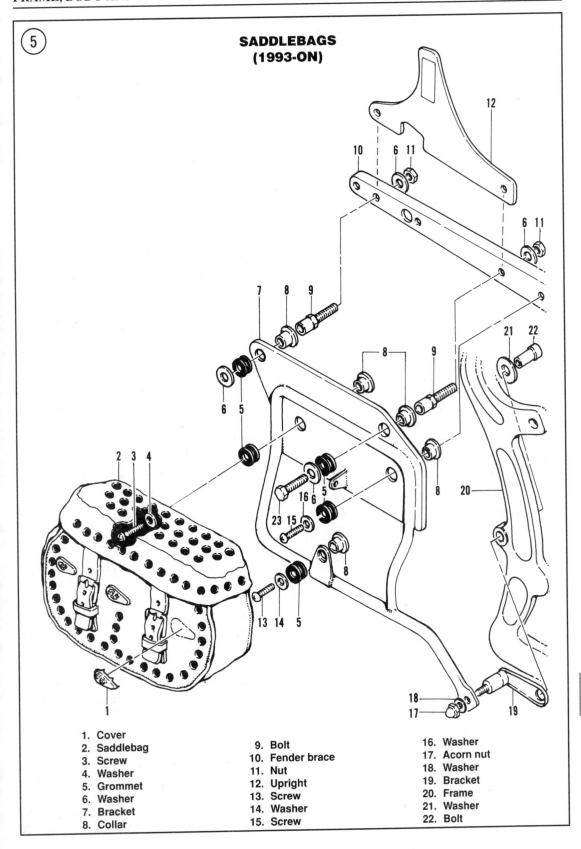

**SADDLEBAGS
(1993-ON)**

1. Cover
2. Saddlebag
3. Screw
4. Washer
5. Grommet
6. Washer
7. Bracket
8. Collar
9. Bolt
10. Fender brace
11. Nut
12. Upright
13. Screw
14. Washer
15. Screw
16. Washer
17. Acorn nut
18. Washer
19. Bracket
20. Frame
21. Washer
22. Bolt

15

frame pivot area for cracks. Check and tighten the swing arm pivot bolts as described in Chapter Thirteen.

6. Check all of the component mounting tabs for cracks, loose mounting fasteners or clamps and other damage. Especially check the mounting brackets securing the footpegs, jiffy stand and rear brake master cylinder.

Component Removal/Installation

If your bike has been involved in an accident, consult with the frame repair shop on how they want the frame delivered to their shop. The following lists steps required to strip the frame completely of all components. When stripping the motorcycle, note the following:

a. If you plan on removing all of the parts from the frame, you will be dealing with a large number of parts. Prepare you work area so that you have adequate storage space that can be left undisturbed for some time. It is especially important to store parts which can be damaged cosmetically (fuel tanks, seat, fenders, etc.), in a safe place.

b. Before removing the first bolt and to prevent frustration during assembly, get a number of boxes, plastic bags and containers and store the parts as they are removed. Also have on hand a roll of masking tape and a permanent, waterproof marking pen to tag and label each part or assembly as required. If your Harley was purchased second hand and it appears that some of the wiring may have been changed or replaced, label each electrical connection before disconnecting it.

c. Note the condition of all threaded fasteners as they are removed from the bike. Replace worn or damaged fasteners with one of the same size, type and torque requirements.

d. Make a list of worn, damaged or missing parts as you work on the bike so that parts can be ordered at the same time. Then keep track of parts as they are ordered and note any missing or back ordered items. You don't want to plan a weekend around assembling your bike only to find that you have to stop because of an incorrect or missing part.

1. Support the bike in a manner that both wheels clear the ground. Double-check to make sure the bike cannot fall in either direction.

2. Remove the battery as described in Chapter Nine.

3. Remove the fuel tank, carburetor and exhaust system as described in Chapter Eight.

4. Remove the primary drive assembly as described in Chapter Five.

5. Remove the engine as described in Chapter Four.

6. Remove the transmission housing as described in Chapter Six or Chapter Seven.

7. Remove the headlight assembly as described in Chapter Nine.

8. Remove the front and rear brake caliper assemblies as described in Chapter Fourteen.

9. Remove the front and rear wheels as described in Chapter Ten.

10. Remove the handlebar, front forks and steering assembly as described in Chapter Eleven or Chapter Twelve.

11. Remove the rear fender as described in this chapter.

12. Remove the rear shock absorbers and rear swing arm as described in Chapter Thirteen.

NOTE
Before removing the wiring harness in Step 13, you may want to take a number of photographs of the harness as it is installed on the bike. These can be used to good advantage during reassembly. Before photographing the wiring harness on the bike, place a piece of blue or grey cardboard behind the bike. This background can help to unclutter the frame and wiring harness in your pictures.

13. Remove all wire guides and other fasteners and remove the wiring harness from the bike. Do not pull on the wiring harness when removing it from a harness guide. If the bike was involved in a crash, check the harness for visible signs of damage. Check each wire for continuity with an ohmmeter.

14. Remove the jiffy stand and all other items left mounted or strapped to the frame.

15. Inspect the frame for bends, cracks or other damage, especially around welded joints and areas that are rusted. Check the frame swing arm pivot holes for elongation or other damage.

16. Check threaded holes in the frame for stripping, cross-threading or deposit buildup. Threaded holes

should be blown out with compressed air as dirt buildup in the bottom of the hole may prevent the bolt from being torque properly. If necessary, use a tap to true up the threads and to remove any deposits.

17. Clean all parts before reassembly.

NOTE
If paint has been removed from parts during cleaning, touch up areas as required before assembly or installation.

18. Make sure all worn or defective parts have been repaired or replaced.

19. Install by reversing these removal steps.

Stripping and Painting

Remove all components from the frame. Thoroughly strip off all old paint. The best way is to have it beadplasted down to bare metal. If this is not possible, you can use a liquid paint remover and steel wool and a fine, hard wire brush.

CAUTION
If you wish to change the color of molded plastic parts, consult an automotive paint supplier for the proper procedure. Do not use any liquid paint remover on these components as it will damage the surface. The color is an integral part of these components and cannot be removed.

When the frame is down to bare metal, have it inspected for hairline and internal cracks. Magnaflux is the most common and complete process.

Make sure that the primer is compatible with the type of paint you are going to use for the finish color. Spray on one or two coats of primer as smoothly as possible. Let it dry thoroughly and use a fine grade of wet sandpaper (400-600 grit) to remove any flaws. Carefully wipe the surface clean and then spray a couple of coats of the final color. Use either lacquer or enamel base paint and follow the manufacturer's instructions.

A shop specializing in painting will probably do the best job. However, you can do a surprisingly good job with a good grade of spray paint. Spend a few extra dollars and get a good grade of paint as it will make a difference in how well it looks and how long it will stand up. It's a good idea to shake the can and make sure the ball inside the can is loose when you purchase the can of paint. Shake the can as long as is stated on the can. Then immerse the can *upright* in a pot or bucket of *warm* water (not hot—not over 120° F [49° C]).

WARNING
*Higher temperatures could cause the can to burst. Do **not** place the can in direct contact with any flame or heat source.*

Leave the can in the water for several minutes. When thoroughly warmed, shake the can again and spray the frame. Be sure to get into all the crevices where there may be rust problems. Several light mist coats are better than one heavy coat. Spray painting is best done in temperatures of 70-80° F (21-26° C); any temperature above or below this may give you problems.

After the final coat has dried completely, at least 48 hours, any overspray or orange peel may be removed with a *light* application of DuPont Rubbing Compound (red color) and finished with DuPont Polishing Compound (white color). Be careful not to rub too hard or you will go through the finish.

Finish off with a couple coats of good wax before reassembling all the components.

It's a good idea to keep the frame touched up with fresh paint if any minor rust spots or scratches appear.

15

INDEX

16

16

1984 FXST

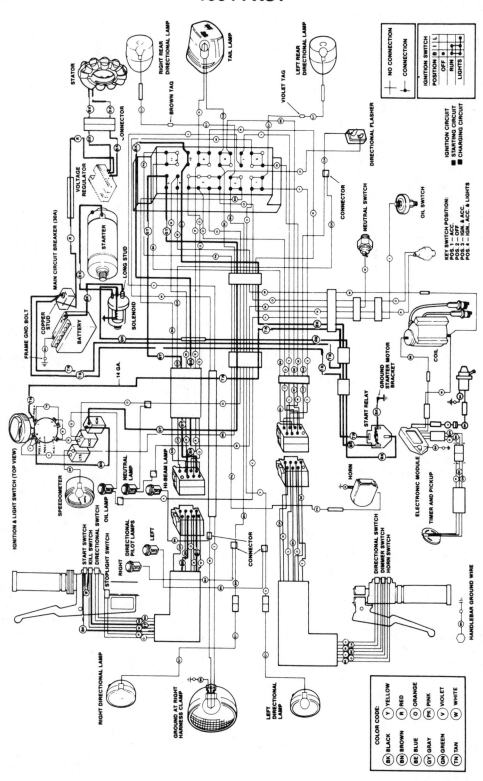

EARLY 1985 FXST/C

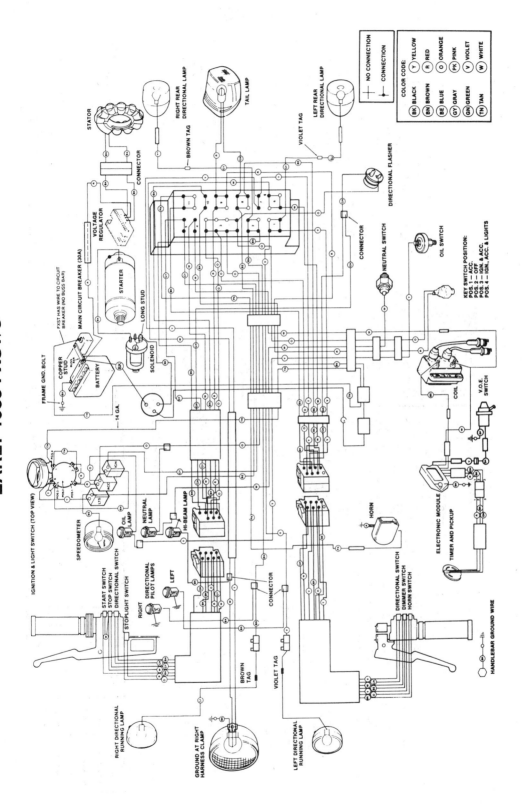

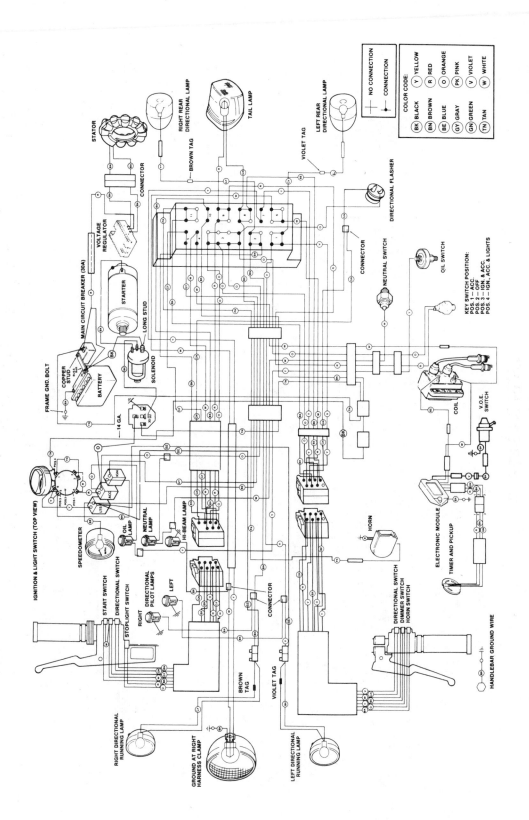

LATE 1985 TO 1986 FXST/C

1986 1/2 FLST

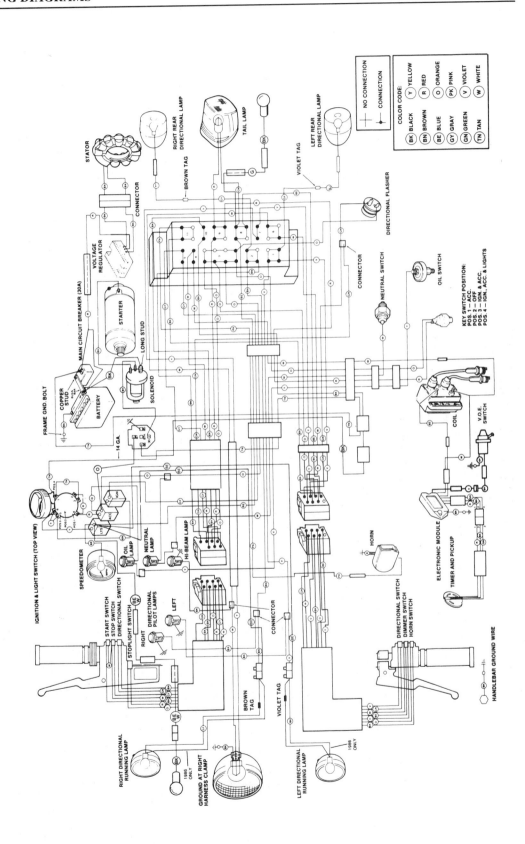

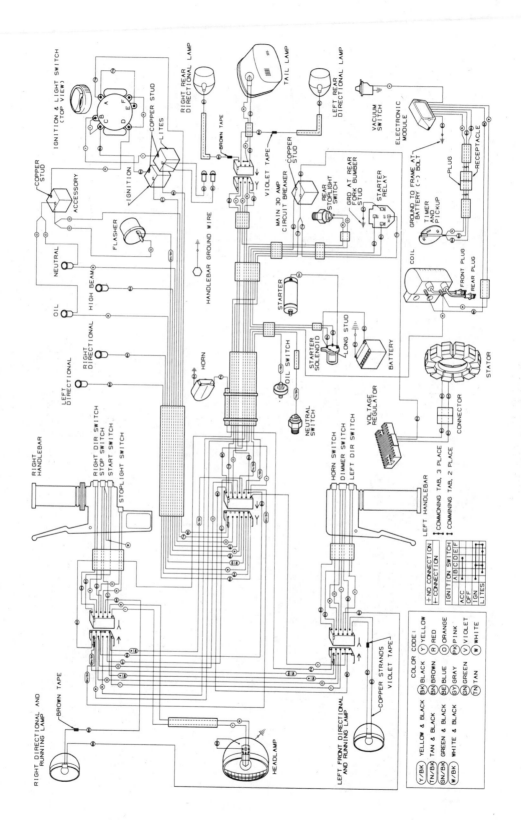

1987 & 1988 FXST/C, 1988 1/2 FXSTS

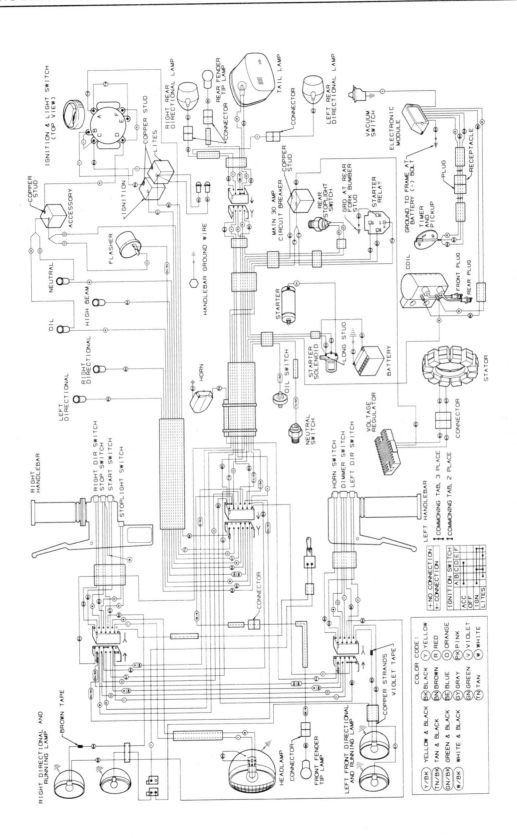

1987 & 1988 FLSTC

1987 & 1988 FLST

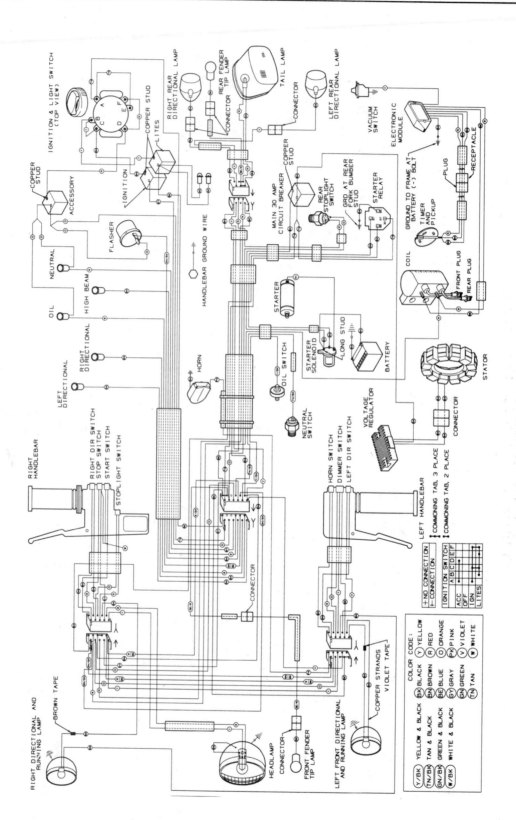

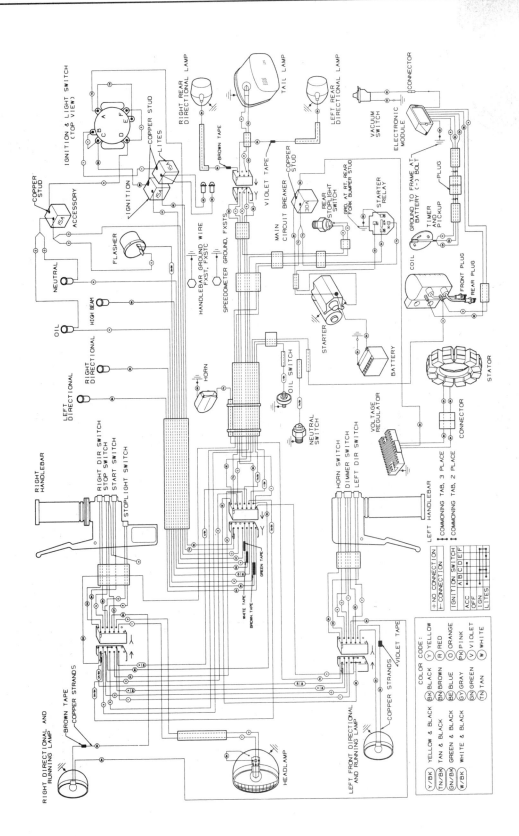

1989-1990 FXST/C/S, 1990 FLSTF

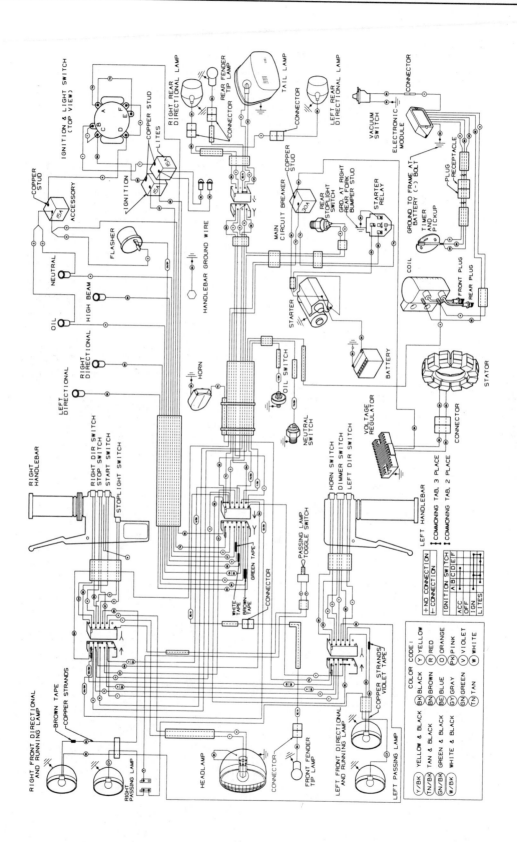

1989-1990 FLSTC

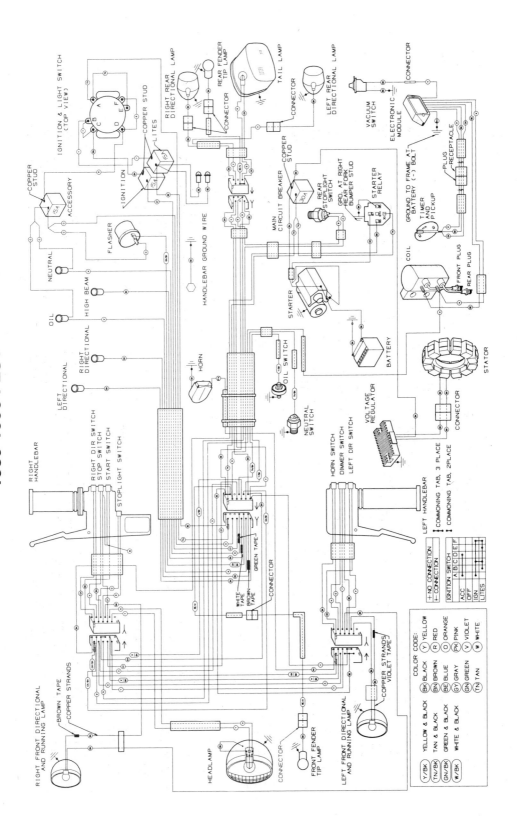

1989-1990 FLST

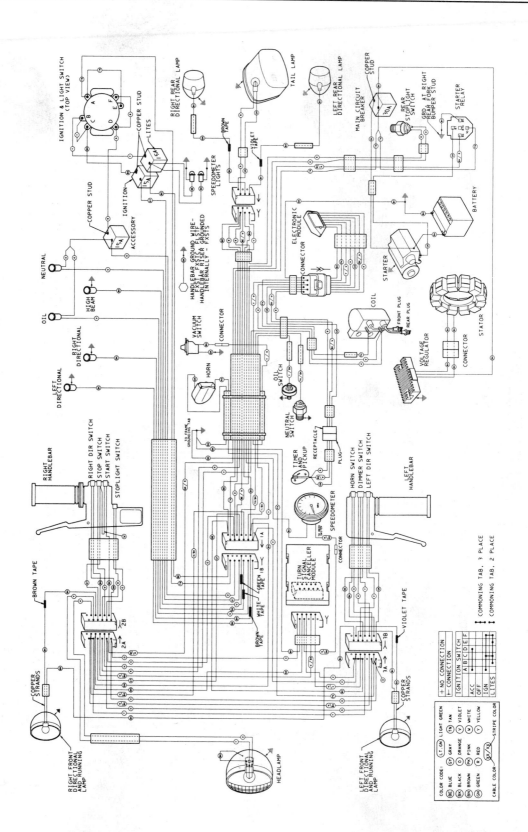

1991 FXSTC, FXSTS, FLSTF

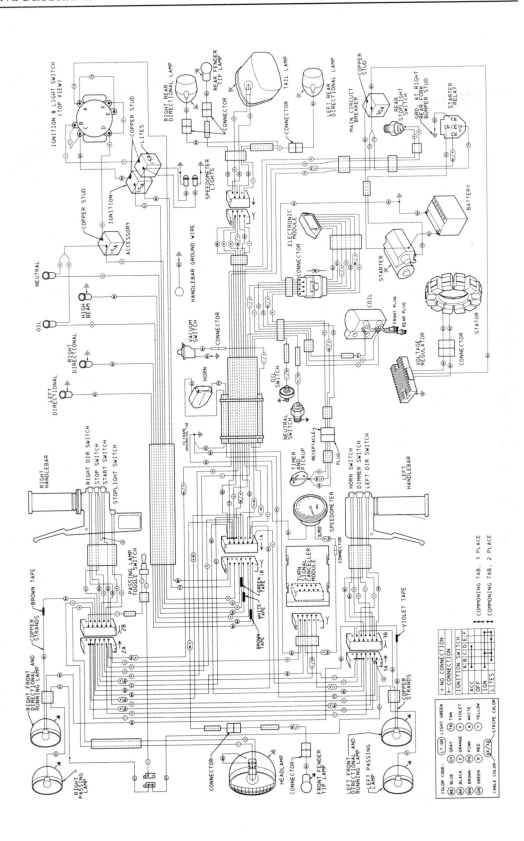

1991 FLSTC

1992 FLSTC

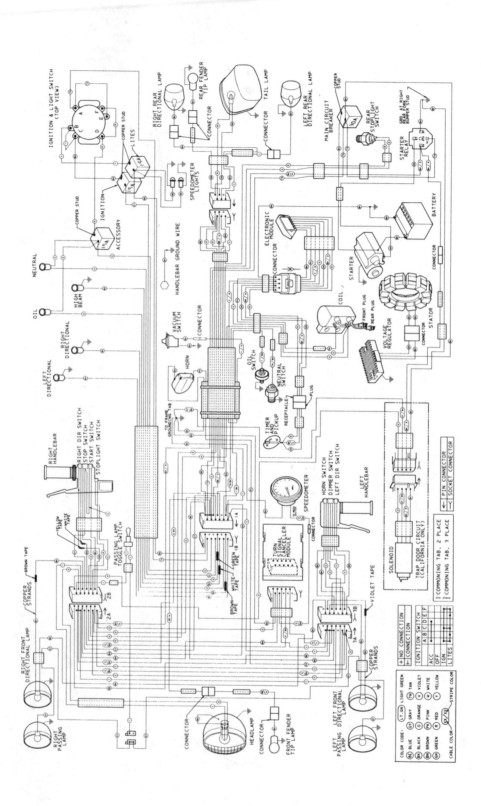

1992 FXSTC, FXSTS, FLSTF

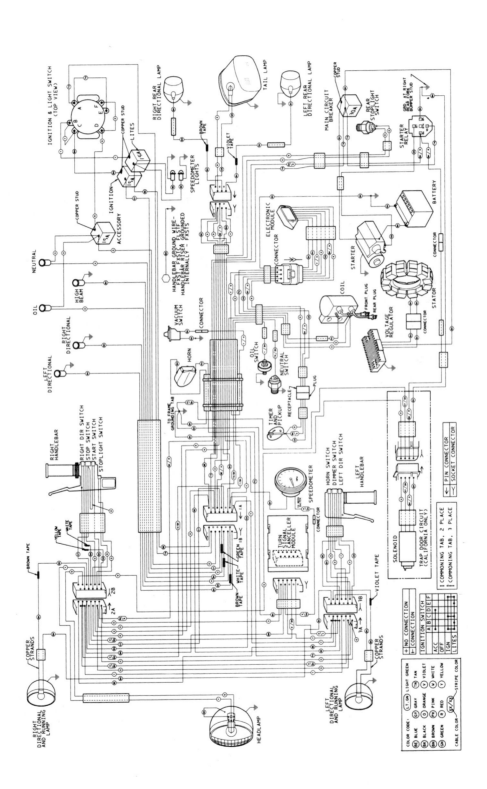

1993 FLSTC, DOMESTIC

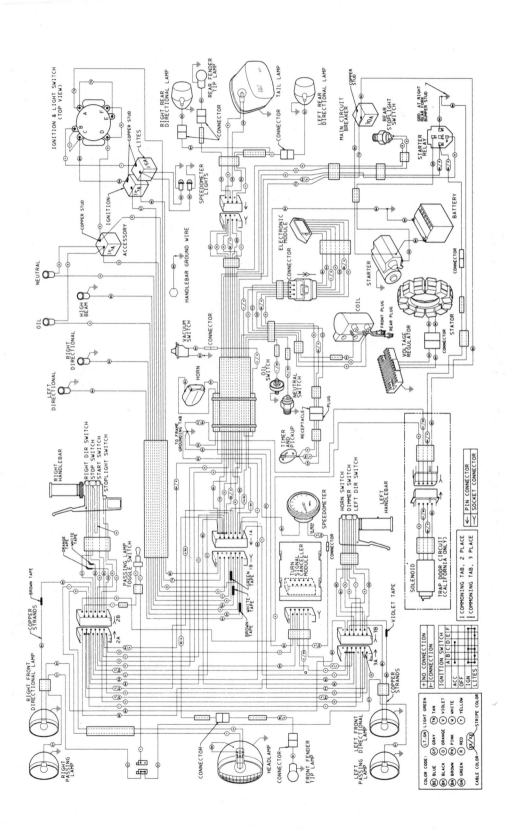

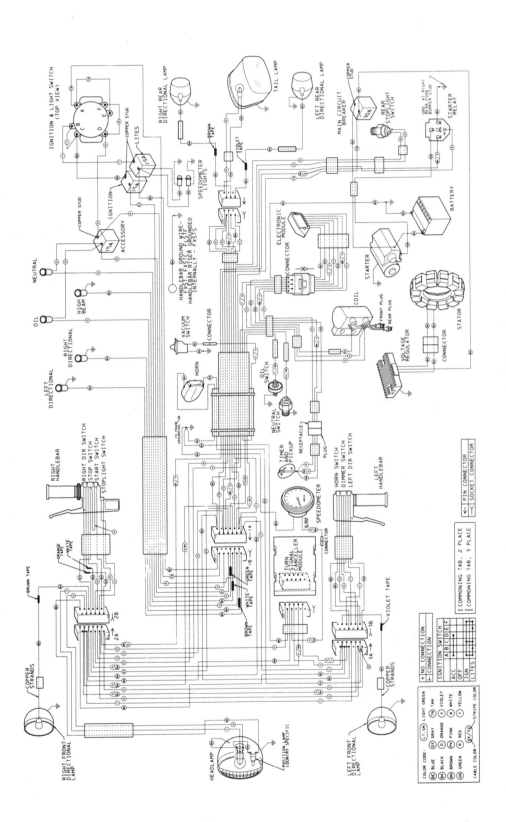

1993 FLSTC/S, FLSTF/N, DOMESTIC

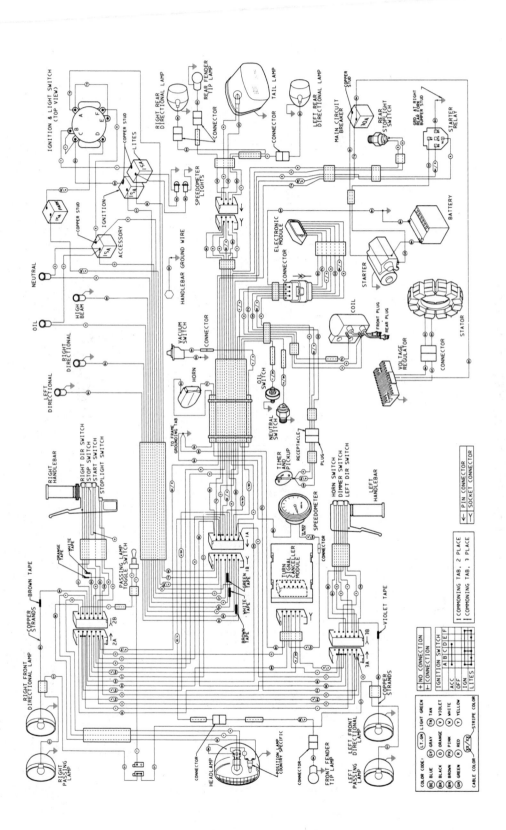

1993 FLSTC, HDI

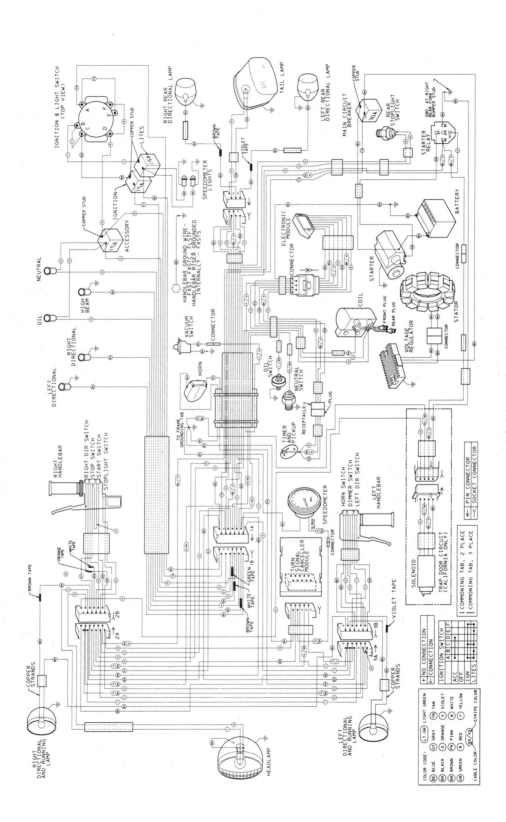

1993 FLSTF/N, FXSTC/S, HDI

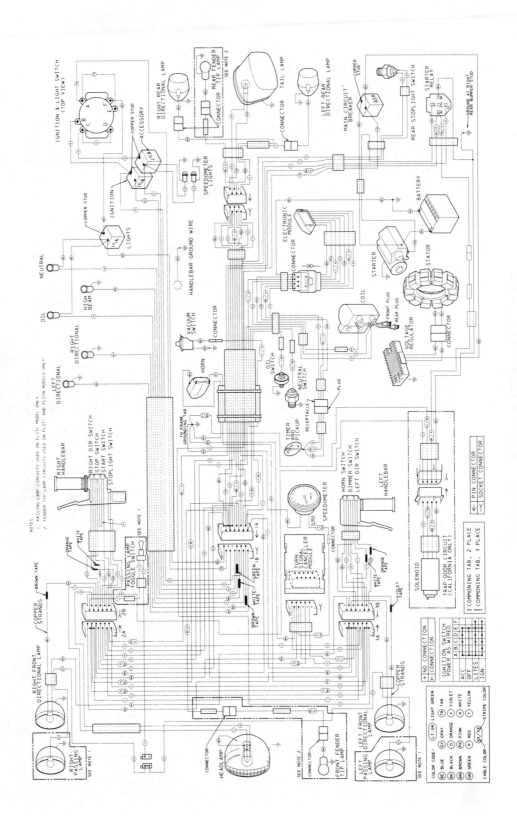

1994 SOFTAIL, DOMESTIC

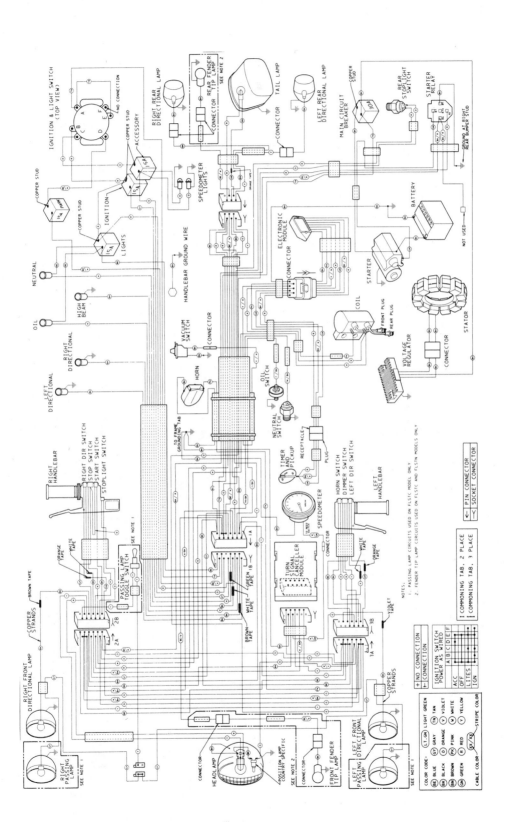

1994 SOFTAIL, INTERNATIONAL

NOTES

NOTES

MAINTENANCE LOG

Service Performed	Mileage Reading				
Oil change (example)	2,836	5,782	8,601		